GUELPH:
PERSPECTIVES ON A CENTURY OF CHANGE
1900-2000

GUELPH
HISTORICAL
SOCIETY

edited by
Dawn Matheson & Rosemary Anderson

Canadian Cataloguing in Publication Data

Main entry under title:
Guelph: perspectives on a century of change 1900-2000-09-15

Includes biographical references and index.
ISBN 0-960594-3-4 (bound)   ISBN 0-9690594-2-6 (pbk.)

I. Guelph (Ont.) – History.   I. Guelph Historical Society.

FC 3099.G83G83 2000   971.3'43   C00-932407-0
F1059.5.G9G83 2000

The Society acknowledges with thanks the financial support of the members of the **Guelph Historical Society**; the **City of Guelph**; Advanced Funding Program, **Ontario Lottery Corporation**; **Guelph-Wellington Men's Club**; and the **Royal City Lions Club (Guelph)**.

Care has been taken to trace the ownership of copyright material used in this book and we welcome any information enabling us to rectify any references or credit in subsequent editions.

Book Manager: Donald E. Coulman
Book Editors: Dawn Matheson and Rosemary Anderson
Printed for the Society by Ampersand Printing, Guelph, ON
Book design contributor and cover design by Dawn Matheson
Original woodcuts by Ryan Price

Cover photos:

(Front: left to right)

Natalizia Marchesano in her garden, 1999
Source: www.deanpalmer.ca

The construction of Creelman Hall in 1914
Source: University of Guelph Library Archives

Maggie McLennan on her porch, 1999
Source: www.deanpalmer.ca

(Back)

Fat Stock Club in front of the Albion Hotel, c. 1910
Source: Albion Hotel

First endpaper:

Panoramic view of the old Atkinson farm, 1915, east of Guelph, on Highway 7.
The only farm in Guelph Township
with a railroad underpass.
Source: Jack Sinclair

Guelph Historical Society
100 Crimea St., Unit A102
Guelph, Ontario
N1H 2Y6 CANADA
www.guelphhistoricalsociety.ca

GUELPH: PERSPECTIVES ON A CENTURY OF CHANGE 1900-2000

Riding the Guelph Radial Railway in 1910.

Introduction

DONALD COULMAN

The city of Guelph was and continues to be built by individuals who have ideas and are willing to take risks.

Guelph was John Galt's idea in 1827. He risked his reputation to make Guelph into a corporation which worked.

Today, not many of us in Canada will have the opportunity to found a city, but each one of us does have the potential, in both the private and public domains, to form a business, a citizens' action group, a music, dance or theatre group, an advisory committee, a charitable organization, a church or a legal firm. During the 20th century in Guelph: Bert Wood had an idea to build the W. C. Wood Company; Oliver and Len Hammond founded Hammond manufacturing; Richard Chaloner had the idea to form the Guelph Big Brothers Association; Frank Hasenfratz thought up the Linamar Corporation; The Guelph Food Bank was Marilyn Worobec's idea; Beatrice Youngman put together the Guelph Music Club; Roy Mason was behind the formation of the Guelph Biltmore Hockey Club; Jean Little had the idea to write a book; Freddy Veri started Freddy's Hairstyling; and, Ed Pickersgill inspired the construction of the Matrix Centre, an affordable housing project.

There is a long list of 20th century Guelph people who are entrepreneurs – entrepreneurs not just in the business sense – but people who have significantly increased our city's physical and spiritual wealth. There is also a lengthy list of individuals who have come forth to say, "it can't be done," when ideas are presented. Usually, these idea-detractors base their arguments on the simplistic and narrow concept of the scarcity of the medium we use for economic trade: money.

The 20th century "Guelph Community" included a myriad of disparate ethnic, spiritual, business and cultural inner-communities. These Guelph inner-communities have come together in a more or less tug-of-war which has provided each one of us with our personal concept of the Guelph Community and our place in it. Reading each author's work and looking at the pictures in this book will not only inform, entertain and sometimes provoke you, but, will also help you to sharpen your personal viewpoint of Guelph and its future.

As Guelph grows in population and geographic size, a major issue facing 21st century municipal councils will be the inclusion of Guelph in a regional government scheme. The danger in amalgamation of political jurisdictions is the subsequent diminution of the individual and the ordinary citizen's loss of easy access to those who govern. Each one of the authors of this book, whether stated openly or covertly, worries about the reduction of the "sense of place" possessed by each Guelph citizen. Concomitant with this, they feel, would be the subtle, but inexorable, elimination of artifacts and traditions unique to Guelph.

Guelph: Perspectives on a Century of Change 1900 – 2000 is the result of an idea Ross Irwin had while he was president of the Guelph Historical Society (1997). I was asked to turn the idea for a book into a reality. After accepting the challenge, I became engaged in thoughtful guesswork to develop some of the ideas I had for a book of this type. The book had to be very different in appearance and writing style than the usual local history book. It had to be an appealing, easy-to-read book which would inform, entertain and provide strong visual stimulation to a wide variety of people.

I decided that no one individual could adequately write about the complex 20th century history of Guelph. As well, the variation in perspective that different authors would bring would result in a more interesting and informative book.

In my mind, I divided the book into possible sections; while, at the same time, mentally scanning the city of Guelph for potential authors and editors. The authors and editors had to be Guelphites and the book had to be printed in Guelph.

Each author would have to bring to the task an in-depth knowledge of Guelph's history, broad historical perspective and just a hint of thoughtful opinion to stimulate the reader's mind. I wanted authors whose words would force the reader to think about Guelph's past, make an assessment of the present Guelph and then think about the Guelph of the future.

The author-editor selection took considerable time; but, once completed, there were numerous exciting and sometimes colourful author-editor exchange-of-ideas meetings to discuss the makeup of the book and minimize overlap. (Sometimes, I wondered if the book would ever happen!) Since, "not everything could be told," each author had to make very thoughtful decisions about what would be included in his or her section.

The name for the book, *Guelph: Perspectives on a Century of Change 1900-2000*, was determined after a long and sometimes agonizing process. Some of the possible titles presented resulted in much laughter, others garnered an abundance of scoffing!

Critical to the writing of this book was the editing process. Editors Rosemary Anderson and Dawn Matheson capably faced this often overwhelming task with thoughtfulness, very hard work and a generous dab of good humour. To ensure that the overall objectives for the book were maintained, Rosemary and Dawn met innumerable times with the authors, both individually and collectively, to discuss re-writes, deletions and additions. They accomplished this difficult task with perception, sensitivity and empathy.

Dawn Matheson, with inspiration, enthusiasm and great energy, was responsible for the overall design, layout and picture placement in this book. Dawn could best be described as an irresistible force – just what was needed to accomplish this huge task!

This book was capably printed at Ampersand Printing in Guelph. Carolyn Klymko, who prepared this book for printing, and Mike McDonald, the owner of this firm, provided much wise and helpful advice throughout the writing and printing processes.

I know that you will be entertained and informed about 20th century Guelph by looking at the pictures and reading the words in this book. Enjoy!

Donald Coulman
Project Manager
Summer, 2000

CHAPTER 1

CULTURAL LIFE IN TWENTIETH-CENTURY GUELPH

GLORIA DENT

THE OLD ANCHORAGE – GUELPH IN 1900

"The Whole City Ablaze," read the headline of the *Guelph Daily Herald* on March 2, 1900. "Never before in the history of Guelph has there been a greater manifestation of loyalty to the British Empire or a more spontaneous outburst of patriotic enthusiasm."

The occasion was the relief of the city Ladysmith by British forces in South Africa. Guelph's other newspapers, the *Daily Mercury and Advertiser* and the *Advocate,* also described the city's jubilation: flags flying in every direction, banners stretched across the streets, homes, shops, and factories bright with lights and decorations. Church bells rang merrily and "whistles tooted in rhyme and out of rhyme." At noon the city's First Brigade, aided by gunners from the Ontario Agricultural College, fired a 21-gun salute and the mayor proclaimed a half-day holiday. Factories and shops closed for the afternoon.

During the morning, six board of education trustees addressed the students in the collegiate's fourth-form room. They justified the reasons for war and spoke of splendid heroism, indomitable British pluck and glorious imperialism. When the chairman promised the pupils a holiday if they cheered well, "the rafters of the building rang again and again with Young Canada's recognition of the Empire's victory."

Students at Central Public School assembled in the drill hall at 11 a.m. They applauded seven patriotic speeches, one of which observed that young women, as nurses, were taking part in the war as well as men. Trustees and aldermen, including such 19th-century stalwarts as James Innes and

Col. Nathaniel Higinbotham, visited the Ward schools. At Victoria Public School, trustee Anderson treated the scholars to oranges in honour of the day. By instruction, encouragement and benevolence, the celebration of a glorious victory was invoked.

At three o'clock, the 30th Battalion Band marched from the Armoury up Wyndham Street to St. George's Square and, in front of the post office, played the *British Grenadiers, Soldiers of the Queen, The Red, White and Blue* and other patriotic airs. As evening drew on, an impromptu procession formed. St. George's banner, held high by six society members, headed the line. Close behind came the Citizens' Band, followed by city council in sleighs; trustees of the two school boards, also in sleighs (separate ones); the Fire Brigade with hook-and-ladder wagon and hose-wagon brilliantly decorated; war veterans and a detachment of artillery; Sleeman's Band; the Wellington Rifles and buglers of the 30th Battalion. After a tour about town, they arrived at Market Square. As a bonfire burned behind the market sheds, "a *feu de joi* was fired ... and a steady volume of rockets soared into the heavens."

The correspondent for the *Guelph Mercury* during the Boer War had been Lieut. John McCrae. His return with the Guelph contingent, expected in the morning of January 11, 1901, was delayed due to platform celebrations at every stop on the journey from Lévis. They did not arrive, as reported the following day, until 10:58 p.m. sharp. A religious service and a banquet had been cancelled, but "all of Guelph" was out to meet its heroes at the station, brilliantly lighted for the occasion by the Guelph Light and Power Company. The snow was falling lightly; the Citizens' Band playing; the

1. R.C. Church.
2. School
3. Church where I sang
4. Post office
5. Episcopal church. —
   The Higinbotham's line beyond this church
The window marked was my room for years most of my life was spent there. King Edward is corner of Market Square and Wyndham St. (the main street

Panoramic postcard of the city of Guelph about 1900 with a view of Church of Our Lady and environs, Loretto Abbey, Central and Alexandra Schools and the church spires, sent by Edward Johnson in 1907 to a friend in Paris. He has marked his room in the King Edward Hotel with four X's.
Source: University of Guelph Collections

Another Reception

When Private Barber returned from the Boer War on September 4, 1900, his friends from the 30th Battalion staged their own welcome. They gave him a shoulder ride through the station crowd and pulled him about town in a cab (horses unattached). They then started a bonfire in St. George's Square from cast-off boxes. When the constable on duty attempted to quench the fire and rescue the boxes, onlookers objected and added more when his back was turned. A young man caught hauling a box was arrested by Sergeant Kickley and put in jail. When the duty sergeant refused to release him, the "rowdy element" threw stones into almost every window in the police court. Another group besieged the CPR telegraph office with stones and broke the front plate-glass window. Order was restored by Mayor Nelson and the chief of police, but not before "Chief Randall had received a bad crack on the head, Constable Borthwick was struck on the nose and Mr. Archibald Clark was hit in the eye with a large stone that dazed him." Later, at the request of Private Barber, the young man was released. *Guelph Evening Mercury and Advertiser*, July 20, 1927.

Visit of the Duke and Duchess of York, later King George V and Queen Mary, at Jubilee Park, October 10, 1901. The platform at Jubilee Park stood on the site of the present C.N.R railway station. Source: Guelph Museums

train's whistle blowing in the distance. Then, as members of Hespeler's 29th Battalion controlled the excited crowd, the train rounded the turn into Guelph and "cheer after cheer went up." Boys and even girls blasted "hundreds of horns," and the old folks made as much noise as the youngsters did. Order was eventually restored, and a large procession, this time led by reception-committee chairman Ald. J. J. Drew, Mayor Nelson, mayor-elect Kennedy and Lieut. McCrae, circled the illuminated streets to the sound of firing rockets and church bells. It reached City Hall at 11:30 p.m., and only after nine speeches and rousing cheers for the Queen did the crowd disperse.

Occasions such as these revealed important facets of Guelph's culture. Other aspects were less obvious. The dominant culture reflected the taste and proclivities of the majority of its residents who were immigrants from the British Isles or their descendants. The city prided itself on loyalty to monarch and empire, but cultural activities generally arose from the citizens themselves who wished to be involved in life beyond their work and family. When certain initiatives coincided with civic ideals, municipal officials sometimes supported them, but most events resulted from the dedicated work of society members and the funds they could raise by selling tickets. Individuals formed or joined a host of voluntary organizations and institutions that sometimes cut across class lines, but more often reinforced social and racial divisions. They donned various hats as

they participated in church functions, worked with a fraternal order or benefit society, promoted labour organizations, or attended a concert or sports event. Many of these voluntary groups proved permanent, others were ephemeral. Not a few assumed new guises under different names, but with purposes similar to their antecedents. Although Guelph's culture was exceptionally vibrant at the turn of the century, it often enjoyed professional performances from beyond the border. Local artists and musicians had to move to large metropolitan centres if they wished to gain a livelihood from their talent.

Just about every citizen went to church, and Sunday school was a normal activity for children of all classes. Sunday was quiet, a day for prayer and reflection, even though children often broke the rules. On Saturday and other special days, no one could forget that Guelph was the centre of a flourishing agricultural industry. Farmers from seven or eight miles around descended on the city to sell their produce and buy supplies. Thousands crowded the streets during the Central Fair at Exhibition Park, the Fat Stock Show and the Provincial Agricultural Fair, held in Guelph for the first time in December 1900. Hotels were filled and retail merchants happy. Major events as these began and ended with special church services that emphasized the keywords of cultural life: duty, loyalty, sacrifice, education and benevolence. These values were taught by the church, reinforced by the schools and exercised by leaders of the community – British Christian men, who had worked hard to establish themselves and who had the

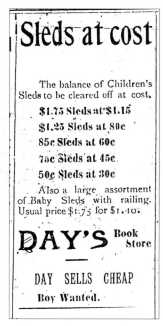

Day's Book Store – not just
books.   Source: *Guelph
Advocate*, March 3, 1900.

welfare of the city and its people at heart. Their authority was God and their example, the Empire. The church had power over the people, the school and parents over the children, employers over the employees and property owners over the general population.

This is not to say that citizens did not enjoy themselves in Guelph in 1900. The front page of the *Guelph Advocate* on February 23 advertised the performance at the Royal Opera House of *For Fair Virginia*, "a southern play of romantic interest." Below it, the Haymarket Theatre (a fancy name for the auditorium at City Hall) boasted a week of dramatic performances by the Marks Brothers Company. William C. Thain's orchestra was playing "excellent music" that week at Petrie's skating rink, located at Wellington Street near Gordon. Mr. Charles Kelly had resumed teaching at his vocal studio and was available for concerts. A. J. Small was offering free use of the Royal Opera House to the newly formed Guelph branch of the Red Cross Society for patriotic concerts. Charles Nelles' Big Book Store was taking stock and customers were asked to kindly settle their accounts. Day's Book Store was selling sleds, doll carriages, and wagons at cost. Knox Presbyterian Church was sponsoring "Canada's brightest elocutionist," Miss Teresa MacCallum, reciting Kipling's *Absent-Minded Beggar*. Popular preacher, the Rev. Mr. Palmer,

riding on the success of a series of lectures at Trinity Baptist Church, would be holding a mass meeting on Sunday afternoon for men only. Dublin Street Methodist Church, celebrating its 25th anniversary, promised special sermons on Sunday and an "Old Fashioned Tea" on Monday, with addresses by several reverends and music by the choirs of 1875 and 1900. At the bottom of the page and not easily missed was the catchy heading "Where to go Tonight." Recommended was a lecture by the Rev. F. A. Cassidy at the Congregational Church and a meeting of the Young Liberals' Club. As for literature, the title of the new daily serial was *For Queen and Country: the Story of the South African War*. The church, the Boer War, and the principles they evoked were not easy to avoid. They were a driving force in Guelph's cultural life at the beginning of the 20th century.

Visitors approaching Guelph in 1900 would first see, as they would now, the Church of Our Lady on Catholic Hill, as it was called. Its towers, completed only to the top of the nave, dominated the city. On the streets below, the established Protestant religions each had one or more solid stone churches that flourished by reason of increasing membership, or differences of opinion.

Dublin Street Methodist, originally called the Second Wesleyan Church, was built as an expansion of Norfolk Street Methodist. Both had a thriving membership. The more radical Primitive Methodists on Paisley Street still worshiped in a white stucco chapel. St. Andrew's Presbyterian had spawned the building of Knox. The erection of Chalmers Presbyterian, some 20 years later almost next door to Knox, was the result of a disagreement regrettably ignored by historians. That the new church was named after the Rev. Thomas Chalmers, leader of the Free Church Movement in Scotland, provided a partial explanation, but the story lingered among descendants of those who knew that the problem concerned the use of alcohol. St. George's, the stronghold of Anglicanism for most of Guelph's 19th century, was faced with dissension when 73 members declared their intent to follow the ideas of the Oxford Movement in England. The Bishop of Niagara consented to the division of the parish, and St. James was formed. In the summer of 1890, "the smouldering embers of disharmony burst into flame" at the First Baptist Church on Woolwich and, in September, 100 members withdrew to build the Second Baptist Church, also on Woolwich Street.

Smaller Protestant congregations had also established permanent places of worship. The Congregationalists owned a dignified stone building at Norfolk and Liverpool streets. The Disciples of Christ occupied the former Zion

The *Guelph Census* provided a breakdown of professed religious denominations in 1901:

Methodist	2839	Brethren	69
Presbyterian	2744	Salvation Army	69
Roman Catholic	2403	Christian Science	68
Church of England	1933	Lutheran	55
Baptist	662	Mennonite	37
Congregationalists	241	Miscellaneous	23
Church of Christ Disciples	158	British Methodist Episcopal	15
Christadelphians	70	Hebrew	13
No church	6		

Miscellaneous included five Adventists; five Old Catholics; four Spiritualists; three Greek Church; two deaf and dumb persons [sic]; a Universalist; an Old Believer; a Latitudinarian; and a Free Thinker. In the manuscript census, 76 entries were illegible.

Evangelical Church on Bridge Street. It was the second oldest stone church in Guelph, having been built by the Congregational Independent Dissenters or "Morrisonians," who disbanded in Guelph around 1880. It was called Zion Chapel in 1900 when, after 25 years of financial aid from the Ontario Cooperation, it was able to pay its own way. The Salvation Army, residing since New Year's Day 1885 in barracks at the corner of Paisley and Dublin streets, was described in the *Guelph Weekly Mercury* as a "new force in religious life." With a combination of faith and good works, it supplied basic help and comfort to those not under the aegis of other institutions. Salvation Army women, too, worked equally with the men. The Canadian Commander from 1895 to 1904 was Evangeline Booth, second daughter of William Booth, the army's founder. The British Methodist Episcopal (BME) Church on Essex Street was the centre of Guelph's black community, a lively church where, about this time, the first BME conference in Ontario was held.

The Salvation Army Band marching through St. George's Square, 1912.
Source: Guelph Museums from a photograph in the Salvation Army Heritage Centre, Toronto

Small groups met in homes or halls. Lutherans held services in Templar's Hall, the Mennonite Mission Hall was on Gordon Street, and the Brethren, in Guelph since the mid-19th century, worshiped in a hall on Waterloo Avenue. Known then as Quakers and later as Plymouth Brethren, they held annual general conferences on Arthur Wells' property south of the River Speed, off Edinburgh Road. Bible students came from other parts of Canada, the United States and England. In 1900, the Brethren consisted of a small exclusive group, mostly members of one family, who gathered to break bread and worship in a lodge hall above the Royal Bank on Wyndham Street. The Christadelphians met in a room over the bank of Nova Scotia. The First Church of Christ Scientist was held at Mrs. Wickham's residence on Woolwich Street and the Second over the rear of the Dominion Bank. The two Hebrew families had not enough male members to form a *minyan*. For the first Hebrew marriage of Charles Freeman and Bella Zecilman on May 9, 1901, a rabbi was brought to town.

Knox's Home Mission Sunday School had met since 1889 in St. Patrick's Ward School. It was now held in a new building at the corner of Toronto and Short streets, known as Knox Church Branch Sunday School. The Congregational Mission to Brooklyn, organized in 1887 in an area between the city and college hill, had moved several times but, by 1901, was held in a house on Brick Terrace off Martin Avenue. When Anglicans realized a "certain leakage going on in Brooklyn, due to the distance of both Anglican churches and the nearness of other

[Sunday] schools, a Church of England Sunday School was opened in Brooklyn under the auspices of St. George's and St. James." Another Anglican mission was established at Watson's schoolhouse and one at Farnham, which was bodily moved to Arkell village in 1901. A Beulah Mission was operating at 144 Quebec St. Although not recorded in the census, a small group of International Bible Students was meeting and delivering Bible Tracts to individual homes.

Protestant churches, in general, held Sunday services at 11 a.m. and 7 p.m. with Sunday school at 3 p.m. Norfolk Methodist held Bible classes before and after the Sunday morning service and Tuesday evenings, with a prayer meeting Wednesday. Pews were still allotted to families of the Protestant congregations. In most churches pew rents were charged. Although Chalmers Presbyterian added "Seats Free" to their newspaper advertisements, a weekly donation to the 'sustentation fund' was required from regular members. Strangers and the poor were welcomed in all churches, but were required to sit at the side or the back. The precentor was gone from the Presbyterian churches and they, like other large congregations, had certain types of organs, full choirs and resourceful choir directors. Concerts with choirs, soloists, musicians and elocutionists were regularly performed at celebrations, annual dinners and fundraising events. Church choir members were the mainstay of choral societies and the musicians were part of the city's small orchestras and bands. When Charles Kelly directed the *Feast of Belshazzar* at Knox Presbyterian on December 6, 1901, he united singers and soloists from most of the churches in town. The Salvation Army Band also contributed regularly to community events. Conductor Captain Keeler added special interest to regular concerts by playing, in addition to the cornet, guitar and mandolin, a musical selection from a salmon tin.

Missionary auxiliaries, mission circles, leagues and mission bands of women and youths met weekly to raise funds for home and overseas missions and for spiritual benefit and entertainment. The Methodist's Epworth League, named after John Wesley's hometown in Lincolnshire, was originally a group of young men dedicated to Christian works, who met Saturday nights for Bible study, lectures and literary evenings. By 1902, women were permitted to join. They pledged to visit the sick, cheer the lonely and be friendly to strangers. Temperance groups and supporters of the Lord's Day Alliance held regular meetings. A Twentieth Century Fund was a popular way of raising money. At Norfolk, $3,500 was raised in 1900 to relieve the church debt and apply to renovations already underway. A New-Century Young Women's Auxiliary was formed at Knox as part of the 'forward movement' in the Presbyterian church. The Girls' Friendly Society at St. James had been in operation for a number of years, and the Brotherhood of St. Andrews was an equivalent society for young men. Most churches also had a young people's organization that was, like those at St. James, inventive in planning programs of "musical recitals, orations, games, sports, plays, debates, slide shows, socials and sleigh rides." The dramatic group from Paisley Methodist, the Paisley Players, travelled the countryside to churches and schools within horse-and-buggy driving distance of Guelph. After a rough trip, they often had to improvise a stage.

Selected Sunday sermons were presented almost verbatim in the Monday newspaper. Topical subjects were popular. Readings from the Christian Science pulpit on February 10, 1900, were on "Mind," and that evening Congregational minister W. J. Hindley spoke on "The Dual Personality," with slides illustrating Stevenson's *Doctor Jekyll and Mr. Hyde*. They frequently dealt with contentious issues, provoking letters to the *Mercury*, or editorial rebuttals. The Rev. Hindley believed the pulpit should legitimately influence every condition of public and private life with a view to remedying abuses and mapping outlines of reform. In a sermon reported on May 4, 1902, no aspect of Guelph life escaped examination. He was particularly disturbed about the discipline at the collegiate where "boys had to be so severely flogged that they bore the marks on their hands for days." Principal Davison objected, the press questioned, but Hindley stood his ground.

He also claimed that churches were "too conservative for the spirit of the 20th century, too idealistic and other-worldly and not sufficiently concerned with things that are," and that they should "catch the spirit of union."

A feeling of co-operation among churches certainly existed. The second week of January 1900 was declared a week of prayer, an event that continued throughout the century. Combined services were held each evening in a different church with excellent attendance, even on stormy nights. By 1902, every Protestant minister belonged to the Ministerial Association in Guelph, although not all attended regularly. The Church of Our Lady was invited, but declined.

Church unity, however, was different from church union. The formation of the United Church of Canada began with the request of the Home Mission Committee to the General Assembly of the Presbyterian Church that a committee be appointed to find a way to prevent rivalry and unnecessary waste of ways and means in the mission work to newer districts of the country. The Methodist Church appointed a similar committee, and the two worked together to find an answer. In 1902, at the General Conference of the Methodist Church in Winnipeg, a proposal was put forward for the organic union of the Presbyterian, Methodist and Congregational churches in Canada. Discussions followed throughout the country. Session minutes of a meeting at Knox Presbyterian in Guelph reported that "the elders showed little enthusiasm for it." A general meeting about church union was held in the city on January 26, 1906. Although the *Mercury* the next day affirmed "some hesitation among Guelph Presbyterians," the article continued, "On the whole, the evidence of the leading ministers and laymen goes strongly in favor." As soon as the problem was fully understood, it concluded, "little opposition would be heard from the solid old stock in Guelph." Lt. -Col. David McCrae, an elder in St. Andrew's and a member of the Presbyterian Home Mission Board, made it clear, however, that "he was orthodox in his opinions and would stick to them union or no union." But he did see many advantages to the new proposals in newly-settled districts and the mission fields, where it would contribute to making the "best type of Canadians."

Guelph's Roman Catholic community was served by members of three religious orders: the Society of Jesus (Jesuits) in charge of the Church of Our Lady Immaculate and its parish; the religious of the Society of the Blessed Virgin, known as the Loretto Sisters, who operated the Catholic schools; and the Sisters of St. Joseph of the Diocese of Hamilton, founders of St. Joseph's Hospital and the House of Providence, later to become the Home for the Aged. Sunday Mass was held at 7, 8 and 10:30 a.m. and 7:30 in the evening, with Sunday school at 3 p.m. On weekdays, Guelph's Catholics climbed the hill for mass at 7:30 a.m. and on holidays at 6 or 10 a.m. Like all churches in Guelph, it was a centre of music, drama and social life.

Latent Protestant prejudices against the Catholic minority sometimes flared into verbal assaults. When a guest preacher at Knox Presbyterian coupled praise for the Loyal Orange Association and the Protestant Protective Association with a severe attack on the Roman Catholic Church, he was condemned in an editorial for narrowness and want of tolerance and Christian spirit. Guelph's Orangemen usually travelled to other cities to celebrate the 12th of July. Their first big parade of the century in Guelph (1906) was reported to be a record breaker in visitors (3,000 by train) and length of parade (led by the Guelph Musical Society (GMS) Band and the Mohawk Reserve Band). Thousands lined the streets with a crowd of 2,500 in Exhibition Park. Speeches were long and historical, but concilia-tory in nature. The Loyal Orange Order aimed to make all men equal, subject to the same laws and enjoying the same freedom. They desired to live in peace with all their fellow citizens. "It was one of the most enjoyable days ever provided for the citizens' entertainment and education," wrote the *Mercury*. "There were no drunks, no fights and no unseemly disturbances."

While a few disturbances might have been expected, other forms of prejudice were less obvious. On April 10, 1908, the *Mercury* headlined an article, "Little Italy on a Tour," when a small Italian child was reported lost. The minstrel show was accepted as an art in a society so secure in its superiority. The Lord's Day Act made no provision for a Jewish Sabbath, and when police visited the establishment of Charles Freeman and found four men sorting rags on a Sunday, the law prevailed, and a charge was laid the next day.

EDUCATION

Three schools shared Catholic Hill with the Church of Our Lady. Loretto Convent, a day and boarding school for girls of all ages, was the only educational institution for ladies west of Toronto. By 1900, regular certificate courses were being taught. With special attention paid to the refinements of a convent education, it had achieved an excellent reputation in music and art. An elementary boys' school, St. Stanislaus, sat on one side of the church and an elementary girls' school, St. Agnes, on the other. The girls were not allowed to walk home past the boys' school. If they lived on that side of town, they had to go the long way around. The sisters of

Guelph students receive instruction in the early part of the century.　　Source: Guelph Historical Society

St. Joseph established a school for nurses at St. Joseph's Hospital in 1900. Nine student nurses were taught six subjects by six doctors during a two-year course. The following year, a third year was added and, in 1904, lay pupils were accepted.

Sharing the skyline with the Church of Our Lady were Central School, Guelph's first senior public school and, nearby on Dublin Street, a two-roomed stone building known as the Senior Girls Public School that, at the time, housed Guelph's first kindergarten. Central boasted 16 rooms, including three in the basement, half underground with poor ventilation and lighting. Classes were taught from Junior I to Senior IV (Grades 1 to 8), as well as a two-year commercial course. It was the first in Ontario, possibly in Canada, to have physical training, although this was strictly of a military nature, consisting of bar-bell and rifle exercises, drills, marching and Indian club-swinging. In charge was Captain Clarke, a previous instructor in the gunnery school at Kingston's Royal Military College. Employed by the public school board since 1882, he had proven himself a master of his art as well as a stylish showman. He founded Guelph's first school cadet corps, including a junior cadet corps and a band at Central, and a group of 120 boys at the Guelph Collegiate Institute (GCI) as the Highland Cadets. They were uniformed in regulation Highland costume, purchased in Glasgow. His corps of 100 girls, known as Daughters of the Regiment, wore scarlet skirts trimmed with six rows of yellow braid, blue tunics with hussar braids and epaulets, and French caps with plumes. Through his 'entertainments,' in the Guelph area and in major cities in Ontario, he raised money for equipment, students' costumes and, among other things, for the complete construction of the gymnasium at the high school, thus raising it to collegiate status.

Five other elementary schools served Guelph's ward areas: St. George's, teaching Senior I to Senior III, St. Patrick's, St. John's, St. David's, St. James and Victoria, a one-roomed school in Brooklyn, all teaching Junior I to Senior II. Weekly examinations were held in the higher classes and weekly reports sent to the parents. Promotion to the next year, however, depended on the teacher's recommendation. Pupils were required to pass an entrance examination to high school at the end of June. In 1900, 117 candidates presented themselves, and 98 were successful. Two hundred and thirty-one pupils were registered at GCI that year, with an average attendance of 148. Only a very small portion of children proceeded to secondary education. They were needed either to help at home or to earn extra income for the family.

Guelph's collegiate building, completed in 1879, remained essentially the same in 1900. Steam heating had replaced the fireplaces, but a pump near the east door still furnished the only drinking water, and a high fence separated a line of outdoor privies from the main building. That a tradition of academic excellence had already been established is illustrated by the report that the recovery of Ladysmith was announced on the blackboards in English, French, Latin and German. The curriculum also included Greek, English grammar and rhetoric, English composition, poetical literature, supplementary reading in English literature, Canadian, English, and ancient history, geography, arithmetic and mensuration, algebra, geometry, trigonometry, physics, chemistry, botany, zoology, writing, book-keeping, drawing, drill, calisthenics, gymnastics and stenography. It had been broadened enough to prepare some pupils for the work force, but other than producing a well-educated citizen, it mainly led to teacher training or the university's traditional professions.

Innovations in music and art depended on the initiatives of individual boards. In 1900, Prof. Charles Kelly was appointed instructor of vocal music. His success was evident in the robust choruses and vocal numbers presented at the annual commencement exercises at the Royal Opera House from 1900 to 1914. His daughter, Hattie Kelly, an accomplished musician and teacher, provided piano accompaniment and arranged music for the choruses. Programs regularly concluded with one of her medleys. Although music was not listed in the GCI curriculum, two persons were recorded in the annual report of 1902 as having matriculated in the subject. A concert was also presented at the annual Conversatione. The advertisement of 1900 announced to GCI ex-pupils:

Assembling at 8; Concert at 8:30; Conversazione at 10; Dancing at 11. It has formerly been assumed that a conversat allowed only promenading, but GCI was more advanced than the Ontario Agricultural College, where the tradition was strictly held when it started in 1904. In keeping with a philosophy of a healthy body and mind, sports programs were organized at GCI, particularly in soccer and football. Games were mostly inter-school, but sometimes against a school from out of town. As with the public schools, gymnastics were of a military nature, directed by Captain Clarke.

Neither adult education nor special education were key words at the beginning of the century. The public school board had made several attempts, and the Loretto Sisters had operated a night school for a while in the 1880s for students unable to attend classes because of daytime employment. But Malcolm MacCormick's Guelph Business College, founded in 1885, continued to thrive. As explained in his *Annual Circular*, courses were open to girls and boys over 14, and were "advantageous to middle-aged men." *Integrity, Intelligence and Industry* was its motto. Situated on "Upper Wyndham Street in the centre of the finest block," it occupied 10 large rooms, including a main hall and a gymnasium. Room and board were arranged in town for the students at $2.50 to $3.00 a week, and they were expected to attend divine service at least once every Sunday. The comprehensive commercial program included French, "a language of evident utility if not an imperative duty," and instruction by the ubiquitous Captain Clarke in physical training, "the value of which, as an accompaniment to mental training, is now everywhere recognized." The college also had a football club. A Scottish vocalist was on staff, teaching piano, violin and voice culture, and a medical doctor lectured on anatomy, physiology and sanitary science. The pastor of Guelph's St.

Several stores in Guelph sold books in 1900, but not exclusively. Some were stationers. Day's Book Store had a lively trade in ice-hockey equipment. Chas. L. Nelles' Big Book Store sold wallpaper and baby carriages. The World Publishing Company was established at 1 Douglas St. with J. W. Lyon as proprietor. The books, with ponderous titles and sub-titles, covered a wide range of topical subjects in 500 to 900 pages and were distributed 'world-wide.' Queen Victoria (1901) with 709 pages in three sections, included one of her journals. This might have been a sensational acquisition, but to the modern reader, it would appear wordy and non-eventful. *The Story of Africa* (1901), with a sub-title of eight lines, was criticized because an American had been hired to write the section on Canadians in Africa. Citizens also enjoyed the benefits of the Free Public Library. Guelph had been the first city in Ontario to take advantage of the province's Public Libraries Act and, in 1900, books could be found upstairs in the Masonic Block on Wyndham Street.

Andrew's Presbyterian Church was professor of political economy, and the president of the Law Society of Guelph instructed in commercial law. Another business establishment, the Royal City Business College, affiliated with Hamilton, Galt and Berlin, occupied rooms in the Traders' Bank building. It claimed to give special attention to "backward pupils," an early innovation.

Although the board of education's earlier ventures into evening classes for adults had been discontinued due to lack of interest, education was a prominent term in the philosophy of the churches and in everyday life. The newspapers also assumed a high degree of literacy on the part of their readers. Articles on foreign news, particularly British, were thorough and extensive. In January 1901, when the empire was saddened by the death of Queen Victoria, the *Mercury* devoted several pages of black-lined columns to details of her life and family, as well as a comprehensive history of world events during her reign. Local topics were reported in detail. All ranks of citizens in town or country discussed them.

The relationship between the city and the agricultural college was one of varied mutual benefit, with interchange on several levels. Agricultural advantages to the city were, of course, immense, and affected both cultural and commercial life. The Central Exhibition, Winter Fairs and annual meetings of the

The ladies experiment, possibly in preparation for Ladies' Day. Source: Liz Gray Collection

'Ladies' Days' were enjoyable occasions when large numbers went up to the college on streetcars, operated partially by ladies of the town. The event occurred twice during the summer, once for the benefit of the General Hospital and once for St. Joseph's. Through the generosity of George Sleeman, all fares on the trolleys that day were donated to the hospital concerned. "The ladies, for sweet charity's sake," wrote the *Mercury* in 1901, "are occupying the street-car platforms today, while the regular motormen and conductors are letting the cars run wild in an honest attempt to entertain their fair assistants and take care of the cars at the same time." There was some censure of the Protestant ladies for being reluctant to give change. High tea was served in the college gymnasium to the music of Thain's orchestra, and a baseball match between city council and school boards was featured in the afternoon. In the evening of August 22, 1901, a tug-of-war took place between the city team and the Cobb dairy. Between each of the three pulls, the crowd retired to the gym for refreshments. Not everything was perfect. "Some contestants," reported the *Evening Mercury*, "showed more control over their muscles than their tempers." And the City Band (GMS Band), on hand nearby, found the one gasoline lamp, erected for the reading of music, "totally inadequate."

Fat Stock Club brought thousands of people to the city for several days. The Central Exhibition provided opportunities for city artisans to exhibit their crafts and to compete with others from Ontario. Information concerning food and gardening was always available. College professors attended city churches and were influential in civic affairs and educational decision-making. Furthermore, the advent of the Guelph Street Railway in 1895 had made special events at the college more accessible to "our city friends," as they were frequently called in the *O.A.C. Review.*

Members of the public and of the collegiate's literary society were invited to OAC's Literary Society meetings and debates. Judges for their annual oratorical contest often came from the city, as did musicians to provide the customary musical interludes. The Crowes, the Kellys and Maud Stevenson appeared regularly. Lady friends from the city attended the Hallowe'en Costume Ball, the 'Conversazione,' 'At Homes' and other celebrations. Annual indoor sports events attracted large numbers from the city. The program in the gymnasium at the end of March 1903 interspersed boxing and wrestling bouts, fencing, parallel bars, tumbling, sabre exercises, and the presentation of medals with musical performances. Two comic songs by Guelph's American ambassador, the Hon. Mr. Daly, were particularly popular.

Guelph sports teams found eager rivals in the college's football, soccer, baseball, cricket and hockey clubs. Road racing was a crowd favourite, with the OAC's one-miler E. C. Hallman, who broke the inter-varsity record (1902), held in high esteem. Students were regularly entertained by young peoples' groups of the city churches. On November 1, about 80 college boys formed in line and marched into town, "disturbing the domestic peace of the citizens with their yells and songs," to attend the Speed Canoe Club concert. They apparently added to the spirit of the evening and the concert was enjoyed by all. A few days later on election night, however, when about 120 students paraded into town carrying torches and horns, they were attacked with mud and stones by a "crowd of ruffians." The college boys seemed to have won their point and, after watching the election results at the bulletin of the *Guelph Herald*, returned to the college, muddy, but again in good spirits.

Because the college was dedicated to the practical over the theoretical, it was to have considerable influence over Guelph's educational system. At the 25th anniversary in 1899, President Mills spoke of an "agricultural discipline, unadulterated by association with university disciplines, that must be kept practical, with emphasis on manual labour." He also advocated education for rural women on the "bread and butter side of life." Adelaide Hoodless must have impressed him when, in a speech at Guelph in 1896, she called for the creation of a department of domestic economy at OAC. By 1900, she had established the Ontario Normal School of Domestic Science and Art in Hamilton, where, she claimed, nothing was taught that was not practical. Her common aim with President Mills was "to improve education in what was commonly defined as the feminine sphere in the home and on the farm." In early January, the *Mercury* reported an "Institute" meeting between members of the college, the Guelph Board of Education and interested citizens. A Mrs. Kinney delivered a lecture on domestic science in which she claimed the subject would "bring the riches of science into the household to upbuild and dignify home life and place home-making on a level with other

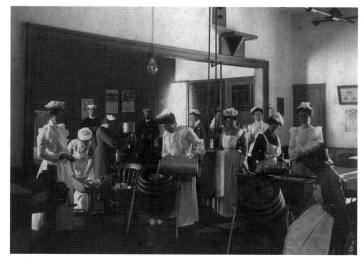

The Dairy Class at OAC, 1904. Before the establishment of Macdonald Institute, the short dairy course was the only one open to women.
Source: Guelph Museums

professions." Dr. Mills agreed, saying he had more letters in the last nine months than in 15 years from daughters of farmers wanting to go to college to learn domestic science. "It is safe to predict," wrote Guelph Public School Inspector Torrance in his end-of-the-year report, "that, ere long, many cities and towns in the province will make a beginning in this direction."

It was providential that the aims of tobacco philanthropist Sir William Macdonald coincided with those of Mills and Hoodless: to improve the living standard in rural Canada and to build schools that provided instruction in practical subjects. That he was aided in the allotment and distribution of funds by former OAC professor of dairy science, Dr. J. W. Robertson, was an additional benefit. Mills, having failed to secure a women's department at OAC, now enlisted Hoodless and Robertson in his cause. Hoodless, who had obtained support from the Department of Education, met Macdonald in October 1901, and from that meeting emerged a "concept for a unique educational institution intended to stand in the forefront of Canadian educational reform." In 1902,

Illustration of the Difference in Form of Man and Woman from *A Complete Medical Guide for Women* by Mary R. Melendy MD, PhD., published by the World Publishing Co., Guelph, Ontario, 1901. "Men may rule the race, but women govern its destiny," confirmed the publisher in his preface.
Source: Guelph Museums

Adelaide Hoodless was a prime example of a paradox. She had freed herself from the very life for women that she advocated. She had carved a career outside her home, seeking to better the lives of women by practical education, but had no message for women who sought careers in other fields. Journalists' attitudes were just as ambiguous. That they mention girls as well as boys blasting horns, or women as well as men serving in the war indicates an acceptance and even a certain pride that the opposite sex was capable of contributing to society in new and commendable ways. An advertisement for Doan's Kidney Pills (*Daily Herald*, February 10, 1900) seemed, in a back-handed way, to acknowledge some women's rights unthought of before. "Why shouldn't a woman enjoy life?" it asked. "Why shouldn't she be strong and vigorous as an all-wise Providence intended?" Rather oddly, the healthy woman in the ad carried a rifle

over her shoulder. An ad for Paine's Celery Compound in the *Guelph Mercury and Advertiser* of the same date claimed in headlines that the remedy "Bestows on women what they most require – Full Nervous Energy and Rich, Nourishing Blood!" In other words, they should be healthy for raising children.

Women may have been slowly forging their way into areas of public life, but the general cultural view placed them in the home. In the preface of *Perfect Womanhood for Maidens, Wives, Mothers: A Book giving Full Information on all the Mysterious and Complex Matters Pertaining to Womanhood: A Complete Medical Guide for Women,* published by Guelph's World Publishing Company, they would have read, "While we admire her in her new role, with her efforts towards success in society, literature, science, politics, and the arts, we must not lose sight of her divine and sublime mission in life – womanhood and motherhood." The author, Mary R. Melendy (MD. PhD. of Rush Medical College, Chicago) was firm in her introduction to her 556 pages of medical advice: "Childbearing and rearing should be a woman's chiefest study, as well as her crowning joy." With such romanticizing of motherhood, a discussion of birth control was naturally not included. It was not a subject discussed, even in families. Information was scarce and inadequate. Whatever was practised in private, the general rule accepted by Christians was abstinence and silence. As a result, women were uninformed and families large.

Sir William gave $125,000 for the building of an educational facility and a women's residence. The objectives of the new institution were to train teachers for rural schools and provide instruction and training for farmers' daughters and others in household science. One-year courses as well as summer courses were to be offered in manual training, nature study and home economics. In February 1904, the *O.A.C. Review* reported, "Arrangements are almost completed whereby senior classes from the Guelph public schools will receive afternoon lessons in domestic science in the Institute. Their instructors will be senior Normal teachers-in-training, assisted by the regular staff." This "will no doubt lead to a permanent department of Domestic Science in our city schools."

Outside the home, church work was an acceptable area for women's work, but one seldom acknowledged in print. The ladies of the First Baptist Church quietly worked for years in many capacities with only vague references to a Ladies Aid in the annual report. When, in 1899, they efficiently raised funds to pay off a note and donated a healthy surplus to the finance committee, they were asked to "reform" the Ladies' Aid and take over the responsibility for the interest on the church's debt. Hospitals were another respectable area for women's work. The Women's Hospital Aid at the General Hospital was formed in 1897. Members canvassed the city for money and materials to make sheets, pillow cases, doctor's gowns and other needed items. The sisters at St. Joseph's Hospital had always relied on an enthusiastic group of women for help and support, but it was 1935 before a formal ladies auxiliary was organized. The founding of the Ontario Women's Institutes, inspired by Adelaide Hoodless's Stoney Creek speech in 1897 and firmly established by OAC President Creelman, marked the beginning of continuing education for Canadian women. Although this was specifically attuned to rural women, the progressive ideas would have been well noted by their city friends.

FRATERNAL ORDERS AND SERVICE ORGANIZATIONS

Community services were few in 1900, but Guelph branches of 19th-century voluntary organizations still fulfilled important needs in the community. These were, in many ways, extensions of church activities. The St. George's, St. Andrew's, St. Patrick's and St. Vincent De Paul societies raised money for the benefit of the poor and needy, mainly those of their own religious affiliation and background. The fraternal orders, with their special form of spiritual mystery and benevolence for members, provided cheap life insurance, funeral aid and relief for widows and orphans. The City Directory of 1901-03 listed six Masonic Lodges; three

Independent Orders of Odd Fellows; one Canadian Order of Odd Fellows, and the Daughters of Rebecca (the only women's branch of a male order existent at the time); two Ancient Orders of Workmen; one Ancient Order, two Independent Orders, and two Canadian Orders of Foresters; three Canadian Orders of Chosen Friends; a Knights of the Maccabees of the World (KOTM); a Royal Arcanum, a Home Circle; a Woodmen of the World, one Catholic and one Protestant Temperance Society; a Catholic Union and a Guelph branch of the Catholic Mutual Benefit Association (CMBA). Some were unlisted, the Orange Lodge, for example, and the labour unions. Under the umbrella of the Trades and Labor Council, the unions were the benefit societies of the working class. They provided insurance at a low cost, raised funds for impoverished families and strove for better wages, housing and working conditions. The first Labour Day Parade took place in 1902.

The YMCA, started in Guelph in 1886 and meeting on Upper Wyndham Street, was essentially a Christian social club. A 'Prayer and Praise' service was held Sunday, 9:30 to 10:30 a.m., Bible Class Tuesday evenings, and Gospel meetings every Saturday night. Reading and recreation rooms were supplied with newspapers and social games. The elite men's club, the Priory Club of Guelph Ltd., occupied a club house at 18 Douglas St., furnished with a billiard table and a bar with wine and spirits. It was open from 9 a.m. to midnight every day except Sundays, when it opened after church at noon. Politics and religious questions of every kind were positively excluded from discussion.

As Leo Johnson observed in the *History of Guelph, 1827-1927*, social initiative had shifted from the individual to the organization and from spontaneous to planned action by the middle of the 19th century. But, at the beginning of the 20th, many areas still required the inspiration of one or more persons before they could be developed. Absalom Shade Allan, Sheriff of Wellington County in 1901, helped draft the original Children's Protection Act (1893) when he was Liberal Member for West Wellington. Col. Nathaniel Higinbotham was instrumental that year in the organization of the Guelph Humane Society, one of the oldest in Canada. Its mandate then, as in 1900, was for the welfare and well-being of children and animals, and it sought adoptive parents for orphaned children. A branch of the Canadian Red Cross was organized in January 1900, presumably by Mrs. Stephen Lett, a woman active in community life and in missionary activities at St. George's Church. Within a few days, they raised $500. This was matched by City Hall, and a large portion was dispersed to families of men fighting in South Africa. A Grand Patriotic Concert with Military Tableaux was presented in February to raise money

Four Children for Adoption.

THE Guelph Humane and Children's Aid Society have for adoption 3 boys, aged 8, 8 and 9 years. Also, wanted a Roman Catholic home for a boy 3 years old.

Further information may be obtained by calling at the Society's Shelter, Waterloo Ave. All correspondence to be addressed to J. SHARP, Sec. Guelph Humane Society, Guelph.

Four children for adoption: The Guelph Humane and Children's Aid Society.
Source: *Guelph Weekly Mercury,* May 17, 1900

for Red Cross hospital supplies. Other health organizations were rare, although the Guelph Association for the Treatment and Prevention of Tuberculosis met regularly.

The cultivation of gardens, conservation and civic improvement received earlier organized attention than destitute animals and children. The Guelph Horticultural Society was originally formed in 1851. An early function was to plant shade trees on Waterloo Avenue. For every surviving tree, city council paid the society 25 cents. As a result, maple or elm trees eventually shaded all the streets in the city. Members then devoted time to their private gardens. In 1900, a reorganized society, with James Goldie as president, clearly defined its aims for the 20th century: to promote the love of horticulture and to educate the citizens to beautify their homes and the city. In 1901, they repaired and beautified Trafalgar Square, only to have pedestrians trample two paths across it. Closely allied with the Horticultural Society was the Field Naturalists Club, founded in 1900, to further biological research in Ontario. Its journal, *The Ontario Natural Science Bulletin,* an annual devoted to the flora and fauna of Ontario, was published in Guelph. Members conscientiously added metal identification tags to trees in the city parks and installed bird-feeding stations.

SPORTS AND LEISURE

Long before most sports clubs were organized, Guelphites skated, played hockey, curled on the river, and slid down hills on sleds or icy trouser seats. In warmer weather, they played with ball and bats, raced, ran and swam. The river belonged to everyone and so did the grass. It was so in 1900. Those who could not afford fees for a specific club, or those too young to work, found the river and quarries for

swimming in summer and for ice games in winter. Open places were plentiful for impromptu baseball and soccer games. Factory and Sunday school picnics, sports days and fairs were held on Exhibition Park's 35 acres, then entirely enclosed by a high board fence. The park's unique octagonal building was used for exhibitions and concerts. Large areas at the OAC were also favourite places for summer pastimes. Coffee's Field, named after a friend and employee of J. W. Lyon, and Idylwyld Park are also mentioned in newspaper reports. The Turf Club exercised horses on the race track at Exhibition Park, or out of town at Hood's farm.

The Guelph Road Race Association (1895) sponsored a major athletic event – the five-mile Thanksgiving Day race to Arkell and back. Runners were cheered in the city streets by spectators and accompanied through the fields by members of the Guelph Hunt Club on horseback. In May 1901, organizers, already working on that year's event, warned that the courses would be extended and anyone wishing to take part would be wise to start practising at once. The Queen's Birthday Games were held on May 24th on the Petrie grounds by the cadets and pupils of the public schools. That a healthy competition existed between various sections of society was evident in the popularity of the time-honoured tug-of-war. The flour, feed and seeds salesmen and drivers challenged any other line of salesman and drivers in the city to a tug of war at the Salesmen Association Picnic in July 1901. Inter-city teams played on OAC grounds at Ladies' Days and the Guelph Central Fairs. "This is for Blood," ran the headline announcing a tug to be held on the Maple Leafs grounds to settle old disputes between the Puslinch and Guelph teams. Proceeds from the 10-cent entrance fee were shared between Guelph's two hospitals.

Guelph druggist A.B. Petrie had built the Petrie Athletic Park on Gordon Street at Wellington in 1898. The provincial cycle races were held there in 1899, and the park soon featured a large range of events, skating carnivals, ice-shows and hockey games. It also offered an indoor bathing pool, gymnasium, tennis courts and a bowling green. On the night of February 28, 1900, the gymnasium was converted into an elegant ballroom for the assembly of the Victoria-OAC Hockey Club. Thain's orchestra played on the encircling balcony, and, after a break at midnight when the 175 invited guests were served supper, continued until two in

 August 30, 1934 – Harold Webster, formerly of the Royal City and winner of a marathon at the British Empire Games in July, returns to Guelph. He started his track career in Guelph in 1923 and on March 15, 1926 broke the record for the three-mile race.

Boys swimming at Pipe's Mill Dam, later Riverside Park, c. 1910. J.W.Lyon wrote to the *Mercury* in October 1904, that he and the other directors of the Guelph Radial Railway had made offers on two properties fronting about 1/4 mile on the Speed River, an ideal spot for boating, bathing, sports, a bandstand and games and amusements.

Source: J. Keleher Collection and Ross Irwin

Oh, But Did You See the Game?

Two hockey teams led by President Bob Dowler and Vice-President Greg Franks of the Young Conservative Association came together last night at the Petrie Rink with a crash. Neither team scored the first half and it required ten minutes of overtime to break the tie of 2-2.

To say the least, the game was of a very bloodthirsty nature. It was rumoured that Mr. Dowler gave the game to his opponent out of pure sympathy for the latter's face which had been badly battered and required a half pound of beef to take down the swelling. Greg Franks' and Will Conway's rushes were marvellous and it required the full strength of the end of the rink to stop them. Johnny Franks was ruled off twice for injuring the ice. He kicked up his feet at intervals of two minutes. The referee was obliged to rule no less than 15 off the ice during the game. After the game both teams limped to the Wellington and enjoyed a sumptuous oyster supper, after which they were entertained in the parlour by a couple of boarders.

The Guelph Advocate, February 23, 1900

the morning. More characteristic of the general population was the less pompous affair reported in the *Guelph Advocate* on March 1: "Last night Bond's hockey team went up against the men in Mrs. Gibson's boarding house, and as a result, had a big hole punctured in their reputation – being defeated by 5 to 0."

A war between the Anglican and Presbyterian teams provided a lively

summer for cricket fans in 1901. On Dominion Day, doctors of the town took on the lawyers – "a highly successful operation for the sawbones," reported the *Mercury*. Baseball, too, was being played by all walks of life. The tailors challenged the barbers, the Yorkroaders took on the Brewery Hustlers (in Coffee's Field), and the boarders of the City Hotel contested the inhabitants of the Commercial Hotel. Guelph's Maple Leafs baseball team, having reached heights of fame in the 19th century, was having difficulties living up to its reputation. Jimmie Cockman was one of a few Canadians to play in the major leagues in the United States and in Toronto (1896-1912).

The Union Curling Club, organized in 1836 after an influx of Scottish immigrants, was a founding member of the Ontario Curling Association. By 1888, the Royal City Club had come into existence with George Sleeman as president. He chaired the building committee for the construction of the Victoria Rink at the corner of Baker Street and Chapel Lane in 1892 and became the founding president of the Guelph Curling and Skating Rink Company. In 1900, the two teams resisted amalgamation and maintained what was termed a friendly rivalry.

Rivalry existed among Guelph's hockey teams, too. It wasn't until 1897 that a local club, the Victorias, first played in the Ontario Hockey Association. They made the semi-finals in the junior series. A second team, the Nationals, reached the intermediate finals in 1899, but were later suspended for 'professionalism.' A third club, the Wellingtons, emerged in 1900, making lively competition for the newly-allied Victoria-OAC Hockey Club. In 1902, the Wellingtons won the city championship. The Shamrocks' Lacrosse Club played in a junior circuit that included Galt, Preston, Berlin, Hespeler and Elora in 1900. Guelph and Elora invariably reached the finals and fought a battle royal for the winning prize. Soccer continued to be popular, with city, college and collegiate clubs reaching various championships. The Guelph National team, formed in 1902 of Guelph businessmen, played successfully for a few years until its members moved to other clubs. A church hockey league was organized at a meeting at Chalmers Presbyterian Church in December 1905, with Methodists, Presbyterians, Anglicans and Baptists participating. This league and a factory league kept hockey alive

 January 25, 1933 – Four lawn bowlers from Guelph are representatives in a tournament in St. Petersburg, Florida. It's the first time a local team goes to an international tournament.

 1929 – Oral Duffy of Guelph becomes the North American Speed Skating Champion in the under-14 category.

until the Guelph Lyons and the Taylor Forbes Company teams were formed in 1909 and 1910.

The Guelph Lawn Bowling Club on the Baker Street Greens was well established by 1900. In 1904, George Chapman won the Novice Singles Championship of Canada. In 1908, after playing a week-long contest with George Creelman to win the doubles honours at Woodbine, he won the Dominion Singles. The Guelph club won the Seagram Trophy that year and many other awards between 1910 and 1915. Golf received little attention. "People began to play golf in Guelph, spasmodically, about the beginning of the century," recorded the *Mercury's Centennial Edition*. "An apology for a course was more or less laid down near the rifle ranges."

The City Tennis Club (1892) made a home on courts on the old Maple Leaf grounds and in the Goldie property on Cardigan Street. The club was mainly of a social nature, with inter-club tournaments. The Rifle Association was set up in 1901, under instruction from the Department of Militia and Defence, to encourage young men of the city to learn the practical use of the rifle. The ranges, laid out on the Howitt farm on Waterloo Avenue, were convenient for students at OAC and the collegiate. The Guelph Off-Hand Rifle Club and the Guelph Driving and Hunt Club were in existence. The Royal Billiard Parlour held regular tournaments.

The Speed Canoe Club was a flourishing organization with about 240 members and 60 canoes during its fleeting existence from 1895 to 1902. It met every Thursday evening at Johnson's boathouse, and members canoed a mile and a half up river to Victoria Park to be entertained by musically-talented members, or special guests from the city. Edward Johnson, Professor Kelly and his sister Hattie were frequent performers. Returning at midnight, they formed an armada, locking arms and canoes together with only the persons at the rear paddling, and singing lustily until they reached the boathouse. In winter, they held dances at the City Hall and meetings in a room at the Victoria Ice Rink. The club also conducted aquatic sports in the OAC outdoor tank when it was first built, and, in 1902, produced *HMS Pinafore* at the Royal Opera House. With local talent, it ran successfully for four nights.

ENTERTAINMENT AND LEISURE

Choral and orchestral concert reviews in the *Mercury* often began: "In musical and

The Guelph Musical Society Band, 1907. Joseph Dawson, conductor, first row third from the left, with prominent city officials in the foreground.

Source: J. Keleher Collection

social circles..." implying a certain refinement to arts. A brass band though, popular for all events, was military in nature, uniformed, male and athletic. Although enjoyed at leisure by all social circles, it was not always pleasure for the bandsmen. Band musicians were office or factory workers who often played in several groups in their spare time. The City Band and the 30th Battalion Band, both conducted by Wyatt Trendall, consisted mainly of the same musicians. A bandsman was paid about a dollar a night, but worked free for civic events and charitable causes. Drummer Arthur H. Parker recorded in his diary that when he played for the Kleopfer Employees' Annual Excursion to Hamilton, from which he returned 12:30 a.m. the following morning, he was only given bare expenses because he was an employee of the firm. When the Guelph Radial Railway Company opened an open air rink on the Sheriff's Pond behind the Power House,

---

From Arthur Parker's Diary, May 24, 1905

This day opened our summer season. We played an hour each on the Jubilee Park and Trafalgar Park [band] stands, our city engagements for which the GMS receives a grant of money from the city. At Trafalgar Square we played for the flag-raising ceremony on the Opera House, after which we were entertained by Mrs. Craigmille to a light lunch and cigars, several of the prominent men making short speeches.

In the afternoon we paraded to Exhibition Park where a lacrosse match was played between a team of Indians and the Shamrocks of Guelph, the latter winning. We played selections between quarters and had an easy afternoon. We played a concert in the evening which was largely attended.

"we went down and played in the open air standing on the ice which was very cold work." Or, July 6, 1905, "we took an open car at St. George's Square and played all the way up to the Street Railway Park. They had a fine bandstand erected, but very badly lighted." Parker's diary illustrates a kaleidoscope of events at which the Guelph Musical Society (GMS) Band entertained the people of Guelph. It tells also of many hours of marching, long hours of playing, and the cheerful dedication of the GMS Band to the service of the city and spectators. Some band musicians played in the Opera House orchestra, but were paid little, if anything at all.

By 1900, the Opera House had become the centre of Guelph's cultural life. It was the scene of large political meetings and fundraising events, patriotic rousers, concerts, local musicals, GCI commencements and imported entertainment. The latter was handled by Ambrose Small and consisted mainly of imports from the United States, with a rare tour from London, England. If it had fallen short of its original purpose in the past, by now it was assuring patrons that there was not a line in the play that was not clean and wholesome. One wonders what deceptions the *Mercury's* advertisement in 1901 held for *The Queen of Chinatown,* featuring "The Haunts of Highbinders and Opium Fiends; A Chinese Gambling Den in Full Blast; The Doyer Street Mission School; An Oriental Opium Joint and its Patrons; Rabble and Riot in Mott St." With a different play every night at City Hall where there was "not a seat to spare," and three different shows at the Opera House with "good attendance," during a winter week of 1900, one can say a fair portion of Guelph's population enjoyed its leisure time. Prices at the Opera House ranged from 25 to 75 cents a seat. Yet workers, with wages $8.50 a week or less, had little to spend on such entertainment. Admission to ice-skating rinks was 10 and 15 cents, with special shows included. On February 27, 1900, Victoria Rink had "the Speediest Skater on Ice," skating five miles against five men in relays to the music of the City

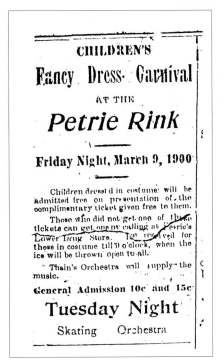

CHILDREN'S
Fancy Dress Carnival
AT THE
Petrie Rink

Friday Night, March 9, 1900

Children dressed in costume will be admitted free on presentation of the complimentary ticket given free to them.

Those who did not get one of these tickets can get one by calling at Petrie's Lower Drug Store. Ice reserved for those in costume till 9 o'clock, when the ice will be thrown open to all.

Thain's Orchestra will supply the music.

General Admission 10c and 15c

Tuesday Night

Skating Orchestra

Children's Fancy Dress Carnival at the Petrie Rink. *Source: Guelph Advocate,* March 3, 1900

A stone-cutter's winter's pastime: stone clock cut in Guelph in 1910. Source: J. Keleher Collection

Band (GMS), while, at the Petrie Rink, "John Nillson, Champion of the World," exhibited his prowess to "unequalled music by Thain's orchestra."

PRACTICE OF THE ARTS

Little or no support could be found for a professional career in the arts. Art was still supposed to serve a purpose. Music was to uplift, painting to inspire, or, in the case of the lantern slides of Parisian painter Tissot, whose Biblical scenes were shown at Norfolk Street Methodist in January 1901, to illustrate. Dr. Melendy informed her readers that one of the best uses of art was "to contemplate statues beautiful and graceful in form and noble in expression," because "the works of the great masters have more effect than the world knows in producing and multiplying forms of beauty and manliness through impressions made on the minds of matrons." William Torrance, inspector of schools in 1900, asked the board of education to set aside a small sum for the purchase "of pictures of the right kind" for the decoration of the schools. "Such adornments," he wrote, "have an educational influence which is too generally underestimated." In answer to his request, Captain Clarke donated funds for the purchase of busts of Shakespeare and Sir John A. Macdonald. Adelaide Hoodless, always practical, promised that making country homes more attractive would ease the crossing of social bridges between city and country life. One wonders how convincing Dr. Melendy was when she wrote, "The children of Italy are beautiful, because they are confronted in the churches by so many beautiful Madonnas."

The only professionals in the arts were those needed by the community: organists and church choir conductors, bandmasters, orchestra leaders, music teachers, and the odd drawing mistress. They received a minimal sum, supplementing it by teaching music, or holding a full-time job in another field. Support was sometimes given by the community in the form of complimentary concerts.

Roberta Geddes-Harvey had come to Guelph in 1876 as organist for St. George's Church. With William Philp, she had established Guelph as a music centre in the latter half of the 19th century. She was also a composer of merit. Anthems, hymns, some instrumental pieces and about 20 songs were published by Whaley Royce and C. W. Thompson. Her opera *La Terre Bonne or the Land of the Maple Leaf* was performed at the Opera House on February 9, 10, and 21 (a complimentary concert) in 1903 and was scheduled to be performed in Boston. Although Guelph-born Laura Lemon (1886-1924) had long departed from her native town, she should be mentioned, as her song *My Ain Folk, a ballad of home* (1904) is considered one of the best known songs by a Canadian composer. J. Wyatt Trendall, conductor of the GMS Band from 1895 to 1900, was also director of the Guelph Amateur Orchestral Association. Ernest Shildrick, later in charge of music at OAC, led the Guelph Philharmonic Society from 1901 to about 1913.

Seven female pianists, determined to practise their art, formed the Ladies Musical Club in February 1898. By April, they were calling themselves the Presto Piano Club. They met once a month in a member's home or studio and each was expected to play a solo. Their meetings were conducted in a dignified manner and according to parliamentary rules. A certain composer was selected for each meeting and one member presented an essay on the subject. Membership fee was five cents. Hoping to share its musical taste with others, the club sponsored its first public concert at the City Hall on March 28, 1901, with tenor Adam Dockray from Toronto. The response was gratifying. The years that followed were interspersed with members' meetings, usually with local guest performers, and one or two public concerts held in the new library's Carnegie Hall or the Opera House. The Presto Choral Club, formed in 1906 with the support of Charles Crowe and Edward Johnson, consisted of 125 members, few of whom had been trained musically. Two successful concerts were presented in 1907 and 1908 at the Opera House. Although music education was a principle aim of the Presto Club, the Choral Club was not their 'cup of tea.' It did not survive, and the ladies, now

numbering 12, continued as the Presto Music Club with their original mandate.

The Presto ladies practised, taught and shared their art. Another aspect of 'old Guelph' was illustrated by a slim volume entitled *The Social Register*. Published by the Watchful Circle of the King's Daughters at St. Andrew's Church, it was a list of the days that certain ladies were 'at home.' When they were not 'at home,' calling cards could be left on a silver tray near the front door. On certain evenings of the week they entertained at whist or progressive euchre. These ladies, usually Guelph-born and bred, were wives of successful businessmen. They contributed to society in other ways – in church functions, service clubs and in fundraising for worthy causes. They also had time to practise several forms of art. The *Mercury* accounts of the Central Exhibition for any of the early years of the century record remarkable entries of oil and water-colour paintings, sometimes copied, but not always. Marine, landscape, floral and animal subjects were abundant. An art-supplies shop existed in Guelph in 1900, and instruction was available at the studio of Miss Scroggie on Oxford Street. Hand-painted china, exquisite lace work and embroidery were also considered art. Patchwork quilts, rag rugs and mats, mitts and hosiery were classified as domestic work. Special mention was made in 1901 of the Upper Wyndham Street photographer, Hurndall, for his medallion photographs and excellent work with colour tinting.

Anyone with single ambitions in the art world or on the concert stage was compelled to go to the United States or Europe to study, to practise and to be seen

Edward Johnson was gifted with a rare voice and singing ability. Music was common in his home, where his father played the clarinet. Later he took piano lessons at Miss Maclean's private school. He learned his trade singing in church choirs under such professionals as Charles Kelly and Roberta Geddes-Harvey. He practised it at benefit concerts, graduation exercises, in Kelly's Scotch Quartette and at GCI, where he led a school choir. As an amateur he would have been paid something occasionally, but even after studying in New York and several years in Florence, he never sang in Guelph 'professionally.' Whenever he returned during his career as a leading tenor or as manager of the Metropolitan Opera, he sang freely at his old school, at the opera house for the Presto Club or at the college. Guelph, like other small Canadian towns, did not yet understand professionalism in the arts. Edward, though, understood civic responsibility.

Edward Johnson, 1906, was gaining a reputation in New York at this time, but returned frequently to Guelph to sing at GCI commencements and Presto Club concerts.
Source: Edward Johnson Collection, Special Collections, University of Guelph Library

and heard. In 1977, Judith Nasby, curator and art historian, used the word 'exile' to characterize the second 50-year period in the history of Guelph art. Rolph Scarlet, 1889-1984, was discouraged from his early ambition to be an artist and designer by his father. For several years he worked for the W. A. Clark firm of jewellers in Guelph. After winning a prize in a country-wide art competition, he was invited to study art at Loretto Convent for a year, perhaps privately as it was strictly a girl's school. He worked independently in New York from 1907-1912 and returned to Guelph, hoping to practise his art and earn a living. We catch a glimpse of his multi-talents in a *Mercury* account and editorial in February 1914, as he is praised for his ability to write the libretto and design the costuming for the Guelph production of the *Gay Pierrots*. Guelph, a fertile ground for amateur talents, provided little nourishment for a professional. Rolph returned to New York in 1918 to enter a career of non-objective art, jewellery design and stage design. Sixty of his works hang in the Guggenheim Museum.

When Governor-General Earl Grey wrote to Lord Mountstephen in 1906 that "there had not been sufficient time to develop the artistic and idealistic qualities of a people which are still lying to a great extent dormant," he could not have been thinking of small cities like Guelph, where, as we have seen, a rich cultural life existed. Perhaps the term 'culture' was irrelevant at the time because it was unconsciously possessed. Every person who emigrated to Canada had a culture. For Guelph, founded on Canada Company policy, it happened to be that of the British Isles. Grey's vision was a broad one with the whole country in mind, a country that would be a great strength in and a credit to the Empire.

THE OLD ANCHORAGE SECURED – GUELPH: 1902-1945

Although the end of the Boer War and the crowning of Edward VII brought visions of a new and prosperous age, they were but preludes to disruptions in the old society. Waves of immigration up to 1914 and the First World War were followed by a brief return to normalcy in the 1920s, when old practices were reaffirmed. The 1930s' Depression and a return to war in 1939 brought dire threats to security and progress. New groups emerged to serve a greater variety of citizens, but many of their presuppositions and those of the city's religious denominations rested on late 19th-century views. Education simply struggled to keep pace with population

☞ May 15, 1915 – Guelph Austrians, Hungarians and Austrian-Poles are rounded up and sent to detention in Toronto. Only married men with families remain in the city.

growth and to implement a few innovations. Not until 1937 did the province issue a program of studies intended to curb attrition by making the curriculum more fully child-centred. While sports continued to provide entertainment for viewers and enjoyment for participants, amateur sports activities were slowly drawn into larger frameworks. The advent of the motion picture, cheap and accessible, set the basis for new expressions of mass culture, primarily American ones. Local citizens enjoyed the old spectacles as before, but music and the arts retained amateur status, unable to generate the revenue reaped by mass entertainment.

Guelph's churches flourished in the first prosperous decade. Knox's interior, destroyed by fire in March 1904 with $6,200 damage, was re-opened in time for its Diamond Jubilee in mid-July. Sparks from the neighbouring Guelph Stove Works set Paisley Primitive Methodist alight in April 1907, and a brand new church on Margaret Street in St. Patrick's Ward was dedicated in less than a year. By 1911, Knox's Branch Sunday School on Short Street had become St. Paul's Presbyterian Church.

Changes took place in St. Patrick's Ward as a steady stream of immigrants from southern Italy arrived, attracted by J. W. Lyon's industrial plan. In 1908, the Jesuits set up a schoolroom at 158 Ontario St. – the first Catholic school away from Church Hill. The upper floor was used for a chapel, and when Father Grick travelled from Hamilton to say mass in Italian, he was well received. The Church of Our Lady was a long walk away, particularly when, like all strangers, they were required to enter by the side door and sit at the side of the altar. In 1911, a log house was bought on Alice Street and replaced within the year by a two-roomed brick schoolhouse, named St. Patrick's School. In the upper room, the Jesuits established a mission. They used a small altar on wheels that could be moved aside when school space was needed.

St. George's Church gathered the Ward's Anglican children for Sunday school in Edwin Wilson's home on Ontario Street. By 1908, the Rector was holding weekly services, using the Wilson's small organ. When the house became over-crowded, the Vestry gave permission for a mission church. J. W. Lyon offered a lot on Harris Street and gave $100 toward the building of a hall. The cornerstone was laid on so cold a day in November that Archdeacon Davidson and his choir had to change into their robes at Mrs. Pudge's on Johnston Street. The first service was held on St. George's Day, 1911. In March 1918, a parish was formed and St. George's Mission became St. Patrick's Church.

In late 1922, a Catholic Mission opened on land donated by the separate

A Royal Welcome from the Royal City: Old Home Week, 1908, with a banner of King Edward VII and Queen Alexandra flying in St. George's Square. Source: J. Keleher Collection

At the bandstand in Exhibition Park on Peace Sunday, July 1919. Source: J. Keleher Collection

school board. St. Patrick's School, next door on Alice Street, provided the heating. It was named Sacred Heart Chapel in order to avoid confusion with the Anglican St. Patrick's. By 1930, the Sacred Heart community was large enough to become a parish. The first pastor, Italian-speaking Father O'Brien, initiated the Corpus Christi procession and an annual garden party on the school grounds, events that engendered a feeling of unity among the parish's various ethnic groups. The 13th Ontario branch of the *Ordine D'Italia* (Sons of Italy) was established in April 1937 at a meeting in the school. In 1941, St. Patrick's was the largest-populated ward in the city.

Also serving the people of this area was the All Peoples' Mission, sometimes called the Friendly Mission to Foreigners, on Morris Street. For about four years until 1915, Alexander Saison, a self-styled missionary of the Hebrew and Christian faith, ran it. A learned scholar, he spoke many languages and was able to help Italians and other immigrants to settle in the area. He formed and directed the first Italian Band in Guelph that was hired by the manager of the Guelph Radial Railway to play at Riverside Park during the summer of 1913. Saison also organized fortnightly concerts of chamber music to help pay for a piano and other furnishings at the mission. On May 14, 1913, Professor Gondio from Rome took part in a program of violin, piano, flute and 'clarionette' music and songs by an Italian chorus. It was sponsored by the Women's Christian Temperance Union and the Royal Templars of Temperance. When D. D. Christie, owner of the building, died, he willed the property to the First Baptist Church on

Woolwich Street. Renamed the Christie Memorial Mission, it was run by missionaries from the Home Mission Board, assisted by members of the Woolwich Street congregation. In later years, it served as a summer mission field for McMaster theology students, but was closed after the Second World War.

Between 1905 and 1908, the parishioners of the Church of Our Lady raised funds to complete its interior. The white marble and onyx altar from the Rouillard studios of Angers, France, was a gift of the Ladies' Altar Society. Also from Rouillard came the delicately wrought marble altar rail that stood with the altar on a platform of Italian Terrazza Mosaic. The interior decoration of murals and stained-glass windows illustrated the life of the Virgin. The Men's Mission was formed in 1915, and the St. John Social Group later sponsored a tennis club, with courts in the space between St. Stanislaus and the church. The club's social events included 'at-home' dances at Wyndham Inn, a drama group and an orchestra. The Columbus Players were renowned for religious plays and lively entertainment. In 1924, the City Tennis Club played a series of games with Church of Our Lady Club, using each other's courts.

In Brooklyn, Miss Nellie Goodeve's post as Sunday school superintendent at the Congregational Mission was taken over in 1903, first, by Prof. Mervin

 July to October, 1911 – The Christian Commercial Travellers' Association, commonly known as The Gideons, place Bibles in the local hotels for the first time.

Cumming and, later, by Dr. Creelman, president of OAC. When Chalmers Presbyterian assisted in management a year later, it became known as the Brooklyn Mission. By 1905, attendance had reached 200, and a move to Albert Street was negotiated. Dr. Robert Harcourt, head of OAC's chemistry department, was then appointed superintendent, a position he held for 35 years. The college provided valuable helpers. Professor Ruhnke directed plays and his wife was active in the Sunday school and scouting program. Students also assisted, including Alfred Hales and Norman High. The OAC Male Quartette often sang at services. When Llew Little, father of children's author Jean Little, was a medical student in Toronto, he preached at evening services at Brooklyn. In 1920, he organized the Brooklyn Young People's Association. A choir was formed as well as a dramatic group, whose play *The Ring of Singapore* ran successfully three nights in Guelph and two nights in neighbouring towns. The move in 1923 to newly-built premises at 60 Martin St. was partly financed by Harcourt's wife, Caroline. Activities for all age groups grew and prospered, including Tuxis, Trail Rangers and boys' basketball team that won the Junior Church League championship three years in a row. When the United Church Mission Board discontinued support, Chalmers engaged an assistant minister to direct the Sunday school and hold evening services at Brooklyn.

The black community was small, but flourishing. In 1903, the Rev. King held the second BME Ontario Conference in the Essex Street church. His successor, the Rev. Lucas, widened the community's influence through musical activities. He conducted the Jubilee Singers, a group popular throughout the city. The Salvation Army continued to attract members. On May 23, 1913, the band paraded with all new silver instruments and the next year received a grant of $350 from city council. The army's first Christmas kettles were on the street in December 1926. By then, a gabled roof replaced the Citadel's battlements.

The January week of prayer, the sharing of churches for large events and during summer vacations, and the combining of choirs for musical events continued between different denominations. The Church of Christ Disciples and the Baptists worked closely, as in June 1907, when the Disciples hosted an Ontario Convention in the First Baptist Church. The Congregationalists and the Disciples sought unity for a number of years. When, in 1919, a final decision was made, it was thwarted by minute details of an old trust deed.

More hopeful about organic union, the Congregationalists in 1910 and the Methodists in 1912 declared themselves ready to proceed. Presbyterians, however, were not ready to commit. A straw vote, taken at Guelph's St. Andrew's in 1915,

resulted in 72 elders, members and adherents for union and 222 against. After the war, however, the pro-union element in the Presbyterian church at large became stronger until, in 1923, the General Assembly agreed to ask parliament to create the United Church of Canada. "This action polarized the two elements in every Presbyterian congregation," wrote historian W. Stanford Reid, "with the result that the controversy increased in heat and volume, if not in light." The Rev. H. E. Abraham at St. Andrew's (1912-1926) actively opposed union. On December 22, 1924, as a result of a petition by 320 members, the Session prepared a ballot for another vote. The result was 356 against, 90 for union, with 4 spoiled.

Knox had an even more influential leader in Dr. A. J. MacGillivray, a member of the Presbyterian Church Association, formed in 1916 to preserve the Presbyterian Church in Canada, but which had subsequently lost steam. MacGillivray had been a supply minister at Knox in 1912 during the illness of the Rev. Arnold and succeeded him at his death in 1913. In March 1923, he began to help local branches across Canada organize against the proposed legislation. Roberta Clare explained the other factors at work in the reactivation of the Presbyterian Church Association. Presbyterian women, like those of other churches, had built a reputation for efficiency in raising funds and managing property. Although they sought closer connection to the church, they were independently organized, not supported by the church, and had no representation on the Home and Foreign Boards. Methodist and Congregationalist women both sat on their church's courts. Presbyterian women could not, and, furthermore, had been instructed to remain neutral in the question of union. When, after the General Assembly of 1922, they realized that, without being consulted, all their funds and property were to pass into the United Church of Canada, they formed their own organization, independent of the church. The Women's League became so successful that little was done without their consultation. MacGillivray was asked to organize a Women's League in Guelph "to counter-act the vote of your Commissioners in the Assembly," but no record of it has yet been found.

In 1925, Chalmers Presbyterian, Norfolk, Dublin and Paisley Methodists and the First Congregational Church joined with each other as part of the United Church of Canada. At St. Andrew's Presbyterian, 346 were against and 90 left to join the United Church. Some members of Knox departed; others came to them. St. Paul's voted 90 to 25 to remain Presbyterian. The Congregational Church became Trinity United, but merged with Chalmers in 1929. The stone building, used for some years for church activities, was sold in 1942.

While the large Protestant churches debated union, smaller religions acquired their own centres of worship. The year 1907 was the first *minyan* year of the Jewish community and, with 10 male members and their families, an official religious congregation came into being. The first marriage ceremony of this group was that of Ezra Smith in 1908. As yet, there was no place in Guelph for the Jewish community to bury their dead. That year, the body of a Mrs. Rozen was conveyed to Toronto in an undertaker's wagon, followed by her mourning relatives in a bobsled, drawn by a single black horse. As the years passed, religious traditions of the *shabas minyans* were strictly observed, whether conducted in private homes, a small building on Farquhar Street or the old Gas Works on Surrey Street. On January 25, 1925, an expanded Jewish community was able to purchase a red-brick building on the corner of Surrey and Dublin, which they remodelled into a synagogue. An extension was added in 1935. The women's Hadassah Ir Shalom

Chapter originated in 1928 with six members. In April 1942, Harry Brown became the first president of the Guelph branch of B'nai B'rith, its male equivalent. Annual sports nights and Brotherhood Week were among their important events, as Jews and Christians sought reconciliation in light of the war's devastation.

A group of Lutherans first worshipped and held Sunday school in the Royal Templars' Hall in 1907 and, later, in the public library's Carnegie Hall. When the Second Baptist Church reunited with the First Baptist Church in 1908, the Lutherans purchased their red-brick church on Woolwich Street. It was consecrated as St. Paul's Evangelical Lutheran Church. As usual, two ladies' groups were quickly active, and the young peoples' Luther League became a founding member of the Canadian Luther League, begun in Galt in 1908.

The Guelph Brethren had continued to meet in small halls. George McAllister, owner of the Guelph sawmill, sold his home on Woolwich Street to

James Johnson about 1907, and purchased 15 acres at 490 Waterloo Ave. When John, eldest of his six children, moved to Guelph in 1914, George purchased a lot on Eramosa Road, and the group of Brethren moved from the upper room on Wyndham Street to a meeting place of their own – the Eramosa Road Gospel Hall. In 1918, he held a three-day conference on the Waterloo grounds during the Dominion Day holiday weekend. Two large tents were erected, one for dining and one for Bible readings and preaching. Successful conferences continued each year until the last summer of his life in 1931. John MacAllister then purchased the property from the estate and donated it as a permanent Bible conference site to be administered by a committee of Brethren from various Ontario and U.S. assemblies. For the 1934 conference, a 400-seat auditorium was built of hewn logs and lumber from the mill. Over 1,000 attended, and so crowded was the auditorium and surrounding grounds that the guest speaker had to be hoisted through

the window to deliver his message. A loud speaker system was soon installed and further additions included the McAllister Memorial Dining Hall and individual log cabins. In 1935, when work with young people commenced, the Guelph Summer Bible School was founded.

By 1914, the International Bible Students were meeting in a home on Northumberland Street. During the 1920s they rented Moose Hall, over Keleher and Hendley's Men's Furnishings (now Budds), but after fire damage, moved to a larger facility at 72 Carden St. above a liquor store. In 1931, the world-wide assembly of the IBSA adopted the name of Jehovah's Witnesses. In 1915, members of the Reorganized Church of Latter Day Saints rented a former butcher shop at the corner of Norfolk and Edwin streets. It became a branch in 1918. Two years later, two lots were purchased on Mitchell Street for $500. Using hand-made cement blocks, members worked evenings and Saturdays until 1922, when their new

The Choirs of the Church of Our Lady, 1922.
Source: Church of Our Lady Archives

church was completed. Over the years, the little grey block building was transformed into a structure of modern design.

In the summer of 1927, several families of Baptists, "not in sympathy with liberal concepts," met at different homes once a week for prayer and on Sunday afternoons for the Sunday school lesson. They eventually converted the living room of a home at 200 Liverpool St. into a hall. A year later, a small building at 17 Suffolk St. became Suffolk Street Regular Baptist Church. Members were also involved in the First Baptist Church's mission operating in the Matthew Wells Pickle factory and later in the Dominion Linen Mills on the east side of Victoria Road. Realizing a

An episode in Guelph's history towards the end of the First World War revealed strong undercurrents of prejudice under a seemingly rosy surface. Clarification was provided by Brian F. Hogan in a well-documented paper. In 1917, faced with strong opposition to conscription, Prime Minister Sir Robert Borden sought to broaden his wartime base by bringing several Liberals and other public figures who favoured conscription into his government. Guelph's loyalty to British ideals and traditions was evident in its support of Borden's Union Campaign. With the help of the citizens' union committee, Toronto based, but chaired by Guelph's J. W. Lyon, Borden's Coalition Government won a decisive victory in December 1917. With the Military Service Act confirmed, the process of call-ups began in January 1918. Questions had been raised about the novices at St. Stanislaus Novitiate. Most were answered adequately, but not to the satisfaction of the Guelph Ministerial Association. In a letter to London headquarters, noting that Protestant colleges had made great sacrifices and that military authorities had failed to induct the novices, they declared their intention to take action. Consequently, an incident that occurred at 9:30 p.m. on June 7, 1918, brought national notoriety to Guelph and highlighted latent prejudices and inconsistencies existing in its religious community. When an "impatient and hastily forwarded memo" was sent from the office of Militia and Defence to the local Assistant Provost Marshall in London, Ontario, giving the impression that the Novitiate should be "cleaned out," Deputy Captain Macauley was dispatched to Guelph with a body of men to search for the evaders. After deploying men around the building to prevent any escape, the captain and two assistants announced their arrival. They were admitted to the building and met by Father Bourque, who was ordered to have all inhabitants presented within five minutes, or submit to a thorough search. Five hours of arguments and telephone consultations with various officials followed. Macauley arrested three novices, but was then ordered by authorities in Ottawa to suspend operations. To complicate matters, one novice was the son of Justice Minister Charles Doherty. In order to allay the exaggerated stories circulating in the Guelph area, a censorship ban was imposed on news items. This was interpreted by the Guelph Ministerial Association as an attempt to muzzle truth and protect the Jesuits and the Justice Minister. After a thorough investigation, the judges concluded that all Jesuits at the Novitiate were legally exempted from service. In the

Robert Donnell

Robert Donnell was born in Toronto in 1920. Raised and educated in Guelph, he became a member of St. George's Church where he learned to play the tubular chimes. The chimes required eight to ten boys standing in a circle with a numbered rope in each hand. Each rope was to be pulled when its number was called. Those chimes were capable of simple folk and hymn tunes only. In 1926, a 23-bell carillon, a gift from Arthur Cutten, replaced the simpler chimes in the tower. Soon after, Donnell, who had studied carillon music at Hart House at the University of Toronto, was chosen as St. George's carillonneur. His reputation as a carillonneur grew and in 1932 he was invited to play at the Peace Tower in Ottawa. In 1938, he graduated from the Mechelen Carillon School in Belgium and in 1939, was appointed Dominion Carillonneur in Ottawa, a position he held until his retirement in 1975. Donnell coaxed the bells in the Peace Tower into singing each Christmas on the commonwealth broadcast. He also composed the music for Canada's official citizenship song, *This Canada of Ours*. Throughout his more than 50 years as a bell ringer Donnell gave concerts in many different countries. When he died in 1986 he was considered one of the most famous bell ringers in the world.

– *Ceska Brennan*

meantime, stories had so grown in intensity that the Guelph Ministerial Association would not let the subject rest. The *Toronto Daily Star* scooped the stories, breaking the ban, and a flood of frontpage versions swept across Canada. The Guelph press, sympathizing with the Ministerial Association, published the Sunday sermons at length. The *Ottawa Citizen* printed eight sermons, noting that "all but the Anglican pastor preached on the incident, for which he was chastised by Jack Canuck." As Ontario and Quebec presses raged forth, Macauley and Father Bourque were transferred to Winnipeg, and Burrows to Vancouver. When the new National Registration required everyone over the age of 16 to register, "except cloistered nuns, persons on active service and inmates of asylums, penitentiaries and prisons..." the Rev. Kennedy Palmer of St. Paul's Presbyterian was not satisfied. Assuming the leadership of a campaign for a parliamentary investigation, he toured Western Canada, speaking 'by invitation' in every city from Winnipeg to the coast. To back him up, the Orange Lodge organized a national writing campaign that resulted in more letters being sent to the Prime Minister than all other business combined. A Royal Commission Enquiry in 1919 concluded that the Jesuit novices had all been legally exempted from service. It noted that one year after the war had ended, only one novice had left the society, and that had been due to ill health. Palmer's plan to denounce the hearings and tour the province did not materialize and the episode was quickly relegated to the back shelves of history.

greater need in that area, the Suffolk Street church moved to York and Victoria roads and, in April 1933, became known as York Road Regular Baptist Church. A new building was completed within a year. Anglican historian John Heap recorded that the Baptist church became popular in the area during the ministry of Pastor Chipchase (1931-1947], except with St. Patrick's Anglicans just down the road, who, under the Rev. Field, had become very "High Church." Chipchase was "quite a rouser," wrote Heap, referring to a current dispute between High and Low Anglicans and the Roman Catholic Church. "St. Patrick's did lose a few souls to the Baptists, but, when the controversy died out in the 1940s, most of them returned to us." During those years the newspaper advertisements of York Road Baptist were the largest and liveliest of all. Musical groups and charismatic speakers performed regularly at "great rousing rallies." Four services took place on Sunday, a Fireside Hour every weekday evening at 8:30 and a Sunrise Service once a month. In 1953, when the Independent Baptist Churches and the Union of Regular Baptist Churches amalgamated to form the Fellowship of Evangelical Baptist Churches, York Road voted to join.

In 1921, the First Baptist Church had also established a Sunday school at Meadowview and Inkerman streets, known as the Meadowview Mission. It was serviced by students from McMaster University and eventually full-time pastors, provided by the Baptist Home Mission. As the congregation gradually became self-supporting, a division arose concerning compromises made by the Baptist Church. When those agreeing with them returned to the First Baptist Church, others asked Pastor Stoll, an evangelical fundamentalist, to be their minister. The mission was closed, and the small group became the Carden Street Baptist Church, meeting in Orange Hall opposite the railway station. Their first service was held in December 1934. The following March, a constitution was drawn up and Calvary Baptist Church chosen as a name. It was subsequently recognized by the Fellowship of Independent Baptist Churches. In 1936, they purchased a lot on Glasgow Street. Their own church, built by its members, was dedicated in December 1937.

In the early 1920s, another gospel hall appeared in Guelph at 4 Yorkshire St., unrelated to other churches or missions in Guelph. The Rosedale Alliance was founded in a house on Cork Street in 1924 by Mr. B. Hocking for the purpose of 'bringing evangelical Protestant work to Guelph.' The first Pentecostal meetings were held in 1937 in tents along the river and, by 1939, were established in the Stone Church at 37 Gordon St.

During the first few decades, as throughout the century, churches were beautified by memorial gifts of altars, windows, pulpits, lanterns and altar cloths to list a few. The Church of Our Lady acquired a Casavant organ from St. Hyacinth, Quebec in 1919. The spires were completed in 1926, giving Guelph an even more distinguished skyline. That year, A.W. Cutten, who had paved St. George's chancel with marble, provided a new organ, choir stalls, a choir loft and a carillon. The 23-bell carillon, made in England, was a memorial to his mother and father, William Hoyt and Anna Margaretta Cutten. The four-manual, 3,000-pipe organ was installed in five weeks by the Frères Casavant. Edith Kidd noted that these gifts changed the focus of music in St. George's and gave the church great prominence in the city and province.

EDUCATION

The question of how to gain and keep the attention of children was a constant problem for teachers, inspectors of schools, who usually sympathized with teachers, and boards, who controlled available funds. The child-centred philosophy of American John Dewey did not fit in with Ontario's firmly entrenched 19th-century system. There was, however, a growing awareness that public education should not only prepare for the professions but also equip more young persons with skills beneficial to them in the home or the working world. Formal education virtually ended at Grade 8 or, as it was then called, Fourth Reader. Those graduating from Central's two-year business course were trained for office jobs, but the many who left during high school were ill prepared for new industrial jobs. The Ontario Department of Education's new theory of 'sense-training,' as opposed to 'mind-training,' promised some solutions, and Guelph schools were in a position to practise them. In 1903, OAC President Mills offered to introduce manual training in Central School, placing at its disposal the services of Mr. Evans, an instructor at Macdonald Institute. The board of education accepted. Carpentry equipment was acquired and installed on the first floor of the new Alexandra School. While the basement was being equipped with gas stoves, tables and a water supply, girls from Central's higher forms were sent by electric streetcar up to Macdonald Institute, where domestic science teachers-in-training needed pupils to instruct.

Nature study and art were included in the new curriculum. "Some think it takes more time than they can afford," wrote Inspector Tytler in his 1909 report. "The reason is probably because they have no training in those fields." Principal Long of the new East Ward School on Waterloo Avenue, built in 1910 and later named after Inspector Torrance, made sure his experiment in school gardens was

Student's garden plots at Macdonald Institute, c. 1905.   Source: Card Family Collection

One experiment did not fare well, although it had been successful in the United States from 1864. Guelph was the first in Ontario to attempt the consolidation of small rural schools into larger well-heated, ventilated buildings with modern facilities and qualified teachers. Sir William Macdonald, hoping to give Canadian rural children the same advantages as those from the city, had built several consolidated schools in eastern Canada. At the urging of Col. David McCrae, who saw the advantage of having such a school near the OAC and Macdonald Training Institute, James Robertson surveyed the area and found that it was an ideal site. Pupils would have the advantage of a school garden, manual training and valuable object lessons to be learned from visits to the college. Five school sections endorsed the plan. Macdonald Consolidated School was opened in 1904 on three and a half acres of college hill near Macdonald Institute. The land and the building had cost Macdonald $38,000. He also paid for horse-drawn vans to transport the pupils from sections one, four, six and seven of Guelph and School System 2 in Puslinch. Unfortunately, the money limited the builders to a plainer design than that envisaged by Macdonald, and word has it that when he saw it on opening day, he refused to leave his carriage and returned *poste haste* to Montreal. Funding was as much the reason for the experiment's failure as were parents' objections to hauling their children over long distances in inclement weather. In 1907, when costs were discovered to be one third higher than the old system, consolidation was turned down by four of the six participating districts. The school was then absorbed into the Guelph Township School Board.

a success by staying in Guelph during the summer to look after them. The new Victory School was completed in 1920 with 10 rooms. All grades were taught, including a special class for those who found academic work difficult or impossible, but who had ability in handicraft and practical work. A similar class was started at St. John's School the following year. This proved a success, and two

years later another was organized at Tytler. The progress of reform was slow to take root, but foundations were being laid.

In the meantime, the physical condition of Guelph schools was a primary concern, and Inspector Torrance's plea for a pleasant and healthy atmosphere was carried on with even more fervour by his successor, William Tytler. Overcrowded classrooms and unsanitary conditions were the subjects of his complaints, particularly in the basement rooms at Central School where, in contravention of provincial regulations, young children were subjected to poor lighting and ventilation. Sixty-three pupils at St. John's Ward School worked in one classroom, 50 in the other. Central's corridors were dark and gloomy, the desks were old and damaged and single desks were needed. A restroom for the 16 female teachers was thought advisable. A truant officer was desperately needed to ensure that all children followed the law by attending school.

Several changes were effected. King Edward School replaced the West Ward School on Suffolk Street in 1904. The stone structure adjoining Central School (the old senior girls' school) was completely remodelled and the small children moved to the second floor from Central's basement. Lavatories were built in St. James School in 1906, and a new four-roomed school was constructed in St. Patrick's Ward in 1908 (later called Tytler), but overcrowding remained. In 1907, 'penny banks' were introduced in the public schools to teach economy and thrift. A school nurse was appointed in 1914, who made recommendations for dental care.

"There were no dull spots" wrote the *Evening Mercury* reporter of the formal opening of the new two-storey and basement addition to GCI on January 26, 1906. "The exercises by Captain Clark[e] and his pupils were delightful and the speeches were humorous, spicy and suggestive." The reporter felt that the plainness and lack of harmonious style was compensated by the amenities inside: roominess, light, modern heating and ventilation and indoor lavatories. Hugh Guthrie MP and J. P. Downey MLA also criticized the architectural appearance of the new building, but C. W. Kelly's presentation of a bust of Queen Victoria restored optimism and confidence. All historian Greta Shutt could remember of the ceremonies were vast quantities of bread, butter and ham made into sandwiches, the amazing competence of the art teacher, whom she had previously thought impractical, and the spontaneous school cheer at the end of the program. The addition of four large classrooms, two smaller ones and two auxiliary rooms were satisfactory for a few years. By 1912, the attendance had increased 65 percent, resulting in desks in the hallways and classes in the gymnasium.

In 1913, the provincial Department of Education began a summer school training course for music teachers and supervisors that continued until 1941. It also devised a grants system, matching a local board's cost of hiring trained music supervisors and buying equipment. This proved inadequate because concern was more focussed on vocational subjects and those that fed the universities. The teaching of art and music relied entirely on the whims of an individual board, principal or teacher. In 1916, Tytler wrote, "instruction in art and music will never achieve a high degree of success because the quality of instruction varies so greatly."

As early as 1908, Guelph's MP Hugh Guthrie had introduced a resolution for the appointment of a commission to investigate the need for technical education. A bill was not passed at the time but, after the First World War, pressures for technical and vocational training were heightened by the policies of Education Minister Henry J. Cody. The Guelph Board of Education began working more closely with industrial leaders, particularly members of the newly-formed Chamber of Commerce, who had issued a 15-point strategy to boost the city's business and industrial profile. The new GCVI, built in 1923, was described in the Canadian Club's magazine *The Maple Leaf* as "a model Collegiate Institute and Technical School – the last word in modern school construction and equipment – a building for Guelph's generations of the future." It boasted 44 classrooms, a gymnasium, swimming pool and an auditorium capable of seating 1,200. The vacuum-heating system allowed for a change of air every 20 minutes and the 65 plumbing fixtures distributed throughout were of "the latest improved make."

In spite of Tytler's prediction, the Guelph board hired Mia Murray in 1920 as art, music, and folk-dancing instructor, apparently with no overall increase in expenses. In April 1921, a GCI orchestra, directed by William Morlock, played in the YMCA rotunda at a boys' hobby exhibition and were highly praised by the *Guelph Evening Mercury and Advertiser*. Georgina Barton was hired in 1922 as a singing instructor and did the work of a music supervisor. The orchestra continued under her leadership, although in 1926 with only seven members.

Edward Johnson had already broached the subject of music in the schools in a speech to the Rotary Club when Barton enlisted his help in petitioning the board to make use of children and their music in the 1927 centennial celebrations. When nothing much resulted, he made a remarkable gift. He offered $25,000 in equal instalments over five years to launch a program of music in the schools. Headquarters were set up in the vacant St. John's School, and Joseph Yule, director of music for the Kitchener Philharmonic Choir and school programs there, was

Second Annual Boy's Hobbies Exhibition at the YMCA, April 12 -14, 1917.

Source: J. Keleher Collection

hired as music director in Guelph, with Barton as his assistant. Working throughout 1928-29 with all the public schools, the GCVI orchestra and Glee Club and a massed choir of 200 children, Yule was ready to partake in the three-day May Festival planned by Edward Johnson, who now specified that the separate school board should be included in his plans. Shortly before the festival, a public school singing competition was held. All three winners were members of church choirs – two from St. George's and one from the Church of Christ, Disciples. Then, on opening night, May 7, 1929, the school choirs, orchestras and individuals performed before a large audience in the collegiate, and the contest winners were awarded medals. On the afternoon of the second day the Toronto Symphony Orchestra presented an educational concert, in which the music and the instruments were introduced and explained. To the delight of all, Edward Johnson sang. He was also soloist for the evening concert with the TSO and the newly formed Vogt Choir of Guelph. "My great ambition for Guelph," he said, "is to see it represented by a spirit of community in music as well as in everything else."

Although Johnson had encouraged the Presto Club to present "culturally significant concerts," the idea behind his gift to the schools was fundamental to

GCVI Orchestra 1929, with David Ouchterloney on double bass.

Source: *Acta Nostra*, 1929. GCVI Archives

Edward Johnson and the Musical Festival, May 2 and 3, 1929. Two thousand crowded into GCVI's auditorium to hear the Toronto Symphony Orchestra and youthful violinist Bettina Vagara.

Source: *Acta Nostra,* 1930. GCVI Archives

every child's well-being. It had both aesthetic and practical undertones, influenced probably by his years in Italy, where music was a heartbeat in everyone's life. Canadian children, educated in music, would provide not only the country's future artists but also its audiences and supporters. The art provided many advantages, and one of them was something new: enjoyment.

Joseph Yule, who drowned in the Saugeen River in April 1930, was succeeded by Capt. William Bishop, and the program was continued for another two years. In October 1932, Johnson sent the last $5,000 cheque to the school board, begging its members to continue their effort for the advancement of music in the community. "With infinite regret," he added, "this cheque must be, at least for the time being, my last." A year of salary cuts and trustees' ambivalence towards the music program followed, but Johnson's experiment was not a failure. In April 1934, the Guelph board, tackling the problem of keeping alive the Edward Johnson Foundation, appointed a ways-and-means committee to consider future policy. It then granted $15 to the Collegiate String Quartet for trips to Toronto and the Stratford Music Festival. Captain Bishop also offered a one-year vocal scholarship. In 1935 the board provided the funds ($20 for up to eight teachers) for three-week, summer master classes in music at the University of Western Ontario. Bishop was succeeded in the fall of 1934 by Frank Cheeseman. The May Festival concerts, featuring competition winners who had been judged by the provincial music supervisor, and the annual Christmas programs under Cheeseman's direction from 1934 to 1939 indicate that a high standard of music education was being upheld in all Guelph's public schools. When Herbert Peachell assumed the post of music supervisor of public schools in 1939, he inherited a healthy system

and vowed to carry on the work started by Johnson's donation.

Diversification with subjects such as art, music, nature study, manual training and home economics had been introduced into the curriculum in Guelph schools in an attempt to keep children there as well as to prepare them for leaving. But, "for every innovative classroom there were 10 or 20 more closely attuned to 19th- rather than 20th-century pedagogical theory," claimed author Robert Stamp. In 1936, over 40 years after John Dewey had pointed out the supreme importance of the child in the classroom, most educators felt Ontario should move its system into the 20th century. Accordingly, the Department of Education issued a new program of studies in September 1937. The school "must follow the method of nature, stimulating the child, through his own interests, into activities guiding him into experiences useful for the satisfaction and development of his needs." Rote memory was to be a thing of the past. History and geography would be taught as social studies and, like all subjects, by activity-oriented or 'enterprise' methodology. The old *Ontario Reader* (editions of 1880s and 1910) was replaced by the attractively designed *Mary, John and Peter,* precursor of many readers to come. Free expression was encouraged in art. Opposition came from teachers untrained in the method, from those who felt its democracy was too close to the Co-operative Commonwealth Federation (CCF), and from parents and community leaders who wanted stability, not innovation.

Physical changes continued. The boarding school run by the Loretto Sisters was discontinued in 1924 to make space for the increasing number of day

A significant advantage to the community was the founding of St. Stanislaus Novitiate by the Jesuits in 1913 on 600 acres four miles from the city on the Elora Road. As explained by Father Edward Dowling, Jesuit Father Bourgue and a staff of 13, including some lay brothers, provided two types of training for English-speaking men wishing to enter the Jesuit Order. The novices were young men with a high school background who studied Latin, Greek, English, French and mathematics and participated in a two year 'boot-camp'– a concentrated training in spiritual life and social work. These men usually completed their scholastic training in Toronto with a BA in philosophy. Another group of young men was trained in farming, construction work and nursing. Some of these arrived with experience, some with little formal education. Not destined for the priesthood, they were called brothers. The Novitiate was self-sustaining, with one exception: no provision for laundry tubs. Laundry was labelled and sent out. The farm was an important element in everyday life, with milk, eggs, vegetables and fruit produced on the premises. Jesuit training also included spiritual work in St. Joseph's Hospital and at the Ontario Reformatory. Short retreats were held at the Novitiate for Catholic men.

High-jinks in the square during Centennial Celebrations, 1927.

Source: J. Keleher from Wally Beadle Collection

students. In 1921, a group of former pupils and friends formed a Guelph branch of the Catholic Women's League for the purpose of raising funds for their Alma Mater. St. Patrick's teas became a tradition and garden parties flourished. They contributed $10,000 towards an addition to the convent in 1926. The Knights of Columbus raised money for a Heintzman piano and donated a substantial cheque.

In 1909, a second storey had been added to St. Agnes, and, in 1914, St. Stanislaus was renovated and given a second storey. St. Patrick's overflow senior students could now be accommodated. A new school was then constructed in the Ward next to the old one. They were collectively known as St. Patrick's School until 1932, when six classrooms were added and it was renamed Sacred Heart School. That year, primary classes of boys joined primary girls at St. Agnes, and senior girls went for the first time to St. Stanislaus. For recess the playground was divided into two sections. The Loretto Sisters continued to teach, but were joined by an increasing number of lay teachers. A boys' choir was formed at St. Stanislaus in 1918. It won second prize at the Toronto Music Festival in Massey Hall (1924) and first at the Hamilton Eisteddfod (1926).

While the practical dominated the theoretical at OAC, the aesthetic was never ignored. Doses administered by the Literary Society were small at first, with musical numbers by students or city friends included in its programs. In 1905, the Philharmonic Society was organized. By 1911, it had assumed charge of an orchestra, choir and the college's musical and dramatic entertainment. The Opera House was sometimes used for College Theatre Night, but it was not unusual for over 700 college and city bodies to cram into the gymnasium for the society's annual concert. "Excellent" and "delightful" were the verdicts in 1911, and the OAC reviewer continued, "the programme, although of considerable length, was never the least monotonous." The word monotonous was never even mentioned after the arrival of Agnes (Scotty) McLean, who stunned Guelphites and students with her debut dramatic recital January 31, 1925. After being asked to help out, she directed campus theatre for over 30 years. "Gone were farces and melodrama. In were classics, operetta, verse drama, and modern works," wrote Terry Crowley in his update of Alexander Ross' *College on the Hill*.

Other individuals stimulated the cultural life of the college and community. English literature professor O. J. Stevenson organized students and housekeepers to save scrap paper for selling and to buy Canadian paintings. Proceeds from a Canadian authors' series of lectures also went into the picture fund. Among the speakers were Stephen Leacock (1920), Bliss Carman for two evenings (1921), Charles D.G. Roberts (1925), Agnes McPhail (1931) and Edwin Pratt (1933). All evenings were sold out with students and city-folk attending. In 1925, Stevenson purchased Tom Thomson's *The Drive* for approximately $500. In 1927, an inter-college art club was formed and the development began of the Canadian Collection that included books, art and music. Stevenson's successor, G. E. Reaman, continued to bring art exhibitions to the campus. He was the prime mover in the organization of the Ontario Genealogical Society in 1961. Reaman was also instrumental in beginning the Sunday Night Nine O'clock Musicals and, in 1939, introduced a course in radio broadcasting, another first in Canada.

The year 1922 brought the oldest veterinary school in North America to Guelph. The advantages of the Ontario Veterinary College were inestimable, as researchers, farmers and city residents reaped the benefits of the latest advances in veterinary science. In 1927, the Bread and Cake-Makers Association of Canada established a school of baking on the OAC grounds that became Trent Institute. Short courses in baking were offered, but were discontinued in 1940.

Adult education in the city continued to be sporadic. Evening classes in household science were conducted in 1908 and 1909. They were successful, but the OAC instructor was forced to resign because of overwork. In 1913, classes recommenced at Central, this time with both sexes and no fees. Dressmaking and sewing were most popular. Other courses included mechanical drawing, building construction, machine shop practice, woodworking, business and industrial English, cookery, home nursing and millinery. Guelph's night-class system was established and, after 1923, was moved to the new collegiate.

A larger and more accessible public library was needed at the turn of the century, but funds and a site were not readily available. When James Watt, chairman of the library board, wrote personally to Andrew Carnegie, he received a reply offering $20,000 for construction and $2,000 a year for maintenance, provided that the city donated a site. The council offered Nelson Crescent on the corner of Norfolk and Paisley streets and, despite usual objections to the destruction of parklands, the project was completed and officially opened in September 1905. The total cost, risen to $24,000, was paid by Carnegie. The library's auditorium and lecture rooms were immediately put to use by Guelph's clubs and organizations. The 1,637 adult members demanded books primarily of a religious

Dorothy Dix's Letter Box

A College Degree Cuts a Girl's Matrimonial Chances in Half. Since Most Men Want to Be More Intelligent Than Their Wives, and But Few Realize That the Better Mind a Woman Has, the Better Wife She Makes

Recently compiled statistics show that a college degree decreases a girl's chances of marrying by half, and that if she has an M.A. from a particularly highbrowed institution of learning the likelihood of her ever being a MA is even slimmer. Even going to a coeducational college doesn't take the curse off the higher education for women, apparently, as they turn out from 40 to 48 per cent. old maids.

Now college girls are, taking them by and large, quite as good looking, quite as peppy and a shade above the intelligence of the average run of femininity, hence a preferred risk in matrimony. This raises the interesting question of why a superior education should be a matrimonial handicap to a girl.

Dorothy Dix's Letter Box: early 1930s advice to women.
Source: *Guelph Mercury,*
January 1933

or poetic nature. In 1910, a few children's books were circulated, but it was not until 1921 that a boys' and girls' library was established. By May 1914, though, the books and bookcases weighed 50 tons, too much even for sound floors. An addition was built, costing over $5,000.

The *Mercury* made gradual efforts to educate women. A second section appeared on Saturdays in 1910 with a 'Social Life by Doris' column and one called 'Woman's World.' By 1912, however, editors were helping women to enjoy their position in the home and stay there. Formerly for society women, they were now designed to appeal to the modest class of wife and mother. 'Points for Mothers' and advice on cooking and baby care were predominant. Mary Marsden and Dorothy Dix appeared later to advise and console.

Education of a revolutionary kind was instigated by a Guelph man, Joseph P. Downey, and his work was outlined in articles written by W. J. Waines for the Guelph Historical Society. A Conservative member from Guelph in the provincial legislature (1902) and member of Ontario's first Conservative government (1905), Downey was appointed chairman of the Special Committee on Prison Labour (1908). His report recommended a change in the prison system, based on rehabilitation. The result was the closing of the Central Prison in Toronto and the establishment at Guelph of the prison farm system. Downey and his committee concluded that prisons should not be solely for punitive purposes, and that it was the "duty of the state to improve the character of the well-disposed prisoner and, if possible, revive or create in him a proper appreciation of his duties and responsibilities." To achieve this physical and moral improvement, the institution should include programs and facilities for education, trades training, callisthenics and military exercises. Employment in the open air would be productive, remunerative and produce goods that might compete least with products of free labour (although this practice was soundly denounced by organized workers). In an article in *Saturday Night*, May 1, 1926, Hector Charlesworth claimed that, under Downey's influence, the "first practicable steps toward reform of reclaimable prisoners to be adopted in Canada were taken." His ideas achieved wide notoriety and praise, as investigators came from England, Japan, Australia, the U.S. and Germany.

Inmates, housed in temporary quarters on 800 acres near Guelph, were engaged in clearing, draining and cultivating the land. A stone quarry

```
COMMUNITY   SINGING        JAZZ   ORCHESTRA
      S P E C I A L    A D D E D    A T T R A C T I O N S

           MUSIC              BY

      GUELPH      PIPE        BAND
      ──         ──          ──
      ──         ──          ──
```

Afternoon Events at the inmates' 11th Annual Field Day, July 1, 1931, at the Ontario Reformatory, Guelph.
Source: Frank Dobias Collection

```
A F T E R N O O N   E V E N T S
─────────────   ──────

          1. 30 P.M.


TRACK FINALS          AND          BASEBALL GAME

1.  Running The Bases........ open to ball players only
2.  Finals................... 100 yard dash
3.  Finals................... Tug-O-War
4.  Water-melon Race......... open to colored boys only
5.  Relay Race............... open to gangs only
6.  Finals................... 220 yard dash
7.  Special Event........... Tug-O-War -- Inside Industrie
                             s vs Outside Gangs -- teams
                             to be picked at end of tug-O-
                             war finals.


        B A S E B A L L   G A M E


          ONTARIO REFORMATORY NINE

                   VS

          THE KIWANIS OF TORONTO


        G R A N D E   F I N A L E


    C L O W N S   A N D   J E S T E R S
```

was opened, a limekiln erected, a concrete bridge built over the river and a small railway laid to facilitate the construction of the buildings. By 1917, wood, broom, tailoring, shoe, paint and machine shops were operating as well as a woollen mill, abattoir and laundry. Prisoners worked the quarry, farmed the land and milked the large herd of Holstein cattle. Although built for 500, usual occupancy was 300. With the war and the passing of the Ontario Temperance Act, the number of inmates was severely reduced and the normal operation of the institution was hampered. In 1917, the provincial govern-

ment turned the Reformatory over to the Military Hospital Commission for hospital accommodation and vocational training for returned soldiers. It was re-opened within four years as the Ontario Reformatory. In 1928, a 'school of letters' was created, whereby illiterate and semi-illiterate men were required to attend day school. Night-school classes were made available to those wishing to improve their education. The Jesuits, the York Road Baptists, the Congregationalists and the Salvation Army were among the churches involved in Sunday morning and afternoon services and chaplaincy there.

SERVICE CLUBS AND ORGANIZATIONS

In 1910, Walter Buckingham wrote that Guelph was "a thriving, attractive, homogeneous but withal conservative community about 13,000 people with a preponderance of old country stock, a city of churches, but with no focal point for its youth, no common meeting place for its people." After stirring up interest at local churches and in the newspapers, he persuaded a few conscientious citizens, including Caroline Forbes (later Mrs. Robert Harcourt), J. W. Lyon, A. W. Cutten and D. D. Christie, to donate large amounts of money to the building of a new YMCA. Charlie Yeates parted with his lot at the corner of Quebec and Yarmouth streets at the price it had cost him – much less than its value. The universal response throughout the city, Buckingham felt, was "the rebirth of civic pride and enterprise and community effort which had its repercussions in the success of the many appeals made during the world war." The cornerstone was laid in May 1912, and the building completed within a year. The mandate had changed

Laying the cornerstone of the new YMCA, 1912, with city and church officials in attendance.

Source: J. Keleher Collection

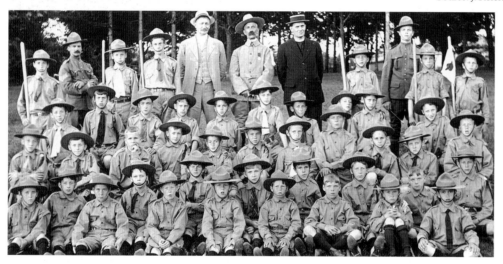

First Boy Scout Pack formed 1910, by Major Merewether, flanked by Mayor George Thorpe, and the Rev. Caleb Buckland, pastor of St. James Anglican Church.

Source: J. Keleher Collection

emphasis: programs were now to be physical, educational, religious, and social in that order. In the first year, 564 men and boys registered. Five gymnastic exhibitions were presented; an Industrial Indoor Baseball League was formed; 247 males underwent medical examinations; over 40 members used the swimming pool each day; and courses in English were given twice a week for 16 weeks to Armenians and once a week to the Chinese. At the cornerstone laying, MP Hugh Guthrie suggested that the city had "been a little backward" in not supplying a similar organization for women, and that he hoped to soon see a YWCA on the corner

across the street. The YWCA was organized as the Blue Triangle YWCA in 1915. On April 1, 1921, clubrooms on St. George's Square were occupied by the Business Girl's Club, the Sterling Dramatic Club and the Dalyte Club. The YWCA moved to new headquarters on Macdonell Street in October 1929, where they also ran a hostel for women coming from out of town to work in the city.

The first Boy Scout contingent in Guelph was organized in 1910 by Major H.D. Merrewether, a faithful parishioner at St. James Church. His capabilities were noted by the *Mercury* when, as chief parade marshal, "resplendent on a white charger, which pranced along in time with the music," he kept a multitude of marchers and 55 bands in order on Orange Day in 1922. The Girl Guides were started in 1936.

The Knights of Columbus Society (1910) met in various places until 1931, when they opened a clubhouse at the corner of Dublin Street and Waterloo Avenue. Like most fraternal orders and benefit societies their immediate aim was to care for the widows and orphans of its members, but as the years passed their mandate broadened. The first issue of the local council's journal *The Knight* was published in January 1921.

Guelph enjoyed the first Canadian Club, but as it neither went national, nor lasted long after it was formed in 1888, it can only be viewed as an antecedent to later developments. When the Hamilton club, begun in 1892, laid claim to being the first Canadian Club in Canada, Guelph's founder and president, Malcolm MacCormick protested, but unsuccessfully. After the formation in Guelph of a sister club to Hamilton in February 1907, with OAC President Creelman presiding, MacCormick rose to the occasion with a splendid dinner and rostrum of speakers to celebrate his club's 19th anniversary. It ended with the singing of *Auld Lang Syne*.

Women continued to promote organizations for their own interests. The first meeting of the Imperial Order of the Daughters of the Empire was held in New Brunswick in January 1900. Inspired by the needs of the Boer War, its purpose was to promote patriotism, loyalty to the Crown and Empire and service to others. Guelph's first chapter, formed in peacetime 1909, adopted the beautifying and improving of the city as its initial work. As the Victoria Guelph Chapter, they provided the City Parks Commission with $200 for the planning of city parks. A landscape architect was engaged, all Guelph's parks were landscaped and a new one, the Royal City Park, was created. Their next project was the erection of a fountain in remembrance of King Edward VII. In 1914, after two years of fundraising, it was constructed and placed in Trafalgar Square. The Captain Frederick Bond Chapter was formed in 1920, with emphasis on youth in Guelph and northern schools. In 1942, they opened an Opportunity Shop which raised substantial funds for projects throughout the century. The Rundle Chapter, no.108 of the Order of the Eastern Star (1920), organized for women related to a master mason, became the largest subordinate chapter in Ontario. The Major Robert Mutrie Chapter of the IODE, formed in 1939 by a group of younger women, immediately began work in aid of the Red Cross. The Guelph IODE Chapters also became adept at arranging annual charity balls, usually at the Armoury and later at Paradise Gardens.

Women enjoyed getting together for reasons other than service. Faculty wives at the OAC formed a Fireside Circle in 1903, where members presented short talks to each other on authors, art, music and architecture. In 1915, study was abandoned in favour of war relief work, and they formed a group for all the ladies in the neighbourhood. Although the College Heights Relief Workers disbanded after the war, the College Women's Club continued on. The Guelph Women's Canadian Club was organized in 1914, with education primarily in mind. It called for patriotic Canadian women to attend, claiming that too little was known of Canada's history, its natural wealth and its prospect for development. They did practical duty during the war years by raising money for the Red Cross and the 153rd Battalion. Shortly after the First World War they went on record as favouring a civic centre in the heart of the city to commemorate the fallen heroes of Guelph and Wellington County, but plans for OAC's Memorial Hall forestalled this. OAC librarian Florence Partridge made a connection between college and city women to form the Business and Professional Women's Club (1928). This club was also primarily for the interest of the members, although it supported good

Menu MacCormick's Canadian Club's
19th Anniversary Party, December 6, 1907
Blue Point Oysters   Lemons
Brown Bread Fingers
Celery   Radishes
Consomme Royale   Croutons of Bread
Roast Beef   Creamed Cauliflower
Mashed Potatoes   French Peas
Roman Punch
Roast Chicken Cranberry Sauce
Creamed Potatoes
Apple Pie or Minced Pie   Whipped Cream
Roquefort Cheese   Wafers
Café Noir

May Day celebrations at Macdonald Institute, 1910.   Source: J. Keleher Collection

causes when necessary. It was an early network club for women, one in which ideas could be shared. Women representatives from most of the churches and organizations met in November 1931, in the interest of peace and disarmament. Their purpose was to organize in the months before the World Conference at Geneva under the name of the Women's League of Nations Association of Guelph. In 1945, Partridge was again at work, this time bringing city and area women who were graduates of other universities to the college by founding the Guelph Chapter of the Canadian Federation of University Women.

Rotary and Kiwanis clubs, emanating from the United States, served to provide male networking while financing support for worthwhile civic causes. Martin Barry, Walter Buckingham, Fred Kelly and Evan Macdonald (father of the artist), were among the original 25 members of the Rotary Club of Guelph, formed in 1920. They met in Charlie Yeates' Royal Canadian Café on Wyndham Street. Annual reports at the meeting, held in the Kandy Kitchen in 1921, recorded the development of the Boys' Work Movement, the presentation of silver cups to various athletic clubs, and work with returned soldiers. Their minstrel show of 1922 played at Griffin's for two nights to full houses. Their purpose was to provide clean amusement, develop their members' talent, and raise funds for the needy and, in particular, the crippled children of the city. The shows of 1929 and 1931 were financially successful, as were future carnivals, garden parties and New Year's

GCVI Girls' Softball Team, 1928.   Source: Donald Coulman Collection

GCVI Basketball Team with Coach John F. Ross, 1933.

Source: Donald Coulman Collection

the YMCA building. In 1927, the Children's Aid Society separated from the Humane Society. The Welcome Wagon was established in 1928 to help newcomers enter into the community. Travellers' Aid was active a few years later during the Depression. Hobby clubs were also beginning to appear. The Guelph Stamp Club, attached to the YMCA, was led by Walter Tyson in 1928. In 1935, he organized an adult club of about 25 members that met during the Depression, but later disbanded. The Guelph Amateur Radio Club was started 1939. The first support group, Alcohol Anonymous, was formed locally in 1945.

dances. Ladies' Night, discontinued during the Depression, was re-instated in November 1937. On that night, Walter Buckingham and Martin Barry played a piano and violin duet.

The Kiwanis Club of Guelph obtained a charter in 1921, with J.M. Kearns QC its first president. Aiming to render altruistic service and help build a better community, it established a camp at Rockwood, provided Christmas welfare and tonsil operations. They also organized a K-boys Club of 20 boys, each under the guardianship of a Kiwanis member. In 1932, they united with the Argos Bible Class in a minstrel show. Roy Austen had formed a small Bible-study group called the Argos that grew into the second largest Bible class in Canada. The Argos carried on an active welfare program that provided dental and eye care for underprivileged children. By 1937, over 800 members had spread to other churches and the YMCA. The less-known fraternal organization, the Royal Antediluvian Order of Buffaloes, formed locally in 1929 to give aid to fellow men.

The late 1920s saw the development of community services separate from service clubs and churches. In 1925, the Red Cross began home nursing courses in

 March 9, 1926 – A near riot occurs at the Guelph-Galt intermediate team hockey game. Police were there when Clarence Boucher, "Galt's big defence man," injured Guelph's George Grant in a crushing move on the ice. The extent of feeling was such that Boucher had to escape out a rear window onto Paisley Street where the police found him and took him to the station. Galt had beaten Guelph 5-2 in the game. They also beat Guelph at court. After considering the circumstances the judge dropped the charges.

SPORTS

Guelph had many notable athletes over the years. Freddie Meadows won the middle-distance running championship of the world in February 1910. Jack Purcell was a world badminton champion from 1932 to 1945. Rod Lamont boxed from 1924 to 1936 and won the Ontario championship in 1924. In 1936, he coached the Canadian Olympic boxing team and founded the Guelph Boxing Club. Cosmo 'Cutts' Carere, also on the Guelph Maple Leaf baseball team, won the Ontario heavyweight boxing championship during the 1920s.

The Royal City Curling Club was provincial champion in 1918, winning the province's highest curling honour, the Ontario Tankard. In 1923, the club was runner-up for the Governor-General's Cup. After years of alleged friendly rivalry, an amalgamation between the Union Curling Club and the Royal City Curling Club created the Guelph Curling Club in 1926. The Union Club then reorganized with a new set of officers, but had a sketchy existence until 1931, when curling began to decline in Guelph. When the Guelph Curling and Skating Company surrendered its lease from the city, businessman David E. Kennedy and his wife bought the property. The first artificial ice plant was installed in 1936.

The Cambridge Ice Palace, built on the corner of Paisley and Norfolk streets in 1919 by a number of Guelph's prominent citizens, provided a home for hockey after the First World War. The Guelph team made the Ontario Hockey Association finals in 1923, but lost to Stratford. Roy Mason's Junior 'AB' team reached the OHA finals in 1936. Because they were getting past the age level, Mason reformed them into an 'A' team, and they surprised Guelph fans by out-playing top-grade junior 'A' teams and constantly reaching the play-offs. In 1942, the entire team joined the armed forces. Working in the background during these years was hockey coach Bill Lindley. In 1940, he was instrumental in the formation of the Guelph Minor Hockey Association and Guelph's Referees' Association.

Before the First World War, competitive baseball was played by the Church Baseball League. Afterwards, it became the Guelph City Senior Baseball League. When the Inter-County Senior League was formed in 1919, the Guelph team won the title in its first round of play-offs. Between then and 1941, it won the league championship four times and was runner-up six times. The Guelph Softball Association was organized in 1923 with industrial and church leagues. In 1925, games between the Guelph Creameries and the Stove Company rose to a high level, with the latter competing for the Ontario championship. Soccer had been popular for many years, with GCI, OAC and city teams enjoying some success. The Taylor-Forbes Club, originally formed in 1911, won five cups in 1923, including the Ontario and Albert Plenty Cups. During the Second World War, a three-club soccer league was created by the Guelph Maple Leaf Athletic Association for service men and members of the Royal Netherlands Army.

With golf increasing in popularity, in 1912, a group of citizens decided to purchase 75 acres of the Hood Farm beyond Riverside Park. With a handsome clubhouse, nine-hole course, three tennis courts and a noisy but useful flock of sheep, the Country Club was opened in 1913. Through the courtesy of the Street Railway, the club was allowed to establish a footbridge just above the dam to allow members going out by streetcar to walk through the park grounds to the club's gate. Competition came when OAC President George Christie met Arthur Cutten at a conference in Chicago in December 1927. Cutten told him about his vision of a huge sports complex located in Guelph's college area that would be

 July 18, 1912 – "A Coloured Ball Team" is announced in the newspapers as having formed in Guelph. The team members all worked at Pipe Mill. Their first game was Dominion Day at Lyon Park.

Ladies playing golf on the third green at the Guelph Country Club, 1938.
Source: Guelph Museums

accessible to students and citizens alike. He was prepared to underwrite the costs and donate the complex to the city. Christie lost no time. Lawyers were appointed, 230 acres acquired and the work begun. Although plans were scaled down, the clubhouse and golf course were reputed to have cost Cutten $750,000 – a staggering sum in the Depression year of 1931, when it was officially opened. Mayor Robson and city council declined Cutten's offer, feeling maintenance and deficits should not be borne by the taxpayers. The property was held in trust by the lawyers and the Cutten family continued to support it. In 1939, three years after Cutten's death, it was sold to Stanley Thompson and Donald Ross and became the Guelph Golf and Recreation Club Ltd. For many years it was known as Cutten Fields and later the Cutten Club.

The Guelph Rifle Association reorganized after the First World War with George Sleeman as president, but, when all rifle associations were disbanded at the request of military headquarters, it was absorbed into the Guelph Garrison Rifle Association. The Guelph Riding and Driving Association boasted some "Classy Entries" for their Dominion Day meet in 1912, as well as "some high class music." Horseracing was discontinued in Guelph shortly after, but meetings continued, with members enjoying success on other Ontario tracks. A light-harness horse business had been established at Springfield farm, four miles from town.

In 1924, Guelphites approved a money bylaw to erect a steel-structured grandstand at Exhibition Park and to lay out a new athletic ground costing $40,000. The Maple Leaf Baseball Club moved to the new diamond, and the old grounds were converted for other sports, including softball. Softball was also played at a park donated by J.W. Lyon in 1908 and at the Armoury. In 1926, the Lyon Park soccer field was enclosed and admission charged.

Sparks Circus Parade, June 29, 1927: elephants, horses and camels.

Source: Dr. R.L. Mahoney, courtesy of Liz Gray

ENTERTAINMENT

With its propensity for parades, Guelph always loved a circus. With exotic animals, colourful wagons and performers from another world, it would clatter through town to Exhibition Park, to grounds at the corner of Paisley and Edinburgh, or on Sleeman's flats off Waterloo Avenue between the car barns and the River Speed. The Ringling Brothers came in 1903, Barnum and Bailey about 1904, and, in 1916, the Latena Trained Wild Animal Circus, named for Guelph-born Tina Hewer, married in 1888 to Andrew Downie of Malville and Downie, circus aerialists.

The greatest pre-war public entertainments, though, in many an opinion, were Guelph's Home Weeks during the summers of 1908 and 1913. There was something for everyone, including reunions with relatives and old friends. Sunday was preparation day, with pulpits occupied morning and evening by former city clergy. Two parades left Market Square every day of the week and marched through crowd-lined streets to Exhibition Park. Daily, too, were band concerts, baseball and football matches and tug-of-war contests between Guelph's Russian, Armenian, Italian, "Scotch" and Irish teams. Monday was Citizen's Day, with gatherings and public receptions, addresses galore, and a Grand Citizen's Parade marching to the music of 10 or 12 bands. On Tuesday in 1908, spectators were entertained by the famous acrobatic family, the Kishizumis. In 1913, it was the day of the Grand Tally-ho Horse Parade (including two trained elephants), with horse races and free simulated "airplane" rides. Wednesday was Military Day or Manufacturer's Day and Thursday was Athletic Day or Automobile Day. That evening in 1913, a Grand Burlesque Parade was headed by "the world famous one and only original" Rube Band. Home Week in 1913 was two days longer than usual, with more athletics, more parades, and a Horticultural Society exhibition in City Hall.

Movies came next in popularity. Guelph's first movie house, Wonderland, was situated on Carden Street opposite the old Weigh Scales building that stood a little west of City Hall. It started operating in 1906 or 1907. Each side of the ticket box was a penny arcade of about eight machines, where, for one large Canadian copper and the turning of the handle, customers could view a continuous action of bathing beauties of the day. The walls of the theatre were painted with lavish waterfalls and forests. The seats were wooden kitchen chairs, nailed together so they could be moved all at once for cleaning the floor. Background music for the black-and-white silent films was provided by Guelph's blind musician Albert Kaiser. His 'illustrated songs' such as *Whisper my name in your dreams* and *I'll get you yet, little Girlie* were worth the price of admission. As the first reel was being rewound on to the spare, Kaiser would play or a guest artist would sing current songs or old-country ballads. Five or six pictures were presented each evening. On the evening of April 5, 1910, the program included a drama *The Masterpiece*, four comedies (*The Man with Three Wives; The Happy Widower; The Good Doctor; The Bridegroom's Joke*), and *The Aero Club Meet*.

A year or two later, the Coliseum opened on the west side of Wyndham above St. George's Square. The Apollo Music Hall was next, operating by 1910, on the west side of upper Wyndham. It presented matinees (5 cents) and evening shows (10 cents) of vaudeville acts and silent movies. The International Bible Students made news at the Apollo by presenting "the world's first colour motion picture with sound," the *Photo-Drama of Creation*, a combination of hand-painted slides, motion pictures, and synchronized sound from phonograph records. In 1917, the Regent Theatre (subtitled the Temple of Silent Art) opened on the grounds of the old Regent Hotel stables. It stretched from the box office on Macdonell Street to the screen, backing on to Cork Street. The projectionist had to use field glasses to focus the film on the screen. Judging from the advertisements, Griffin's, the Apollo and the Regent did well during the war. The Apollo was shut down in early 1920, when the Castle Theatre was erected next to it on the site of the old American Hotel. Then, in May 1922, Griffin's Royal Opera House closed. Eleven months later, the New Capitol Theatre held a grand opening with a thousand good seats, every one with full view, 35 cents anywhere. The Castle burned down in 1928 and the Regent closed shortly after, leaving the Capitol as the only theatre until 1934, when the Royal opened in the old Bell Piano and Organ Company premises. The first

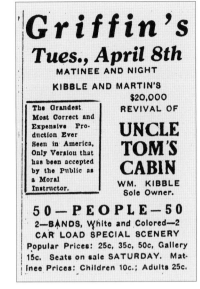

Left: Uncle Tom's Cabin, April 8, 1913.
Right: Empire Concert by the Philharmonic Society of Guelph, April 9, 1913, at Griffin's.
Source: *Guelph Evening Mercury,* April 5, 1913

talkie starred Al Jolson in the *Jazz Singer*. The Royal and the Palace, built in 1941, were operated by Famous Players Ltd. American culture was not new to Guelph, but it came in full force with the Hollywood movies.

The Philharmonic Choir had continued Guelph's 19th-century choral tradition, reaching at least an equivalent with a 110-voice choir in an Empire Concert, April 9, 1913. Led by James R. Pears, described by the *Evening Mercury* as "the peppery little Briton," it presented national airs with "vigour and harmony, giving one of the best programs heard in the city for a long time." Amateur musicals continued to be produced, and, in 1913, a new Guelph Dramatic and Operatic Society was formed with J. Burlington Rigg as musical director and stage manager. *Geisha*, the *Merry Widow*, and *Florodoro* were planned as productions.

Two days after Britain's declaration of war in August 1914, a spirited meeting was held in the Armoury during which 107 of Guelph's army and navy veterans sent wires to Prime Minister Borden and the Minister of Militia indicating they were ready to serve. On the 13th, a muster parade was held. On the 14th, the GMS Band gave a concert in Exhibition Park under the auspices of

Curtains and side boxes of the Royal Opera House, opened in 1894. Under new management in 1910, it became Griffin's Royal Opera House (sometimes simply Griffin's) and, in 1923, the Capitol movie-house. It was demolished in 1953. Source: Guelph Museums

The Guelph Jazz Band shortly after its formation in 1919. They were more often seen playing about town on the Radial Railway.
Source: Guelph Museums

the Ladies of the Garrison, and the *Evening Mercury* observed that "long before the enlisted men paraded from the armouries, the streets were alive with people, who crowded up to the curbing, anxious to see the boys who would represent Guelph at the front." St. George's and St. James churches held a special military service on August 19 in Exhibition Park. Prepared for the occasion by the Archbishop of Canterbury, instructions had been received in Guelph that afternoon. The following morning, the first overseas contingent of 80 men left for Valcartier, each supplied with two suits of woollen underwear by the Ladies' Garrison Club. The Winter Fair building was immediately put to use as barracks and, during the war, housed five artillery batteries.

The Catholic Women's League, at this time known as the Confraternity of the Holy Family, organized the voluntary registration of women in the parish, placing their services at the disposal of the country in any capacity required. The Prime Minister replied, and their communication was brought to the immediate attention of the Voluntary Service Registration Bureau. The Red Cross executive, having folded in 1902, reorganized. Their first urgent one-day-appeal for funds, produced over $1,880, with an appreciable amount, it was noted, coming from the Italians in St. Patrick's Ward, the poorest area in the city. Guelphites continued to be whole-hearted in their giving. When the Guelph branch of the Canadian Patriotic Fund undertook to raise $15,000, they received $26,000. On another

occasion, aiming for $60,000, as was noted in the King's Daughters of the Empire edition of the *Mercury,* they raised $91,000.

Musical and social circles were continuously active. Every week Kelly's Music Shop advertised new comic songs: *Sister Susie's Sewing Shirts for Soldiers*; *Something Seems Tingling-Ingling*; or *Mary Pickford, She's the Darling of them all.* The Knights of Columbus regularly entertained Catholic members of the forces with games, euchre, dancing, musical programs and refreshments. The rest of the churches took care of the Protestants. Ambitious fundraising events were staged, ranging from the Daughters of the Empire's talent night in Tovell's Hall for the Belgian Relief Fund to the massive production called 'Fifty Fifty'(50 percent to the Red Cross, 50 percent to 'Wellington Battalion Colors') in Griffin's Opera House. The program featured everything from vaudeville to the second act of *Madam Butterfly*, and from the YMCA acrobatics class to the most classical of Guelph's musicians.

"In the good old days," said Guelphite Trudi Becker ,"the GMS Band played every Sunday night in Exhibition Park. Everybody went. Parents sat in the benches around the bandstand and any family who had a car took it and parked at the perimeter. The young girls walked one way around the band stand to the music and the boys the other. You always tried to stop opposite someone you liked. The cars all honked at the end of the piece and stopped when the band started up again."

The GMS Band held patriotic concerts Sunday evenings in the Opera House, although complaints were voiced in a *Mercury* editorial (June 30, 1915) that the band was "militating against church services." The suggestion was made that if the concerts began at nine, "church-goers would have an equal chance with others in the rush for seats." In answer to criticism and lack of support, the band outlined its work during the war in a letter to the *Mercury*. It listed dozens of recruiting parades, military church parades, Red Cross parades, sacred concerts and fundraising events for which they were not paid, nor did they charge. Civic parades, circus parades and their dutiful weekly concert in the park were also enumerated.

In the effort to get the job done, there was a feeling of reconciliation among groups. Management and labour even tried to understand each other. On Labour Day, 1918, after a speech-filled luncheon, the Guelph Board of Trade and the Trades and Labor Council co-operated to sponsor a Gala Day of Sports at Exhibition Park. Thanksgiving races were revived, with the opinion expressed that they would continue in future years.

Amidst all the activity there was, of course, anxiety, suffering and dreadful personal losses. In January and February 1917, a scarcity of fuel closed nearly all the schools. In the latter part of the year, they were closed for three weeks due to the epidemic of influenza. During the severe winter, teachers volunteered in the hospitals. Sunday services were held in church basements. The epidemic was more severe in the fall of 1918. Schools and churches were closed, meetings curtailed and the local hospital crowded to capacity.

After the war, certain services were obviously needed. The Guelph branch of the Great War Veteran's Association was started by seven returned soldiers in April 1917. Working first from a room in the Queen's Hotel, they attempted to help other veterans re-enter civilian life and find employment. The offer of free rooms in the YMCA made work there easier. They also supported a group of veterans who wished to start a band independent of the GMS. With instruments loaned from the Armoury, they played at a victory celebration in 1919, two days after their first rehearsal. Their soccer team that year was reputed to be the finest ever organized in Guelph. The Red Chevron Club also sought to provide support and financial assistance, when needed, to veterans and their families. Their group was the fourth in existence after Toronto, Peterborough and London. Their weekly newspaper column voiced news and encouragement for veterans. Red Chevron members formed a Guelph Legion Bugle Band in 1932. "They wore old Army Service Corps uniforms, " wrote historian Ross Irwin, "used short model army surplus bugles and rehearsed in the Armoury, in the Legion and on a hill in a field at Victoria Road near the Keleher Foundry, which drove the cows to the other end of the field." Under Matt Conners' direction they won prizes at the Canadian National Exhibition for several years. The year they entered at Waterloo, Irwin relates, "they came home too drunk to realize they had won until the next morning." They became the Guelph Veterans Trumpet Band in 1938 and took part in Guelph's Victory Day celebrations in August 1946. After the formation of the Royal Canadian Legion in 1926, Guelph veterans organized into two branches, numbers 234 and 257. The John McCrae Memorial Branch grew out of number 234. The two groups eventually amalgamated and established themselves at 34 Elizabeth St.

Tovell's Hall and Singular's Hall were popular pre-war sites for dances. Markle's Orchestra provided medleys from old songs and comic operas. The Royal City Waltz Club sometimes indulged in square dancing. New dance bands were being formed, notably the City Jazz Band led by Bobby O'Connor, that played through the city in open cars on special occasions. But the moral code had

changed for some men returning from the war. One *Mercury* columnist warned Guelph parents in 1921 that three dance halls existed in Guelph with "no chaperones and not even a chuck-er-out." Chaperones had become obsolete, she explained, but it was time they were revived. Her solution: the appointment of a policewoman or a morality officer backed by a secret advisory committee, to put a check on the alarming growth of prostitution. Pastor Hind, although admitting his knowledge was second-hand, chose to awaken the civic conscience to the debauchery and degrading circumstances in the city. In the "reeking atmosphere" pervading the city, "failures in classroom and physical culture" were festering in "the absolutely inevitable stirring of sexual passion." The guardians of culture were worried, and tried to do something about it.

In 1918, a group of enthusiasts from various churches met at Chalmers Presbyterian Church to listen to representatives from the Social Service Council of Canada. Its aims, listed in the *Mercury*, September 25, 1918, were multiple: child welfare; suppression of venereal disease; abolition of partisan patronage in politics; enforcement of all laws bearing on morals, especially with the view of having the U.S. and Canada permanently dry by 1920; the suppression of the white slave trade; and the promotion of women's franchise. A resolution was passed for the formation of a Guelph branch and a provisional executive elected. Motions by Guelph's MLA Sam Carter and the Rev. Konke were then passed, pressing for the immediate action by the legislature to provide pensions for dependent mothers, adequate provision for farm workers, cottages for the "feeble-minded" and adequate, sanitary housing for working people at reasonable rentals. Professor J. W. Crowe addressed the regular meeting of the Trades and Labor Council on the aims of the group. The election of officers took place in February 1919, when resolutions were passed endorsing several principles of social welfare. Bi-monthly meetings followed in which health, welfare and housing were discussed, and guest speakers from the national council were invited. What was done immediately is not clear, but the Social Service Committee was active during the Depression and responsible for the Travellers' Aid and a Mothers' Club that mended and distributed clothes and quilts.

The Guelph Choral Society was formed in the fall of 1920 because, according to a concert programme, "music had sunk to the lowest ebb possible during the years of harrowing war, when people sought distraction in picture houses that did not always tend to uplift." The programme also stated that music in theatres, music halls and ballrooms was "of such a character as to call for

Alexander Saison and Guelph's first Italian Band, 1912.   Source: Private Collection of Ruth Saison King, Toronto

censure rather than approbation," and because young people were "revelling in the birth of jazz and ragtime." The choir, under the direction of James Pears, organized festivals for Armistice and Christmas celebrations and raised substantial sums for the unemployed. Mrs. Powell Hamilton's Guelph Opera Company produced successful Gilbert and Sullivan operas for a few years in the early 1920s.

However, "the motion picture activities [in Guelph]," wrote Lawrence Mason in the *Globe*, September 12, 1925, "seem to prevent regular acting companies from using the town's only real stage, so that dramatic activity is practically at a standstill. The poor acoustic properties of the collegiate stage made the recent performance of the Dumbells very unsatisfactory."

In 1922, the Daughters of Scotland financed the founding of the Highland Pipe Band that, two years later, was renamed the Guelph Pipe Band. An Italian band had continued to exist since the days of Alexander Saison and, in 1925, 'Professor' Giovanni Sartoria arrived from Sicily (via Hamilton) to form a Sons of Italy Band and to give music lessons. He was found work in the Northern Rubber Shoe factory on Alice Street. New instruments and highly decorative uniforms were ordered from Italy, and the city provided a grant. The band was greatly loved, but not very good, claimed Ross Irwin. At concerts in Lyon Park, it was

often augmented by the Robinson Bakery Band (1920-1938). Its demise is not certain. It either folded two years after the death of Sartoria in 1931, or at the beginning of the Second World War.

During the First World War, Presto Club donated the proceeds from several concerts to the Belgian Relief Fund and the Red Cross. The first young student's program was held in 1918 at Idlewood. By 1920, the cost of the Opera House had become prohibitive, and concerts were held in Dublin Street Church. On October 6, 1921, they risked renting the Opera House for a recital by Edward Johnson. Despite daringly high ticket prices ($1.50), the theatre was packed. The following year, they filled the Armoury with a concert by the Cleveland Orchestra (with Johnson as soloist). As active membership had risen to 41, meetings were forcibly switched from individual homes to Norfolk Street Methodist Church. The auditorium at GCVI became the concert venue as soon as it was built. For the next two decades, a variety of famous artists graced its stage: The Hart House Quartet; Vladimir Horowitz; Gregor Piatigorsky; the Don Cossack Chorus; Harold Bauer; Georges Enesco; Artur Rubenstein; Trudi Schoop and her Dancing Comedians; and the Volkoff Ballet. During his tenure as general manager of the Metropolitan Opera (1935-1950), Johnson saw to it that many of his company sang for Presto. This is not to say that Presto neglected Canada's talent or promising students. Betty-Jean Hagen, the Canadian Trio (Ernest Macmillan, Kathleen Parlow and Zara Nelsova), artists from the Hambourg Conservatory, the Pach Duo, and youngsters like Marion Grudeff and Guelph's David Ouchterloney and Beauna Somerville were given opportunities to perform.

The Depression affected everybody. St. Patrick's Anglican Church survived, although half the congregation was unemployed and those fortunate to work had to do so on 'short time.' St. Paul's Presbyterian, in the same area, found itself in financial straits and accepted the services of students from Knox College. In 1936, it joined with Eden Mills. Membership at Dublin Street continued to grow, reaching a high of 930 in 1938. Some families could not attend church, however, because they had no decent clothes to wear. School attendance rose because those who had left could either not find work or were let go. Unemployment insurance did not exist, factory benevolent funds were depleted and the government was forced to establish a relief system of vouchers for food and clothing. Interviews made by Guelph Social History Project in 1998 illustrate how some were affected. Dorothy Farquharson remembered the chain of men riding the railroads and those knocking at the door, asking for a meal. Her family grew as much as they could and kept chickens, but money was very short. An orange and a banana were Christmas treats. Bootlegging constituted a principle means of earning money, as was fishing for shiners in the Speed River or picking mushrooms in the garbage dump. Youngsters collected hot coals when trains dumped their ashes at the railroad junction at Sackville and Alice streets at seven in the evening. "Charlie Barber's butcher's shop," said Dorothy Lazzari, "would give free pigs' ears, tails, liver, heart and bones and chicken wings," not thought good in those days, but made excellent sausages. Dave Kennedy Jr. remembered his father's words: "You must never forget you are a very privileged person and, as such, you have a responsibility to help those who are less fortunate." Almost every night a man knocked at his door looking for food. He was fed in the kitchen. Arrangements were made with the 'Y' for a place for him to sleep and with the Peacock Restaurant to hire him for some work.

Money raised by concerts was mainly to help the unemployed with food and clothing. A packed crowd in GCVI's auditorium appreciated Edward Johnson's return to Guelph in 1931 to perform in aid of the *Guelph Daily Mercury* Relief Fund. The *Mercury* also played a large part in keeping the community together. An editorial, complimenting the Horticultural Society for instilling a pride in well-kept grounds and kitchen gardens and for other activities beneficial to the city, brought over 200 out for the society's annual meeting – the largest number ever. Nearly a page was devoted to boys, featuring church, school, YMCA activities and opportunities for work. Even more space was allotted when the Boys' Work Board suggested the inclusion of girls. A 'Young People's Page,' appeared the following week (January 16, 1933) covering both girls' and boys' activities and suggesting the formation of a Girls' Work Board to oversee girls' activities.

Several hundred citizens were active in amateur theatricals throughout the city, raising money and displaying thespian abilities. OAC's productions, directed by Scotty McLean, attracted large audiences from the city. Her January 1933 production of *St. Joan* received high praise. The play-reading group at the YMCA was always well attended and the Columbus Players were presenting a variety of plays in the Church of Our Lady Hall. No wonder that the first Western Ontario Drama Festival in London, March 1933, aroused considerable interest. "Why," asked the *Mercury* (January 10, 1933) "was there, as yet, no Little Theatre movement in Guelph?" Before long, resources were pooled. City folk provided the executive, the first president being Royal Bank manager Arthur Wilkinson. Actors were drawn from various groups, including the Columbus Players, and McLean directed the

The Robinson Bakery Band was organized in 1920. They played at lawn socials, parties and fairs and, in 1926, won the class B family award at the Canadian National Exhibition.

Source: Guelph Museums

first production *Yellow Sands* in November 1935. Rehearsals were held wherever there was space large enough. City Hall was the main venue for performances, augmented by GCVI, Memorial Hall and the Capitol Theatre. In 1937, at the seventh annual Western Ontario Drama League Festival, GLT won the Meredith Trophy for showing the greatest promise for future achievement. The award was based on the productions of *The Skin Game* by John Galsworthy and A. A. Milne's *Mr. Pim.*

Guelph was dressed up and all ready to go at least a week before the coronation of King George VI and Queen Elizabeth in May 1937. Flags, streamers and buntings decorated the streets and buildings. Store windows were filled with symbolic scenes, and a great arch of red, white and blue lights hung over City Hall doorway, draped with the Empire's insignias. On Sunday, May 9, overflow crowds attended special church parades to hear sermons and music suited to the occasion. A commemorative service was conducted in the collegiate by the Ministerial Association. Against the background of a huge, draped Union Jack, Frank Cheeseman directed a massed choir from the churches, assisted by the GMS Band. The following day, the biggest parade for many a year took place as over 3,000 marched through flag-bedecked streets from the Armoury to Exhibition Park. Guelph was enjoying itself again. At the time of the actual coronation, St. George's carillon pealed out the notes of *God Save the King*, and the city cheered.

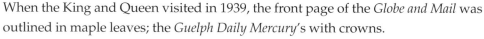

King George VI and Queen Elizabeth visit Guelph, 1939. Mayor William Taylor is being introduced to them by Prime Minister Mackenzie King.
Source: J. Keleher Collection

Victory Bond Parade passes through St George's Square, c. 1940.
Source: Guelph Museums

When the King and Queen visited in 1939, the front page of the *Globe and Mail* was outlined in maple leaves; the *Guelph Daily Mercury*'s with crowns.

National organizations were highly organized and ready to work when war broke out in 1939. Due to frustrations over allocations of funds between the national and local organization, Guelph Red Cross work was delayed until September 1940. For the first time since its founding the executive consisted entirely of men. As the city had now decided to raise money through a single fundraising organization, the Community Chest for War and Welfare Service received its charter October 1940. In May 1941, $70,000 was raised.

Space allocation was the next problem. The college made adjustments. From 1941 to 1945, the No.4 Wireless School of the RCAF occupied Watson Hall, Macdonald Hall, Macdonald Institute, Creelman Hall, Mills Hall, the maids' dormitory, the students' dormitory, Trent Institute, the administration building, the gymnasium, Memorial Hall, the farm mechanics' building, Bursar Hall, the skating rink and the laundry. These buildings were fenced off from the rest of the campus. Students had to find lodgings in the College Hill area or downtown. The president, bursar and registrar moved into the horticultural building. When the

RCAF station was enlarged to accommodate a training school for the Canadian Women's Army Corps, they took over the Cutten clubhouse. An annex was built for sleeping quarters and a mess hall. The club operated from the stone house on the 13th fairway.

The Guelph Branch of the Navy League of Canada, founded in 1941, took up residence in James Johnson's old boathouse. The Armoury and the market buildings were barracks and training centres for five artillery batteries. The City of Guelph made 500 plots of ground available for Victory Gardens, and under direction of the Horticultural Society, citizens turned their flower gardens and lawns to the production of vegetables. Patriotic work groups were organized in the churches and thousands of garments and boxes of food sent to Guelph boys in Canada and overseas. In a frenzy of fundraising, organizations and clubs co-operated. B'nai B'rith held Saturday night dances for service men in Columbus Hall. The Horticultural Society staged an 'Old Country Flower Festival and Carnival' in Exhibition Park (June 1941). It featured a 'Monster Bingo' on the Grandstand, a 'Giant Parade' of cadets and military bands and street dancing on Exhibition Street. An electric V sign was erected in front of City Hall (July 1941) for a 'Monster Street Carnival' and open-air concert and bingo, sponsored by the 2/11th Field Ambulance. Tag days, old-time fiddlers' contests, a 'Mile of Coppers' drive by the Kiwanis Club; old forms of entertainment and new ones devised raised money for individual causes or the Community Chest. Presto presented student concerts and famous artists, including Gladys Swarthout and Thomas L. Thomas. In October 1942, it held a 'Week of Music in Wartime.' Events, co-sponsored by the Kiwanis Club and Business and Professional Women, provided a week of concerts, lectures on the benefit and joys of music and special church music. Proceeds went to the *Mercury's* British Distress Fund and the Kiwanis East Coast Fund for Merchant Seamen's Comforts. In December, in Memorial Hall, Presto presented a series of Sunday evening 'Musicales' for the men and women of the No. 4 Wireless School RCAF.

Infantry marching down Woolwich Street during the Second World War. Source: Liz Gray; photo by E. H. Austen

In the schools, health and physical education was revamped into a defence-training course and the languishing cadet corps was revised. Teachers and children were to play their part in the preservation of democracy. Empire Day was reinstated and every child prepared for it weeks ahead. High school and college years were shortened, enabling boys and girls to work longer on farms. In October 1942, when an afternoon 'Musicale' was held in Massey Hall at OAC as part of the Presto Club's Music Week, over 100 OAC boys were still out west, helping with the harvest. Small children also did their best to help. Melba Jewell and friends collected newspapers in thick bundles (to get into a movie free), and silver paper from discarded cigarette boxes. In 1943 pupils at GCVI contributed $1,610 towards the Red Cross, the Veteran's Poppy League, the Navy League, the British Distress Fund, Aid in Russia, the School War Service Club and War-Savings Stamps.

A large section of Guelph's population was severely distressed during the war. Members of the Italian community, although born in Guelph, were treated as aliens. Their organizations folded. Some had to carry alien cards, some found it impossible to get a job, and a few spent time in detention centres. Interviews by Robert Hainey with Guelph's Italians (in Italian) showed that many were sympathetic to Mussolini. Beliefs in the benefits of fascism served to distance that community from the mainstream. Teresa Marucci told *Mercury* reporter Hilary Stead in a 1991 interview, that she was offered a job at the spinning mill on Alice Street in 1939, but never worked there, because the other employees threatened to strike if she were hired. She was accepted in the Canadian Army, though, and served as a sergeant until the war ended.

THE PRACTICE OF ART

Guelph's cultural life remained too small and provincial to support indigenous professional talent. Musicians could supplement their income as organists and choir conductors, or by giving private lessons. David Ouchterloney (1914-1987) took this route and established a fine reputation as a performer, composer, adjudicator, CBC and CFRB radio host and principal of the Toronto Conservatory of Music from 1968 to 1977. Other successful careers were the result of personal

Market day at City Hall and Carden Street, 1935.　　　Source: Guelph Museums

initiative. Guelph's Beauna Somerville became a first violinist with the Toronto Symphony. Anne Jamieson, who performed for Presto in 1933 and 1939, gave concerts in New York, on the air, and sang opera in San Francisco and Los Angeles. Ivy Dale, billed as 'Guelph's own soloist and operatic star' for her Presto concert in 1933, studied in Toronto and enjoyed a limited career in the rest of Canada and the United States.

Trumpeter Bob Hamilton described work done in Guelph to "keep boys off the street" that eventually produced some fine professional musicians. When, in 1941, Police Chief Harold Nash asked Sid Ecott to form a junior boys' and girls' band, the Canadian Women's Service Force, at that time in Guelph, agreed to sponsor it. Used instruments were supplied, and between 30 and 40 joined. Private lessons were available from John (Pop) Denver, who was in charge of the boiler room at the Court House, where rehearsals were held. The Guelph Y's Men's Boys' and Girls' Band was formed in January of 1942, quickly gaining 40 members. Bandmaster was Arthur C. Robinson of London, brother of Guelph's Chris Robinson, well known in Guelph for his work with the Robinson Family Band.

Two Guelph painters were gradually establishing themselves as artists. After five years at the Putney School of Art and the Royal Academy in London, England, Guelph-born Evan Macdonald (1905-1972) returned to Guelph in 1930 to work full-time at his father's store. He had become known as a portraitist and illustrator, but practised his art in the evenings and on weekends. In the early

1940s, he rented part of a department store on Wyndham Street to exhibit his works. After serving from 1943 to 1945 in the Royal Canadian Engineers as an instructor and designer of camouflage in B.C., he returned to Guelph as president of D. E. Macdonald Brothers store. In 1945, the Business and Professional Women's Club sponsored an exhibition of his work. Gordon Couling, also born in Guelph (1913-1984) studied at the Ontario College of Art and did post-graduate work at New York University. While also serving with the Royal Canadian Engineers, he had a one-man show at the Vancouver Art Gallery in 1946. He returned to Guelph to become art instructor at Macdonald Institute. Effie Smith, who had studied art in Hamilton and Chicago, was giving classes in china painting and watercolours.

The connection between religion and victory had been emphasized during the war by the churches, schools and cultural organizations. In the past, schools had not strictly enforced the opening exercises of a Bible reading and the Lord's Prayer. Whenever they did, many were dissatisfied with the choice of scriptural passages. An interdenominational committee had been established in 1922, but its three graded books *Bible Readings for Schools,* although well received, proved too expensive for wide use. By 1940, about 10 percent of schools had voluntarily added religion to their curriculum. As interest grew in the subject, in October 1943, 15 Guelph clergymen volunteered to teach a course for one half-hour a week. It was prescribed by the Religious Education Council of Ontario and approved by the Ontario Department of Education. Bibles were donated by the Gideon Society. Then, in 1943, Premier George Drew advocated a return to the traditional aspects of education that had been de-emphasized with the progressive curriculum of 1937: the Three R's (reading, writing, and arithmetic); the British Empire; and the Christian religion. In the speech from the throne in February 1944, two half periods a week were to be devoted to study of the scriptures with an aim to set up ideals, build attitudes and influence behaviour. Robert Stamp, education historian, concluded that "in Drew's mind a 'Christian society' and a 'democratic society' were closely linked, if not synonymous, and both were central to his vision of a post-war society." Many in his hometown thought the same way.

The old anchorage held firm in Guelph well into the first half of the 20th century. Without two world wars it might have lost grip; but it was needed by circumstances it created. Those wars could not have been fought and won with vigour, without strong faith in God, unswerving loyalty to king and empire, responsibility to fellow humans and a belief that goodness would prevail. Old values and disciplines were bulwarks against many foes and thought necessary for a healthy and useful life. They were inherent in the words, "be yours to hold it high. If ye break faith with us who die, we shall not sleep." Having been schooled in the city of Guelph, founded and nurtured by 'old country stock,' Drew's friend, John McCrae, knew of what he spoke.

LOOSENING THE ROPES – GUELPH 1945-1967

The siren's shrieking message was followed by peals of peace from St. George's carillon. Everyone who could, went downtown. The streets were filled with singing, dancing and impromptu music. Shops closed and church doors opened, and many entered to give thanks: the boys were coming home and life would return to normal!

The afternoon parade was dignified with uniforms, ribbons and flags. Old men with medals marched, followed by bright-eyed Brownies and Cubs. Dignitaries kept time with Salvation Army hymns. Army and Sea Cadets, Guides and Scouts led Legionnaires and the wives and mothers of servicemen. The traditional costumes of the Polish Friendship Society swayed in time with the Field Ambulance Pipe Band, while strains of military music could be heard in the distance. Nick Antonelli's Accordion Band brought up the rear as crowds turned to follow. Five thousand were reported by the *Mercury* to have arrived at Exhibition Park for the victory celebrations. The words of pastors and priests praised God in eloquent terms, for "without Him we could not have won the war." Looking across the jubilant throng, Mayor Rife held up his arms with the warning: "We will not be any better for this victory, unless we build the better world we have discussed so much."

Few had doubts that a new and better world would not be built. Guelph had entered the post-war world with its economy strengthened by the conflict. Workers earned better wages during the war, servicemen sent regular incomes home, farmers retired to buy city homes and new industries were attracting young families. In March 1946, the relief roster counted less than 100 compared to 3,000 during the Depression years. Residents had more money to spend, and contributions to the Community Chest went over the top.

Returning military personnel brought both a baby boom and a desire to return to normal life. A search for sure methods and stability in education persisted, accompanied by a determination that every child should receive an education according to his ability. The federal government entered the provincial field of education to help returning servicemen. Voluntary organizations expanded, new facilities were constructed and more attention paid to the needs of youth and the disadvantaged. New churches formed as waves of immigrants arrived and, with Guelph's mosaic changing, an interest arose in the city's own past. The municipal government assumed a greater interest in leisure activities. Hockey was king, its popularity promoted through the city's new radio station and the spread of television in the 1950s. The theatre scene was stimulated by the arrival of British immigrants after the war. Musical and artistic groups benefitted from federal initiatives to support Canadian culture and by the founding of an arts college at the University of Guelph in 1964. Although more professional qualities were incorporated into amateur productions, the advent of television was stiff competition to local events. Guelph was a small city (with a population of 27,386 in 1951), and cultural life still depended on the inspiration and vision of a few citizens.

The churches welcomed ex-servicemen home with receptions and banquets, and organized new clubs for them and their families. Church nursery departments were formed to care for children and infants, allowing young parents to attend the morning service. Guides and Brownies began a series of mother and daughter banquets at St. James Church, and the tennis club thrived there until the Church of Our Lady opened larger courts to the public in 1948. With financial worries lessened, new buildings and parking lots appeared. Dublin Street paid off the mortgage in 1949 and completed a Christian education wing in 1956. Sunday school attendance at St. James exceeded that of St. George's as the post-war babies grew, and they converted their courts into a badly-needed parking lot. The electric Wurlitzer organ, purchased in 1952, was worn out by 1959. A better choice was made in 1961, when another Casavant came to Guelph, one constructed specifically for St. James to last for generations.

Paisley United, too, had paid off the mortgage and its now 1,000 members celebrated its centenary in grand style for three weeks. A Christian education addition was completed in 1960. Gordon Couling redecorated the church interior, including the ceiling, by hand. The first of 12 stained-glass windows that he designed was installed that year. Paisley also held an early morning Hungarian service. The Church of Christ (Disciples) organized a Canadian-Girls-in-Training (CGIT) and renovated the church basement to make more room for the Sunday school. From 1958, any person professing faith in Jesus Christ regardless of baptism would be accepted into the church. The next year, the name was changed to the Christian Church (Disciples). In 1963, adjoining property was purchased, and an educational building, minister's study, library and nursery were built in time for the church to host a five-day all-Canada convention.

Exceptionally fine organists and choirmasters invigorated the choirs. At St. James, J. R. Pears directed a large ensemble with 20 juniors. A choir mother would "bop them on the head if they misbehaved," wrote historian Terry Crowley. Madeleine Kelly, daughter of cellist Charles Kelly, conducted a large and ambitious choir at Dublin for 23 years. Ralph Kidd, appointed organist and choirmaster at St. George's in 1941, provided exquisite church music with a senior and boys' choir during his 30-year tenure.

Home missions began to assume greater importance. The United Church's maritime project in 1946 involved the support of supply boats and missionaries travelling Canada's eastern and western coasts in aid of the native peoples. On White Gift Sunday, Paisley's entire choir loft resembled the front half of a ship. The bow protruded over the pulpit, with a mast and rigging reaching heavenward. St. James Parish Guild made nightclothes and bedspreads for an Anglican Indian school at the Brantford reserve, contributed to disaster relief and sent food parcels to Britain. The parish supported the building of a chapel at Guelph General Hospital in 1954.

The growing population of Ukrainian Catholics held a special service in the Church of Our Lady in 1953 to acquaint English-speaking friends with the rites of their ancient religion. They also expressed gratitude to the church for allowing them to conduct a service once a month until they had a space of their own. A site on Bridge Street (now York Road) was consecrated in October 1952, but the building was not completed until 1963. In July that year, the Byzantine church, with three copper and brass cupolas and a central dome, was consecrated as St. Mary's Ukrainian Catholic Church of the Holy Protection of the Mother of God.

The Guelph Reformed Church, a branch of the American denomination, was organized in 1953 to serve the large number of immigrant Dutch families. The first services in Dutch were held in the YMCA, then in St. Paul's Presbyterian and later in the larger Paisley Memorial United. In June 1956, a lot on Speedvale Avenue was purchased and the official opening took place in April 1959. The Christian Reformed Church was based on Calvinist tradition. Eleven immigrant families from Holland first met in the Orange Hall in 1953 and later in a building at the corner of Albert Street and Martin Avenue. When, by 1960, membership had

grown from 25 families to more than 100, a new church was built at 287 Water St. Renamed Ichthius Christian Reformed Church, it was more often called the First Christian Reformed Church.

The Brooklyn Mission also expanded. When Caroline Harcourt died in February 1953, she left 31 James St. as a rent-free home for the mission caretaker and 63 Forbes for a manse. She also provided an endowment fund of $35,000 for maintenance of the two houses and for annual Christmas gifts for the Sunday school children. When the hour of Sunday worship was changed to the morning, the substantial increase in the congregation indicated the need for a permanent church. The mission was recognized as Harcourt Memorial United Church in February 1956. For Sunday services, the Royal Hotel and the Canadian Legion lent chairs (to be returned every Monday morning), an antique pump-organ was borrowed, and old theatre seats from the Capitol Theatre were used for the choir. One hundred and forty names graced the charter membership roll. Larger quarters were soon needed and, in May 1960, a two-and-a-half acre plot on Dean Avenue was purchased for the building officially dedicated in 1962.

A large portion of post-war growth took place in the northeastern section of the city. Responding to inquiries from the Stevenson and Speedvale area, workers from Chalmers set up Trinity United Church Sunday School in Edward Johnson School. After the first church service there in February 1956, attendance grew rapidly. Funds were raised, and Trinity United Church dedicated its new building in October 1959. St. Paul's Presbyterian separated from Eden Mills in 1954 to return to its old Guelph home, but found the area not as populated as in the past. Knox, on the other hand, started a Sunday school in Ottawa Crescent School in September 1956. Church services began in 1957 and, the next year, the first congregation and minister were formally accepted. When plans for a new church on Victoria Road were underway, St. Paul's was pleased to amalgamate. The first service in Westminster-St. Paul's Presbyterian took place in March 1960.

During a financial campaign in the 1960s, St. Patrick's on York Road discovered that over 70 percent of its congregation no longer lived within the parish and that more than 40 percent were in Green Acres, a new housing development within St. George's Parish. As a large number of St. George's also lived in that area, the diocese had purchased a lot on Speedvale Avenue, just east of Victoria, for a new church and parish hall to be called St. David's. Discussions and disputes followed at St. Patrick's, but financial realities prevailed, and the congregation voted to move. The old church was sold, its memorials transferred to the new church and, on the third Sunday in June 1967, the first services were held in St. David's and St. Patrick's. St. Patrick's old rival, York Road Baptist, also moved to the same area. Having needed larger quarters since 1959, the congregation decided on a Victoria Road location. The dedication service of Crestwicke Baptist Church took place in October 1966.

The Roman Catholic Church ventured into the northeast in 1956 when Bishop J. F. Ryan invited the Holy Spirit Fathers (Spiritans) to celebrate mass in the corridor of Holy Rosary School in November 1956. As the parishioners increased in number, Sunday mass was held in the auditorium of John F. Ross Collegiate. A parish hall was constructed a year later. Scouts, Guides, Cubs, Brownies and a Holy Name Altar Society were quickly organized. When the parish numbered 700 families, it was given permission to build a church and a rectory. The official opening of Holy Rosary Church took place in June 1964.

St. John's Parish was created in July 1966. A small green and white cottage on Victoria Road, owned by the Hamilton diocese, became the parish house and a tiny building, formerly used as a cooling house for milk, was converted into a chapel. Only six or seven parishioners could attend mass at a time. A weekly bingo night, several dances and a bazaar were successful fundraisers that year. By early 1967, a general financial appeal had provided sufficient funds to purchase land in front of St. James High School on Victoria Road. As the church building fund continued its work, Father Sienna and parish committee member Pacific Valeriote went to Italy to purchase a pipe organ, church bells and a large bell. The official blessing of the church took place in March 1969. In 1978, after eight years at Sacred Heart Parish and 12 as the administrator of St. John's, Father Sienna was assigned to a teaching post in Florida. A new era began at St. John's under the spiritual care of the Barnabite Fathers.

Other developments were progressing in the west and southwest. By 1958, the Guelph Brethren had outgrown Eramosa Road Gospel Hall, their meeting place since 1916. In 1960, they opened the Guelph Bible Chapel on the Bible Conference Centre grounds at the end of Waterloo Avenue. Although grounds and chapel had separate administrations, they co-operated on many events. St. Joseph's Catholic School was built in 1949 on a plot of farmland, donated to the Hamilton diocese by the Schario family. In 1950, the Church of Our Lady established a mission parish in two of the schoolrooms. It spread west of Edinburgh Road, stretching from

Moving the old synagogue, May 1951.
Source: *Guelph Mercury*

Breaking the sod for the new Beth Isaiah Synagogue, October 1948.
Source: *Rosh Hashanah, Vol. I, Issue I*

Highway 7 to the southern city limits, and included about 330 families. The first pastor was appointed in 1952, and the Church of Our Lady and Sacred Heart Church contributed funds for a rectory on Paisley Road. Because a family member still occupied the house on the property, the building of a large church was not possible. A prefabricated church, suitable for about 400 was therefore purchased. The white clapboard building with Gothic-shaped windows came in a series of sections from a London firm. As the population increased in the southwest, mass was held in Stone Road Mall and, later, in the Mary Phelan School gym. The year 1969 saw the building and consecration of the new St. Joseph's Church.

Another Catholic establishment was settled in Guelph when Jesuit property in Oakville, intended for a lay retreat house, was requisitioned for a golf course. The Catholic Diocese of Hamilton selected a new site on land adjacent to Ignatius College in the north end of the city. Loyola Retreat House was officially opened in June 1964. Indicative of growing ecumenicism, all faiths were welcomed.

The Jewish congregation, now 55 members strong, completed the building of a new synagogue in 1949 on the same lot as the house they had bought in 1925. Named Beth Isaiah, it was dedicated to Isaiah (Sidney) Acker, who died serving his country in the Royal Canadian Air Force in the Second World War. It also honored the memory of all Jews who heroically gave their lives for humanity and freedom. Regular Sabbath services were held and Bar Mitzvah exercises introduced. The yellow double-brick building provided a house of worship, a religious school and a community centre. Their former edifice was bought by Len Ariss in 1951. Weighing 100 tons, it was equipped with rollers, set on rails and moved about 100 yards further east to be converted into a duplex. By this time, the Ir Sholom Chapter of Hadassah had become active in the community, supporting the Retarded Children's Fund, the YMCA boys' camp, St. Joseph's Hospital, the Red Cross, the Salvation Army's Eventide Home and other causes. Their fall tea and bake sale evolved into an annual bazaar, held at the Armoury, that attracted large crowds from all walks of life. The Sisterhood of Beth Isaiah Synagogue was the ladies' auxiliary of the synagogue.

In 1945, the Christian Scientists, meeting in the YMCA, were recognized by the mother church in Boston. A Sunday school was formed in 1947 and, soon after, property was purchased at the corner of Woolwich and Suffolk streets. Sunday services and Wednesday evening meetings continued until 1967, when larger premises were acquired between James Street and Forbes Avenue. The reading room was open to the public. In 1962, radio station CJOY began broadcasting regular Sunday morning programs dealing with the teaching of Christian Science. Pastor Boyd of Calvary Baptist also began a weekly broadcast on CJOY.

The black community was so small at this time that the BME Church struggled to survive. In 1964, after several years without a resident minister, the Rev. Addie Aylstock was given the task of building up the congregation. As many of the young had left Guelph for larger centres, she expressed hopes of attracting some white members to her church. She roundly deplored the racial stereotypes perpetrated by the current minstrel shows and, a year after her arrival, the Kiwanis Minstrels were performing without black faces.

Church bells rang in salute to the Salvation Army at 2:45 p.m. on Saturday, October 29, 1966, when a new citadel on Waterloo Avenue was dedicated. The army's Christian service and welfare work of many years was honoured by city officials and friends: food and clothing for the destitute; Christmas hampers and treats for needy families; practical help for unwed mothers and alcoholics; a suicide prevention bureau; a tracing service for missing relatives; the Clarke Street Eventide home for men; activities for youths, children and seniors; and joy and good cheer spread throughout the city by the band.

In a desire to escape the dogma of traditional churches, the Guelph Unitarian Fellowship, affiliated with the Canadian Unitarian Council, was established in Guelph in 1961. Membership included thinkers of all persuasions who respected the inherent dignity of every person. An action committee, established by Tamara Puthon, launched the Guelph Memorial Society for inexpensive funerals, largely free of commercialism.

Public meetings were held by evangelist Elizabeth Sharpe, who had come to Guelph in 1943. Originally called the Faith Clinic, the group met in the Orange Hall and, by 1957 in the BME Church. In September 1960, St. Paul's Presbyterian on Short Street was purchased by the group and named the Life and Glory Temple. A.J. Willoughby introduced the Baha'i faith to Guelph in 1956. His message was carried on by OAC students and, in 1960, Mr. and Mrs. William Hodge began holding 'firesides' in their home. By 1967, a small group was meeting at 26 Eramosa Rd., the Brethren's old Gospel Hall.

Women were slowly allowed positions of authority in the church. Mary Hales was the first of her sex to be appointed to the committee of stewards at Chalmers, where Dr. Flora Little was the first to be inducted as a member of the Session, both in 1962. Women's groups, though, were widening their influence. The Mothers' Union at St. James, formed in 1967, stressed the multicultural character of Anglicanism. Their program included a one-day retreat conducted by a sister of St. John the Divine, visits to the Beth Isaiah Synagogue, and continuing discussions with Harcourt United Church on union between their churches.

In spite of a religious vitality in these years, adjustments had to be made. St. Andrew's Church, having experienced poor attendance at evening services for about 10 years, dropped them in 1965 (except for preparatory service, communion and special services). Competition from Ed Sullivan and other TV spectaculars on a Sunday night was blamed. Attempts to attract interest with laymen's services, including Stanford Reid's series of lectures on church history and doctrine, failed to revive evening attendance. Sunday school was gradually switched to mornings before or during church, resulting in only one service on Sundays. Although church buildings were now occupied all week with related activities, concerns still existed. In the *Centennial History of Chalmers Church* the Rev. D.G. Paton quoted from the 1962 sessional statement, "Modern life is confronted at every turn with new situations and problems that cry out for solutions. A materialistic outlook on life, created in part by our affluence, is impinging on our church loyalties. The old traditions have ceased to have any meaning for a preponderant part of our membership and are being questioned."

Intense examination of Christian truths followed. The United Church's new Sunday school curriculum quickened an interest in Sunday school work. Dublin teachers enjoyed the new ideas that emphasized the essential truths behind Biblical stories and lessened the importance of facts or inconsistencies. Some city churches were slow to adopt new directions; some teachers never did. Further agitation was caused by Anglican Bishop A. T. Robinson's book, *Honest to God*, that caused the 'Death of God Theory' to rock pulpits and even surprise free thinkers. The Anglican Congress, in which a bishop, priest and layman from every diocese in the world took part, counteracted in 1963 by developing the 'Mutual Responsibility and Dependence in the Body of Christ' document. It expressed a change of attitude, an opening of minds within the church that recognized so-called missionary areas as places to be respected from which much of value could be learned. Pierre Burton's *The Comfortable Pew* (1965) raised more discussions and apprehensions.

Unity again became a keyword. In 1962, the New Life Mission's series of interdenominational evangelistic meetings received strong support in Guelph. Singers from several churches joined the mission choir. The Anglican and United churches ventured to agree on the principals of union. To discuss the implications, St. George's was paired with Chalmers and St. James with Harcourt. On occasion the two churches exchanged ministers at their regular Sunday morning services. The Brotherhood of Anglican Churchmen, promoted by the bishop of Niagara, Walter Bagnall, formed at St. James. Each year during Brotherhood Week, they held a dinner in conjunction with B'nai B'rith of the Beth Isaiah Synagogue.

In 1959, the *Book of Common Prayer* was adapted and simplified for modern church-going persons. Name-changing seemed a good idea. 'The Church of England in Canada' acquired the more unifying and convincing appellation, 'Anglican Church of Canada.' In 1962, United Church women's associations were amalgamated with the women's missionary societies into 'United Church Women.' Women's auxiliaries of the Anglican Church became 'Anglican Church Women.' Many were not happy as it meant loss of identity for auxiliaries honouring deserving individuals. In 1967, 'Anglican Young Peoples' changed to 'Anglican Youth Movement,' with greater contemporary significance. Discussions of union between the Anglican and United churches subsequently lost impetus.

Education

In his government's 22-point program of July 1943, Ontario Premier and Minister of Education George Drew vowed to revise Ontario's educational system so that every child would have the opportunity to be educated to the full extent of his or her mental capacity. Vocational training would be made a more important part of schoolwork so that children could be prepared to earn a living, and health measures would be established, making medical, dental and health protection available to all.

The Department of Education developed a booklet on vocational guidance that John F. Ross, principal of GCVI in 1944, was quick to implement. One period a week of vocational group guidance was introduced to Grade 9 students in September 1944, with all other grades receiving approximately one period every three weeks. Home-room teachers 'guided' pupils with the department's booklet in hand until 1950, when a guidance office was established with Gordon Reid as director. He provided information and advice concerning placement in business and industry and supervised counseling given in the classrooms. IQ tests, carried out in Ontario for about 20 years, were used to determine a student's ability to learn. From now on, experts agreed, every child would be educated according to his or her intelligence.

Health was another issue. Until 1950, there was no sanitary inspection of schools and no nurse or dental care, although some students had been X-rayed for tuberculosis. A change came that year with the establishment of a health centre in room 210, with a doctor and nurse visiting three times a week. Technical advances were few. Lantern slides were the only method of illustration, besides blackboards and photos. A public address system existed, but no films, silent or sound, and no radio until 1947.

In 1944, the Committee on Planning, Construction and Equipment of Schools in Ontario was established, offering extra financial encouragement for the building of large school sites, landscaping, art and music rooms, gymnasiums and auditoriums and other amenities. A new provincial grant structure also aided Ontario boards. Guelph, however, was slow to take advantage. By 1950, facilities at GCVI were strained, especially in the shop area, and the suburban townships needed more access to vocational training. Not until 1953 was another vocational school officially proposed. A sense of urgency further developed when Canadian General Electric revealed a plan to bring 400 employees to Guelph before June 1954. A site at Eramosa Road and Stevenson Street was chosen, but progress was stalled by city councillors who disapproved of issuing the required debentures. Only after an energetic publicity campaign, did council reverse its decision and acquire Ontario Municipal Board approval for $822,000 in expenditures. It opened in September 1956 as a small vocational school for technical and commercial courses. Students numbered 460, the staff 25. Eramosa Road had no sidewalks, there was no bus service within reasonable distance and no parking spaces provided at the school. Classrooms had no doors, lockers were piled in hallways and construction dirt covered almost everything. At the opening in September 1956, the Victoria

Opening of Edward Johnson School, November 29, 1955.
Edward Johnson, his daughter, Fiorenza, and her husband, the
Hon. George Drew, with Fred Hamilton, chairman of the board
of education and L. McQuaid, principal of the school.
Source: *Guelph Mercury*. Edward Johnson Collection,
Special Collections, University of Guelph Library

St George's Public School, built before 1900, was destroyed by fire 1963.
Source: J. Keleher Collection

number, graduated. In 1964, *Hamlet* was produced and the band won first prize at Stratford Festival in 1965.

GCVI's gym was torn down in 1960. Two years later, the old GCI building was replaced by a 24-room addition that permitted a range of technical courses from hairdressing to restaurant management. As a result of Herbert Peachell's efforts to continue the work started by Edward Johnson's donation, the string program at GCVI was revitalized after the war. In June 1950, all Grade 8 students underwent a musical aptitude test, and those who indicated they would benefit by instruction were given the opportunity to learn. The board of education purchased two bass violins, three violas, four cellos and 19 violins. An additional number of violins were loaned or given outright by interested citizens. Instruments were taught by a class system, a method, said Peachell, unthought of 20 years before. When Peachell retired in 1964, Charles Wilson, organist and choir director at Chalmers Church, was hired.

Provincial Minister of Education John Robarts attempted to improve the system in 1962. Under his plan, high school courses were reorganized into three branches: arts and science; business and commerce; science, technology and trades. Students were streamed after Grade 9 into either a five-year academic course leading to university or to professional business administration for boys and secretarial work for girls. A four-year arts and science option provided a general course, while a two-year occupational program led to the service industries. The four-year arts and science program was popular at GCVI, probably because of the new courses it introduced – world politics, theatre arts, speech arts, geology and 'man in society,' an interdisciplinary social science course. The objectives were to educate for every pupil's needs, to prevent premature dropping-out by average or below-average pupils, and to provide an easier route to professions. Cadet Corps training, so essential to the old regime, was dropped in the same year due to lack of instructors.

Public schools had been seriously overcrowded in early 1948. Space was rented in two churches, and basement schoolrooms in Central were re-opened, as well as the long-obsolete St. John's School. The first post-war public school, Paisley Road, was built in 1948 as a low-cost experiment in a wartime housing neighbourhood. It consisted of three white metal buildings costing $5,000 each.

Chapter of the IODE, upholding the spirit of the Empire, presented the school with a framed photo of Queen Elizabeth and the Robert Mutrie Chapter unfurled a new Union Jack. Early extra-curricula efforts included a Glee Club, a newspaper and Christmas drives for the needy. John F. Ross was one of the first schools in Ontario to use electric typewriters for the training of typists.

In 1959, an addition along the south side, allowed the school to offer a collegiate general course to Grade 12, with Grade 13 added in 1960. The students now numbered 900. The 877-seat Ross Hall, 32 new rooms and a large double gymnasium at the east end were officially opened in September 1963, increasing the school's capacity to 2,090 students. Because, as a small vocational school, it had suffered humiliating defeats against GCVI's sports teams, a system of intramural sports was devised whereby the school was divided into four houses, each competing with the other. Within a few years the school was able to enter CWOSSA and win titles in volleyball, badminton, gymnastics, tennis, basketball, hockey and football. Harry Jacobi's 1969 curling team (Fred Osburn, Rob Sinclair, Bob MacGregor and Ian Robinson) won the Ontario crown and went on to the All-Canada Bonspiel. Ted Denver became the school's first music teacher, and, with Rae Stuart, wrote the school's song. In 1960, girls were taught to understand football and 'powder-puff games' were initiated. The school year book *Ross Echo* became the *Rostrum* in 1960. Orchestral music was not available as at GCVI, but Martin Bauer's band and Keith Conrad's new combo and dance band, the Mello'aires, excelled in their duties. In 1962, the first Grade 13 students, 41 in

King George School, however, was constructed in 1950 at a cost of $400,000. In 1953, three new classroom units were added to Paisley, and a new school commemorating John McCrae, was constructed on Water Street to replace Victoria School. Edward Johnson was honoured in 1955 by a school, shaped in a T, housing 13 classrooms and eventually 20. The next year, Ottawa Crescent was built as a twin of Edward Johnson, with 12 classrooms in two wings, a large auditorium, a kindergarten and offices. Laurine Avenue (1958) was followed by June Avenue, Brighton Street, and College Avenue (1959). Students were housed in Trinity United Church and the Pentecostal Tabernacle on Speedvale Avenue while Waverley Drive School was being built (1963). Six more classrooms, a kindergarten, nurse's room, store room and washroom were added in 1965, through a critical path method by which every phase of construction was strictly timed and every deadline met. It was the fastest addition ever built in Guelph. Waverley's seven acres also comprised the city's largest elementary school site. When a two-room addition was constructed at St. George's School in 1962, classes were carried on for several months at St. George's Church. After the 1963 fire, during which pupils were housed in the as yet unpopulated addition at John F. Ross, the old part was demolished and four new rooms added to the two-room addition.

Little had been done for the education of children with disabilities in Canada until 1952, when a class was started in Toronto. The Guelph and District Association for Retarded Children was organized in 1954 by the efforts of interested parents and citizens, pre-empting the founding of the Canadian Association for Retarded Children by two years. In 1955, with the help of individual donations and support from city council and the public school board, a school was opened at the Brooklyn Mission with 24 pupils and four teachers. It was held there until the building of Sunnydale on Waverley Drive was completed in April 1959.

Rapid expansion of the separate school system began in June 1951 with the opening of St. Joseph School on Guelph Street. Its six rooms were constructed in a novel L-shaped design, allowing for a maximum amount of natural lighting. A new parish was subsequently formed and Sunday mass held in one of the schoolrooms. Holy Rosary School, at the northern end of Church of Our Lady Parish, served the same purpose. It opened with six classrooms and 150 pupils from Grades 1 to 8 in 1955. Sisters of Loretto were in charge, although a number of lay women were among the teachers. Four classrooms were added in 1957 and again in 1961. Loretto Academy became co-educational in 1953. In the following year, co-educational Notre Dame High School (Grades 9 and 10) was built at the

bottom of the hill at the corner of Cork and Norfolk streets. In 1962, Loretto and Notre Dame became Bishop Macdonell High School, the only Catholic high school in the county. Their buildings were joined by an addition in 1967.

By 1958, the parish of Sacred Heart Church had grown to over 1,500 families, and school facilities were inadequate. Persuaded by Pastor Bodendistel and his assistant, Father Sienna, the board bought 10 acres on Victoria Road. A four-roomed school, St. John, was built. When Father Sienna came from Sacred Heart to serve mass on Fridays, principal Mary Phelan and her sister Alice served him breakfast afterwards to allow him more time in classes. St. John was increased to 12 rooms and, in 1964, a junior high school, St. James, was built on the Victoria Road property. In the meantime, St. Bernadette had opened near St. Joseph's Hospital in 1959, and St. Paul, a six-roomed school, heated electrically (the first time in Guelph), was erected on Forest Street in 1964 to serve the university area. Major building programs continued when the Guelph Separate School Board combined with Nichol Township in January 1965. Kindergartens operated mornings and afternoons, and 'opportunity classes' for slow learners were held at St. Paul School and St. John. After intensive investigation of the advantages of senior elementary schools, Our Lady of Lourdes was built on Westmount Road in 1965 with comprehensive facilities for Grades 7 and 8. Similar accommodations were erected at St. John and St. Bernadette. All other schools under the board's jurisdiction became junior elementary. In September 1964, Donald Ewing was hired as the first music supervisor. The rotation system was then established, by which Grade 7 and 8 students, after a morning in home room, moved to classrooms especially equipped for art, music, home economics and manual training. The sisters of St. Joseph taught in St. Bernadette and Our Lady of Lourdes.

The existence of Roman Catholic separate schools in Ontario had been constitutionally guaranteed by Canadian confederation in 1867, but Dutch immigrants wanted formal schooling infused with the particular Calvinist bent of their Protestant theology. In 1961, they opened Guelph's first modern alternative school in the basement of the Reformed Church on Water Street. Although John Calvin Christian School started with only two teachers and without government support, it slowly expanded, gathering the offspring of parents from different ethnic backgrounds who shared its views about God's plan for humanity. Funds were raised from private sources and school fees. The establishment of the city's first private day care had opened in an old Victorian house at 32 Arnold St. in 1954. Founded by a Mrs. Smith, the Jack and Jill Day Care Centre and Nursery was taken over by Grace Doherty, and has remained in her family ever since.

For some adults, particularly immigrants, fundamental language education was needed. Teachers themselves required training in English as a Second Language (ESL). A few large companies set up in-house training schemes for jobs, but many areas were left uncovered. A federally funded Manpower Retraining Program for the unemployed was launched by the Guelph board in 1963-4 and held in GCVI. Then, in 1969, after the provincial government set up 20 schools of Applied Art and Technology (community colleges), Guelph's Manpower Retraining Centre was transferred to the jurisdiction of Conestoga College and became its Guelph branch with a campus on Speedvale Avenue. Academic upgrading and post-secondary credits and courses in many new areas were available, including nursing-assistant training. In 1971, nursing itself was transferred from the hospitals to the community colleges, giving nurses a much broader educational experience.

OAC also provided initiatives in adult education. Many Guelph citizens took advantage of a series of lectures on communications offered to the public by the department of extension education in 1962. Speakers included an anthropological linguist, a sociological communications expert, a specialist in propaganda techniques, the chairman of the department of communications at Michigan State University and Marshall McLuhan, whose second book *The Gutenburg Galaxy,* was about to be published. Through lectures and small group discussions, a large number of professionals, faculty and townsfolk were introduced to the implications of communication and information technologies. Workshops in programmed learning and positive reinforcement techniques, relevant to current movements in education and business management, were also presented to Guelph teachers and business managers.

The college continued to influence the artistic life of the community, especially through Gordon Couling, who had begun teaching art and design courses at Macdonald Institute in 1949. He encouraged donations of art to the college collection and developed it into a valuable teaching resource. He took students on bus trips to art galleries in New York and, along with Wilfred Tolton and Romeo Lacasse, was instrumental in the formation of the Creative Arts Association in 1948. Through a Canada Council grant, the Institute began purchasing Canadian Art. *Mercury* columnist 'Pen 'N Brush' was impressed in July 1956 by the number of works by area artists in the collection and wrote that the travelling exhibits on show each month at Macdonald Institute "put the city to shame." The formation of an art department in 1965 with Couling as chair turned

the tables. Within the next few years, Walter Bachinsky, Gene Chu, Judy Coxe and Elton Yerex joined the art department and also set up studios in the city. In 1968, Judith Nasby was appointed curator of the now large and prestigious art collection. Exhibitions were moved to the main floor of the McLaughlin Library, where they were accessible to the public. Ian Easterbrook's invitation to Eric Cameron and his fine-art students to come to the university's audio-visual services and TV studio ultimately led to the integration of fine arts and the media at the university and, with the subsequent founding of Ed Video in the city, further exploration into the 'medium as the message,' as coined by Marshall McLuhan.

SERVICE CLUBS AND ORGANIZATIONS

During the war and soon after, new service clubs were formed, each one energetically serving the cause it favoured. Boys' work was the main project of the 77 Optimist Club of Guelph (1940). The Boys' Workshop to train young mechanics was held for 10 years in the City Hall basement without fees for instructors. In the Christmas season of 1950, the Boy Scouts joined them to make toys for needy children. In January 1951, they sponsored the show *Going Places,* staged by local talent. The interest of Guelph Lions Club (1944) was to help blind and underprivileged people. In 1951, they helped build the Kitchener headquarters of the Canadian National Institute for the Blind. They provided transportation for blind citizens in Guelph, furnished a room in both hospitals and installed bleachers at the baseball diamond in Exhibition Park. No. 105 Order of the Scottish Clans (1946) and the Jane Kennedy Auxiliary No. 105 to the Order of Scottish Clans (1947) provided social and charitable activities. The first meeting of the fourth Guelph IODE chapter, named for Edward Johnson, was held in November 1949, and the Guelph Lioness Club first met in 1950.

Kiwanis now covered many aspects of everyday life. The Sunshine committees gave old folks' dinner-parties at the Y and sent baskets to those unable to attend. Their first Junior Achievement concert was held at Memorial Hall in April 1959. The annual Minstrel Show, started in 1952, ran for 18 years. The imagination of director Norman was infinite. Shows were set in Dodge City, Chicago and Paris with appropriate costumes and music. Professional performances by Burt and Gladys Hanna, Ken Jeans and Harry Kelly thrilled full houses every night and provided funds for the Belwood Camp, 4-H Club work, music awards, minor baseball and the training school. The first project of the Royal City Kiwanis Club, formed in 1960, was a children's swimming pool area in Riverside Park.

Rotary's Easter Seal Campaign for the Benefit of Crippled Children was started in Guelph in 1947. In 1953, new work was commenced to combat cerebral palsy. With the co-operation of the Rundle Chapter of the Order of the Eastern Star, a July clinic and training program was held at John McCrae School. Rotary also co-operated with the YWCA in programs for underprivileged girls and with Kiwanis to send the Y girls to a camp at Lake Belwood. The result of their continued work with children with disabilities was the building of a permanent training centre on Beechwood Avenue, opened in February 1955. Later that year, when the Guelph and Wellington Society for Crippled Children was incorporated, the centre came under its jurisdiction and was operated as a treatment centre and school. An outstanding teacher was children's author Jean Little. As government programs grew, the need lessened and, in 1968, the building became the Rotary Children's Centre.

The Kinsmen Club of Guelph was created in 1953 to get younger men interested in helping those in need. Their first projects dealt with individual needs such as a TV for a bed-ridden boy with muscular dystrophy and Beta-Cortisone drugs for an arthritic mother of eight children. Major projects were two children's wading pools in the city and a physiotherapy department in the new St. Joseph's Home.

The Guelph Red Cross carried on peacetime work with two new programs: the homemaker's service and the loan cupboard. Qualified women were sent to homes where the mother was sick or hospitalized. For those who could pay, the fee was nine dollars a day; for those who could not, it was adjusted or free of charge. The loan cupboard, an invaluable service, lent hospital beds, wheelchairs, crutches, canes and other articles needed for recuperating patients, free of charge, on recommendation of a family doctor. These services were taken over by the Victorian Order of Nurses in 1965. The Red Cross started swimming and water safety programs in September 1948, the year that the Lyon Memorial Swimming Pool was opened in Lyon Park by the recreation commission. Only those with a Red Cross instructors' certificate were hired. Admission was one nickel.

St. John Ambulance, part of the International Order of St. John, was established in Guelph in 1947, with 27 men in the ambulance division. Seeing a need to help new immigrants settle into community life, Evelyn Graham instigated the Council of Friendship in 1948. In 1951, Guelph's Canadian Save the Children Fund was founded by Trevor Lloyd Jones and Ruth Saison of the veterinary college and a number of prominent city women. An early fundraising project grew to national proportions – the production and sale of Christmas cards.

Harry Worton

Harry Worton's reputation as a "man for the people" was earned through a long and successful career in public service. Born in Guelph in February 1921, he started his business life in the family bakery in 1937, therein establishing a lifelong pattern of working long, hard hours. He also met hundreds of customers over the years who became first his friends and later his constituents.

He was only 23 years old in 1944 when he was first elected alderman – a position he held until 1947. This was followed by an appointment to the newly-formed parks' commission in 1947, re-election as an alderman for two terms in 1949, and as mayor in 1951. He continued to serve Guelph in that position through the post-war industrial boom. In 1955, he accepted the Liberal nomination to run for the Ontario legislature. In 1980, when he celebrated 25 years as a member of the legislature, a fellow politician remarked, "The only promise Worton ever made was to put more raisins in the buns." That and his service to the people of Guelph had him re-elected as Liberal MPP for 30 years. Those years, he sat on several committees making significant recommendations such as universal auto insurance, drug benefits and geared-to-income housing.

"One of the highlights of my time in municipal council," said Worton, "was receiving an invitation to the coronation of Queen Elizabeth. I still have the invitation hanging on my wall today. I asked the High Commissioner what I could take with me as a gift for the British people. He told me silk stockings were in short supply so John Rennie gave me 48 pairs and I handed them out in the hotel. I also took a cheque for $1,000 raised by the police, fire and old timers hockey group. I presented the cheque to the Lord Mayor of London to help repair storm damage that had recently happened in the English Channel."

While he was overseas, Worton made a point of visiting and laying flowers at the graves of Canadian soldiers in France. In 1984, on the 40th anniversary of the Normandy landing, Worton returned to visit those graves again. He retired from politics in 1985. Over the years, Worton continually supported advances for the aged and the sick and fought hard and consistently for the small independent business people.

– Ceska Brennan

Working on an idea of Val Henderson, local art student Marion Paton designed a card (four angels carrying a giant candy cane through a starry night). Costs for supplies and local printing were partially covered by donations, and the first year they broke even. After advertising in *Chatelaine* the next year, the project became a

The Cheese Roll: One of many events at Festival Italiano, 1999.   Source: *Guelph Mercury*

year-round concern. Designs were contributed by Guelph artists Hazel Runions, Roy Lefneski and Paul Buchanan and later by Jack Bush and A. J. Casson. In 1961, the net profit from sales across Canada was $8,000. In the late 1960s, the project, too large to be handled by a small group, was transferred to the national organization.

Three worthy historians, Hugh Douglass, Greta Shutt and Verne McIlwraith, took executive positions in the Guelph Historical Society, formed in 1961. With the preservation of Guelph's history in mind, they published annual volumes in typescript. Having collected a number of artifacts, they opened a small museum in the old Light and Heat building in 1961 with the co-operation of the recreation commission. When this burned down the following year, they and the commission moved to the old Isolation Hospital on Delhi Street. The city was persuaded to take an interest in 1964, and a board was formed with Mrs W. Stanford Reid as chair. Fred Grundy was appointed as the first curator. The society began a tree-planting program in 1964 in co-operation with the Department of Parks and Recreation. Each year on St. George's Day, trees were planted in honour of notable persons, industries or institutions. In the summer of centennial year, the museum was open in Tovell's store on Wyndham Street. Later in 1967, a permanent home was found in part of the new market building and an official opening took place in December.

Hobby and activity clubs were becoming popular. Guelph Gremlin Model Airplane Club was formed in 1945. The Stamp Club was revived in 1946 by John Heap and Harry Norton. The Cameo Club, an early self-improvement organization formed in 1951, emphasized public speaking, human relations and personality development. The Camera Club reorganized about 1959, the Guelph and District Coin Club in 1963 and the Guelph Model Railway Society in 1969. In 1966, the Hunt Bridge Club dedicated itself to teaching and promoting the activity. For those wishing physical activity, there was the Guelph Scottish Country Dance Club [1957], the Royal City Squares [1962], the Merry Eights Square Dance Club [1966] and the Guelph and District Highland Dancer's Club, active by 1969.

The YM-YWCA and the recreation commission were now stressing the importance of recreation for the well-being of the citizen. In 1965, Riverside Park was expanded north to Woodlawn to join the 17 acres already owned. With the co-operation of the Grand River Conservation Authority, Royal City Park was extended westerly and roads were opened to picnic, playground and sports areas. Summer activities for children on school playgrounds and three two-week day camp adventures at the Barber Scout camp site were organized for children. Adult social clubs, hobby clubs and arts and crafts exhibitions were well attended.

The old folks were beginning to have some fun and to enjoy a new identity. A Golden Age Club, formed in 1951, met at the YWCA. A popular non-denominational Over-Sixty Club was founded by the Salvation Army in 1964. Within three years, it had grown to 150 members. The YMCA amalgamated with the YWCA in 1961 and a new facility was built on Speedvale Avenue in 1966. The Legion Hall offered leisure-time activities for veterans of both wars.

"Guelph's biggest influx of Italians took place between 1951 and 1957," said Monte Cirotto, one of the founders of the Italian Canadian Club in 1952. Speaking to a *Guelph Tribune* reporter in July 1999, he told how social gatherings at home grew so large and impractical that an Italian community centre became a necessity. Fundraising dances were held at Paradise Gardens (now the Desert Inn), and the first big picnic took place in 1953. Five years passed before land was purchased. Although some sub-trades were hired, most of the work was done by the members. When completed, the club became a major asset to the community at large. Concerts, visiting speakers, political meetings, weddings, gatherings of all kinds were welcomed, and the Italian food was always a success.

SPORTS

In 1947, the Guelph Curling Club occupied the indoor curling rink on Baker Street that doubled as the Victoria Skating Rink by day and a roller-skating rink in the summer months. It backed on to Knox Church on Quebec Street. "You had to be careful there was no curling on Sundays," observed Murray MacGregor. The club purchased the rink from David E. Kennedy that year, and a holding company,

 July 21, 1938 –The first pro-wrestling show is staged at Mason's Cambridge Street arena.

Victoria Rink (Guelph) Ltd., was formed to operate the entire property, including the bowling greens. A junior curling club, set up in 1945, was active by this time. The Ladies' Curling Club was reorganized in 1948, and a figure-skating club operated a summer skating school in 1951. The club hosted the first National Schoolboy Championship in 1962 and the next year, for its 125th anniversary, held the Canadian School

The Guelph Biltmores and the Memorial Cup, 1952.
Source: Donald Coulman Collection

Curling Championship in Memorial Gardens. Business girls' curling started in 1965, with 68 members who played after work three days a week.

The Cambridge Street arena was in disrepair in the late 1930s, but to prevent its closing, Roy Mason purchased it and, for a while, known as Mason's Arena, it was used as a training ground for intermediate and NHL players. In 1940, a sheet of ice was put on the floor of the old market building. This was used until the building was needed for the Netherlands troops in 1943. In 1946, when planning for a large memorial project began, some wanted an enlarged winter fair building. Many exhibitors had been turned away from the fair before the war, and the provincial government had offered to pay one third of the cost if Guelph would continue to hold it. Serious arguments arose in favour of Guelph's maintaining its profitable agricultural tradition. In April, however, city council voted eleven to one to accept the recommendation of the special committee on recreational facilities to proceed with an ice rink with artificial ice and to remodel the existing market building to incorporate a recreational hall. Memorial Gardens was dedicated on November 11, 1948, to the memory of Guelph's war heroes. It was equipped with modern ice-making machinery, ventilation systems and was, according to goalies who played there, one of the best lighted arenas. The building was fireproofed and offered an unrestricted view from any seat. The players could enjoy large, airy dressing rooms, steam-heated showers and toilets. A manager was appointed in 1948, but, as the mood swung to greater municipal support for leisure activities, the recreation commission was established and a full-time recreational director

appointed. Arts and sports specialists were also hired. Their first so-called offices were cubicles at the rear of City Hall auditorium.

After the war, Roy Mason persuaded nine other businessmen to invest with him in a Junior 'A' hockey team. They created the Guelph Biltmore Hockey Club in 1947. For the first year, while Memorial Gardens was being built, they made Galt their home base. Hugh Bowman used the term 'Fabulous Fifties' in his reminiscences of his four decades as sports writer and broadcaster. Hockey, for certain, saw its most glorious days of the century. It started, Hugh wrote "with Alf Pike's Biltmores upsetting a loaded Windsor Spitfires in a series that ended in an overtime sixth game, and the whole town went stark, raving hockey mad." The city went further berserk when the Biltmores won the Memorial Cup in 1952. After the Junior A franchise was shifted to Kitchener, John Prigione kept hockey alive by forming a senior team that gave Guelph one Ontario Hockey Association championship and lots of laughs. "They played for a few bucks, gas money and all the beer you could drink after the game," wrote Bowman. "On the ice they played like there was no tomorrow."

Ken Marshall, director of recreation for the city, was instrumental in starting minor hockey in 1948, not with the purpose of producing a small group of stars, but to promote and supervise hockey for the boys of Guelph without regard to race, creed, colour or ability. When they joined the Ontario Minor Hockey Association in 1952, 600 members were active in five age groups. In this voluntary effort, the Memorial Garden Commission provided free ice time, with financial backing by the Biltmore Hockey Club.

When the Guelph Country Club integrated a curling rink and lounge into its facilities in November 1964, the ice was tested by a group of Scottish Rotarians and only after their approval, so they said, was it opened a few days later. Seven bonspiels were sponsored in the inaugural season. The Cutten Club underwent a major facelift in 1965, increasing its golf course in length, beauty and complexity. Three of the new holes bordered the river, and the 17th was on an island in the river, giving the golfer two opportunities to avoid the water. The planting of trees enhanced the beauty of the course and also the degrees of difficulty.

ENTERTAINMENT

The Capitol, Palace and Royal movie theatres had, by 1948, been joined by the Odeon. Guelph's radio station, CJOY, founded by Fred Metcalf and Wally Slatter,

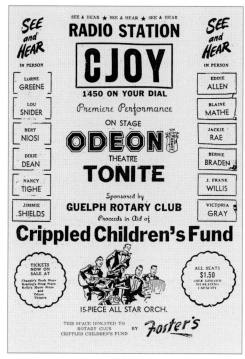

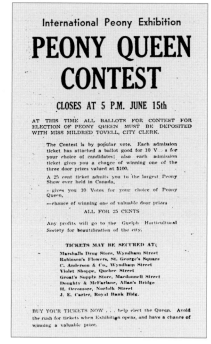

CJOY's first broadcast: from the Odeon Theatre, June 1948.
Source: *Guelph Mercury*

International Peony Exhibition in the market building, June 1948.
Source: *Guelph Mercury*

first went on the air in June that year with a variety show broadcast from the Capitol Theatre. The Guelph Rotary Club was sponsor and proceeds went to its Crippled Children's Fund. Twenty-five radio stars appeared on stage, including Lorne Greene, J. Frank Willis, Bert Niosi, Dixie Dean and Percy Faith with a 15-piece all-star orchestra. Among CJOY's first programs were Gordie Tapp and his Serenade Sunset at 6:45 on Monday, Wednesday and Friday, and a radio auction sale by the Guelph Kiwanis in aid of boys' and girls' work. Hugh Bowman broadcast all the Biltmore's home and out-of-town games. Gordon Sinclair wrote in the *Toronto Star*, November 16, 1950, "Several letters to this column say that a youngster in Guelph (CJOY) is Ontario's best hockey broadcaster outside Foster Hewitt, but unhappily, I've misplaced the lad's name. If he's the one who handled the finals of last year's Biltmores, he is indeed good!"

 1959 – Chuck Jemmett opens The Jem Drive-In Theatre. Operating today as The Mustang Drive-In, the theatre is one of only 69 drive-ins still in business across Canada. (Source: Ceska Brennan)

Norm Jary

Born in Toronto in 1929, Jary moved to Guelph in 1954 to become the voice of hockey for the local radio station.

Jary recalls memorizing all the names of the Guelph players and their sweater numbers because he was unfamiliar with the team. "I didn't know the team well enough to recognize them at the game," said Jary. "My wife, Jean, tested me. She'd call out the sweater number and I'd reply with the name of the player or she'd call out a name and I would yell out the number on the sweater." Jary thought he was ready for the play-by-play broadcast but, when the Biltmore Mad Hatters came on the ice, they were all in new sweaters and numbers. Jary didn't recognize a soul. Apparently his play by play satisfied the audience for Jary's familiar voice delivered the news and sports to generations of city residents over the local radio station CJOY.

Jary signed off his radio broadcasts with "My name is Norm Jary - just in case you need me for something." Jary remembers that one late night someone actually telephoned saying he did need him for something - to change a tire! In 1966, Jary was the television voice of the New York Rangers Hockey Club and announced the scoring of Bobby Hull's 51st goal of the season breaking Maurice Richard's long-standing record of most goals per season.

Jary was elected to council in 1964 and was mayor from 1970 through 1985. During his term, city retail increased with the building of Stone Road Mall and Willow West Mall. The Exhibition and Centennial arenas and Victor Davis Pool were opened and the Guelph Lake project got underway.

From the voice of hockey to the voice of Guelph, Jary attempted to open the doors of City Hall to the democratic process. "I always tried to have people recognize that city council was their council," he said.

In 1994, more than 300 people packed the Italian Canadian Club to honour Norm Jary, the former member of the Police Services Board and Guelph's popular politician and celebrity, to mark the day of his retirement from radio. In 2000, he retired from city council.

– Ceska Brennan

Guelph residents now sought a greater variety of leisure-time entertainment. Five hundred and fifty-four dogs, including 19 international champions, arrived in Guelph for the International All-Breed Dog Show in June 1948. Cutten Fields Golf Club entertained 250 guests for the Toronto Railway Club's summer outing on the 12th. From the 14th to the 18th the college's annual Farm and Home

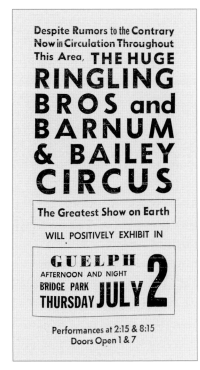

Despite Rumors to the Contrary
Now in Circulation Throughout
This Area, **THE HUGE**
RINGLING
BROS and
BARNUM
& BAILEY
CIRCUS

The Greatest Show on Earth

WILL POSITIVELY EXHIBIT IN

GUELPH
AFTERNOON AND NIGHT
BRIDGE PARK
THURSDAY **JULY 2**

Performances at 2:15 & 8:15
Doors Open 1 & 7

Advertisement for The Greatest Show on Earth: the Ringling Bros and Barnum and Bailey Circus. July 2, 1953.
Source: *Guelph Mercury*

LIFE

"He came upon the screen in Argentine costume, with Gaucho boots and a sash around his waist. He danced the tango; he strode up to women masterfully; he bent them back from the waist like lilies to kiss them, and when he whispered to them it was a breath of pure passion."

THE
"Valentino"
STORY
IN COLOR BY
TECHNICOLOR
by EDWARD SMALL

ELEANOR PARKER
ANTHONY DEXTER

"MAKING MOUNTIES"
Color Cartoon · News Reel

STARTS
TODAY **ODEON**

Cecil B. DeMille's
Samson and Delilah

Cecil B. DeMille's "SAMSON AND DELILAH"—Hedy Lamarr·Victor Mature·George Sanders
Angela Lansbury·Henry Wilcoxon   A Paramount Picture

Starting Today

FEATURE   TIMES
2.25 — 6.55 — 9.30
Last Complete Show 9.00

PALACE

FOR THE FIRST TIME AT REGULAR PRICES!

Exciting movies in Guelph at the Odeon (left) and Capital Theatres in May, 1951 (right).
Source: *Guelph Mercury,* May 2, 1951

horses, floats and clown-carts, a herd of elephants with lovely ladies atop, and a steam calliope brought shouts of joy from the children. They were followed by Shetland ponies with colourful trappings, jungle beasts in cages, a two-ton hippo in a cage with a tank of water, monkeys and clowns and more clowns and a trampoline wagon with comedy acrobats in action. Hundreds lined the streets and attendance at the performances was estimated at 5,000. Another June adventure took place in 1961 when the merchants of Guelph

Week broke the previous year's record, when over 21,000 Ontario farmers converged on the city. The same week, the General Hospital celebrated jubilee events throughout the city, and 2,000 junior farmers from 20 countries met at OAC for judging contests and competitive games. The Horticultural Society raised excitement on the 24th and 25th with the International Exhibition of the American Peony Society and the elaborate election of a Peony Queen. Over 38,000 votes were cast in Guelph and the county. An Elora girl won, defeating five Guelph contestants. The beautifully bedecked queen, surrounded by equally adorned attendants, was crowned in the market building amidst the perfume of 10,000 blooms.

A circus had not come to Guelph in over 20 years. When the King Brothers and Cristiani Circus rolled into town in the middle of June 1953, children were given a half-day holiday. The big tent was set up on the Bridge Street circus ground in the early morning and at 11:30 the circus parade proceeded 'in review' through the town. Red and gold glimmering bandwagons drawn by teams of

decided to boost sales by organizing a three-day Jaywalkers' Jamboree. For the first time since Guelph's centennial celebrations in 1927, Wyndham Street was blocked off for a special event. All traffic was stopped at 6 p.m. on Wednesday, the 21st. Shops were decorated with flags, banners and coloured lights to give the street a Mardi Gras air. Children's rides were set up in the centre of the street, including the carousel, later made famous by Ken Danby's painting. Shoppers arrived before opening time the next day ready for bargains. The weather was good and the newly opened Baker Street parking lot was filled. Organizer Les Love was encouraged. Guelphites liked a little fun and friendliness along with value when spending their money.

Back in 1945, Presto Music Club membership had reached 1,252 and, over the next 10 years, outstanding programs were presented. Signs of strain became evident in 1955. Membership had declined, work was becoming more difficult and expenses had risen. When the New York-based Community Concerts made overtures to the city, Edward Johnson urged Presto to renew and revitalize their own membership. He also emphasized the need for generous public support. The club struggled valiantly for two more years, but without success. Minutes of those years reveal that Johnson not only donated student memberships and financed the student concerts but, in 1958, also paid all artists' fees. As the season ended, Presto urged members to support Community Concerts.

Edward Johnson had never lost sight of his vision of Guelph as a musical city and Canada as a musical nation. When, in early 1954, Herbert Peachell's ideas of a community orchestra were permeating musical circles, and Ralph Kidd and

> Sunday sports and movies became legal in Guelph on January 4, 1965. A good crowd watched the Guelph Regals being defeated by the Woodstock Athletics at Memorial Gardens that day. Others took in Sean Connery in *Goldfinger* at the Odeon's afternoon or evening performance or the Palace's feature *Rousabout* with Elvis Presley. Outdoor sports had to be staged between 1:30 and 6 p.m. Moving pictures, theatrical performances, concerts and lectures were permitted indoors between 1:30 and 11:30. Outdoor evening and morning activities were eliminated to avoid noise and flood-lighting nuisances and conflict with church services. Extra measure had been taken to counter-act the all-embracing leisure-time activity of television.

Hildo Bolley had gathered a group of interested citizens, he joined forces. He had retired as general manager of the Metropolitan Opera Company, but was still on the Toronto Conservatory of Music Board, and these connections made the hiring of conductor Ernesto Barbini possible. Forty-five amateur musicians and a choir of 75, mostly from church choirs, rehearsed for five months under Barbini's direction and, on June 5, 1955, the Guelph Civic Symphony and Chorale presented a concert. Memorial Hall was packed, with 200 persons turned away at the door. "Royal City on Musical Map" wrote Dick Brimmell of the *Mercury*. John Kragland of the *Globe and Mail* called it a major triumph. Both quoted Edward Johnson's words, "I hope to live to see the day that Guelph will have a musical festival."

The following year, when a shortage of string players was apparent in Guelph, Johnson immediately decided to remedy the situation for the future, by offerring to finance the musical education of any child who wished to study. Fifty-five answered the 1956 advertisement and, under the direction of Dorothy Farquharson, classes began in violin, viola and cello. Instructors were Jennie Lamb, Rudy Roth and Jennie's brother, John Wideman. In 1958, with Johnson's encouragement, Lamb formed the Crusade for Strings Orchestra and, in 1961, the

Guelph's performing artists donated their services in aid of the Civic Centre Association in 1959. Three evenings were filled with music, dance and drama.

Source: James Schroder

Guelph Academy of String Music. Johnson managed to interest his fellow Rotarians in the crusade, and they responded by obtaining a charter in November 1957 for the Edward Johnson Music Foundation. Its mandate was to provide facilities and instruction in music; to encourage appreciation of and interest in music; to accept donations, gifts, legacies, and bequests; and to invest and re-invest any principal in such investments. Always in mind was a wish to re-instate Johnson's May Music Festival. The opportunity came when Nicholas Goldschmidt, another man with a vision of Canada as a musical nation, brought *Les Jeunesses Musicales* vocal competition to Guelph in 1967 as part of Canada's centennial celebrations. He saw Guelph as a perfect site for an annual music festival, reminiscent of the small European towns of his youth. His enthusiasm inspired Dean Murdo MacKinnon of Wellington College and OVC's dean, Trevor Jones, president of the EJMF, into action. The Foundation sanctioned the idea and, with its mandate in mind, MacKinnon's office became the hub of festival organization. Members of the English department and their wives needed little persuasion to join in the venture. Barbara Wolfond, director of publicity, was allotted space in the arts building. Ticket sales and other aspect of administration were handled by the university's box office and concert manager, Edith Kidd. Not only did the university hire Goldschmidt as director of music, thus giving him a reason to stay in Guelph, by agreement with President Winegard, it also underwrote all overhead and unseen costs. The University of Guelph played no small part in the initiation of a festival that was to bring national and international renown to Guelph.

Bill Winegard

William (Bill) Winegard, born in Hamilton in September 1924, moved to Guelph in 1967 from the University of Toronto to become president of the University of Guelph, a position he held until 1975.

Winegard served as Minister of State (Science and Technology) in 1989, and, in 1990, became Canada's first Minister for Science. A Privy Council member from his years as a Federal Cabinet Minister, he has received honorary degrees from around the world. He has earned medals, awards and honorary memberships in countless organizations and is an Officer of the Order of Canada.

In 1993, Winegard retired from his position as Conservative MP for Guelph-Wellington, a post he had held since September 1984. During his term he spent countless hours meeting with constituents, touring local factories and learning about his community in order to better represent Guelph interests while in Ottawa. Bill Winegard is an internationally-known engineer, scientist and educator. With all these accolades, Winegard still jokes, "The only really special achievement I've had is getting married to the right woman."

Winegard's careers in the military (navy), in education, in politics and on various boards dealing with research, farming, technology, trade and international development have put him in contact with Canadians from every walk of life.

– Ceska Brennan

In 1947, Ted Denver assumed the leadership of the Guelph Police Boys' Band in which 95 boys, aged 8 to 16 were enrolled. As well, Denver continued in his father's tradition by giving free lessons to those who needed it. Seventeen youngsters captured 22 awards at the Waterloo Music Festival in June 1948. Fourteen were from the Guelph Police Junior Band, and three from the Guelph Metronome Accordion Band. Operating at a deficit in 1952, the band acquired the Red Chevron Club as a sponsor. It continued to win prizes at the CNE, the Waterloo Festival and other competitions. Most of the boys had little formal education, but, as a result of Denver's training, doors were opened to them in the military as musicians and in local band groups. Many became professional musicians or music teachers. Members included Ron Petitt, Ernie Scott, Charles Merry, Bob Hamilton, Bill Phillips, David Poulton, John Wilkie, David Drew, Ed Barlow, Fred Mills, Nick Kefalis, Bob Emberson, Ted Cote, Don Singular, Walter Radlowski, Buddie Huth, Alf Cunningham, Fred Leadiston and Bruce Lemon. The Red Chevron Boys' Band ceased in 1954 when the 11th Field Regiment Bugle Band separated from the regiment to form the Royalaires, which many of the older boys joined.

By the end of this period, a new form of entertainment had become firmly entrenched in the homes. In the early 1950s, Wally Slatter and Fred Metcalf had heard about the development of cable television in the United States. As Metcalf had done with radio, he visualized what he could do for Guelph. It was not as simple as it sounded; but with co-operation from Guelph Hydro, his first TV signals in 1953 were the beginnings of community cable television in Canada.

PRACTICE OF THE ARTS

Guelph continued to provide opportunities for the professional church musician. Charles Wilson came to the city at the age of 23 as organist and choirmaster at Chalmers Church. His studies included organ with Charles Peaker, composition with Godfrey Ridout, Lucas Foss, Aaron Copland and Carlo Chávez, and conducting with Leonard Bernstein. He obtained a doctorate at the University of Toronto with his *Symphony in A*. His founding of the Guelph Light Opera and Oratorio Company in 1958 was a stimulating contribution to the musical life of the city, with local singers, musicians, choreographers and theatre experts joining forces. After the initial success of *The Pirates of Penzance* that year, Wilson directed one light opera and one oratorio a year for the next 15 years. *This Happy Land*, composed by Wilson with libretto by poet D.G. Jones, was presented in 1960 and repeated the following year by popular demand. He also conducted the Bach-Elgar Choir of Hamilton and the Guelph Civic Symphony and Chorale.

After the war, Guelph Little Theatre presented or sponsored up to six plays a year, often assisted by groups such as the Hamilton Players Guild, the Melville Players of Fergus, the Kitchener-Waterloo Little Theatre or Galt Little Theatre. In spite of difficulties with funding and rehearsal space, they brought live theatre to the public at City Hall, Memorial Hall and the GVCI auditorium. Their 1947-8 production of *Quiet Weekend*, directed by John McElderry, was selected for entry in the Western Ontario Drama League (WODL) competition. Scotty McLean's guiding hand and Dolly Nunan's inspiration kept the company alive during the 1950s. The old dance hall at the Old Mill in Riverside Park was christened Dolly's Saloon in Nunan's honour. In 1950-51 season, GLT sponsored a One-Act Play Festival with local groups competing and, in 1953-4, was host to the WODL Festival. Public support began to waver, though, and membership declined. In 1955, GLT dropped out of the WODL until Nunan's 1957 production of the *Solid Gold Cadillac*, starring Hugh Bowman and Gertrude Hutton, restored new confidence in the company. By then, several theatre afficionados from Britain,

Guelph Little Theatre production of *The Broken Jug* by Canadian playwright and humorist Don Harron won an award for the best English-speaking play at the Dominion Drama Festival, 1967. Phyllis Dodson; Terry Doyle and Michael O'Brien; Kathy O'Brien and Catherine Renwick.   Source: William and Kay MacKie

including Trix Davies, the Dodsons and the Briggs had arrived in Guelph, as well as the McKies from Toronto. With Kay McKie's direction of *Witness for the Prosecution* in February 1958 came new life and greater appreciation of GLT's voluntary activities. The production, with Elizabeth Gruen, Terry Doyle, Hugh Bowman, John Weston and Trix Davies among cast members, was praised for a "flawless presentation" in the *Guelph Daily Mercury*, February 7, 1958.

The Creative Arts Association had been formed to create an atmosphere in which genius could develop and grow. The hall above Ryan's store was the first locale for the association's annual exhibition. Others followed, including Norfolk Church, City Hall auditorium and the Armoury. Joseph Drenters, a sculptor from Rockwood, was an early exhibitor with the association, as was the architect Karl Briestensky. The first known outdoor art exhibition in Ontario was organized by Peter Briggs in 1960 and held at the Parkview Motel. Success insured its continuance, and every June those practising their arts and crafts could exhibit, be judged and sell their work at the Painting-on-the-Green on the grounds of the Dehli Street Recreation Centre. A permanent gallery for collected works was created in the new public library in 1966. It opened with an exhibition of 40 paintings by Guelph's Evan Macdonald.

Gordon Couling remained active in many areas. In addition to his contributions to creative arts groups, he set up the Central Ontario Art Association and a five county teachers' council that aided in the development of adequate teachers for art

groups. As president of the Ontario region of the Federation of Canadian Artists that emphasized the need for the Massey Commission (1949-51), he made a significant contribution to the establishment of the Canada Council for the Arts (1957).

Guelph's cultural activities were often only amateur because those practising the arts were volunteers, or working for a low fee. Opportunities were rising for the one who excelled, but competition across Canada was becoming greater. The popular mood was changing to advantage, though, and support was more forthcoming. Guelphites were beginning to appreciate the beauty of their city through the paintings of their artists, as Canadians had seen Canada through the eyes of the Group of Seven. Ontario's Stratford had brought recognition to Canadian actors, and a life sustained by the arts, although a struggle, was a nearer possibility. A Canadian culture was beginning to exist. Grants from the Canada Council of the Arts were available, and Guelph's practitioners of the arts were moving positively.

Ostensibly, the old anchorage was still firm. "There was no doubt remaining as to the loyalty of Guelph's citizens," observed the *Mercury* in an extensive coverage of Governor-General and Madame Vanier's two-day visit in September 1966. Crowds lined the streets as they made their way to Holy Rosary Church, where they celebrated mass. Five thousand school children were primed to give a rousing welcome at Memorial Gardens. The John F. Ross CVI orchestra played, the Tytler School choir sang and, at the end of his speech, the Governor

General told his audience that, as representative of the queen, he had the right to grant them a holiday. The roar of cheers assured his popularity. Clearly enjoying himself, he took time to speak and shake hands with many children and accepted a candy apple from one of them. In the afternoon, Vanier placed a wreath at the McCrae Memorial Shrine and, in the evening, he opened Guelph's annual United Appeal 'kick-off' in St. George's Square. At an official dinner at the Cutten Club he praised Guelph for the fighting men who had served Canada in the Northwest Rebellion, the South-African War and the two world wars, words that had been heard many times before. He continued, speaking of Canada's "prodigious destiny," its vast natural resources, its versatile and varied human resources, and added, "To whom much is given, much will be required."

Four 105-millimetre Howitzers thundered a 100-gun salute the following day as the Vaniers participated in ceremonies honouring the 100th birthday of Guelph's 11th Field Artillery Regiment, the oldest artillery regiment in Canada. In the evening, the vice-regal couple attended an all-ranks ball in the Guelph Armoury. The visit was a success. Children, parents, the religious, the military, the elite, all were happy. The harbour seemed safe enough.

ANCHORS AWAY! GUELPH: 1967-1999

Guelph celebrated its 140th birthday in Canada's centennial year by organizing a 15-mile trek from Galt to Guelph to 'replace the tree cut down by John Galt'. Over 600 persons, aged 7 to 81, made the effort. Bone-chilling winds and a 30-degree Fahrenheit temperature dampened enthusiasm for Confederation costumes, although some were donned in time for the television cameras. Stopping in Hespeler for coffee and biscuits, mayors Smith of Guelph and Kerr of Galt were 'arrested' for crossing the Macdonald-Cartier Freeway without a licence, intent to create a riot, and carrying a concealed weapon (John Galt's axe). When Mayor Kerr arrived in Guelph, he was sentenced in the name of the people's court never to allow an invasion of Guelph by anyone named Galt and never to cut down a tree without permission of the Guelph Public Works Department, unsurpassed as it was in tree-demolition skills. Dominion Day festivities that year lasted 16 hours. Rotary's parade took an hour to pass any given point. The 11th Field Regiment sounded the traditional 100-gun salute at noon, but rain flooded out a game between the Guelph Green Ghosts and the Kenmore New York baseball teams. The Cutten Club's Invitational Golf Tournament and the Church of Our Lady's Tennis Tournament carried on. In the evening, Guelph's multicultural groups

entertained in St. George's Square. Street dancing followed and continued after a brilliant fireworks display by the Italian Canadian Club.

Journalist Verne MacIlwraith and his centennial committee made sure that no week passed without a special event to stir the spirit and revive historical pride, but festivities only partially obscured the severity of problems at hand. Guelph, like most Canadian cities, was faced with a growing population, expanding industrial and technological development, and a drastic adjustment in cultural values. The 'Statement,' of the Student Democratic Society in 1962 at Port Huron, questioning the inconsistencies in American society, made small impact on Guelph. The Woodstock rock festival of August 1969 received greater media coverage. By then, many Guelphites were wondering what was happening to their children. Time-honoured values such as loyalty and responsibility seemed to have disappeared. Authority in all areas was being challenged. Powers from the top had become irrelevant. Culture was coming from the grass roots, and the 'me' generation had been born.

Guelph's traditional churches struggled to keep the young in the fold, probably more successfully than in larger centres. With the help of the press, though, they were forced to contemplate what seemed an ultimate indignity – the foundation of the Church of the Universe in 1969 at Clearwater Abbey by Wally Tucker, whose sacrament was marijuana and vestment, the naked body. (By the early 1990s, the church's new headquarters was in Guelph, at the site of the International Malleable Iron Company, dubbed 'Hempire Village' by its new tenants.)

Educators, stretched to the limit with child or student-centred programs, found their credentials challenged by the brash self-confidence of the new generation. Misunderstandings wrought solid families apart. Denim jeans, a statement of rebellion, became a new uniform for all. The lyrics of rock and roll, incomprehensible to older generations, were subliminally suggestive of free love, free drugs and freedom, even from life.

For those who survived the first decade, the flower-child motto 'make love not war' became the catch phrase sifting through a multitude of rigid conventions and presuppositions. Barriers were eventually lowered as the older generation stopped blushing when mentioning the companion status of their children. Old

Guelph band, The Fabulous PJ's, performed at the British Methodist Episcopal Church and throughout the city in the 1960s and 1970s.

Source: Guelph Museums

Guelph had virtually disappeared, and few cared, except the likes of old Mr. Goldie, the lawyer who was reported to have mumbled on Wyndham Street that Guelph had been a nice town until the university came. But, as contemporary culture worked its way into everyday life, a new tolerance emerged and a new concern for the less fortunate, the sick and the aged. Guelph's escalating multi-racial population became simply Canadian. Women were accepted as equals in many fields. Although organizations still depended on individual initiatives, funds were becoming available from provincial and federal agencies. Flower power blossomed in the arts and, as help became available from the Canada Council and Guelph's own arts' council, a new art was seen and a new music heard.

When reaction set in, as it was bound to do, pressures from technological changes and emphasis on economic advancement forced a different mind-set on the young. Those with excessive freedoms on their mind were left behind; some were lost. The statement made by a young offender, interviewed by the *Globe and Mail* in April 1999, that someone should help kids to make something of themselves, illustrated the predicament of many youths. In the 1990s, great efforts were made by churches, educational institutions, and social and leisure-time organizations to do just that. In the city of Guelph in 1999, nobody needed to be left by the wayside. If they sought help, it was there to be found.

Knox's peak membership of 1,870 in 1968 made it the third largest Presbyterian congregation in the country, but from then on it experienced a steady decline. In 1970, St. James Sunday School had dropped to a quarter of what it was in 1950. "The congregation was at its lowest point in 1969," said Rev. Hedley-

Smith of St. George's, "and since then [1976] it has increased." In 1976, many churches claimed that attendance had either slightly risen, or that it had remained constant, not that it had decreased – an illusion caused by failing to take account of Guelph's population growth. The Church of Our Lady took positive action by increasing Sunday masses to four and introducing a Saturday evening mass for those with changing working conditions. Whatever the Protestant churches wished to admit, they realized some action was required to retain present membership and attract a new and younger one.

The Religious Census of 1961, with Guelph's population at 41,767, was as follows:

Roman Catholic	12,939	Greek Orthodox	246
United Church	8,959	Pentecostal	192
Anglican	6,992	Disciples	164
Presbyterian	5,668	Ukrainian Greek Catholic	81
Baptist	1,605	Christian Science	43
Lutheran	942	Mennonite	28
Christian Reformed	274	Evangelical United Brethren	19
Jewish	258	Confucian	3
Others, and non-religious	1,936		

Thirty years later the population had more than doubled to 97,213. Individual denominations were no longer itemized in the census, and only the following statistics were available: Catholics: 31,640; Protestants: 47,700; other religions: 3,290. The number citing 'no religion' in 1991 was 13,540, or approximately 11 percent, slightly less than the Canadian statistic of 12.1 percent. An article in *Statistics Canada*, Autumn 1991, concluded, "while most Canadians still have formal religious affiliations, there is an overall trend toward declining religious activity in Canada." Religious activity is here equated with church attendance.

Adjoining property, where possible, was acquired for parking lots. The Christian Church (Disciples) demolished an educational building, built in 1963, to make way for one. In 1971, St. Andrew's set up a bus service. When joined by Knox, Chalmers and St. George's, they rented three buses from the Guelph Transportation Company. Elevators were installed, if space permitted, to make the sanctuary accessible to the elderly and handicapped. Ladies' parlours were redecorated. An inter-church softball league was organized and folk music encouraged. Younger members of St. James' choir formed a group called the Apostles. St. Andrew's appeal to its young people resulted in a walkathon to Rockwood to help bolster the church's dropping donations. In 1969, the first

Presbyterian Summer Day Camp was organized at the MacLean Estate in Crieff. Although Scouts and Guides continued, groups of Beavers, Pathfinders, Rovers, Venturers and Travellers were created to excite young, modern minds. Teachers at St. James wrote a new curriculum in 1976 with lessons illustrated by examples from everyday life. Services were held Wednesday evenings and Thursday mornings to reach weekend holiday-makers or those on shift-work. A liturgical renewal took place. St. George's young curates and radical youth groups introduced folk masses, rock bands and secular music into the service. Older persons tried to understand, but were seldom impressed or comfortable. Unable to "wholly relate to it," organist and choirmaster Ralph Kidd took early retirement in 1971.

Church buildings and sanctuaries were put to use for non church-related events. As early as 1947, Knox had granted permission to the Christian Business Men's Association and to the Kiwanis to hold conferences in the church auditorium. The Business and Professional Women's Club presented the Leslie Bell Singers there in 1949. The initial concert of the Guelph Spring Festival in May 1968 was the first time admission was ever charged at St. George's Church. Church seating plans and rental policies soon became a necessity.

Women were emerging as leaders in the church. In 1969, three women were admitted to St. Andrew's board of management and two were elected as elders. Two were on the advisory council at St. James in 1970. The first woman lay delegate to the Synod was elected there in 1972, the first deputy warden appointed in 1978 and the first warden in 1980. The late 1970s saw women lay assistants at Holy Communion. Constance Williston was the first woman to be priested in Guelph, at St. James in April 1979. Gail Dawson became the first minister's wife to establish her own identity separate from that of her husband by seeking employment and interests beyond the confines of the parish. Contrary to age-long expectations, women were no longer appendages to their life companions. Martha Smith Wood, minister of Guelph's Mennonites, was the first woman ordained by the Mennonite Conference in Ontario (1982). In 1986, Guelph's Elinor Knight was re-elected to the presidency of Canadian Unitarian Council.

Much of the church's progress was based on outreach, a term encompassing the virtues of duty, responsibility and loyalty. It first meant to bring new members into the church and old ones back for the benefit of their souls as well as the church coffers. The legacy of St. Andrew's year-long sesquicentennial celebrations in 1977 was an outreach committee, set up to bring people in contact

The Daughters of Scotland march through St. George's Square in the Sesquicentennial Heritage Day Parade, 1977. Source: Donald Coulman Collection

with the church. An outreach of Crestwicke Baptist Church in the 1970s and 1980s, on the other hand, was Sunday school held in various schools in the area with more than 1,000 children attending. As many as 20 buses were used for transportation. Knox's congregation addressed the issue of declining membership by hiring an expert on growth and outreach in 1981. There was a "lower than average turnover and an aging congregation," he reported, "and, unless the normal inertia pattern was halted, a gradual decline would result." All downtown churches were painfully aware of this, but the positive note was that "in such a central location, there were opportunities for outreach as a welcoming community." After solving its financial problems by a strenuous campaign, Knox hosted the 111th General Assembly of the Presbyterian Church in 1985 and erased the deficit in 1986. A welcoming community became a key phrase for the 1980s.

Compared with 'bringing in,' outreach became 'going out' into the community. One way was to continue the ecumenical spirit. The Rev. Michael Shields, head of Ignatius College, participated in a service at St. James in 1970 – a first for the parish and the city. The new combined hymn book of 1971 was accepted by Anglican and United churches. The pairing continued and, although union was not possible, unity was. Harcourt and St. James united to form a branch of FISH, a society in England using the ancient symbol of Christianity as its name.

In an effort to help the lonely and depressed and the suicidal, they established a 24-hour telephone service in which 89 volunteers from several Guelph churches took part. Although FISH only lasted from 1969-74, it helped many for whom no immediate support was available at the time and was the predecessor of the drop-in and crisis centres in Guelph. Sister Christine Leyser initiated the Welcome In Drop-in centre for the jobless downtown in 1983, with St. James providing moral and material assistance. Within five years, it had expanded to include emergency shelter and rehabilitation. The Parish Guild and the Mothers' Union continued to help. The Parish Pantry food bank was started to help those in need. The Women's Crisis Centre developed with support from St. George's Parish. Archdeacon Peter Moore saw those years as one of a ministry of outreach and pastoral concern.

Outreach also meant expanding into new areas. Guelph's three Anglican churches, more united after the failure of union with the United Church, instigated a new style of team ministry in which outreach teams worked with small groups in each parish. Named Project House Church, it found its theme in Koinonia, a form of the Greek word for fellowship and enrichment. On teachers' professional-development days, a Creative Christian Experience program was held for children. An informal Family Eucharist and coffee hour with care for pre-school children in the gym of Priory Park School became the first service of the Mission of St. Matthias in February 1978. In November 1980, with permission to be called St. Matthias Church, the group moved to the chapel on Arkell Road with their own pastor. Within six years, they had built a church on Kortright Road. A day-care centre, Kortright Playschool, was soon operating. The Vacation Bible School, formed in 1984, linked with Kortright Presbyterian Congregation in 1991 and, in the following year, with a Baptist congregation. Five hundred children attended with 60 to 70 teachers. In September 1992, a joint service of St. Matthias and St. Paul's Lutheran was broadcast on CBC's *Meeting Place.*

The South Guelph Mission Unit began to worship in the gymnasium of Fred. A. Hamilton School in October 1990. It became Southwood United Church in January 1991. When the school closed for the summer of 1992, St. Matthias proposed that its congregation join them in worship, using the Anglican order of service. Southwood's minister was given an office. Finances remained separate, but a one-year contract for sharing the church was subsequently extended and a financial agreement settled. As both churches were subsidized, the advantages of the new arrangement were many. Social services, counselling, community projects, office equipment and even subsidized housing could be offered more efficiently. St. Matthias began services at 9:30, Southwood at 11:15, and services were combined on special occasions.

During a discussion at St. Matthias of the national program *Hearing Diverse Voices, Seeking Common Ground,* a gay man was asked what he would like to see in a 'welcoming' congregation. His response lit a spark, and he was encouraged to attend church the following day. He and his companion found the congregation amiable and with a welcome that did not wear off. Wishing to share the experience with others who felt uncomfortable elsewhere, he formed the Rainbow Community Church, a mission of the Metropolitan Community Church congregation. The members of St. Matthias voted in support of MCC Rainbow also sharing the building, with services at 7 p.m. Sunday nights.

In a similar way to St. Matthias, Kortright Presbyterian began as a new church extension of the Presbyterian Church in Canada. The first worship service was held at University Village Public School in September 1980. It was officially recognized as a congregation in March 1981 and, on Thanksgiving Sunday, moved to a larger facility at Centennial High School. With the help of denominational grants and a large amount of volunteer work, a service of dedication was held in a new church on Kortright Road in March 1984. The mortgage was burnt in December 1995. Cedarbridge Christian Fellowship was founded in 1997 as an evangelical outreach of Kortright Presbyterian.

The incentive to build Westwood United Church came from a core group who saw a family need in the Willow Road area. A small pastoral charge held services in Westwood School from 1976 until 1981, when a store-front church in the Westwood Court Plaza was opened. The church, finally built in 1987, was smaller than originally planned, but when the congregation doubled in two years, an expansion project was possible. The enlarged building was dedicated in December 1994.

In 1987, after nearly 80 years at 200 Woolwich St., the congregation of St. Paul's Evangelical Lutheran moved to a new, spacious building on Silvercreek Parkway North. One form of their outreach was the building of Lutheridge, a senior residence of 34 units. Another was their involvement with St. John's Parish Social Awareness Group in the ecumenical movement to bring Roman Catholics and Lutherans closer together. A significant event took place in the Church of Our Lady on October 30, 1999. While the Doctrine of Justification was being signed in Augsberg, Germany, Pastor John Fogleman of St. Paul's and Father Frank Rizza of St. John's signed affirmations of the historic document on behalf of Guelph's congregations. Present were dignitaries from the Eastern Synod of the Lutheran Evangelistic Church and the Roman Catholic Diocese of Hamilton.

The Unitarian Church, having outgrown the house on Bristol Street to which they had moved in 1986, bought the old St. Patrick's Church on York Road in 1992. A YM-YWCA day-care centre, still operating on the premises, continued to use it five days a week. The church could now offer separate Sunday school classes for three groups of children and a new youth group for teens. In the controversies of the 1970s and 1980s, Unitarians confirmed their respect for women and homosexuals as ministers.

Reform churches were also reaching out. The First Christian Reformed Church enlarged its auditorium in 1980 and built eight classrooms. In 1996, several families parted amicably to form the New Life Christian Reformed Church on Victoria Road North. Along with usual activities for all ages, it hosted a Community Clothing Closet for the first time in 1998 in partnership with the Waverley and Brant neighbourhood groups. It also organized the annual March for Jesus, started in Guelph in 1993. That year, the Guelph Reformed Church on Speedvale Avenue made its building wheelchair accessible and added elevators to three levels.

With outreach came 'inreach.' In October 1975, Koinonia themes became popular with several denominations, and church clubs were formed for the purpose of fellowship and Christian nurture. 'Cursillo,' an ecumenical undertaking involving the United and Roman Catholic churches, by 1987, included Lutherans, Anglicans and other denominations in Guelph. It enabled individuals to deepen faith and express growth in small groups, often involving a weekend retreat. Guelph was fortunate in this respect because, by 1969, Loyola House had developed as an interdenominational centre for spirituality. Its approach to an individual's specific spiritual needs by providing an opportunity for contemplation and readjustment were appreciated by a widening variety of religious organizations. As the Novitiate section of the college became smaller, the novices, needing companionship and contact with a larger number of fellow students, were accepted for training by two groups of American Jesuits in St. Paul, Minnesota. The old building became a residence for priests and others working in Loyola House, with space available for

March for Jesus along Gordon Street heading for Riverside Park, 1994.
Source: Impact Guelph

those making retreats. Meanwhile, the Ignatius Farm Community had, by 1974, developed as a halfway house for inmates released from prison, operating on "a farm-based philosophy of helping a person to recover and heal." This philosophy was the forerunner of the healing aspect of church ministry in the late 1990s.

Due to the efforts of a few faithful families, the British Methodist Episcopal Church was still in operation. In celebrating Black History Week in February 1998, it was packed, with many standing. "How nice to see you all here," said Minister Erica Davis. "Hands up who'll be here next week!" She laughed and the audience laughed with her, saving embarrassment on both sides of the pulpit. Guest speaker was Dr. Benjamin Ayanbadejo, chief of obstetrics and gynaecology at Guelph's hospitals. Giving examples from his own life, he asked the children, "Are you ready? Are you prepared? No matter how smart you are, you have to do your own work. Western society recognizes only one thing, and that is excellence." Two congregations used the building, Bethany Baptist and the BME Sunday School.

Jehovah's Witnesses' congregation grew steadily, splitting into new groups when it became too large to provide personal assistance to all members. The former bakeshop on Edinburgh Road was Kingdom Hall until 1965, when property at 639 Eramosa Rd. was purchased. A new building was opened in October 1967 and, with renovations and enlargements in the 1970s, was used by two congregations. After outreach into Guelph's Italian district, an Italian congregation was formed and separate Italian meetings held in the Eramosa Hall. These were eventually assimilated into English-speaking congregations. On Victoria Day weekend, 1987, a group of volunteers cleared and leveled the land and installed the foundations and floor slab for a new facility. Then, over two weekends in August, approximately 500 volunteers completed the major construction, including decorating, fixtures, furnishings and landscaping of Torch Lane Kingdom Hall. Two halls now served four congregations: Guelph Lakeview, Central, Hanlon and Willow Park.

Two churches, in particular, did not survive. Christian Science, still flourishing in 1986, was gone by 1997. The Mennonites first met again in 1979 at the Victor Davis Pool in the Victoria Road Recreational Centre. House meetings continued until 1981, when they assembled in Priory Park School. They disbanded in 1992, the majority going to Breslau.

In the search for certainty in a troubled age, more persons turned to fundamentalism. The older churches expanded and new ones were created. A new church auditorium and Christian Education building were constructed at Calvary Baptist in 1971. More renovations in 1983 accommodated the church's rapidly expanding activities, including a vacation Bible school, Pioneer Boys' or Girls' Brigade, Young Peoples' and adult and senior groups. Crestwicke Baptist continued to support their academy, surviving financial and administrative difficulties. A Jolly Sixties group and a TV ministry were active in 1974. While expansion and renovations were being considered for the Victoria Road property, the YMCA building on Speedvale was offered for sale. Crestwicke quickly purchased it and began renovations. Most remarkable was the conversion of the swimming pool area into a well-appointed church auditorium. The Bible Chapel, too, was rapidly expanding and, by 1989, was so overcrowded that 40 families decided to start a new church. They raised a million dollars, purchased a farm off Victoria Road, just north of the city, and built Lakeside Bible Church. With contemporary music (guitars and drums, no organ), sermons relating to today's world, active missionary work and an innovative children's program, they attracted over 300 families within 10 years. In 1998, heading a staff of 120, were a senior pastor, a youth pastor, a music director and a children's ministries director.

A number of new denominations were established in the latter part of the century. Rosedale Seventh-Day Adventists first met in Guelph in 1967 at the Guelph Reformed Church on Speedvale Avenue. In 1974, they purchased the church at 114 Lane St. from the Rosedale Alliance Church. Rosedale Alliance reappeared in 1983 as the Guelph Alliance Church. A new group of Pentecostals began to meet in 1960 and built Parkview Pentecostal Church on Speedvale Avenue in 1976. Ten years later it had a licensed day-care centre for 70 children, a

library and a fellowship hall that doubled for a gym. In the late 1990s, five families living in the south side of Guelph formed a branch church, meeting in the Holiday Inn until a new building could be found. It became the Southside Christian Assembly, the only church to advertise a Web site in the 1999 Guelph phone book. Emmanuel Canadian Reformed Church, a daughter of the Fergus Canadian Reformed Church, founded in 1956, took up residence in 1974 in the old St. Paul's Presbyterian Church on Short Street. It was not related to the Christian Reformed Church. Outreach included a radio broadcast on Magic FM and a street mission in Hamilton.

A small group of United Brethren began meeting in homes in 1976. They were members of the first denomination to be born in America (in Pennsylvania on Pentecost Sunday, 1767). Parkwood Gardens Community Church of the United Brethren of Christ became an official church in Guelph on Whitelaw Road in 1985. By 1998, their original membership of 180 had quadrupled. Parkwood shared a youth pastor with Kortright Presbyterian. "It is not a big organic union," explained Pastor Brian Magnus, "but we have found areas where we can partner around common goals and purposes." In 1999, while retaining a 9:30 a.m. service on Sundays during the summer, the Community Church moved its 11 a.m. service to 7 p.m. on Thursdays, partly to allow church members to enjoy the rest of a Sunday summer in other activities, partly to solve an increase in number of persons converging on the small church. The Rev. Elizabeth Long of Kortright Presbyterian thought it a good idea. Prayer meetings and family worship were held Wednesday nights in early years. Her church, too, was introducing a special summer service in addition to the regular 10:30 one – a quick half-hour service without music, "geared toward people with time constraints." Neither Chalmers' Rev. Dianne Clark nor Harcourt's Rev. Jean Wright thought it radical. Harcourt, in fact, had offered an outdoor service, 'Worship on the Green', at 7:30 p.m. each Wednesday for several years, replacing their 9 a.m. Sunday service.

In 1969, the Church of Jesus Christ of Latter-Day Saints (Mormons) renewed missionary efforts in Guelph. They attended church in Kitchener on Sunday mornings and held Sunday evening services at the Guelph Orange Hall. A church on Marksam Road was built in 1979.

A rise of independent evangelical, fundamentalist churches occurred in the 1990s. In 1988, David and Marilyn Worobec, ordained by the Canadian Fellowship of Churches and Ministries (CFCM), started a small Gospel group in the unfinished basement of their home. In their garage, they had collected a supply of groceries for those in need. As the mission, named Spiritwind, grew, new space was found in the Edward Johnson and Fred F. Hamilton schools. Spiritwind's food supply, the Guelph Food Bank, established at 95 Crimea St., became the most visible of all outreach in Guelph, recognized in every home by its brown paper bags, and giving every homeowner an opportunity to donate to its work. In 1997, both the church and the Food Bank moved to larger premises at 100 Crimea. The Royal City Evangelical Missionary Church (1992) ordained its own pastor. A basic outreach philosophy linked it with local organizations and benevolent couples' club assisted with care for members in the community. Also in 1992, a church plant from the Cambridge Vineyard denomination settled in Guelph, believing in its great commission to preach to all the world. They eventually found a home in the 3-Star Cinema Plaza on Woodlawn, with a congregation of 250. Services at the Christian International Restoration Centre (1995) took the form of a folk gospel. The pastor, ordained in Florida, had one Guelph outreach, a downtown Second Choice Thrift Store. The Word of Life Church (1996), organized in St. Catharines in 1990, established itself in the plaza at Woodlawn and Victoria roads. This Pentecostal church aimed to help the homeless in Guelph. A small school was established in 1998. The Evangelical Free Church in Guelph (1998), although prominent out west, was the first in Ontario. The church model, Ross Creighton claimed, "is a new concept for Canada in which cell groups meet during the week for prayer, worship and discussion and unite on Sunday for celebration." Grace Community Church was founded in 1975. Its pastor claimed to be an "on-the-job man," not formally trained, but learning with his congregation to live out faith in a modern world through the authority of the Bible. The Church of Christ, a denomination that divided from the Disciples at the turn of the century, gathered occasionally in Guelph in the 1970s and, in 1988, formed a congregation meeting at first at Conestoga College and later at the Evergreen Centre.

In every decade and for many reasons groups of people had left their native lands. Whether fleeing from discrimination, poverty, turmoil, oppression or seeking a new start, they brought to Guelph their skills, their art, and a mosaic of values and customs. Many joined existent churches, but some needed new churches of their own. The Guelph Chinese Alliance Church was established in April 1988. Services in Mandarin, Cantonese and English were held at John McCrae School for 50 regular attendants. East Indians began to settle in Guelph in the early 1970s. By 1982, close to 500 Hindu residents were looking for a spiritual meeting place. In 1982, plans were made to convert a former restaurant on York

T. Sher Singh

Faith, and faith in people, are fundamental for Guelph lawyer T. Sher Singh. Born in Patna, India in 1949, Sher Singh came to Canada in 1971 to study. Upon completing his education, he worked as a stockbroker but developed a fascination with the law. He eventually pursued the profession and began practising at age 35 in Toronto.

While visiting a friend in Guelph, he fell in love with the city. "There is an incredible decency in small town Canada that can be found nowhere else in the world," he said. A local law firm, Nelson and Watson, had an opening and he was hired. Five years later in 1995, Singh established his own local practice and began writing.

His wide interests, life experiences and optimistic outlook on life provide him with material to fill his newspaper columns and television broadcasts. Singh writes about community issues, politics, travel, personal life experiences and multi-faith issues, reflecting his interest in the faiths of the world and his own personal faith as a Sikh. Schooled by nuns in a Catholic monastery he is familiar with Christianity and appreciates beliefs other than his own. He encourages others to do the same.

"You only do justice to your own faith when you respect another's," says Singh. Although not specifically active in the multicultural community in Guelph he is very involved in the multi-faith community.

"A blending of the cultures is happening," says Singh. "When minorities read my column I remind them, with my words and with my picture, that it is possible to be different and be a Canadian."

The Sikh community, numbering two and three thousand in Guelph, calls him "The Lion of Guelph" in recognition of the English translation of his name and the issues he takes on.

In October 1999 Sher Singh travelled to Italy by invitation of the Pope to share in the millennium celebrations at the Vatican. He carried with him a bronze sculpture as a gift from the Sikhs of Canada to the Catholic Church to mark such a special celebration.

– Ceska Brennan

Road into a Hindu temple. Chandrakant Kothari, property owner, said that non-Hindu persons would be welcome, and Yoga and Hindu philosophy classes would be provided. No Hindu temple existed in Guelph in 1999, but as Hindu pundit Oma Persaud explained to a *Mercury* reporter on the eve of Shiva-Raatri, there were no prescribed rules and it was enough to pray in one's own home.

Sikhs began to arrive in Guelph in the late 1960s. Most were professional men, who worked at the university or practised medicine. Bhangra dance and music was performed in Memorial Hall in June 1975 by Raj Pal Singh's top group, celebrating the 10th anniversary of the university's India Student's Association. By 1975, 25 families lived in the city. They met with Sikhs from Cambridge and Brantford to worship in Kitchener. Eventually they held services once a month in Paisley Road School. In August 1990, now numbering about 150, they applied for permission to use property they owned on Regal Road for a Gurdwara, a Sikh church. City council denied their request because four surrounding manufacturing businesses opposed the re-zoning. The Sikhs claimed discrimination, but the city insisted it was trying to restrict industrial land for industrial uses. The property was sold, and the search for another site begun. In the meantime they continued their services every three weeks in the school and, later, were able to buy and renovate a former beer store on Stevenson Street.

In the case of the Greek community, the planning board overruled advice from City Hall and recommended approval of their plan to build St. George's Hellenic Community Centre and Greek Orthodox Church on Silvercreek. In 1993, city council changed zoning in the industrial area to allow building of a Hellenic community church. The Guelph Islamic community at this time was renting facilities at 74-76 Regal Rd.

Sunday services at the Ontario Reformatory, conducted by chaplains from various churches had continued. In the mid 1970s, with the initiation of a Native Sons program, a liaison officer was appointed to counsel individual inmates of aboriginal heritage and to provide opportunities for their participation in the customary spiritual rituals and cleansing ceremonies of the sweat lodge and medicine pipe, or smudge ceremony. Originating from Laurentian University in Sudbury, the Native Sons program in Guelph was the first for a correctional centre in Canada. The ceremonies helped one "to be in a relaxed state of mind, to be open to learning, seeing and hearing with heart and mind as one, and to prepare the next seven generations to look after the earth," explained Mary Ann Cheesequay, who arrived in Guelph from the north in 1977. With the help of Mary Ann Saunders, Linda Thomas and Edith McKee, she tried to gather Guelph's aboriginal people together. At first a small social group met for coffee. Networking was difficult because many aboriginals were transient. Cheesequay persisted, and when a Native Women's Circle was formalized in 1982, a surprising number came forward to announce they were aboriginal or had been adopted. The Men's Circle followed, a Guelph Native Men's Drum group and, eventually, a Native Women's Drum group. Although sweat lodge ceremonies in the area were conducted by a

Toronto person, the Guelph native community regularly held feasts to celebrate the seasons. In the mid 1990s, they took place at the Matrix Cente and at Dublin United Church.

A general shift in charity had taken place from foreign missionary services to organizations or foundations helping closer to home. But when actual pictures of the hungry and suffering entered homes through television, outreach suddenly became every person's responsibility. Funds and donations could be channeled to specific places by a variety of national organizations. Two operated in Guelph, both church-related. The Pentecostal Assemblies' Centre for donated goods for Third World aid at 161 Regal Rd. was known as ERDO (Emergency Relief and Development Overseas). A B.C. benefactor held a mortgage on the property, and it was operated by 150 senior-citizen volunteers from city churches. In 1994, 30 beds were sent to Indonesia, a 40-foot container of winter clothes to Paraguay and a shipment of school books to Zimbabwe. "The organization only sends goods to missions that can ensure they get to intended destinations and not the black market," said warehouse manager Don Moss, when interviewed by Hilary Stead (June 9, 1994). ERDO also worked with the Canadian Food Grains Bank, started by Mennonites for farmers to donate a percentage of their crops to the Third World. The Mennonite Central Committee in Guelph arranged to have thousands of pounds of meat sliced at the University of Guelph, federally inspected at the meat science laboratory, then cooked, canned with a mobile canning machine, labeled and loaded on transport trailers by Mennonite volunteers. In 1987, 30,000 cans were sent to Eastern Europe, Asia, the Caribbean, Mediterranean, Middle East and Asia. In 'Cans for Kosovars' 600 volunteers prepared 50,000 pounds of beef for the relief camps bordering Kosovo. Related to overseas operations, the Mission Aviation Foundation Canada (MAF) moved to Guelph from Alberta in 1975. Canadian planes, pilots, aircraft engineers and radio technicians were

In 1990, the Historic Sites and Monuments Board designated the Church of Our Lady as one of four exceptional examples of the Gothic revival style in Canadian churches and offered a plaque to commemorate its architectural significance. Others were Nôtre Dame Basilica in Ottawa, All Souls' Chapel in Charlottetown and Tryon United Church, also on Prince Edward Island. In 1998, a committee of concerned parishioners expressed disfavour with certain modernization plans for the church and were successful in halting them. A restoration architect who entered the church during unsettling times of discussion remarked, "This church is a prayer in itself." Plans were soon made for the plaque to be accepted in the spring of 2000.

deployed in Africa, Indonesia, Papua New Guinea and Brazil to assist church and development workers of dozens of non-profit organizations. MAF supply lines enabled workers to stay in isolated areas working on community projects, disaster relief and health and training programs.

As the gap between the well off and the poor widened, Chalmers Church Food Bank was launched at Thanksgiving 1997. Renamed the Fair Share Food Shelf to distinguish it from the Guelph Food Bank, it quickly attracted interest and aid from other Guelph churches. The emphasis, as in the many humanitarian efforts, was on need rather than religion or ethnicity. Trust was involved. "We don't demand anyone to prove his need," worker Pat DeVries was quoted as saying. "We treat people as if they wouldn't be here if they weren't in need."

EDUCATION

Within four months of publication in 1968, *Living and Learning*, the report of the Provincial Committee on Aims and Objectives in Education (the Hall-Dennis Report), had become a bestseller. The book was an up-to-date analysis of a child's predicament in Ontario at that time. The committee had listened to students' opinions before drawing conclusions. In pointing a new way to democracy, responsibility and moral convictions, its ultimate aims were similar to Drew's reforms of the 1940s, but the methods were different. Instead of memorizing content, a child would learn by experience, through methods of discovery, exploration and inquiry. In this child-centred program of learning, one would realize one's full potential.

In keeping with an activity-oriented curriculum, school interiors had to be changed. They would accommodate the skills of communication arts, including dance, pantomime, drama and movies and the improvement of special learning situations. More attention would be paid to mental and physical health and leisure, with tours to outdoor sites for education or recreation. A fresh approach to Canadian Studies was recommended, with concentration on the importance of bilingualism in a multi-lingual world. Technology was seen as a route rather than a goal. Corporal punishment was an unacceptable method of discipline. According to Robert Stamp, "it was the most radical and bold document ever to originate from the bureaucratic labyrinth of the provincial department of education." Mac Irvine, acting principal of College Heights observed that vocational schools were already geared to students' needs. Enterprise methods may be new to academic fields, but they had been in practice in Ontario in special education since 1933. Stamp, too, pointed out that many of the innovations had been implemented in

some schools before 1968. Guelph, in fact, had been a leader in several areas.

In accordance with plans to amalgamate several communities into county-wide systems, the Guelph District Board of Education was changed to Wellington County Public School Board. On January 1, 1969, it took control of 10 secondary schools and 53 elementary schools with an enrolment of approximately 22,000. Nearly 16,000 elementary and high school students returned to public schools in Guelph in the fall. At the same time, the Guelph Separate School Board became the Wellington County Separate School Board with 4,950 students under its care in three senior schools and 14 elementary ones. The objective was to provide equality of education throughout the county, to raise the standards of teaching and to supply a continuous and integrated program of elementary education. While dealing with a myriad of logistics, the Wellington board began to complete their adaptation of Hall-Dennis Report. Their first concern was to accommodate the city's ever-increasing population, keeping in mind the current approach to educational needs and the growing demands for technological improvements.

Guelph's 60-acre education-recreational complex on College Avenue West was a massive centennial achievement that included a junior vocational school, a new collegiate-vocational institute, and an ice arena operated in co-operation with the recreation commission. Improvements and additions to College Avenue Public School, built in 1959, were planned at the cost of $250,000. The fall of 1969 saw a new gym, the conversion of the old gym to a library-resource centre, new health, staff, guidance and speech-therapy rooms, and additions to the industrial arts and home economics rooms. English and French classes were held in open-concept rooms and art, music, and science in regular classrooms.

College Heights Vocational School, completed in 1969, was the first of its kind in Wellington County. "We are producing the bulk of the citizens of Guelph," explained Mac Irvine, defending the school against those who thought it was degrading for their youngsters to attend. "Young people who go into service trades and skilled and semi-skilled labour force are the ones who stay here. Students who go on to universities most often move away [when they graduate]. We turn out a marketable product with 90 percent of graduates hired immediately." In March 1970, it was thought to be the first secondary school in Ontario to venture into closed-circuit broadcasting. College Heights' cafeteria was a day-long classroom as students prepared meals for two lunch hours, catered to special luncheons or dinners and cleaned up afterward. By 1987 it had developed a radio station.

Centennial CVI, opened in 1967, was an outstanding achievement for the gala year. Its $3,000,000 cost, dispersed into three distinct zones, provided academic, vocational and athletic opportunities for the development of healthy, well-rounded students. A major addition in 1969 expanded its capacity from 750 to 1,500 students. Featured were seminar rooms for small groups, a group-instruction room for larger ones, a library with a basement ready for expansion, and a cafetorium for 600 in which the bench-like seats could be changed to ones suitable for the auditorium with the flick of a switch. A track and football field and a state-of-the-art swimming pool with a six-foot-square underwater window for better coaching were part of the athletic facilities. The city shared the $300,000 expense of the pool, ensuring that the recreation commission would use it twice as many times as the school. A small bombshell was dropped when the county's health officer, Dr. Dale, failed to give approval of the pool on the grounds that the floor, according to Health Act regulations, sloped too suddenly and was dangerous. After a series of recriminations and justifications, the squabble was resolved when the provincial health minister simply changed pool regulations. In 1969, Centennial, competing with 38 other schools, won the first Ontario high-school girls' swimming championship.

Flutist Karen Gaettens accompanies the Gael singers during the Christmas Concert at GCVI, 1998. Other school groups performing included the Junior Concert Band, the Senior Band class, Stage Bands A and B, a String Quintet and several vocal ensembles.
Source: *Guelph Mercury*

In 1969, the old swimming pool at GCVI, used for one year and idle for 45, was converted into one of the most modern resource centres in Ontario. Supported on deep concrete footings, the 6,000 square-foot area contained 13,000 books, with room for another 20,000, forty study carrels with electrical facilities for audio-visual equipment and room to house the archives. Principal Gordon Reid hoped the installation of a photocopier would stop students ripping wanted pages from a book. A year later, after complaints about weather conditions inside the school, a modernized heating and ventilation system was installed. New flooring, lighting, windows, plastering and a rebuilt roof were approved in 1972 at a cost of $250,000.

Douglas Long, superintendent of curriculum at the time, listed several instances in which the Wellington County Board of Education was a leader in the province. Foremost was the concept of co-operative education. With the help of GCVI principal Jack Burns and approval of the board and the Ministry of Education in 1974, George King initiated a program whereby a student was allowed to work in a community service, business or technical setting for half days for one semester. For this, the student would earn two credits. The course received community co-operation and support and, by 1980, had rapidly grown to be the largest offered in any school in Ontario. King became the co-ordinator of co-operative education in the entire county. Part of the success was due to the link he forged between the public and separate school boards. The success of the venture was evident in 1998 when over 500 employers took students for part-time work in the program.

Summer-time continuing education was also an innovation. Dorothe Fair, night-school principal at GCVI, was instrumental in establishing the upgrading concept for students, managing to do it without cost to the taxpayer. Through her people and management skills, she presented summer-school and night-school opportunities with credits for children and adults for the whole county at a reasonable cost, without the board having to pay for it. A new model for contin-

Guelph's high schools continued to excel in the arts. They participated annually in the Sears Drama Festival and the Wellington County Drama Festival. In 1993, John F. Ross hosted the Sears Regional Festival in which both Ross and GCVI had been selected to enter and, in 1999, Tom Slater's school production of *Reflections* was one of 10 plays invited to an international drama festival in Nebraska. Centennial's Meistersingers, directed by Niklaus Kaethler, won first prize in the CBC national amateur choir competition in 1976 and came second in the finals of the European Broadcasting Company competition, 'Let the People Sing.' No Canadian school choir had ever progressed that far. Of Meistersingers' performance of Norman Symonds' *Four Images of Nature* at St. Laurence Hall, Toronto, in January 1977, William Littler of the *Toronto Star* wrote, "to hear the spirited way they performed it, was to appreciate how contemporary Canadian music can function as a tonic in our schools." Both boards of education supported the Guelph Spring Festival in the training of children's choruses for opera and choral productions and by giving art students time to design posters or paint scenery. GCVI students in Sharyn Seibert's Grade 11 sculpture class spent four weeks creating imaginative sculptures to illustrate the festival's 1999 theme 'A Matter of Time.' They were exhibited at the River Run Centre. A massive collaboration between the schools and the festival in 1977 produced the children's historical satire *The Return of the Tiger* by Edwina Carson and David Archibald. Although a success that year, such an enterprise was found too exhaustive for the school curriculum and not repeated.

uing education was set up in 1983 with night school and summer school co-ordinated for the county under one administration, headed by Fair. With a 'take it to the site' policy, community contact persons (CCPs) were hired in each far-reaching centre. Their job was to select teachers in local schools, produce brochures, and register and run programs for those who could not come to larger centres. Of note was the women's program that allowed them to update their education and re-enter the work force. The board was happy: the more people, the more money.

Fair was also a pioneer with her idea of providing education in the workplace. Staff was hired to teach literacy training on site for new Canadians and regular workers who wished to upgrade their language skills. Another first was recorded with the establishment of a transition program for high-school students entering the University of Guelph unprepared for math and science programs. It was taught at the university under continuing education administration. In 1985, the Wellington board became the first and only board to run child-care centres to encourage young parents to return to school. With the co-operation of the ministry of community and social services, a grant was acquired to set up early-learning centres at College Heights, John F. Ross, Arthur District High and Central. The program was designed to operate on a break-even basis, with fees covering the cost of equipment and meals.

The Wellington board was also provincial leader in outdoor educational programs. In good weather this entailed trips to the country or city summer-school programs. In other times a van or truck was set up with outdoor educational supplies for classroom instruction or a schoolyard experience. Broader programs were gradually developed such as a three-day, two-night experience of living in 17th-century conditions at Sainte Marie Among the Hurons.

The board attempted to advance special education 'for autism, the hard of hearing, the mentally retarded and gifted' – in later terms, children with special needs. The Retarded Children's Education Commission, established in compliance with the Schools Administration Amendment Act, gave assistance to such programs. Ron Corbett, superintendent of special education, was also the leading consultant for the Rotary Children's Centre. Priory Park School was built in 1976 on one level in order to integrate special-needs students into regular classrooms. Wide doorways and open hallways insured accessibility to students with a variety of needs. When Bill 82 became an amendment to the Education Act in 1980, the Wellington County board was already in line. A special education class was set up in John McCrae School for autistic children in 1982, and plans were underway to accommodate both the handicapped and the exceptional child. Sunnydale, originally under the aegis of the Guelph and District Retarded Children's Association, was taken over by the board of education in 1983.

The Wellington County board gave early encouragement for French immersion. In 1972, with Cliff Whitfield as superintendent, French immersion was set up with commitment from kindergarten to Grade 13 at Edward Johnson, Victory, John McCrae and Waverley Drive. Parents who wanted it were keen with ferocious loyalty. Students, at a dead loss at first, adjusted as the program built. The separate school board initiated a French language school for kindergarten to Grade 8. L'Ecole St. René Goupil was established at St. Patrick's School (Victoria Road) in 1978, and children from many parts of the city attended. With increased enrolment after two years, the students were transferred to larger quarters at Sacred Heart. Installed in the old St. Patrick's building, they shared the gym and the schoolyard, already encumbered with five portables. With the help of the English trustees, St. René Goupil was bumped to number one for capital grants and, in 1988, received $2.1 million from the Ministry of Education for relocation. A new St. René opened on Scottsdale Drive in 1990. In 1998, the provincial government created a network of public and Catholic French-language boards as part of its restructuring program. St. René Goupil was transferred to the new French language Catholic board. French

Computer and audio-visual support was readily available for teachers. As early as 1945, an Ampro sound-projector was used at Tytler. On January 6, 1966, Victory, Edward Johnson, Ottawa Crescent and Tytler were ready to receive the first coast-to-coast Canadian school telecast by the CBC from 3 to 3:30 p.m. Other schools quickly hooked up, including St. James and Our Lady of Lourdes. At Central's first showing, a stunned principal Carson Allen reported that the pupils sat in dead silence – without any pressure! At an audio-visual workshop on Teacher's Institute Day, October 20, 1967, teachers were urged to use tapes and tape recorders, film strips, overhead projectors, educational television, and a closed-circuit system along with books, maps and chalkboards. In 1971, Paisley Road and GCVI were two of 288 Ontario schools producing motion pictures of their community. Their three-minute films were shown at Ontario Place in May. When King Edward closed in 1976, the board's Education Media Centre moved in, delighted at last to have space for over 2,000 pieces of audio-visual equipment. Teachers flocked to computer courses in the summer of 1982. At the beginning of the school year in 1999, those at Guelph's new model for high-tech learning, Mitchell Woods Public School, were still undergoing training on its newer technology. Wellington County was also one of few boards to have a teacher-librarian in every school, and it led the county in co-operative transportation between the public and separate schools.

Fred A. Hamilton

Fred A. Hamilton Public School is named after a man who made the business of education his life's work. A member of the Col. John McCrae Legion and a long-time member of the Guelph Garrison Officers' Mess, Dr. Fred A. Hamilton was born in Fergus in 1909. He entered high school at age 11 and gained his teaching certificate when he was 20.

In 1964, he was appointed Guelph's first director of education. A man of boundless energy, he was a member of a number of organizations and clubs. He co-founded the National School Boy Curling Associations in the 1940s to encourage sportsmanship and camaraderie for young boys. He was re-elected three times to the Wellington County Board of Education, where he served as chair. Hamilton was president of the Ontario Directors of Education, Superintendents and Federation of Secondary School Athletic Association. He received an honorary doctorate of law degree from Queen's University and was a fellow of the Canadian College of Teachers.

He was considered a classics scholar, a respected school trustee and a keen sports enthusiast. From his activities within the community "Mr. Education" was probably one of the best-known citizens of Guelph in his time. Daughter Suzanne recalled that no matter where the family went in Canada someone always recognized her dad and genuinely wanted to tell him what sort of impact he had had on their lives.

Guelph's first 'Citizen of the Year' died on January 11, 1989. His funeral was held at Chalmers Church as the funeral home could not handle the number of people who came to pay tribute to such a caring man.

– Ceska Brennan

---

immersion continued in Brighton, John McCrae, University Village, Paisley Road and Victory schools under the public school board.

Recommendations for the tearing down of Central School had been made in the early 1960s. In the midst of indecision, the board decided to repair the old belfry, only to remove it the following year. After several architects had proclaimed that the $400,000 cost for renovations would be a waste of taxpayers' money and Principal Allen had stated, "if I were a businessman, I don't think I'd want to invest money in a building of this vintage," the decision was made. Closing-out ceremonies were held in June 1968, with former pupil George Drew as speaker. That summer both Central and Alexandra schools were torn down,

with disastrous effects to Guelph's skyline. A new Central was opened in 1969, fully equipped with record players, tape recorders, earphones and no walls between classrooms. It was Guelph's first open-concept school. Shelldale (1970) and University Village (1971) soon followed, with kindergarten to Grade 6 in one large classroom. By that time, at Central, piles of books and other materials had become makeshift dividers.

Public schools continued to be built to satisfy rapidly growing areas and the guidelines of the report. A two-storey 24-room school was built on Willow Road in 1967 for Grades 7 and 8. With students from Victory, June Avenue, Paisley Road, Torrance, Central, Marden, and eventually, Westwood Junior School, it represented a cross-section of social, economic, racial and ethnic backgrounds.

Brant Avenue had been operating since March 1971, but officially opened in November, giving parents an opportunity of seeing the school in operation through slides and movies of classroom action. Brant's proximity to the development of the Guelph Lake sports complex in the mid-80s gave it an advantage over other city schools. With baseball diamonds and wooded trails, recreation and nature were near at hand. A breakfast club, started in 1988 to make sure the children had a nutritious breakfast, evolved into a social club with a community room open to the public for morning coffee.

A general view emerged around 1973 that the school had a role as a central institution in the community and should consciously build firm connections with it. Westwood School, opened in November 1976 as a junior school, was especially designed for that purpose, the only one in Wellington County. Outside doors, leading to the gym and change rooms, could be left open for community use during evening hours, and the door from gym to school, closed. A distinction was not made at first between educational purposes and social or recreational use of gymnasium or an auditorium, and difficulties arose regarding fees. In 1982, the board settled the matter with a comprehensive and clearly understood policy.

After the building of Gateway Drive in 1981, eight years passed before another school was needed. Fred A. Hamilton School (1989), the first in many years to be named after a person, had, in the words of reporter Hilary Stead, "the dubious distinction of 200 percent occupancy and more portables than classrooms." Other unique features were two storeys, a mezzanine and a balcony, eight permanent classrooms, and an elevator fully accessible to the handicapped. It was also the first local school subject to new Ministry of Education regulations requiring day-care facilities to be built in all new schools. Jean Little School, named after the Guelph children's book author, opened in 1991, with electronic encyclopedias replacing books on shelves and computer terminals in every classroom, including kindergarten.

It cost $5.6 million to build Taylor Evans School. Completed by 1992, it featured the following: a separate section for developmentally-handicapped children to be integrated when possible; a non-profit day care with before and after school care; elevators; hook-ups for multiple computers; eyewash stands in case of accidents in the science room; computerized sewing machines in the family studies room; practice booths in the music room; special preparatory room adjoining the science room; fully equipped design and technology room with space to add computer-assisted design manufacturing; and an adult-sized double gym with full change-rooms and showers.

The separate schools' building boom continued with a new St. Patrick School opening on Victoria Road in 1968. Three years later the first school to be completely planned and built by the Wellington County Separate School Board, St. Francis of Assisi, was opened on Ridgewood Avenue. It was the board's first open-concept school, its "innovative design, allowing a greater degree of flexibility in instructional grouping." Mary Phelan School, in 1975, serving the Priory Park and University Village areas, was the first local separate school named after a person – the well-loved teacher at Sacred Heart and the first principal of St. John School. Mass, usually said for the area's Catholics in the foyer of Stone Road Mall, was transferred to the gym at Mary Phelan. In the fall of 1976, a change took place on the historic hill. The 123-year-old St. Stanislaus School was torn down and replaced by a plain white, modern building. New ground was broken in 1976 with St. Peter School, in the Willow West subdivision near Hanlon Parkway, serving kindergarten pupils to Grade 4. Originally built for 80 pupils, it had two rooms, a small gym, offices, and a library, all entirely portable. Six portable classrooms and one relocatable gym were on the site by 1982 and in 1998, it was filled with a dozen portables and 518 pupils from junior kindergarten to Grade 8. A new school was planned for September 2000.

In 1984, the provincial government decided to extend full support to Roman Catholic schools, enabling students to complete their high-school education within the separate school system without paying heavy fees. In September 1985, St. James and Our Lady of Lourdes were upgraded to high-school status. Bishop Macdonell, still with financial difficulties in spite of an energetic Heritage Fund Campaign, was unable to discharge its debts and

Jean and Flora Little

Guelph is home to internationally-known author of children's books, Jean Little. She was born in Taiwan in 1932 to missionary parents. Born with poor eyesight, her sight improved marginally in the first years of her life but gave way to blindness in later years. Jean learned the power of words at an early age and decided then to become an author. Her parents bought her a large-print typewriter when she was seven and had her taught to touch-type when she was 10 years old. Jean was 15 when her first book, a collection of poems entitled *It's a Wonderful World*, was published. Her first novel, *Mine For Keeps*, won the Little, Brown Canadian Book Award in 1962.

She earned a B.A. from the University of Toronto and trained as a teacher of disabled children, but turned to writing full-time. She writes about orphans, foster children and handicapped children to illustrate their similarities to, rather than their differences from so-called "normal" children. To date, she has written 29 children's books which are available in 10 languages and has had a television movie based on one of her books. She has earned eight literary awards and received three honorary doctorates. She was inducted into the Order of Canada in 1993 for her books, her work with the Canadian National Institute for the Blind, and her work with children in schools to promote a love of reading.

Jean's mother, Dr. Flora Little, was Guelph's first woman doctor. Born in Taiwan in 1902, she entered the University of Toronto at age 16 and graduated from medical school in 1923. Shortly after, Dr. Little returned to the country of her birth to work as a medical missionary. Flora and her husband Llew, also a doctor, returned to Canada in 1939 and, one year later, the couple set up a medical practice in Guelph. During the war she was one of the few doctors who remained in the city and for years was the only practising woman doctor in Guelph.

Dr. Little often made house calls to farms. Jean fondly recalls one time her mother returned home at 3 a.m. after delivering a baby. The doctor was so enthralled with the experience she made a snowman outside their home before she went to bed. When Jean and her siblings got up in the morning they were mystified as to where it could have come from.

Flora Little was named Guelph's first woman Citizen of the Year in 1949-50 and received the Glenn Sawyer Service Award from The Ontario Medical Association in 1975. She died in July 1991.

– Ceska Brennan

continue with rising costs. In 1991, the Catholic Secondary Education Committee recommended its closing and the expansion of St. James and Our Lady of Lourdes as the best way of reducing costs and providing improved services to students.

Dissatisfaction with the existing system of education was expressed in the rise of alternative schools. The board's audio-visual equipment had to be moved

In 1966, the Ontario government appointed a special committee, headed by J. Keiller Mackay, to review the teaching of religion in the public schools. After three years of public hearings, reading of briefs, letters and petitions and intensive study of the subject, the committee advised the total elimination of the 1944 requirements for religious instruction. They should be replaced by an informal moral or ethical education that permeated the entire curriculum to encourage students to make their own value judgements and moral decisions. A formal course of study of the world's religions was suggested as an option in Grades 11 and 12. It also advised that the acquisition of information about and respect for all religions be recognized as an essential objective of the educational system from kindergarten to Grade 13.

out of the old King Edward School when it was bought in 1977 by the Canadian Reformed School Society of Fergus and Guelph, a Dutch Calvinist denomination associated with the Canadian Reformed Church. It reopened as Emmanuel Christian High School with about 45 students. Courses were in Bible history, English, mathematics, physical education, health, French, geography, church history, home economics, drafting, typing and business practice. They did not condone sex education, the theory of evolution, or lack of discipline, believing them not in accordance with God's word. The school celebrated its 25th year in 1986 by planning a two-room addition for a new classroom and a library-resource centre. Crestwicke Baptist Academy, founded in 1973 with Crestwicke Baptist Church carrying about 70 percent of the cost, was incorporated in 1994 with a separate budget and account. Although closely associated with the church, the Academy accepted students from many faiths and ethnic backgrounds, concentrating on religious principals rather than religious doctrine. John Calvin Christian School, on the other hand, was firm about accepting only children from Protestant families.

Other alternative systems of education were being established. The Guelph Montessori House of Children held an introductory meeting in May 1977 at Victory School. The program was based on teaching methods developed in the early 1900s by Dr. Maria Montessori, Italy's first female doctor. "Between two-and-a-half and six are crucial years when children are receptive to new ideas," explained instructor Dawn Reynolds. "Although the school is a learning [and] not

a play experience, its thrust is to make learning a pleasure." The school, owned by Rubina Alidina, was held in a rented room at Holy Rosary School, then in St. Patrick's School. As the Guelph Montessori School, it was housed in a renovated stone home on Woolwich Street and included an elementary program for ages six to nine. In 1989, it was transferred to new owners and, in 1998, moved to larger quarters on Ignatius College grounds. Enrolment in 1999 was 80, with an extended program to the age of 12. The Montessori School of Wellington was established in 1997 in the basement of Dublin Street United Church. In 1996, the Trillium Children's School opened in the basement of Westwood United Church, following the Waldorf Method taught by Rudolf Steiner in the 1920s.

Two groups of parents, who felt they had a better system of education to offer, were given serious consideration by the public school board. The Wellington Community Co-operative School was set up in Waverley Drive in 1993 as a three-year pilot project for kindergarten to Grade 6. Operated mainly by parents wanting to be involved in the education of their children, it was the epitome of child-centred education. In a relaxed environment, pupils learned what they were interested in and helped make the rules and develop the curriculum. Beyond literary and academic standards, the focus was on interpersonal communications skills. Forty-nine pupils were enrolled at the beginning, but a gradually dropping enrolment forced the board to close the venture at the end of three years. In the meantime, another parental group petitioned for a traditional values or back to basics school. Theirs was a structured approach to learning with a balanced curriculum and an emphasis on basic skill building. Their vision included competition, grading, traditional teaching methods and discipline and a teacher-centred classroom with students sitting in rows of desks. According to founding member Lori Clarke, 260 children were pre-registered, but the board reversed a decision to hold registration early in 1996, ostensibly because of reductions in provincial funding.

Finding appropriate child-care was difficult in spite of an increase in licensed home operations. Aladdin Day Care opened in 1967 in the basement of Trinity United Church and accommodated 56 children. As chairman of the Community Service Council Child-Care Committee, Dorothy (Sheri) Dixon was responsible for the establishment of the Wee Y's in 1971 at the Guelph YM-YWCA with a supervisor and two staff members. She was also instrumental in initiating a private day-care program in Guelph to raise the quality of care given in private homes. In 1974, noting the increase of single parent families and working mothers, she recommended that the city expand day-care resources by taking advantage of a government program that covered 100 percent of the capital costs for renovations of old buildings or construction of new ones. City council responded. In November 1975, Guelph's first municipally owned day-care centre, fully equipped for 42 full-time children between two and four-and-a-half, was officially opened on Willow Road. As welcomed as it was, it could not satisfy an increasing demand. "Space for babies triples with $1.4 million centre," reported Hilary Stead at the opening of the University of Guelph's child-care centre, the only one in Ontario owned and operated by a university. Of 104 spaces, 10 were for infants three to 18-months-old. The headline pointed out the need for infant care in Guelph, and as three quarters of the spaces were to be are allocated to children of university faculty, the advantage to the community was not great. The YM-YWCA, however, increased a number of sites across the city, becoming its largest day-care provider. More expansion occurred with the move to a new building in the city's south west end in 1996. In a modern kitchen, meals could now be prepared for all sites. The Y's child-care program had grown from 22 spaces in 1972 to 660.

Neither the public nor the separate school board was enthusiastic about the 1989 throne speech proposal for mandatory junior kindergarten, even though half the capital cost was to be paid by the province. Although the education ministry indicated junior kindergarten (JK) was likely to become law in 1994, Wellington County board members could not agree to begin phasing in the program in 1991. Many thought of it as positive step toward increasing the quality of life of children, but Donna Lero, child development expert at the University of Guelph, outlined some of the problems. Decisions had to be made on curriculum, staffing (teachers or day-care workers), physical design, and child-to-teacher ratio (eight-to-one in day care and 20-to-one in kindergarten), and adjustments with working parents' time schedules. Aware of the fact that 18 schools would require renovations, 20 would need portables and renovations, and six would have to build additions as well as add portables, the board rejected the JK proposal, hoping that the government would change its mind. Parent expectations were high again in 1998 when the government offered a choice between JK and an early-learning grant for educational enhancement from kindergarten to Grade 3. In March 1999, the board chose the latter. The literacy initiative program included funds for extra teachers, greater resource support, and professional development for kindergarten and Grade 1 teachers.

In the 1970s and early 1980s, problems had mainly been physical ones concerning the building of the right kind of school and the implementation of approved curriculum. Although working mothers and single-parent families were cited as the main cause of behavioural problems, a small but active body of parents attended board meetings, voiced their opinions, and submitted petitions and proposals. One concern was a healthy environment for their children. The popular *modus operandi* in an attempt to influence board decisions was to form a committee with a significant anagram. The Parents Against Retrofitting Excluding Natural Terrain and Sunlight, otherwise known as PARENTS (1982), failed to halt the board's plans for filling windows with concrete blocks in order to conserve heating and save the price of drapes. They were more successful as CARE (Coalition Against Retrofitting Excesses) in reducing the number of windows altered. Later problems arose concerning asbestos at John F. Ross, weed spraying at Central, air quality at King George, mould in many of the portables, and rashes from the new desks at Centennial. King George, originally built for Grades 1 to 6, became a senior elementary school in 1969. By the 1990s, the gym was inadequate and unsafe for rigorous sports games and the library too small and outdated. After working two years on new proposals, teachers and parents started to fundraise. During 50th-anniversary celebrations in 1999, a board trustee, impressed with their endeavours, announced that their strategy report would be accepted. Parents of Paisley Road students had lobbied persistently in 1990-91 against leaky roofs, small crowded rooms and the 19 separate units between which their children travelled each day. The board hired an architect who agreed with the parents that the school was in a dilapidated state. In 1993, their children entered a brand new school.

Boards also found themselves involved with problems with which they

Instruction on the dangers of drugs was intensified in 1990. When a Guelph teacher asked her Grade 3 class if anyone could name an illegal drug, she discovered they knew them all. A way to assist in drug education was found in videos, aimed at three different age groups and distributed to each school by the Canadian Association of Police Chiefs as part of the Canadian Offensive for Drug Addiction. *Open Flame*, a video examining the effects of drugs on the mind and body that had been produced by a Grade 13 drama group at North York Collegiate, was circulated in secondary schools.

had no prior experience. A large number of parents were asking for assistance from the school in raising their children. Both teachers and parents were confronted with sexual promiscuity, drug abuse, depression, suicide attempts, disruptive or violent behaviour and racism. The former approach to sex education under the title of health education or family life studies now had to deal with contraception, abortion and pregnancies. In 1989, 158 pregnancies were reported in Wellington

County among girls ages 15 to 19. In 1990, the board supported the establishment of three 'teen clinics' to be operated by the Wellington-Dufferin-Guelph Health Unit at GCVI, College Heights and the Centre Wellington District High School in Fergus. A group of girls interviewed by Hilary Stead welcomed the new counselling services with the following remarks: it will be wonderful because parents don't listen; it will help keep the kids in school, because teachers don't care; maybe it will provide information about being kicked out of the house so you don't have to drop out of school; there should be information about drug use – there is a lot (of drug use at GCVI) although not as much as at Centennial; it would be great if they supplied birth-control pills for a small fee instead of $30 a month. Two years later the drop in teenage pregnancies was attributed to the information supplied by clinics and seminars. In 1993, John F. Ross students attempted to dispel myths and dispense information about sex in a hilarious production *Live on Stage Uncensored,* written by drama teacher Tom Slater and four students.

In an attempt to curb rowdyism, the board installed cameras on the buses. This was successful to a degree, although it did not stop the slashing of

seats. Violence was more difficult to control. "We have changed the name from the old 'Safety in the Schools' policy to the 'Task Force on Youth Group Violence,'" reported Dave Clark, superintendent of schools. "Groups and gangs there have always been, but not the number of weapons and violence." In accordance with a Ministry of Education mandate, a policy of 'zero tolerance' was adopted in Wellington County schools in 1990. The aim was 'violence-free schools.' Punishment for acts of violence and bullying varied from a three to 20-day suspension to expulsion or police charges. Three days off school often meant three days to watch television. With expulsion, a child would simply quit school, and police charges would label him for life. Randy Norris, a parent volunteer at John McCrae School, believed a 'zero tolerance' attitude towards conflict was not realistic. "Conflict is out there," he said. "We need to learn to manage it, not ignore it, and certainly not run from it." The school's parent council initiated a peer-mediation program in early 1999 to teach students how to solve arguments. In December 1999, the Upper Grand District School Board approved a new policy requiring each school to have a violence-free school plan with mandatory training of staff, codes of behaviour for students, violence prevention, conflict resolution programs and an expanded plan for responding to a crisis.

No educational act for reform ever caused such uproar in Ontario as did that of the Harris government in 1997. Public and separate school boards were united in their reactions. They had customarily raised funds through property taxes, topped with provincial grants when possible. With the enactment of Bill 160, the province assumed the raising of educational taxes, relieving the local boards of control and autonomy. It also presented a new funding formula based on the enrolment of 1,000 pupils per school. A school with fewer pupils would get only a percentage of support positions such as guidance counsellors and librarians. College Heights, with 550 students, two librarians and two guidance counsellors, would now have 1.5 of each. The library was therefore closed for one period a day, reducing a student's chance to do extra work during a spare period. Libraries in smaller schools had to close for half a day; some would have no librarian. Most counselling jobs disappeared. The boards, however, could obtain long-term funding for new schools and additions by closing exiting schools that were inefficient or under-utilized. Renewal grants were based on 96 cents per pupil per 100 square feet, but if a school were closed, the board would get $11 per pupil per 100 square feet from a "new pupil place grant." The small enrolment at Torrance Public School could generate only $12,000 a year, and it needed costly renovations. Its fate was immediately sealed, with no thought of its historic and unique structure designed by local architect W. Frye Colwill. Protestations were vociferous enough to save the building from the wrecking block. Within the year the old building was bustling with community activity. Leased from the city by Sue Richards, founder of Art Jam in Guelph, it housed four artists' studios on the top floor, Art Jam's activities on the first floor and the Guelph International Resource Centre in the basement.

After initial parental angst and anger over the proposed closing of Shelldale School, some advantages became apparent. As a small school with four portables and 219 pupils, it could not have a full-time principal, librarian or other support staff. When about 200 Grade 7 and 8 students, living west of the Hanlon, transferred to the new Mitchell Woods Public School in September 1999, half of Shelldale moved into neighbouring Willow Road, gaining the advantages of a larger school, including cafeteria, large gymnasium-auditorium and design and technology facilities. Future plans called for an addition to Willow by September 2000, when all pupils would be transferred, with Shelldale offered for use by community social services.

Because less money was available for school administrators (one for every 1,000), not all schools could have a full-time principal. The solution was to twin June Avenue with Victory and Laurine Avenue with Ottawa Crescent. The Catholic School Board consolidated six Guelph schools. Six principals of small schools were required to teach one half or one fifth of the time. Many teachers took early retirement on the advice of their unions. With the new formula requiring an average of 25 pupils per class and with an increase in enrolment expected, new teachers and more portables would be required. There was now a shortage of both.

Further changes involved the amalgamation of the Wellington and Dufferin County boards into the Upper Grand District Public School Board and the complete reconstruction of public and high school curriculum with a back-to-basics, no-nonsense agenda. Hours of teaching and the number of school days were outlined specifically. Teachers would have to teach more hours and have less preparation time. "We enacted reforms that teachers had long wanted," said Premier Harris to the *Guelph Mercury* editors, "new textbooks and other supplies, a standard curriculum and more help in the classroom." Teachers and their unions did not agree. Strikes and work stoppages followed, resulting in school closures, work-to-rule methods, and cancellation of extra-curricula activities, but with little result. After the Conservative government was re-elected in 1999, educational reform moved ahead as planned.

Two hundred and forty-six graduates from Wellington School of Continuing Education in June 1998 – the largest class to date. Source: *Guelph Mercury*

Adult education or continuing education had become an integral part of society in the latter years of the century. Sharing and networking were keywords when Wellington County's public and separate school boards joined to form the Wellington Centre for Continuing Education in 1994, housed in the vacated Bishop Macdonell High School. One example of the co-operation between boards was the development of the International Language Program to provide free instruction for elementary school children in any of 19 languages. Classes were held Saturday mornings and at a three-week summer camp. Crafts, music and cooking lessons emphasized the fun of learning. A vibrant parent's association assisted with special events and also produced two cookbooks.

Courses offered throughout the county included English as a second language (ESL), literacy training, secondary-school credits, computer schools, international languages, after-school programs for elementary school children and general interest and leisure courses. Two hundred and forty-six adult students received their Secondary School Diploma from the Wellington Centre in 1998.

Education was not only taking place in the schools. Several non-profit community-based organizations had been founded in Guelph to deal with basic literacy training. Statistics had revealed that 24 percent of adult Canadians were functionally illiterate. Although Wellington County's rate was lower at 17.3 percent, the information was startling. It indicated that the educational system, highly rated as it was, was not reaching a large number of citizens. With provincial funding, Action Read began in 1987 as a small group connected with the Centre for Employable Workers. One of their first ventures was an eight-week, family-literacy program at St George's Church. Action Read grew rapidly over the next 10 years. With a staff of 100 volunteers in 1999, young adults over 16 and no longer in school were given one-to-one training in reading, writing, and basic mathematics. Project READ, based in Kitchener, provided a literacy network covering Waterloo and Wellington counties to assess the needs of young adults and direct them toward areas of help. Second Chance Employment Counselling, in Guelph since the early 1970s, changed from trying to find work for applicants to teaching them how to plan a job search and providing necessary skills for writing resumes and cover letters and handling an interview. Sixteen graduated from their Young Entrepreneurship Programme in 1999. Funded federally, it helped young adults with skills, talents, and ideas to launch a business of their own. Lutherwood Coda, a branch of a Kitchener-Waterloo association that came to Guelph in 1997 assisted unemployed adults over the age of 25. As these and private organizations continued to grow, Dorothe Fair and Don Drone again saw a need to share information. In 1998, they set up GRACE, the Guelph Regional Association for Continuing Education, amalgamating all organizations in the area that offered opportunities in the field. GRACE also provided assistance to adults with financial restraints. Included were the Guelph Recreation and Parks Department and other sources more recently perceived as belonging to continuing education: Guelph Museums, the Guelph Public Library, the Wellington Dufferin-Guelph Health Unit and the Guelph and District Multicultural Centre.

The Guelph Civic Museum came into prominence when it moved from the market building to the Knights of Columbus Hall in 1980. With space to display its growing collection, it could now store, accept and catalogue the artifacts, photographs and archival materials donated by public-spirited citizens. It could offer special exhibitions and install a gift shop. By 1999, its artifacts numbered 30,000, including 4,000 photographs on the history of Guelph. Extensive educational programs were developed as well as education kits for teachers to use in the classroom. In 1968, McCrae House was opened, the result of years of planning and work by the Col. John McCrae Birthplace Society, organized for that purpose. Furniture, photographs, letters and documents, displayed in John McCrae's family house, revealed the story of his life and a history of his time. Children's programs on the Great War, Victorian life, and gardens were offered and, during Remembrance Week, the Guelph Amateur Ham Radio Operators could be seen sending Remembrance Day messages around the world. In 1983, McCrae House amalgamated with the Civic Museum to form Guelph Museums.

September 7, 1998 – University of Guelph students set a Guinness World Record during Frosh Week for the longest human conveyor belt ever.

Also a member of GRACE was the Office of Open Learning at the University of Guelph. Successor of many years of extension education from the hill to the community, it now could function nationally and internationally. Non-degree courses, workshops and certificate programs for professional and personal development were still taken at the university. Distance education provided university courses that could be studied at the office or at home, using a variety of technical learning aids. In 1999, 39 courses could be taken on-line via the World Wide Web, by any age, at any stage, from anywhere, any time. Gilbert Stelter's *Reading a Community* (1995), the first regular university course to go on-line, used Guelph as a basis for a wider historical study of urban development, thus providing an up-to-date study of the city.

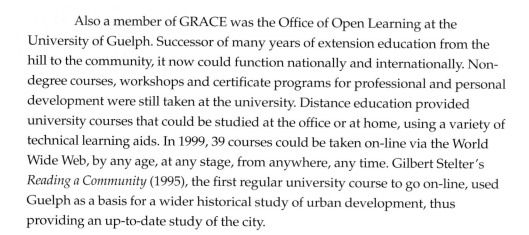

Headlines made by the university for its great achievements paled in the summer light of an afternoon in July 1991 when student Gwen Jacob contributed significantly to its course on women's rights. By taking her shirt off and, bare-breasted, walking home from classes, Jacob became a catalyst of change and a challenger to existing laws. Unlike the men on the street, she was charged with indecent exposure. The press had a field day, the issue was argued, controversy raged, and eventually, with her conviction overturned, the law was changed. Bowser and Blue's popular song concluded,

We compare ourselves with the U.S.
And often they come out the best
But they only have the right to bear arms
And we have the right to bare breasts.

The university opened many special areas to the public, including the Arboretum, with its mandate to facilitate understanding and respect for the earth, and the new Health and Performance Centre, where individuals could test and improve their physical condition. A multitude of events every year at the College Royal provided enlightening experiences for all family members. Thursday noon concerts continued to showcase professional and student performances, town and gown joined in the choir, orchestra, band, and jazz band presentations, art students exhibited their work in MacLaughlin Library or at the Macdonald Stewart Art Centre, and drama students attracted audiences for their regular productions. Professors from all disciplines continued to contribute to the city's multifaceted cultural life.

Macdonald Consolidated School had continued on its disparate course. In 1969, it came under the newly-created Wellington County Board of Education.

When boundary changes occurred in 1971, its pupils were relocated at the newly-built University Village School. With the second floor structurally unsound, the school's first floor was used for a few years by the university's psychology department as an experimental educational clinic for four-year-olds. By this time, the limited gallery space in the university's McLaughlin library was too small to display its now sizeable art collection. With encouragement from university president Donald Forster, who wished to make the collection more available to the public, and members of the Macdonald Stewart Foundation, who cared about the old building, an assessment was carefully made. When renovation as a public art gallery was considered feasible, the Foundation provided a naming grant, and a capital campaign was launched that proved successful. The Macdonald Stewart Art Centre was established in 1978 through a private member's bill in the provincial legislature. Its four contributing sponsors were the University of Guelph, the Wellington County Board of Education, the City of Guelph and the County of Wellington. The university's art acquisitions, representing 75 years of collecting by the founding colleges and the university, were then placed on permanent loan to the gallery. The centre's new director, Judith Nasby, wrote, the "dream of building a survey collection of Canadian art has been achieved," and "by providing professional and program support staff, the university ensures that its collection has proper care and is developed as an educational resource for the entire region." By 1997, the collection, amounting to over 4,000 works, represented a 300-year survey of Canadian art. Approximately 15 exhibitions were mounted each year, accompanied by an educational program for the public.

Under Nasby's leadership the art centre developed several areas of specialization. A collection of contemporary Inuit drawings began in 1980 and, in 1987, the art centre's touring exhibition became the first survey exhibition from settlements across the Canadian Arctic, bringing attention to drawing as a major artistic medium among the Canadian Inuit. In August 1994, the art centre opened an exhibition of 43 drawings by Baker Lake artists in the community hall at Baker Lake in Nunavut. This was the first survey exhibition of Baker Lake drawings to be organized and the first touring exhibition produced by a southern gallery to open in an Arctic settlement. An accompanying symposium program focussed on the

Agitato. Oil painting on canvas by Guelph-born artist of many talents Rolph Scarlett, 1943.   Source: Macdonald Stewart Art Centre

Untitled work of Baker Lake artist Irene Avaalaaqiaq, felt applique and embroidery, 1989, exhibited at the Macdonald Stewart Art Centre in 2000.
Source: Macdonald Stewart Art Centre

artists, the community, and the tundra landscape. The show toured to Japan, Iceland, Phoenix and Jaipur, India. The MSAC's Inuit collection contained over 500 drawings as well as sculptures, prints, print-stones, wall-hangings and clothing. In 1999, the University of Guelph awarded Baker Lake artist Irene Avaalaaqiaq an honorary degree.

A second specialization developed in 1983 when the garden plots, ice rink, grove of trees and playground of the old Macdonald Consolidated School were transformed into a landscaped site for a sculpture park. Individual outdoor sculptures representing the cutting edge of contemporary Canadian art were gradually acquired by national competitions or commissions and placed in fitting areas of the landscape design. At the century's end, the park contained 20 sculptures and was recognized as a major Canadian cultural resource. Nasby's specialized research into the paintings, design drawings, stage designs and jewellery of Guelph artist Rolph Scarlett revealed his genius

Canadiana/Begging Bear by Karl Skeleton at Macdonald Stewart Art Centre's sculpture garden, 2000.
Source: Dawn Matheson

Young cellists rehearse at the Suzuki String Institute, August 1991.
Source: Christine Nightingale

Early members of Ed Video Media Arts Centre, 1978. (l-r)
George Young, President Teri Chmilar, Jeremy Blackburn, Julie
Sommerfield and Nick Hall.　　　　　　Source: Ed Video

Sally Wismer, executive director of Guelph Arts Council, is
seated by the Blacksmith Statue in Priory Square, March 18,
1999. The statue, a work of art included in GAC's recently published
guide to Public Art in Guelph, was donated to the city by J.B.
Armstrong, one of the city's early industrialists and stood in St.
George's Square from 1885 to 1922.　　　Source: *Guelph Mercury*

and assured recognition of his work at home and abroad. An international touring exhibition was launched in March 2000, with an extensive catalogue in preparation.

Guelph had never suffered from a lack of fine music teachers. For many years most belonged to the Royal Conservatory of Music Teachers Association. With an active younger generation of teachers emerging in the early 1980s, the Guelph Independent Music Teacher's Association was formed. Jenny Lamb's String Academy continued successfully with traditional string instruction and an annual concert until illness forced her retirement. In 1972, Daphne Hughes had started the Suzuki String School of Guelph, and Gail Lange followed with the Suzuki piano program. The teaching of an exciting new method involved serious parental commitment to the extent that some parents learned to play an instrument along with the child. Young string players were soon more visible as they readily entertained at local gatherings. Concorde, a group of senior students, reached professional levels. Weekly string group lessons provided participants for a larger enterprise – the Guelph Youth Orchestra, formed in 1977 by Guelph Arts Council. The Guelph Orff Music Studio, Children's Recorder Group, and Music for Young Children were smaller groups with the same purpose, but different programs. The Guelph School of Music, opened in 1997 introduced an early childhood program based on the Kodaly method. Extra motivation for all music students, choirs, and instrumental

groups was provided when local Kiwanis officials, inspired by Niklaus and June Kaethler, agreed to revitalize the Kiwanis Music Festival. No longer having to take students to Stratford or Toronto to compete, parents and teachers enthusiastically supported the festival and, with the hard work of the Kaethlers, it grew from 600 entrants in 1981 to over 2,500 in 1998.

Guelph has enjoyed a variety of qualified dancing instructors and many annual recitals. The philosophy of Patricia Plummer R.A.D, who took over from Anne Richmond in 1963 and formed the Patricia Plummer School of Ballet and Related Arts, later the Royal City School of Ballet, was particularly suited to the latter part of the century. "Parents gave so much time and worked so hard with costumes and accessories to put their kids on the stage," she said, "that I never felt I could take the proceeds of the concerts we put on." Starting in 1979, she used profits from annual ballet recitals to send students on scholarship to Banff. Since 1985, all proceeds have gone to the Guelph Arts Council to use for arts scholarships in the schools. "This way, the money is back in circulation," she added, "and is working for the arts." During her years in Guelph, Pat Plummer McLeod choreographed over 30 musicals for schools, the Guelph Light Opera Company, Little Theatre, the Road Show, and was a founding member of the Royal City Musical Productions (RCMPI). Anna Marie Oliver and Bonnie Dyer have each contributed responsibly to the city's cultural life, with the latter's Canadian National Tap Team awarded a gold medal at a 1998 World Tap Dance competition in Germany.

The creation of Guelph Arts Council in 1975 was a major stimulant to continuing education in the arts. Artists in all fields were encouraged to make themselves known, to communicate with each other, and to use GAC as a resource centre. Through *Arts in Guelph*, a monthly newsletter, the public was alerted to artistic activity in the city. Workshops, either sponsored by GAC or on an individual's initiative, took place throughout the year. A later inspiration was the 1998 Arts Schmoozefest, regular evenings of socialization and networking between groups and individuals. The council was also involved in the founding of Guelph Tourism Connection, later Guelph Visitor and Convention Services, that emphasized the value of culture and heritage in attracting tourists to the city. Discover Guelph: Be a Tourist in your own Town was a joint venture of both organizations. Twelve venues, 20 artists' studios, and eight galleries were featured in a panoply of art, history, performance, leisure and nature, all available on a five dollar passport for the day.

The close relationship of education to the arts was clearly illustrated in the founding of Ed Video Creative Community Television, after several name changes, Ed Video Media Arts Centre. In applying for a Local Initiatives Program grant in 1975, the federal government liaison officer recommended a change from 'Art Video' to 'Ed Video,' as any reference to art might have jeopardized their chances to receive funding. Their mandate was to teach the creative use of video, and to use its potential to develop and enhance personal expression in the schools and institutions in the Guelph area. As they refined their methods with new and better equipment, technology and techniques, they continued to educate with public performances and exhibitions on the intricacies of the world around them, always encouraging individual expression in paths previously unexplored. The 1999 exhibition *Digital Me*, illustrative of art entering a new dimension and involving audience participation, was on-line for a year.

As education led into the arts, it also enveloped many clubs and organizations. Education, in fact, could not be separated from any aspect of contemporary life and society.

Garbasauraus: A work of 'found-art' after the 20th annual Speed River Clean-up, 1999. Sculpture by Greg Elliot.   Source: Dawn Matheson

CLUBS AND ORGANIZATIONS

"In today's economy, the most precious commodity seems to be time," wrote *Mercury* reporter Alan Ferris about the 1990s. Service clubs were having difficulty recruiting new members with time to spare. Brad Herron, president of the Optimist Club agreed, stating that the Royal City Lions Club, the Royal City Kiwanis Club and the Kinsmen were also having difficulties. "People commute to work or are on shifts and many members are old and feel they have done their part." Technology had also played a role in declining membership. "People used to join clubs to interact with other business people," said the president of the Royal City Kiwanis Club, "but with e-mail and faxes, they have constant contact."

Time was indeed a commodity, but more, not less of it was being spent by citizens in community-related activities. In Guelph, one in every three adults was a volunteer in 1998. Over 20,000 persons contributed as much as three hours a week, about 24 million dollars worth of labour to the local economy. In the past, the term 'volunteer' generally meant the younger woman with children at school, or the well-intentioned older woman whose children had left home. In the 1990s, one third of Canada's volunteers were young people, male and female, who wished to learn new skills and improve their job opportunities. Most other volunteers were employed, well educated and short of time. They also had to be committed and dependable because they were filling gaps caused by government

Sister Christine Leyser

The Loretto Sisters, known as the Society of the Blessed Virgin Mary, came to Guelph in 1856 to teach and give aid to the poor. Although the Loretto Convent closed its doors in 1996, Sister Leyser stayed in Guelph with others of her order to work for the people in need in the community. Many Guelph residents know Sister Leyser as Sister Christine and are familiar with her work at the downtown drop-in centre. The sister's Welcome In centre opened in the summer of 1983 to provide food and drink as well as company and temporary shelter for the disadvantaged. On Thanksgiving and Christmas, Sister Christine arranges for turkey dinners with all the trimmings. Welcome In stays open 24 hours over Christmas and holds a gift exchange for the regulars.

Sister Christine does not allow loitering or criminal activities in or around the centre. Guelph police have come to rely on it as a resource for everything from assisting people in need of bus fare to supporting mental health patients who need to be reminded when to take their medication. Receiving funding from the United Way and community support, the original Welcome In has since become the Welcome In Drop In Centre Corporation and is a vital part of the community.

Under the compassionate eye of Sister Christine, the corporation opened Stepping Stone, a short-term residence accommodating 10 people, and Yorkhaven. Yorkhaven, consisting of 13 family units and 24 bachelor units, is owned by the Guelph Non-Profit Housing Corporation, but is run by the drop-in centre. The centre also sponsors 'The Workshop,' started by Sister Christine, which provides training in woodworking and hairstyling for the people from the centre.

In honour of her services to the Guelph community, Sister Christine received the Good Citizenship Medal in 1992 and was named Guelph's Citizen of the Year in 1999.

– Ceska Brennan

cutbacks. Volunteering, therefore, became a serious business and training was needed. In 1974, the Children's Aid Society hired Paul Young as its first co-ordinator of Volunteer Services. An annual volunteer training workshop was established in 1981 in honour of Mannie Birnbaum, an industrialist, tireless in his efforts to educate the community in the need to support hurting families and single mothers. These workshops, implemented by the Social Service Council in 1989, evolved into the Guelph-Wellington Network for Volunteer Administration. Education, training and support for volunteers was offered, as well as help in finding a suitable position. Public appreciation of volunteer work was expressed in 1976 when Bess Rosenberg became the first recipient of the James Wexler

Award for her volunteer work in the city. In the 1990s, volunteers were recognized as never before. National Volunteer Week was established to honour and award them though special events and tributes. In 1997, the mayor of Guelph inaugurated an annual awards ceremony in which three volunteers were to be honoured.

Two women, who received the province's highest medal awarded a volunteer, the Ontario Medal for Good Citizenship, represented different aspects of volunteering, both essential to the well-being of society. Pat McCraw was awarded the medal in 1999 after 50 years of volunteer activity with Save the Children, the YM-YWCA, Children's Aid (now Family and Children's Services), the United Way, the Guelph Spring Festival, the Canadian Federation of University Women, the Zonta Club of Guelph, and as a member of the steering committee of the Guelph Community Foundation, an organization designed to take on a fundraising role for social groups in the city. Involved in the administrative, financial, organizational and fundraising aspects, she worked in the upper echelons encompassing many areas of need. Loretto Sister Christine Leyser, who received the award in 1992, worked on the spot with the homeless and the poor with her Welcome In drop-in centre.

Sister Christine's initial efforts mushroomed into wider social services with government support, although that support was seriously lessened by the end of the century. Guelph's Women in Crisis, a haven for women and children fleeing from violent situations, began in a cramped basement apartment in 1977 and later moved to a dilapidated, insecure building on Gordon Street. Forced to keep a low profile because of threats from abusers, they worked quietly and without advertisement. In 1992, with help from the Ministries of Housing, Community and Social Services, and Disabilities, a long-planned new residence, Marianne's Place, was opened. Although its client capacity had not increased beyond 18, the space was now a bright and supportive environment with an adequate kitchen, a quiet room, several playrooms for children, including a creative outdoor playground, and a pleasant ground floor office for the 24-hour Crisis-Line volunteers. In 1999, in keeping with strong community support, the agency installed a sign in front of the administrative building, unafraid to advertise their existence. "Violence in all forms is wrong," asserted executive-director Joanne Page. "Women in Crisis is responding by being much more visible. This is really a sign of the times."

Wyndham House was first established in 1973 by Bev Darnell and Sheila Cowton, staff members of Homewood Health Care Centre, as a transition home for women leaving the centre. It operated for 10 years on Homewood grounds, then moved to Suffolk Street. After a period of closure due to government cutbacks, it re-opened in 1987 as a co-operative residence for seven women, aged 16 to 21, who were unable to live at home while completing their education. The Change Now drop-in centre was created in 1991 to help young men and women deal with drug and alcohol problems and other life issues by discussion and referral if necessary. Victim Services Wellington, founded by police services and Women in Crisis, was in operation with trained volunteers by 1996 to help those suffering trauma from crime or tragedy. The Sunrise Equestrian and Recreation Centre, founded in 1982 and later operating on a 105-acre farm in Puslinch, needed 100 volunteers a week to operate its therapeutic riding programs for adults and children with mental and physical disabilities. Difficulty in finding $250,000 a year to fund the operation in 1998 was overcome by over 500 regular donors, interested individuals, service clubs, business concerns and government grants.

Fundraising was obviously the other occupational necessity of the 1990s. For institutions that could afford it, a fundraiser was hired, but volunteers often did the footwork. While clubs and churches still successfully employed the older methods of bazaars and benefit concerts, modern fundraising moulded itself to popular taste. The appreciation of good food and new lifestyles of eating out, the quest for exercise and good health, and a growing interest in the arts became prime avenues. Giant fundraisers headed the list. 'A Taste of Guelph,' was a garden-party affair on the grounds of Riverslea mansion. Four hundred guests attended as 20 local restaurants served up appetizers, entrée teasers and desserts. Local breweries and wineries chipped in with refreshments and local musicians entertained. Thirty thousand dollars was raised for the General, St. Joseph's and Homewood hospitals. A less auspicious affair but no less noteworthy was the carnival in the parking lot at Willow West Mall, sponsored by the neighbourhood group, Onward Willow. With a number of merchants contributing, the day was filled with prizes and giveaways. Money made from the sale of hot dogs, sausages and pop at nominal prices went toward the group's work in making life easier and more enjoyable for members of the community.

A show of strength, agility, or endurance proved a popular way of raising funds. A participant fulfilled a pledge for a certain amount of money by engaging in an ordinary or extraordinary task for an abnormal length of time. Two young cyclists led a 100-kilometre ride through the countryside raising money for cancer research. The Victorian Order of Nurses collected $2,000 for community-based

The Victorian Order of Nurses annual bus pull, June 21, 1998.   Source: *Guelph Mercury*

health-care programs at its fourth annual bus pull in June 1998, with 12 teams competing. Centennial Park became a tent city during the 'Hot Foot Happening' as individuals or companies supported their teams, running, walking, jogging, or crawling in a 24-hour relay around a 2.5 km. track. One hundred and fifty volunteers donated their time to organize and run the event in 1997, and to provide team cheer, massage therapists, music, food, a beer garden, children's activities and a trivia tournament. The 1,600 participants raised $215,000 for special hospital equipment and research. The University of Guelph held its 11th annual Aerobathon in 1999 with 200 healthy lifestyle enthusiasts doing the Tae-bo step and boxercizing in a three-hour-long jazz, hip-hop and aerobics combo. Ten thousand dollars was raised for the Big Sisters Association and the University's Child Care Centre. Booths, lining the room with information about fitness education and various health clubs, provided advertising value to the university and the organizations that had sent instructors. School children pledged to run for Kosovo. Seniors walked for Parkinson's Disease; mothers and daughters for heart disease; and thousands to raise money for AIDS victims. Drama and art were combined when 300 characters from Oz marched along a yellow brick road in the Wizard of Hope Walk for Schizophrenia.

The business community became involved in volunteer work in many ways. The Guelph and District Home Builders Association held its fifth annual Business Community Luncheon in April 1999 at the Italian Canadian Club to raise $10,000 for Women in Crisis. From the Investors' Group's second annual charity golf tournament came $20,000 for Guelph Teen Housing. The 'Black-tie Bingo,' a strictly formal affair at the River Run Centre, was an innovative way devised by the General Hospital Foundation to garner funds towards a patient monitoring system in the critical care unit. Hairstylists donated their services at a Cut-a-Thon for Parkinson's Disease at Guelph School of Hairdressing. For contributions to the GSF and other arts and educational programs in Guelph over the past 25 years, the Co-Operators Development Corporation won a national award in 1998 – the *Financial Post's* award for the Most Effective Corporate Program in the Business in the Arts. In a unique twist, striking Bell workers of Local 44 of the Communications, Energy and Paperworkers of Canada set up a Guelph Food Bank barrel at their Campbell Road picket line in May 1999. Managers who brought along food got a shorter wait before being allowed to enter the building.

Finally a stable reality, the arts community now contributed significantly to charitable events.Twenty-four Guelph and area artists imaginatively decorated small chairs to raise funds for the proposed civic centre and the Macdonald Stewart Art Centre. Further ventures with fanciful boxes and trays were even more successful. Robert Batemen, Ken Danby, Carl Brenders and Carol Evans were among those contributing to the Humane Society's first art auction in 1998, and artists transformed simple frames into works of art for the benefit of the MSAC. The proceeds of the seventh annual 'A Day with Art' Gala Auction (1999) with works of art donated by local and area artists were donated to the local AIDS Committee.

Musicians also gave freely of their time. In 1995, Dave Teichroeb, co-founder with Lewis Melville of DROG (Dave's Records of Guelph) produced a CD *Guelph Happens: The Wyndham Sessions*, a collection of songs performed by 11 local bands to raise funds for Wyndham House. Amateur and professional female artists shared their creativity in a 'Women in the Groove' benefit concert for Guelph-Wellington Women in Crisis. Black Sheep Morris Dancers, Goldie Sherman and the Barefoot Rhythm Dance and Drum Collective, Vicki Fraser, Tanya Hobbs, Kate Richmond, Choral Stimulation and the Women to Women Choir were among those performing in 1999. These groups were popular and the sums raised, substantial.

Many fraternal organizations, active at the beginning of the century, were operating at its end, but some with membership slowly diminishing. Distinctive rites and loyalties aside, their work now resembled that of regular service clubs. Chapter 1331 of the Loyal Orange Lodge held Christmas Craft sales for the benefit of the Pediatric Speech and Language Pathology Program at St. Joseph's Hospital. The Freemasons started a Charity Coat Drive for the needy in Guelph and Wellington. The Rundle Chapter of the Eastern Star, part of the largest fraternal

organization in the world to which both men and women belonged, were visible to the public at Christmas time, wrapping gift parcels at the Stone Road Mall in aid of local charities. The IODE, with a national membership of nearly 300,000 after the Second World War, experienced a steady decline to fewer than 8,000 at the end of the century. A change in tradition occurred when the Royal Wyndham Chapter of the IODE was formed by young working women in 1985. The 162 women of Guelph's five chapters combined their efforts for many new projects. "It is still an organization of considerable drive and impact," wrote member Helen Brimmell, citing the current project to provide $5,000 to furnish a room at the Guelph General Hospital for assault victims. The International Order of Job's Daughters, Bethel, was established in 1981 for the development of character and responsibility in young women.

Guelph Sertoma amended its charter in 1985 to allow women to join. Organized in 1970, and seeing a need to help boys in the area around St Joseph's Catholic Church, Sertoma hired Pat O' Brien as supervisor of the Boys' West End Club. Service to Mankind Awards were presented annually. Rotary filled the years working with youth and students and the Travelogue Series; Annual Car Draws; Easter Seal Campaigns; Skatathons; Prima Festa (1969); the first international student's exchange program (1972); and a $410,000 donation to Victoria Road Recreation Centre to insure proper amenities for the handicapped (1973). The Wellington Men's Club (1977), inspired by Ken Greenaway, was organized for senior Kiwanis men as a relaxed coffee club with speakers and companionship, the first of its kind in Guelph. After it reached its limit of 120 members in 1982, a new Kiwanis Club for men of pre-retirement and retirement age was developed. Rotary Club of Guelph-Wellington was formed 1985 for men and women. Prominent among the Kiwanis' later achievements were the continuation of Camp Belwood for mentally and physically-challenged children, Family and Children's Services projects, the Sports Hall of Fame and the spectacular success of its annual music festival. The Kinsmen, aided by the Kinettes, continued work for Cystic Fibrosis, ran Santa Claus parades and, in 1996, organized the first Christmas Lights tours for seniors. Royal City Lions Club formed in 1987 with a focus on Canine Vision Canada training for seeing-eye dogs, sports teams, Highway 7 clean-ups and an annual Christmas phoning session for seniors in seven nursing homes.

Two organizations, separate for men and women, worked together for the same aim. Big Brothers Association of Guelph and Wellington County began in

1968 to give one-to-one help to boys, six to 16, who had no male role model in the home. Case worker Kay Thurtall helped devise policies in the society's formative years and many were adopted nationally. The Big Sister Association of Guelph became incorporated in 1975. They provided role modelling for girls and young women, aged five to 19. Both groups expanded over the years to meet contemporary issues by volunteer screening and training, teen programs, guest speakers, workshops and community events.

As professional women began to define themselves in groups, they formed power bases from which they could improve their working conditions and status. Wellington County Medical Secretaries united in 1967 as the local branch of Ontario Medical Secretaries Association. Credit Women International (1982) educated members in sound practices and procedures of credit. Professional Secretaries International learned more about their jobs and their bosses. Guelph Women in Networking (1983) helped make connections – a form of self-advertisement. The Soroptimists International of Guelph, established in 1967, allowed only one executive or professional woman from each specified classification. Activities in 1982 centred on helping the deaf and hard-of-hearing, providing wheelchairs for Guelph Services for the Physically Disabled, Youth Citizenship Awards Program for high-school students and programs for women requiring specific training for re-entry into the labour market. Zonta International received its Guelph charter in 1980. Its members, also executive and professional women, worked for the advancement of all women. Their annual Distinguished House Tour supported Wyndham House and the YM-YWCA´s Teen-age Parent program.

Hobby Clubs blossomed in the 1980s with calligraphers, chess and bridge players, star-gazers, astronomers, miniaturists, coin collectors and porcelain painters adding to their numbers. Old and antique car enthusiasts formed 'Cruisin' the Past' and made regular visits to senior homes. In 1999, the Guelph Historical Railway Association ran the first train in 40 years on the Guelph

The 12th annual Take Back the Night march through downtown Guelph started with a rally in Marianne's Park and ended with a social evening at the Boathouse Tea-room. September, 1999.
Source: *Guelph Mercury*

Junction Railway to raise funds for the restoration of a 1927 wooden CPR caboose.

'Thinkers' kept active. After the Canadian Club lost impetus in the 1960s, the Club of Guelph, founded in 1975 by Ken Hammond, was a think-tank of a small group of scientists, professors, economists and other experts, most with international reputations. They met to deliberate on topics related to man's survival such as population, energy, food, nutrition, pollution, and to bring their concerns before the people of Guelph. The Royal City Toastmasters were dedicated to 'better thinking, better listening, better speaking.' In 1987, they hosted the Canada Speech contest open to all Canadians 18 years and older. The theme that year was "What it means to be a Canadian." In 1995, Robert Munsch was presented with the club's first annual Communicator of the Year Award. The humanists, the scientists and the field naturalists continued their activities.

Action groups multiplied, particularly social ones. Some were in opposition to government cuts to social assistance programs and the existence of poverty in Guelph. Others became a voice for women's status in education, justice, labour, and social services, or for same-gender family rights. Quiet protests against violence were seen in the vigils held every year in St. George´s Square in memory of 14 female engineering students killed in Montreal in 1989, or for those in Tianamen Square. In the 1970s, the Guelph Citizens for Peace and the Guelph Peace Coalition educated citizens on the subject of disarmament and peace-related issues.

By 1996, 20 organizations were actively helping newcomers to adjust to social conditions in a foreign land. The Anishnabeg Outreach, a satellite of the Kitchener organization, was set up in Guelph in 1997. Following a mandate to build bridges for Aboriginals in urban communities, it provided employment and education information as well as assistance in overcoming the barriers existent in the social and economic infrastructure. Environmental issues were the concern of 14 organizations. Professional associations, existing for the promotion, networking, education and betterment of their work, numbered 46. The Humane Society was in greater prominence with more focussed fundraising activities. As the old established Horticultural Society continued to encourage the beautification of the city, individuals such as Sandra Pady, founder of the Donkey Sanctuary of Canada, strove to improve animal welfare policies, to educate the public on humane animal care and the love and preservation of nature.

At least two dozen seniors' clubs existed by 1995. Golden Agers were now Keenagers, or the Young in Spirit (Holy Rosary) or Jolly 60s (Crestwicke). The *Troizième Age* lectures enjoyed by Mark Waldron after a visit to France inspired him to instigate, with the help of John Hurst, Ross Pauli and others, the Third Age Learning series in Guelph. An outstanding success from its first lecture in 1987, it indicated that seniors were vitally interested in the acquisition of knowledge. Lecturers who, on rare occasions, talked down to the audience, were confronted with serious complaints. A year after the Evergreen Senior Centre opened in 1992, 4,000 members had registered and 300 volunteers were assisting in the programs. From 9 a.m. to 4 p.m., five days a week, the centre was a hub-bub of activities: arts and crafts, bridge and cribbage, line-dancing, carpet bowling, shuffle-board, badminton, computers and snooker, to name a few.

Most noticeable in the latter part of the century was the rise in number of support groups. "People don't want to look after themselves anymore," said David Kennedy Jr. for the 1998 Guelph Social History Project. "They used to stand on their own two feet." Many would have agreed. The 'stiff upper lip' and 'grin and bear it' stances were old society's ways of dealing with serious illness, tragedy and disaster. In most cases, no other help or information was available. In the 1990s, support groups disseminated knowledge, promoted discussion, helped with understanding, and offered companionship and encouragement. The ultimate aim of all support groups was self-help. By the end of the century, there was hardly an illness or human problem that did not have a corresponding support group.

Another characteristic of the 1990s was the development of at least six neighbourhood groups to oversee the health and well-being of children and families in a particular vicinity. They held educational programs for adults, children summer activities, sponsored fundraising events, and dealt with food and clothing emergencies when necessary. Proudly protective of their heritage, they became a voice in questions of traffic direction, housing development, or bylaws concerning the community. Two volunteer groups, Block Parents and Neighbourhood Watch, worked with Guelph police throughout the city for protection against crime.

Guelph's excellent reputation for successful fundraising campaigns had been proven from Boer War appeals through the Community Chest and Red Feather campaigns to the United Appeal. In 1972, working on earlier inspirations of Mannie Birnbaum, Guelph made the unusual step of combining fundraising with social planning under the Community Service Council. Its three components were the United Appeal, the Social Planning Council and Guelph Information Services. The Social Planning Council surveyed the city to discover areas of true need, while Guelph Information provided a link with the community and a 'direct service' aspect. Differing from its predecessors, the Community Service Council did not allot funds to organizations to deal with as they wished, but to certain needed projects within the scope of that organization or to ones arising from the community itself. Changing its name with the times and broadening to include the county, the organization became the United Way Community Services of Guelph and Wellington. In spite of the new long name its headquarters remained as in 1972 – the caretaker's small stone house on the Torrance School grounds.

Executive Director of Community Services for many years, Morris Twist became concerned about its limitations. Many groups and projects, vital to a healthy community, were operating outside the framework of social services. No capital funding was in place, nor were there opportunities for bequests or endowments. With these objectives in mind, a group of interested citizens were spurred into action to form the Guelph Community Foundation.

SPORTS

"Sports are a huge part of the fabric of Guelph society," said Dave Pollard of the *Guelph Mercury*. "Every Sunday we feature a high-profile athlete and have no trouble finding one in Guelph and area. Top-calibre athletes are being produced in minor sports and the schools. Baseball, for instance, is a hotbed of youngsters with great possibilities." Pollard's only complaint was the lack of enough ice surfaces or lighted ball parks and soccer fields for the number of teams. He regretted, too, that Ontario universities provided no athletic scholarships. Guelph's best athletes were welcomed at U.S. institutions, where they received free education and quality training.

The Minor Sports Association, supported by local businesses and run by volunteers, offered challenging opportunities for boys and girls from the age of four to 17, and for parents, who had to get them to the game on time. Guelph minor hockey celebrated its 50th anniversary in 1999 'bursting at the seams.' Sixteen hundred youngsters were enrolled in 80 teams, 24 of which travelled to compete in other centres, with the rest playing in house league competitions. Guelph Girls' Hockey Association, formed in 1997, registered 230 girls in

September 1999 and planned to host its first tournament in January 2000. Minor baseball with 1,800 children (down from 2,400 in the last few years), sponsored 140 teams, including Double A and Triple A travelling teams and boy's and girl's rep. Two Guelph girls played on Baseball Canada's Team Ontario at the first peewee women's Canadian Championships in Winnipeg in 1998.

The decline in baseball popularity was attributed to the boom in Guelph Youth Soccer, with over 3,000 enrolled in 1998. Paul Osborne, sports writer of the *Guelph Tribune,* described a night in May at 6:30 p.m., as 33 teams of four and five-year-olds descended onto the fields, wearing every colour of the rainbow, looking for their practice area. (In the middle of practice, his son sat down in the busy field, fascinated by the grass). That year, the Guelph Youth Soccer Club brought the Canada versus Bolivia under 20 test match to the university, where it was attended by 1,499 fans.

Interest in basketball picked up during the last decade. Minor enthusiasts could learn with Hoops 'N Hustle while three rep teams, the Catholic Youth Organization sponsored by the Knights of Columbus, the Guelph Oakes and the Guelph Rebels competed for titles in various leagues. A Guelph Minor Lacrosse Association and Guelph Minor Track and Field Club sponsored by the Royal City Optimists were also operating. In the 1990s, when the youth subsidy was reduced by city council and the cost for youth sports rose considerably, Kids Can Play, a non-profit organization, was formed to help underprivileged kids participate in local sports.

Guelph's high schools were vigorous in their sports programs. Delays, caused in the 1998-99 year by teacher-government disputes and the resulting work stoppages, had little effect as the century closed. Titles won the following year by the St. James' Lions, the Centennial Spartans, the GCVI Green Gaels, the Ross Royals and the Lourdes Crusaders were too numerous to mention. St. James' senior boys basketball team won the Ontario High School AAA Championship, the first time ever won by a Guelph team, with two boys from the team winning American Division I scholarships worth $125,000 each.

"The interest generated in high school programs leads to a club team which in turn feeds into a university team," claimed Guelph Gryphon's women's rugby coach, Jim Atkinson. The women's rugby team had been the dominant

Thanksgiving Day Races, 1981.   Source: Donald Coulman Collection

force on the Ontario women's rugby scene since the sport was granted official varsity status in 1994. They won the first five provincial titles, and in 1998, the Canadian championship. That same November, the Gryphon's men's rugby team won their first Ontario championship since 1974. Canadian university championships have been won in the past by the men's basketball team in 1974, the football team in 1984 (Vanier Cup) and the men's hockey team in the 1997-98 season.

Guelph's baseball team, although a direct descendant of the famous Guelph Maple Leafs, was renamed several times. It played as the Royals in the 1960s and, as the C-Joys in 1970, won the Inter-County Major Baseball League championship. In 1993 and 1997, it won it as the Guelph Royals. Many players received scholarships in the U.S. from this top Canadian amateur baseball league.

In the late 1960s, senior hockey gave way to an outlaw junior league. "It was wild and woolly," claimed Hugh Bowman. "Lou Fontinato was the coach and he was as fiery behind the bench as he was on the ice." When the Southern Ontario Junior Hockey League was formed in 1970, Guelph found itself playing teams from St. Thomas, Brantford, Chatham, Detroit and Welland. It reached a championship series with the Detroit Red Wings, but lost by a fluke goal. In 1972, they won the Centennial Cup with a sweep over Red Deer in Guelph. As the Biltmores (the old Biltmores were now the Kitchener Rangers), they went to the finals in 1975 and, in 1978, with Joe Holody operating the team, they again won

 June 2, 1993 – The first inductees are named for Guelph's Sports Hall of Fame. They are Rachelle Campbell Clausen, Victor Davis, Joe Kaine, Roy Mason, Huck O'Connell and Ted Wilford. The 1951-52 Biltmore Mad Hatters are inducted in the team category.

the Centennial Cup. Bowman concluded that, in 12 seasons in Tier Two Hockey, Guelph teams never failed to make the playoffs and only once failed to go to their league final. They were now ready to move up to the Ontario Hockey League. With Holody's patience, fortitude and funds, they became a major force at the top level of junior hockey, winning a league champion in 1982 and the Centennial Cup in 1986. By 1989, however, the Platers were losing support in Guelph and therefore money, and Holody moved them to Owen Sound.

The Guelph Storm Hockey Club came to Guelph from Hamilton for the 1991-92 season. They won the Ontario Hockey Championship in 1995-96 and in 1997-98. They reached the Memorial Cup finals in May 1998, but lost to Portland. Dave Pollard calculated, however, that since the 1994-95 season they had won 196 games and lost 88, the best numbers in the OHL. In April 1999, the Storm made a five-year commitment to the Guelph Minor Hockey Association. The partnership included naming the city's 23 rep hockey teams the Junior Storm and allowing them to wear uniforms identical to those of the Storm. The Storm also pledged to use its marketing expertise to attract new sponsors for the GMHA and to provide seminars for coaching and training. "We'll be teaching more than power and play systems' said Storm general manager Alan Millar to Alan Ferris, "We also want to talk about life skills and values."

In 1999, the Storm declined to bid for Guelph to host the Memorial Cup. They had tried three years previously, but Memorial Gardens was then judged unfit to host a tournament of such high calibre. After nine years of political wrangling, decisions were made and plans completed for the construction of a new downtown arena to be called the Guelph Sports and Entertainment Centre. In February 1999, the Storm agreed to be its major tenant for 20 years and expected to play its first game there in September 2000. Closing ceremonies for Memorial Gardens took place during the last week of March 2000. Friday night hockey games had been a tradition for 52 years, but entertainment had included wrestling and boxing, ballets and bingos, orchestral concerts and western jamborees, circuses and

One last Gardens Party: Andy Bathgate and Lou Fontinato of the Biltmore Mad Hatters, Paul Brydges of the Holody Platers and Chris Madden and Eric Beaudoin of the Storm display winning banners at the Memorial Gardens' closing ceremonies, March 24, 2000.
Source: *Guelph Mercury*

Ice Capades, George Formby, Bob Hope and others, and yearly Remembrance Day services. Too small and antiquated for today's commercialized game and lacking the comforts of modern design, the Gardens' great days will not be easily forgotten.

With the development of organized sport, skating, ice hockey, baseball and swimming, still pastimes of youngsters and adults alike, were not as spontaneous as in the early part of the century when more natural open spaces were available. Over the winters, though, volunteers around the city spent many cold hours creating and maintaining 30 neighbourhood ice rinks. It took 20 alone several hours a week in 1999 to flood, scrape and shovel the two popular rinks at Exhibition Park. Cross-country skiing became popular in the 1970s with enthusiasts breaking ground across farmers' fields or Guelph's snow-covered golf courses. As new trails were groomed on the outskirts of the city, the sport, inexpensive once the equipment was bought, continued to make winter a desirable part of the year.

In 1973, Grand River Conservation Authority announced plans to create a 1,000-acre water reservoir for the purpose of flood-river flow control and to provide a safe, quiet place for swimming and boating. Its completion in 1977

Between 1970 and 1971, a group of hikers forged a trail along the 33-kilometre Guelph Radial Line from Guelph to the Bruce Trail near Limehouse. The Guelph Trail Club, formed the following year, aimed to stimulate more interest in hiking and in conservation. In 1973, they completed the Speed River Trail from Guelph to Cambridge and, in 1975, the Arkell Trail running off the Radial Line near Guelph. The club joined the Federation of Ontario Hiking Trail Association when it was formed in 1974. Although more than 80 km. were maintained from Limehouse through to Cambridge, the club had none in the city. It did, however, persuade Florence Partridge in 1984 to write *A Walk around Guelph,* the first of a series of books, later sponsored by GAC. A walk through Guelph by the river, a dream for many years, was realized in 1999 though a joint venture of the city and the Grand River Conservation Authority (GRCA). Named in honour of Guelph's long-time MP, Alf Hales, the trail will span the city, eventually hitching up with the Elora-Fergus Trail and, in turn, link with the Trans Canada Trail.

within the 4,000-acre Guelph Conservation Area (Guelph Lake) brought new meaning to leisure-time activities and summer sports to families in Guelph and area. At last, youngsters had a beach and a place to swim and camp, and Guelph had a site on which to host water-sports events, camping conventions and festivals. Those members of the Guelph Sailing and Canoe Club, who moved from Belwood Lake to Guelph Lake, became part of the Guelph Community Boating Club, officially opened in 1979. With 65 members, it was a low-key, family-oriented, co-operative club with 14 sailboats for the use of any member who did not own a boat. The Guelph Lake Aquatic Society became the umbrella organization under which a number of groups functioned, including the Sea Scouts, the Army Cadets, the University of Guelph Rowing Team and the Y Camping programs. The expansion of other facilities and programs by the city, the schools, the Y, the university and private enterprise during the latter part of the century afforded opportunities for persons of all ages and at all levels to enjoy the sport of their choice for a reasonable fee. For those wishing to test their abilities to the limit, Guelph Lake was a prime site for a triathlon. On the occasion of the 1998 President's Choice Triathlon Series, over 1,000 athletes were expected to swim 1.5 km., cycle 40 km. and then run 9.5 km. in the Sunday Olympic competitions. The two-day event also featured "try a tri" in which children and teens with a few weeks of training could test their abilities.

When the city purchased the old Baker Street property for a parking lot in 1968, the Curling Club moved to 10 acres on Woolwich Street north of Woodlawn Avenue and new curling facilities were opened the following year. Guelph hosted the Ontario Men's Provincial championship in 1972, the last time a provincial event was held in a club facility. In 1985, the city agreed to build and maintain two ball diamonds and a soccer pitch on the land at no cost to the Curling Club, and the Guelph Curling Club Sports Complex was born. In 1997, the Guelph Club won the Ontario Men's Curling Championship.

Centennial CVI's swimming coach David Clutchey organized a competitive speed swimming club in 1968, named the Guelph Marlin Aquatic Club after the fast-swimming game fish. The team worked out at Centennial's 25-yard pool,

Canoe Race on the Speed River, 1982.   Source: Donald Coulman Collection

and later at the Y and the university pool. A full-time coach was hired in 1973 and, in 1975, the club moved to the new Victoria Road Recreation Centre with its six-lane, 50-metre pool with a moveable bulkhead, a warm up pool and an exercise weight-training facility. By this time, the city had entered into a two-year arrangement: it would hire coaches, set programs and fees and the parents' auxiliary would take care of meets, transportation, clinics and other details.

Marlin swimmer Victor Davis brought international attention to the club by winning a gold medal and setting a world record in the 200-metre breast stroke at the 1984 Olympics. He also earned silver medals in the 100-metre breast stroke and the 4 x 100 medley relay, and countless other awards. The memorial fund, established in his name after his accidental death in 1989, provided scholarships for high-performance swimmers with national ambitions.

Guelph Saultos Gymnastics Club formed in 1975 to promote gymnastics for all levels from the age of 18 months, and members successfully competed in various categories at the provincial meets. In June 1998, the club hosted a training camp for national women gymnasts. Guelph's Intrepid Gymnastics was a competitive club created in 1998 for boys training out of the Saultos facilities. Four of its members made the team representing the Central Region in the provincial championship in 1999 and one competed in the national championships.

By the late 1990s, golf had made great strides during the century and was, according to the *Guelph Mercury,* on the upswing across North America . The DeCorso family had purchased land on Victoria Road South in 1964. Working on a centennial project, they managed to open a course on the west side of Victoria in 1968, a par 61, that encouraged leisurely play in which a complete set of clubs was not needed. Land on the opposite side of Victoria was developed into a 71-par championship course and opened in 1974. This became the Victoria Park Golf Club East, the other, the Victoria Park Golf Club West, both flourishing in 1999. Guelph's fifth golf course, Guelph Lakes Golf and Country Club, is situated on 145 acres of rolling green land overlooking Guelph Lake. A five-bedroom stone farmhouse (and 2,400 square feet addition) was transformed into a clubhouse and

In-line skaters invade Crimea Street in July, 1999.
Source: *Guelph Mercury*

Controversy arose when two new sports hit the streets in the 1990s. In-line skating and skate-boarding seemed particularly hazardous when exercised in the shopping areas downtown. Merchants complained of damage and discourteous behaviour. A city bylaw was enacted, prohibiting both types of skating on city property. Influenced, however, by a teen group called the Royal Zoo, Guelph Recreation and Parks set up a temporary facility in Memorial Gardens in the summer of 1998. It attracted 1,200 users in the 35 days it was open. Thirty community sponsors and donors then helped stage a skateboard contest and demonstration that raised funds towards a future facility. As city council pondered amending its bylaw to designate in-line skating as a viable mode of transportation, the parks and recreation department worked with the Royal Zoo and its skateboard action committee on the development of a facility. Progress was slow, but in the interim, local youths were allowed to skateboard in the Memorial Gardens arena during July and August of 1999. In the related sport of snowboarding, Guelph native Mike Wood was team leader for the Canadian contingent at the 1998 Winter Olympics.

Skateboarder masters the ramp at the summer skateboard park in Memorial Gardens, August 1998.
Source: *Guelph Mercury*

of the Ontario Billiards and Snooker Association, announced that Guelph would host the National Pool Championships in 2000 and 2001. Four full-sized snooker tables and eight smaller ones would grace the River Run Centre stage, with players wearing tuxedos. In May 1999, the Woodlawn Bowl produced a provincial bowling champion in 14-year old John F. Ross student, Michelle McKay, and Guelph's Rob Veltman headed for world championships on the Canadian Jui-Juitsu team. The Sealy Karate School held a kick-a-thon to raise money for Kids Can Play. The Guelph Grotto Club encouraged fun for children and serious training for mountain climbing. The National Youth Frisbee Challenge was held at Riverside Park in July 1999, when youngsters and adults took part in a cross-country three-minute Frisbee throw and catch to enter the Guinness Book of Records.

The addition of women members added lustre in unexpected areas. Guelph's women wrestlers earned a silver, bronze and a fourth place finish at the Investors Group Canada Cup international meet in July 1999. Predictions of head coach Doug Cox, former Olympian and national Greco-Roman coach for the 2000 Olympic Games, were beginning to come true. In April 2000, after coming second in the junior women's freestyle and winning the junior men's freestyle and Greco-Roman crowns at the Canadian junior championships, Guelph's Wrestling Club was on the way to being the best in Canada. "The rising popularity of women's boxing is causing a problem," said Rob Pelletier, owner and coach at the Back Street Boxing Club, "because you don't have the strong amateur base you have for men and a woman gets put into a ring before she has really learned the sport." Nevertheless, he believed that Canada's future success in boxing would be achieved by women. Both sexes of all ages made up the club's 400 members, many appreciating boxing as a new stress-relieving fitness exercise.

The Ontario Special Olympics Championship was held in Guelph in June 1982 and, in August 1998, more than 2,600 athletes converged on the city for the Ontario Summer Games. Over 1,800 volunteers worked to make it a success. The games featured sports included track and field, rowing, canoeing, cycling, sailing, soccer, tennis, field hockey, basketball, lacrosse, softball and events for disabled athletes. Rogers Cable channel 20 provided coverage, and information was available on the games' website.

other attractions included computerized software for course operation, a par 71, 18-hole full size, public championship golf course, practice areas and a chipping green. The course opened in 1998.

As the interests of Guelphites broadened, excellence was achieved in time-old sports and new ones. The Lawn Bowling Club was still in action on Gordon Street by the river. Tom Gallina of the Guelph Horseshoes League, formed in 1977, won the Canadian Horseshoe Championship in 1997 and 1998, and the Guelph Horseshoe team won the B division of the Golden Triangle Horseshoe League in 1998. After participating on the Darts Ontario provincial team, Andre Carman earned a place in the World Embassy Championship and the World Masters tournament, both in Britain in December 1999. The Knights of Columbus were dart team champions in the Royal City Dart League. Guelphite Dutch de Boer, president

ENTERTAINMENT

Fred Metcalf sold his cable television company to Maclean-Hunter in 1968 and, in 1994, it was taken over by Rogers Community Television. CJOY radio station celebrated its 50th anniversary in 1999, giving a party for everyone in Riverside Park with a live broadcast, free rides for the children, and a barbecue to raise money for the General Hospital's new dialysis unit. As TV stations increased in number and variety and the rapid development of the Internet began drawing viewers into the World Wide Web, apprehensions were cast by those in the performing arts. Who, now, would attend a live performance? Fundraising and marketing efforts, indeed, had to be revalued, but other factors were to be considered. At work in Guelph was a strong musical and artistic tradition, the influence of Edward Johnson, pride in his achievements and the conviction to carry on his work and that of others by ensuring that all phases of the arts should survive and be practised to the enrichment of Guelph's citizens.

The musical tradition was upheld by the Guelph Concert Band, direct descendent of the 19th-century City Band. Renamed the Musical Society Band at the turn of the century, it provided entertainment in good times and bad. But the old bandstands gradually disappeared, and the removal of the one from Exhibition Park in 1964 marked the end of an era. In 1968, with the Guelph Musical Society no longer functioning, the name of the band was changed to the Guelph Concert Band and a new constitution adopted. In 1999, the band suggested, as a millennium project, the building of a replica of the turn-of-the-century Exhibition Park bandstand with a few modifications for better sound projection. With approval of the Grand River Conservation Authority, fundraising began with plans for its construction in the Royal City Park by 2001. The Salvation Army Band had also crossed the century bringing music and service to the streets, hospitals, concerts and parades. The Guelph Pipe Band maintained tradition since 1922, and in the 1970s placed fifth in the World Pipe Band Competition in Scotland. In 1983, they won the Intercontinental Championship at the Canadian National Exhibition. The Royalaires, having evolved from the Great War Veteran's Association Band of 1919 and the 11th Field Regiment Bugle Band until 1954, continued the tradition, winning

The Guelph Concert Band, direct descendant of the old City Band and the Guelph Musical Society Band, Bill Hughes, conductor, in bow-tie. Paisley Memorial United Church, 1994. Source: Guelph Museums

many awards and championships in Canada and the U.S. A group of 'old-timers' started rehearsing as a dance band in 1983. Known as the Twilites, their popularity in Guelph led to performances in other major cities, including Toronto's Roy Thomson Hall.

The Presto Club tradition was restored when music lovers decided they preferred choosing their own concert musicians to those prepackaged by Community Concerts. In 1975, under the leadership of Beatrice Youngman, they formed the Guelph Music Club. As a result, many remarkable Canadian artists were included in the rostrum of stars brought to the city. Also in 1975, members of Chalmers United Church launched the Merry Organ series to celebrate the restoration of the church organ. It continued successfully for five years. In 1980, realizing the need for a more broadly-based chamber music organization in the city, Eleanor Ewing, co-ordinator of Guelph Arts Council, and the Chalmers' Music Committee established the Guelph Chamber Music Society, later *Musica Viva*, that, in turn, created the Guelph Chamber Choir. With Gerald Neufeld as musical director, this award-winning choir achieved professional status and became an essential factor in the city's musical celebrations.

The Choral Union of 1880s had proven the city to be a centre of music, and the tradition was sustained in the churches and by individuals who wanted the people to sing. In his 1992 article "Guelph, the Musical City" musicologist Gerald Manning concluded, "Edward Johnson would have liked the place." Johnson, who believed in the efficacy of community choral singing, would have liked it even more in 1999, when choirs for every age were entertaining the public and experiencing enjoyment while doing so. In addition to public, high-school, university and church choirs, choral activity was offered by Today's Family Choir, led by Margaret Benson-Hendricks; the Guelph-Wellington Men's Club Choir and the

 November 23, 1993 – The staff from the TV show "A Current Affair" arrives in Guelph to check out rumours that Michael Jackson had checked into Homewood.

"Where is Love" sang nine-year-old Chris McCracken in *Oliver*, RCMPInc.'s first production, November 1979.   Source: Beth McCracken

Final audience at the old Citadel: members of GLT and friends watch as firefighters battle to save the theatre, 1993.
Source: *Guelph Mercury*

active in John Ross Collegiate's theatre arts program, founded the Royal City Musical Productions, later incorporated as RCMPInc. The mandate of the non-profit organization was to provide high quality Broadway-style musicals, using amateur singers, dancers and technicians and, in doing so, 'make life more fun.' The first production, *Oliver* in 1979, heralded a yearly production of first-class Broadway musicals that involved over 1,250 persons during the first 20 years. Those who went on to professional careers included dancers Kathy Akin and Janet Ksenych, stage manager Jeff Norman, television host Carla Collins and actor Terry Doyle.

"I've had fun doing it all," said a surprised Guelph Little Theatre director, Kay McKie, in July 1999, on hearing she had been awarded Theatre Ontario's Maggie Bassett Award for her contributions to the development of theatre in Ontario. "She took us all up a notch," said Terry Doyle, interviewed during a brief respite after five months in London's West End production of *Beauty and the Beast*. "Finding a home in the old Salvation Army Citadel in 1967 also helped," he added, "and our first production there was Don Harron's play *The Broken Jug*, that went on to win the Dominion Drama Festival in Charlottetown." Sustained by other theatre-loving couples, the Snowdons, the Slaters, the Doyles and countless individuals, GLT gave Guelph 25 years of excitement with award-winning plays, yearly musicals and one-act festivals. Even the devastating fire that gutted their citadel, destroying sets, props, costumes, scripts and archives in November 1993, did not stop them. The respect they had earned from the community and other Ontario theatre groups was revealed when, with their help, a full production of *Blood Relations* went on in time in the GCVI auditorium. After a reasonable insurance settlement, major fundraising efforts and the help of scores of volunteers, a former welding plant on Morris Street was purchased and transformed into GLT's new home. A Gala Opening took place in January 1997 with a nostalgic performance of *The Broken Jug*.

Smaller groups have presented plays that GLT would not attempt. The Road Show Theatre started in 1974 as a summer program at the University of Guelph. These student productions, directed by Rex Buckle of the drama department, went on the road, hence its name. In 1975, with help from the Ontario Arts

Guelph Male Choir, both conducted by Niklaus Kaethler; the Italian Cultural Choir); Coro Cantitalia, a multicultural choir for all ages; the senior women's group, the Silvertones; and the Rainbow Choir for gays and lesbians. Smaller groups with professional experience included the Overtones, originally the Barbershop Belles, and Royal City Ambassadors who have served the community faithfully since the 1960s. The Guelph Children Singers, established in 1991 by the GAC in conjunction with the Guelph Chamber Music Society and directed by Linda Beaupré, achieved excellence in performances, competition and recordings. After the debut of the Guelph Youth Singers in 1997, the Children Singers amalgamated with them, becoming Choir II for 14 years of age and under, while the older singers, from late teens to early 1920s, became the touring choir. Both choirs won first prizes in the Provincial Music Festival in 1999, and Choir I was the highlight of the American Choral Directors Association's convention in Chicago.

Light opera had flourished in the early part of the century, but resources for a full-scale production had diminished during the Depression and the Second World War. In 1972, after 15 successful years, the GLOC disbanded and was sadly missed. In 1978, Ross McLean, Kay McKie, Pat McLeod and Dave Rogers, all

 1974 – Adam Furfaro, an 11-year-old Guelph boy, sets a Guinness World Record for hand-clapping for 15 hours, breaking the old record of 14 hours and 31 minutes.

Council and a federal Local Initiatives Project grant, Buckle established his group as a professional acting company in the old York Road Baptist Church. Although the actors were paid, they did not belong to Actors Equity, a factor that partly contributed to its closure in 1980. Nevertheless, a remarkable number of careers were forged in a short five years, including those of actors Peter Donaldson, Paula Barrett, Jim Millington and Eric Coates. The latter gained his first professional engagement with the Road Show at the age of 14. Road Show's production manager, Douglas Lemke, became head of production at Stratford, Ontario's Shakespearian festival. Ken Albanese's Theatre Alive (*Ladies' Night*), Kim Renders' Theatre Out and About (Winter Solstice Celebration), Obsidian Theatrical Productions (*Kiss of the Spiderwoman*) and For The Love Of Louis Productions (George Walker plays**)** provided innovative experiences for actors and audiences alike during the 1990s. Local actors also took part in plays produced for Theatre in the Trees by John and Margaret Snowdon. Staged in the Arboretum, it provided a unique dining-out experience. Many of Guelph's productions, musical and otherwise, have profited from the work of freelance choreographer Sarah Jane Burton, who, in 1998, was nominated for a Dora Mavor Moore award for a notable career in show business.

Guelph's early festival tradition was revived in 1968. When the Edward Johnson Music Foundation presented the first Guelph Spring Festival, there was nothing like it for miles around. Visitors and critics from Toronto, Hamilton, Kitchener and Scotland praised the city for creating such a jewel in the crown of entertainment. The success of this cultural and social event resulted from the genius of Nicholas Goldschmidt, the acuity of Murdo MacKinnon and the hard work of a brigade of women and men who transported, entertained and fed the artists and organized public and private receptions. For its first opening day, it reverted to some of Guelph's beloved traditions – a street party with international dancers, clowns and road races and, in the evening, an illuminated parade. Although it struggled to be perceived as a peoples' festival with block parties, streetfests, fringe festivals and the inclusion of jazz and popular artists, it was often labelled elitist. Yet there was diversity as well as high quality amongst the artists it brought to Guelph. Yehudi Menuhin came

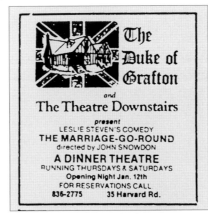

Where the action was in February 1984.
Source: *Guelph Mercury*

The Guelph Spring Festival's Gala Opening Concert, 1972, in the Church of Our Lady. Conductor Charles Wilson with Alan Monk, the Guelph Concert Singers, the Bach Elgar Choir and the Hamilton Philharmonic Orchestra.
Source: Colin Clarke, photographer. Edward Johnson Collection: Special Collections, University of Guelph Library

twice. Jon Vickers, who seldom appeared in Toronto, came five times. Oscar Peterson, W. O. Mitchell, P.D.Q. Bach, the Borodin String Quartet, Dave Brubeck, the National Ballet, Tatiana Troyanos, *I Musici Di Roma*, Robertson Davies and Woody Herman provide a small sample. John Murrell's play *Memoir* with Siobhan McKenna was premiered at the festival in 1977 and later translated into 15

Guelph Spring Festival Block Party, Carden Street 1992.   Source: Gloria Dent

languages and performed in 25 countries, including a three-year run in Paris and an Edinburgh revival in French in 1998. Dozens of young Canadian singers and musicians enhanced their careers in the yearly production of chamber operas, and by 1999, with the help of Canada Council, Ontario Arts Council and interested patrons, 60 Canadian works had been commissioned.

The festival achieved notoriety on several occasions. Most amusing was that aroused by the commissioned production of *Operetta* (1970), choreographed by David Earle for the Toronto Dance Theatre. As a quartet of amorous dancers cavorted to the tune of Beethoven's bassoon and clarinet duo, they began to undress. The stage immediately blackened and a short film episode revealed them in the nude, carrying large red flowers and skittering into verdant foliage. "Oh, not in Guelph!" cried a board member, horrified for the festival's reputation. Toronto critics made the most of it: "Glimpse of skin in Guelph!" "GSF goes Nude!" "Guelph rolling in the aisles!" Strangely, it was the *Mercury's* Constance Howitt, who sounded more like a flower child: "They tripped off into the distance happily free of shame and inhibition."

Churches provided an aesthetic experience for the audience in spite of uncomfortable pews, but they were less than ideal for the staging and viewing of chamber operas. The school auditorium or college gymnasium was not built for professional entertainment companies and, as *Financial Post* columnist Arnold Edinborough once asked, "How can anyone listen to music with the redolence of sweat and running shoes still faintly present?" Interest in a performing arts centre had been growing since the demolition of the opera house in 1953. The Civic Centre Association had been formed in 1955, and funds were raised by a National Ballet performance in Memorial Gardens in 1959 and a three-day festival of Guelph talent in 1960. Nothing more of note was done until 1972 when Ann Godfrey inspired a group of citizens to contact the Ontario Arts Council. With the influence of Godfrey, elected to city council in 1974, and that of fellow councillor Margaret MacKinnon, the city commissioned Edith Kidd to investigate the feasibility of a civic centre in Guelph. Substantiated by preliminary reports of Woods Gordon and David Scott, the detailed Kidd Report of 1974 indicated that "Guelph's busy and diverse arts' scene was frustrated by poor facilities and lack of co-ordination." Guelph Arts Council (GAC) was incorporated the following year. "Guelph must have a vital, unique life of its own," wrote John Hearn, "or degenerate into a garden suburb of Toronto, or even Kitchener." The creation of GAC coupled with this warning heralded a turning point for arts in the city. GAC became a focal point of resources, support and encouragement that brought organizations, old and new, together in a common goal. When a 1984 survey by the Recreation, Parks and Culture Committee revealed that a lack of cultural facilities headed the list of recreational needs in Guelph, the city asked Woods Gordon to conduct another feasibility study for a multipurpose centre. The final report of October 1985 concluded that such a facility was definitely needed in Guelph. In response, GAC called together a group of interested citizens from various sectors of the community to form the Citizens' Committee for the Performing Arts Centre. This committee was recognized by the city in March 1986. Intensive planning and fundraising began, but a false dichotomy, fostered in the press as a war between sports and the cultural elite, and a small group, expressing North American anti-fine-art sentiment and tax-rise concerns, delayed the city's approval of the centre for nine years. "I'm for Bach and beer and baseball and Beethoven and Mozart and minor hockey," Jim Schroder told the GAC Annual Meeting in April 1990. "I watch baseball and NHL hockey and curling. I go to symphony and choral concerts. My wife and I have attended the Grand Ole Opry in Nashville, Tennessee. I like jazz and blues, Anne Murray and

Pavarotti, k.d. lang and Beverly Sills. I like comfortable seats. I like to see and hear when I go to a game or a concert. About the only thing I don't like is being called 'elitist' because I want something good for our city." He was ready to fight and so was the Citizens' Committee under the leadership of Margaret MacKinnon. The community aroused, it came forward with $5.6 million. The public was then invited to name the building, and a competition was set up for artists and craftspeople to design and execute an artwork on a free-standing copper wall in the entrance lobby. The name, River Run, chosen by judges from 1,200 unduplicated names, was submitted by drama and media teacher Stephen

Ballet Creole perform at Hillside Community Festival, 1999.
Source: Melanie Gillis; www.melaniegillis.com

Guelph's Mambo Nation band, a popular entertainer at the Guelph Jazz Festival, September 1999.
Source: *Guelph Tribune*

Norton who felt that, because Guelph was becoming a leader in the arts and culture, the centre should have a progressive name that would reflect all that was unique about it. The winner of the art competition was Peter Johnston's 'Passages,' an imaginative and fascinating capture of Guelph's history through time. In April 1997, the 170th anniversary of Guelph's founding, riverbank celebrations were held as the centre opened its doors for guided tours. The Guelph Spring Festival was held the next month in the uncompleted building with record audiences. The official opening of the River Run Centre took place in October with a homegrown dramatic and musical variety show, based on James Gordon's song *Home is Where the Heart Sings*.

Other venues were occupied with festivals during the last decades of the century. In 1978, at the request of the city, Lorraine Scott organized a weeklong Guelph and District Multicultural celebration. For 10 summers, residents enjoyed a trip downtown on a June evening for refreshments and music. For merchants, it was good; for bars and restaurants it was not, and in 1988 the festival was asked to relocate. In the meantime, a multicultural centre was created to provide settlement services to immigrants. In 1997, when a $2,000 city grant sanctioned an Asia-Pacific Festival in Riverside Park, nearly 5,000 persons attended, making it an unqualified success. By 1999, the Multicultural Festival had become an annual event, featuring culinary delights from around the world. The food tent was "a cornucopia of culinary creations," wrote Hilary Stead, "inviting visitors to use food to break down cultural barriers." The opening ceremony included Aboriginal drumming and the national anthem sung by Coro Canitalia, Today's Family Choir and members of the International Languages program.

Driven from its chosen site on Hillside Farm by a zoning bylaw two weeks before its initial event in July 1984, Hillside Festival moved to Riverside Park and, with a dozen lively acts, entertained from noon to 11 p.m. Families were attracted by the children's activities, craft tables and food concession as well as a place to picnic and enjoy music. Two years later, incorporated as a non-profit organization, it moved to the Guelph Lake island, where it grew into the perfect community summer festival. In 1996, it was named one of the top 25 best festivals in the world by *Guitar Magazine*. Success lay in its community orientation; it was accessible to everyone. Camping and parking were available in the park with music and fun directed to all tastes. As for the food bazaar, it received the unprecedented rating

Old cars as good as new at the Antique Car Festival, 1998.

Source: *Guelph Mercury*

Hi-Steppers swing in time at the Evergreen Centre's annual Variety Show, 1999.

Source: *Guelph Tribune*

Scottish dancing and square dancing had been an essential part of celebrations for many years and other forms of dance were no longer confined to the studios and annual concerts. In 1998, the Contemporary Dance Festival was founded by Catrina von Radecki and Janet Johnson. One attraction of its 1999 festival was its Site-Specific Series, with performances at open-air sites in downtown Guelph, including a demonstration of Egyptian-Oriental dancing (belly-dancing) in St. George's Square. **(See centre colour section)**

of five forks in the *Mercury's* 'Local Restaurant Review.' Unfortunately, Tim Middleton's rave review could not be substantiated until the following year. Approximately 4,500 attended each of the three days in 1999. A village of tents formed a make-shift mall with vendors selling tie-died clothing, artwork, jewellery and silver work. A display inside a large teepee gave insight into Aboriginal culture. Sixty-two performers ranged in style from various multicultural and historical develop-ments of jazz, blues and traditional folk music to popular rock and alternative.

Hillside was unique among festivals; it was not in debt. It also functioned with a mandate requiring one third of performers to be from Guelph. That the festival could fulfil that demand and maintain a high quality of performance confirmed the city's credentials as a nourishing arts community.

Guelph's Jazz Festival, founded in 1994 by university English professor Ajay Heble, was the only jazz festival in Canada offering an educational colloquium as part of a regular schedule of events. The workshops that provided a broad context for the music were free. Artists talked about their music and their theories, and debate was invited. The main jazz concerts were held in Dublin Street and Chalmers churches, the MSAC, local restaurants, and a jazz tent on Carden Street. The Jazz Festival was awarded the Lieutenant-Governor's Award for the Arts in 1997.

Not all festivals involved the performing arts in the true sense. A classic car was a work of art in the eye of the beholder, as was the driving of it. Autofest, founded in 1996, drew hundreds downtown to admire the entries on Father's Day. The sauce and the cooking of the ribs at the Rotary Club-Trillium's Ribfest was an art and, although the eating was not, it was often a great performance. Forty-three thousand persons attended the three-day event raising $30,000 for local charities. Tours of elegant and interesting houses, garden tours, and trips around the Ale Trail or a wine-tasting spree at Wellington's wineries combined education, entertainment and social pleasures. All forms of entertainment included the practice of an art.

PRACTISING THE ARTS

"Composers can't eat music," wrote Hilary Stead after interviewing Charles Wilson in 1991. At that time, the amount of money earned by Canadian composers was approximately $400 a year. Wilson was supplementing his earnings by teaching creative composing as composer-in-residence at the university. Up to that point, more than 50 of his works had been performed. His centennial oratorio

Angels of the Earth was presented in Guelph and Hamilton by the Guelph Light Opera Company and the Bach Elgar Choir. His opera *The Summoning of Everyman*, with libretto by Eugene Benson, was commissioned by Dalhousie University and performed in Halifax and at the Stratford Festival. Benson, a professor of English at the University of Guelph, also provided a libretto for *Heloise and Abelard*, commissioned by the Canadian Opera Company. Performances took place in Toronto and Ottawa. Wilson and Benson collaborated again for the opera *Psycho Red*, commissioned by the Guelph Spring Festival under a grant from the Ontario Arts Council in 1978. An 'interiorized' drama, *Psycho Red* was the most advanced of all his works, difficult to perform and not generally understood by its audience. Before retiring from the university, Wilson introduced his students to electro-acoustic music and produced several compositions in that field.

From 1968 on, the Canada Council for the Arts awarded $3,636,388 towards cultural life in Guelph, and several of Wilson's earlier works had been commissioned with its help. The main recipients were organizations promoting the study or performance of the arts: the university for special projects such as the *Canadian Theatre Review*, the *Canadian Journal of Fiction* and the university choir; the EJMF; the Macdonald Stewart Art Centre; and Ed Video Media Arts Centre. Tamarack and the Guelph Chamber Choir received considerable help. Thirty-seven individuals received one or more grants over the years that helped establish their careers. The Ontario Arts Council awards were mainly to Guelph individuals, although the total amount given to organizations was significantly more. Statistics showed that $1,542,889 was contributed to Guelph's cultural life between 1993 and 1999. Help was certainly available, but competition across Canada was stiff.

Musicians, for the most part, achieved success through hard work and determination. Bill Phillips, one of Ted Denver's trumpeters in the Police Boys' Band, became a founding member of the Canadian Brass Ensemble and continued a career as conductor, composer and soloist. In 1972, Frederic Mills, also a protégé of Denver, replaced Phillips in the Canadian Brass. Joseph Macerollo began playing the accordion in 1950 at the age of six and soon became a popular entertainer. At the age of 11, he formed his own band. Because his instrument was not taught, or even recognized as a vehicle for classical music at the University of Toronto, he was forced to major in piano. "It was only when I proved myself as a musician that I was able to bring the accordion out of the closet," he said. While teaching at the Royal Conservatory of Music in Toronto(1969-85), he collaborated on the first free-base accordion syllabus. Through 30 years of virtuoso performances with Canadian orchestras and chamber groups, teaching at Queen's University, the University of Toronto and Sir Wilfrid Laurier, writing, recording, composing and premiering new works, he established the instrument's legitimacy in a classical repertoire as well as its effectiveness in a wide range of media. John Barnum, musical director and conductor of the Mississauga Symphonic Association for the last 18 years, and Paul Pulford, cellist in the Penderecki String Quartet, began their studies at Jenny Lamb's String Academy, and numerous professional instrumentalists have emerged from the Suzuki School including cellist Jeremy Hughes, violinists David Gillham and Mitch Huang and violist David Samuel, winner of a Juilliard Scholarship.

Small venues were important in the development of the popular arts. As young people responded to new musical beats, country and western, jazz, blues, folk and rock resounded in the Factory, the Woodshed, the Chooch, the Copper Kettle, the Albion Hotel and Paradise Gardens. Saturday afternoon competitions were held week after week, as budding artists tried until they could win. The Carden Street Café, opened in 1977 by James Gordon, Jamie MacKinnon and Pam Cross, and later owned by Hilary Stead, provided an early stage in the coffee house tradition for individual performers. Nationally acclaimed professionals emerging from these environments included Jane Siberry, James Gordon and Tamarack, the Bird Sisters, and Rick Avery and Judy Greenhill.

In 1973, Doug and Barb Minett opened a small, independent bookstore on Macdonell Street called the Bookshelf. They moved to Wyndham Street in 1975, but, after a few years, realized they needed to create more excitement to stay in business. In 1980, they moved to Quebec Street and, catering to the new coffee or lunch downtown culture, became the first book shop in Canada with a café. In 1988, they added a floor to the building and opened an art-house cinema, a bar and a rooftop terrace – the first in Canada to do so. In creating this unique and

 May 5, 1993 – Frog returns. The small statue of the frog from the drinking fountain in St. George's Square – missing for almost two years – shows up at the front door of Guelph's Public Works Department in excellent shape.

During the 1980 Quebec Referendum, Guelph entertainer Mark LaBelle wrote a song *Do not leave us if you love us*. His arrest, while 'attempting to drop it off' at 24 Sussex Dr. and subsequent questioning by the RCMP, provided the press with a national story. LaBelle was recorded in both languages by MCA Records, with the French rendition receiving excellent exposure and popularity in Quebec.

highly successful combination, they quickly became the centre of a vibrant cultural life. Keeping pace with the technological world, the Minetts created their own on-line site, launching it in September 1998 to become the first Internet bookstore in Canada. Indigo Books knew a good thing when they saw it and the Minetts saw an advantage to selling. "We parlayed our investment in the Internet," said Barb Minett to Vik Kirsch of the *Mercury*, "into a reinvestment of our roots. We believe in downtown and we believe in community." Meeting the challenge of Chapters in the Stone Road Mall, they enlarged the bookstore (wider aisles, more books and reading places) and the restaurant (café, bar and summer courtyard), added a bar/billiard room and Internet café upstairs with ample space for book readings and music performances. Wall space throughout qualified the building as an art gallery, once paintings were hung.

Johnson's old boathouse on the Speed River was restored into a tea house in 1997, with a cozy ambience for storytelling and comfortable concerts. Goldie Mill became a park and a theatrical and festival site. Old hotels were refurbished and defunct buildings renovated, thus providing unique spaces for clubs and cafés that catered to a wide range of cultural activities.

Guelph's first recording artists, the Velvetones, started with a London company in 1962. In the 1963 recording of two of their own songs, *One Little Minute* and *Dreaming of You*, another Guelph group, the Condors, accompanied them. By the end of the century, several small recording studios existed in Guelph. DROG was producing 10 CDs a year. In 1996, they began to focus on specific themes such as *Truck Songs* and *Music for Peace*. The latter was the brainchild of singer-song writer Lewis Melville, co-founder of DROG and a University of Guelph research scientist. One hundred area musicians participated in the 33-track double compact disk. Costs were donated and proceeds went to Doctors

Maestro Orpheus and the World Clock, a CD produced by Joanne Grodzinski, owner of the Carden Street Music Shop, and colleague Robert Pennee in 1997, was nominated for a Juno award and received gold star recognition from the Canadian Children's Book Centre. Actor R.H. Thomson narrated the story of a little boy's musical adventures, and the carefully selected classical music was performed by the English Chamber Orchestra. Its possibilities of being a successor to Peter and the Wolf became apparent when a stage version was performed at the Guelph Spring Festival. In 1999, a stage performance with live music by the Kitchener-Waterloo Symphony, played to a sold-out house. Maestro Orpheus received an award from the American organization Parents Guide to Children's Media in October of that year. A classroom teacher's guide was developed by Grodzinski and Carolyn MacMillan in 1998.

Popular storyteller, Robert Munsch, with his book, *Mmm, Cookies!* The children's book author received the Order of Canada in 2000.
Source: *Guelph Mercury*

Without Borders, the International Red Cross and other charitable organizations aiding people in conflict. *Songs About Food*, featuring Guelph and area song-writers and musicians, was the first in DROG's ambitious concert series at the River Run Centre in 1999. By then, Guelph was bursting with record-release parties. In August, Boo Radleys featured 'the kramdens' and the Albion Hotel launched the Jim Guthrie Quartet. The Guelph-based, nationally acclaimed folk group Tamarack released its 14th album of traditional songs and original creations, recorded at a River Run performance in December 1997. Guitarist Bob MacLean, the Royal City Saxophone Quartet, Woofer, Boogabee and Mumphrey with album *Music Makes the World Go Round*, and Jeremy and Jay Shute were among Guelph's many other recording musicians.

For many years, Guelph benefitted by its proximity to Eden Mills and its annual writers' festival in which University of Guelph professors were prominent among organizers and guest speakers. Thomas King, who made Guelph his home in 1995, was a 'hot attraction' there in 1999, having just released his third novel *Truth and Bright Water* to critical acclaim. He was also in his fourth season of writing and performing in CBC Radio's *Dead Dog Café Comedy Hour*, set on a native reserve. "My characters may be First Nations," he said, identifying with his Aboriginal heritage, "but they are just as off-beat as people anywhere." Guelph's authors of children's literature, cook books, travel and sports books have published successfully and have enjoyed opportunities to read at mini-festivals and cafés about town.

Two prolific, award-winning children's authors made significant contribu-

In 1999, a busload of people from Taiwan paid tribute at the graves of Jean Little's grandparents, Rev. William and Margaret Gauld and her parents, medical missionaries Drs. Llew and Flora Little. Margaret Gauld introduced written music to the Taiwanese and Llewellyn Little was once director of the Sin-Low Christian hospital in Tainan City.

tions to Guelph's cultural life, while achieving international acclaim. Long-time Guelph resident Jean Little, a favourite guest at children's groups and adult conferences, has published 29 books (See profile on page 77). Robert Munsch came to Guelph in 1975 to work at the university's day-care centre and began telling stories. His refreshing approach in *I'll Love You Forever* (1986) was the delight of every grandmother. Tackling themes attuned to contemporary society, he often invited controversy. In 1989, the Middlesex County School Board banned *Giant, or Waiting for the Thursday Boat* because of "undue violence with reference to religion." God, in the book, was a little girl. "It's about living together with difference," explained Munsch. Judy Coulman, teacher and librarian at Edward Johnson School agreed, believing it "extremely appropriate for children who want to talk about how they see God." Shortly after the release of his 35th book, he received word that he would be inducted into the Order of Canada in April 2000.

Sue Richards of Art Jam.
Source: *Guelph Mercury,* 1998

Guelph's artists rejoiced when Otto Ahlers and son Chris opened Wyndham Art Supplies in 1992. "Before we moved to Guelph," said Otto, "we checked census and economic development surveys of Ontario cities and discovered that 10 percent of the Guelph and area population derived income from art-related work." It was a good move for the Ahlers. Within six years, they had doubled their business volume and floor space and made inroads into markets and mail-order services previously dominated by chain stores. "Most of the staff are practising artists," said Chris, "and we maintain a high level of customer service based on expert advice." Space was allotted for art exhibitions, and courses were offered by Guelph artist, Nan Hogg.

Small art galleries, like small cafes, were often ephemeral. The Barber Gallery, however, an off-shoot from Barber Glass, began exhibiting mostly local paintings in the early 1970s and, in 2000, hosted an exhibition of the Canadian Society of Painters and Watercolourists. Art Etc., on Woolwich Street, was formed

Stephen Lewis is supported by his sculpture during the Guelph Studio Tour, 1999.
Source: Dave Carter

in 1998 as a collective of seven artists sharing the expense of operating a gallery in order to display their work and to deal directly with the public. Art-in-Guelph started as a Website in 1997 and opened as retail space at 3 Paisley St. in 1998.

The Guelph Creative Arts Association continued to hold an annual Painting-on-the-Green and to provide workshops in the community. In 1977, to celebrate Guelph's sesquicentennial, members commissioned a watercolour painting of Guelph by Ken Danby. He chose the carousel in Riverside Park, with his son standing by one of the horses. An edition of prints of the painting, commissioned with great foresight, was a successful money-raiser. In 1984, the association inaugurated an annual scholarship to a student in fine arts at the University of Guelph in honour of Gordon Couling. Prominent among the craft organizations was the Canadian Embroiderers' Guild Guelph, founded in 1977 as the St. James Embroiders' Guild by Caroline Oldacre, Virginia Buchanan-Smith and Elizabeth Litch. Open to anyone interested in learning the techniques of liturgical embroidery, it was soon to enrich the parish of St. James with delicately-worked banners, vestments, church fabrics and a magnificent cope. In 1992, they joined the Hand-Weavers and Spinners Association and the creative arts association in the cooperative venture of over 40 artists and crafts persons – the Guelph Artisans Store in the Eaton's Centre.

Lois Etherington Betteridge, known for her innovative hollowware, ecclesiastical silver and jewellery, had practised her art for over 50 years and in Judith Nasby's words, "is without doubt Canada's most highly honoured and most influential silversmith." Having already received the Prix Saidye Bronfman and the Jean A. Chalmers award, she was made a member of the Order of Canada in 1997. Her work and her influence on several waves of students and apprentices was recognized in a tribute exhibition at the Macdonald Stewart Art Centre in March 2000.

The versatility and variety of the visual arts in Guelph was illustrated annually by the Guelph Studio Tour. Starting in 1985 with a few painters and crafts people, still only a small percentage of those actively working in the city, it grew to 30 artists in 1999. The first Guelph Arts Festival, operating on the same October weekend, augmented the Studio Tour with 87 artists and 18 performing groups. Working together, the two events celebrated the city as a centre of practising art. Four local artists on the 1999 tour appeared nationally on Life Network's *Sue Warden CraftScapes*, giving examples of their work and methods: bookbinder Joan Rentoul, textile artist Lynda Grinnell, fibre artist Karen Dueck and creative crafts-woman Alison Bailey Smith, who made hats out of television wires.

Some artists worked for a lifetime in Guelph; some came to teach at or to graduate from the university's distinguished art department; others arrived because they liked the city. "Many artists who live in Guelph," said Nasby, "are exhibiting nationally and internationally and have work in important collections." The practice of the arts in Guelph, then, was no longer the question of how many went on to careers in larger centres. It was about how they were staying, or returning, to earn a living and a reputation in their chosen field. It was also about those who came from larger centres and found a city attuned to the artistic spirit.

Art Jam, a pilot venture funded by the Laidlaw Foundation, Ontario Arts Council and Canada Council and organized by Guelphite Sue Richards, was designed to give individuals the experience of creating art without fear of making mistakes. The finished products, always made from recovered, recyclable objects, were to be exhibited in public places. Children in the school program were encouraged to learn the use of brushes, but adults painted with sponges, corks,

Buddhist meditation, guided by Ken Hood, held at the Living Yoga Centre. One of many 'alternative' spiritual groups in Guelph.
Source: Dawn Matheson, 2000

kitchen utensils, feathers, or their hands and feet, if they wished. The result of the first session, in which 15 adults decorated four bi-fold doors (rescued from the wet-dry facility) with colourful fruits and foods, was displayed in the vacant site of the old Salvation Army Citadel for several weeks until it disappeared. "That's fine," said Sue Richards. "If someone wants it, all the better." An old chair imaginatively painted and left at a bus stop also disappeared, but not before it had been used, enjoyed and become the subject of discussion on the street. Centred in the spacious rooms of the old Torrance School building by arrangement with the board of education, Art Jam also presented Spirit Connection, a summer day camp that recognized the art and spiritual values of the native community and the preservation of and respect for the natural world.

Similar values were inherent in the Guelph Unitarian Fellowship's winter solstice celebration for women, or in Harcourt United's Sacred Circle Dance and in their healing ceremonies, in the sunrise services at the Guelph Turfgrass Institute, or 'Morning Light' breakfasts and meditation at Ignatius College. Theatre, song, dance and stories were part of the winter solstice celebrations at Goldie Mill Park. They were part of Earth Week '96/Tomorrow's Children, a weeklong blitz of activities by the Guelph-based non-profit Future Earth Research Organization. Tree-planting and field nature workshops, art exhibits and ReUsed art contests, Aboriginal crafts and traditions and Japanese floral art demonstrations, creative African dance, theatrical expression and mime, storytelling and music – all were offered with a goal of linking the arts, cultures, sciences and social sciences to the themes of environmental awareness and service to the community.

By the end of the 20th century, the arts had become entwined with new concepts of religious activity, education, family life and with the grass-roots energy of volunteers, fundraisers, support groups and scores of clubs and organizations that existed for the welfare of Guelph's citizens. Over the years, the cultural elements had confronted the negative aspects of society. Now, facing new social realities, they were still working for the betterment of all. Guelph was a caring community with new visions of cultural life. In the first half of the century, it had kept up its "quarrel with the foe." In the latter half, opportunities abounded for every citizen "to feel dawn, see sunset glow."

"Canada will not become great by a continued display of her virtues, for virtues are – let us face it – dull. It must have art, if it is to be great."

Robertson Davies, 1951, quoted in *Canada Year Book 1999*.

SOURCES

The Old Anchorage: Guelph in 1900

100 Years of Service: Sisters of St Joseph, 1861-1961. Guelph, 1961.

1901 Census: microfilm of original, Guelph Public Library.

The Advocate

Annual Reports 1898-1918. Guelph Board of Education.

Archives: Church of Our Lady Immaculate; GCVI; Guelph Historical Society; Guelph Museums; Guelph Public Library; University of Guelph Library: Archives and Special Collections.

Canadian Encyclopedia World Edition, McClelland and Stewart: Toronto, 1998.

Daily Mercury and Advertiser

Encyclopedia of Music in Canada, 2nd ed. Helmut Kallman, Gilles Potvin, Kenneth Winters eds., University of Toronto Press: Toronto, Buffalo, London, 1992.

Guelph Daily Herald

Guelph Daily Mercury, Centennial Edition, June 20, 1927.

Guelph Evening Mercury and Advertiser

'Guelph Presto Music Club,' programs, minutes and newspaper clippings. Archival and Special Collections, University of Guelph Library, Guelph Public Library, Guelph Civic Museum and Mary MacKay's 'Notebook.'

Guelph Weekly Mercury

O.A.C. Review. 1900-

Arthur H. Parker's Engagement Book. Guelph Musical Society Band, 1904-1911, in Ross Irwin, *Bands of Music in Guelph,* Guelph, 1993.

'A Brief History of the Union Movement,' in *Church Union: Documents approved by the General Conference of the Methodist Church as a Basis of Union.* October, 1911. MacLaughlin Library, University of Guelph.

First Baptist Church: One Hundredth Anniversary, 1853-1953. n.d., author unacknowledged.

Sesquicentennial History, 1844-1994: Knox Presbyterian Church, Guelph, Ontario. Sesquicentennial History Committee: Guelph, 1994.

Seventh Annual Circular of the Guelph Business College. Jas. Hough Jr., Guelph, n.d.

Social Register. Watchful Circle of the King's Daughters, St. Andrew's Church. Guelph Civic Museum Archives.

Unidentified handwritten notebook, 1874-1918. Archival and Special Collections, University of Guelph Library.

Ambrose, Linda M. *For Home and Country: The Centennial History of Women's Institutes in Ontario.* Boston Mills Press: Erin, Ontario, 1996.

Ashton, Emily. *The Story of Brooklyn Sunday School-Harcourt Memorial United Church,* 1887-1975. Guelph, August, 1975.

Collins, Catherine. *A History of Guelph Separate Schools: A Sesquicentennial Project of the Wellington County Separate School Board,* Guelph, 1977.

Crowley, Terry. *For All Time: A Centennial History of St. James the Apostle Anglican Church.* Guelph, 1990.

— .'Madonnas before Magdalenes: Adelaide Hoodless and the Making of the Canadian Gibson Girl,' *Canadian Historical Review* LXVII, 4, 1986.

— .'Adelaide Hoodless, Women's Education and Guelph.' *Historic Guelph* XXV. Guelph Historical Society, 1986.

— .'The Origin of Continuing Education for Women: The Ontario Women's Institutes.' *Canadian Women's Studies* 7:3, Fall, 1986.

D'Alton, John. 'William Philp and Guelph's Cultural Awakening,' *Guelph and its Spring Festival.* Gloria Dent and Leonard Conolly eds. Edward Johnson Music Foundation: Guelph, 1992.

Farquharson, Dorothy H. 'Roberta Geddes-Harvey Mus. Bac. (1849-1930), Composer and Organist.' *Historic Guelph* XVII. Guelph Historical Society, April 1978.

Graesser, Mary D. 'St George's Parish, Guelph, 1832-1932.' *St. George's Church, Guelph 1832-1982.* Peter B. Moore ed., Guelph, 1982.

Irwin, Ross. 'The Priory Club,' Guelph Historical Society Meeting, October, 1998.

— . *Bands of Music in Guelph.* Guelph, 1993.

Johnson, Leo. *History of Guelph: 1827-1927.* Guelph Historical Society: Guelph, 1977.

Kallmann, Helmut. *Encyclopedia of Music in Canada,* 2nd. edition. Helmut Kallman, Gilles Potvin eds. University of Toronto Press: Toronto, Buffalo, London, 1992.

Koop, Alvin. *To Celebrate Children: A History of the Children's Aid Society of the City of Guelph and the County of Wellington,* 1883-1993. Guelph, 1993.

Nasby, Judith. M. *Visitors, Exiles and Residents: Guelph Artists since 1827.* University of Guelph, 1977.

Paton, D.G. *Centennial History: Chalmers Church, 1868-1968.*

Ross, Alexander M. and Crowley, Terry. *The College on the Hill: A New History of the Ontario Agricultural College, 1874-1999.* Dundern Press: Toronto, Oxford, 1999.

Shutt, Greta Mary. *The High Schools of Guelph.* University of Toronto Press: Toronto, 1961.

Tippet Maria. *Making Culture: English-Canadian Institutions and the Arts before the Massey Commission,* University of Toronto Press: Toronto, 1990, quoting Earl Grey's letter to Lord Mountstephen, March 13, 1906.

Vaughan, Carol. *The History of the Guelph Red Cross.* Guelph, 1977.

Whitehead, Jim and Thompson, Janet. *Christian Church, Disciples of Christ: History 1876-1976.* Guelph Public Library Archives.

The Old Anchorage Secured: Guelph: 1902-1945

Archives: Jesuit Archives, St. Regis College, Toronto; St. David's and St Patrick's Anglican Church Archives, Guelph.

'The Early 1900s in Guelph, Ontario, as I remember.' Unsigned, undated MS, Guelph Civic Museum.

The Globe. December 11, 1917.

Guelph Evening Mercury. 'King's Daughters of the Empire Edition.' December 1, 1916.

Guelph Social History Project. Video Interviews. Guelph International Resource Centre, Guelph, 1998, 1999.

The Maple Leaf. January, 1923.

New York Clipper, October 27, 1988. Circus World Museum Archives, Baraboo, Wisconsin.

Presbyterian Church Association Papers, Presbyterian Church Archives. 'Letter from the Rev. J. A. MacNamara to the Rev. J. A. MacGillivray, July 9, 1923,' quoted by Roberta Clare.

R.F.W. *Guelph Bible Conference Grounds, 1934-1973.* Pamphlet.

Blyth, Joyce. 'Victory Gardens,' *Historic Guelph* XXXV. Guelph Historical Society, 1996.

Bowley, Pat. 'The Italian Community in St. Patrick's Ward, Guelph, Ontario, 1990-1939: Development of a Chiaroscuro.' *Historic Guelph* XXXIII. Guelph Historical Society, 1994.

Brett, Frank. *Cutten Club: Fifty Years, 1931-1981.* Guelph, 1981.

Brimmell, Helen. 'The IODE in Guelph, 1909-1997.' *Historic Guelph* XXXVI. Guelph Historical Society, 1997.

Buckingham, Walter. 'Address to the YMCA Annual Meeting,' January 25, 1944. Guelph Civic Museum.

Campbell, Douglas. 'Putting Women in their Place: Women and Church Union,' Working Paper no. 19, Presbyterian Church Archives, quoted by Roberta Clare.

Clare, Roberta. 'The Role of Women in the Preservation of the Presbyterian Church in Canada: 1921-28,' in *The Burning Bush and a Few Acres of Snow: The Presbyterian Contribution to Canadian Life and Culture.* William Klempa ed. Carleton University Press: Ottawa, 1994.

Clifford, N. Keith. *The Resistence to Church Union in Canada 1904-1939.* University of British Columbia Press: Vancouver, 1985.

Connolly, J.J. *Church of Our Lady: Handbook Descriptive of Interior Decorations, Paintings, Windows, etc.* Guelph, 1908. Church of Our Lady Archives.

D'Alton, John Patrick. *Edward Johnson and Musical Education in Canada.* MA Thesis, University of Guelph, 1996.

Durtnall, B.M. 'Children at War: Guelph Youth during World War II,' *Historic Guelph* XXXV. Guelph Historical Society, 1996.

Hamilton, Robert F. *Guelph's Bands and Musicians.* Hamilton Art Studio: Guelph, 1996.

Heap, John. *A History of St. Patrick's (Anglican) Church, York Road and Harris Street, Guelph, Ontario.* MS. St. David and St. Patrick's Church Archives, n.d.

Hogan, Brian F. 'The Guelph Novitiate Raid: Conscription, Censorship and Sectarian Stress during the Great War.' paper given to the joint session of the Canadian Catholic Historical Society and the Canadian Society of Church History, May 29, 1978.

Keleher, John W. *The Sacred Heart Parish of the Ward.* Guelph, 1980.

Kelly, Peter. 'Guelph's World of the Flicks.' *Guelph Historical Society Publications* X, 1970.

Kidd, Edith. 'Music in St. George's: 1932-1982.' *A History of St. George's Anglican Church, Guelph, Ontario, 1832-1982.* Peter B. Moore ed., Guelph, 1982.

Mason, Lawrence. 'Music in Guelph,' *The Globe,* September 12, 1925.

Morrison, Barbara. *A History of Crestwicke Baptist Church.* Pamphlet n.d.

Nasby, Judith M. 'The Macdonald Stewart Art Centre.' *Canadian Collector* 5, Sept./Oct., 1980

Oakes, Gregory. 'Gunner Town: A Brief History of the 11th Field Regiment,' *Historic Guelph* XXXV. Guelph Historical Society, 1996.

Parker, Verne. 'Paisley Memorial United Church.' *Historic Guelph* XXVIII. Guelph Historical Society, 1989.

Paterson, David. *A Century of Worship: The History of the Guelph Congregation of Jehovah's Witnesses.* MS. Guelph, 1999.

Pollard, Ruth and Eber. 'Walter Tyson and the Circus.' *Guelph Historical Society Publications* XII, 1974.

Reid, W. Stanford. *A Century and a Half of Witness 1828-1978: The Story of St. Andrew's Presbyterian Church, Guelph, Ontario.* Guelph, 1980.

Shaman, Tony. 'Royal City Soccer: Its Associations, Clubs and Leagues.' *Historic Guelph* XXXVI. Guelph Historical Society, 1997.

Stamp, Robert M. *The Schools of Ontario, 1876-1976.* Ontario Historical Studies Series, University of Toronto Press, 1982.

Stead, Hilary. 'Italian Connection,' parts 1, 2, 3 *The Mercury,* April 18, 19, 20, 1991.

Stelter, Gilbert. 'A Historical Sketch of Dublin Street United Church, Guelph.' Introduction to *Dublin Street United Church: One Hundred and Tenth Anniversary Booklet.* Guelph, 1984.

Stewart, H.E. and Walker, M.C., *Guelph Church of Christ (Disciples) 1876-1969,* Guelph, 1969.

Waines, W. J. 'Joseph P. Downey and Prison Reform: Proposal to Establish the Ontario Reformatory.' *Guelph Historical Society Publications* XVI, nos. 1, 2, and 3, 1976.

Loosening the Ropes: Guelph 1945-1967

Archives: Centennial CVI; John F. Ross CVI; Guelph Arts Council.

Arts in Guelph. Guelph Arts Council, 1975-

The Guelph Tribune

Bowman, Hugh. 'Sweet sixties,' *Guelph Daily Mercury.* April 10, 1986.

Brimmell, Helen, *et al.* 'Guelph Creative Arts Association,' *Guelph Historical Society Publications,* XII, 3: Guelph, 1973.

— -, ed. *50 Years of Fine Arts and Crafts: A Scrapbook of History.* Guelph Creative Arts Association, 1999.

Crawford, Suzanne. 'Save the Children - Canada in Guelph,' *Historic Guelph* XXXVI. Guelph Historical Society: Guelph, 1997.

Crowley, Terry. *For All Time: A Centennial History of St. James the Apostle Anglican Church, Guelph, Ontario.* Guelph, 1990.

Distinguishing Features: 15 Years of Artist's Video at Ed Video Media Arts Centre. Ed Video Media Arts Centre: Guelph, 1993.

Emslie, James J. *A History of St. John's Parish: 1966-1991 The First Quarter Century*: Guelph, 1991.

Irwin, Ross. *Trinity United Church: A History, Part One: From the Beginning of the Sunday School to October 29, 1959*. Guelph, 1959.

Larter, Betty. *The First Twenty-five: Westminster St. Paul's Presbyterian Church, 1958-1983*. Guelph, 1983.

MacKay, Mary. 'The Presto Music Club: Last Meetings.' MS notebook.

Nasby, Judith M. 'Building the Collection,' *The University of Guelph Art Collection*. Judith Nasby ed., University of Guelph, 1980.

Putz, Sylvia. 'Novitiate Marks Anniversary.' *The Daily Mercury*, June 11, 1988.

Scott, M.G. Rev. 'The Holy Ghost Fathers,' *25th Anniversary History of the Parish of Holy Rosary, Guelph, Ontario, 1956-1981*. Guelph, 1981.

Stuart, Rae. *The Story of a Great School: 25 Years of Service and Progress in the City of Guelph*. c.1977. John F. Ross CVI Archives.

Anchors Away! Guelph 1967-1999

Archives: St. Matthias Anglican Church Archives.

Living and Learning. The Report of the Provincial Committee on Aims and Objectives of Education in the Schools of Ontario. Newton Publishing Company: Toronto, 1968.

Religious Information and Moral Development. The Report of the Committee on Religious Education in the Public Schools of the Province of Ontario. 1969.

St. Matthias Parish Council Minutes. May 11, 1992.

Baker, Sid. Rev. 'The Search for a Welcoming Church,' *Niagara Anglican*, January 8, 1996.

Baril, Alain and Mori, George A. 'Leaving the Fold: Declining Church Attendance,' *Canadian Social Trends*. Statistics Canada: Autumn, 1991.

Bibby, Reginald W. *Fragmented Gods: The Poverty and Potential of Religions in Canada*. Irwin Publishing: Toronto, 1987.

Contini, Anna. 'What's in a Name? Civic Centre Named,' *Arts in Guelph*, 22:5, Sept./Oct., 1997.

Dent, Gloria. 'The Guelph Spring Festival, 1968-1992,' *Guelph and its Spring Festival*. Edward Johnson Music Foundation: Guelph, 1992.

Irwin, Ross. 'The Guelph City Band,' *Historic Guelph* XXXVII. Guelph Historical Society, 1998.

Nasby, Judith M. 'Preface and Acknowledgements' and 'Celebrating the Opening of the Exhibition at the Baker Lake Symposium,' in *Quamanittuaq: Where the River Widens: Drawings by Baker Lake Artists*. Marion Jackson, Judith M. Nasby and William Noah. Macdonald Stewart Art Centre: Guelph, 1994.

Stead, Hilary. 'Junior Kindergarten.' *Guelph Mercury*, June 25 and 26, 1990.

Vigor, Frank. *Municipal Involvement in Recreation Services*. MS. May, 1999.

Extract from 'Busting the Breast,' words and music by Bowser and Blue, with their permission.

Interviews

Trudy Becker
Rev. Mary Ellen Berry
Hugh Bowman
Richard and Helen Brimmell
Mary Ann Cheesequay
Catherine Collins
James Colnan
Dr. Terry Crowley
Fred Dack
Father Edward Dowling
Terry and Joyce Doyle
Donald and Eleanor Ewing
Dorothe Fair
Dorothy Farquharson
Lorna and Eva Fisher
Ann Godfrey
Aubrey Hagar

Anna Jackson
Madelaine Kelly
Daryl Kennedy
Douglas Long
Margaret MacKinnon
Pat Plummer McLeod
Florence Partridge
Dave Pollard
Archdeacon John Rathbone
Dawn Reynolds
Sue Richards
Rev. and Mrs. Donald Sinclair
T. Sher Singh
Joan Smith
Rev. Dr. M. Jean Stairs
Sally Wismer

Guelph Social History Project Videos

Dorothy Farquharson
Melba Jewell
James Kelso
David Kennedy
Dorothy Lazzari
Savina Scammell
John Snell

Research Assistant: Bonnie Durtnall

My special thanks to Ellen Morrison and Darlene Wiltsie (Special Collections, University of Guelph), and Beverly Dietrich and Kathleen Wall (Guelph Museums) and the librarians at the Guelph Public Library.

CHAPTER 2

GUELPH TOWNSHIP

TED MITCHELL with BONNIE DURTNALL

A Farmer's Outlook

"Only the land is forever." This line taken from *Gone with the Wind* (1936) captures the special bond between the farmer and the soil.

When A.E. Byerly wrote *The Beginnings of Things* (1935) he made this comment about the people of Guelph Township: "They are men and women of sterling quality and they have contributed greatly to the progress and development of this county." At the time he wrote, the original families were in their fourth generation and Guelph had recently celebrated its 100th anniversary, in 1927. In the 65 years since Byerly wrote, there have been huge changes. In Ontario, the population of those living on farms has dropped from about 60 percent to less than four percent over the last century. Guelph Township, originally 42,338 acres, has been reduced to about 30,000 acres due to the growth of the city of Guelph.

Pioneer family names have all but disappeared from the township map.

Reflections on Farm Community Life

THE WAY IT WAS

The first half of the 20th century was the era of the family farm. Grandparents lived out their lives on the farm where they themselves had farmed. Often an elder son inherited the farm and his children became contributing members to the farm workforce. Even a young child could help with farm chores. By age 10, most farm boys could be trusted to drive a team of horses on the hay wagon, hoe root crops, assist with the care of livestock and even drive the farm tractor. Girls made comparable contributions, more often related to the mother's sphere, looking after

Farming- a family affair. Young Bob Heming sitting backwards on horse-drawn cultivator.
Source: Heming Family Collection

the garden, cleaning the house, milking the cows and picking berries. However, many girls helped with the farm tasks along with the boys. These were significant labour contributions, but no remuneration was expected. The young person was making a contribution to family well-being. Food, clothing, and shelter were one's entitlements, with occasional extra allowances for special needs. A child could have a sense of accomplishment without money changing hands. A few would supplement allowances with a trap line. The good of the family was being served and the family's progress was of greater value than that of the individual member. Unless the reader has actually experienced it, this concept may be hard to grasp. There was a happy sense of fellowship, which was an incidental aspect of working as a family group. Farm people who succeeded have always valued resourcefulness and frugal tastes. It was the age of those eternal homilies such as "a wilful waste will bring a woeful want."

At the beginning of the 20th century mixed farming was practised by most Guelph Township farmers. At this time farms were carefully fenced with a secure gate at the end of the lane. Anyone beyond middle age can remember getting out of an automobile to open and close gates in order to enter a farm property. Often cattle or sheep would graze the grass along the lane way, and this grazing sometimes extended to the roadside. Someone would be assigned to direct and control the herd outside the fenced property. One's time was not deemed so valuable as now, and automobile traffic along the road was not so concentrated and fast.

The fenced farm may be considered a metaphor for the self-contained family farm.

Sisters Ida and May Card with Hubbard Squash, 1905.
Source: Card Family Collection

The typical mixed farm had a herd of cattle, a flock of sheep, a pen of hogs and a flock of chickens. Many farms had a large garden to supply the family with fresh produce. In addition there was often an orchard with 20 to 50 apple trees, as well as a few plum, cherry and pear trees. Several township families had a stand at the Guelph Farmers' Market. The farmer's income was not hugely remunerative, but his expenses were not ruinous.

By mid-century the fences and gates had disappeared.

There is no denying that some farm children grew up with no real love of farm life. These young people took an opportunity to leave the farm for the city as soon as possible. In 1920, Canadian writer Peter McArthur addressed this very topic in an essay "Why I Stick to the Farm."

"To be born on a farm is the greatest good that can befall a human being," he wrote. "It satisfies the human sense of wonder at the beauty of nature and the sense of tradition with one's family."

RURAL NEWS

In the first 50 years of the 20th century rural communities recorded the ebb and flow of rural lives through columns in the local newspapers. On a weekly basis, write-ups reflected the spirit of fellowship and neighbourly concern,

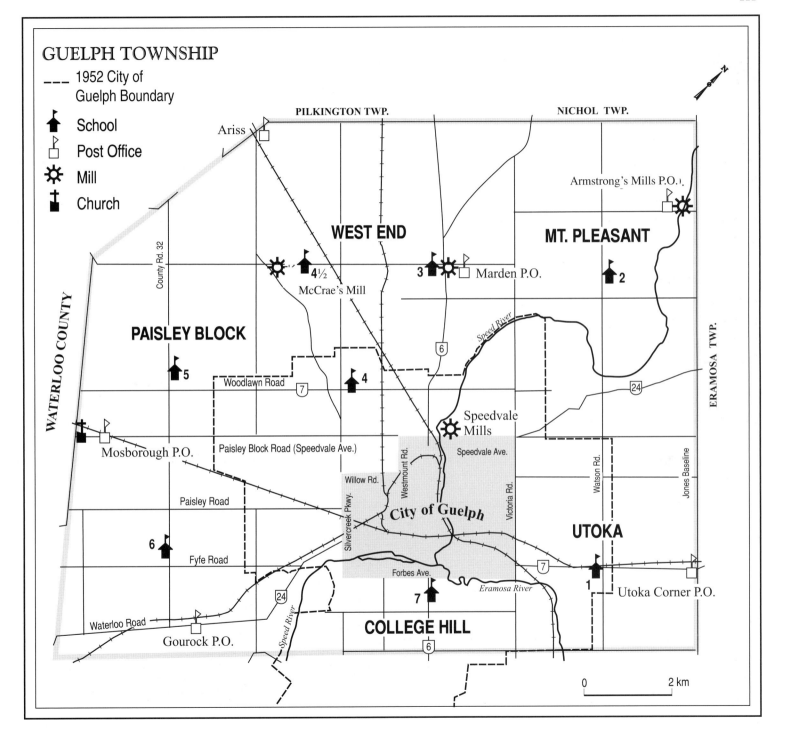

GUELPH TOWNSHIP

- - - 1952 City of Guelph Boundary

School

Post Office

Mill

Church

PILKINGTON TWP.

NICHOL TWP.

Ariss

Armstrong's Mills P.O.

WEST END

MT. PLEASANT

County Rd. 32

4½

McCrae's Mill

3

Marden P.O.

2

PAISLEY BLOCK

Speed River

6

WATERLOO COUNTY

5

Woodlawn Road

7

4

Speedvale Mills

24

ERAMOSA TWP.

Mosborough P.O.

Paisley Block Road (Speedvale Ave.)

Speedvale Ave.

Watson Rd.

Jones Baseline

Willow Rd.

Westmount Rd.

Paisley Road

City of Guelph

Victoria Rd.

UTOKA

6

Fyfe Road

7

Forbes Ave.

7

1

Utoka Corner P.O.

24

Eramosa River

Waterloo Road

Speed River

COLLEGE HILL

Gourock P.O.

6

0   2 km

Holstein cows coming in from pasture for milking, 1953. A time when grazing the roadside was possible. Source: Card Family Collection

Katherine Cleghorn of the Paisley Block, correspondent for the *Guelph Mercury*.
Source: Cleghorn Family Collection

present. Fall apples are plentiful." The Marden column for November 17, 1922 notes that "threshing is almost complete, roots are all in, fall plowing well underway, apples picked and stored away, while storm windows are being put on and wood supplies estimated...." On November 22, 1922 the Ariss reporter remarks on the shipments of turnips (10 carloads) and hogs, as well as the engine problems experienced while threshing. Side by side with these reports on farm chores were notices of marriages, funerals, social gatherings, club meetings and departures. When the Derby family of Mosborough, for example, took their leave for Saskatchewan in 1924 there was a community gathering. In her column for that week Miss Cleghorn wrote: "We will often think of you - may this gift [a little settee] evoke fond memories of happy times spent here in the Paisley Block." The annual picnic held by the Marden community also reinforces the idea that these farming communities had sturdy ties during the first half of the century.

which was typical of that era. Reporting of events tends to cement feelings of community, and such columns caught the happiness and sadness of people the readers knew and cared about.

For over a decade, a weekly Mosboro (abbreviated from Mosborough) column appeared in the *Guelph Mercury*, written by Katherine Cleghorn. She lived with her parents and brothers on the "Old Concession Road" in the heart of the Paisley Block. The events reported in her column were not, in essence, different from those of other rural reporters. There were newspaper columns from Mount Pleasant, Marden, Ariss and Gourock whose words express a similarity with the Mosboro column in subject and treatment. They also reveal an intriguing sense of community based on social rather than political boundaries. A good example of this is Miss Cleghorn's reference to several Waterloo County families, such as the Fisks, Berners, Taylors, Tucks, Jacksons, Reeves and Pringles, within the context of the Mosborough community. Many of these people took part in Mosborough events and attended the Mosborough Church although they lived and farmed in Waterloo County.

The columns produced over this time period by rural women provide an interesting glimpse of farming life during the past century. The everyday activities were often reported: turnip shipping, the shipping and receiving of cattle, the cutting of wood for sale or home use and the planting and harvesting of various crops of the region. The Mosboro column for October 8, 1918 stated "turnip shipping, corn cutting and making of apple butter are the occupations of the

Mills and Post Offices – The Hub of the Regions

At the turn of the century the citizens of the township needed the frequent services of both mill and post office, and in some cases they were located in close proximity.

Prior to 1912, when rural mail delivery in the township began, the mail was picked up at the closest sub post office located at Gourock, Mosborough, Utoka and Ariss, and at Marden and Armstrong's mills. **(See township map for locations)**. Armstrong's and Marden had a mill as well as a local postal station. The local postmaster or someone close by kept a stock of items most commonly needed on a farm, while at Ariss, Marden and Armstrong's mills there was a general store, and at Mosborough and McCrae's Mill there was a small store.

The local post office was another factor that encouraged a neighbourhood orientation as one met friends and relatives picking up mail and supplies. Though Guelph was never further than five miles away, even that was a consideration in times of horse and buggy, wagon or sleigh.

Flour could be processed at McCrae's or Armstrong's mills in the early part of the century, but by 1950, even the bigger Guelph mills such as Goldie and Speedvale (Pipe's) were no longer competitive with larger and more specialized mills.

Grist, a coarsely ground cattle feed, was a more important farm service and one that lasted into the latter half of the century. A few farmers had a

Regions Within Guelph Township

Guelph Township had five regions within its boundaries, shown in shaded areas on the map on page 111.

Paisley Block	Concessions south-west of Guelph, named after birthplace of earliest settler, John McCorkindale.
West End	Concessions north-west of city, includes the Scotch Block, area within the West End where the Guayran settlers located.
Utoka	Concessions east of the city, beyond the Correctional Centre to the Jones Baseline.
Mount Pleasant	Concessions centred around Armstrong's Mills in the north-east part of the township.
College Hill	Located on the south-east side of the township. Since annexation of the university area by the City of Guelph did not occur until 1965 this part of the township was semi-urban in the early decades of the 20th century.

Having just defined these regions, it should be added quickly that the demarcation lines are mainly in the minds of the inhabitants. In 1999 under provincial government mandate, Guelph and Eramosa townships were merged forming a new Guelph-Eramosa Township. The amalgamated township is now under a single administration based in offices on County Road 124, east of Eramosa.

Miller Charlie Hattle hands Joe Kirby a bag of feed, 1935. Hattle's Feed Mill, Marden.   Source: C. Hattle

chopping mill but the majority would bag up grain and take it to the mill to have it turned into either rolled oats or chop – the oats for the horses and sheep, the chop for the cattle and hogs. By the 1950s large feed companies were selling supplements to be added to the feed during the milling process. The grain was poured into a grill-covered opening in the floor from which a conveyor lifted it to a hopper, gravity carried it down to the chopper or roller where it was then re-bagged to be taken home by the farmer. In the 1930s cost for this service ranged from three to five cents a bag.

While at Marden, one might have arranged to have the horses shod or metal fabricated at Murdock's Blacksmith Shop. One could also pick up confections and some supplies at McIntosh's General Store, formerly Blyth's Tavern. Near Armstrong's Mills there was a small brewery producing East Kent Ale; this may have been made under agreement with Holliday's Brewery of Guelph, since East Kent was their trade name. There was also a small cheese processing plant nearby. Anyone who has been to Armstrong's Mills must be impressed by the beauty of the location in that pretty valley on the Speed River.

At McCrae's Mill, steam was the source of power. McCrae's had a sawmill as well, although its last service was as a cider mill. At the beginning of the 20th century each farm had an orchard with a variety of trees: Pippin, Spy, Astrakan, Snow, Russet, Wealthies, Yellow Transparent and Tolman Sweet. Some of the apples were stored, or sliced and dried for winter use. Most farmers made a trip to the cider mill and came home with fresh cider and apple butter. It comes on good authority that a few farmers made hard (alcoholic) cider.

That the city of Guelph still depended on the agricultural trade at mid-century was evident in the big grist mill, Doughty and McFarlane, at Allen's bridge. Harvey Groat on Woolwich Street did an extensive business, particularly with the horse and poultry customers, while Smith's Feed Mill was located on Quebec Street East.

Nearby mills did business with Guelph Township farmers: Wheeler's in Eramosa, Eden Mills, Maryhill and A.J. Shantz at Fisher Mill in Waterloo County. The Shantz Mill had the distinction of providing all the usual farm mill services but with an excellent seed grain cleaning and treatment service.

All the older mills of Guelph Township are now inactive. The closest active flour mill still in use today is in Cambridge (Preston). The grist mills fell victim to the large tractor-driven mills which farmers bought for their own individual use. The United Co-operatives of Ontario and Sharpe Farm Supplies remain the only large feed mills still in the livestock feed business.

THE TOWNSHIP SCHOOLS – A COMMUNITY GATHERING PLACE

Most families in Guelph Township were in their third generation by 1900. The

Winter at Marden Hotel stables and public weigh scale, 1910.
Source: W. Husband

Artist Ken Danby's home, the former Armstrong's Mills, 1999. Source: E. Mitchell

pioneering phase of farm life was over. The pioneer log schools such as the Paisley Block School on Speedvale Avenue West had served their purpose.

A series of education acts in the latter half of the 1800s had ensured publicly funded primary education in Ontario. The very fact that these township school buildings still exist today is testimony to both concern for education and the skills of the builders. Five of the schools were of stone construction, three of brick. The name of one school, No. 4 1/2, is evidence of a human miscalculation in demographics. Seven schools had been designated for Guelph Township, but by the turn of the century it was found that the population of the area around the Marden-Maryhill Road had been underestimated, and, in 1902, No. 4 1/2 had to be fitted in. The present building was erected in 1909.

In retrospect we know that the local schools were to play a very important role in the development of a strong sense of community - as the nucleus is to the cell. A publicly-owned and permanently-located building, the school was to become the focal point of community activity.

The school's first service was to provide for the primary education of the children within the geographic jurisdiction – a radius of about two miles. From the very beginnings of formal education each child in the community came into contact with his peers. For the next eight years they studied and played with these classmates, walked or biked to school with some of them. When school reunions are held now, it is apparent that many lifetime friendships were started in the community school.

Teachers taught six subjects in eight grades to a school enrolment which varied from 15 to 40 students. It was a huge responsibility and yet many teachers did an excellent job. The township schools made possible the primary education of all farm children at a time when transportation was more limited, with

S.S. No. 6, Guelph Township, 1938.

Source: Ida Merkley

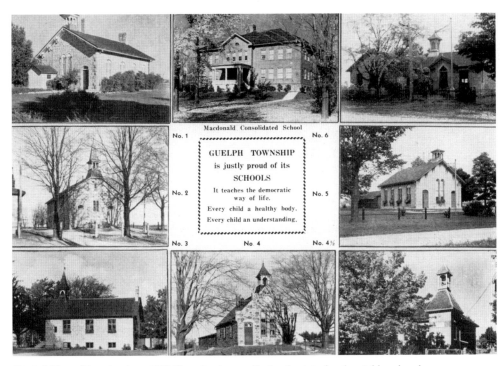

Guelph Township schools, c. 1950. The schools were the focal point of each neighbourhood.

Source: M. Campbell

GCVI Latin teacher, 1925-1960. Township girl, Ella Sinclair, was a favourite teacher for generations of students. Source: J. Sinclair

horse-drawn vans to the consolidated school. However, in 1907 those farm communities opted to return to the local schools. Again, in the mid-1940s, senior students from the rural schools were bused to the Macdonald Consolidated School on Friday afternoons for classes in manual training/household science and agriculture. This was more in the nature of an enrichment program, but again, the experiment lapsed. However, today all rural children are bused to schools in the city of Guelph.

Sunday Schools – The Community at Worship

Most Guelph Township communities had vigorous Sunday schools during the first half of the century for adults and children alike. The Sunday school movement had been started in England much earlier (1780) with the object of promoting Christian knowledge and literacy. For some families the distance from the city might have precluded regular worship in Guelph, thus the schools doubled as a place of worship for all ages.

Meetings convened at the local school on Sunday afternoons. The general pattern was to meet spring, summer and autumn, although at Watson's School, No. 2, Sunday school was held during the winter as well. Each year a superintendent and secretary-treasurer were elected, and pianists and teachers were chosen to serve that year. A committee was established to arrange for special speakers and music.

Meetings assembled between 2:30 and 3:30 p.m. The meeting would come to order with a hymn, usually from Sankey's Gospel Hymns, a prayer and announcements. If space allowed, the adult Bible class would then gather in another room (hall or cloakroom) to be addressed by a speaker. More often, curtains would be used as dividers in the big one-room school. Children were grouped into classes of approximate age and an adult would teach a short Bible lesson. Sunday school newsletters such as *The Messenger* were available as a take-home sheet. A Bible verse would be recited and possible applications of the lesson in daily life were considered.

At No. 6 School, Professor Frank Schofield of the Ontario Veterinary College was a frequent speaker, as were two Christian laymen from Guelph, J. Oakes and E. Pettifer. A. Habermehl of Waterloo County was a frequent visiting

school buses 75 years in the future. Students who went on to high school in the years between 1870 and 1950 often boarded in Guelph with a relative or friend.

It was in primary school in the local community that many children had their intellects awakened. While the first purpose of the rural school was primary education, it was also the nurturer of community awareness. Whenever a community activity was conceived, those people who initiated it saw the school as the meeting place.

The rural school system was terminated in 1964 when the county boards were created. Only one township school, Marden (No.3), was given a reprieve, until 1999. Township school reunions have thus been held at Marden School. Four generations of many farm families had attended the same township schools.

At the time the township schools were phased out, many reasons were put forward to suggest that the one-room school could not provide as good an education as a larger, graded school. In fact, centralized education had been tried in an earlier period, 1904-1907. The Canadian tobacco magnate, William Macdonald, had subsidized the Macdonald Consolidated School with $38,000. Pupils from the designated township schools, Nos. 1, 4 and 6, were transported by lay preacher, while local farmers, J. Fisk and F. Pinder, were speakers from within the community. At the conclusion of the service all groups would re-assemble for a closing hymn and prayer. At dismissal people did not leave for home immediately – children played and adults talked. Members were long-time friends as well as assembled Christians. It was Sunday and nobody did manual labour, the cattle were on pasture, and essential chores were down to an absolute minimum.

For others, Sunday school was integrated with a local church service in Guelph. The Mosborough church held a

West End United Farmers of Ontario, c. 1925. Note the fur coat on the gentleman seated at right.   Source: West End Tweedsmuir History

special Harvest Thanksgiving each autumn and local Sunday school services at No. 5 and No. 6 schools were suspended for that day. Mid-week prayer meetings were held in some communities, associated with local churches or Sunday schools. Some township residents were members of Bethany Church in Pilkington and Barrie Hill in Eramosa. These congregations were part of the United Church of Canada after Church Union in 1925, and continue today as vigorous congregations. The longest lasting Sunday school was at No. 4 1/2 School (1961). Its longevity may be attributed to the dedication of people such as Alex Anderson, a farmer and community organizer, Grace Bowman, a public school teacher and Flora Cleghorn, who ran the Sunday school. It can be said that the local Sunday school was the "community at worship." Each year, a Sunday school supper, often in the autumn, and a Sunday school picnic were held. Riverside Park in Guelph Township was a favoured site for all the community picnics, although occasionally they were held at Puslinch Lake, Victoria Park in Kitchener or Waterloo Park.

Community Organizations
United Farmers of Ontario and United Co-operatives of Ontario
In this year 2000 the letters UFO do not automatically bring to mind the United Farmers of Ontario, but during the first half of the century there were UFO branches in every community in Guelph Township. The local UFO branches were both social and political, offering economic fellowship. They usually met in the local school.

The UFO had evolved from an earlier American farm federation called The Grange. It was dedicated to the idea that farmers should organize to achieve greater incomes. In March 1914, a group of 300 farmers met in Toronto to form two closely-related organizations: the United Farmers of Ontario and the United Co-operatives of Ontario (UCO). The UFO was established on the premise that the middlemen (wholesalers and retailers), with whom the farmers did business, always took a large cut out of the price of the final product, while the farmers, the producers of the food commodities, could not count on a fair market value. It remains a familiar theme even in 2000. The farmer gets so little remuneration for his inputs, without which there could be no end product. The UFO therefore planned to cut out the middleman through the use of consumer co-operatives which would buy directly from the producers.

In the provincial election of 1919 the UFO ran candidates in some areas and although they did not get a majority, they did elect 43 members, a number that constituted a plurality. They chose Barrie farmer E.C. Drury, a graduate of the Ontario Agricultural College, as premier. Since the UFO did not have a majority they were dependent on the support of members of other parties. They lost power in 1923 when the Conservatives returned to office.

Disillusionment with the UFO as a political force set in during the 1920s. The spunky Agnes Macphail publicly berated farmers for being faint-hearted in their convictions. It was during this unstable time in 1928 that Guelphite Herbert Henry Hannam was elected education secretary of the UFO. He was born in 1898

United Co-operatives of Ontario creamery truck and driver Earl Reeve, c. 1960.   Source: J. Keleher

Milk tank truck arriving at Gay Lea on Speedvale Avenue, 1999.   Source: E. Mitchell

Provincial office of the Federated Women's Institutes of Ontario, 1995. Road 30, west of Marden.
Source: FWIO

near the hamlet of Swindon Park in Grey County, and his family moved to Guelph Township in 1920. This family had long been active in rural causes. Hannam remained dedicated to the idea that conditions must be improved for rural people. He was instrumental in the formation of the Farm Forum in the late 1930s whereby families within a community would gather in neighbours' homes to listen to a CBC program presenting a farm issue. At the end of the broadcast there was a discussion among the local members of their responses to the issue.

In 1933 Hannam became secretary of the UFO, then in 1936 secretary of the United Co-operatives of Ontario and, in 1939, he was elected president of the Canadian Federation of Agriculture.

The UCO, Guelph branch, opened a retail store on Neeve Street across from the Canadian National Railway station, in the former Walker's Fruit Wholesale building. An economic fellowship dedicated to getting a better financial deal for the farmer, its roots are in the UFO. During the 1940s when farmers began using more commercial fertilizers, the UCO opened a mixing and retail fertilizer outlet in the former Goldie Flour Mill, renting space on two floors. Guelphite Alex Anderson managed that facility with the assistance of George Dickieson.

In 1954 the UCO opened its retail store on Speedvale Avenue. The location allowed them to maximize customer usage from both farm and urban buyers. A new feed mill was opened at the rear of this site. In 1958 a distinct charter was given to the United Dairy and Poultry Cooperative. In 1966 the poultry group withdrew as the dairy producers "wanted to bring together all the dairy co-operatives in Ontario in one organization in order to develop the resources needed to become a significant force in the (dairy product) market."

It was soon to become known as the Gay Lea Cooperative, and they

gradually bought up other creameries in southern Ontario. Guelph was to become a major centre for research and production for dairy products.

WOMEN'S ASSOCIATIONS

In the early 20th century, rural women became members of various women's groups. The most prominent and well known of these was the Women's Institute (WI). The Wellington South District WI originated on June 11, 1903. Its founding member and first president, Bella McIntosh, was also founder of the Marden WI established earlier that year. The importance of Marden was to become evident by its choice as the location for the Ontario headquarters of the Federated Women's Institutes of Ontario (FWIO) in 1994.

The Wellington South WI was to act as an umbrella for the several groups that were to emerge as an integral part of a woman's life in the township. Mosborough (1947) was the last of a group that included not only Marden but the Paisley Block (1905) and the West End (1915). While each group acted independently in terms of their own types of issues and reforms, the Wellington South District provided an overall voice for events that affected all farmers and their wives in south Wellington County. In a meeting held on July 7, 1932, they were told:

"In its social work the WI has united the communities and brought its source of enjoyment into the community. Marvelous work has been done in providing common halls, rest rooms, and libraries, in beautifying schools and school grounds, but...there is a need to co-operate with and aid in every possible way the efforts of the agricultural representative."

As it can be seen, the WI groups were not merely social. According to Linda McGuire Ambrose, a social historian and author of a book on the subject, these groups were formed for three reasons: educational advancement, social outings and community activism through local projects. This is certainly true of the township branches. They held public speaking contests, hemmed sheets for the Guelph General Hospital, did mending at local shelters, gathered money for the relief of the Armenian boys' home, petitioned and raised money for a rest room at Guelph Farmers' Market, and provided money and clothing for various agencies at Christmastime. In 1938, The Royal WI (formerly Riverside, which was formerly Marden) sent help to Ratcliffe, Saskatchewan for drought victims. In particular they were thanked for "the bale of toys sent the children in the drought area." At WI meetings they held socials but they also heard various papers on different issues facing the world. The Riverside WI listened one afternoon in March 1926 to a paper by Mrs. Burnett titled: "Modern Conveniences in the Farm Home."

In 1940, at the suggestion of Lady Tweedsmuir, wife of the Governor General (1935-1940), the Institute members undertook the Tweedsmuir History Project: the recording of local history through the history of their own families and community activities. The project is still underway in 2000.

For nearly 100 years, the Federated Women's Institutes of Ontario have been dedicated to the principle that women working together can improve living and working conditions for their families, their rural communities and the world. Their diverse accomplishments are the result of co-operation and the collective visions of women from many walks of life. In 2000 they are achieving their goals in partnership with a variety of other agencies, for example, their efforts in health promotion in co-operation with the Osteoporosis Society of Canada and the Canadian Cancer Society.

Yet the WI was not the only group a farmer's wife or rural dweller could turn to for both social and moral purpose within the community. There were several United Farm Women's Organization (UFWO) groups. The West End UFWO Club held meetings throughout 1926 in spite of the bad weather. (Rural roads were not plowed after snowstorms until plows became available in the late 1930s). It was a mixed audience that came to hear W.J. Moreland speak on grading and marketing of eggs. This particular UFWO club seems to have been the most active and long lasting, as it was still around in 1932.

Women could also belong to a sewing society such as one in Marden in 1926, or various church-based organizations, as the Panton Missionary Auxiliary or the Women's Missionary Society of Paisley Block. Such groups had a specific target and speakers tended to deal with religious and missionary work, providing further opportunities for women to get together.

Youth Groups

As was the case with women, youth also had their own groups and associations. A Guelph Township branch of the Junior Farmers was formed in 1948-49, about the same time as Eramosa Township organized their own group. The 4-H program, pioneered in the United States, was designed for children and young adults aged 10 to 21 years to develop skills in communication, leadership, problem solving and goal setting. Guelph Township young people have been active in 4-H with projects selected from a huge range: from foods to forestry, calf clubs to computers. In 1967, members of the female branch of the Wellington County club, the 4-H Homemaking Club, included two national award winners from Guelph Township: Nancy Carroll of RR 3 and Jane Harris of RR 7. There was also an active youth branch of the United Farmers of Ontario in Marden during the 1920s until at least 1934.

Literary and Debating Clubs

In the 1920s several communities had active literary and debating clubs. The community clubs associated with the United Farmers of Ontario occasionally produced plays which they presented first to a local audience and then took to other communities for presentation around the township. As an example, in mid-December 1921 the No. 5 School's Young People's Society put on a play entitled *The Young Village Doctor*, a production involving 16 local young actors.

Even more common were debates held under community or UFO auspices. A theme particularly significant to the Guelph area was a topic at No. 5 School in March 1922: "The usefulness of a college education to a practical farmer." The opponents argued that such education was often impractical, extravagant and irrelevant, but the proponents nevertheless won the debate. Debating topics were sometimes more whimsical. In early May 1922, the West End debaters considered "whether one should marry for love or money." The love side won,

 1934 – The Ontario Agricultural College Literary Society holds a speaking contest. The winner, J. M. Jackson, year '34, spoke on "Rural Poverty applied to Large Areas." Second prize went to E.T. Parker whose topic was "A Rural Problem."

West End Literary Society, 1908.   Source: West End Tweedsmuir History

Jock Clark

One of Guelph's master gardeners, Jock Clark managed the parks in the city from 1948 until his death in September 1973. Clark, a Scottish emigrant, was chosen for the position of parks superintendent as a result of the recommendations and testimonials from his Scottish associates. Under his careful guidance, Guelph soon became renowned for its parks. It was Clark who arrived at the idea for a floral clock in Riverside. The concept, three years in the making, grew out of a former hobby. As a young Scottish sailor he had collected old clocks from distant ports. The original clock, built in 1949 was rebuilt and mechanized in 1955 and patented in 1956. At 28 feet in diameter with the numbers on the face at four feet high, it requires more than 6,000 plants to achieve the effect. Though the clock was Clark's main legacy to the city, he ensured in other ways that the parks would always pleasure Guelphites. In 1966, he bought a carousel and miniature train from Conklin's Amusement Parks. Both are still operational and have been magnets to the city's children. Clark was also responsible for the construction of the greenhouses at Riverside Park, where, even today, parks staff cultivate the flowers and plants necessary to keep the city beautiful. Yearly, Clark and his staff designed and planted flowerbeds and arrangements throughout the city to honour various organizations and groups.

When Jock Clark died in 1973, Mayor Norm Jary eloquently summed up Clark's contribution: "Every time we look at a flower or walk through a city park we will be reminded of him."

– Ceska Brennan

although the lead affirmative speaker, Alf Dawson, a bachelor, avowed he "knew little of either love or money." That same year, a UFO-sponsored debate arguing whether "a good-natured wife/housekeeper is preferable to one with only the ability to cook or sew" took place. Hibbert Campbell and Gladys Jackson upheld the affirmative while Mamie Pringle and Stanley Bechtel took the negative and scored the most points. On December 11, 1923, the West End Women's Institute debated the issue: "women occupying the same positions as men should receive the same salary." Janie Garland and Katherine Cleghorn spoke for the affirmative, while two men, James Campbell and Alf Dawson, took the negative. The affirmative side won.

Such social events were very popular at a time when radio was new and television was 30 years or more in the future.

THE GUELPH TOWNSHIP HORTICULTURAL SOCIETY

The Guelph Township Horticultural Society has made a significant contribution to the beautification of Guelph Township from 1922 to the present time.

In 1897, an act of the Legislature of the Province of Ontario provided a broad endorsement for organizations which would "encourage Agriculture, Horticulture, Arts and Manufactures." A provincial act of 1906 specifically encouraged the formation of horticultural societies and a committee formed in the township in February 1921 resolved to apply for membership within the Ontario Horticultural Society (OHA). The initial meeting was held at No. 4 1/2 School with 35 members present. Professor J.W. Crowe of the Ontario Agricultural College, William Laidlaw and J.E.Carter discussed the benefits of membership

 1919 – Guelph Horticultural Society tries to get Guelph citizens to work for the title "The Aster City."

 January 9, 1972 – Guelph is officially given the title "The Poppy City" due to the special efforts of the John McCrae Birthplace Society.

Ontario Reformatory

On September 25, 1911 Sir James Whitney laid the corner stone at the "farm" located on the grounds of what is now the Guelph Correctional Centre. The headlines of the *Guelph Mercury* claimed the "event marks a new era in history of prison reform work in the Dominion of Canada." This was a time when farm work was considered part of the reform system of prison life.

The Guelph Farm, located on the east side of Guelph Township, consisted of several "model" barns. These included a horse barn, an up-to-date piggery, a creamery and a dairy barn. Perceived as a model of efficiency, the grounds were included as part of a visiting official's tour of Guelph. Everyone from labour trade unionists to Australian cricket players visited the reformatory farm. They admired the acreage of fruit trees: 1,800 apple, cherry, plum and pear trees comprised the orchards. Over 80 Holsteins were stabled in the barns. These cattle gained national attention with the awards that accompanied them. It was, in fact, to these herds that the Ontario Agricultural and Veterinary Colleges at the University of Guelph turned for various studies. In May 1971 W.C. Winegard, president and vice-chancellor of the university, expressed appreciation for the significant contributions of the herds as both a teaching tool and a research resource.

This had not originally been the intent for either the herds or the crops. The 830-acre farm was intended to provide meaningful work and reform for the prisoners while producing sufficient amounts of food to feed inmates of Ontario institutions. In 1911 alone, 6,000 bushels

Ontario Reformatory prisoners dig the ponds at the OR site as part of the prison reform movement, c. 1933.
Source: Frank Dobias

of potatoes were harvested. Together with other crops such as turnips, mangels, pumpkins and wheat, provided early proof of what the farm could do, and did, until the end of the Second World War.

Besides growing crops and raising cattle the management introduced trades. In addition to the manufacture of such goods as woolens, men were taught the workings of a slaughterhouse. The farm's abattoir was constructed to handle both farm animals and local livestock. It did not, however, exist without controversy. In 1934 two buyers for the abattoir were involved in a scandal. After having purchased sheep, hogs, lambs and cattle over a five-year period, the buyers made $95,000 and $475,000 respectively. This was an excessive amount when compared with the farmer's profits who received 25 cents commission per hundred-weight of livestock they brought in.

However, the abattoir weathered the storm and was still active in 1978. In fact during 1977 and 1978 this program of work was commended. A study of the Guelph Abattoir Program felt that the benefits of this "innovative approach to correctional industries" far outweighed any negatives. In spite of this encouragement, the program was eventually discontinued and replaced by a private enterprise known as "Better Beef." In fact, the entire farm system of reform was ended. The fields were no longer worked and, ignoring the support for the livestock resources from the University of Guelph, the dairy herd was sold. The provincial government had concluded: "farms no longer have the significance for corrections that they once had."

 January 18, 1937 – Rioting erupts at the Ontario Reformatory on January 17. Heavy steel doors were used as battering rams by prisoners and one huge barracks was created by the destruction of all barriers such as doors and walls. Police used batons (obtained only in 1934 when they tried to control the garment workers' strike). Many provincial police were called in from Kitchener-Waterloo, veterans from the Canadian Legion also were suited up as well as provincial traffic officers. The greatest effort was expended to keep the disorder contained within the jail. Hundreds of citizens reportedly flocked to view the site of the disturbance. Quiet reigned on the 18th.

According to the reports the riot started over food. One inmate told the *Guelph Mercury* "We wanted butter." It was a question of quality and not quantity. Sixteen were arrested and the total damage was pegged at around $200,000. Judge James Madden of Napanee was appointed to conduct an inquiry. In an unorthodox move he actually listened to the complaints of the prisoners and followed this up by tasting the food himself.

Arnold Jensen

Known locally as "the flower man,"Arnold Jensen indulged in his love of flowers and people for more than 27 years. Jensen was born and raised in Sudbury, where he had worked in the mines as a young man. When he and his wife Margaret moved to Guelph from their 100-acre farm, Jensen soon became known for the bouquets of cut flowers and the many annual and perennial plants that filled the front porch of his little white house on Woolwich Street. More interested in daisies than dollars, he left a cash box on a table for customers to drop in payment for an arrangement or for their choice from the various jars and buckets of flowers. He made sure to have tulips ready for Mothers' Day and his specialty, gladiolas, came into bloom shortly after. His snapdragons and daisies beckoned to drivers as they passed. Jensen told the story of an out-of-town visitor who commented on his method of payment – the old honour system – as a marvelous thing, especially in this day and age. She added, "It's a Guelph thing though, don't you think?" Jensen agreed. It never occurred to him to believe otherwise. Jensen died in 1993.

– *Ceska Brennan*

and the group endorsed the application to become a branch within the OHA, which was approved by the provincial committee in 1922.

The hope was that: "Guelph may be known as a beauty spot within Ontario. At present Guelph is well known as the home of the leading agricultural college. Let us now make it known as the leading agricultural and horticultural district."

One of the strengths of the horticultural society was that it sold memberships to any resident of the township even though not all residents took an active role in the organization. Membership allowed the cardholder to qualify for a small

 1950s - The farm at St. Joseph's Hospital, which had operated on the 42-acre site, is phased out. For years the institution was supplied with milk from cows raised on the property. The sisters did the milking until 1948.

At the turn of the century two workers tilled the ground, and a team of work horses were kept as well as a driving horse. Chickens were many and eggs plentiful in those days and one year the sisters undertook to raise ducks and geese but abandoned this as the noise disturbed the residents and patients. All the vegetables needed were grown on the farm and stored in sand in the root house to last through the winter.

The first barn was destroyed by fire early in 1882. This was rebuilt, and in 1941 was replaced by a larger barn to hold up to 12 cows and four horses. True to type, the sisters kept one old horse, worn out and homeless. They called him Charlie. (Source: Gordon Guthrie)

discount at many garden retail centres within the township. Incidentally as active members traveled about selling memberships in their neighbourhoods it was another factor making for a sense of community.

Horticultural beautification projects within the township were favourite activities. For many years each public school would receive a package of tulip bulbs to help beautify schoolyards. Small prize incentives were awarded for "lawn and roadside improvement with the township."

In 1922, J.P. Henderson won the award for the best kept vegetable garden and Walter MacDonald won the award for lawn and garden. In 1927, there were 111 adult memberships and 23 youth memberships sold. In 1932, the township society had four executive meetings, a show and the annual meeting. There were occasional social and money-raising events: in 1932 a dance was held and a silver collection was taken at the annual meeting. In 1936, it was reported that a "very successful euchre and tea was held at Marden School." There was a charge of 20 cents and the lunch committee served currant bread, cake, strawberries and ice cream. In 1944, J. Taylor and S.B. Stothers were judges at the annual flower and vegetable show held at No. 4 School. A dance with refreshments ended the evening. Between 1950 and 1956 a rock garden at Marden located on the road allowance of Highway 6 beside the William Small farm, commemorated the "Guelph Township Horticultural Society" in floral display. Unfortunately, when the highway was widened, the rock garden was lost.

At various times the society sponsored essay contests to foster horticulture awareness especially among the youth. There was always a close association with the Ontario Agricultural College. At a 1958 meeting at the Macdonald Consolidated School, Professor H.W. Goble gave an illustrated talk on insects and their control as related to lawn and garden. The society developed a photo competition program to appeal to a wide segment of the township residents. The program goes on essentially the same today to encourage public and private efforts to beautify the township.

COMMUNITY CLUBS

In the 1930s community clubs were still active in each school section and monthly meetings were the norm. A committee established at the beginning of the year

 1932 – William Garnett, an Ontario Agricultural College student, becomes the first ever agricultural student in North America to win a Rhodes Scholarship.

would decide the monthly format, which might be a euchre, a social evening of music or a speaker. Invariably there was a hearty lunch at the end of the evening.

Dances were held at special occasions throughout the year: New Year's, Valentine's Day and Halloween. Local orchestras including Dawsons, Bradleys, Fletchers and Parkinsons performed, with a caller in attendance to call off square dances. Occasionally a fireworks display would honour Victoria Day. In June there was often a garden party in the schoolyard, featuring strawberry shortcake and ice cream.

The individual community clubs were thriving right up to the time of the closure and sale of the rural schools in 1964. Most farm people foresaw that the loss of the schools would result in erosion of the sense of community, and they were, of course, correct.

The rural community of Guelph Township did indeed change. It is true that many rural young people were drifting off the farm to higher-paying jobs. Farming had changed irrevocably. Mechanization had rendered the labour-intensive family farm close to obsolete. Industry and technology were expanding and beckoning young people away from the farm.

Many rural lots were severed for people who wanted "to live in the country." These were people who did not make their livelihood from farming, and some did not really want to integrate into a rural neighbourhood.

Animal Husbandry

BEEF CATTLE

F.W. Stone, whose first farm was bought by the Province of Ontario to become the nucleus of the Ontario Agricultural College (OAC) in 1873, was among the noted importers and breeders of top quality cattle. His Shorthorn and Hereford cattle were among the best in Canada. The old British beef breeds were regarded as the best foundation stock in the first half of the 20th century.

In the March 1890 issue of the *O.A.C. Review* mention is made of the "celebrated herd of Hereford cattle owned by F.W. Stone ...a splendid herd of Devons owned by Mr. Rudd of Arkell...Galloways of first class quality owned by Mr. McCrae on College Avenue West." The *Review* went on to say that farmers'

James Bowman of Elm Park farm on Paisley Road, 1925, famed for his Angus cattle and Suffolk sheep.
Source: S. McColeman

One high-priced bull! 1920. Millhill's Comet was purchased in Scotland for $34,000 by J.J. Elliott.
Source: Florence Frey

sons could learn a great deal by attending the Ontario Agricultural College and that they might become first-class farmers such as those named in the article.

Another noted livestock breeder was James Bowman of Paisley Road. He bought the Sandilands farm in 1891, naming it "Elm Park" to honour a fine stand of elm trees that grew along the south boundary of his farm. Bowman is credited with keeping the first systematic records of the Aberdeen Angus breed in Canada and was a pioneer breeder of Suffolk sheep in Ontario. His breeding stock was in demand across the country and he exhibited widely, taking awards in Toronto, Chicago and St. Louis.

The Angus tradition, which Bowman began, was continued by Thomas Henderson, who became known as a breeder who gave meticulous attention to the feeding and care of his animals. James Hasson has since continued the Angus tradition, with his sons taking the Queen's Guineas at the Royal Winter Fair.

J.J. Elliott of Mount Pleasant (Mill Road at Watson) made a profound impression in Shorthorn circles in the early decades of the century and by 1920 he had won several awards at the Canadian National Exhibition. The show circuit is appealing to many and it took Elliott to the leading shows in Western Canada,

 1911 – While in the year 2000 people complain about dogs roaming free in Exhibition Park and making a "mess," the problem in 1911 was much larger. A number of cattle had been allowed by their owners to run at large on the grounds. The police in November of that year were threatening that if the problem wasn't remedied they would impound the cattle.

 1934 – Two horses, King and Major, make the letters page and continuing newspaper headlines when the city decides to sell them after 10 years service with the fire department. Maud Pentelow starts a campaign to raise the $125 asked for them. Letters of support praise her action and condemn the city for insisting on selling the animals instead of retiring them after their years of excellent service.

Feedlot-fed beef cattle on Arnie Bruce's farm, 1985.   Source: Arnie and Vera Bruce

Draught horses at work on Alf Dawson's farm on Woodlawn Road, 1938. Another farmer is stooking (not pictured here), keeping up to the pace of the binder.   Source: West End Tweedsmuir History

Beef Ring

In the first two decades of the century, the meat co-operative system known as the "beef ring" was in operation with several "rings" within the township. During spring, summer and autumn when temperatures made storage impossible, a co-operative group of neighbourhood farmers would butcher an animal and share the beef. Although refrigeration had been invented in the 19th century, there was as yet no practical application in the form of refrigerators or freezers. Commercial freezers were available in the late 1920s, and the home refrigerator in the forties.

When freezer technology allowed the walk-in freezer, small neighbourhood butcher shops came on the scene, including Cheevers at Paisley and Arnold, Cremascos on York Road, Hawkins at Waterloo Avenue and Yorkshire Street, Hewer's on Wilson Street and Dollery at Highway 7 and Silvercreek Parkway. By the late 1930s, it became the norm for a farmer to rent a freezer locker, one of the largest of these being located at the Guelph Creamery at Baker and Yarmouth streets behind the old YMCA. For a small annual rental fee a family could rent one or more lockable containers, each of which would hold about 200 pounds of packaged meat. Since most farmers were in town once or twice a week, it was not inconvenient to pick up meat, especially when there would be a weekly crate of eggs and a can of cream to be sold to the Guelph Creamery. Other locker facilities were available by the 1950s, including the Hales Lockers on Lower Wyndham Street.

where he took awards with his senior yearling heifer, Rosa Hope. In 1920 he was present at the Perth Sale in Scotland, where he bought the highest-priced bull calf that had ever come to Canada at that time. Millhill's Comet was purchased for 6,600 guineas (approximately $34,000) with a loan from the bank. Upon arrival in Canada, another Shorthorn breeder, Sir Frank Bailley, offered to pay Elliott a premium over cost price, but Elliott refused the offer. Cattle prices declined in 1921, and Comet did not get as much use as expected. There was no insurance on the bull, and his death caused considerable financial hardship for the owner.

The Shorthorn Association in Guelph Township remained strong, although inbreeding tended to decrease the size and quality of the breed for some decades. Shorthorns may be white, roan or red, and were sometimes called Durhams. Until mid-century there was a dual-purpose Shorthorn strain producing both milk and meat. Other Guelph breeders included A.D. Thomas, J.R. Elliott, and C. Blyth while J. Dunbar and J. and D. Hasson raised Herefords. In recent decades, European beef breeds such as Charolais, Limousin, Simmental and Chianina assumed new importance in Guelph Township.

Barber abattoir on Elizabeth Street in Guelph, c. 1920. Famous Bacon!

Source: J. Keleher

T.K. Henderson with a Suffolk ram, 1938.
Source: G. Henderson

challenging. With any human pressure in one direction, a reverse reaction from the hogs could be expected.

During the first half of the century, the Charles Barber abattoir on Elizabeth Street processed much of the local pork and C. Barber bacon became famous, at least within the region. The Barber Butcher Shop on Upper Wyndham Street retailed much of the Elizabeth Street product and the Barber delivery wagon became a common sight around Guelph. Another large plant that operated in the 1930s and 1940s was Wellington Packers, located on York Road just beyond Victoria Road where the railroad crosses York Road. Rail facilities were needed because some hogs were shipped in from North Wellington County. At least one existing grocer, Upsdells, bought products from Wellington Packers back in the 1930s. These hog products were quality meat that won a niche market even in Britain. Wellington Packers was the main Guelph market until the 1940s, after which Burns of Kitchener handled most of the township hogs. Other packers who got some stock were Essex (Fearmans) of Hamilton and J.M. Schneider of Kitchener.

A hog marketing agency was created in the 1960s. The main thrust of this effort was the requirement of Guelph Township hogs to be marketed through a facility at the Waterloo Farmers' Livestock Market. This ensured that the pork processors would have to bid to acquire the hogs. The marketing agency also used advertising in newspapers and television to promote the use of pork. However, the fact that the Ontario Pork Marketing Board had no authority to establish quota, limit production or have any initiative in establishing price meant that it was not a very effective program for pork producers. At the present time prices for live hogs are very low.

The pork industry is subject to overproduction since gestation of pigs is only three months and the time period from birth to market is only five to six months. If the market price is strong the pork producer needs only eight to nine

Horses

In the sphere of draught horses, the Sorby brothers, Walter and Oswald, were developing some of the best bloodlines of Clydesdales at "Woodlands," their farm a few miles south-west of Guelph on a property that straddled Guelph and Puslinch townships. They bought the best breeding stock that Britain could provide, and practised a systematic breeding program at Woodlands, selling to markets in the United States and Canada. The Sorbys also imported Hackneys, a combination riding and carriage horse, also in great demand at the beginning of the century. They stayed in business for only one generation, and in 1911, Woodlands was sold. The property eventually was to become Vimy Ridge Farm.

Hogs

Almost every farmer kept a few hogs, and some as many as 100. It used to be standard practice for the farmer to plan to have hogs go to market just before his property taxes were due, so as to be sure to have cash on hand. An experienced farmer could estimate weight very well with market weight being 200 pounds. Marketing was simple: the farmer phoned the drover with the information that he had hogs ready to go to market. The drover set aside at least one day per week to transport hogs. Of all livestock to load on a truck, hogs are among the most months to increase production. This is the stage where there is a tendency to overproduce and glut the market.

SHEEP

At mid-century, T.K. Henderson was active in the sheep business, especially the Suffolk breed. He was in demand as a judge at the agricultural fairs. In the late 1940s he arranged for the sale of several train car loads of Suffock breeding stock to California.

Milk and bread delivery was commonplace up until the Second World War. Here, the Canada Bread delivery wagon is seen on Elizabeth Street at Huron in 1938/39. Source: J. Keleher

Many township farmers kept a flock of sheep, but this became less common in the last part of the century, in part due to accessibility of air freight to import fresh lamb from Australia and New Zealand, where 12 months of grazing allows cheaper production costs. However, there are a few flocks in evidence in the township and fresh Ontario spring lamb still commands a premium price.

DAIRY FARMING

Dairy farming has been important in Guelph Township during the entire century although dairies were first developed in nearby Oxford County. Ayrshire, Jersey, Guernsey and even dual-purpose Shorthorn breeds were commonly used as milk producers until mid-century. The Holstein-Friesan breed now accounts for at least 80 percent of dairy cattle.

Milk, cheese and butter were the early dairy products while at the end of the 20th century, concentrated (condensed, evaporated) milk, powdered milk, yogurt, cottage cheese, ice cream and other related products are important to the dairy industry.

In a study called *Guelph Milk Bottles, Dairies and Dairymen 1900-1999*, local historian Joyce Blyth identified 22 small dairies existing in Guelph between 1900 and 1950. Each had several suppliers and a home delivery system: horse and cart and later, trucks.

At the beginning of the century, many people, even in the city, still kept a

cow to supply their own milk and churn their own butter. Most farmers hand-milked a few cows, separating the cream to be marketed for butter, while using the skim milk to fatten hogs.

Among the early milk producers in the township were Tom Gilchrist, Bill Fair, Albert Dunk, Alf Husband, Jerry Fox, Walter MacDonald, James and Hibbert Campbell, Doug Cleghorn, Rich Hannam, Doug Hodgson, the Allisons, Jess Gale and William Friendship.

One of the first milking machines in use locally was a Hinman, which took its power from a power shaft driven by a one-cylinder gas engine since most farms did not have hydro until the late 1920s. Naturally, not all farms got electricity at the same time since it involved running poles and lines to a much less densely populated area than in the city. The Beatty Company of Fergus developed improved milking machines. By mid-century the Surge milking system eventually replaced virtually all others.

Milk was cooled in a cold-water trough. Several milk producers delivered their milk to the dairy either in a trailer behind a car or in a pick-up truck. It was the era of the milk can. The W.C. Woods Company of Guelph developed coolers that allowed exact control of temperature while the milk was in storage. By 1954, a major milestone was achieved with the transportation of bulk milk in truck tanks and trailers, but it was not until 1965 that the milk cans were entirely replaced. The venerable old cans were destined hereafter to become only objects for collectors' nostalgia.

When in town, milk producers could also sell milk products, such as butter, to local processors like the Guelph Creamery at Yarmouth and Baker streets. This practice did not always exist without controversy though, as illustrated in a series of letters to the *Guelph Mercury* in 1908 concerning Chief of Police Randall and his crackdown on butter weight. He was seizing butter that was purportedly underweight and giving it to charity. Several farmers complained that if the harassment continued they would reconsider their market choice. One writer pointed out that most farmers were now near a railway station that could easily ship their cream or butter to a factory or to another city. As butter

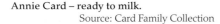

Annie Card – ready to milk.
Source: Card Family Collection

Milkshakes – 10 cents! Mrs. Gus Mano at Goody Sweets on the corner of Wyndham and Quebec streets, 1935 to 1968.
Source: Florence Rilett

creameries and dairy processors in and around Guelph provided farmers with an alternative to direct sales to the public. Dairy farmers began to sell directly to city dairies, which processed and marketed milk to homes and stores.

Changing expectations by the public brought about a growing concern with health issues. In Guelph, initially, local farmers could sell consumers "raw" (unpasteurized) milk. The initial move towards a "pure" milk concept involved the Board of Health in Guelph. It also created an increased interest by the board in changing acceptable milk practices. It began to regulate the processors and therefore the suppliers. In 1912 a "City Dairy" was selected from among the local township farmers to supply milk for Guelph. It also marked, with a bylaw, the licensing of all people who could sell their milk in Guelph. The licensing cost was $1 annually. The bylaw also stipulated the temperature for milk and the conditions of cows and their environment. Moreover, it impacted upon small producers, particularly women. It stated that anyone who offered milk for sale within the city must be sure that their dairy or such premises were located in a store room or milk house separate from any other residence. In other words, milk, butter or cheese could not be prepared within a kitchen, summer kitchen or any other room within the home. Furthermore, all milk that was not "pure" must be marked with a red label. The annual report of the municipal health organization for the year 1912 supplied some justification for the measures taken. It revealed that not only had improved milk conditions decreased infant mortality in that year, but also raised the actual standards of Guelph's milk suppliers. The Barrett Dairy Company (later to become the Model Dairy) received the highest ratings while Eckstein's, the lowest. This resulted in Barrett's emphasizing that they were 'number one' because they pasteurized their milk.

After 1912, the market for milk continued to be increasingly regulated. In 1922 an even larger step was taken. Movement was made towards mandatory milk pasteurization, but not enforced until 1934, when Ontario law required all milk to be pasteurized, prompted by a concern to eradicate diseases such as tuberculosis. But by far the most significant piece of legislation was the Ontario

churning was often a chore performed by women, the writer quite rightly asked why a farmer's wife should labour with butter, drive several miles to the market, and then pay Chief Randall to weigh her butter and then donate it to the hospitals. Another letter signed by a "Working Mutt" took the other side stating he would like to see the names of dishonest butter women "in print."

The butter question pointed out several things: the importance of women in the farm economy, the friction between city rules and rural realities, and the growth of an alternative market. As the century progressed farmers were to be affected by changes in urban policies and consumer demands. Public health concerns became an issue. The perception of what constituted a "good" product was to alter. In the industry some felt that the newer methods of production were better because they were "much more scientific." This is particularly obvious in milk production. The direct sale to the consumer from the farm of such products as milk, cheese and butter was to be altered dramatically. The arrival of larger

 1934 – A cow, Pauline Atlas Fancy The Third, holds a record of performance of enviable proportions. For milk over a year the six-year-old Holstein, owned by J.J. Fox, produced 17,566 pounds of milk yielding 711.25 pounds of butter. Over a one-month period she produced 2,181 pounds of milk.

Milk Act of 1965. Countless commissions and agencies had tried to regulate the dairy industry without great benefit to the producers. William Stewart, Minister of Agriculture, was committed to permanent and substantial change in the milk industry. The Ontario Milk Marketing Board was empowered to periodically review prices in such a way that the milk producer was assured a permanent and reasonable return on investment. The board awarded dairy farmers quota, and only those farmers with quota could market milk. In the long term, quota has

Combination wagon, c. 1930. Used as either field crop wagon with sides down or as a small animal stock rack with sides up. Source: J. Sinclair

Livestock drover Lloyd Dickieson of Speedvale Avenue West stands beside his 'International Truck,' 1967. Lloyd was a well-known drover from 1950 to 1980. Source: T. Dickieson

acquired value since it assures the producer of a profitable market. In the year 2000, quota sells on the open market at approximately $22,000 per cow. Thus, the dairy farmers of Ontario achieved a security of income envied by most other farmers. Only the poultry producers achieved a comparable accommodation.

Virtually every agricultural commodity now has an agency and/or marketing board. The international trade movement has objected to price setting, most recently through the North American Free Trade Agreement. To this point, however, the federal government has refused to change its policy regarding the dairy industry.

During the late 1960s the Gay Lea Cooperative bought up regional dairies in southern Ontario: Hanover, Chesley, Paisley and Teeswater to name only some of the significant old businesses purchased over the years. By the 1970s they were the largest dairy co-operative in Ontario. They were also processors of traditional products such as butter, cheese, skim milk powder and ice cream.

When the milk producers achieved price stabilization through the Milk Marketing Board, the Gay Lea plant on Speedvale built a sophisticated food laboratory and new product development facility. In a society which had become increasingly health conscious during the 1970s the new Gay Lea products, including yogurt and the Nordica line of cottage cheeses, met a receptive market.

 February 1965 – A Honey Quality Control Conference, first of its kind in North America, is held at the University of Guelph.

LIVESTOCK TRANSPORTATION

Cattle drives were common in the first part of the century. Until the mid-1920s cattle were commonly driven (walked) to the stock pens at the closest rail yard. Even after the advent of trucks, it was common to drive cattle: gates were closed along the route, and traffic was much slower and willing to cede the right of way. The author remembers helping drive 50 cattle about 15 miles in 1945. It took most of the day and involved crossing Highway 6.

Until about 1925, virtually all livestock that had to be transported any great distances went by rail. Each rural railway station had a siding with stock pens for cattle to be driven and loaded into stock cars. There were a few combination stock-racked farm wagons, such as the "Bain" which could be hauled by a team of horses, but they were only practical for a few hogs, calves or sheep going a short distance. After 1925, most livestock went to market by truck. In each community, some enterprising person would see the need and fill it. In Guelph Township those with trucking services included Jack Curtis, W. Telford, J. McAninch, Dan MacKinnon, Charlie Hurren, Lance Dickieson, Lloyd Dickieson and E. Mitchell.

REPRODUCTIVE TECHNOLOGY

Since the Second World War there has been tremendous progress in reproductive technology. Artificial insemination, initiated in the 1940s, has proven itself in both the dairy and beef industries. In 1968 United Breeders was formed as a co-

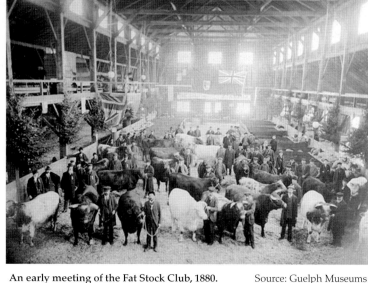

The Guelph Fat Stock Club

Guelph, 4th November, 1913

C. L. NELLES,
President
JAS. BOWMAN,
1st Vice-President
E. V. THOMPSON,
2nd Vice-President
J. M. DUFF,
Secretary

CITY OF GUELPH
SAMUEL CARTER,
Mayor

BOARD OF TRADE
GEO. J. THORP,
President

Guelph Fat Stock Club letterhead.   Source: Steve Thorning

operative, located just north of Marden, where an impressive stable of dairy and beef bulls is maintained.

In 1996 United Breeders amalgamated with Western Ontario Breeders to form GENCOR, which owns 750 acres and houses 680 sires. The organization has also taken a position in embryo transfer services and sales. GENCOR is associated with SEMEX, located in

An early meeting of the Fat Stock Club, 1880.   Source: Guelph Museums

the Research Park on Stone Road, the organization concerned with marketing the services and products on an international basis. Together these organizations have built an international reputation for superior genetics in livestock.

The Fat Stock Shows and the Ontario Provincial Winter Fair

Guelph Township has always been a leader in the livestock industry. Before the completion of the Grand Trunk Railway the reader can easily appreciate the difficulty of getting breeding stock into an area at least 30 miles from Lake Ontario. After the completion of the railway from Montreal in 1856, imports from Britain and Europe were easily arranged, although still expensive. In 1862 the *Mercury* reported that Lazarus Parkinson of Eramosa brought cattle to Guelph intending to show them at a fair, but such was the demand for breeding stock he sold his cattle before ever even reaching the fair.

The term Fat Stock Show seems somewhat incongruous at the beginning of the 21st century. We have just come through more than 40 years when animal fat has had very bad press as a health factor. In pioneer days this was not so. With good breeding stock in short supply, it was a real achievement to have raised a carcass of beef with good conformity to the strengths of the breed, and withal having a nice "finish" or "bloom" which inevitably meant a liberal marbling of fat. There were many fat stock clubs around Ontario. Any breeder was proud of having a carcass

well fleshed in the loins and hind-quarters, since this meant top grade. In photographs and artistic depictions of 19th century cattle, the depth of the carcass is astonishing. The carcass "rolling in fat" was a sign that the stock had the right genes and the owner provided first-class feed. Guelph had a Fat Stock Club before 1880. Fairs were held in the great pavilion at Exhibition Park or the fairgrounds where the Armory is now located.

The first Christmas Fat Stock Show was held in Toronto in 1883 with William Whitelaw of Guelph Township as president. It was funded by a $500 grant from the Toronto Agricultural Societies. Following this beginning, the shows of successive years were held in Guelph, Woodstock or Toronto. When in Guelph the competition was in the Drill Shed, a building across the tracks from the CNR station.

Successive years indicated that a show without a permanent location or proper accommodations could never hope for the kind of success to which the members aspired. Thus in 1899 Guelph was chosen to be the permanent site of the Ontario Provincial Winter Fair and suitable buildings were erected, beside the City Hall on Carden Street.

The show was a great success right from the start. It was planned for early December so as not to conflict with the Chicago Exposition. It helped that Guelph was on the Grand Trunk Railway main line and had Canadian Pacific Railway access via the Guelph Junction Railway.

The *Globe and Mail* reported that the "Guelph Winter Fair had suddenly become an exposition of at least Canada-wide fame. It was well supported by both the rural and urbanites of Guelph." The horse barns, now the Guelph Farmers' Market, were built in 1909 with a connecting tunnel under the Grand Trunk Railway tracks.

Year after year the *Mercury* would carry headlines, such as "Bigger and Better than Ever" (December 2, 1914) but it soon became apparent that the number of exhibitors and visitors overtaxed the facilities. Indeed, entries came from all over Ontario and beyond. By 1910, the breeders associations, dairy, beef, swine, poultry and grains, were urging larger facilities but still returned in increasing numbers each year.

While in Guelph most of the breeders' associations held their annual executive dinner meeting here. The Kandy Kitchen on Wyndham Street became a favourite meeting and dining place, even providing a small orchestra for the enjoyment of the farmer-businessmen.

It is extraordinary to read that in 1914 one of the best-attended shows had 11,000 people in attendance on one day, December 9. The total attendance for the year was 37,200 for the four-day exhibition. The railways offered special fares to Guelph from any place in Ontario; for example, a return fare from Toronto to Guelph was $1.95 via Canadian Pacific Railway. It was touted as "Canada's Greatest Stock Show." An article in the *Mercury* for December 5, 1915 described excursion trains disgorging their travellers at the Grand Trunk Railway Station and at the Canadian Pacific Station on Trafalgar Square, who then hurried on down Wyndham and Carden streets to the fair. The *Mercury* writer enthused: "This is the greatest event of the year for the people of the Royal City. People are here from all over Canada and the United States."

Representatives of the local banks staffed one room at the fair building in order to expedite the business transactions that were concluded at the event. Guelph merchants were not slow to realize the potential market and offered special pre-Christmas prices, "just a small mark-up over cost." Cole Bros. and Scott welcomed visitors to Guelph and invited them to shop at the "People's Store." D.E. MacDonald & Bros. invited visitors to a store where "our standard is quality."

Farm machinery companies such as DeLaval invited dairy farmers to visit their exhibit at the fair. "Look over our goods and get acquainted," they urged. In 1916 the New Idea Company had an exhibit for a "self unloading manure spreader" available from two local dealers, Penfold Bros and John Daniels.

It was an event for the whole community. From the beginning school-children in the city and township were given a day off. Monday, December 7, 1914 was "Schoolchildren's day at the Winter Fair. Every youngster in the city has

Dinner upstairs at the Kandy Kitchen, 1910.   Source: Kent McPhee

approached dad with a request to fork over a nickel." Also in 1916, the fair was favoured by a musical ride by the members of the 64th Battery, commanded by Major Wallace. It was reported that "there wasn't a flaw in their performance."

Each year the awards lists were published in the *Mercury*. Guelph Township entrants were well represented with annual entries from A. and W. Whitelaw (Leicester sheep), Parkinsons (Lincoln sheep), G. Henderson (Suffolk sheep), C. Blyth (Shorthorn) and J. Bowman (Angus), among many others. Most of the dairy awards went to Oxford County until 1922 when there was a prize awarded to J.D. Gale of Guelph Township.

Due to the smaller investment required, it should not be surprising that the poultry show assumed immense proportions. There were 7,000 entries in 1918. Consider that this class included not only chickens (eggs and meat), turkeys, and geese, but all the exotic birds and carrier pigeons. Of note was Walter Baulk, a Cork Street tobacconist who took a lifetime total of over 200 ribbons in the pigeon class. For many years Guelph held the North American record for entries in the poultry class.

In 1918, C.L. Nelles, the Guelph Fat Stock Club president, noted that the facilities were barely adequate to accommodate the "greatest show ever." There was some grumbling that the central executive was pressing some municipality to put up facilities which would cost an estimated three-quarters to one million dollars. The question was "why should Guelph put up all that money for a government show for Canada?" "I, for one, cannot see it that way," said Mr. Nelles. Guelph would be willing to spend $15,000 to $20,000 but that was it. He allowed that Guelph is the only proper place for the fair, "since it is the agricultural centre for the whole of Ontario."

"Couldn't we just carry on for another five years?" he asked.

In 1922 Toronto chose to put up the money to become the home of the Royal Agricultural Winter Fair, a national agricultural competition. It should be

 1934 – Guelph Township posts a bounty of $5 a head on dogs chasing livestock.

noted that it did not replace the Guelph Winter Fair, which always had promoted itself as Ontario's fair and continued on for another 17 years.

The Ontario Provincial Winter Fair in Guelph continued to thrive in the 1920s and 1930s. In 1929 it was again noted "every department will be taxed to the limit of capacity," when Dr. G.I. Christie of the Ontario Agricultural College declared the show open. Newspaper comment was that "for nearly 50 years the fair has been held in this city and interest is as keen as ever, notwithstanding the competition of similar fairs in nearby cities, notably the one held in Toronto just a few weeks prior to the Guelph fair." In fact the organizers were careful not to conflict with already established fair dates and again the *Mercury* reported Guelph's Winter Fair to be the outstanding show this year. Premier Hepburn was in Guelph to open the show in 1938, and predicted:

> "The present buildings may be rehabilitated and adequate accommodation for all entries should be provided for all who wish to come to the fair."

It was evident the fair had become a major social event in Guelph by this time. In the same year, fair president Dr. W.J.R. Fowler and his wife gave a fashionable dinner to mark the beginning of the riding competitions reflecting a growing emphasis on riding, dressage and horsemanship.

The following year (1939) the fair enjoyed further success, but in October a notice was posted sealing its fate.

> "The Winter Fair Building has been taken over for the accommodation of troops stationed here. It is no longer available for Fair or market use."

It is doubtful that it was realized at the time the fair would never be revived. At the end of the war, revival was considered but the buildings still would have required large expenditures of money, a major consideration in allowing the fair to die. Thus without a whimper the Ontario Provincial Winter Fair came to an end in 1939. It had been a colourful episode in the history of Guelph.

Plant Husbandry

In the early part of the century mixed farming was the common practice. Thus, in addition to animals, many farms harvested crops and had a large garden to supply the family with fresh produce and sometimes a stand at the market.

The first hayloader in Guelph Township, 1902. Thompson Farm, West End.
Source: West End Women's Institute

HAY

Hay is a nutritious animal fodder, used by farmers for millennia and is essential for horses, cattle and sheep. Initially cut with a scythe, by 1900 the horse-drawn mower was in use. A team of horses pulled a mower which took power from cleated wheels. A gear mechanism "harnessed" this power to a pitman shaft which operated a reciprocating cutting bar with knife sections. Once the hay was cut the farmer was dependent on nature for the sun and wind to reduce the moisture content. Drying time varies from two to five days. Side rakes, capable of turning the drying hay, put it into a windrow from which a hayloader could elevate it to a man on a wagon. Among the first hayloaders in the township was one owned by the Thompsons of the West End in 1902. The load was built in such a way that it could be removed by a large fork suspended from the ridgeline in the barn. A rope and pulley mechanism allowed the wagonload to be removed in four large bundles, deposited in any mow the farmer chose. Those who remember those times will recall "tripping the hayfork." The men in the mow had to stand clear when the great bundle of hay dropped from the track at the peak of the barn, ready to be leveled. This method of hay harvesting was time-consuming and it required lots of help for there were many different facets to the process. Fortunately it was ideal for a family farm. One of the author's first farming responsibilities was driving a team of horses on the hay wagon at age seven.

The technology for baling or "pressing" hay had been invented, but was used only to supply hay to remote lumber camps or for sale. The practical adapta-

Dump rake with Eva Thurtell at the reins on the Westholme farm, 1929.   Source: M.E. Campbell

Marshall Day's ditching machine, c. 1920.   Source: V. Bruce

tion to a mobile baler, usually powered by power take-off had to wait until the 1940s, when baler technology developed rapidly. The result of this revolution in baler technology was to make it possible for one person to harvest the hay which previously required the labour of many. The hay crop remains important for Guelph Township farmers.

WHEAT

The technology for harvesting wheat and other small grains was developed by Cyrus McCormick in the United States in 1834. Originally a reaper, and later a binder, by the turn of the century this machine could turn a field of grain into a field of sheaves bound with binder twine. These sheaves then had to be "stooked." No one who has done it will forget stooking. It was the manual and systematic process by which the sheaves were collected into "stooks" or "shocks" of eight or 10, grain end up, to facilitate further drying. If there happened to be a week or two of dry weather, and if one could obtain the services of a thresher, it was possible to have a "stook threshing" in the field. However, the more usual method was to store the sheaves in the barn until autumn, when the threshers' time could be reserved. This method involved more work but had the benefit of all the proceeds - grain, chaff, and straw, which were left in the barn where the farmer had immediate access during the winter.

Early in the century Goldie Mill in Guelph was a substantial user of local wheat, as was Pipes' Speedvale Mill. Local wheat was also marketed in Preston

and St. Jacobs; Preston has undergone many name changes but remains the one local mill still in operation from an earlier time. Distance to the mill is of little concern now, whereas at the beginning of the century one reads of horse-drawn wagons lined up at Goldie Mill waiting their turn to weigh in and unload.

At mid-century there were many good farms achieving yields of 70 bushels of wheat per acre, still considered an excellent yield in 2000.

OATS AND BARLEY

Oats and barley sometimes sown together as mixed grain were the standard grains for animal feed. These were planted in the spring as soon as the ground was workable, and were harvested in the summer, a few weeks after the wheat. Each barn had a granary for storage, and when required, during the fall and winter, grain would be bagged and taken to the grist mill to be ground.

Some farmers in the 1930s bought a grain grinder from the W.C. Woods Company of Guelph. It was powered by an electric motor. This could be installed beneath a chute from the granary and would deposit chopped grain in a feed box in the stable where it was fed to the livestock. By mid-century, a few farms had their own grinders powered by a farm tractor.

Other grain crops that were grown to a lesser degree included buckwheat, rye, millet, flax and canola. Kale and rape/canola were usually planted in June to provide a pasture supplement in late autumn. If milking cows were being pastured on kale or rape/canola, the taste of milk was affected.

1968 Ploughing Match on Nichol and Guelph Township boundary.
Source: W. Husband

Turnip pulling time at the Nessner farm, c. 1960. The top was removed from the turnip with a deft cut from a turnip knife. Four rows were then collected into one for loading.
Source: *Chemagro Courier*

Since hay was a very important crop, failure due to drought was indeed a real disaster. This often happened in a late spring when rainfall was scarce, and 1949 was just such a year for Guelph Township. May is an important growth month but the rainfall was lacking for hay. The crop was only a fraction of normal and this meant a shortage of cattle feed for the next winter. Many township farmers planted sorghum as a hay alternative. It is a plant related to sugar cane and may be planted in late May. By the end of August it had achieved a growth of approximately 48 inches with foliage similar to cane leaves. It was harvested with the grain binder which tied it into sheaves. It did involve a great deal of work but the cattle liked the sweet leaves and small stalks as fodder during the next winter. Fortunately years like 1949 were relatively rare.

Root Crops

Most farmers grew some root crops: turnips, mangels, and of course, enough potatoes for the winter. Turnips were labour intensive since they had to be hoed by hand, but they offered the prospect of cash returns in early November. The two township turnip processors at mid-century were John Houser's plant and the Ryder plant in Woolwich Township just north of Ariss which marketed many county turnips. The Houser waxing plant was located at Woolwich and Speedvale on the railway line. John Houser Jr. remembers that as many as five train carloads per week were exported to New York City during the 1950s.

Surplus and "culled" turnips were fed to the livestock after chipping or slicing in a pulper.

By the 1960s, a combination of factors affected the turnip trade: mainly farmers' reluctance to do the intensive work and the failure of processors' organization. George Nessner created an integrated turnip-marketing unit on the west side of Guelph Township, where he grew, processed and marketed turnips. Nessner says that the development of the Stanhay Precision Turnip Seeder in the 1960s was the most important factor in reducing the labour component. Furthermore, a turnip harvester adapted from a carrot harvester was developed. Sprays took care of weeds and aphid control.

There is an interesting anecdote on how Wellington County turnips became a favourite vegetable in Boston, Massachusetts and surrounding area. A Rockwood turnip producer named McKeon was also a sheep farmer, and when showing sheep at a Boston Fair in the 1930s, he took several bags of turnips for his sheep. A Bostonian took one home, cooked it and found the taste excellent. Brad Kurtz of Kurtz Produce says the local turnip has a sweeter flavour because of soil nutrients and a sharper frost which mellows the flavour. A niche market remains in the Boston area. Kurtz Produce of Ariss is currently the only producer of turnips in Guelph Township.

Corn

Until the middle of the century most corn grown in the township was ensilage corn (chopped and stored in a silo) and there was relatively little grain or cob corn grown. However, new varieties, which were suited to soil type and heat units, were developed and grain corn became a major crop.

The production of grain corn has more than doubled since 1975 in Guelph Township. Yields have quadrupled during that same time period. It is said that 10 percent of the items sold in a supermarket derive from corn including starch, oil and sugar. One use, which has not realized its full potential, is fuel ethanol, again derived from corn. Ethanol production plants exist in Ontario, but there has been a resistance on the part of automobile manufacturers to endorse ethanol as an alternative or even a major component of fuel for use in internal combustion engines. Gasoline containing ethanol today may be purchased locally at the UPI Gas Bar, formerly the Co-op Gas Bar on County Road 124, and at Sunoco stations.

The Farmers' Market

At the beginning of the 20th century farmers had little choice in market systems. Essentially Guelph Township farmers could sell their products locally to the stores or the various farmers' markets, or ship it to processors and other more formal dealers.

The Guelph Farmers' Market was a destination for many local farmers every Saturday morning, and in the past on Wednesdays. It provided a service for urban and rural dwellers alike. Farmers could sell the garden produce and such goods as butter, eggs and flowers; urbanites could stock their pantry with fresh goods and even acquire fodder and bedding for their own livestock. In other words, the early relationship was a reciprocal one.

The occasion was also a social event, as it is today, with buyers and sellers developing a relationship that extends beyond that connected with the commercial trade of supermarkets and their customers. In August 1934, a writer with the *Guelph Mercury* noted this in the weekly article about market prices and conditions:

> "Guelph citizens who do not visit their own market on Saturday morning miss something that is of real value. It is a glorious place, a delight to the housekeeper. There may be something about the sunshine that floods the square in front of the market, where produce is spilled around the booths in rich maturity, that raises the spirits, for there is always an air of happiness and camaraderie about the place."

A more recent article (1984) in the *Mercury* simply stated that over time "its reputation for quality and hospitality remains unchanged...the mainstay of the community."

For farmers' wives, the market provided a chance for them to mingle as well as to make some extra money. It was the women, after all, into whose realm fell the chores of milking and the making of butter and cheese. Women were also mainly responsible for the vegetable gardens, and it was these goods that made their way to the local market. Until the First World War, hay was sold in the market loose or baled on a regular basis. Special and seasonal crops such as maple syrup and cherries also made their way to market. Farm men were not available to attend markets in the peak labour periods of spring and autumn when sowing and reaping took up their time. During such times Guelph citizens relied more upon people known as "market gardeners." These included J. Fleming of Elizabeth Street, J.K. Skinner of Grange and the Franchettos of Grange Road East who had 20 acres of market garden. There were also hawkers and peddlers who made their way up from as far away as Hamilton.

The prices, like the products, varied in accordance with availability and economic factors. The sale of produce at the Guelph Farmers' Market rose steadily over the first decade of the 20th century to peak in the late 1920s. In January 1903, for example, butter fetched 21 cents a pound; eggs, 20 to 30 cents a dozen; chickens, 40 to 80 cents a pound; apples, 40 to 65 cents a bag; and potatoes, $1 a bag. In 1912 they were purchased at 25 to 28 cents; 40 to 43 cents; 15 to 20 cents; $1.50; and $1.25 to $1.60 respectively. By January 1922 prices had increased again slightly. The bottom fell out of the market, however, with the arrival of the Depression. Butter was now bringing in only 23 cents a pound; eggs could be had for 20 to 25 cents a dozen, while chickens had fallen to 15 cents a pound; apples to 50 cents a bag; and potatoes to 60 to 90 cents a bag. One farmer stated that during this time period, with a stall costing 25 cents, a farmer could leave the market with much of the produce unsold and actually lose money. Even the return to "good times" with the war did not result in prices commensurate with those of the 1920s.

The year 1912, the date of the beginning of increased separation between producer and consumer in the dairy market, also marked the growth of legislation related to meat production. The Guelph Board of Health pushed towards greater control over the meat processors in the city. This, as in the case of milk, was to affect farmers selling their products at market. In both cases it was a matter of "sanitary" conditions for all parties. Cattle to be slaughtered or milked had to be "healthy." This included animal inoculation as well as healthy living conditions. The city tried from at least 1908 to establish a municipal abattoir. As late as 1927 they had still failed to do so. Even shipping methods were being questioned. The Humane Society saw that poultry cages were changed to become more humane for their occupants during their trip to market

Eggs were also to fall under government jurisdiction. In 1925 the federal government through the Department of Agriculture began to set standards for egg sellers based on the method known as grading. All people selling eggs even on local markets after the summer of 1925 were expected to take them first to a grader. In Guelph the grader was located at the Farmers' Market. Farmers complained of lineups and lost customers. Even the Women's Institute objected to city council about the law. The city, for once, could blame someone else. In fact, by 1932 both levels of higher government had aligned their legislation in favour of grading. Although the governments claimed it benefited the producer and the consumer, there was one group for whom it did not - the small casual producer, usually a farmer's wife.

At the end of the century, the vendors at market are once again the focus of the health board regulations, which may threaten the existence of the local market. Baked goods have to be prepared in a separate kitchen in the home, and eggs have to be properly graded.

Products of the Matthews-Wells plant on Victoria Road, 1930-1970.   Source: N. Raithby

Sacks of wool, c. 1900, near the present-day site of the police station.   Source: J. Keleher

CUCUMBERS

The Matthews-Wells Company, founded in 1931, was the primary purchaser of cucumbers in the township. Located on Victoria Road, south of York Road, they operated an extensive plant, manufacturing food products. Some of their raw produce was imported from farms in Prince Edward Island, but many township farmers were contracted to supply gherkins and cucumbers. After some decades of successful operation the company was bought out and gradually phased out production.

BEANS

The soybean has become a very popular crop in Guelph Township. As a legume it tends to enrich the soil by fixing nitrogen in its root nodules. The oil produced from the mature bean is widely used in margarine, salad oil and mayonnaise. Soybeans are also widely grown in the United States, China, and Brazil, and as a consequence, a crop failure anywhere else in the world means the price tends to rise, while a world surplus causes prices to fall. This is a crop that requires relatively little care and we do have heat units suitable for the production of many varieties. As a

component in so many foods, intensive research is on-going and new varieties are being developed constantly.

Though not as widely produced as the soybean, white beans do well in Guelph Township. Their cultivation and harvesting generally requires more expense and work: they have to be sown more widely apart, and in harvesting, they must be cut, dried, then combined.

Most cereal grains today are harvested by the producer and stored either on the farm or at a comprehensive grain supply company. In Guelph Township these are Woodrill, First Line Seeds and Sharp's Farm Supply. Drying and elevator storage is available. The grain may be sold, or if one expects the price to rise, it may be stored in the elevator. A phone call on any day will effect the sale of the grain. Some farmers choose to use the futures market when even before the crop is planted one agrees to sell a certain amount at a specified price. This marketing practice gives the producer more price stability on a long-term basis.

At the beginning of the 21st century producers are entering a new phase of cereal grain production with the arrival of genetically modified seed, but this new innovation is being met with some concern.

Conversely, there is a popular return to organic farming with home delivery of organic produce as well as a selection of organic goods being sold in grocery stores locally and at the Guelph Farmers' Market.

Alternative Farming

FURS

There are two aspects to the fur business: harvesting of wild furs and fur ranching. The wild-fur trade was one of the earliest reasons for the exploration of North

America. Even after the settlement of Guelph Township the trapping of fur-bearing animals continued to provide a supplementary income for some farmers. The heart of the fur-marketing business was on lower Spadina Avenue in Toronto. The only licensed local fur buyer in the township was E.D. Mitchell. The trapper could send his furs directly to the Spadina furriers but most chose to sell them locally. A trapper's license cost $5 up until mid-century, although the farmer-trapper did not need a licence if the animals were taken on his own property.

Furs were a seasonal trade with muskrat in the spring, and wild mink, fox, raccoon, skunk and weasel in late autumn and early winter. There was a consistent demand for these furs until mid-century. The fur trade, like all other businesses, ultimately relies on market demand for its existence, and fashion is the arbiter for the demand for furs. By the 1950s the wild-fur trade was being challenged by the advent of artificial fibres, and by the import of furs from northern Europe. At the end of the 20th century there is still some harvesting of raw furs by people who enjoy the activity, but as a means of supplementary farm income, trapping is virtually extinct.

Mink ranching in Guelph Township is associated with the Parkinson name. Archie Parkinson started his mink ranch near Armstrong's Mills in 1933. In the early years Archie combined trapping of wild furs and mink ranching. Ranch mink had to overcome a certain bias in favour of wild mink, but in competition it became evident that ranch mink could provide pelts of more even quality, consistency and colour. By careful selective breeding "mutation mink" was developed, allowing certain variations in colour. Although in limited demand domestically, as the century advanced, an international market opened up for Canadian mink and today most is sold in the Far East. Several other Mount Pleasant farmers took on mink as a sideline but Ross Parkinson and his sons have carried on the family tradition most strongly.

O.W. Thompson Fox Ranch on Highway 7 East, 1929.

Source: I. Morrision

Archie Parkinson's autumn catch of raccoon with a few fox pelts at extreme right, c. 1940.

Source: Vera Parkinson

Long furs, such as fox and raccoon, enjoyed a period of popularity from the 1920s to 1950, and fox was very much in demand. Archie Parkinson raised some fox before turning his attention to mink, but the O.W. Thompson Company had two large fox ranches in Guelph Township: the larger one on Highway 7 East across from the present Guelph airport, the smaller on County Road 124 near the Lake Road (County Road 34) junction. Fox ranching had been pioneered in the Maritimes, and it was from Prince Edward Island that Charlie Morrison was recruited to be manager of the larger ranch. Each ranch had an elaborate wire netting structure to enclose pens. An observation tower allowed the manager surveillance of the area. The Thompson Company also had fur ranches in Waterloo County. Fox fur neckpieces, jackets, and even coats were very popular, with fine silver and black pelts commanding prices from $300 to $400. By 1950 there was no longer an effective demand.

Labour

Farm labour can be divided into two types: family and hired. Family labour comprised the backbone of the family farm throughout the first 50 years of the 20th century. It was the family who planted, weeded, hoed and gathered in a never-ending cycle. Women tended to milk the cows and gather the eggs, make the cheese and churn the butter. Men often fed the livestock, cleaned the stables, cultivated the land, put in and harvested the crops.

Arthur Cutten, "The Little Wheat King"

Born in Guelph in 1870, Arthur "Buzz" Cutten left his home at the age of 18 to seek work in Chicago. There, in his first job as a messenger boy for the Marshall Field Department Store, he earned $7.50 weekly. Two years later he joined the Chicago office of grain brokers A.S. White and Company as a bookkeeper and learned the grain and trading business. In 1897, he purchased a membership on the Chicago Board of Trade. Cutten quickly gained prominence as a speculator in corn and wheat. By the time he expanded into Wall Street in 1925, he was a 54-year-old multi-millionaire.

Cutten is described as a bespectacled, stiffly-collared, unassuming type of man; always the gentleman but with a dry sense of humour. The *New York Times* wrote, "compared to him the Sphinx was a blatherskite."

This intense nature is reflected in a tale his nephew, James Cutten, recalls of a robbery at the Cutten home. Arthur, his wife Maud and several servants were locked in a vault as the robbers fled with some loot. Other servants quickly set them free so Arthur and his men were immediately able to apprehend some of the suspects. After this episode he kept a pistol tucked under the cushion of his favourite chair "should the need ever arise." Over the years, Cutten sought the remaining robbers at his own expense, not because they had robbed him but because they had used inappropriate language in front of his wife. He tracked the last one to Alberta. The old robber asked what Cutten now planned to do. "Nothing," Cutten replied. "I just want you to know you did not get away with it."

Cutten may, arguably, have got away with one of the most devastating 'robberies' of the 1930s. When the big crash came in 1929, the "Wheat Baron" lost heavily on paper but not as much as many investors in the stock market. Because of this, it was rumoured he had a part in causing the great stock crash. In fact, the *Toronto Star* called Cutten "the Samson who pulled down the pillars of the exchange."

The economic climate in those lean years did, however, interfere with Cutten's plans for Guelph. On one of his visits to the Cutten home, "Tranquille" at the corner of Grange and Stuart streets, he announced plans to build a golf course and a recreation complex, complete with a football and a cricket field, and baseball and tennis facilities, to be located in the area of the Ontario Agricultural College. He also had plans for a downtown luxury hotel operated by the Canadian Pacific Railway. The announcement of the project caused a great stir in town. The golf club was completed, costing Cutten three quarters of a million dollars, a staggering sum in 1931 when the country was in the midst of a depression. Unfortunately, other events intervened to prevent the completion of his other elaborate plans.

In 1934, the Grain Futures Commission in the United States accused Cutten of making false reports of his grain-holding to manipulate the price of grain and subsequently barred him from trading on the grain market. Although he was later acquitted on appeal, in 1936 a federal grand jury in Chicago returned an indictment against the speculator on another charge - income tax evasion. The internal revenue department claimed Cutten owed almost a million dollars in back taxes. A few months later Cutten died in Chicago. He was buried in Guelph's Woodlawn Cemetery, a property of which he had been a benefactor over the years.

Local legend says that Arthur buried his fortunes somewhere on the Cutten Club site. About a year after his death, U.S. revenue agents visited the club searching for a suspected 90 million dollars. Nothing was found. While the rumour is completely unsubstantiated, it hasn't stopped people from digging on the grounds for the treasure.

– Ceska Brennan

Other Land Uses

GOLF

Increasing popularity of golf and the growing population in Guelph made the development of three golf courses feasible in the township.

- Arthur Cutten opened Guelph Township's earliest golf course, the Cutten Club, in 1931.
- Ariss Valley Golf and Country Club was developed in 1993 on a farm owned by David Hasson. The headwaters of the Hopewell Creek run through a corner of the former farm.
- The Guelph Lake Golf and Country Club on County Road 124 North, formerly the Stephen Lewis farm, enjoys an attractive elevation across from Guelph Lake. The old stone farmhouse was converted into an attractive clubhouse for the 1998 opening.

During the wars this division of labour was affected. The shortage of available farm labour meant that women and girls became more active in what were perceived as male roles. In a look at the situation in August 1942 one reporter wrote: "Girls are driving tractors, doing hoeing, even building the loads of hay. On some farms even the farmer's wife goes out and drives the binder."

For men and women alike it was a life that demanded skill and energy. Help for such work as planting and haying could be gained from neighbours and relatives, sometimes one and the same. Next door neighbours helped one another in the major chores or in times of sickness and worry. Guelph farmers, such as George Holmwood, who farmed on Highway 6 across from the Novitiate, helped his neighbours and they him; his diary tells of him helping the Kennedys, Jerry Fox and Harry Hayden with the threshing. It was a reciprocal arrangement with sometimes no money changing hands.

Where money did come into question was in hiring workers. Farmers did frequently employ people to help out on the farm. These could be permanent or casual hired hands. Some even viewed themselves as "apprentice farmers." A Major Smith who worked for the Watson family at their farm "Cottingham" was one such man. In a collection of his writing, he describes a typical day in 1919 as beginning at 6:30 a.m. and ending 12 to 13 hours later. During that time period, he fed 31 cows and calves, (milking at least one); prepared the milk; cleaned the separator; pumped water for the stock; turned the cows out; watered and bedded the horses; cleaned the stalls; put hay down for the sheep; and fed turnips to the horses, cows and pigs. At the end of the day he was expected to repeat some of the chores and prepare the animals for the night. The tasks varied according to the farm and the farmer who employed him. In some instances hired hands were treated well, being housed in the same type of conditions as the farmer and his family. Hearty meals and laundry were included and the hand was allowed to take part in other aspects of family and community social life. This seems to have been the case with Major Smith. The Watson family provided him with a small cottage (in somewhat rough shape), Mrs. Watson invited him to meals on a regular basis, and Mr. Watson took him to such events as the Guelph Winter Fair. At other farms such hospitality was not always the case, as Guelph historian Terry Crowley noted in his study of hired hands.

The source of such labour varied. Previous to the First World War, Guelph Township farmers utilized their neighbours' sons and drew from a pool of various men, some just passing through. Wages were around $15 to $20 per month. In the 1930s wages and hours both declined after a surge in the 1920s. In 1933 a hired hand could expect the sum of $10 to $15 a month for a period of three to four months. This increased to $15 to $20 per month in 1934 for a seven to eight-month period.

Between the wars another source became available in the form of Vimy Ridge Boys. In 1926 the Ontario government revamped the old Vimy Ridge Farm, located off what is now called Niska Road. They changed its original purpose of veteran rehabilitation to training immigrant youth farmers from England. An agreement between the British and Ontario governments was entered into that gave them about 300 boys between the ages of 15 and 17 to train and settle on Canadian farms. They would be trained by members of the Ontario Agricultural College and given actual experience on local farms for three years. Tom Gilchrist and T.K. Henderson were among the local farmers who hired these workers to help run their farms. In the early 1930s there is mention of a good demand for their services, in fact at this point the demand was greater than the supply. The money the boys received was originally intended to be the going rate. In actuality the amount varied from farm to farm and from circumstance to circumstance. The Vimy Ridge Farm experiment did not survive beyond the Depression. It was bought out in 1932 by the Walker family and returned to private farming. Today, most of the old farm has been excavated for gravel.

Guelph Township diarist, George Holmwood.
Source: Ted Fox

THE THRESHING BEE

A "bee" in this sense means a time of communal activity. The term came into use in the 18th century, and is derived from Old English "ben boon," meaning neighbourly help. It was adopted for silo filling, and in some areas for cutting wood, and of course, the barn-raising bee.

The threshing bee, which disappeared by mid-century, is a fondly remembered aspect of farm life since it represented that spirit of co-operation and community effort that reflects a very positive aspect of rural life. Each community would have a family who had established a business as threshers at harvest time. The Berner family in the Paisley Block, and the Smiths in West End and Mount Pleasant were the owners of a tractor and threshing machine. Other township threshers at various periods included Andrew Smith, Jack McCrae, Matt Kirby and Morris Fitzjohn. A stook threshing sometimes took place in August, in which case six neighbouring farms would each send one man with a team and wagon. If not stook threshing, there would always be a barn threshing in late autumn. Once the grain had been stored inside, threshing could be arranged without concern for the weather. An endless drive belt powered the threshing machine from a distance of about 50 feet. Only the tractor was exposed to the elements and since it was sitting there with only the pulley at work it really did not matter a great deal if it might happen to rain.

The threshing machine was located on the drive floor of the barn. One man was positioned on a platform beside the feeder and a group of four or five men forwarded the sheaves to him in relay style. He was to be judicious enough to

Barn raising at the Card farm after the original barn was destroyed by lightening, 1904.   Source: Card Family Collection

Threshing equipment, Marden, c. 1910.

Source: West End Tweedsmuir History

feed the sheaves at the appropriate rate, even though, in theory, an automatic feeder would stop if fed too heavily. The great straw pipe at the rear of the threshing machine would be aimed off to a mow where the straw, stripped of its grain, was to be stored for bedding. Another person had to be in the granary to ensure that the grain did not plug the pipe at its end and that the granary bins were appropriately filled.

Threshing usually started at 7 a.m., and if everything was working well there would be a short break at 10 for coffee and a pastry. Threshing was resumed at 10:15 and continued to noon, at which time even the tractor was shut down for the lunch break. The threshers by this time were usually coated with dust; men would take off their shirts and shake them, and a fellow thresher would use a broom to clean away dust from his co-workers. Usually a wash tub was placed on a side lawn with soap and ample towels.

Lunch, in truth, was a full-course dinner. Since the threshing circuit took each man to his neighbours' table for several meals, only the best food would do, often a roast of prime rib as entree and several types of pie for dessert. The afternoon would pass in the same way with a coffee and pastry break at 3 p.m. and dinner at 6. With a gang like this, often a nine-hour threshing would complete the work for a year, but it might take another half or whole day.

This was the threshing bee that prevailed during most of the first half of the 20th century. The threshers' charge in 1940 was $5 per hour. For this the farmer got tractor, threshing machine and the two men who travelled with the outfit. The six men who constituted the labourers for the threshing bee simply exchanged labour;

such an arrangement was to the mutual benefit of each farmer, since he too would get his threshing done. Threshing day was a time of great excitement, lots of work and fellowship.

The coming of the Second World War meant other measures had to be taken. In some instances an exchange system between Western Canada's farmers and those in Ontario took place. Although in existence prior to the Second World War, the practice gained the status of necessity during the war years, when the shortage of farm labour reached crisis proportions. In 1942, 27 farmers from out west arrived in the Guelph area. They were to remain until August 5, at which point, or shortly thereafter, Guelph Township farmers were to head out west to help them in their harvest. In 1943, for example, Simon Bruder, James C. Kurtz, Wilfred L. Kurtz, R. McDonald and Allen E. Hayden all went out west from the area.

Another source of labour for Guelph farmers came from a less conventional source. The prisoners from the Ontario Reformatory were sent out to the farms. This lasted only for one year, 1942. The service was discontinued without a reason in the following year.

However, the war also encouraged other innovative means of coping with the shortage of labour. This included the early release of many school children and the extension of their summer vacation in order to help out on farms. Although school-aged farm children had been doing this since youth, governments at the time urged urban children to help out. In 1940 it was announced that students who volunteered for farm work would receive special permits. In 1941, 100 students (70 boys and 30 girls) from Guelph Collegiate Vocational Institute were released early to go to local farms.

A further measure, the Farm Labour Agreement, negotiated between the Dominion and Ontario governments in 1941, set the standards for non-traditional farm labour. Farmerette Brigades, Women's Land Brigades and the Farm Girls'

Brigades were part of this concept. City workers were encouraged to take their vacations on a farm. Local farmers had mixed reaction to these suggestions. J.L. Doughty of RR 1, Guelph, felt that it was a "wonderful idea" but also noted that it would be difficult for "city boys." S. Gray of RR 6, Guelph, agreed, stating that "these school boys could assist greatly right now, even if they couldn't do more than pitch the sheaves." W.B. Bailey of Ariss was less optimistic. He felt the "season would be over before they knew what they were doing. Yet, again maybe it would be alright if someone was always there to oversee their work."

Mechanization

In the latter half of the 19th century there were several small farm machinery manufacturing shops in Guelph. Louden, Gowdie, Cossitt, Tolton and Gilson each were making some limited lines of equipment. With the exception of Gilson, which was a more diversified company (washing machines, and later, refrigerators), these companies were to pass out of existence as competition from more specialized companies developed. Steam tractors had replaced the "horsepower" (a gear ratio device) as a source of pulley power.

The Guelph Novitiate

Relaxing on the verandah of the villa in 1914. Left to right:
H. Gauthier, H. Bourque, Tom Bedford, Mr. Bedford.
Source: Father Joseph Leahy, S.J., Ignatius College

The Guelph Novitiate was founded in 1912 by the Society of Jesus on a property north of the city of Guelph, part of which was once known as "Langholm." It had been a working farm when it was purchased by the society and has continued to be so. The idea of the farm was to make the community it served self-sufficient. The result was the approach common to farming in the area: mixed farming. There were cattle, dairy cows and chickens. Crops such as apples and vegetables were grown. Hay and oats were produced for animal fodder.

Everything that could be was put back into the farm. What could not be made was bought locally. The United Co-operatives of Ontario in Guelph provided the Jesuits with seed and animal feed. At one time such local dairies as the Royal Dairy in Guelph bought the milk. While cream may have been produced on the farm in the early days, excess milk and products such as butter and cheese were best made elsewhere. There was also a need for updating or repairing farm machinery. The local dealers such as Hanna's in Guelph and McKinnell's in Marden supplied equipment to keep the farm running. Still, much of the work was done manually. Brother Leo Voisin milked the herd by hand until the purchase of a milking machine in 1944. Brother Alvin Brady ran the orchard, seeing to the pruning of trees when he grew older and could no longer continue the work in the fields. Apples continue to be sold to the people of Guelph and surrounding areas.

In essence the community was a closed unit for much of the first half of the century. Interaction with the local farmers was small but the township around the community occasionally served as a source of farm labour. While the students at the Novitiate helped out with the farm chores, times were financially lean during the 1940s. A local boy, Frank Morn, was hired in 1946. He received a wage, lived in the residence, ate and worked alongside the brothers in the fields. The cattle were butchered on the farm, and Frank Morn was particularly adept at this task. Not all cattle were killed for meat or retained, however. The farm kept only the amount sufficient to their needs. All others were sold, and in the 1940s this meant shipping them to the stockyards in Kitchener.

Although Frank Morn was not the only hired hand to work among the Jesuits he was one of the longest standing. He worked on the land from 1946 to 1966 when he died. He is buried there. With his passing a change came to the farm. The chickens were soon dispensed with, more mechanization took place and the farm began to lose its viability.

In the last three decades, the Jesuit Community has shifted its focus away from a self-sufficient farm to an outreach program. In 1976 Doug McCarthy, a Jesuit and chaplain at the Ontario Reformatory, began to welcome men and women with learning disabilities and social problems to stay at the "Red House" across from the property. By the winter of 1979 the program had expanded, as had the need for residential space. The farmhouse was incorporated into McCarthy's program, the two homes accommodating 15 to 16 persons. In addition, several "day-timers" came regularly to take part in the project. The purpose of this program was to help men and women with learning and psychological problems, many of whom had difficulties with the law. A return to farm work was seen as a means to help them develop their potential. Since 1970 Bob Donaldson has managed the farm. The tasks vary. There is a large cow-calf beef operation with between 80 and 120 beef cattle to be cared for, as well as some pigs, a few sheep and 180 laying hens. The apple orchard must be pruned and tended. Although the Jesuits help out, the residents of this program now perform the work. They have also created a store on the grounds to sell the various wares and products, including eggs, apples, apple cider and a few crafts. All produce is organically grown. At the end of the 20th century the property also served as a centre for spiritual retreats.

Guelph farm machinery ad in the *Guelph Mercury*, 1924.
Source: *Guelph Mercury*

Hanna and Sons letterhead, Guelph, 1938.
Source: Steve Thorning

Guelph Township. Gasoline for tractors cost 11 cents per gallon in 1944 (no road tax). The Farmall had been developed as a row-crop tractor that was adaptable as a general-purpose tractor.

New types of tillage equipment were being developed. A trail-type plow came on the market in the 1920s,

Cockshutt, and later Massey Harris, built manufacturing plants and used mass production methods in Canada. Ed Thompson of Ariss speculates that what really ended the small manufacturer was the formation of International Harvester, a company formed by McCormick-Deering out of a host of smaller companies in Chicago in 1902. In the following year International Harvester Canada established a manufacturing plant in Hamilton, Ontario. Naturally most of their product engineering was developed in the United States. John Deere followed the same course establishing a plant in Welland, Ontario in 1913. In the last third of the 20th century, Deere was to emerge triumphant in the quest for market share in the farm machinery business.

The earliest tractors were powered by one or two-cylinder engines whose momentum was maintained by large flywheels on either end of the crankshaft. Fueled by kerosene, these tractors and stationary engines could produce impressive power at a very low cost.

Henry Ford had great success in the early 1920s with a Fordson tractor powered by a four-cylinder engine. A few of these tractors found their way into Guelph Township, William Fair being among the early owners.

However, it was International Harvester that was to assume an astonishing lead with its Farmall line of machinery. By 1929 they had a commanding 60 percent of all tractor sales in North America, and many of these machines were used in

capable of turning four or five furrows with each passage. The Ford Company made a radical breakthrough with its versatile 9N model in 1939. This tractor with its three-point hitch and hydraulic system was destined to set a trend in tillage machinery. In 1941 the Ford dealer in Guelph was Heber Little and the price for a 9N tractor with a two-furrow plow was $995.

By the late 1930s, the heavily-lugged steel tractor wheels were replaced by pneumatic tires, for increased efficiency and decreased damage to road surfaces. The decade of the forties was one of relative prosperity and many farmers in the township bought their first tractor. The technology was so good by this time that even the most dubious farmers were convinced that a tractor would increase their productivity.

An interesting experiment in farm power was the "Autotrac." Because of a shortage of new tractors during the Second World War, Otaco, a company near Orillia, had designs to make a tractor-like machine. It used a car motor and a bus or truck transmission and differential. It greatly helped to be a mechanic, since few of these pseudo-tractors were reliable. At one time there were at least 50 of these machines in Guelph Township.

Two new pieces of equipment did come on stream and were destined to truly change the whole nature of farming: the combine and the mobile baler. Virtually all the major machinery companies were marketing a combine by the 1940s. These were powered by the power take-off from the farm tractor. They were capable of harvesting any small grains – wheat, oats, barley, rye, plus grass seed. The Allis Chalmers All-Crop 60 sold for $750 in 1948; several township farmers

Ted deVries combining soybeans on J. Mitchell farm, Paisley Road, 1999.
Source: E. Mitchell

Self-tying baler on the Gilchrist farm, 1943. International Harvester Company dominated the farm machinery market to mid-century.
Source: J. Gilchrist

owned the Allis Chalmers but all makes were in evidence. However, the threshing machine was still the preferred method of harvesting in 1950. As a matter of interest, though no longer used in this township, one need only go into Mennonite country near Guelph to see binders and threshing machines still in use.

Mobile baler technology had been pioneered in the 1930s. The Gilchrists of Mount Pleasant had one of the first International Harvester Company self-tying balers in the township in 1942. This technology revolutionized the harvesting of hay and the collection of straw after the combining process. Baler technology has gone from the small rectangular bale weighing 40 pounds to the large rotary bale, at 800 pounds, and the large rectangular bale at 1,000 pounds.

Combine technology progressed rapidly in the last half of the century. The self-propelled combine made increasingly efficient by the use of diesel engines, hydrostatic transmissions and rotary separation technology has largely replaced the pull-type combine. Prices have increased along with size and technology. Most fully-equipped combines top $225,000 in 2000.

 November 1913 – Three lawsuits are launched against the City of Guelph for flood damages that occurred in the freshet floods of 1912-1913. Two occurred by the Guelph Carpet Mills and one by the Guelph Worsted Spinning Company. On January 16, 1914 the "lordship" finds in favour of the complainants stating that the "new bridge (Neeve Street) built in such a manner that it impeded the flow of the river when swollen by the spring freshets." Damages of $41,500 are awarded. The city initially decided to appeal but later changed its mind.

Guelph Lake, 1999, former farmland. Source: *Guelph Mercury*

The dam on the Speed River, which created Guelph Lake, was completed in June of 1976 under the Grand River Conservation Authority (GRCA). The dam was the local effort of a water conservation project started much earlier with the completion of the Shand Dam at Fergus. It was designed for flood control, low-flow augmentation and recreation. Many readers may be surprised to learn that it was not uncommon for part of the city along Wellington Street to experience flooding as late as the 1960s. The GRCA records many floods that wreaked havoc on the mill dams of Guelph as early as the end of the 19th century. In 1929 the records tell of one of the worst floods when heavy snowfalls and spring rains combined to cause flooding of the Speed River carrying away the dam at Goldie Mill.

Negotiations to acquire the land for the Guelph Lake project caused much friction at the time. Farmland and homes had to be expropriated. Twenty landowners were affected, some of them re-locating in entirely new areas of the county. Arriving at an acceptable cash value was a process that took years and caused considerable acrimony.

Guelph Lake is currently the site of an annual music festival, Hillside, dragon boat races, camps and many more activities. It provides Guelph with a recreation facility complete with an interpretative nature centre.

The only remaining log house in Guelph Township, built in the 1830s. Located in the West End.   Source: E. Mitchell, 1999

The old Griffith's Tavern at the junction of the roads to Elora or Fergus. Shown here just before demolition for road restructuring, 1984.   Source: M. Campbell

The Bow Bridge, built by the township in 1916. Located on Stone Road.   Source: E. Mitchell, 2000

Epilogue

Rapidly changing technology has revolutionized farming during the 20th century. The social patterns that had evolved over several generations were challenged at mid-century by economic and technological developments. It would be incorrect to depict life in the first 50 years as something of a rural idyll. People have never been able to devise a utopia in this world. However, those people who lived in the earlier years recall a quality of community life that has been lost.

As noted earlier, community life suffered when the rural schools were closed but it had even more to do with changing economics and political circumstances. Social patterns change relatively slowly whereas economic and political ways change quickly. The fundamental consideration is that in earlier times quality of life took precedence over economic circumstances. Furthermore because of the government's increased involvement in the lives of the individual, people have allowed government to assume responsibilities that once belonged to the family and the community.

In the winter of 2000, police have just broken up a demonstration of Saskatchewan farmers who had occupied the Legislature Building in Regina for over a week. The same problems related to the food grains of Western Canada could be cited in other parts of Canada, even Guelph Township. The farmers' share of the retail dollar is only six percent; this works out to $0.09 cents on a loaf of bread costing $1.50.

In an article in the *Globe and Mail* (February 7, 2000), Canadian Federation of Agriculture President Bob Friesen stated that Canadian farmers are providing "one of the most affordable grocery baskets in the world."

Friesen says "while farmers have worked hard to improve productivity and efficiency, they continue to struggle to eke out a living." The dairy and poultry farmers are protected by both supply management and by control over market price, but this is not true for grain, hog and beef producers.

One bright spot in this is the resilience of the human spirit and the constancy of the land. In 1924 Peter McArthur, Ontario essayist writing about Oxford County, defined the constancy of the farm: "It is solid right down to the centre of the earth. It stays right where it is through depressions, panics, wars, and every other kind of human foolishness. Even an earthquake would only joggle it, and this is not an earthquake region." Neither is Guelph Township.

SOURCES

Ambrose, L.M. *For Home and Country: the Centennial History of the Women's Institute in Ontario.* Boston Mills Press, Erin, ON. 1996.

Bloomfield, E., Stelter, G.A., Turner, J. *Guelph and Wellington County: a Bibliography of Settlement and Development since 1800.* University of Guelph, Guelph, ON 1988.
A catalogue of the various sources of information relating to Wellington County.

Byerly, A.E. *The Beginnings of Things.* Guelph Publishing Company, Guelph, ON 1935.
The author was an interesting personality. Born in Iowa, he trained as an osteopath and eventually settled in Guelph.

Hannam, H.H. *Pulling Together for 25 Years. A Brief Story of Events and People in the United Farmers' Movement in Ontario 1924-1939.* United Farmers of Ontario. Toronto, ON 1940.

Illustrated Atlas of County of Waterloo (1881) and County of Wellington (1877). Reprint edition. Port Elgin: Ross Cumming 1972.
This atlas is often overlooked by modern readers. It does not have biographical sketches, but has interesting photographs and advertisements.

Historical Atlas of Wellington County. Historical Atlas Publishing Co. Toronto 1906. Reprint 1972.
A useful source of maps and biographical information. Since it was published on the basis of subscription, not all families are included.

Johnson, L.A. *History of Guelph 1827-1927.* Hunter Rose Co. Toronto, ON 1977.

Middleton, J.E. and Landon, F. *Province of Ontario. A History 1615-1927.* Dominion Publishing Company. Toronto, ON 1927.

Report of the Ontario Milk Industry Inquiry. Province of Ontario, Toronto, ON 1965.

ACKNOWLEDGMENTS

My thanks to the many people who contributed to the Guelph Township unit, with special recognition of the assistance of Vera Bruce, Marian Campbell, Marjorie Durnford, Gord Guthrie, Robert Lyon, Warren Husband and cartographer Marie Puddister.

NOTES

Mills There is little printed on the individual mills of the township. A student's essay on Armstrong's Mills is included in the Riverside Women's Institute Tweedsmuir History. The West End and Mosborough Tweedsmuir histories have some related material.

Schools Some records in custody of the Upper Grand District School Board exist. A few Sunday school records are available.

Ontario Provincial Winter Fair The yearly accounts of the fair in the *Guelph Daily Mercury* 1900-1939 are the most valuable sources. An article in the Guelph Historical Society Publications volume IX, No.1, 1969 by Roberta Gilbank deals with fairs before the Ontario Provincial Winter Fair.

Mechanization A major theme in agriculture during the entire century. Many books on the subject have been published, among which are :

Broehl, W.G. *John Deere's Company: a History of Deere and Company and Its Times.* Doubleday. New York. 1984

Wendel, C.H. *International Harvester - 150 Years.* Motorbooks International. Osceola, WI. 1992.

Co-operatives Archives, University of Guelph.

Field Husbandry Ontario Ministry of Agriculture, Food and Rural Affairs is an excellent source of data on farm acreage, returns, prices, etc.

Animal Husbandry Each breeders' organization has published in whole or in part its own history.

Guelph Township Horticultural Association The organization has had a historian from its beginning (1922). The original records are held by Betty Larter and records are also on microfilm at the Wellington County Museum and Archives.

Women's Institutes The Tweedsmuir histories are maintained by each branch as a repository of information about each area - Riverside, West End and Mosborough.

CHAPTER 3

DOING BUSINESS IN GUELPH

STEVE THORNING

THE SHADOW OF THE NINETEENTH CENTURY

To claim that the city of Guelph was poised, as the year 1900 heralded a new century, on the starting line of a new economic era, is simultaneously an exaggeration and a truism. Historians, in common with the larger aggregation of people best identified as history buffs, are fond of dividing the past, as a matter of convenience, into segments of centuries and smaller fractions of decades. Business cycles only rarely encounter sudden disruptions, either up or down. To understand what happened in the first decade of the century, it is necessary to comprehend the trends and trajectories of the economic forces at work in the decades before, and in particular, the 1890s, when Guelph's business leaders strove to build their city into an industrial centre deserving of wide notice.

The final generation of the 19th century had not been, in the comparative context that so enamoured Victorian observers, an outstanding one for the Royal City. In 1870, Guelph had ranked sixth in size among Ontario cities. Nearby Brantford overtook Guelph about 1890, and by the turn of the century Windsor had done so as well, with Berlin and Peterborough coming up fast.

Guelph's stoutest economic roots ran back to the 1850s and 1860s as a regional market town, and vestigial health still remained on these roots in 1900. Of the flour mills, only one remained as a producer of any significance. The People's Flour Mills, operated by James Goldie and his sons, Lincoln and Roswell, had survived narrow profit margins and cut-throat competition to become a major producer, turning out some 100,000 pounds of its popular Dictator and Snowdrift brands of flour each day. At the same time, its local ties had diminished. Grain in carload lots from the prairies replaced queues of local farmers' wagons as the prime source of inputs. The flour, much of it destined for eastern Canada, now left the mill in cloth bags, rather than the traditional wooden barrels manufactured by a once substantial cooperage industry in Guelph, employing some 75 coopers.

The cattle business, sustained by the prosperous stock-raising farmers of Guelph Township, bolstered Guelph's position as something of a cattle town, but the rambunctious cattle market and monthly cattle fairs had receded into history by 1900. The Guelph Armoury was to rise in a couple of years on the land once dedicated to cattle sales. Increasingly the cattle buyers visited farms to make their purchases. They preferred to ship their cattle from the smaller stations surrounding Guelph: Mosborough, Gourock and Marden. It was possible in 1900 to encounter grizzled veterans of the city's changing fortunes, only too delighted to regale the stranger with tales of the old cattle market days of the 1850s and 1860s.

Still, in 1900, the rural presence remained. Wagons loaded with grain, wool and livestock trundled up and down the major streets. From a compound at the corner of Wilson and Carden, woodsmen peddled cordwood chopped from unlogged portions of township farms. Farther down Carden, at the corner of Wyndham, the old farmers' market shelter had only recently been demolished to make room for Jubilee Park, which itself would soon be claimed for a new station by the Grand Trunk Railway.

John Galt and the Canada Company had intended the market grounds, a large triangle bounded roughly by Carden, Wilson and Surrey streets, to be the centre and focus of the town. Indeed, many of the first businesses and hotels had clustered around the west and south edges of this tract. Civic leaders could not contain their glee in 1856 when the first Grand Trunk trains plied the new railway line which neatly bisected the market grounds.

The merchants, though, voted with their feet. Wyndham Street began to attract the major stores in the 1860s. A decade later St. George's Square had become the commercial focus of Guelph, and a building boom in the 1870s pushed the shopping district farther north on what was then known as fashionable Upper Wyndham Street.

Guelph, in 1900, could boast a population of a little over 11,000, roughly the equal of Fergus in 2000, and an increase of only about a thousand from 20 years previously. The new downtown commercial blocks had been constructed on the promise of a prosperous rural trade and a growing industrial sector within the city itself. Neither materialized to the extent of other towns, and most pointedly, those nearby in the Grand River watershed: Berlin, Galt and Brantford. Some of these merchants had supplemented their retail trade with a substantial wholesale business, supplying smaller stores to the north and west: James Massie in groceries, John Hogg in dry goods, Nathan Higinbotham in drugs, and John Horsman in hardware, for example.

But in 1900 the days of the wholesalers had passed. Merchants such as George Ryan, and up-and-comer D.E. MacDonald, represented the new era. They filled their large stores with ample stocks, and took advantage of the prosperity of the late 1890s that put more money in farmers' pockets. The commercial core of Guelph had been overbuilt in the 1870s. In the 1880s, Guelph merchants had chartered trains for Saturday shopping excursions from Elora and Fergus to the north. When the Grand Trunk discontinued these trains after a barrage of protests from those good burgs, Guelph merchants began refunding the price of railway tickets for their out-of-town customers. Offsetting these sales was the business diverted to the Toronto mail order houses, which grew to alarming proportions in the 1890s, adversely impacting local retailers everywhere. But let us take a closer look at the Guelph of 1900. It was plain that business volumes had finally caught up with the available retail space. The downtown seemed fresh and new, which it was. Many of the buildings had been standing only about 25 years or so, and their new plate glass windows, shaded by colourful canvas awnings, awed the public with bountiful stocks of consumer goods.

Three successive good years had produced a feeling of optimism in the commercial sector, and with it a renewed belief in the beneficence of progress. Visibly symbolizing the new era were the streetcars, converging on St. George's Square all day from four directions at 20-minute frequencies, as they had done since September 1895. The system, owned and operated by Guelph brewer and businessman George Sleeman, whose expansive gestures, ebullient optimism and all-round confidence had buoyed the city through its ups and downs for more than two decades, provided not only a practical service, but demonstrated to anyone who cared to glance at the shiny rails that Guelph had become a real city. In 1900 Sleeman was still in full stride, with a major role to play in the coming decade of Guelph's history.

 February, 1914 – Norman Ryan of the G. B. Ryan and Company Department Store of Guelph becomes the very first Guelphite to fly. While on a buying trip in England he "goes up in an aeroplane." Later he tells the *Guelph Mercury* it "was delightful, but that it was something he would not want to try every day."

Boosting local business: Faced with competition from shoppers who travelled to Hamilton and Toronto, and with intrusions by mail order houses such as Eatons, downtown Guelph merchants aggressively promoted the downtown core in the early years of the 20th century. Among other things, they offered rebates on railway tickets for customers from Elora, Fergus and other nearby towns, and ran free streetcars for Guelph residents. This conspicuously decorated car, with banners and the Guelph Jazz Band, ran around Guelph about 1920. Source: J. Keleher

Industry and manufacturing had played second fiddle in the marketing and commercial centre that was the Guelph of the middle years of the 19th century. Over time this had become a diverse sector, with some 175 enterprises in the mid-1870s. Barely a half dozen of these were manufacturing firms of major consequence, the vast majority employing only one or two men, and most with lifetimes that rarely spanned two decades. The proprietors of the larger of these establishments, with their allies from amongst the commercial sector, constituted a small group of nabobs who embraced industrial growth as the imperative for Guelph.

Virtually to a man, these were dour, stoic characters, neither exciting in their ideas nor excitable in their personal demeanor. Charles Raymond, the tight-lipped American-born Congregationalist whose sewing machines spread the Guelph name across the continent, and William Bell, the stone-faced manufacturer of equally famous parlour organs, typified the group, which pitched its tent under the banner of the Guelph Board of Trade, with a membership roll, shifting over time, that numbered a couple of dozen.

In comparison with smaller centres such as Elora and Fergus, where industrial employment declined in the late 19ᵗʰ century, the Guelph Board of Trade's success in building the industrial sector of the city can look reasonably impressive. The number of manufacturing firms in the city had declined to 75 or 80 in 1900, but employment, both in absolute numbers and in the percentage of the population employed in industry, stood at all-time highs. Compared to other cities of the same size though, particularly the nearby rivals of Brantford, Galt and Berlin, the Guelph record looked dismal.

Despite the striving of a quarter century, rivals had managed to outpace Guelph. In the 1870s the Guelph Board of Trade nabobs had sought city status as soon as they could qualify – indeed, they began lobbying the provincial government before the city had the requisite 10,000 in population. The designation of city, which brought with it increased powers, particularly those permitting the subsidization of industry, came in April 1879.

A steady stream of subsidy bylaws ensued – some 19 of them between 1880 and 1899. Most exempted manufacturers from the payment of property taxes, normally after meeting minimum requirements for building or employment. During this period, the Guelph Board of Trade, with a few notable exceptions, had little difficulty in guiding city policy. More bonus and subsidy proposals lay ahead in the post-1900 period.

Transportation loomed larger than municipal subsidies in the minds of the business bigwigs. Roads had built Guelph as a market town in the 1850s, and then railways in the 1870s had eroded its vitality, not only diverting business to nearby towns to the north, but also in levying freight rates that, in the certainty of Guelph minds, gouged its shippers. Guelph had boasted two competing lines, the Great Western and the Grand Trunk, but these lines were prone to rate fixing agreements, traffic pooling, and other acts of collusion so popular with 19th-century railway managers. All pretense of competition disappeared with the amalgamation of the two systems in 1882.

The Credit Valley Railway, built to the south of Guelph through Puslinch in 1879, and acquired soon after by the Canadian Pacific Railway, offered the promise of relief, only some 10 miles away, from the Grand Trunk's ruinous rates. When the Canadian Pacific showed no interest in the projected Guelph branch line, Guelph's leading lights incorporated the Guelph Junction Railway, and, under the incessant cheerleading of James Innes of the *Guelph Mercury*, and the urging of

William Bell, convinced the voters to approve the financing of the project by the city. Its promoters, notwithstanding their constant advocacy of the line, invested only $1,000 in aggregate of their own money in it. When the line was finished in September 1888, they leased it to the Canadian Pacific Railway.

In its first dozen years, the line earned some $70,000 for the city– far less than the $150,000 or so expended on debenture payments. Defenders of the line stated that, by forcing the Grand Trunk to lower rates, the project had paid ample dividends. Even so, the Grand Trunk, in 1900, still managed to retain approximately 75 percent of the carloadings in and out of Guelph.

Whatever its concrete benefits, the Guelph Junction Railway project set the tone for business development in Guelph for the following two generations. Piloted by a cross-section of business and civic leaders, its purpose was not to advance a particular firm, but to provide transportation facilities that would allow smaller firms to become established. Most members of the group that pushed the project through to completion operated small and medium-sized firms, and felt most comfortable with others like themselves. They saw the city as a place to live as well as one in which to do business, and all felt an affinity with the prosperous agricultural sector surrounding the city; a feeling strengthened by the presence of the Ontario Agricultural College in Guelph. This tended to discourage both large enterprises and branch plants of American firms. Most

The Guelph Junction Railway Company

PRESIDENT—J. W. LYON.
VICE-PRES—HIS WORSHIP, THE MAYOR OF GUELPH.
SEC.-TREAS.: A. H. MACDONALD

Guelph, Canada, Nov. 26, 1913.

DEAR SIR:

I notice by the list of entries for 1912 that you were an exhibitor at the Ontario Provincial Winter Fair and Fat Stock Show, held in Guelph. I anticipate that you will also be an exhibitor at this year's Fair, which will be held from Dec. 9th to 12th, inclusive.

If you are only a visitor we ask you to secure your transportation via Canadian Pacific and Guelph Junction Railways, if an exhibitor we would ask you to have your freight shipped via Canadian Pacific Railway, and your express by the Dominion Express Company. Both freight and express companies will provide sufficient help, so that your stock will have proper care and attention on their arrival at Guelph, and on their departure from the Fair.

Furthermore, the Canadian Pacific Railway is the best route for your stock to be shipped by, so as to insure prompt delivery and careful handling.

We have a reason for asking you to have your transportation, freight and express routed via Canadian Pacific Railway. The City of Guelph owns 16 miles of this road and they are very largely interested in the earnings, and as Guelph has contributed largely to the success of the Ontario Provincial Winter Fair, we do not think that we are asking too much from you when we ask you to patronize the road. The earnings of this road are very substantial and are increasing year by year.

As the City Council agent for the G. J. R., I am desirous of securing all the business possible for our own road, and would solicit your business. You will find this a safe and convenient route to reach Guelph by.

Thanking you in anticipation of your hearty co-operation,

I am,

Yours respectfully,

R. McDONALD.

Town and Country

No one is more identified with the industrialization of Guelph than J.W. Lyon. But he, like his Guelph Board of Trade associates, fellow Guelph Junction Railway directors and circle of business friends, desired to maintain strong ties between the City of Guelph and agriculture. The Guelph Board of Trade devoted much energy to boosting the Provincial Fair in Guelph and to providing adequate facilities for it. This request, sent to prospective visitors and exhibitors at the 1913 fair, asks for business to be routed via the Canadian Pacific to provide more business to the Guelph Junction Railway. It is a vivid demonstration of the old slogan: one hand washes the other.

Source: Steve Thorning

importantly, the Guelph Junction Railway gave the city's businessmen a taste for public ownership. After 1900, public ownership of the city's utilities headlined all promotional efforts by Guelph council and the Guelph Board of Trade.

Guelph's 19th-century businessmen liked to grumble about the lack of adequate banking facilities in the city. Although they had their choice of three or four banks, the orthodox opinion was that the banks did not provide sufficient credit or banking facilities to underwrite the expansion of business in their city.

The Bank of Montreal was, and still is, the oldest financial institution in Guelph, though the Bank of Commerce could claim an earlier antecedent – it had taken over the Guelph branch of the failed Gore Bank in 1868. These two bank branches dominated the financial sector until the 1890s, with a branch of the relatively weak Ontario Bank a distant third.

It is impossible at this date to say whether banking in Guelph in the pre-1890 era was truly inadequate. Credit availability was only one factor. Local interest rates could rise through lack of competition, or for no apparent reason. There was also a perception that some banks – particularly the Montreal – would reduce credit lines to customers in places such as Guelph in order to employ their funds more profitably elsewhere.

Personal relationships mattered a great deal. Another factor, largely forgotten in today's homogeneous banking climate, is that 19th-century banks differed greatly in their administration of lending accounts, and in their manage-ment of branch banking. A disagreement with his banker could mean hard times for a businessman. Even the largest chartered banks had not yet grown to the point where they had internal departments and layers of middle management. Only two people mattered for the borrowing customer: the local manager and the general manager at head office.

William Bell, with his piano and organ factory the largest industry in the city by the mid 1880s, began to see himself as something of a steward for the general welfare of industry in Guelph. In 1885, Bell met with a group of businessmen from across Ontario who shared his views about inadequate banking facilities. The eventual result was the chartering of the Traders Bank of Canada. The other shareholders elected William Bell vice-president. Though Toronto-based, the Traders intended to concentrate its business in the smaller centres. Guelph would not get a branch until 1890.

Besides the Montreal and the Commerce, two other banks had operated Guelph branches: the Central and the Federal. Weak institutions, they both failed – the Central in 1887 and the Federal in 1888, the latter taking down with it the private Guelph Banking Company, owned by Walter Cutten. Two years later, the faltering Ontario Bank closed its short-lived Guelph branch.

The closure of three of the five Guelph bank branches in a period of less than three years had fewer repercussions than might be expected, though it was a circumstance not experienced by the other cities in the Grand River basin. The Dominion Bank took over the accounts of the Federal Bank in 1888. Of far greater significance was the opening of the Traders Bank in February 1890, which took over the office and accounts of the Ontario Bank branch.

Six months after the opening, the Traders Bank transferred A.F.H. Jones to Guelph as manager. Unlike previous Guelph bankers, who generally preferred a quiet lifestyle spent socializing amongst the social and legal elite, Jones felt more at home with ambitious young businessmen whose accounts he pursued on behalf of the bank. As well, he plunged into civic work of various sorts, serving a term as president of the Guelph Board of Trade, and as a director of a dozen societies and organizations.

The expansive and dynamic personal style of A.F.H. Jones won many new customers for the Traders Bank, and forced the competition to respond. The others began to play a game of catch up. The Bank of Montreal responded to the upstarts by renovating and enlarging its building on St. George's Square in 1892 and beefing up its staff. Nevertheless, Jones continued to recruit new customers, no doubt aided by the fact that William Bell moved up to the presidency of the bank in 1895. The appointment of a second Guelph man, Christian Kloepfer, to the board of directors of the Traders Bank underlined the importance of the Guelph branch. By 1900 the Traders was the leading bank branch in Guelph, and one of the largest in the Traders branch network.

The four Guelph banks of the 1890s – the Montreal, Commerce, Dominion and Traders – provided a competitive but stable financial service sector well in advance of Guelph's economic boom in the first quarter of the 20th century.

The typical bank customer of 1900 was a factory owner or merchant. The majority of Guelph residents at that time seldom entered a bank branch. Bank savings accounts, as we now know them, were still a novelty. Businesses usually paid their wages in cash, and few individuals operated chequing accounts.

For those wishing a safe haven for their money, the post office operated a savings bank that was used by most people with only small sums to save. Another alternative, especially for those with larger hoards of cash, was the Guelph and

Maconell Street, 1903: Downtown Guelph's mix of commercial and industrial activity is clearly evident in this view, which shows the water towers at Bell Piano and Organ, whose factory dominated the block south of Macdonell and east of Wyndham. At the left, the carriages are parked in front of the Albion Hotel's livery stable, now the site of the *Guelph Mercury* offices.　　Source: Wellington County Museum and Archives

Ontario Investment and Savings Society. Established in 1876 as a joint-stock company, with well-known Guelph names such as David Stirton, Alex Petrie and J.E. McElderry dominating the list of shareholders, this institution was a continuation of the old Waterloo Building Society, founded in 1850, which had evolved into the Wellington Permanent Building Society in 1855.

The Guelph and Ontario operated savings accounts, paying one percent more in interest than the chartered banks, and sold debentures to those with larger sums to invest for long terms. These funds were loaned on mortgages to local residents and farmers in the area.

William Bell's active role in the affairs of the Traders Bank helped give that chartered bank a local face, one quite in keeping with the goals and ideals of the group of businessmen who came together in the late 1880s and the 1890s, in large part under Bell's leadership, and who set the tone for the major industrial boom in the years after 1900.

The generation of William Bell and Charles Raymond succeeded in establishing a climate in which Guelph's industrial base could expand and prosper: a group of businessmen with shared goals, who dominated the Guelph Board of Trade and influenced strongly the policies pursued by the city council; a

willingness to subsidize new businesses and expansions with tax concessions and loans, and a growing fondness for public ownership of utilities. As the 20th century began, the Royal City was eager to capture its full share of economic expansion, and to make up for ground lost.

THE OPTIMISM OF A NEW CENTURY

The generation of William Bell and Charles Raymond established the conditions for an economic boom, but the new era would be dominated by others. Raymond died in 1904, having sold his sewing machine factory to a local syndicate in 1897, and Bell had sold his firm a decade before that to a joint-stock company based in England, though he continued to influence its affairs. Dominating the first years of the new century was J.W. Lyon, the American-born book salesman, who levered his success at publishing and distributing religious and inspirational tracts into a career as a land speculator. Lyon made real estate investments in more than a dozen cities, but locally he is best known for his development of a 400-acre tract in St. Patrick's Ward, commencing in 1906, as a combined industrial and residential subdivision. Lyon gave land to factory proprietors, and made his money on the sale of nearby residential lots. The Guelph Junction Railway neatly bisected the land, providing a further inducement to new industries to locate there.

Several times Lyon considered running for mayor, but always backed out, seeking, successfully, a seat on city council only once, in 1906. His milieu was Guelph's Board of Trade, Junction Railway and Board of Light and Heat. An intimate of Sir Adam Beck, the father of Ontario Hydro, he became a tireless advocate of the necessity of public ownership for small industries to prosper. Though prone to wild exaggeration, compulsive optimism, and occasional self-promotion, Lyon enjoyed applying his abilities to boosting the Royal City. Personally, his character contrasted sharply with those of Raymond and Bell. Lyon enjoyed living life to the fullest. In his late sixties he became an enthusiastic motorist, and enjoyed nothing more than taking a carload of his white-knuckled associates for a high-speed joy ride.

A good portion of the industrial growth after the turn of the century came from existing firms. George Sleeman expanded his empire when he opened the Spring Bank Brewery on Edinburgh Road. At the edge of Guelph on Waterloo Avenue, the Standard White Lime Company, formed in 1901 as the continuation of two older firms, began the production of lime products. Its quarry would remain in production for the entire century. In 1902 there were further expansions:

The Raymond Sewing Machine Company: One of the pillars of late 19th century industry in Guelph, the Raymond Company was in decline when this photograph was snapped about 1910. A saturated market for sewing machines, and a rise in store-bought clothing over homemade togs reduced the firm to a minor Guelph industry, despite an attempt to expand the production line to include bicycles and cream separators. The Cleveland-based White Sewing Machine Co. purchased the sprawling complex on Yarmouth and Baker streets in 1916, and closed the operation down permanently in 1922. Source: Donald Coulman

Sam Carter, owner of the Guelph Knitting Company, put up a new factory on Norwich Street. The spring maker James Steele let a contract for a new factory on Woolwich Street, east of Eramosa. It would be one of many moves for this long-lived Guelph firm. In 1904 the Guelph Carpet Company expanded its line to include tapestry carpets, made in a large new addition to its plant on Neeve Street.

Later in 1904, the Taylor-Forbes Company, operating from a complex that included portions of the old Allan distillery, announced another addition to increase its production of lawn mowers and hardware. This firm outpaced all other Guelph industries in its growth after 1900. Taylor-Forbes had its roots in the old A.R. Woodyatt foundry. Originally located on the present site of the Guelph Public Library, Woodyatt purchased the old Allan distillery property in 1898. It had been occupied by the bankrupt McCrae Woolen Mills, which in its day had

 1902 – Guelph forms the first Breweries Union in Canada.

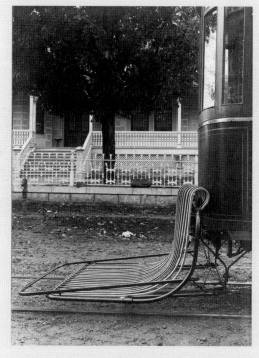

James Steele typified the craftsman who built his business slowly and steadily until, at the end of his career, he could be classed as an industrialist. Beginning in 1885 with two employees, Steele manufactured coiled wire springs and other spring steel products for a market that evolved over the decades. An inventive craftsman, he devised a bumper for the front of George Sleeman's streetcars in 1897 that saved inattentive passengers from being run down. It was so successful that streetcar lines across North America adopted it. As Steele's business expanded, it moved to ever larger quarters, including two locations on Woolwich Street, and in 1926, under the management of his sons, to a former Raymond Sewing Machine building that is now the site of the Baker Street parking lot. Though modest in scale, this would become one of the longest lived of Guelph industries.

Source: Wellington County Museum and Archives, left; 1943 Canada Trade Index, right

been one of the major Guelph employers. When Woodyatt died in 1901, a well-financed group of businessmen, headed by John M. Taylor and George Forbes, purchased the business. Taylor-Forbes began with 75 employees, and the number increased steadily. Seven years later, with more than 325 employees, Taylor-Forbes overtook Bell Piano as Guelph's largest employer.

There were changes as well at the venerable old Bell Piano and Organ Company on Carden Street. The firm expanded its capacity for parlour organs, at the time enjoying a fad, with an addition in 1902. A year later, pipe organs

The Gilson Manufacturing Company on Victoria Road, 1912: One of the major new Guelph industries to arrive in the years before the First World War, Gilson's initially produced farm equipment and engines (and for a time tractors and a few automobiles), before switching to furnaces and refrigeration equipment. Source: J. Keleher

Gilson employees, 1911. Source: Donald Coulman

THE GILSON STANDARDIZED KEROSENE TRACTOR

10-20 H. P.
15-30 H. P.

"The Ultimate Tractor"

Today's Collector's Item

The Gilson Manufacturing Company, for a brief period, supplemented its line of portable gasoline and oil-fueled engines and other farm-related equipment with a tractor, built to the designs of its Wisconson-based parent company. Though it appears cumbersome, this 4-cylinder model rode on roller bearings. The line proved to be unsuccessful. Today a restored example is a valuable and much-admired collector's item.

Source: Steve Thorning

disappeared from the company catalogue.

Two new industries arrived in 1902. The Louden Machinery Company, makers of barn cleaning equipment and hardware, began modestly in the old Drill Shed building with five employees before moving to new premises on Crimea Street. More important was the new Page-Hersey factory on York Road, established when the city provided a $42,500 loan. This industrial subsidy became a hot political issue. Manufacturing light tubing, pipe, and later, automobile parts, the factory employed about 100 men. The Page-Hersey subsidy again became a public issue in August 1906, when American interests purchased the firm.

Two important industries arrived in 1907. The Canada Ingot Iron Company, better known as Armco, set up production in the old Inglis and Hunter foundry beside the Norwich Street bridge. Initially, the firm produced road graders and scrapers, as well as the culverts that later became its specialty.

J.W. Lyon liked to boast that he lured the Gilson Manufacturing Company to Guelph, after the management of the Wisconsin-based company had first decided to locate its Canadian branch plant in Kitchener. In any case, the Gilson plant on Victoria Road in Lyon's St. Patrick's Ward subdivision became one of Guelph's longer-lived industries. Initially, the firm produced farm equipment, including portable engines, tractors for a time, and even an ill-fated motor car. Employment at Gilson's soon reached the 100 mark, quickly making this an important Guelph industry.

Horace "Horrie" Mack

In 1905, a little boy began to keep a daily record of the wild birds and animals he found around Guelph. In 1910, the boy, Horace Mack, went to work for Edward Barelman who had an unusual collection of birds and animals on his property in Eden Mills. Thus began an interest in rare species, particularly wild fowl, that was to remain with Mack his entire life.

Mack joined the Gilson Manufacturing Company in 1911 as an office boy. By 1927 he had worked his way up to president. Not only is he credited with the slogan "Goes like Sixty" that headed the company's ads, but he also gained attention for the pheasants and pea hens that graced the company's Guelph property. Mack was one of the first Canadian naturalists to raise the birds.

The majority of his birds were raised at a game sanctuary located in Eden Mills where he kept his own large collection of ducks, geese, pheasants and peafowl. Many of the birds, domestic and exotic, roamed free on the land. The need for open water that could be maintained year round caused Mack to move his collection to the Niska (Cree for Grey Goose) land bordering Guelph Township where the open water allowed waterfowl to breed successfully. In 1952 he worked towards the designation of the Niska area as a federal wildlife sanctuary. Mack erected a house, barn and fenced paddocks on the property. When he died in 1959 he left a remarkable record of achievements. He had built martin houses and helped establish a wildlife management course at the agricultural college. He had advised officials at Stratford, Ontario, on the care of their swans and helped to create Crown reserves and local parks in area townships and at Rockwood and Elora. The Niska property was bought by the non-profit Ontario Waterfowl Research Foundation. Their main interest was, and still is, wildlife research. The foundation renamed part of the park as the Niska Waterfowl Research Station. The name Kortright was given to the park in 1965 in honour of the late Frank H. Kortright, one of Canada's leading wildlife authorities. Kortright's wife was a great-granddaughter of John Galt, the founder of Guelph. A plaque was laid there in 1967. In that year, approximately 1,000 birds of 50 different species resided at the park located where the ecologically unique Hanlon Creek flows into the Speed River. A thriving tourist destination whose main direction is conservation and study, Kortright Park has played a remarkable role in North American breeding and research programs. Park officials have been credited with the revival of wildfowl species that were once considered threatened. In 2000, it may be Kortright itself that is on the endangered list, as it is now part of the city of Guelph. The surrounding farmland has been urbanized and the park sits in the suburbs, a small oasis in a sea of houses.

– Ceska Brennan

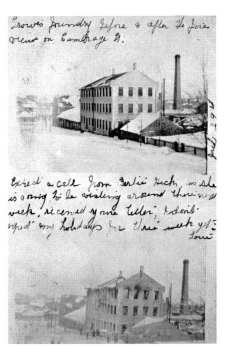

Crowe Foundry: One of the pioneers of Guelph's metal working industry, the Crowe Foundry survived a major fire at its Norfolk Street premises on March 23, 1906. Industrial fires could have a positive element: after this blaze, the Crowe firm moved to a larger and more efficient new plant on Suffolk Street in 1908 that permitted a doubling of production.
Source: Wellington County Museum and Archives

There were several other new industries in Guelph in 1907, some of which prospered for decades. Among the latter was the Guelph Paper Box Company, established by Tolton Brothers, manufacturers of farm implements. The Toltons sold the box company in 1915. It was still a minor industry with less than a dozen employees at that time. Under new owners, the business grew. Another 1907 newcomer was the Guelph Elastic Hosiery Company, with two employees on a second floor flat on Wilson Street. Almost forgotten today are the old Imperial Biscuit Company, founded in 1907 on Cardigan Street, and Barber's Pork Packing Limited, established about the same time on Elizabeth Street.

An economic downturn spooked businessmen in 1908, slowing new industrial investment. The biggest project that year was a new factory for the Crowe Foundry on Suffolk Street, which doubled the capacity of this old Guelph firm, established in 1872. The factory produced grey iron castings, most of which were components for goods manufactured by other companies.

Guelph's boom resumed in 1909, with the incorporation of the Guelph Cotton Company and the Flexible Conduit Company, better known by its later name, Dalyte Electric Company. Originally producing insulated electrical wire and cable, the firm branched into light bulbs in 1914. The factory used a portion of the old Allan's Mill building on the Speed River.

J.W. Lyon attracted three industries to his St. Patrick's Ward subdivision in 1911 and 1912. One was an existing firm, the Guelph Stove Company. Established in 1897, the company had outgrown its cramped premises at the corner of Paisley and Norfolk streets. The new plant on York Road produced a full line of stoves and heaters, including enameled models. Most of the production went to the T. Eaton Company. The Dominion Linens Company, organized by Guelph

Guelph Stove Company, c. 1920s: Long a fixture in St. Patrick's Ward, the Guelph Stove Company produced lines of wood-fired, gas and electric stoves and ranges. This is the casting floor of the foundry department, where workers poured molten iron into moulds of sand to produce some of the components for the firm's products.

Source: Liz Gray

Guelph Stove Company employees, 1916.

Source: Guelph Historical Society

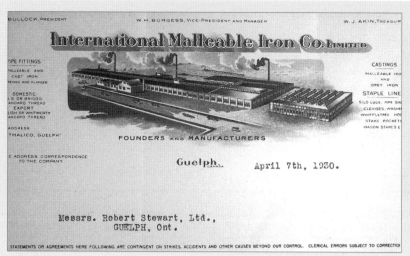

Heavy Industry

When International Malleable Iron began production in 1913, adding its output to that of the half dozen other foundries in Guelph, the Royal City had been irrefutably transformed into a metal working and foundry town. Though the new boy on the block, IMICO soon outpaced the other Guelph foundries in output and employment, becoming, after five years, the largest employer in Guelph. A state-of-the-art facility when new, the business would fall on hard times in the 1960s and 1970s. After its closure, the environmental problems with the property would provide a decade-long headache for Guelph council. Source: Stewart Lumber Collection, University of Guelph Archives

businessmen Robert Dodds and Christian Kloepfer, but including well-connected figures such as railway magnate Sir William MacKenzie, set up shop in 1912 in a new building on Victoria Road, producing towels and household linens.

The other new firm, the International Malleable Iron Company, would ultimately have a far greater impact on the city. The plant began production in 1913 with a range of malleable and grey iron pipe fittings, with customers across Canada and around the world. Three years later, another Guelph foundry opened on the other side of town. The Crimea Street facilities of the Callander Foundry produced small castings in grey iron, brass and aluminum, much of it for the electrical industry.

Industrial growth and expansion in the first half of the 20th century completely altered the face of the city. The once dominant Bell and Raymond firms still operated at the outbreak of the First World War, but they had been completely overtaken by the upstarts. The population of Guelph, hovering at 11,000 in 1900, topped the 16,000 mark in 1915, an increase of 45 percent.

The growth came with problems. The municipal water system, parts of which dated to 1878, supplied increasingly poor water, largely as a result of sewage and surface water infiltration, and increasing demands on the system. The city had offered unlimited free water to several industries as an inducement to locate in Guelph. Eventually, though, the reputation for poor water began to discourage growth. The answer, fully supported by the Guelph Board of Trade, was a sewage system, parts of which were installed in 1903.

The sewage system did not solve the difficulties with the water supply, which suffered worsening quantity and quality problems. Typhoid cases overloaded the Guelph hospitals. Engineer W.M. Davis and City of Guelph engineer James G. Lindsay determined that springs near Arkell could provide Guelph with an immense supply of high-quality water. The city issued $125,000 of debentures to finance the four-mile pipeline, a new water tower, and other improvements made in 1908 and 1909.

The water and sewer systems were municipally owned from the beginning. Such was not the case with gas and electricity. A private company, the Guelph Gas Company, founded in 1870, provided gas which was generated from coal and distributed through a system of underground pipes to various commercial and residential properties, mostly for lighting purposes. This system fueled the streetlights in Guelph's downtown core, providing dim but valuable illumination. At the request of the city council, the company installed a water-powered generator in 1887 to provide electricity to carbon arc streetlights. A new coal-powered generator, supplying both streetlights and other customers with electricity, went into service four years later, and the company changed its name to the Guelph Light and Power Company.

Dissatisfied with the prices and service, city council decided to purchase the system in 1902. A long and acrimonious debate ended with approval by ratepayers in January 1903. In the meantime, several Guelph businessmen, among them J.W. Lyon and Christian Kloepfer, became involved in a scheme to bring electricity from Niagara Falls to smaller cities such as Guelph. Their efforts would soon result in the formation of the Hydro Electric Power Commission, better known as Ontario Hydro.

 1912 – In January, the garbagemen complain. Now that pick-up service is established for such things as ashes they say people are taking advantage of them. While it is a weekly service many people pile up the ashes in their cellar or elsewhere and then expect the garbagemen to carry away some very heavy and awkward loads.

Guelph council unanimously backed the connection with Ontario Hydro. In May 1908, Guelph became one of the first 14 municipalities to sign an agreement for Niagara power, fulfilling the desire of J.W. Lyon and others for cheap reliable power for industry. Guelph switched into the Ontario Hydro system in September 1910, and the old coal-powered Sussex Street plant closed forever. Taylor-Forbes became the first industry to acquire most of its power from the municipal system. One by one, emissions from belching factory smokestacks lessened as industry switched to purchased electricity for energy.

The acquisition of the Guelph Light and Power Company in 1903 had involved major additional expenditures. New lines were needed for the electrical system, and inadequate gas piping had to be replaced. A short time later, the city issued still more debentures to acquire the Guelph Radial Railway. Constructed by George Sleeman in 1895, Guelph's streetcar system had not been a good investment. Losses mounted year by year. In 1902 the Bank of Montreal and the Traders Bank seized the property when Sleeman could not meet loan payments.

The banks wanted $100,000 for the Guelph Radial Railway property. Several proposals by individuals got nowhere. Eventually, J.W. Lyon was able to negotiate the price down to $78,000, which was approved by the ratepayers in a plebiscite in September 1903. The purchase gave the city eight miles of track, 11 streetcars, Sleeman's holdings at Puslinch Lake, and what several Guelph businessmen considered vital: control of trackage into the city.

Most Guelph businessmen regarded the purchase of the streetcar system as a wise defensive move. There had been a growing fear that electric railways controlled elsewhere might build into the city, or take over the Guelph system. At the time of the purchase, studies were in progress on extensions to Puslinch Lake, and on an electric line north of the city. Neither would ever get off the drawing board. Beginning in 1906, the streetcar system generated an operating profit, and did so for the next 11 years, but each year the debt servicing costs on the debentures exceeded the profit. An additional benefit of the Guelph streetcar system was that it handled freight cars, switched from the Grand Trunk and Canadian Pacific, to provide direct railway service to industries not located along one of the railway lines. Eventually, about a dozen firms had sidings connected to the streetcar lines, and freight traffic provided between 15 and 20 percent of the gross revenues of the system.

 1912 – Guelph becomes enamoured with the "taxi cab." An ad for "Johnson's Service" stated: Same price for a cab or hack [horse-drawn vehicle], except by the hour. Phone 899 or 828L.

Heady Days at the Guelph Post Office

As with industry in Guelph, the local post office, located in a building constructed in 1876 on the present site of

the Bank of Nova Scotia, experienced change in the first decade of the 20th century. Work began in 1903 on a third storey to the building, bringing it into scale with other Wyndham Street buildings. Construction ended in 1906 with the installation of a new clock. On August 15, 1907 the staff began using a machine canceller to process mail. Three months later, a staff of letter carriers began door-to-door delivery, twice daily for everyone, and three times a day in the downtown core. The Guelph office forwarded mail for more than a dozen small offices in the area, and beginning in 1909, provided the base for rural routes, which ultimately numbered seven. With a staff numbering about 40 in all, the post office ranked as a medium-sized business in its own right. Illustrated is an impression made by the machine canceller on its first morning of service.

Source: Steve Thorning

In a short period of time, the acquisition of the streetcar, gas, and electrical systems, as well as major work on the water and sewer systems, had placed a considerable debt burden on the city. Looking only at the financial statements, the purchases of the utilities made little sense. The champions of the policy, though, defended them on the grounds that they provided cheap and reliable services to residents and industries big and small. More important than anything was the issue of local control. Though they often argued among themselves, Guelph's prominent business and political leaders in this era believed steadfastly in the principle of public ownership of utilities and natural resources.

Back in 1888, when the city built the Guelph Junction Railway, there had been much talk about extending the line west, with an ultimate goal of Lake Huron. The Canadian Pacific had no inclination to build the line then, but the project never faded in the minds of Guelph's boosters. William Bell, as president of the Guelph Junction Railway, made several trips to Montreal to lobby William Van Horne and Thomas Shaughnessey at the CPR head office. In 1900 Shaughnessey added a Guelph-to-Goderich line to the company's long-term plans. Under further prodding from Bell, the CPR made preliminary surveys over the summer of 1903.

From this point, events moved quickly. The railway awarded tenders for construction in August 1904. Rails and ties began arriving in July 1905 with over 100 carloads in one week. The first locomotive on the line reached Elmira in May

The Grand Trunk Station, c. 1905: Guelph city council constantly criticized the old 1856 Grand Trunk Railway station as hopelessly small, decaying and musty. The railway first promised to replace the structure in 1888. After three years of bitter contention between the railway and the city, the new station opened in 1911 in what had formerly been Jubilee Park. Today, preserved steam locomotive 6167 reposes on the approximate site of the old station. Directly behind the old station in this view is the Bell Piano and Organ's 1902 pump organ factory, constructed at the peak in popularity of those instruments. It was the last example of 19th century-style industrial architecture to be constructed in Guelph. Farther back is the distinctive cupola that originally graced Guelph's City Hall.

Source: Wellington County Museum and Archives

The new station: Both the Grand Trunk and Canadian Pacific Railways opened new Guelph stations in 1911. This view, looking across the Speed River immediately upstream from the Eramosa Road bridge, shows the CPR edifice soon after its construction. In its heyday, passenger trains left here for Toronto, Hamilton and Goderich, with connections at Guelph Junction for other points. The opening of the extension of the Guelph Junction Railway to the Port facilities at Goderich in 1907 greatly increased the volume of traffic on the line. Today an apartment complex sits on this site, facing Cardigan Street.

Source: J. Keleher

1906. Regular service on the entire line to Goderich commenced in August 1907.

William Bell and his associates desired the line to increase traffic over the city-owned Guelph Junction line, of which the Goderich line was a continuation. As well, they believed it would capture traffic and business that previously had gone to Waterloo and Stratford.

It was natural for Guelph, with its Guelph Junction Railway under lease to Canadian Pacific, to prefer that line over the Grand Trunk. The Grand Trunk had attempted to throw roadblocks in the way of the Guelph Junction when it was built, and relations with the city had been cool at best ever since. To placate Guelph, the Grand Trunk had in 1888 promised a new passenger station, to replace the existing one at the east end of Allan's Bridge. Twenty years later, there was still no station, and its inadequacies began to produce constant complaints from Guelph. In addition, Guelph maintained a steady stream of other complaints about GTR service, ranging from slow delivery of cars to blocked street crossings.

In July 1908 the GTR announced plans to build the new station near Edinburgh Road, close to the junction of its four lines into Guelph. Howls of protest resulted because this location was then at the western extremity of the city. The GTR immediately withdrew this proposal. A month later, city officials were conferring with the railway about plans for a downtown station, largely as the result of a ruling by the Board of Railway Commissioners over blocked crossings in the downtown core. The GTR wanted bridges over Neeve and Gordon streets, with only a passenger walkway at Wyndham, and the new station in Jubilee Park, at the corner of Wyndham and Carden streets.

This ambitious project soon stalled over the design and the costs. The GTR considered the city's price for Jubilee Park to be exorbitant, further delaying the work. There was also a major change to the design, with overpasses at Wyndham

Another rail link: The date is August 26, 1907, and the Canadian Pacific's new line west of Guelph to Elmira and on to Goderich has just opened. The scene is the original CPR station, The Priory, which was the first building constructed in Guelph. Four years later the railway moved to its modern new station at Eramosa Road.
Source: Wellington County Museum and Archives

1906 Labour Day parade: Trade unions in Guelph got off to a rocky start in the 1870s, and struggled for more than 20 years to become solidly established. The major breakthrough for unionists was the organization of the skilled workers at the Bell Piano and Organ Company in the 1890s. Other union locals became established in succeeding years. By the time of this photograph, the Labour Day parade of 1906, unions had become a solid part of the social and economic fabric of Guelph. Political leaders gladly rode in the parades, and union locals vied with one another to decorate the best float.
Source: Wellington County Museum and Archives

and Wilson streets, and a pedestrian subway at Neeve Street. Guelph had to pick up 75 percent of the cost of the overpasses.

Anxious to proceed, the GTR announced expropriation proceedings for Jubilee Park in September 1910, along with its design for the new station. Seven weeks later, Canadian Pacific announced plans for its new station, to the west of Eramosa Road. The new passenger stations, both opened in 1911, became immediate sources of pride for the Board of Trade and civic boosters in Guelph.

Year by year, with new stations, new factories, improved utilities and the beginning of street paving in the downtown core, Guelph began to look more and more like a bustling city. The business climate attracted, among other businesses, new banks to vie with the Montreal, Commerce, Traders and Dominion for a share of the business. The Bank of Nova Scotia and the Merchants Bank opened Guelph branches soon after the turn of the century. A couple of years later the fledgling Metropolitan Bank opened in Guelph, hiring Guelph businessman C.L. Nelles as its manager. The Union Bank opened in 1912. Two years later the Metropolitan Bank merged with the Bank of Nova Scotia. Banking facilities in 1900 were thus a vast improvement over what had existed even a decade previously. It should also be noted that the five major Canadian chartered banks, with their antecedents, have done business in Guelph through the entire 20th century.

With the rapid industrial growth between 1900 and 1915, Guelph's boosters could take a measure of pride. Even with the growth, they had managed to keep pace with public utilities and services. Labour unrest had surfaced occasionally, but to a lesser extent than in other small cities. Along with publicly-owned utilities, free industrial sites, good water and parks, the Guelph Board of Trade liked to advertise contented labour as one of the attractions of the Royal City. This idyllic vision would sustain a few bumps during the First World War and its economic aftermath.

THE QUIET YEARS OF THE 1920S, 1930S AND 1940S

The First World War and its aftermath in 1919 and 1920 had a surprisingly minor impact on the industries of Guelph. There were, of course, the wartime problems of materials shortages and scarcity of labour. From the time the first volunteers signed up in August 1914 until the Guelph recruiting office closed in March 1918, more than 3,300 men enlisted at Guelph. Within months of the declaration of war, military personnel could be seen everywhere, and even more so after the federal government took over the downtown Winter Fair buildings in January 1915. Businessmen enthusiastically supported the local Patriotic Association, led by J.M. Taylor of Taylor-Forbes and miller Lincoln Goldie, raising huge sums for war bonds and charity.

Guelph's factories, despite the scarcity of labour, operated at close to full production, a number of them on war contracts. Largest of these came at the very end of the war late in 1918: a two-million-dollar order to the Page-Hersey Tube Company from the United States government for munitions.

Rapid inflation, especially after 1917, more than doubled the price of most goods. Rising prices taxed the business abilities of factory managers and store-keepers, but for workingmen the problem was more acute, as their wages fell behind the increases and their wives had difficulty balancing the household budget.

This situation produced labour unrest in many centres across the country, but such was not the case in Guelph. There had been labour unions in Guelph since the 1870 era, but these early activities had been sporadic at best. Labour unions achieved a more permanent presence in Guelph with the organization of

Guelph Carpet Company, c. 1920: Photographs of factory interiors are not common, and this one is especially valuable because it portrays some of the employees. The Guelph Carpet Company and the associated Guelph Spinning Mills employed large numbers of women and teenagers in the early part of the 20th century.   Source: J. Keleher

the Guelph Trades and Labour Council in 1898, drawing support from perhaps a dozen union locals active at that time. A major milestone was the organization of the piano workers at the high-profile Bell Piano and Organ factory.

The decade immediately preceding the war had witnessed a growing union movement in Guelph, paralleling the growth of the industries in this period. By 1912, Labour Day had become a major holiday, observed by the entire city.

The war years hurt organized labour in Guelph. Many of the most energetic and ablest leaders had enlisted. A handful of doctrinaire socialists, convinced of the absurdity of the conflict, had taken a vehemently pacifist stance, which thoroughly enraged patriots, of which Guelph had more than its share. The situation had degenerated further with rumours of various socialist sabotage plots, duplicity and deceit by Catholics, and general bullying of anyone not perceived to be pro-British. Guelph had not seen such ugly sentiments expressed since the Orange Order riots of the 1840s. Several incidents, well publicized across the country, gave the city a black eye.

When the war ended, everyone wanted to forget the bad feelings. The 1920 Labour Day parade – the first large display of unionism since the pre-war period – signalled the return of social cohesion when the mayor, in company with the leaders of the Trades and Labour Council, rode proudly at the head of the procession. Union members overwhelmingly eschewed radicalism: Independent Labour and socialist candidates invariably suffered crushing defeats when they presented themselves as candidates for office. Once again, Guelph could boast on its promotional literature that labour peace was one of its enticements to prospective industries, as it did in 1924:

> Guelph's twenty thousand inhabitants are uniformly prosperous and real poverty does not exist. In the latest figures issued by the Canadian Government, Guelph is shown to have the second lowest percentage of unemployment in the Dominion. Strikes, as a result of these stable conditions, are practically unknown. The general moral atmosphere of the community is excellent. Its foreign population has been well absorbed, and prosecutions for criminal offences are few.

Post-war industrial Guelph looked remarkably like the pre-war tableau, but there were some changes, some affecting Guelph's oldest industries. In 1916 the American-based White Sewing Machine Company bought the venerable Raymond firm, which had been in decline for about 10 years. Two years later, Robert Dodds, the majority owner of the Guelph Carpet Company, sold the firm to British interests, as well as an associated company, the Guelph Spinning Mills. The new owners merged the firms. Later in 1918 the Goldie family sold their large flour mill to F.K. Morrow and Co. of Toronto. The Bell Piano and Organ Company, British-owned for 30 years though strongly identified with the Bell family and the city, suffered the indignity of a bankruptcy in 1916, a victim of the combined forces of the wartime closing of export markets and of the phonograph, which, after 1905, gradually replaced the pump organ as the parlour favourite in most households.

The Canada Temperance Act put an end, temporarily at least, to Sleeman's beer in September 1916. For the next decade the firm would rely on malt and ginger ale for its income.

For the Guelph Carpet and Goldie firms, the loss of local ownership had little adverse impact on the operations. Both expanded under the new owners. New equipment at the Goldie Mill, all electrically powered, increased production

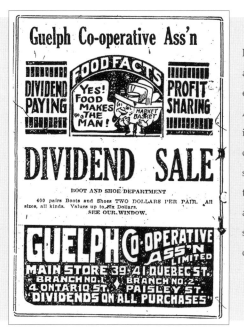

For the Working Man: A visible sign of the appearance of labour unions in Guelph was the establishment of the Guelph Co-operative Association, to provide basic goods at low cost to its members. At its peak, several hundred families carried membership cards, and the Co-op had stores on Paisley and Ontario streets in addition to its main store on Quebec Street. Prices did not always beat those of other stores, but the Co-op's supporters argued that its mere presence in the city prevented gouging by other stores.

Source: *Guelph Mercury*

Armco Drainage: Established in 1907 as the Canada Ingot Iron Company in a stone building adjoining the Norwich Street bridge, Armco, now known as Armtec, has prospered to become a major Guelph industry, producing culverts and drainage components, largely for road construction projects. Growing demand forced the firm to seek larger premises. This is Armco's George Street plant in 1949.   Source: J. Keleher

 January 15, 1935 – On this day a Russian picture titled "Golden Mountains" is shown in Workers' Hall. The subject was the working conditions in Russia of 1914. It was a Soviet-made talking picture described in the *Guelph Mercury* in a colourful way. "The cast is typically Russian, heavy and serious, deep in pathos and rising, at times, to the heights of Slavic humour and music..."

Fred Hammond

Born in Guelph in 1912, Fred Hammond was one of Canada's best known amateur radio operators. His name and call sign, VE3HC, is recognized around the world. It all started in 1923 when at age 11 he built his first radio after falling in love with this new technology. Fred was also instrumental in founding Hammond Manufacturing Company which today is a major innovator in the electronics industry. Its predecessor, O. S. Hammond and Sons, began as a small shop on Yarmouth Street in 1919 and manufactured radios until 1925. It has since gone on to produce everything from radar equipment during the Second World War to transformers for cancer treatment in the 1990s. Fred Hammond, however, still retained a fascination with radio in all its forms. He founded the Guelph Amateur Radio Club in 1946. He also provided, at his own expense, much-needed radio components to amateurs all over the world, including the Jamaican Red Cross. Hammond donated equipment for China's first amateur radio station and visited there in 1984, becoming the first amateur to transmit signals from communist China when he called home. In 1986 he provided special equipment for the Canada/USSR Trans-Polar Ski Trek Expedition.

During his lifetime Fred collected old radio equipment dating back to the turn of the century and by 1978 had opened the Hammond Museum of Radio in Guelph, the largest and finest private collection of its kind in the world. The museum collection depicts more than 80 years of wireless and radio progress, old TV sets from the early days of television and even a working spark transmitter. Hammond's hard work and dedication was recognized in 1996 when he was inducted into the Radio Amateurs' Hall of Fame. Fred Hammond died in 1999.

– Ceska Brennan

to the point where the mill could grind and bag 200,000 pounds of flour every 24 hours, sufficient to fill five or six railway cars for shipment to points all over eastern Canada. The firm liked to boast that it was the only flour mill in Canada served directly by private tracks from both the Grand Trunk and Canadian Pacific. And Goldie's produced sufficient traffic to keep both smiling, easily ranking as the best customer in Guelph for the railways in the 1920s.

Things weren't quite so rosy over on Baker and Yarmouth streets at the old Raymond factory under the White ownership. Production, which in the past had often hit 100 sewing machines a day, dropped to a mere half dozen. In 1922 orders came from Cleveland to shut down the factory.

Northern Rubber: One of the major additions to Guelph's industrial sector in the period immediately after the First World War was the Huron Street complex now operated by Uniroyal, but originally the Northern Rubber Company, and later, Dominion Rubber. At its commencement, the factory was locally controlled, producing rubber boots, among other things, for a national market. Source: J. Keleher, 1950

Despite wartime conditions and post-war economic instability, a number of firms decided to set up shop in Guelph. Alex Callander augmented Guelph's metal working sector with a new foundry in 1916 on Crimea Street. Later that year the Tolton Manufacturing Company took over the Colonial Knitting Company plant on Cambridge Street as the city's textile industries continued to evolve and change.

The following year saw the arrival of the Dominion Casket Company, and an announcement by the Fried Lee Hat Company that their factory would move from Toronto to a Suffolk Street location. This firm began Guelph production of men's hats on a modest scale in 1919, but did not begin to prosper until a local group, led by Frank Ramsay, purchased the business and renamed it Biltmore Hats – named after the prestigious New York hotel – and added lines of straw hats and panamas, both very popular in the 1920s.

A modest operation, but one which eventually would become a major industry, began making battery chargers in 1926. The Hammond Manufacturing Company soon introduced lines of transformers for radios, prospering through the 1930s and 1940s with the rapid growth of the broadcasting industry.

Expansion of older firms provided premises for new ones. When Canada Ingot Iron (Armco) moved to a large new plant on George Street, its old location at the Norwich Street bridge provided space for the Sterling Broom Company. With larger facilities, Armco expanded from its line of iron culverts to highway guardrails, traffic signs and road graders.

The major addition to the post-war industrial sector was a locally organized company which reinforced Guelph's predilection for locally controlled industry. Among the directors of the Northern Rubber Company were J.G. Smith, F.W. Kramer, George Drew and members of the Kennedy family, who were connected by marriage to William Bell. Several of the group also held blocks of shares in the Guelph White Lime Company and the Dalyte Electric Company. Northern Rubber began producing rubber footwear in April 1920. Well financed and managed, the business mushroomed in five years to first place among Guelph's industries in employment, with a payroll near the 600 mark in the late 1920s. The firm's five-storey factory on Huron Street, a state-of-the-art facility when it was constructed, boasted more floor area than any other Guelph industry. The company set up eight sales branches across Canada and engaged agents in a score of locations worldwide.

Ranking second among Guelph's employers in the mid-1920s was the Taylor-Forbes hardware firm, operating from a sprawling complex on the banks of the Speed River, portions of which had originally been Allan's Distillery. The

The Famous Tolton No. 7 Jointer Plow

Price 30.00 complete
includes 1 wheel, 1 coulter, 1 skimmer & 1 extra share

CHAMPION PRIZE WINNER AT ALL THE LEADING PLOWING MATCHES

Having arranged with Tolton Bros., Ltd., for the manufacture and sale of this far-famed Jointer Plow, we are now prepared to furnish same on short notice.

Therefore, would say to all good Plowmen, SEND IN YOUR ORDERS EARLY AND SECURE ONE

Rae's Wagon & Truck Body Works

Yarmouth Street   GUELPH, ONT.

All Kinds of Wagons, Bodies and Sleighs, etc., in Stock and Made to Order

The Tolton Brothers firm prospered in the early years of the 20th century, but its roots went back to the 19th. For virtually its entire life it was dominated by sons of William Tolton Jr., who came to Guelph Township in 1830, with his father, from England. A 17-year-old lad at the time, William Tolton quickly adapted to the new land. Two years later he married Hannah Parkinson of the well-known Eramosa family. They would ultimately raise a family of 14 children.

Of the sons, Andrew and David were the most important in the life of the Tolton Brothers firm. A skilled mechanic and inventor, Andrew experimented and developed a number of innovations in farm equipment. The brothers began building farm implements in 1866, but the firm was not properly organized for another 11 years.

In 1875 Andrew and David Tolton joined with their brothers John P., Benjamin and Andrew Luke, in establishing the Tolton Brothers partnership, with a factory on what is now lower Wyndham Street, just north of the present Guelph firehall. Like many of the firms of that era, they attempted to make as wide a range of implements as possible, but achieved their greatest success with plows and tillage equipment. Most of these employed improvements developed by Andrew Tolton. David soon took charge of the sales and financial side of the business. Though the name remained constant, the firm went through several incarnations. The first was the resignation of John and Benjamin in 1887. Later, after Andrew's death, David Tolton took in W.H. Conway and George Dickieson as partners. The firm enjoyed modest success during the 1880s and 1890s. Eventually, following the trend in the industry toward specialization, David decided to concentrate on plows and harrows, and on a pea harvester developed by his brother Andrew.

The Tolton Brothers business was able to take advantage of the boom years either side of 1900. Guelph capitalist Christian Kloepfer became involved with the growing firm, and guided it through incorporation in 1904, serving briefly as president. A director of the Traders Bank of Canada, Kloepfer was in a position to tap outside sources of capital to finance the expanding business. By 1906 Edward Tolton, another brother, had joined the firm as president, with Benjamin back as vice-president. David, with the most experience, was secretary-treasurer and general manager. In 1907 the Toltons branched out, establishing the Guelph Paper Box Company. With about a dozen employees, this firm made shipping cartons used by a number of Guelph industries, particularly textile firms. Guelph Paper Box eventually became an important industry, but by then it was guided by other hands. The Toltons sold it in 1915, desiring to concentrate their attention exclusively on farm implements.

The Tolton Brothers firm enjoyed its best years from about 1910 until the early 1920s. Its popular models of horse-drawn plows enjoyed a brisk market in this period, and the factory's payroll ballooned to the 100 mark during busy times. The increasing use of tractors, though, soon doomed the horse-drawn Tolton plow. The pea harvester also suffered from declining sales. As a family-owned business, there were problems with succession and direction, and there was no one on staff to design new models to keep up with changing technology. Agricultural prices remained sluggish at best during the 1920s, putting strains on farmers, and this had adverse effects on the entire farm implement industry. By the late 1920s, the Tolton firm was a pale image of its prosperous years. Alex Rae, head of Rae's Wagon and Truck Body Works, took over the remnants of the Tolton firm about 1930. For several years he continued to make and sell the horse-drawn Tolton plow and its harrows. He also serviced these implements and sold spare parts for them. Tolton plows were in production for some 60 years, and today surviving examples are proudly-held artifacts of Guelph's heritage.

The advertising sheet shown here is from March 1931, near the end of the line for Tolton plows. The handwritten price quotation is from the pen of Alex Rae.   Source: Steve Thorning

Muller's in 1903 and 1930: Some firms coped well with the transition from horses to automobiles. These two views show the Muller's long-lived business over the interval of a quarter century: based on carriages in 1903 (with a lone automobile in front), and automobiles in 1930. For decades the firm's shop at the corner of Woolwich and Eramosa was a readily recognized landmark.
Source: Wellington County Museum and Archives

foundry, machine shop, assembly, and warehousing personnel totalled 500. The International Malleable Iron Company, only established in 1913, maintained a payroll of about 450 in the mid-1920s at its plant in St. Patrick's Ward.

A short distance down the Speed River from Taylor-Forbes was the fourth of the major Guelph employers, the Guelph Carpet and Spinning Mills Limited, with 80 power looms, a product line that included wool yarn, Brussels, Wilton, tapestry and velvet carpets, produced by some 400 employees.

These four large firms accounted for 35 or 40 percent of the industrial employment in Guelph in the 1920s, but much smaller firms dominated the list of 75 or so manufacturing establishments. The Gilson Manufacturing Company and the Guelph Stove Company both maintained payrolls near the 200 mark. Perhaps a dozen plants employed 100 or so, including the Page-Hersey Tube, Lander Brothers Limited, Biltmore Hats, Colonial Whitewear and the Tolton Manufacturing Company, among others. A much larger group employed between 30 and 50: Griffin Foundry, Callander Foundry, Louden Machinery, Guelph Casket, Imperial Biscuit, Canada Ingot Iron (Armco), Holman Luggage, Regent Textile, Guelph Spring & Axle, Sterling Rubber and Guelph Paper Box. At the bottom of the list of industries were approximately 25 firms with a dozen or so employees.

There were, of course, seasonal variations in the employment figures. The Gilson payroll could balloon up to 250 at times. Demand for specific products could push employment up and down, particularly in the textile sector, where fashion more and more ruled the day.

The textile business enjoyed prosperous times in Guelph during the 1920s. Lander Brothers, makers of silk stockings, came to Guelph on the strength of a $20,000 loan from the city, approved in 1923. Established in 1922, Joseph Cartledge's Guelph Elastic Hosiery Company produced elastic sporting goods, and elastic surgical hosiery and supports. About 40 people worked in the factory, but another 75 worked out of their own homes in a putting-out system that is usually associated with immigrant workers and big city ghettos.

All in all, Guelph had unarguably become an industrial city in the 1920s, with more than 5,000 of its 20,000 population working in manufacturing. A factory culture characterized the city, and would do so until the 1950s. Several hundred women worked in manufacturing, particularly in the textile trades, and there was ample work available to youth who desired to leave school as soon as the law allowed. Many households had the income of more than one pay envelope, which, in the absence of unemployment insurance, provided security during layoff periods, which occurred frequently in all manufacturing during the 1920s.

The concentration of metal working and textile firms in Guelph tended to attract others in the same lines. The pool of skilled and semi-skilled labour made the start-up of a new firm easier. The presence of other firms in the same field improved employment opportunities and stability: when one firm laid off employees, there was usually work at another in the city. Over time, a degree of integration introduced itself. The Guelph Pattern Company, for example, sold a good portion of its output to the foundries in Guelph. On the output side, the International Malleable Iron Company sold a portion of its castings to local manufacturing firms. Another example was the Live Wire Company, established in 1919 with six employees in the basement of the Partridge Rubber Company. Initially, the firm produced building wire, buying bare copper wire and procuring the rubber insulation from the rubber plant upstairs. Soon eclipsing its supplier, Live Wire moved to a vacant plant on Dublin Street in 1930, and changed its name to Federal Wire and Cable. Continuing to expand through the Depression years of the 1930s while other factories suffered massive layoffs, Federal moved to the old Crowe Foundry property in 1936.

The locations of manufacturing firms emphasized the way that industry had become interwoven with Guelph's character. There was no large industrial

Out To Pasture: Irrefutable evidence that the motor car had arrived to stay was the closure of Guelph's downtown livery stables, both the independent ones and those associated with one of the hotels. The old buildings were converted to other purposes, such as the movie theatre in the Commercial's livery, or demolished to make way for other structures. In their place, automotive dealerships appeared in the downtown core, and service stations sprouted on corners all over the city. This ad, from April 1920, announced the demise of Guelph's largest livery and the sale of all its sleighs, carriages, harness, and its horses, already down to 15, but which once had been twice that number.

Source: *Guelph Mercury*

area. Rather, factories stood singly or in pockets throughout the city, surrounded by residential areas. Even J.W. Lyon's large subdivision in St. Patrick's Ward continued this tendency: he located factory sites on the Guelph Junction Railway's line and on York and Victoria roads, but all intermingled with residences. A number of factories ringed the downtown commercial core, including Taylor-Forbes and the Guelph Carpet Company and several textile plants.

Industry in the very core of Guelph, though, waned during the 1920s, first with the closing of the Raymond factory, and later with the demise of Bell Piano and Organ on Carden Street. With foreign ownership and inept management, the Bell firm had failed to adjust to changing markets. The factory had turned out about 900 pianos in 1918. Five years later the number had fallen by half, and there was an even greater decline in parlour organ

production. In 1926 there were new lines of phonograph cabinets, which went into production just as phonograph sales began to plummet as the public shifted to radio from records for its amusement. Brantford interests purchased the Guelph plant in 1928, and a short time later, the Lesage Piano Company of St. Therese, Quebec acquired what was left of the assets.

Though the Bell Piano and Organ factory was moribund, downtown Guelph bustled with commercial activity during the 1920s. Except for a dozen or so corner grocery stores, virtually all of the retail trade of Guelph was conducted in the downtown core, including car dealers such as Daymond Motors on Quebec Street. Cars had taken over the streets by 1920, leading to the closure of livery stables and new uses for them. The Commercial Hotel's livery underwent renovations and reopened as a movie theatre, one of three in the downtown core.

The Bank of Hamilton became the eighth chartered bank in the city when it opened a branch in 1920, but mergers would soon reduce the number to five by 1925: The Merchants Bank with the Bank of Montreal in 1922, The Bank of Hamilton with the Bank of Commerce in 1924, and the Union Bank with the Royal Bank in 1925.

Retail chains had made their appearance by the war years when McKee's Drug Store became part of the Rexall chain. The grocery business saw a major shakeup during the 1920s. At the start of the decade, Guelph's grocery stores had all been independents. Only one, Jackson Brothers, pointed to the future by advertising a list of weekly specials before 1920. Dominion

Chain Stores on the Corner: The major grocery chains – Dominion, Loblaws, A&P and Carroll's – all opened stores in downtown Guelph, eclipsing the old independent grocers. Outside the downtown core, other chains acted as suppliers to older neighbourhood stores and newer corner groceries, offering bulk purchasing power and advertising support. Red & White was one of these chains, but the biggest in the late 1920s was Superior Stores, with a dozen Guelph locations in its chain.

Source: *Guelph Mercury*, May 17, 1928

The first Canadian artist to make Red Seal Records is Guelph's Own

EDWARD JOHNSON

Her Bright Smile Haunts Me Still
64839—$1.25

On With the Play—Pagliacci—Italian
64840—$1.25

Are two of the most beautiful Tenor Solos ever recorded.

New February Records on sale today.

C. W. KELLY & SON

A Downtown Cornerstone: C.W. Kelly and Son was already one of the older downtown businesses when the 20th century began, and the store would be a familiar sight for most of it. Beginning as an outlet for musical instruments and sheet music (including the Guelph retail outlet for Bell pianos and organs, manufactured up the street), Kelly's kept up with the times, adding phonographs and recordings, electrical appliances, radios and televisions when these became popular consumer items. This ad, from 1920, announces the first Victor recordings made by Edward Johnson, Guelph's most famous musical export, who had just returned from a lengthy stay in Europe, where he had been billed as Eduardo Di Giovanni to overcome the Continental bias against colonials. On the immediate horizon for Johnson was a triumphal career with the Metropolitan Opera in New York.

Source: *Guelph Mercury,* March 23, 1920

Stores led the parade of grocery chains into Guelph, opening a store at 38 Carden St. in 1923. The independents were driven into insignificance, as other chains followed over the next six years: Carroll's, A&P, Loblaws, and the Eaton Groceteria, all with stores on Wyndham Street by 1930, and a second downtown Dominion Store at 41 Quebec St. The chains captured most of the grocery market that at the start of the decade had been held by local independents such as Jackson Brothers, Benson Brothers, and J.A. McCrea.

Local clothing and dry goods stores more than held their own during the 1920s. G.B. Ryan and Company, dating from 1886, already ranked as one of the oldest retail firms in the city in 1920, with a staff of 50. Larger, older, and even more successful was D.E. MacDonald and Brothers Department Store, established in 1882, and expanded several times, most recently in 1920. Their store, staffed by an army of 65 to 70 employees, occupied the entire block on the east side of Wyndham between Macdonell and Carden streets, with a second store on upper Wyndham Street. A victim of the combined forces of aging ownership and Depression conditions, MacDonald's closed in 1932 after a lengthy sale. Evan MacDonald, the best known of the younger generation of the family, preferred an artist's paint brush to a merchant's apron. Immediately filling the niche left by MacDonald's was Walker's Department Store, part of a small chain, which opened in 1931.

Though the city reached a new plateau of prosperity during the 1920s, higher labour and operating costs doomed some businesses. These were hard years for the newspaper business generally in Canada, and Guelph was no exception. The *Guelph Daily Herald,* which had commenced publication in 1847 as a weekly, fell behind the *Guelph Evening Mercury* in the early 1920s. The *Mercury* purchased its old rival, and the last *Herald* rolled off the press on the final day of 1923.

Railways in Guelph reached their peak in usage in the early 1920s, and by the end of the decade, the beginning of their seemingly irreversible decline was already apparent. A new rail system opened to Guelph in April 1917: the Toronto Suburban Railway, carrying passengers and express by electric streetcars. Controlled by the Canadian Northern Railway interests, the line from West Toronto to Guelph had been conceived as a competitive service to that of the Grand Trunk. Construction had taken six years, and by opening day, the Canadian Northern system was collapsing into bankruptcy. Guelph welcomed the line, which used city streetcar tracks from the Gordon Street Bridge to Carden Street.

Along with parent Canadian Northern, the Toronto Suburban Railway was nationalized into the Canadian National system. Traffic levels showed promise for a couple of years, with ridership peaking in 1921. The line proved a great convenience for farmers, along the line, and a handful of people employed in Guelph.

Conditions with the city-owned Guelph Junction Railway were very rosy in the early 1920s. The leasing agreement signed by the CPR provided for 40 percent of the gross revenues to be paid to the city. Inflation had raised the income to levels much higher than had been foreseen by Canadian Pacific. For its original investment of some $170,000 in 1888, Guelph received $1,300,000 in dividends by 1930. As with the Toronto Suburban, traffic peaked in 1921, when the city's 16 miles of railway paid almost $87,000 in dividends. The fall to $59,000 in 1929, a decline of 32 percent, is an indication of the amount of traffic lost to trucks during the decade. Still, city officials continued to pat themselves on the back for this windfall, which went into the general revenue of the city and reduced property taxes.

Relations between the city and the Grand Trunk had been rather quarrelsome for many years. The absorption of the Grand Trunk into the Canadian

 1926 – Guelph merchants host a contest: "Guelph Shoppers' Club Popular Lady Shopper Contest." Every contestant had to get votes between January to April from specific stores. Supporters included Guelph Bakery, Royal Dairy, Guelph Motor Car Company, George Williams, Cosford the Shoeman, Castle Theatre and Hewer Seed Company. Each purchase at a participating store resulted in a specific number of coupons which were then translated into "votes." For the week of March 18 all shoppers received double value coupons.

Guelph Farmers' Market.

Source: Dave Carter, 1999

City Hall at night.

Source: Dave Carter, 1999

A Native Drum Circle, Guelph.

Source: Dale Hamilton

Music in the square, conductor Niklaus Kaethler.

Source: Fred Dahms, 1996

St. George's Church.

Source: Dave Carter, 1999

Left: **Sergeant in the First Howitzer Brigade Canadian Field Artillery which was named in 1911 and operational by the beginning of the First World War; c. 1914**
Source: Major Robert Lyon

Right: **Rifleman of the 30th Regiment Wellington Rifles: part of the reorganized militia; c. 1918.**
Source: Major Robert Lyon

Note: Both of these images, printed on silk, were available in cigarette packages.

Royal Canadian Sea Cadet Corps Ajax, Guelph, Navy League of Canada. The Battle of the Atlantic Parade, Wyndham Street, May 7, 2000.
Source: *Guelph Mercury*

Inside the covered bridge.
Source: tom klinger, 1999

Dancers from the Royal City School of Ballet rehearse for the opening of the River Run Centre, October 4, 1997.
Source: Archives, the River Run Centre: Photo by Ross Davidson-Pilon

Mud Kids at Hillside Festival.　　Source: Tony Leighton, 1996

Guelph Storm winger Eric Beaudoin about to score his 33rd goal of the season on Sault Ste. Marie goaltender Jason Flick. OHL contest at Memorial Gardens.　　Source: *Guelph Mercury*, 2000

Guelph's British Episcopal Church celebrations for Black History Month, February 2000.

Source: *Guelph Mercury*

Burning of the Paisley Street Methodist Chapel, 1907.
Stained glass window detail by Gordon Couling in the Paisley Memorial United Church.
Source: Stelter, 1986

A wedding ceremony at St. James Church 2000. (Danielle Bertrand and Peter Pickfield.)

Source: www.deanpalmer.ca

The old Bank of Commerce on St. George's Square in the 1950s. Detail of oil painting by Evan Macdonald.
Source: Private Collection

The Wellington Hotel (1876) in the 1930s.
Source: Guelph Public Library

ST. GEORGE'S SQUARE, GUELPH, ONT.

St. George's Square, circa 1908. The post office, with its third storey added in 1904, dominates the square in this panoramic scene. Upper Wyndham had only become a major shopping area in the previous two decades. Virtually all the buildings shown here were less than 30 years old when this photo was taken. The streetcars originally circled the small park in the centre of the square.
Source: Steve Thorning

Potter Jessica Steinhauser in front of Stonehouse Pottery, 2000.
Source: www.deanpalmer.ca

Lawnbowler Jim Moore.
Source: Pete Kelly, 1992

Guelph Multicultural Festival at Riverside Park.
Source: Downtown Board of Management, 1997

Guelph Egytian dancer Kara Culp Wenman at the Guelph Contemporary Dance Festival. 1999.
Source: Melanie Gillis, www.melaniegillis.com

Audrey Palmer Steinhauser at Strom's Sweet
Corn Farm, Fall 1998.
                    Source: www.deanpalmer.ca

Butcher Jack Upsdell of Upsdell's Food Market.
                    Source: Scott Hammond, 1992

Workers at IMICO, c. 1917
Source: Guelph Public Library

National system in 1923 heralded a fresh start to the relationship. In May 1923, the president of Canadian National, Sir Henry Thornton, visited Guelph to discuss service, and potential improvements, with local residents and shippers. A champion of passenger service, Thornton authorized increases in train frequency: seven a day to Toronto, four each day to Hamilton and Palmerston, and six to Kitchener and Stratford.

The Canadian Pacific offered similar frequent service on the Guelph Junction line. There were five trains a day each way: three to Hamilton, two to Toronto, all via Guelph Junction. Two daily passenger trains ran northwest to Goderich. Altogether, some 34 passenger trains left the Royal City each day, in the mid-1920s, not including the frequent electric service on the Toronto Suburban.

This high level of service was not enough to forestall the inroads being made by motor cars, buses and trucks. Vehicle registrations increased fourfold during the 1920s. The provincial government assumed a major role in the road network during the 1920s, establishing the basic network of provincial highways. The provincial Department of Highways, established in 1915, brought with it a new class of road, the Provincial County Highway, which provided a 40 percent subsidy for designated roads brought up to the required standard. The old county road from Hamilton through Guelph to Fergus and Owen Sound was so designated in 1918. Two years later it became a full provincial highway, though the county still had to pay 30 percent of the costs until 1926. A second route through Guelph, from Toronto and continuing to Kitchener and Stratford, came into the provincial highway network. These routes, later in the 1920s, were allocated numbers 6 and 7. Both routes were rebuilt and paved in the mid-1920s, providing truck and bus routes into Guelph that paralleled the railways. Guelph's third provincial highway, No. 24, formerly a county road, came into the system in 1937.

As the Depression deepened in 1930 and 1931, railway passengers and express melted away. Faced with mounting losses, the railways drastically cut back their service to Guelph by more than half. Beginning in 1931 on Canadian

Fire!: Downtown Guelph has suffered the devastation of major fires on a number of occasions over the years. This is upper Wyndham Street on July 6, 1921. Guelph fire fighters responded to an alarm at the Stewart Lumber Company's yard and planing mill at 4 a.m. The best they could do was to contain the blaze, which for a time threatened the buildings on the other side of Wyndham Street. Staff roused groggy guests at the Wellington Hotel, at the the corner of Wyndham and Woolwich, to evacuate the building. The federal government later acquired the burned-out Stewart Lumber site and constructed a new post office there in the 1930s.
Source: Wellington County Museum and Archives

National, only three trains ran daily to Toronto, two to Palmerston and one to Hamilton. At Canadian Pacific, a single mixed train ambled daily to Goderich, and a gas-powered self-propelled coach connected the city with mainline trains at Guelph Junction. The two impressive Guelph stations, opened only 20 years before, had lost their place as the primary transportation facilities of the city.

The Guelph Radial Railway, the city's most contentious public utility, again became the subject of controversy at the end of the First World War. The line had made an operating profit every year since the city takeover, though always less than the payments on the debentures issued to acquire the system. These profits disappeared in 1918.

A year later, after much acrimonious debate, Guelph signed an agreement authorizing Ontario Hydro, which ran streetcar systems in other centres, to manage and operate Guelph's streetcars, with the city responsible for improvements and losses. Two years later, Ontario Hydro purchased the system outright.

 April 12, 1934 – "Suspected Bicycle Theft Ring in Guelph," reads the headlines of the *Mercury* this day. Apparently, the police felt that the bikes were being stolen within the city and boundaries, then "disguised" before being sold in other cities.

By then, deferred maintenance had taken its toll on the system. Ontario Hydro engineers recommended that it be rebuilt entirely to reduce operating costs and increase speed and frequency of service. Improvements boosted patronage, which peaked in 1925 at over 5,000 paid fares per day. The system enjoyed the busiest day in its history on December 19 of that year, when Christmas shoppers boosted ridership to 9,400, a phenomenal figure for a compact city of only 21,000 people. Increasingly, though, the heaviest patronage came at rush hours, resulting in crowded cars which otherwise sat idle most of the time.

Paving the streets: The city paved most of the streets in the downtown core before the First World War. Spurred by increasing automobile ownership in Guelph, the street improvement program accelerated in the 1920s. These views show a steam roller of the C&P Paving Company at work on Woolwich Street in 1925, and another crew paving Waterloo Avenue in 1927. Paving these streets required extra work due to the streetcar tracks. Source: left: J. Keleher; right: Giuseppe and Eda Gazzola

Despite mounting losses for the transportation system, there was some expansion. Guelph's first bus went into service in 1926, on a new route along Eramosa Road. Four years later the managers decided against major repairs to the Suffolk Street line, abandoned the track, and substituted another bus on this route, which had the lightest patronage of the streetcar routes.

Time, though, was running out on the entire system. Mounting losses during the 1930s prompted Guelph city council to authorize the abandonment of streetcar service. The last Guelph streetcar rolled into the Waterloo Avenue car barns on September 30, 1937. Freight traffic had been a major source of revenue for the system, but by this time most of the industrial customers, such as Guelph Carpet, could use trucks easily. Nevertheless, freight service remained in place until May 1939. At the end, the major customer was the Ontario Agricultural College, which used up to 250 carloads of coal each year in its central heating plant.

Guelph formally resumed ownership of its transportation system in 1939, when council created the Guelph Transportation Commission as a committee of council.

Part of the cost of upgrading and improving the streetcar system had resulted from street improvements and paving. Guelph council had paved Wyndham Street in 1907, and Quebec, Macdonell, Douglas and other downtown thoroughfares in the pre-war years. The program resumed in 1920, necessitating the

rebuilding of the streetcar lines wherever these ran. Last of the major streets to be paved was Eramosa Road in 1931. These same years also saw a great expansion in water and sewer service, particularly in St. Patrick's Ward, where improvements had lagged behind residential and industrial development by many years. The city's debenture debt, as a result of these projects, peaked in 1923.

The city authorized another major expenditure in 1931, when the Board of Light and Heat commissioners replaced its aging and cumbersome 1906 gas plant with a British-made, automated facility, with a capacity of 450,000 cubic feet daily. The Guelph Light and Heat Commission began an advertising campaign, promoting gas for cooking and water heating. The chief byproduct, coke, 3,500 to 4,000 tons of it each year, was sold to homeowners for domestic heating. In a practice that would horrify present-day environmentalists, coal tar from the plant was used by the city on its streets to keep down dust.

 June 4, 1932 – Mayor O.G. Lye, in an attempt to stimulate the business economy of local shops and services, declares 'Three Guelph Days.' He appealed to locals to "Spend what you can. Help to keep the stores busy." Advertisers of the event and supporters included Acker's Furniture Store, Beatty Washer Store, Zellers Limited, Cole Brothers and Scott, King Edward's coffee shop, Budd's Department Store and the Capitol Theatre. Various street events were planned including a demonstration of the Guelph Fire Department at St. George's Square, jitney dancing in the evening with music by Jeans' Night Hawks, a street parade with a children's bicycle parade, concerts and various sports events. The *Guelph Mercury* posted a $10 reward for the capture of "Mrs. Mercury" as part of a promotional game for the downtown. She was apprehended Saturday afternoon by Miss Myrtle Rae of Kelly's Music Store.

By some measures, the period roughly from 1920 to 1950 could be regarded as one of stagnation for Guelph. The average growth rate in population for the period works out to less than one percent per year. There were new industries, but the number of them matched almost exactly those that closed. The city continued to promote itself through the period, relying on the same themes that had brought success in the first two decades of the century.

The dynamism of that earlier period, though, was missing. The Board of Trade, so active in the earlier years under J.W. Lyon, George Ryan, A.F.H. Jones and others, stagnated after 1915. As well, there were major rifts among the business leaders of Guelph, most involving the city's relationship with Ontario Hydro.

The Guelph Board of Trade went through a major reorganization in 1917, with J.W. Lyon again at the head, and public-ownership advocates such as G. Powell Hamilton and T.J. Hannigan in prominent roles. A couple of years later there was a further reorganization, as the Guelph Chamber of Commerce, with Alderman George Drew as president, two other aldermen as directors, and honorary positions for the old warhorses: J.W. Lyon, J.M. Taylor, Hugh Guthrie and Lincoln Goldie. The old partnership between council and businessmen was back in place by the mid-1920s, but it produced few achievements.

No one could describe the advertising slogans of the period as inspired: "Guelph, Its Past and Present Assure Its Future," and "The Glasgow of Canada." A degree of smugness and self satisfaction permeates the statements of the business leaders of the 1920s and 1930s, as well as the advertising of the Guelph Chamber of Commerce and council's industrial committee. Clearly, they found great satisfaction in Guelph as it was: compact, with its industries, many locally owned and controlled, dispersed throughout the city; a thriving downtown core; excellent public utilities and recreational facilities and a stable population, the overwhelming majority of whom were homeowners.

There were those who found the Royal City a rather dull, sleepy, unexciting, and even an uncultured place during these years. The later decades of the 20th century would be a much happier time for them.

THE BOOM YEARS OF THE 1950S AND 1960S

There are those who recall Guelph's history between 1920 and the early 1950s, and economic and social climate of those years, as one of idyllic stability. Perhaps a larger proportion view this period as one of sleepy torpor. In any case, cracks in the picture began to appear in the immediate post-war years, to explode in a expansionist boom

Owens-Corning: This York Road plant has been a fixture of Guelph's industrial sector from the time it was constructed in 1951 by Fibreglas Canada. This view is from 1965. The complex has undergone considerable alteration under its current owner, Owens-Corning.
Source: J. Keleher

between 1952 and 1954. Events in this short two-year period would determine the shape and direction of the city for the rest of the century and beyond.

The Depression years of the 1930s had affected Guelph less than most small cities. Lengthy layoffs plagued the textile industries and the large metalworking plants such as Malleable Iron and Taylor-Forbes, but most Guelph firms survived. Expansion at some firms such as Hammond Manufacturing and Federal Wire offset the layoffs to an extent, and civic leaders thanked themselves that Guelph was not a one-industry town.

War contracts pushed up employment at the electrical and textile firms, with employment at the metal working plants at all-time highs. A trickle of new industries arrived as well. Armet Industries, a paint producer established in 1936, expanded rapidly in the post-war years, with six extensions to its Sussex Street

Downtown Guelph, 1947: Much of the 19th century, and its mix of retail, commercial, industrial, and residential uses, remained in the downtown core until the 1950s. Demolition and new construction altered much in the downtown core in the second half of the 20th century. This view looks south, with the Wyndham/Woolwich/Eramosa Road intersection in the foreground.

Source: Wellington County Museum and Archives

Hart Products, a 1941 arrival, produced chemical products for the textile, leather, metals and paper industries. With many of its customers based in Guelph, Hart continued the local integration of industry that began in the 1920s. The firm constructed a 650-foot siding to connect its Victoria Road plant with the Guelph Junction Railway to supply bulk loads to customers elsewhere. Hart was important not just in itself, but for its general manager, E.I. Birnbaum, who, through the 1950s and 1960s, became Guelph's most active business leader since J.W. Lyon.

Established in Toronto in 1930, the W.C. Wood Company, a producer of feed grinders, milking machines, electric fencers and milk coolers, migrated to Guelph in 1941. Locating in a Woolwich Street industrial building that had seen several occupants, the firm prospered when it secured some wartime defence contracts. After 1945 it found great post-war success with freezers. With 150 employees by the early 1950s, the Wood Company had become a major component of the Guelph economy, a role it would retain for the rest of the 20th century.

The City of Guelph sold the old Drill Hall to Zephyr Looms who made battle dress, U.S. Army webbing and parachutes from 1939. They employed 1,200 people, mostly women, in their four plants, making them the largest wartime employer in Guelph. The firm later became Textile Industries.

Another Toronto transplant, Rennie Industries set up shop in Guelph in 1945, making hosiery, sweaters, socks, and later, dresses and men's shirts, produced by a workforce composed largely of women. In its early years the firm purchased most of its wool yarn from Guelph Yarns. Also from Toronto, where the firm was founded in 1930, was James R. Kearney Limited. Coming to Guelph in 1948, the firm produced electrical switches, connectors and insulators. Much of the production in the early years was destined for military equipment.

A total of eight firms established in Guelph in 1952, which, with additional hirings and expansion at existing industries, added almost 1,500 jobs in Guelph that year. For the first time the number of manufacturing establishments passed the 100 mark. Most important were Oregon Saw Chain, making replacement chain for saws; Foundry Services Limited, better known as FOSECO, producing chemicals for

plant in four years, spurred by new products based on silicone rubber.

In 1939 Leland Electric arrived, taking over the old Louden Machinery plant on Crimea Street. This firm had been established three years earlier in Toronto as the Canadian branch of an American firm, making motors, alternators and generators up to 30 h.p. capacity. War contracts and post-war demands resulted in several additions to the plant, and production would boom through the mid-1950s supplying new equipment for the 60-cycle electric conversion program in Ontario.

the metallurgy industry; Sheepbridge Engineering, a British-based producer of high quality castings, Harter Metal Furniture; and Valeriote Electronics, headed by the three Guelph-reared Valeriote brothers. This firm commenced the production of communications equipment and antennas at a farmstead on Victoria Road before moving into a new industrial building.

Except for a few arrivals and closures, it seemed a case of business as usual among Guelph's older industries of the early 1950s. Virtually all the major employers had also made the list 30 years earlier. The largest Guelph employer in 1952 was Harding Carpet (the old Guelph Carpet factory, now under new ownership), and its subsidiary, Guelph Yarns, with a total payroll exceeding 600 at times, but much lower during periodic slumps. International Malleable Iron provided work to 525, down somewhat from the wartime peak. This firm installed an automated casting production line in 1952, which greatly increased productivity. After rocky years in the 1930s and boom years in the 1940s, the Taylor-Forbes firm employed about 300 in the early 1950s, but a rocky road lay ahead. Competitive pressures eroded profitability of its radiator, heating equipment, lawn mower and hardware lines, which was not restored by a reorganization in 1953. The end of the road came in December 1955, when Taylor-Forbes closed for good, disposing of its factory property to the upstart W.C. Wood Company, which had outgrown its existing premises.

Two small firms from the 1920s moved to the upper rungs of the ladder after the Second World War. Biltmore Hats' payroll topped the 450 mark after 1950, and would remain high until men's hats went out of fashion in the 1960s. In 1953 Biltmore bought one of its suppliers, Lancashire Felt, located on the corner of York and Morris streets. Biltmore rebuilt the old structure, constructed a large addition, and moved there from its cramped plants on Dublin and Suffolk streets. Federal Wire and Cable, beginning as the minuscule Live Wire Company in the 1920s, had expanded several times since taking over the Suffolk Street premises of the old Crowe Foundry in 1936, increasing its floor area from 20,000 to 150,000 square feet by 1950. An insatiable market for Federal's building wire, enamelled wire for motors, appliance cords, coaxial cables and automotive

Downtown Guelph, 1947: This view shows much of the downtown in the immediate post-war era, when the vast majority of retail and commercial activity was concentrated in the city's core.　　　　Source: Wellington County Museum and Archives

wiring harnesses had pushed employment from 30 in 1936 to 450 in 1952.

Also prospering in the post-war economy was the Callander Foundry on Crimea Street. When war contracts ended in 1945, the firm, still dominated by the second generation of the Callander family, introduced a line of power tools for woodworking and home handymen, designed by the firm's own engineers. Sold under the "Beaver Power Tool" brand, these found a market all over North America. Within five years they constituted over half the production of the plant, and had pushed employment to 330.

Post-war employment at the old Northern Rubber Company on Huron

Long-time employees: The relatively stable industrial sector of the first half of the 20th century meant that employees rarely found it necessary to move or switch jobs. This is the International Malleable Iron Company's Quarter Century Club, taken at a dinner and reception at the Cutten Club in 1947. Commencing with a handful of employees in 1912, this firm ranked high in Guelph's industrial sector in 1947. The employees here all joined the firm in its first decade.   Source: Wellington County Museum and Archives

Start of the boom: This plant, constructed by General Electric at Woodlawn and Edinburgh in 1953, began the boom in Guelph's economy that resulted in continual rapid growth in the second half of the 20th century, and the move of industry to the west side of Guelph. Despite changes in ownership, this factory still produces heavy transformers for high voltage transmission lines.   Source: Dave Carter, 2000

 January 5, 1994 – John Long sells the IMICO property to the Church of the Universe for a dollar, thus beginning a long saga that ended with the expulsion of Reverend Walter Tucker and clan in 1998.

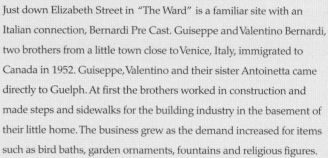

Guiseppe (bottom) and Valentino (left) Bernardi

Just down Elizabeth Street in "The Ward" is a familiar site with an Italian connection, Bernardi Pre Cast. Guiseppe and Valentino Bernardi, two brothers from a little town close to Venice, Italy, immigrated to Canada in 1952. Guiseppe, Valentino and their sister Antoinetta came directly to Guelph. At first the brothers worked in construction and made steps and sidewalks for the building industry in the basement of their little home. The business grew as the demand increased for items such as bird baths, garden ornaments, fountains and religious figures. In 1961, they moved the shop to three acres on Elizabeth Street where it's been located ever since. The Bernardis laboured to make gardens everywhere beautiful and many Guelph gardens showcased a Bernardi statuette. The Pre Cast company began to provide larger items for business and industry. Antoinetta, a registered nurse at St. Joseph's Hospital, created several models and painted the figures and ornaments in her spare time. Valentino's wife Maria kept the office and accounts. The extended family worked together and lived together. "It was a very close family," said Peter, one of Valentino's three sons. "We had one bank account. The money from all sources went into the account and the expenses for everything and everyone came out. It worked well. It was good." All three of Valentino's sons became lawyers, but two eventually returned to the family business. Peter runs the Guelph shop while son Paul manages their second location in Florida.

Guiseppe is still with the family but Valentino died in 1994. Peter's daughter, Valentina (in honour of nonno), is "a little too young yet to go to the shop now," said Peter, "she will in time." Bernardi's soaring Grecian columns and fountains share the dusty yard with rearing horses, elves and story characters. They lure the curious into the shop daily. One of the better known sculptures is a rooster over nine feet tall. It was once rented by a local businessman to surprise a friend. When the friend and his bride returned from their honeymoon they found the farmyard creature decorating their lawn.

– Ceska Brennan

Street, now part of Dominion Rubber, generally hovered in the range of 300 to 400 in the post-war years. Another old Guelph firm, the Gilson Manufacturing Company, had plunged into the boom of the late 1940s with lines of freezers, washing machines and kitchen ranges replacing the gasoline engines and farm equipment that had originally been the products of the plant. Employment at Gilson's, which now had plants on York and Victoria roads, hovered in the 250 range. A rising factor in the Guelph economy was the Ontario Agricultural College, a presence since 1874, but growing quickly with mushrooming enrolments. By 1950 the college had about 175 faculty which, with support, research and maintenance staff, pushed total employment to the 400 range.

In 1952 Guelph council and industrial commissioner Ted Whittaker concluded that the supply of vacant land suitable for industry had become exhausted, but that the city, at that time, possessed a huge potential for growth. The proposed solution, formally presented in July 1952, was a revolutionary one for Guelph: the annexation of some 2,500 acres of land from Guelph Township, which would virtually double the area of the city. Moreover, there would be an "industrial basin." The city proposed to impose strict zoning controls on over 1,000 acres of land west of Edinburgh Road and south of Woodlawn Road that would permit nothing but industrial development. After two lengthy Ontario Municipal Board hearings, where some of the property owners voiced strong objections over the loss of their rights, the proposal received approval, effective January 1, 1953.

This would be the most important event in the 20th century for Guelph, in that it determined the future direction of development in the city. The industrial basin concept overturned the historical mixing of residential, commercial and industrial uses that had characterized Guelph for a century. Not recognized at the time were the long-term implications. The notion of providing large parcels of land at low prices encouraged sprawling industrial development that would be wasteful of land and raise the cost of roads and servicing. The separation of industry from residential areas would mean that virtually no employees could walk to work, and the dispersed nature of development would make good public transit impractical. Perhaps most important, the annexation would ultimately remove the focus of the city from the downtown core.

Barely two months after announcing the annexation, Guelph received word of a major development. Canadian General Electric had purchased the 200-acre Lasby farm on Woodlawn Road, part of the annexed land, and planned to construct a huge factory to construct large high-voltage transformers. The

Dick Stewart

When former chief of police, Dick Stewart, joined the local police force in 1961, officers downtown used call boxes to communicate. The only means of communication, the gray, cast-iron boxes were located at strategic positions in the downtown and were the lifeline for constables on the beat. Each officer carried a brass key as it was a matter of unlocking the box and dialing "0" to reach the station. Conversely, the dispatcher could reach the officer by calling to a box. A light, mounted high on a building closest to the call box, lit up when the phone was ringing. The lights were visible anywhere on the beat and an officer knew he had only a few minutes to answer the call. Stewart jokes his career went "from call box to computers" in the years he spent on the job. Dick Stewart joined a department of 54 officers at age 18 and worked his way up through the force as cadet, constable, sergeant, staff sergeant, inspector and deputy-chief. He was made chief in April 1988.

Stewart felt community involvement was an important part of policing. During his time as chief, the Guelph force was among the first police forces to initiate the "adopt a cop" program, where officers went into the schools and were available if children wanted to speak to an officer about problems or concerns. The "adopt a school" program followed, putting officers into schools on a more casual drop-in basis.

Dick Stewart made serving the Royal City his life's work. In 33 years he unsheathed his gun only once. As a very young officer, he searched a dark and silent building. A figure he'd mistaken for an intruder turned out to be an angel that was part of a Christmas display. No wonder it hadn't responded to his instructions. "I just put my gun back in the holster and got out of there. I sure wouldn't want to have had to write a report on that one," he said. Looking back, Stewart offered, "we've probably had the average number of crimes over the years given our population. But as a city we were envied for our low crime rate." At the time of his retirement in 1994 the force had grown to 139 officers.

– *Ceska Brennan*

proposed payroll was an even 1,000 people. By far the largest construction project ever undertaken in Guelph to that date, the plant took 18 months to build and provided work for up to 300 during this time.

The General Electric project created a general feeling of euphoria in Guelph, and a faith in growth and a better future that dominated the next two decades, and persisted long beyond that. With it came a contempt for the heritage

Lenna Bradburn

In 1994, Lenna Bradburn was sworn in as the chief of police for the Guelph Police Service becoming Canada's first female chief of a major municipal police service. In response to the furore on her appointment she stated: "I like to be where there's a challenge. I'm not just someone who likes to manage the status quo." This is reflected in her employ-ment profile. Born in 1960 and raised in Scarborough, Lenna began her policing career in 1981 as a constable with the Metropolitan Toronto Police. She left this position in 1987 to further her education, obtaining a masters degree in public administration at Queen's University before she became a police services' advisor for the Ministry of the Solicitor General in 1991.

Chief Bradburn was recognized in 1997 for her achievements. She was named as one of "Canada's Top 40 under 40," a national program which recognizes 40 individuals in Canada who have achieved considerable professional and personal accomplishments before age 40. Her achievements were also recorded in the 1997 edition of *Canada's Who's Who* and *Chatelaine Magazine's* 1998 'Who's Who of Canadian Women.'

"One thing that strikes me about this community is the extremely high level of volunteerism here. Is it unique to Guelph? - I don't know, but it certainly is fortunate," said Bradburn. Her own commitment to volunteerism and the community was most overtly expressed in 1997 when she shaved her head as part of the "Guelph Cops for Cancer Program."

Chief Bradburn resigned in 2000 to take a position with the Ontario Ombudsman.

– Ceska Brennan

Huskisson. It opened in May 1955. Interestingly, Dominion was reluctant to abandon the downtown core altogether for its first store, selecting a location on the fringe for its first large Guelph store. Though initially successful, the store would be abandoned 15 years later, to be renovated into Guelph's main fire hall.

Carroll's went in the other direction, announcing in December 1954 that it would build a store on Eramosa at Metcalfe Street, under the Grand Union name. It was the beginning of the end for downtown grocery stores. Dominion followed two years later with its second large Guelph store, becoming a major tenant in the new shopping plaza, the first in Guelph, at Speedvale and Stevenson.

Other retailers, though, still retained enthusiasm for downtown. Walker's renovated its major multi-level downtown clothing and dry goods store, which employed 55 and maintained two delivery trucks by 1953. The popular and high-profile manager, F.V. Garlick, still considered that rural ties were important to the Guelph economy: "Guelph is fortunate to have such a fine rural area to draw from. This has been a chief factor, along with the city's rapid growth, in fostering such extensive expansion on the local retail scene," he told a *Guelph Mercury* reporter.

The same day as the Loblaws opening, Simpsons-Sears, present in Guelph since 1938, inaugurated its revamped downtown store, which occupied part of the old MacDonald Department Store block. In July 1954 the venerable Ryan's store completed renovations that included Guelph's first escalator. Ever-larger suburban shopping centres such as Speedvale and Stevenson in the late 1950s, Willow West Mall in the 1960s and Stone Road Mall in the 1970s would gradually erode the vitality of the downtown retail core.

of the city: the old buildings, the mixed neighbourhoods and the slow pace of life that in the 1920s and 1930s had been Guelph's attractions, and a selling point for prospective industries.

A portent of the future for downtown Guelph came on the last day of 1952. Loblaws announced that it had purchased two acres on the northwest corner of Speedvale Avenue and Woolwich Streets, in the area annexed, for a large grocery store. Legal problems over a right-of-way held up the building permit, but the firm nevertheless proceeded with construction while city officials turned a blind eye. This was Guelph's first major retail location outside the downtown core. Hundreds lined up when the store opened on October 8, 1953.

Other grocery stores followed. Dominion Stores demolished three houses to build its new store and parking lot on Lower Wyndham Street, then known as

1985– Tony Phung opens the first full-size Asian grocery in Guelph. The Oriental Market on Wyndham Street provides for Guelph's Chinese, Vietnamese, Lao, and Thai communities. The business is currently run by the Tran family.   (Source: Dawn Matheson)

Except for the 1930s post office, there had been few changes in downtown Guelph for decades. This began to change in 1952. The city reconfigured St. George's Square to accommodate more city buses and increased traffic flows, and in 1953 repaved and widened some downtown streets to cope with increasing traffic. The *Guelph Mercury* opened its new building in April of that year on the location of what had once been the livery stable for the Albion Hotel. The ceremony, officiated by Roy Thompson himself and federal cabinet minister Paul Martin Sr., was broadcast on radio station CJOY, a post-war addition to Guelph's downtown scene with studios on the second floor of the Bond building on St. George's Square.

The move triggered further construction. Contractor Joe Wolfond purchased the old *Mercury* building on Macdonell Street, demolished it, cleaned up a burned out property next door, and constructed a large four-storey block containing 51 apartments and seven stores. Wolfond followed this project by buying the old 1894 Royal Opera House at the top end of Wyndham, then housing the Royal Theatre, tearing it down in 1953, and constructing a new building for Simpsons-Sears. The opening of this store on December 2, 1954 caused a near riot by excited shoppers.

Previous downtown construction had resulted from fires. These two were the first involving the demolition of solid buildings. Over the next 20 years many more would disappear, including all the 19th century buildings on St. George's Square, as progress and modernity dominated the thinking of virtually everyone.

Local pride and patriotism had long been a feature of the Royal City, and the desire for growth and progress piggybacked upon the older sentiments. The Guelph Board of Trade began staging annual one-day Guelph Industrial Shows in 1945, featuring displays and demonstrations of goods produced in Guelph. These attracted 1,500 people, sometimes more. On August 7, 1953 the *Guelph Mercury* and the Guelph Transportation Commission staged a free bus tour of the city to view the growth and progress that had taken place, particularly in the previous 18 months. Organizers had expected 150 or so to show up. Instead, more than a thousand crowded into St. George's Square to board the buses. Extra coaches were quickly commandeered, but some had to be turned away. A week later another 950 took the same tour.

The tour was an eyeopener for Guelph oldtimers, accustomed to seeing little change in the city for most of their lives. Particularly noticeable was the new housing, with subdivisions mushrooming all around the city. Housing constructed in 1952 and 1953 increased the residential units by more than 10 percent. The building boom had made construction the largest industry in Guelph by far, and it would remain a dominant one for the rest of the 20th century.

Residential growth, plus servicing demands for the new industrial basin, placed a strain on the city's services. Council issued debentures to pay for more than two miles of water main and sewer lines in 1953, and further water and sewage projects in 1954. The city began a program of paving streets that had previously been gravel or sprayed with oil.

The rapid growth created challenges for the Guelph Transportation Commission. In 1952 and 1953, the commision added six new coaches to the system to take over the daily duties of some of the original buses, which dated back to 1937 and only had 21 seats. The system owned 27 buses, including two for charters, but overall ridership hit a peak in 1951, then began a slow decline. The new subdivisions required adjustments to routes to provide efficient service.

As had been the case for decades, city officials continued to issue rounds of self-congratulation each year through the 1950s with the statements from the Guelph Junction Railway. As of 1952, the 16 miles of line had paid $2.2 million to the city's coffers. The dividend that year was $72,600, the highest since 1923, and equal to about five percent of the property taxes levied that year. The trend, though, was downward, as more freight went to trucks. The dividend dropped to $68,000 in 1953. Officials crossed their fingers that new trackage in the industrial basin would boost revenues.

The boom that began with the annexation talks in 1952, and the announcement of the Canadian General Electric plant, slackened late in 1954, following the official opening of the CGE plant in a ceremony that included C.D. Howe and Ontario Premier Leslie Frost. The boom slackened, but never ended. New construction in 1954 included the United Co-operative's feed mill on Speedvale Avenue, a major addition to Sheepbridge Engineering and a new plant for Hammond Manufacturing. There were also two important takeovers, an indication of the rising portion of American branch plants in Guelph. American Machine and Foundry acquired Leland Electric in 1952, and Rockwell bought out the Callander Foundry a year later. Two 1954 announcements pointed the way to the future. The Department of Highways surveyed the route for Highway 401 through Puslinch. When completed, this route would fuel business growth in Guelph. The other was the promise of Alberta natural gas in 1958, at a cost half that of the coal gas sold by the city.

Surprisingly little immediate interest had been shown in the new industrial basin, but the CGE plant did not sit alone for long. By 1960 there were immediate neighbours: Bucyrus-Erie across Woodlawn Road in 1957, and Imperial Tobacco to the east. The industrial basin itself filled up in the late 1950s and 1960s with dozens of new industries, and continued to spread west. The small, compact city of the first half of the century was gone forever.

CONTINUOUS GROWTH: THE 1960S AND 1970S

The industrial developments of the 1950s established a trend of growth that, except for minor pauses, has been continuous for the balance of the 20th century. After 1960 the vast majority of the new growth located in the west-end industrial basin, and later in the Hanlon Industrial Park at the south end of Guelph.

An important arrival in 1963 was an assembly plant for Allis-Chalmers, turning out lift trucks and tractor loaders. Extensions in 1964, 1966 and 1972 made this firm a major Guelph employer by the 1970s, typifying the trend from foundries and heavy metal working to the automotive industry as the dominant force in Guelph manufacturing.

The electrical sector, strong in Guelph since the 1920s, strengthened with several new plants. The Potter Brumfield Division of AMF Canada Limited began producing relays at 135 Oxford St. in 1958, expanding several times in succeeding years. Pirelli Cables began the 1970s with a new 100,000 square-foot plant on Imperial Road.

Fastest growing of all was International Telephone and Telegraph (ITT) on Dawson Road. Established in 1968, this plant, four years later, had three divisions – communications, controls and fluid handling – and employed 450. A major boost for this plant was a contract for $4,400,000 for automated sorting equipment for Canada Post in 1971. Postal mechanization equipment kept the plant humming through the 1970s.

Export business grew in importance for Guelph firms long before the free trade period of the 1990s. Karl Husson established a customs brokerage business in 1957, and another firm, Terminal Customs Brokers, opened its doors on Dawson Road in 1961.

Rivalling the Church of Our Lady spires on the skyline of downtown Guelph: The Co-operators Insurance "skyscraper" initiated a shift in downtown Guelph's employment profile in the 1980s, with hundreds of office workers. The company employs a workforce similar in size to that at the beginning of the 20th century at the Bell Piano and Organ Company, whose factory stood across Macdonell Street from the Co-operators edifice.   Source: Gil Stelter, 2000

The plant that led the 1950s industrial boom continued to lead Guelph's list of industries into the 1970s. The General Electric plant on Woodlawn Road reached a payroll of 740 in 1972 – still the largest in the city – turning out ever-larger transformers for long-distance transmission lines. In 1969 the plant shipped its first 575,000 KVA transformer – a monster 45 feet long and weighing 375 tons – on a specially-designed railway car. Additions to the plant brought its floor area up to 415,000 square feet.

Next door, the Imperial Tobacco plant, constructed in 1959, ran a close second to General Electric in the size of its workforce. New and faster automated equipment went into the plant in 1971 in a continuing program of technological innovation.

In the retail sector, the approval for construction of the Stone Road Mall in 1972 signalled a new era for Guelph. The mall, when it opened in 1973, immediately drew trade away from the downtown core, a trend that the construction of the Eaton Centre was unable to reverse.

The Eaton Centre, constructed on top of the eastern portion of Quebec Street, altered forever the appearance of the downtown core, St. George's Square, and John Galt's original plan for the city. Other changes were in store for the downtown core. The Co-operators Insurance building on Macdonell Street, at nine storeys, towered over its neighbours. A 13-storey building combining apartments and commercial space replaced the old YMCA building at Quebec and Norfolk streets.

The growth-minded spirit of Guelph dominated the thinking of civic leaders. The growth of the population, to 40,000 and then 50,000, were occasions for celebration. The *Guelph Mercury* noted the 60,000 mark with red headlines in 1971. Most people eagerly looked forward to the milestones that would come in the following years: 70, 80, and then 90,000 people.

The Hammond Manufacturing Company: One of the pioneers of Guelph's electrical components industry, the Hammond firm commenced in the 1920s as a small-scale producer of battery chargers. Today the firm, operating from several sites, produces metal cabinetry and small-scale transformers for consumer products and the electronics industry. The firm's founder, Fred Hammond, also established the Hammond Radio Museum in Guelph, drawing on his personal collection of historic electronic equipment. Source: Dave Carter, 2000

W.C. Wood, on Guelph- Hespeler Highway: From modest beginnings, family-owned W.C. Wood Company today ranks as one of the major industrial employers in the city, and as the largest manufacturer of freezers in Canada. Source: Dave Carter, 2000

OMAFRA: The move of the main offices of Ontario's Ministry of Agriculture, Food and Rural Affairs to Stone Road, adjoining the University of Guelph campus, is yet another phase of the trend, beginning early in the century, of spin-off business development from activities at the Ontario Agricultural College and other university components. At this location, ministry staff are close to university technicians and researchers, and to the numerous small businesses that have developed from university-based activities. Despite the changing role of the ministry, and fluctuating staff levels in the 1990s, consulting firms and small plants linked in one way or another to the university account for hundreds of jobs in the Guelph economy. Source: Gil Stelter, 2000

Once a city of homeowners and single-family houses, Guelph took on a big city appearance with the construction of more apartments and townhouses in the 1970s. New single-family houses accounted for only 30 percent of the new housing built in the 1970s. Another record was set in 1971, when 934 new housing units were constructed in Guelph.

Growth put constant strain on the infrastructure services provided by the city. Guelph Hydro saw annual growth in demand of more than five percent per year during the late 1960s and early 1970s, requiring new substations and transmission lines. Electric heating became popular – over 30 percent of new housing units had electric heat in the early 1970s. Concrete and steel poles came into use in 1971, and Guelph Hydro promoted underground distribution lines in areas where this was feasible.

Of all the municipal services, the Guelph Transportation Commission caused the most headaches. In 1970 the system suffered a $225,000 deficit. The solution was a 20 percent increase in fares, and a realignment of the system's nine routes. Ridership remained flat at about 2.7 million riders per year, below the peak reached in 1951 and far below the peak per capita ridership achieved in 1925 on the smaller and more compact streetcar system. By 1970, fewer than 10 percent of the population used the bus system regularly.

The building boom of the early 1950s, and the policy of promoting the west-end industrial basin for new industry, established an economic climate that, with a few minor ups and downs, prevailed for the rest of the 20th century. During this period the population of Guelph almost quadrupled, and the city annexed further tracts of land, most to its west and south. Even with annexations, Guelph's urban development spilled into Guelph and Puslinch townships as industries and homebuilders sought larger acreages and lower taxes, and were willing to sacrifice some of the urban services of the city. There had always been small businesses on the fringes of Guelph, but the movement began in earnest in 1963 when Superior Propane, Crawford Transport and Viceroy Aluminum set up shop near the old hamlet of Gourock on Highway 24 South. The proximity of Highway 401 was a factor in their site selection.

The arrival of new industries diversified the Guelph economy even further. Takeovers, mergers and plant closures made the last quarter of the century particularly volatile. Old names disappeared, as well as some old businesses such as Rockwell International, successor to the old Callander Foundry and operator of two large plants; Federal Wire and Cable, in the expanded Crowe Foundry, and after an ownership change; the Gilson Manufacturing Company; Harding Carpets, whose once immense labour force had dwindled to 100 when it closed in January 1978; and International Malleable Iron. These had been some of the dominant industries for much of the century. Their demise, in most cases with the ensuing demolition of their plants, further concentrated industry in the west end of the city, and later, in the new Hanlon Industrial Park in the south of the city, where more than 50 industries had located by the end of the century.

FROM SLEEMAN TO SLEEMAN: GUELPH AT THE END OF THE 20TH CENTURY

The list of the major Guelph employers in the 1990s bears little resemblance to that of 40 years earlier. At the top of the list by a wide margin was the University of Guelph, with about 5,000 faculty, research and support staff, and maintenance personnel. The Homewood Health Centre employed about 630, and the Co-operators Insurance Company had a staff of about 500 at its downtown "skyscraper" head office. With these and other white-collar employers in the city, manufacturing claimed a much smaller proportion of the labour force.

A surprising fact, but one quite in keeping with Guelph traditions, was the continuing prevalence of locally-controlled firms, and their success in the last three decades of the 20th century. Three of the top five industrial employers had strong local roots. Linamar Corporation, founded in 1966 by Frank Hasenfratz, prospered in the automotive parts business. In the 1990s the firm operated 15 plants in Guelph and area, with a total payroll of 3,500 and annual sales exceeding $800 million. In second place was W.C. Wood, which had become the largest manufacturer of freezers in Canada (a title once held by the Gilson Manufacturing Company), operating from both the former Taylor-Forbes site, much enlarged over the years, and from a new plant in Guelph Township, with a total of 900 employees. Also ranking high on the list was the Hammond Manufacturing Company, with two plants and 600 employees in Guelph, and another one in Alabama. Still largely owned by the Hammond family, this firm strove to meet new competition as a result of the free trade agreement.

John Sleeman Jr.

Sleeman is one of the oldest names in Canadian beer brewing history. The Sleeman family was involved in beer making as early as 1834. John Sleeman and family moved to Guelph in 1847. Three years later they purchased the property for their Silvercreek Brewery. John's son George, born in 1841, became manager of the beer business in 1862 and, incidentally, in 1880, became the first mayor of Guelph after the incorporation of the city. At the turn of the century, with a population of a little over 11,000 people, Guelph had 42 drinking establishments - averaging one for every 274 people - rather fertile grounds for a brewing entrepreneur. George died in 1926. The brewery closed operations in 1929.

In 1985, the great-great grandson of John Sleeman revived the family business, currently known as Sleeman's Brewing and Malting Company. Born in Toronto in 1953, the young John Sleeman left home at 17. He didn't pursue beer making initially, perhaps because the family's brewing history was never mentioned when he was growing up. Instead he was employed by market researchers A.C. Neilson Company, eventually becoming an executive in the firm. Next he established his own company importing British beers and operating a pub in Oakville. Since he was then in the beer business, Sleeman's aging Aunt Florian made the decision to inform him about the family's past. She presented him with the now-famous diary. He has never looked back. John uncovered the old family recipes for his beer on page 64 in his grandfather's time worn, leather-bound diary. To commemorate this discovery, each bottle cap on Cream Ale bottles has the number 64 printed on the underside.

With his engaging smile and down-to-earth attitude, John capitalizes on his image as a little guy taking on the big conglomerates. He once commented, "there are a lot of people who like the idea of buying from a company where they can call up the guy whose name is on the bottle." In 1996 Sleeman was a director of the Brewers Retail and British Canadian Chamber of Trade and Commerce. He was voted American Marketer of the Year, Toronto Chapter, in 1999.

In 1988, John, dressed in a tuxedo, took one of the first clear, long-neck signature bottles off the line. In a Rolls Royce he visited his grandfather's grave in Woodlawn Cemetery. Here he toasted the gentleman whose diary had made his business possible for him. At the end of the 20th century, Sleeman's Brewery is a multi-million dollar international industry.

– *Ceska Brennan*

 November 2, 1995 – Guelph citizens are used for a pilot project for Mondex Cards. The Smart Card System was cancelled in October 1998 and ceased December 5, 1998.

Guelph firms had been suppliers to the automotive industry since before 1920, but this market became much more significant after 1980. Polycon Industries, which commenced production in 1991 as a joint venture between Ford and Magna International, employed about 800 people to turn out automotive body parts.

Better Beef Limited on Victoria Road, established in the 1970s, had become the largest independent abattoir in Canada by the 1990s, employing about 750, and processing some 300,000 head of cattle for the year. Its fresh and frozen beef found markets across Canada and on the export market. The small scale Oregon Saw Chain Company, which began modestly in 1952, had grown into Omark Corporation, one of the dominant Guelph firms of the 1960s, was taken over by Blount Canada in 1985, but remained a major industry in Guelph with 750 employees. The years after 1960 saw further declines in railway usage, as the completion of Highway 401 diverted more and more traffic to rubber wheels. Canadian Pacific's shuttle service to and from Guelph Junction ended in November 1960. CP closed its Guelph freight and express sheds in 1969. The passenger station, for a time the home of the Guelph Chamber of Commerce, lasted until 1983, when an apartment building took its place.

On Canadian National, passenger service to Toronto remained at a level of four or five daily trains to Toronto until the major cutbacks of 1989, when service dropped to two daily trains each way. Passenger service ended to Hamilton in 1959 and to Palmerston and the north in November 1970. Abandonments of CN's line to Elora and Fergus, and CP's line to Goderich, both in 1989, ended freight service to those points.

Both major Canadian railways underwent major restructuring during the 1990s. As a result, the remaining lines to Guelph were spun off to shortline operators. Operation of the city-owned Guelph Junction Railway, which had been part of the Toronto, Hamilton and Buffalo Railway following the expiration of the 99-year lease to Canadian Pacific in 1987, was turned over to the Ontario Southland Railway on January 1, 1998. Later that year, Canadian National leased its line from Georgetown through Guelph to Kitchener and London, and what

The Sleeman Brewery: The successful revival of a 19th century business by John Sleeman, a scion of the original proprietors, is spreading the Guelph name to beer drinkers far and wide.   Source: Dave Carter, 2000

was left of the branches, to RailTex Corporation, to be operated as part of is Goderich-Exeter Railway. This company had been operating between Stratford and Goderich since 1992. Both shortline operators offered the promise of more personal and timely service to shippers.

One unfortunate outcome of the rapid growth, the sheer size of Guelph, and the volatile economic climate in which plants opened, closed and changed hands, was that the firms and their employees showed a weaker identification with the city of Guelph than had been the case at the beginning of the boom. In 1953, almost 10 percent of the population spent an evening on a bus tour to view the progress of the city. At the end of the century, such an outing seems merely quaint, and no one has considered sponsoring such a tour.

Still, there are ties with Guelph's industrial past that are strong, if not numerous. In 1985 John Sleeman, a direct descendent of Guelph's most famous brewer, re-established the old family firm in Guelph, using the old recipes for the beer. The family had been out of the brewing business since 1937, when Jockey Club Brewery purchased the Sleeman's Spring Bank Brewery. It was a happy day in 1988 when the first bottle of Sleeman's Cream Ale passed through the bottling machine. Sleeman beer, sold in distinctive clear bottles, enjoyed a rapidly expanding market that pushed the brewery beyond the microbrewery category. By the mid-1990s, after purchasing Upper Canada Breweries in 1995, Sleeman beer had between two and three percent of the Ontario market, and 100 employees on the payroll. Occasionally inclined to appear in his own commercials, John Sleeman has built a profile for himself and the company in keeping with the traditions of old George Sleeman at the start of the century. Sleeman, John Wood – another businessman who proudly displays his name over the main door of his factory – and a number of other industrialists continue the traditions set at the beginning of the century: pride in a good product that reflects favourably on those who made it, and stewardship of an industry that is a vital part of the economic and social fabric of the Royal City.

SOURCES

This section is an attempt to come to terms with a century of economic development that involved several hundred industries, an even greater number of retail businesses and the role of a municipal government in shepherding change. I have made use of the standard references as starting points. Leo Johnson's *History of Guelph 1827-1927* is still the standard history of the Royal City. A number of articles in the Guelph Historical Society's annual *Historic Guelph* have been most useful. The *1906 Wellington County Atlas* contains information on some of the important figures at the start of the 20th century.

It is regrettable that so few records and original documents relating to Guelph's industrial and commercial history have survived. The notable exception is George Sleeman. Papers relating to his numerous business activities, including the Guelph Radial Railway, reside at the Guelph Civic Museum, the Guelph Public Library, the University of Guelph Library and the Ontario Hydro Archives.

Guelph's evolving economy has attracted the attention of several students at the University of Guelph. Among those whose unpublished theses I consulted included Cathy Wilson, "The Leading Elite of Guelph, 1870-1890" (1980); John S. Warecki, "Charles Raymond and the Raymond Sewing Machine/Manufacturing Company" (1988); Joe Gabriel, "William Bell: A Study of a Business Elite" (1986); Marvin W. Farrell, "The Guelph Junction Railway, 1884-1950" (1951); and A.A. Burbridge, "Guelph: A Study in Urban Growth" (1953).

On the subject of banking I was able to make use of material I gathered for my PhD dissertation: "Hayseed Capitalists: Private Bankers in Ontario" (McMaster, 1994). During my research on the subject of banking I made notes on businesses in Guelph and Wellington County found in *Monetary Times* and *Industrial Canada.*

My first published article was on the subject of railways: "Streetcars in Guelph," *Historic Guelph* (1983). Published material of direct relevance to Guelph includes Robert Stamp, *Riding the Radials* (1989), and the railway theme issue of *Wellington County History* (Vol. 4, 1991). I also used original public timetables and the printed transactions of the Canadian Freight Association.

Overall, the most important source was the *Guelph Mercury.* Historians are fortunate that an almost complete run of the daily exists for the 20th century, as well as many copies of the weekly edition published in the first quarter of the century. Unfortunately, only scattered issues of the rival *Guelph Herald* have survived, and this paper ceased publication in 1924. In my research on other topics I have frequently stumbled upon Guelph items in other papers published in Wellington and elsewhere, and I have a habit of making notes on them. The Centennial Edition of the *Mercury* (July 20, 1927) has become something of a bible for Guelph historians, and items in it act as guides to other sources. This is the best single source for basic information on the industries and businesses of the 1920s. Also useful is the *Mercury's* golden anniversary issue (July 20, 1917). For the 1950s and after, the *Mercury's* annual progress edition, published in winter or early spring, contains useful information on business activity during the previous year.

Finally, it is convenient to have city directories, old telephone books, and the financial reference books published by *Dun and Wiman* available for reference and for establishing dates and locations of individual enterprises.

CHAPTER 4

BUILDINGS AND GUELPH'S CHARACTER

GILBERT STELTER

Guelph was "a solid, prosperous little city, resembling an Old World country town," according to the 1921 *Guelph City Directory*. Guelph's buildings help to define the character of Guelph; they express its values and cultural traditions; they tell us about the dreams of those who designed and built them and of those who used them; their replacement by newer structures reflects the community's changing interests, priorities and needs.

This chapter is about Guelph's buildings and about those who designed and built them in the 20th century. At one level, it is a story of competing visions of how a city should be built. Should the emphasis be on practicality and function only? Or should there also be a concern for style and that elusive quality, beauty? At another level, it is the account of differing attitudes to the past. Twentieth century builders did not create a new townscape on a clean slate, of course. Much of what we still regard as the essential character of the city was already established by the beginning of the 20th century. How was the older built environment to be treated as the city grew? Should the city look to the future and emphasize modernization? Or was the Victorian townscape a valuable legacy, an incomparable heritage to be maintained and appreciated?

Before we turn to the 20th century itself, it might be useful to understand the nature of the city that 20th century Guelphites inherited.

I GUELPH'S 19TH CENTURY BUILT HERITAGE

Nineteenth century Guelph had two characteristics which distinguished it from most other Ontario communities. One was John Galt's imaginative town plan; the other was the practice of building with locally quarried limestone. To these two could be added an observation that Guelph seemed to attract a particularly talented group of architects and builders.

John Galt's radial, fan-like design of the town site in 1827 produced possibilities for dramatic views and focal points in Guelph that were not generally seen in other Canadian cities until the popularity of the "City Beautiful Movement" of the early 20th century. Most Canadian cities and towns were laid out in monotonous

John Galt's plan of Guelph in 1827.
This engraving is an accurate version of the actual survey of the radial portion of the town site. The radial streets, shown at the top of the plan, focussed on the spot where Galt cut down the mythic maple tree.
Source: Joseph Bouchette, *The British Dominions in North America*, Vol. 1 (London, 1831).

grids or evolved rather haphazardly without any central plan. Galt appreciated the dramatic effect of a building on a prominent hill, and his plan provided this opportunity for the future Catholic church. As a result, the Church of Our Lady has become Guelph's foremost physical symbol, visible for long distances – for example, while approaching the city from the southwest on Highway 24, or from the north on Eramosa Road. Focal points that were created by Galt, such as St. George's Square, which was the original site of St. George's Church, later allowed for the prominent placement of key buildings such as the old Post Office/Customs House. Later generations of Guelph residents have not always appreciated or understood the possibilities of Galt's design. If the two most important public buildings of the Victorian era, the court house and City Hall, had been placed in focal points with streets converging on them, their significance as symbols of citizen involvement in local government would have been immeasurably increased.

The use of local, amber-hued limestone was Guelph's other distinguishing characteristic. It resulted in a remarkably homogeneous, unified townscape of public buildings, churches, businesses and homes. While the styles of these buildings were typical of what one could expect to see in other Ontario towns and cities, the use of stone rather than brick or wood gave a restrained and somewhat stolid look,

Queen Anne: George Sleeman's house (1891), 501 Wellington St. W.
Source; Sleeman Collection, University of Guelph Library Archives

Vernacular Classical: The John McLean house (1847), 21 Nottingham St.   Source: Stelter, 2000

The "Ontario House": 7 Heather Ave.
Painting in oil by artist Evan Macdonald, of his home in 1965.   Source: Macdonald Family Collection

The "Ontario Cottage": the James Perry house, 15 Oxford St.   Source: Stelter, 1988

balanced, rectangular building with a central front door. Some classical decoration in the form of door moulding often was present, but many had the classical proportions and only very plain door and window treatments, as in the McLean house (1847) at 21 Nottingham St. From the 1850s a second type of rectangular cottage usually sported a gothic gable over the front door, a style popularized by pattern books used by builders. This second type became the typical rural "Ontario" house; examples in Guelph include a stone house at 254 Edinburgh Rd. S. The third basic type, the "Ontario" cottage, stemmed from the "Regency" or "Picturesque" cottage, a square one-storey with a hipped roof. These ranged from the very modest, as in William Kennedy's "Yankee Cottage" (1847) where Rose and Arthur streets meet, to the more elegant James Perry house (late 1850s) at 15 Oxford St.

II A New Building Tradition, 1900-1945

During the Victorian era, Guelph was the largest city in the Upper Grand River Valley region, but it grew only very slowly after the boom years of the 1870s. In 1901 its population (11,496) was still larger than that of its nearest rival, Berlin/Kitchener, but by 1911, Guelph's population of 15,196 was matched by that of Kitchener which had quickly become a thriving industrial centre. While Guelph was losing its regional status, it actually grew fairly quickly in the first decade of the 20th century when many important buildings were constructed and a major housing boom took place.

Most of the major new buildings were designed by outside architects like George Miller and John Lyle of Toronto, or by federal and provincial government architects. Local architects and builders tended to concentrate on renovations or additions to existing buildings or on the production of homes. They seldom could afford to concentrate only on architectural commissions, so also supplemented their incomes by acting as contractors, or became involved in real estate business and property management. Among the most active local architects early in the century were William Mahoney, W. Frye Colwill, W. T. Tanner, Louis C. Wideman and George Bruce. Some contractors, like William A. Cowan, also acted occasionally as architects. Slow city growth after 1911 probably explains why the number of practising architects dropped and many new buildings were put up by contractors without the involvement of an architect. The *Guelph City Directory* usually listed about 45 contractors from the 1920s to the 1940s.

Churches

Unlike the Victorian era, church building was not a feature of building in 20th century Guelph. The most obvious exception was the Church of Our Lady. In 1907 and 1908 the interior decoration was completed under the direction of architect Arthur Holmes, referred to as a "disciple and successor" of Joseph Connolly. A number of huge murals were painted on the walls, including one of St. Patrick preaching in Ireland. The most sophisticated stained glass windows in the city were produced by prestigious German and French firms, and included some of local historical interest. For example, one depicts the 1854 ceremony in Rome which declared the Immaculate Conception of Mary. Several Canadian prelates

The construction of the towers of the Church of Our Lady, 1925.
Watercolour by Andre Lapine, July 18, 1925. View from Eramosa Road.
Source: Private Collection

present were shown, such as Bishop Bourget of Montreal, and in the foreground, the Vicar General of the Hamilton diocese, the Very Reverend James Keough who donated the window. A marble sanctuary included a statue of Mary after the style of the great Spanish sculptor, Murillo. In 1926 the exterior of the church was finally completed with twin towers with an English look, like that of the cathedral at Canterbury. It is not clear why Connolly's original plan of twin spires, as those at Cologne Cathedral, was not followed. Perhaps in an effort to reduce costs, concrete, rather than stone pinnacles were used to top off the towers.

One of the few new churches built during this period was Paisley Memorial Methodist Church (1908), located on Margaret Street in St. Patrick's Ward, then the fastest growing part of the city. This replaced a former chapel on Paisley Street which had burned the previous year. One of the major contractors in the city, J.W.Oakes, was in charge of construction. The plans for the church were reported to be "very much after the lines" of Trinity Baptist Church (later a Lutheran church, now condominiums) at 200 Woolwich St., which Henry Langley had designed in 1892. In 1941 the church was redecorated by one of the church members, Gordon Couling, who was trained in ecclesiastical art. Couling later designed and installed some of the most original, locally-produced stained glass windows in the city. Of particular interest are those which depicted general church history and some local scenes such as the burning of the Paisley Street Chapel. **(See centre colour section)**

INDUSTRIES

In the world of work and factory production, the 20th century represented a new spirit of functionality and practicality, with little of the previous concerns for aesthetics and attractiveness in buildings. Nineteenth century industrial buildings had been family-owned and located in the downtown core, and were quite handsome in their own right, as in the case of the Raymond Sewing Machine Company or the Bell Organ Company. The new industries were owned by outside corporations who built in the suburbs, especially in St. Patrick's Ward, later simply known as "The Ward." The local architect who became the leading exponent of this new functionality was William A. Mahoney, who gave a rather plain and undecorated look to most of the buildings he designed. An example was the large Standard Valve and Fitting Company complex that was built on York Road in 1907 at a cost of about $35,000. He also designed the various stages of the International Malleable Iron Company (IMICO) on Beverly Street in 1912 and 1917. The same trend was apparent in the Page-Hersey Iron Tube Company factory that Louis Wideman constructed on York Road in 1903, and in a factory that William A. Cowan designed and constructed for the Louden Machinery Company near the Grand Trunk Railway Junction in 1908. An exception was the work of W. Frye Colwill, who managed to incorporate at least a small measure of style into his factory designs. His factory for Guelph Worsted and Spinning Company at the corner of Arthur and Cross streets (now Len's Mill Store) in 1902 still has some artistic flourishes in the medieval castle-like touches at the top corners.

PUBLIC BUILDINGS

As in other North American cities in the early 20th century, public buildings were designed in a style that has been labelled Beaux Arts classicism, after the famed architectural school in Paris where so many North American architects had trained as students. This new classicism, first displayed in an ensemble of buildings at the Chicago World's Fair of 1893, represented a rejection of late Victorian eclectic styles, such as the Queen Anne, with its asymmetrical massing of towers and other forms. The work in Guelph of Toronto architect George M. Miller reflected this transition in taste. Miller was no stranger to turn-of-the-century Guelph. In 1894 he designed a large brick Queen Anne house for G. B. Ryan at the corner of London Road and Park Avenue. When the Massey family of Toronto gave $40,000 for a library and hall at the Ontario Agricultural College campus, Miller was their obvious choice for he had already designed several buildings for them in Toronto, mostly in the Queen Anne style. The Massey Library and Hall (1901-03) at the Ontario Agricultural College (now the University of Guelph) is one of the finest examples of this style, with its irregular massing, the shaped gables and a quaint tower.

When Miller was commissioned in 1903 by Montreal tobacco magnate,

William Mahoney and car in front of his home, 376
Woolwich St.   Source: Mahoney Family Collection

Massey Library and Hall (1901-1903), Ontario
Agricultural College, about 1910.
Source: University of Guelph Library Archives

Homewood Sanitarium (1905-1907) in 1915.
Source: Guelph Public Library

Miller was also chosen to design the modernization of Homewood Sanitarium (1905 to 1907) at a cost of $150,000. Homewood had been founded in 1883 on Guelph's northern outskirts as Canada's first private psychiatric hospital, using the large limestone house of Guelph lawyer Donald Guthrie as its main facility. Miller added major wings to this house, which was renamed the Manor and became the administrative centre. He also built two new buildings of local stone in the classical style, the Colonial, the main patient area, and the Vista, a smaller facility for patients requiring isolation. All were located on the crest of a hill, overlooking the magnificent grounds with their combination of lawns, gardens, and natural forest.

The most splendid structure in the new classical style conceived by a local architect was the Carnegie Library, designed by W. Frye Colwill in 1902, after he had been in practice for only about two years. Guelph was one of the earliest of the 111 Ontario communities to receive a library grant from Andrew Carnegie, the wealthy Pittsburgh industrialist. The grant of $20,000 allowed the local library board to choose Colwill's elaborate classical plans and the board felt that the use of artificial stone rather than brick or stone would enhance the "classic Grecian" style and give "a much finer effect." Carnegie officials sometimes allowed larger cities to build Carnegie libraries in the newly fashionable style, but seemed horrified that a small city like Guelph would have such pretensions. Although the grant had already been sent, officials complained that the board had "chosen a grandiloquent and expensive exterior" including a impressive dome above the entrance. Local residents, however, generally agreed with library board chairman, lawyer James Watt, who predicted that the library building "will be an ornament to our city for many years to come."

Carnegie Library about 1908.
Source: National Archives of Canada

The Post Office/Customs House about 1908.
Note the changes in the square since the photo taken in the late 1890s.   Source: Guelph Civic Museum

William Macdonald, to design two buildings for the new women's part of the campus, he turned to the new Beaux Arts classicism for the main building, the Macdonald Institute. This building is the best example of this kind of classicism in the city, with its dramatic central entrance flanked by columns and pilasters, and its theatrical terracotta decoration over the major windows. It is a modest version of what visitors to Chicago or other large North American cities would have seen in this period. Miller also designed the third Macdonald building on campus, the Macdonald Consolidated School at the corner of College and Gordon streets in 1907 (now the Macdonald Stewart Art Centre). This school building was extremely plain when compared with the Institute building. Director Judith Nasby has written that Macdonald himself was extremely unhappy with its appearance when he arrived for the official opening. He never returned to Guelph as a result.

 October 11, 1905 – Dr. Stephen Lett, the Homewood Sanitarium's first superintendent, dies while he is a patient at Homewood after suffering from mental illness. (Source: Gordon Guthrie)

W. Frye Colwill, 1871-1928

Colwill came to Canada from England in 1890 with his widowed mother, Fanny, brother Tom and sister Fanny Elizabeth. He had attended art school in England and his mother was determined that he would become a professional. In 1896 he trained with Brampton architect John A. Trimble who designed several Guelph buildings. In 1899 he established his own firm, often working together with his brother Tom who had prepared for a parallel profession, civil engineering. Colwill's family life sometimes resembled a soap opera. His mother Fanny's remarriage to insurance agent Herbert Calvert proved disastrous for Calvert was continuously unfaithful and also left Fanny with numerous unpaid debts. Colwill secretly married Minnie Little against his mother's wishes. Fanny used her artistic ability to help Colwill with architectural drawings and plans. Colwill's interest in architecture tended to the artistic rather than the functional; the Carnegie Library and Torrance School were the best examples of his work. The attraction of the Muskoka area eventually led to a move there with his family in 1918 and a change of career. He went into the tourist business, as the host of his Clovelley Inn at Bala Park Island. Photo source: Colwill Family Papers

A greatly enlarged Post Office/Customs House early in the century provided Guelph with an important public monument in one of the popular variations of the classical fashion. The *Mercury* had long argued that Guelph had been "starved" by the federal Conservative government, with smaller places like Napanee and Deseronto given handsome buildings because they supported the right party. With Laurier's Liberals in power, local Liberal Member of Parliament Hugh Guthrie lobbied successfully for both an enlarged Post Office/Customs House and an armoury. Plans drawn up by federal chief architect David Ewart and his assistant T.W. Fuller took into account the rather restricted, triangular lot on St.

George's Square which held the old post office, constructed in the 1870s. The design resembled that in several small cities across the country, a simplified version of what is now known as Edwardian Baroque, then popular in public buildings in Britain. Ewart decided to build in local limestone after being impressed with the quality of the stone in various local buildings, including Sleeman's house. He reportedly wondered why he saw so many buildings in brick when such good quality stone was still readily available. The $40,000 renovation and enlargement was completed in 1904 by local contractor John Kennedy, a former mayor, with Louis Wideman as the local supervising architect.

The Post Office/Customs House became the city's chief physical symbol for the next 50 years, pictured on dozens of versions of postcards which generally emphasized its prominent position at the heart of the city. But the building lost one of its major clients about 1935 when the federal government moved its post office functions in 1936 to a new fashionable building on a less prominent site on Upper Wyndham Street. This Art Deco structure featured stylized decorative motifs over its doors and windows. William Mahoney was the local supervising architect.

While Guelph had a distinguished military tradition in both artillery and infantry, it lacked proper accommodation for military activities. Guthrie's efforts resulted in plans by Ewart and Fuller for an armoury typical of those in many other places – a red brick structure with limestone trim resembling a medieval castle. Plans were enlarged after Guelphites discovered and then loudly complained that

William Austin Mahoney, 1871-1952

Mahoney was the most prolific architect in Guelph in the first half of the century. He apprenticed as a carpenter and about 1900 became a junior partner of Hamilton architect Stewart McPhee who designed several Guelph buildings, including the fine office building at 20 Douglas St. (1903). By 1906 Mahoney had his own practice. His designs tended to be functional rather than ornamental. His enormous number of buildings included factories, homes, businesses, schools, and he often served as local supervising architect for major projects designed by outside architects. Another major achievement was his planning of about 15 Carnegie libraries in Ontario, including those in Fergus, Elmira and Port Hope. Unlike many other local architects, Mahoney was very successful financially and became a major owner of downtown property. He was an avid sportsman, well known for his baseball, curling and lawn bowling. He was a devoted baseball fan, regularly attending games of the Toronto Maple Leafs of the International League. Photo source: Mahoney Family Collection

The Guelph Armoury (1908), shortly after construction. Source: Mahoney Family Papers

The Provincial Winter Fair building from Carden Street, about 1930. Source: Guelph Public Library

Peterborough's new armoury was larger. Finding a proper location was difficult and the final choice next to the railroad tracks left a lot to be desired in terms of space for outdoor activities, but it did provide an impressive southerly focal point for Wyndham Street. The Guelph Armoury was completed in 1908 at a cost of $140,000, with William Mahoney as supervising architect. For many years the large assembly hall was the location for major community festive occasions.

Guelph prided itself as being the centre of provincial agricultural improvement, especially from the time of the founding of the Agricultural College in 1874. The city's status in this regard was enhanced in 1900 when it was chosen as the site of the Provincial Winter Fair for a 10-year term, which, as it turned out, was to be regularly renewed until the Second World War. Guelph had previously been the site of the provincial fair in 1884 and 1886, and again from 1890 to 1896. Accommodation of the fair's displays and showing of cattle used various venues, but especially the Victoria Skating Rink on what is now the Baker Street parking lot. All of these were far too small. To house an enlarged fair, provincial authorities in 1900 constructed a rather plain building on the old market site next to City Hall, but this too was inadequate. By 1909, provincial architect F. R. Heakes designed a large extension complete with four imposing towers on Carden Street, which were meant to resemble those of the great London meat market, Smithfield, for Guelph was styling itself as the "Smithfield of Canada." William Mahoney was named local supervising architect to the consternation of other local architects who felt that they had not been given a fair chance for the commission.

The extended fair building proved inadequate almost immediately, for the fair drew close to 30,000 visitors each winter. The city council had reluctantly paid for half of the cost of the $50,000 renovation and made it clear it would not contribute any additional funds. Occasional discussions about moving the site of the fair from the crowded heart of the city to a less constricted suburban location never amounted to anything. The obvious problem was that the fair's short-term hectic activity did not seem to lead to any appreciable economic benefit to the city for the rest of the year. The fair was suspended during the Second World War, with the building used for military purposes, such as billeting a Dutch army contingent. A strong local belief that the fair was moved to Toronto to become the Royal Winter Fair is simply a legend, for Toronto's fair was national in scope and operated in parallel for more than a decade to the provincial fair in Guelph. After the war there

The Provincial Penitentiary (1909).
Shown here when it served as a military hospital in 1918.
Source: Guelph Public Library

The County and City Jail (1911).
Source: Dave Carter, 1999

was not enough provincial or local interest to revive Guelph's fair, and the building was partially demolished to make way for the War Memorial Gardens.

One of the city's architectural masterpieces from the early 20th century came from an unlikely source, the provincial jail system. Guelph was chosen as the site of what was regarded as the largest and most completely equipped institution of its kind in the country, with a farm, quarries and industries based on prison labour. The Provincial Penitentiary (later the Guelph Correctional Centre) was built in 1909 on an 830-acre site just to the east of the city. It was designed by one of Toronto's most talented architects, John Lyle, who had studied at the Ecole des Beaux Arts in Paris, and who was to design Toronto landmarks like Union Station and the Royal Alexandra Theatre. The centrepiece of Lyle's restrained classicism at the penitentiary was the handsome administration building, with its strong entrance topped by a relief sculpture of the scales of justice. The rest of the prison spread out behind it in an E-shaped plan. Most of the buildings were built of limestone quarried on the site, including some of the industrial buildings which Lyle designed with grand, arched windows. The landscaped grounds provided a park-like setting for this huge complex.

Much more modest was the local county and city jail built behind the County Courthouse in 1911. William Mahoney designed the jail and the accompanying warden's residence in the restrained version of Edwardian Classicism that was to become his personal trademark in the city. Much of the stone was salvaged from the original octagonal jail that had been built in 1839.

When passenger trains were a primary way of travelling, the local railway stations were busy hubs of communities like Guelph. New stations were built in Guelph by the Grand Trunk and the Canadian Pacific in 1910 and 1911 respectively.

The Old Collegiate in 1909.
Source: Guelph Public Library

Zavitz Hall (1914) about 1920.
Source: Zavitz Collection,
University of Guelph Library Archives

The construction of Creelman Hall in 1914.
Source: University of Guelph Library Archives

St. James Ward School (1910).
Later, Torrance School.   Source: Stelter, 1993

Both companies had standard designs they used across the country in smaller cities. In both cases plans were sent to city council for approval and placed on exhibit at their respective, existing stations. The plans for the new Grand Trunk station at Jubilee Park, next to City Hall in the heart of the city, had the standard hipped roof with bell cast eaves. It also had a rather grand tower resembling a Tuscan villa, which fitted in very well with the towers of the neighbouring City Hall and the Bell Organ factory. The Canadian Pacific station was located away from the downtown at the foot of Trafalgar Square, on its line leased from the city-owned Guelph Junction Railway. The first response from the city fathers to the plans was that this station seemed "too low" and lacked any sort of tower. Company officials, however, replied that they were not building towers on any of their stations, presumably because of the cost for an item that would be decorative only.

SCHOOLS

The schools built in Guelph in this period reflected the competing visions of what was suitable architecture for community buildings. William Mahoney's design for St. Patrick's Ward School (now Tytler) in 1908 was a functional, sober rendering of Edwardian Classicism, typical of most other new buildings across Ontario during this period. In sharp contrast was W. Frye Colwill's conception for St. James Ward School (later Torrance) on Waterloo Avenue in 1910. This was a spectacular interpretation of Beaux Arts Classicism, in some ways even more daring than his Carnegie Library about eight years earlier. A classical temple front featured a strong frontispiece of three huge pilasters topped by a shallow dome. The *Mercury* referred to it as "certainly one of the finest of the public buildings in the city."

The diverging approaches were still present in 1922 when schools officials

decided to replace the old collegiate that had been designed by John Hall in 1878 with a new Guelph Collegiate and Vocational Institute. Colwill submitted two dramatic watercolours, one with classical columns, another with strong Gothic features, but the commission was given to Hamilton architects Hutton and Souter, with Mahoney as supervising architect. Their submission depicted a building in the currently popular Scholastic Gothic, widely used on academic buildings, with Gothic touches restricted to an elaborate entrance. Colwill's daughter later recalled a remark of someone to her mother: "I am standing here looking at that atrocity; it looks like a box or factory and our old Collegiate was so beautiful. Your husband would have given us better."

On the campus of the Ontario Agricultural College, construction which took place in the early 20th century after the Massey and Macdonald edifices were completed effectively followed the original master plan of 1882. This design grouped most buildings along a curved driveway, allowing for the maintenance of a great central open space, Johnston Green. Buildings of this period were designed by draftsmen in the provincial government's Department of Public Works who used a variety of styles rather than working toward a unified look to the campus. Among the most important buildings were the new dining hall, now Creelman Hall(1914), a neoclassical structure with an imposing entrance flanked by four heavy columns, and the field husbandry building, now Zavitz Hall (1914), designed to look like a picturesque English cottage.

In 1922 the Ontario Veterinary College moved to the Guelph campus. Government architects designed a Colonial Revival (or Modern Renaissance)

building with a distinctive cupola, and matched it with a very similar dairy building for the Agricultural College. These two additions, across Gordon Street from the original campus, provided focal points for the ends of the semi-circular drive, effectively fulfilling the original campus plan. The most striking change on campus took place in 1931-32, with the demolition of the Old Main, long the centre of campus life, which served as a residence, a classroom building and administrative offices. Its replacement was a new administration/residence building, Johnston Hall, in the popular Scholastic or Academic Gothic. The portico of Old Main had been carved by local sculptor and builder Matthew Bell as the entrance to a farmhouse which became the original venue of the college. The portico was moved to Johnston Green as a memorial to the college's early days.

The "foursquare" house: 31 Kent St. Designed by William Mahoney for his nephew Harley in 1913.
Source: Dave Carter, 1999

The "gable front" house: 300 Suffolk St. W. One of a set of five built by J.A. Turner on Suffolk St. W. in 1907.
Source: Stelter, 2000

The first "modern" house: 49 Metcalfe St. Built by Dario Pagani as his family home in 1936.
Source: Stelter, 1995

HOUSES

The bulk of any city's built form is made up of houses. The trends apparent in other types of buildings were also present in the styles adopted for homes in the early 20th century. Gone was the preponderance of the Queen Anne and other elaborate styles of the Victorian era. The new concern was for comfort and efficiency, with emphasis on the interior rather than the exterior which was usually quite plain. Technological advances usually included indoor plumbing, built-in gas and electrical utilities and central heating. A basement with laundry facilities also became common.

Two general categories of house styles can be distinguished in this early 20th century period. The first could be called the "plain" house, usually built in red brick. It was overwhelmingly the popular choice and consisted of two types, the "foursquare" and the rectangular "gable front." These were usually put up by building firms who constructed several at the same time on the same street. Many were also built by individuals using pattern books. The second category could be called the "elaborate" house. It was often the product of an architect's design and included everything from Tudor Revival cottages and eclectic combinations that are difficult to label, to Art Moderne and Art Deco.

The most favoured type of the "plain" house was the "foursquare," referred to by the *Mercury* as the "solid square style." These two-storey red brick houses, with their pyramidal roofs, still line the older streets of the city. Variations

of dormers, porches and entrance locations gave a small degree of individuality. The interest was in the interior, where woodwork and fittings were "most elaborate and convenient." Some of the more elegant versions of this type were a set of three at 114, 116 and 118 Queen St. N. designed by William Mahoney for contractors Oakes and Stratton. Each has a Palladian window in the centrally located dormer and Ionic columns on the porch. Smaller and simpler versions were often built in larger numbers, as in the set of nine built by Taylor Brothers on Elora Street in 1909, which have some minimal ornamentation in the form of artificial stone trim.

The rectangular "gable front" house was usually referred to by the *Mercury* as the "workingman's house." It could be built on the narrow lots of the inner suburbs at a relatively low cost, usually in multiple numbers. Examples include a set of five houses built by J.A. Turner on Suffolk Street West in 1907. The *Mercury* suggested that these houses "should be in demand by workers in the new Crowe plant." Another example is a set of 12 built by the Robert Stewart Lumber Company along Victoria Road South in 1912. While owners have modified many of them, the original pattern is still apparent. Many of the homes in "The Ward" are of this type, initially built in conjunction with the many industries which located there.

The second category of houses were those which exhibited a greater sense of individuality, often because they were architecturally designed. These include two by W. Frye Colwill, for his houses were frequently planned to take advantage

William A. Cowan, 1875-1960

Cowan was the son of Walter Scott Cowan, an early Guelph contractor. For several years he attended the Art Students League in New York City before returning to his father's business, which he took over in 1905. He designed many homes, businesses and factories. His outside interests were extensive. He served several terms as alderman, was long associated with the Guelph Planning Commission and with Speed River beautification, and was a prize winning gardener. Portrait by Evan Macdonald. Photo source: Private Collection

of a particular site. His Tudor Revival residence for Dr. Edward Wells (of Homewood) at 100 Queen St. N., in 1902 and his eclectic design for the brewer W.H. Halliday at 35 Spring St. in 1909 both had their interiors so arranged that their owners had spectacular views over the Speed River Valley. William Cowan's house designs tended to be Tudor Revivals, as in his own home at 64 Kathleen St. (1906) and the more elaborate home for banker Thomas McMaster at 35 Queen St. (1911). William Tanner specialized in designing houses for the business elite; most were modern and not easily labelled, as in his own home at 31 Oxford Street (1906). William Mahoney tended to design and build in the "plain" style, but in about 1928, he built himself a new house at 380 Woolwich St. (later the Montessori School) which had Art Deco touches. Probably the first truly "modern" house in Guelph was built by contractor Dario Pagani as his own home at 49 Metcalfe St. in 1936. The streamlined design, the smooth surfaces, and the horizontal emphasis of the Art Moderne style were inspired by the great French modernist, Le Corbusier, whom Pagani very much admired.

Guelph remained a city of single family houses during the early 20th century. Terrace or row housing was virtually unknown, with notable exceptions

Dario Pagani, 1903-1986

Pagani was the major builder in Guelph at mid-century. He was born and raised in the Milan region of Italy and migrated to Windsor as a young man. He moved to Guelph with his wife and family in the mid-1930s and quickly established himself as a builder capable of work beyond the ordinary. Pagani's construction firm specialized in larger projects such as the Memorial Gardens, industries such as Omark (now Blount) and the police station. The last two were designed by his son Richard, who trained as an architect at the Massachusetts Institute of Technology in Boston. Photo source: Richard Pagani

such as Louis Wideman's elegant "Hampshire Terrace", a three unit complex built in 1903 on Duke Street (now Regent Street). Apartment buildings were also rare. An early example was the Delhi Apartments, a three-storey block at the corner of Delhi Street and Eramosa Road. It was built in 1936 by Dario Pagani and partner, Angelo Battaglia, with classical proportions and simple, but graceful classical ornamentation. It demonstrated that apartment buildings, if properly designed, could be attractive, positive additions to an existing neighbourhood.

III MODERNISM AND THE REJECTION OF THE PAST, 1945-1975

The new replaces the old. The Odeon Theatre and the Sears store on the site of the Royal Opera House. Source: Stelter, 1988

Guelph grew considerably in the 1950s (27,383-39,838), and even more in the 1960s (39,838-60,210). This growth, combined with a new spirit of modernism sweeping the western world, transformed the look of the city. In an effort to be progressive, Guelph's residents turned enthusiastically to modernism, which led to the demolition of some of the major symbols of the older city. Those architects who practised in Guelph after 1945 were trained in architectural schools where the new International style of modernism dominated the curriculum. The popular icons of this modernism included Walter Gropius, who abolished all courses dealing with the history of architecture at Harvard, and Mies van der Rohe, who specialized in glass and steel towers without any ornamentation. They shared a rejection of the styles of the past and emphasized design principles that were related to industrial form. In practice, this meant that their buildings were often indistinguishable from factories. Two other modernists, Le Corbusier and Frank Lloyd Wright, were more flexible in their designs than their contemporaries, and their innovative creations influenced some of those architects who shaped Guelph in this era.

The earliest post-war buildings constructed were not the product of the new International style. After the Bond building on St. George's Square was destroyed by fire in 1946, a new Bond building was designed by William

Joseph Wolfond, 1905-1978

Born in Russia, Wolfond escaped the pogroms and with his father came to Guelph in the early 1920s. As a Jewish immigrant, he found it difficult to find work and went into the scrap metal and salvage business. Eventually he began a construction company, Wolfond Construction, and became one of the leading entrepreneurs in the city. Three elements of his business activities merit mention. He bought a large number of downtown properties, especially corner locations, and rented them out to various enterprises. He perhaps was most associated with his demolition business for he took down community landmarks like the Customs House and the Carnegie Library. And he built a number of downtown buildings, including the Odeon Theatre, the Simpson-Sears store and the Bank of Nova Scotia. In 1952 a *Mercury* reporter wrote that he "has the reputation of being able to build them up as quickly as he can knock them down" and that he "doesn't pretend to be a sentimentalist." His sons Arthur and Melvyn formed Armel Properties which became the major developer of the west end of the city. Photo source: Melvyn Wolfond

The old Royal Opera House (1893-94).
Source: Guelph Public Library

Mahoney (probably his last major work), and constructed by Dario Pagani. The *Mercury* felt that it was "one of the most impressively modern structures in the entire downtown district." Pagani was also the contractor for the "remodelling" of the Provincial Winter Fair building into the Guelph Memorial Gardens in 1947 and 1948. Jenkins and Wright of Toronto were the architects. The completed Gardens was considered one of the finest facilities of its kind, with a modern ice surfacing system and superior lighting. City council had actually saved up most of the funds for this facility and was able to pay off the rest within a year.

A key figure in the transformation of the downtown core in the 1950s and 1960s was Joseph Wolfond, whose company specialized in demolition as well as construction. Wolfond made a practice of buying under-used buildings and either renovating them or replacing them with new structures before leasing them to a variety of commercial operations. The first building he designed and built was the old Royal Theatre on Macdonell Street in the early 1930s. Perhaps the best example of his approach was the old Opera House site at the corner of Wyndham and Woolwich streets, which he purchased and demolished in 1953. The Opera House had been designed in 1893-94 by Stratford architect Henry Powell in Romanesque Revival style, but the building lacked the presence of many regional opera houses, partly because of its awkward corner site. After 1923, the building was the Capitol Theatre. In 1954 Wolfond designed and built two adjoining buildings on the site; the Odeon Theatre (now the Club Denim), 166 Wyndham St. N., and the Simpson-Sears store (now being renovated as the Ontario Medical Centre), featuring the modernist look by emphasizing glass and unornamented walls of smooth stone-like slabs. This material evidently met the requirements of a 1946 city bylaw which stipulated the use of stone on all facades on buildings on Wyndham Street.

T. Allan Sage

The International style's formal arrival in Guelph can be precisely dated – it was brought in 1951 by T. Allan Sage, a recent graduate of the University of Toronto's architectural program. Sage had heard that Mahoney, Guelph's only architect, was no longer active, and so he saw there was an opportunity for a young architect. His training at Toronto was almost exclusively in the International style, but his clients in Guelph were less interested in the look than in the low cost possibilities of the style. In an interview with the author in 1995, Sage candidly outlined the difficulties of getting commissions in Guelph in the 1950s. For government jobs, one's political affiliations were crucial. For school projects, one's religion was the key. But the most important factor was who you knew. Sage observed that he was

T. Allan Sage, 1923-2000

Sage was born in Hagersville, Ontario and served in the air force overseas during the Second World War. He studied architecture at the University of Toronto from 1945 to 1950, a time when Eric Arthur was the chief professor and the modern approach was taught exclusively. He opened his practice in Guelph in 1951, specializing in school construction for the Guelph Board of Education. During the 1950s he was the major architect in the city. In 1967 he moved his architectural practice to Toronto, where he retired in 1976. He then embarked on a career as an artist and completed a degree in fine arts from the University of Guelph. Photo source: David Sage forced to spend more time chasing commissions than actually designing buildings. He played golf almost every day and regularly attended meetings of the Kiwanis Club. He designed in his office at night, where he usually had about three draftsmen and a secretary working. He provided the traditional full architectural service for a project which involved the initial design, the discussions with the client, handling the contractors, supervising the construction, approving of payments to contractors – all this for fees which ranged from six percent to 10 percent of the total cost of construction.

**The Christian Education Wing of
St. Andrew's Church.**
The limestone used for this addition came from the
demolished Opera House.　　　　Source: Stelter, 2000

Edward Johnson School (1955).
The lighter coloured brick is the result of retrofitting,
that is, filling the large windows of the original
buildings with brick.　　　　Source: Dave Carter, 1999

such as General Electric (1953) and Imperial Tobacco (1958). Cost restraints were a major factor; the local school board insisted on designs that could be built for $9.50 a square foot, although this figure was later raised. The results were one-storey structures which featured smooth, unornamented wall surfaces ("clean" in Sage's words) which were curtains hung over structural steel skeletons. Wall surfaces were broken by long, continuous windows. Interior walls were partitions which could be easily moved.

　　　During the 1950s, the buildings that Sage designed were primarily in the International style. These included the Federal Government building (1958) on Farquhar Street. A federal government architect gave him a rough sketch plan and left him with the impression that the prevailing modernist style was expected, probably because that would be the least expensive. A more complex, H-shaped building was designed for the Guelph Public Utilities Commission (Guelph Hydro) at the corner of Speedvale Avenue and Dawson Road, where the main portion houses the administrative functions and the two symmetrical wings the maintenance departments.

　　　Sage could also design in a more traditional vein, as in the additions to St. Andrew's Presbyterian Church and Knox Presbyterian Church. At St. Andrews, he used stone from the demolition of the Opera House and designed the addition to match the original gothic structure. In his house designs he also tended to stay away from the more extreme modernist versions.

Schools

The International style proved to be particularly popular for the many schools that were built in the 1950s and 1960s with Allan Sage as the most prolific designer in this area. Compared to the older schools of Guelph, which had been central monuments of the community and symbolic of the exalted place of education in society, the new schools seemed to be merely functional, characterless institutions, indistinguishable from the new factories that now appeared along Woodlawn Road,

　　　The earliest school of this type was probably King George (1948), designed by Toronto architect Gordon Adamson. Another was John F. Ross (1955), also designed by Adamson. The major force, however, was Sage himself, who designed most of the public schools, and some of the separate schools for a 12-year period, starting with an addition to Victory School in 1952. Some of his other schools were Edward Johnson (1955); Ottawa Crescent (1956); Paisley Road (1957); Brighton Street (1959); Laurine Avenue (1959); and June Avenue (1961).

　　　Other architects also designed public schools in the international style, including Richard Pagani with College Avenue (1959) and John Haayen with Waverley Drive (1962). In 1962 the original portion of the old collegiate, designed by John Hall in 1878, was demolished and a large modern wing for shop and occupational teaching was added. A third high school, Centennial CVI and College Heights Vocational School were both designed in 1967 by Abram and Ingelson of Toronto. Old Central School, long a landmark on the Guelph skyline, was demolished in 1968 and replaced by a modern version designed by James Craig of Toronto. This building was superior to most of the other new public schools because the school board was now able to spend more money on new buildings. A new feature was the "open" concept, with a minimum of classroom divisions, although the *Mercury* reported some parents had "doubts and worries" about this new approach. Other changes were apparent at Brant Avenue School (1970), designed by William Jarrett. Windows were now smaller and facilities were included for community use, in the form of a multi-purpose room near the entrance.

　　　The plans for the separate school board tended to be slightly more

St. Joseph's Hospital in 1912.
The oldest portion, dating from 1861-1877, is shown at the far left. The 1895 portion dominates the view.
Source: Guelph Public Library

St. Joseph's Hospital, 20ᵗʰ century additions.
One of the 1924 wings is to the left, the 1951 modern structure is to the right. Source: Stelter, 2000

Guelph General Hospital about 1910.
This postcard view shows the three portions of the old hospital. Source: Guelph Public Library

The new Guelph General Hospital.
The 1951 hospital can be seen to the far right. The 1969-1971 building is in the foreground.
Source: Stelter, 2000

adventurous. Holy Rosary School (1955) was designed by Allan Sage in the low, horizontal style that had become his hallmark. Richard Pagani's scheme for St. Bernadette (1959) was also basically in the International style. By the 1960s, the designs for schools moved beyond the purely functional. When Bishop Macdonell High School was built in 1962, the modernistic structure was decorated with gothic touches on the exterior and became a fitting companion of other religious buildings on what was known as "Catholic Hill." John Haayen's design for Our Lady of Lourdes Secondary School (1965) included some Corbusian touches (since removed in a renovation) in the windows of the library, which were of different shapes and irregularly placed, as in Corbusier's famous chapel at Ronchamp, France. And in an obvious retreat from the horizontal look of the modernists, Karl Briestensky's design for St. Patrick's School (1968) featured strong vertical lines in its windows and brick columns.

HOSPITALS

Guelph's two hospitals were given modern facelifts during this period, but each is the product of numerous additions over the years. In the case of St. Joseph's Hospital, operated by the Sisters of St. Joseph, the original building of 1861-62 was doubled in size in 1877 in a matching style with its distinctive gothic gables. In 1895 a large new building was built to the east, designed by local architect John Day, with gables that evoked the spirit of the original which was converted into a House of Providence for "the aged and infirm." Much of the Day-designed building was retained when three-storey wings were added in 1924. A five-storey modern structure was completed in 1951, facing Westmount Street. Designed by

the Toronto firm of Maroni, Morris and Allan, the stepped-back configuration and the monumental look hint at a simplified version of the Art Deco style. In 1959-60, a spacious new home for the aged was added, and the historic 1861-1877 building demolished.

The General Hospital's history is equally complicated. The original public hospital was designed in 1875 by Victor Stewart in the prevailing Second Empire style, with a mansard roof. Wings were added in 1887 and 1897. Three other buildings made up the General's complex: the Elliot Home, a Protestant "House of Refuge" (1904, demolished in 1965 for the new Elliot); the Nurses's Residence (1911-12, now the City and County's Family and Children's Services offices), designed by Hamilton architect Stewart McPhee in Edwardian Classicism; and the Isolation Hospital (1911-12, now the Delhi Street Recreation Centre), behind the nurse's residence, designed by local architect W.T. Tanner in Edwardian Classicism. The badly overcrowded conditions in the main facility were finally addressed in 1950-51 with a new modern hospital in the International style designed by Maroni and Morris. According to Alan Whitworth, former executive

 1951 – The post Second World War baby boom necessitated an expansion of hospitals across the province, including St. Joseph's. An addition is opened with a new ward which included a room for the preparation of formula, while new mothers received instruction on how to care for newborns in the conference room. Fathers, who traditionally did not observe or assist at the birth, had their own waiting room at the end of the ward. (Source: Gordon Guthrie)

 August 16, 1922 – The first X-Ray machine is installed in Guelph at the General Hospital.

Len Ariss, 1922-

Born and raised in Guelph, Ariss apprenticed with J.D. Oakes and formed his own construction company in the early 1940s. He owned his own heavy equipment for excavating and did work for many of the main builders such as Reid and Laing and Brazolot. Even a partial list of the buildings constructed by his firm reads like a history of building in the city for it includes a number of schools such as June Avenue and Waverley Drive, Harcourt Church, factories such as Hammond Manufacturing and Allis-Chalmers, bridges like Allen's and Eramosa, the Guelph Public Library, the Royal Bank, the nurse's residence at the General Hospital and the Guelph Airpark, which he owns and operates. Photo source: Len Ariss

director of the hospital, staff were not consulted in the planning process. Planning concentrated on the number of beds but not the required support facilities, because government grants were based on numbers of beds only.

In 1957 a new nurses' residence located on the site of the original hospital, was designed by the Toronto and Peterborough firm of Craig and Zeidler. Len Ariss, whose construction firm had the contract, recalls working closely with Eberhard Zeidler (who was to become one of Canada's most prominent architects) on what was a very advanced building for its time. Two large columns formed the basic support structure, with reinforced concrete cantilevered out from the centre. This residence is now the Medical Health Centre on Delhi Street.

Craig and Zeidler also had the commission for the large addition in 1969-71, which more than doubled the size of the hospital. While this was also based on the International style, with curtain walls and continuous ribbons of windows, it obviously was different from the earlier portion. Funding was based on a new financial arrangement, with costs split between the federal, provincial and municipal governments on a formula based on square footage, not beds. And in a new spirit of architectural design, Craig and Zeidler researched requirements from the point of view of patients and consulted the staff.

NEW ARCHITECTS

During the 1960s, Guelph-based architects began to move away from a strict adherence to the more sterile forms of the International style. Three new architects

 1949 – The General Hospital appoints its first pharmacist.(Source: Gordon Guthrie)

began to practise in the city: John Haayen, with experience in Europe, the United States and South America; and two local products – Richard Pagani, the son of contractor Dario Pagani; and Karl Briestensky, who would become the most prominent architect in the city in the 1980s and 1990s. Haayen's work included the Westmount medical building, which he designed with his partner Jack Campbell. The building was constructed in 1965 by the local contractor William Parker. Haayen visited several clinics in Toronto before drawing up final plans of a central core with offices arranged around the perimeter. The exterior featured tall narrow windows with concrete louvers or sunshades. As a result of the impact of this building, Haayen was invited by the Omark firm in 1964 to join Richard Pagani in designing their offices and plant near the corner of Edinburgh and Woodlawn roads. The massing and window treatment were similar to the medical building, but at a different scale. In 1967 the same look was applied to the new YM-YWCA building (now Crestwicke Baptist Church) on Speedvale Avenue, where Haayen's partner, Jack Campbell, was in charge of design.

John Haayen, 1927-

Born in Dutch Curaçao, Haayen was trained in architectural engineering at the University of Delft and later in architecture at the University of Toronto. His favourite architects were Eero Saarinen, Le Corbusier and especially Frank Lloyd Wright. Haayen came to Guelph in 1960, but much of his work has been done abroad - in Europe, the West Indies and Africa. His work is primarily institutional, including schools like Waverley Drive and Our Lady of Lourdes, industries such as Omark, Rockwell and Korzite, and for five years, the Guelph Police Station.

His conception of Harcourt Church is on his desk, showing a separate spire which was never built. Photo source: Stelter, 1995

Richard Pagani only practised architecture in Guelph for less than a decade but he produced some notable buildings which indicated a considerable degree of imagination and innovation. A good example was the Guelph Police Station on Wyndham Street which he designed in 1959 and which was constructed by his father's firm. To what was essentially still a modernistic glass and brick box, Pagani added a partial second storey decorated with what locals

Omark (now Blount) offices.   Source: Stelter, 1995   Guelph Police Station (1959).

Source: John Haayen

referred to as "Christmas trees." Pagani recalls being influenced by trends in Boston where he had studied. He felt that perhaps he could get people's attention by designing a building which was "a little bit out of the ordinary." John Haayen was impressed with Pagani's daring design and remembers thinking that "you would need some nerve to design a building like that in good old Guelph."

Richard Pagani, 1930-

Born and raised in Guelph, Pagani is the son of the late Dario Pagani. His architectural training at the Massachusetts Institute of Technology combined an emphasis on engineering and the fine arts, especially modern painting. After a year's apprenticeship in Italy, he began to practise in Guelph in 1957. His designs for schools, houses, institutions and factories were imaginative and beyond the ordinary. In 1967 he left Guelph to work for H.G. Acres of Niagara Falls, partly because of his disappointment at a local tendency (especially on the part of the university) to go to outside architects for the major projects. Photo source: Richard Pagani

CHURCHES

The designs of several churches illustrate a transition to a more dramatic approach to building in the city. The first was Pagani's design for St. Paul's Presbyterian Church (now Westminster-St. Paul's) on Victoria Road in 1959. A curved roof sweeps upwards almost from the floor level, creating a spectacular interior. A second church was John Haayen's design for Harcourt United Church on Dean Avenue in 1962. Haayen consciously distinguished between the lower portion, which he related to the scale of the houses on the street, and an A-frame, spire-like

St. Paul's Presbyterian Church (1959), now Westminster-St. Paul's.   Source: Dave Carter, 1999

Holy Protection Mother of God Ukrainian Catholic Church (1962).   Source: Stelter, 2000

St. John's Catholic Church (1967-69).   Source: Stelter, 2000

main portion, which represented the divine. The original design called for an A-frame of 75 degrees, but church officials insisted on a less precipitous look and the final compromise was 60 degrees. A third church, the Ukrainian Catholic Church on York Road, completed in 1962, provided a new feature to the Guelph skyline, a Byzantine style more familiar on the prairies. A fourth church was St. John's on Victoria Road, built in 1967-69, an early work of Karl Briestensky. This church building was a compromise between the wishes of a local parish committee who wanted to hire a local architect with innovative ideas and that of the Hamilton Diocesan Building Committee who argued for a more experienced and conventional church architect. The Diocesan Committee considered Briestensky's original designs a "departure from current church design" but eventually accepted a redrafting of the plans. Briestensky acknowledges the twin influences of Frank Lloyd Wright and Le Corbusier on his work and says that the pyramid-shaped structure was based on a Wright design and the unusual bell tower was derived from Le Corbusier's design for a French monastery.

THE UNIVERSITY OF GUELPH

Some of the most modern construction in the city took place on the campus of the new University of Guelph as it was being expanded beyond its older functions as an agricultural college in the 1960s. This expansion was guided by a new master plan established by Project Planning Associates, headed by two OAC horticultural graduates, Macklin Hancock and Don Pettit. Both were also graduates of Harvard, and Hancock had just completed a major planning initiative, Don Mills, a development that was to become the prototype for subsequent Canadian suburban planning. One of the consultants they brought in was Jose Luis Sert, the Spanish artist who was the dean of the Graduate School of Design at Harvard. Sert proposed creating a new urban-style campus next to the old agricultural college campus concentrated on Johnston Green, rather than merely adding new buildings to the old campus and thus destroying the character of the old. The new portion was to centre around an urban square, now Branion Plaza, and was connected to the old campus by a broad brick walkway, later named Winegard Walk.

The new buildings of the campus reflected the architectural fashions of the 1960s. The architectural branch of Project Planning designed the first major buildings of the new campus, an arts building and a library, with Sert as a consultant. The McLaughlin Library was designed in what became known as Brutalism, based on Le Corbusier's use of *bréton brut*, a concrete whose surface was left as found after the wooden forms were removed. The building itself is a varied composition of differing shapes and textures, and relies on load-bearing walls rather than the glass curtain walls of the International approach. The Arts building (now MacKinnon) was Corbusian in another sense, based on his striking apartment towers in Marseilles and Nantes which were widely imitated around the world. University faculty were involved in planning the interior functions of the building and chose to divide the academic functions of the building, with professorial offices in the tower, awkwardly isolated from the classrooms located in an attached three-storey wing.

THE FATE OF THE CUSTOMS HOUSE

The interest in the new modernistic styles of architecture was usually accompanied by a lack of respect for the traditional architecture of the city, especially during the 1960s when this destructive trend was North American in scope. In New York City, for example, the demolition of Pennsylvania Station led the *New York Times* to condemn "this monumental act of vandalism... any city gets what it admires, will pay for, and, ultimately deserves... And we will probably be judged not by the monuments we build but by those we have destroyed." This seems a fitting commentary on Guelph's activities in regard to heritage in the 1960s. The major battleground was St. George's Square, the symbolic centre of the community, which was ringed with a number of fine limestone buildings going back to the mid-19th century.

The first and most important building to be threatened was the Customs House, which had long been both a customs house and a post office. After the removal of the post office functions to the new building on Wyndham Street in 1936, the old queen of the square slowly deteriorated. In early 1960 it was declared surplus by the federal government's Crown Assets Disposal Corporation and put up for sale. A lively public debate quickly took place, partly through the editorial pages of the *Mercury*. Many writers referred to European cities and the extent to which they took care of their heritage. One writer argued that Guelph's distinctiveness depended on buildings like the Customs House, for without it, Guelph would be "on the way to the monotonous anonymity of just another small Ontario city." An occasional letter in defence of "progress" was typified by "a downtown business man" who condemned the building as old-fashioned and costly to maintain: "any business man can recognize that this land should be put to far better use."

Melvyn Wolfond, 1933-
Source: Stelter, 2000

City council probably reflected the public's will when it decided to try to purchase the building for civic uses at a reasonable price. The city's bid of $25,000, however, was far exceeded by a bid for $101,000 from an unknown party. Federal officials made it clear that they would sell to the city if it could match the winning bid. In May, Alderman William Hamilton, the chairman of council's special projects committee, negotiated a tentative deal with a local development firm, Armel Properties, Limited, which would purchase the building from the city at cost. Armel was a company formed by Arthur and Melvyn (Mel) Wolfond, sons of local contractor and demolition specialist, Joseph Wolfond. If this deal were completed, the Customs House facade and clock tower would be saved without any cost to the city.

The partially demolished Customs House
in St. George's Square, 1960.
Watercolour by Evan Macdonald.
Source: Macdonald Family Collection

The Bank of Nova Scotia (1961).
The replacement for the old Post Office/Customs house.
Source: Stelter, 1987

The supposedly ideal solution fell apart at the July 18th, 1960 meeting of city council when Armel announced they were withdrawing from the deal. A letter from Mel Wolfond gave two reasons. First, they had received estimates, including one from Allan Sage, which suggested that the cost of renovating the building would be as high as $250,000, much more than the building was worth. Second, they had learned that the highest bidder was a local firm, Tri-County Holdings, a business organization with which they did considerable business. Tri-County's lawyer at the council meeting made it clear that they intended to demolish the building and erect a bank building, which later turned out to be the Bank of Nova Scotia. Alderman Hamilton's attempt to get council approval for talks with Tri-County failed. There was no discussion of the city actually raising the required funds for outright purchase; this would have gone against all local government traditions. The building was surrendered to Tri-County by default.

Much of the real activity in this case took place behind the scenes, according to some of the key players involved. The principals of Tri-County were Philip Gosling and Albert Fish. They had assembled several properties as the site for a new Woolworth's store, which included a building leased by the Bank of Nova Scotia. This move released the bank from a lease and allowed it to become the major tenant of the next stage, Tri-County's acquisition of the Customs House site. Because of delays in the process, which included the city's opposition, Tri-County decided to transfer the purchase agreement directly to Armel. Tri-County thus changed its role from that of prospective developer to that of sales agent.

In October and November of that year, Wolfond Construction demolished the historic landmark. The *Mercury* reported that an estimated 200 people gathered on the street in front of the building on the morning of November 17th to watch as the clock tower thundered to the ground. Early in 1961 Wolfond constructed the new bank building at a cost of $240,000, about the estimated cost of repairing the old customs building. The bank was designed in the Miesien International style by Mel Wolfond who had studied architecture at McGill University. Perhaps no modern building in the city has attracted as much negative response from the public, partly because of what it replaced, but also because most people probably did not really like modern architecture.

THE MODERNIZATION OF ST. GEORGE'S SQUARE

The other banks on St. George's Square all followed the lead of the Nova Scotia. In 1961 the Bank of Montreal began demolishing its premises in stages, beginning with the manager's residence which had been built by George Miller in the French Chateau style in 1892. In 1962 they removed their original bank building which had been built in the mid-1850s, possibly to the designs of the great William Thomas. By early 1963 a stone and glass structure in the modern style was completed. The *Mercury's* 1963 'Progress Edition' featured a full front page spread with the headline: "St. George's Sq. Scene of Big Changes." In a caption a writer argued that while "some people may be critical of this change, we must move with the times... we must accept these changes if we are to keep up our place in this modern world."

Two other banks and a trust company completed the "modernization" of the square in the next few years. The impressive Bank of Commerce building, in Scottish Baronial style with a corner turret and matching stepped corbels, came down in 1968 **(See centre colour section)**. It was replaced in 1969 by a rectangular structure in limestone and granite, designed by the Niagara Falls firm, H.G. Acres Limited, and built by Len Ariss Construction. The Royal Bank's move involved the demolition of two stone buildings on the square. The first was the removal of the Mahoney building in 1970, a Second Empire structure which dated back to 1887, and its replacement by a nondescript modern glass and stone building in 1972. The Royal's previous premises, the Tovell building, was a fine Victorian stone structure designed by John Hall in 1881. It was pulled down in 1974 to make way for a modernistic new stone, steel and glass building for the Royal Trust Company, designed by Karl Briestensky.

The Toronto-Dominion Bank building (1859).
This fine structure was renovated in 1962 and again in 1977.
Source: Stelter, 1995

Carnegie Library tower demolition, 1964.
Pastel by Evan Macdonald.
Source: Private Collection

The Guelph Public Library (1965). Source: Dave Carter, 1999

By today's standards, many of these demolitions on St. George's Square would be considered nothing less than vandalism, demonstrating a particular cultural blindness to the possibilities of historical restoration. Not all of the buildings on the square were worth saving, but the Customs House, the Bank of Commerce, the Bank of Montreal and the Tovell building were structurally sound and probably could have been restored for less than the cost of a new building. That this restoration was possible in the 1960s was amply demonstrated by the decision of the Toronto-Dominion Bank to renovate its premises at the corner of Wyndham and Macdonell streets in 1962. This building had been designed and built by David Allan in 1859 for Nathaniel Higinbotham as a drug store, and represented an excellent example of Guelph's mid-19th century architecture. The $50,000 renovation project was handled by William Parker Construction, well known for his fine stone work. The bank later refurbished the entire building in 1977, demonstrating the practicality of saving rather than destroying the city's heritage.

The Demolition of the Carnegie Library

The case of the Carnegie Library was more problematic. The Beaux Arts design of W. Frye Colwill had helped make it one of Guelph's favourite buildings, but it was poorly and cheaply built of artificial stone. By 1960 it was far too small for the amount of use it received so the library board hired Mel Wolfond to propose plans for an extension. His report suggested that a new library could be built for the same cost as renovation and an addition. Chief librarian John Snell strongly supported this approach, for a new building would be more efficient. Nevertheless, the library board spent almost three years trying to save the building because of strong public opinion that it be preserved. In 1963 they hired

 January 5, 1984 – In its 100th anniversary year, the Guelph Public Library establishes its first branch library at Bullfrog Mall on Eramosa Road.

the Toronto architectural firm of Murray and Fliess, well known for their libraries in the Toronto area. James Murray was the principal involved with the Guelph project. He was a faculty member of the architectural school at the University of Toronto and the teacher of several of Guelph's architects. The following year he told city council that he felt the building could not be repaired. What upset many Guelphites, however, was his conclusion that its demolition "would not constitute a serious historical loss to the city."

Public reaction through the pages of the *Mercury* was heavily in favour of saving the library in some form, for it had become a much-loved local symbol. Many of the writers presented practical solutions. The president of the Guelph Historical Society, Hugh Douglass, suggested that the Carnegie Library be saved in its present form as a reference or special collections library and that a new general library be built in another location. Further engineering reports convinced the library board and city council by the fall of 1964 that demolition was inevitable. With that decided, one writer concluded that "we are going to wake up sometime around 1980 and find that we have become the most nondescript city in Canada."

The sight of Joe Wolfond's crews demolishing an older building in the downtown had become a familiar sight to Guelph residents. Among those who witnessed the dome crashing down on December 7, 1964, was the artist Evan Macdonald. In a number of sketches, watercolours and oils he protested the action by documenting it for future generations.

Demolition revealed a building that probably could not have been saved even with the best of intentions. Len Ariss, who had the contract for the new building, helped in the demolition and recalls being surprised by the shoddy construction. The new building, on the other hand, was also a disappointment to many. Architect James Murray said that he would produce "a traditional, conservative, and interesting building." The result was a modern glass and stone structure completed in the summer of 1965. Unlike its predecessor, it has never become one of the defining elements of Guelph's identity.

Organizing for Heritage Conservation

A local heritage conservation movement eventually took shape, led by Professor Gordon Couling, head of the fine art department at the University of Guelph. In 1969 he was elected president of the Guelph branch of the Architectural Conservancy of Ontario and took on the joint tasks of educating the public about the value of the local architectural heritage, and of organizing resistance to the destruction of older buildings. The first case the Conservancy handled, however, did not bode well for its future. Couling tried unsuccessfully to find another use for the city-owned Allan's Mill which dated back to the earliest days of Guelph. But it was subsequently demolished with only a remnant kept as the centre-piece of Heritage Park. Couling's efforts in another respect had greater long-term impact. In 1974 he worked with city officials to set up an inventory of buildings that Couling felt had historical and architectural merit. The result was the 28-volume *Couling Inventory*, which formed the early basis for decisions on what should be preserved.

Housing

The other side of the coin to the changes in the downtown core was the rapid spatial expansion of the city through the building of new suburbs. This expansion was based primarily on the building of thousands of single-family houses, in which the city maintained its traditional low-rise approach to housing. Apartments and row houses, for rental and then for condominium ownership, first became significant in the late 1960s, then quickly grew in number. The story of housing during this period in Guelph is really a remarkable success story. Houses became larger, were better equipped, and remained affordable for the vast majority of the population. The residential expansion to the suburbs was accompanied by the building of convenient shopping malls which, incidently,

Aerial view of wartime housing, c. 1950.
The housing is located on the outer edge of the city (mid-photograph). The complex to the left is concentrated around Winston Crescent and Franklin Street while the housing to the right is on Dunkirk Street.
Source: Elsebeth Pederson

decentralized the city's commercial functions and threatened the downtown core's primacy in retailing.

A major factor in the rapid expansion of housing in Guelph as elsewhere in the country was the intervention of the federal government during and after the Second World War. The government granted mortgages which made home ownership possible for many people for the first time. It also set building

The "Bevin Simplex," 47 Division St., 1947. Source: Robert Mogk

standards and provided model plans for builders to construct modest but efficient and comfortable homes. This government activity also created a building industry of big and small firms who were able to take advantage of the mortgage system and the standardized plans.

The federal government's involvement began during the war through a Crown corporation, Wartime Housing Limited, which was set up to provide housing for war workers and veterans. These so-called "Victory Homes", or simply, "wartime houses," were modest in size, from 600 to 860 square feet, without a basement. They were pre-fabricated, and then brought to the site for assembly by local builders. Several models were usually available; the most popular in Guelph and across Canada was the Type C, a one-and-a-half storey unit reminiscent of the Cape Cod colonials on the East Coast. Another popular model was a one-storey bungalow. Local examples of each appear in a 1947 development of 60 lots on Winston Crescent and Franklin Street. (Note the first names of the two most famous wartime leaders). In two other developments, the Type C dominated: the 75-lot development on Paisley Road and Memorial Crescent in 1948, and the smaller development on Dunkirk and Cassino avenues in 1948. The success of the program can be gauged by the fact that these houses still represent an important part of the landscape in older suburban neighbourhoods.

Veterans could also take advantage of a federal government program that gave them priority ratings in the purchase of the very scarce housing materials. An example is a house constructed by Robert Mogk at 47 Division St. in 1947. He purchased a pre-fabricated model called the "Bevin Simplex" at a base price of $1,779 from the Halliday Company of Burlington. The company delivered the

materials in sections to Guelph. Contractors were hired to construct the block walls of the basement, to erect the pre-fabricated sections, to put on the roof, and to do the plumbing, heating and plastering. Mogk, who was an electrician, did the electrical work and the interior finishing. The style of the "Bevin Simplex", known as minimal traditional, was one of the most popular house styles in the country during this period.

A second stage in the federal government's involvement in housing came with the creation in 1945 of the Central (now Canada) Mortgage and Housing Corporation (CMHC) which administered the National Housing Act. CMHC also supplied books of approved designs which local builders used extensively. According to local builder Peter Brazolot, the process worked something like this: he would apply to CMHC for a mortgage for a particular house by submitting a house plan and an expected purchase price. If CMHC agreed with the proposal, it approved a mortgage of up to 80 percent of the expected selling price, for 25-year terms at five to six percent.

Another factor in the rapid expansion of residential building was the availability of relatively inexpensive suburban land. There were usually two major stages in the process of developing suburban land for housing: the subdivision of vacant or underused land, and housing construction. These tasks were often divided between those who acted as developers and those who were builders, but in some cases, one firm handled the entire process. Developers initiated the action and gave direction to the city's growth. Local developer Philip Gosling makes the case that developers really shape the city by their activities which include the assembly of land, applying for rezoning if necessary, and determining the economic level of the future neighborhood by the size of the lots that are laid out. Until the 1960s the city installed all services and charged a local improvements levy over a number of years to the purchaser of a house or lot. Later, the developer was expected to put in these services in advance, which increased the initial cost to the purchaser.

Most of Guelph's suburban development was done on a relatively small scale, with many players involved. This activity was confined almost entirely to local entrepreneurs with national companies such as Cadillac-Fairview and Bramalea hardly involved. Builders such as Peter Brazolot or Reid and Laing sometimes acted as developers as well as builders. At other times they purchased land from local developers such as T.T. "Jack" Skov or Albert Fish, or from Armel Properties, the biggest developer who concentrated on west-end land. Mel Wolfond recalls buying land in the west end at very low costs in the 1950s when no one else wanted it because it was across from the sewage plant or was the site of abandoned gravel pits. Armel built houses for four or five years in the suburbs but generally specialized in development, selling lots to various local builders. The character of the western part of the city was determined by their development.

Piecemeal, small scale developments were the norm in the subdivision process in Guelph. As an example of how the system worked, we will concentrate on one small developer, Jack Skov, and his first subdivision, for his methods appear to have been fairly typical. In 1952, the year he began his real estate firm, Skov purchased a 22-acre farm between Eramosa Road and Speedvale Avenue, near the city's northern boundary. This farm had been operated since 1845, first by Andrew Ritchie, who in 1866 had built a one-and-a-half storey, red-brick farmhouse with the familiar gothic gable over the entrance. Skov used this farmhouse as the centre-piece of a little subdivision of nine lots he laid out on a new street, Orchard Crescent. The subdivision itself was called "Sunset View" and was the first of several he laid out on the crest of a glacial moraine that runs through that part of the city. Skov retained several rights over the property he sold. Purchasers of lots had to agree to build in the middle of the large lots (making further subdivision difficult in the future) and their house plans could not be carbon copies of others on the street.

In the following years Skov slowly added new sections to his original subdivision, presumably as the economic circumstances warranted. Five more portions were named "Sunset View" by 1962, numbered consecutively from II to VI. Skov continued to develop property in the general area at least until 1974. Builders competed for the lots which only became available sporadically. One builder recalls a common saying at the time: "When Skov fiddles, builders dance." Architects like Allan Sage, Richard Pagani and William Jarrett designed a number of homes in the area for professionals and businessmen.

The building process itself was dominated by many small builders and several larger, local firms. A typical small builder of the 1940s was J. Douglas Oakes, who had just a few employees including his son Robert who went into the business at age 14. Oakes built about 30 houses in 1948-49 in Bedford Park, a small subdivision laid out by Thomas Bedford on McCrae Boulevard, Forest Hill Drive and parts of James and Water streets. Oakes later went into the manufacture of brick and pre-cast concrete.

The production of the larger building firms in Guelph was modest by metropolitan standards. Peter Brazolot, for example, began building houses in

Executive Members of the Guelph Builders Exchange, 1974.
Left to right. Front row: Len Ariss, Ariss Construction; Ken Bohn, Bohn Tile; Dennis McMurtry, Northeast Engineering and Construction. Back row: Peter Brazolot, Brazolot Homes; Roy Lefneski, General Contractor; Joe Goetz, Goetz Construction; Henry Battaglia, A. Battaglia Construction; Gordon Campbell, Knel Hardware.   Source: Len Ariss

Tage Teilman "Jack" Skov, 1902-1990

Born in Denmark, Skov attended an agricultural college in Copenhagen. He came to Canada in the 1920s and to Guelph in the early 1930s, where he had a variety of careers. Together with a brother, Helge (Joe), he started a dairy. He later farmed about 160 acres to the north of the General Hospital. In 1952 he founded T.T.Skov Real Estate and began a successful career in real estate and land development. As a benefactor, Skov donated the land for Skov Park and contributed to the construction of its tennis courts. A long-time Rotarian, his bequest to the Rotary Foundation made possible the construction of the auditorium of the Evergreen Seniors' Centre which is named after him. According to his former housekeeper, Elsebeth Pedersen, Skov was an inveterate joker about his business dealings, but she recalls one instance in which his humour backfired. In 1988, in an interview with the *Mercury*, Skov told the reporter that he had bought his real estate company for "two bits," and that he had only put down the same amount for his first big land purchase. The reporter took him seriously and made it the basis for his article, to Skov's great embarrassment. Ironically, the same details were repeated in the *Mercury* obituary two years later. Photo source: Elsebeth Pederson

1946, and has built over 1,000 single-family homes. In two early projects – Louisa Drive in 1954 and Julia Drive in 1959 – he acted as his own developer. These houses were about 900 square feet, selling for $4,500. At this time the city was still putting in the services and charging purchasers for local improvements. Brazolot usually had only three employees, who poured the concrete for the foundation, did the framing, shingles, windows and cupboards. The rest was subcontracted, including the excavating (often by Len Ariss), electrical, plumbing and heating, and plastering. An example of a later, larger project in the 1960s was a subdivision he called Crestwicke, part of a larger development by Albert Fish and Louis Klug of Kitchener. Brazolot reserved about 60 lots and paid the developers for about 12 a year, building about that number of houses on streets that were called by very British names: Kingsley Court, Eton Place, Balmoral, Windsor and Inverness. Most of these were built for specific customers. Speculative building, that is, putting up a house and then hoping to sell it, accounted for only about 10 percent of his business. In the early 1970s he bought a number of lots from Armel in the west-end on streets like Rhonda,

Peter Brazolot, 1929-

Brazolot was born in "The Ward" in Guelph, the son of northern Italian immigrants. After high school he worked as a carpenter before starting his own house building business in 1949. He and his wife have raised nine children, some of whom are in the building industry. His community activities include ten years on city council and board memberships with various local organizations such as St. Joseph's Hospital and Bishop Macdonell High School. Photo source: Len Ariss

Marksam and Thistle, and built houses in the $25,000 to $40,000 category.

Another local firm, Reid and Laing, was probably the most prestigious builder in the city. The firm was made up of three Reid brothers – Melville, George and Albert – and William Laing, and operated from 1955 to 1970, during which time they built about 1,000 single-family homes. Although they did several larger projects, most of their construction was infilling specific lots, specializing in custom-built houses in all parts of the city. In their first projects in the 1950s they acted as developers and builders of small subdivisions of one street each

Albert Reid, 1928-
Source: Stelter, 2000

– Glenwood, Oakwood, Barton and Robertson Drive. They had a relatively large crew of 30 to 40 men who built the whole house. These were usually one-storey bungalows of 1,000 square feet, selling for $9,200 to $10,000. In the 1950s and 1960s they were the major developers and builders of the university area, including streets like Hales Crescent, Woodside, Young, Rodney, Heather and Yeadon.

There was a standardized character to the houses built during this era. House design in the 1940s and 1950s was heavily influenced by CMHC guidebooks; in the 1960s and 1970s, the influence of mass taste, especially as disseminated through books and magazines, determined what most people wanted. Most Guelph builders offered their own variants of popular plans, thus providing design as well as construction. Peter Brazolot had studied drafting in high school and drew his own plans. Albert Reid studied drafting and design in night classes. In some cases customers came to them with possible plans from magazines and they adapted these to local circumstances. The result was a vernacular form of housing that was similar across the country. Albert Reid points out that builders simply could not build "way-out" houses as most people would not buy them.

Nevertheless, the transition in styles from the early period of the 1940s to the 1960s, and the later years from the late 1960s and the 1970s, was quite dramatic. In the earlier phase, CMHC plan books emphasized basic, simple houses without garages. As with the wartime house, the two basic styles were the one-and-a-half storey, and the one-storey bungalow (the term used locally for any one-storey), which came with either a gabled or a hipped roof. Builders often alternated these on a street. Slightly more varieties were offered by Reid and Laing in the 1950s on Metcalfe Street North for example. A one-and-a-half storey, a hipped-roof bungalow, and a broken-front bungalow were alternated regularly on the east side of the street.

By the late 1960s and the 1970s, houses were larger and built on wider lots with attached garages. Three basic types dominated the local scene, with some variations possible. These were the two-storey, of traditional classical origin; the ranch, usually an elongated bungalow with a low-pitched roof; and the split-level of two kinds, one with the garage attached to the single-storey portion, the other with the garage and family room below the second-storey bedrooms. This last type, called "the Alberta split" by Brazolot and "the Glebe" by Reid and Laing, was enormously popular and dominates many suburban streets.

The larger builders also produced houses they consciously regarded as "workers housing", scaled-down versions of the two-storey, the bungalow and the side-split. For example, Brazolot bought a subdivision from Armel in 1970-71 and built 30 houses on Dovercliffe, Piccadily and Argyle which were marketed under the name Savecom and sold for $20,000 to $22,000 each. Reid and Laing put up houses on Eastview, Cheltonwood and Hastings that they felt workers could afford.

Architecturally-designed houses tended to be more "modernistic" than the builder-produced houses. Two subtypes of what is known as Contemporary appeared on Guelph streets. The most numerous is the gabled Contemporary, strongly influenced by the Prairie style of Frank Lloyd Wright, which has a very shallow pitched roof with long, overlapping eaves which created covers for patios and carports. Allan Sage designed several early versions of these in the 1950s on Callander Drive, in Skov's second "Sunset View" subdivision. These included his own house at No. 84, and that for his friend J.D. Oakes at No. 88. Unlike the builders' houses which faced the street and featured "picture" windows, Sage's houses had dramatic floor-to-ceiling windows oriented to the backyards.

Less common was the flat-roofed Contemporary, reflecting the influence of the International style. One example on Callander Drive, across from the Sage houses, is No. 81, designed in 1962 for Frank Basso by Elio Stradiotto, an architectural technician who worked in Pagani's office, and built by Peter Brazolot. Mrs. Basso remembers wanting "something different." Stradiotto says he was influenced by Marcel Breuer, a Bauhaus colleague of Gropius. Another example is 6 Tobey Ave., designed in 1960 by Richard Pagani, which features redwood walls and a flat, eaveless roof. This style was obviously not for everyone. When Reid and Laing were completing the construction of the house, the grocer Louis Embro bluntly asked them: "When are you going to put on the roof?" Perhaps the most daring house of this period was that designed by Pagani for himself at 13 Evergreen St. in 1960-61. Pagani and his father Dario were intrigued with the possibilities of barrel-vaulted roofs and together they experimented with bending plywood for the roof. The result is a dramatic building with wonderful interior

The "post-modern" house, 13 Evergreen St.
Designed in 1960 by Richard Pagani as his own home.
Source: Dave Carter, 1999

atmosphere. Pagani recalls that some locals believed that it looked like a gas station; others thought it might be a synagogue.

During the 1960s, Guelph's traditional emphasis on the single-family house began to change with the building of apartment buildings and row houses. An early example was the 46-unit low-rental building constructed in 1961 by Toronto builder Ralph Weber at the corner of Willow Road and Bagot Street. By 1967, apartment construction exceeded all other types, with 601 units built that year. Most apartment buildings were still relatively small by big city standards. In the late 1960s Reid and Laing built one prestige building, the "Georgian", a 23-unit apartment building on Woodlawn Road near Victoria Road. Larger complexes began to appear by the 1970s. A typical example was the 1971 to 1979 Silvercreek Apartments development, 300 units in three tall buildings on Silvercreek Parkway, designed by Karl Briestensky. City council had reluctantly softened its density restrictions to allow them to fit the long, narrow site.

Row houses were introduced relatively late in Guelph, and generally referred to as townhouses. According to Norman Harrison, then a senior planner with the city's planning department, the chief obstacle to the introduction of this housing type was the belief that they would become "instant slums." One hundred and eight units were built in 1968, most of them for rent. The condominium approach initially was not as popular in Guelph as in surrounding communities. In 1970, Reid and Laing began to build the first up-scale examples, a 75-unit complex at 120 Country Club Drive.

As people moved to the suburbs, commercial activity soon followed, but suburban malls came relatively late to Guelph. This was due, in part, to city council's opposition to commercial decentralization, which led to a 1968 official plan policy banning regional shopping plazas. The largest was Willow West Mall, announced by Armel Properties in 1970, several months after the ban was lifted. The mall was anchored by the largest department store in the city, Zellers, the largest Zehrs grocery store in the city, and about 25 other shops. The mall was designed by Karl Briestensky, and Wolfond Construction was the general contractor.

IV THE PAST BECOMES FASHIONABLE: 1975-2000

The scale of development and building increased in the last quarter of the century, matching population growth from the low 60,000s to about 100,000. New ways of thinking were reflected in the kind of city that was built in this era. Larger cultural change at the international level saw the rise of what has been called "post-modernism", replacing "modernism" as the dominant way of designing buildings. At the local level, there was a new search for meaning, a new way of defining the community, demonstrated by the organization of several groups dedicated to the preservation of the city's remaining architectural heritage. A new respect for the past was obvious in many of the new buildings constructed during this period, in the adaptive reuse of older buildings, and even in the use of Victorian vernacular styles in the new suburbs.

New Building

As a style of architecture, post-modernism represents a trend away from the modernism which had rejected any historical allusions in building design. Victorian towers, classical columns and an individualized approach again became fashionable. The great icons of this phase are Le Corbusier, his later works, and especially Frank Lloyd Wright, whose eccentric designs so influenced this era. Locally, this trend is best exemplified in the work of Karl Briestensky, the dominant local architect in shaping the look of Guelph since the 1970s. He has designed a wide variety of commercial, educational, industrial, recreational and residential buildings and has been a leader in historical renovation. Most of Briestensky's buildings display angular gables and towers with a liberal use of glass. A good example is his Turfgrass Institute (1990-1991), reminiscent of local farm buildings, situated on a hill overlooking the city from the east. The dramatic

Karl Briestensky, 1935-

Briestensky was born in Brampton and moved to Guelph with his family when he was five. He studied architecture at the University of Toronto and recalls, in particular, the influence of Eberhard Zeidler in the design studio. While the International style dominated the teaching, he also became interested in the work of Le Corbusier and of Frank Lloyd Wright. Briestensky worked for Allan Sage as a summer student in Guelph, and full-time for a short period after graduation in 1958. After working with Richard Pagani in Guelph and with other architects in Burlington and Kitchener, he opened his own office in 1968 on the second floor of the Bank of Nova Scotia building. In addition to the buildings mentioned in the text, his designs include the Victoria Road Recreation Centre (1973-75); Barzotti Woodworking (1983); the Royal Plaza at the corner of Paisley and Gordon streets (1984); and additions to the College Motor Inn (1987-89). Photo source: Stelter, 1995

The National Trust building nearing completion, August, 1987.   Source: Stelter, 1987

John Haayen's design for the Guelph Police building, 1988.   Source: John Haayen

view from the interior is focussed on his favourite building, the Church of Our Lady, several kilometres away, across the Eramosa River valley.

In the downtown, Briestensky's most prominent design is the National Trust building facing St. George's Square. It was completed in the mid-1980s, at the site of the post-war Bond building which had burned earlier. Briestensky says that he looked for a design that would blend the old and the new, to try to recapture the spirit of St. George's Square that had been exemplified by the old Bank of Commerce and the Post Office/Customs House. Much of the four-storey building is fairly conventional office space, but the roof line and several towers effectively evoke an older Guelph. And like 19th century architects such as Henry Langley, who placed St. George's Church tower as the termination of the vista looking north on Douglas Street, Briestensky located the main tower of the National Trust building at the point where it focuses the view south from Douglas Street. This building provokes strong opposing opinions, from those who think it looks like a grain elevator or a parking garage, to those who feel that it neatly encapsulates the Victorian spirit in a new dress.

One of the main architects of the earlier period in Guelph, John Haayen, continued to be active to the end of the century. An example of recent work is the complete re-making of the Guelph Police building, 15 Wyndham St. S., which Richard Pagani first designed in the 1960s. Haayen's design in 1988 went beyond the modernism of the old, with an angular foyer and a cantilevered floor on the west end (which was dropped from the final building because of the cost). Haayen provided daily supervision during the five-year construction period. The complex building includes a parking and repair garage, a firing range, a gymnasium and offices.

The Edmund C. Bovey building (1991), University of Guelph.
Source: Stelter, 2000

The Bullfrog Mall. Source: Fred Dahms, 1999

Philip Gosling, 1928 -

Born in Birmingham, England, Gosling trained in physiotherapy before immigrating to Canada in 1955. He began his career in Guelph as a physio therapist at St. Joseph's Hospital, then moved into real estate with Albert Fish. He eventually went into development on his own, specializing in commercial development, including malls such as Bullfrog Mall on Eramosa Road, the Willow Plaza on Willow Road and the Evergreen Plaza in Kitchener. In a parallel career as a naturalist, he was a founder of the Bruce Trail which he established in 1962. He worked for seven years to set up the organization and lay out the routes. Photo source: Stelter, 2000

Construction of the University of Guelph slowed down during this period, but did produce the major new facilities of the Edmund C. Bovey building in 1991 on Gordon Street, part of a great expansion of scientific laboratory space. This hi-tech building was designed by the Toronto architectural firm of Robbie, Young and Wright, with Ann Percival in charge, as she has been on several other projects on campus by the same firm. As with other university buildings, the choice of architects and much of the detailed planning was done by a building committee appointed by the University president, which included faculty and students. The large structure looks rather plain and utilitarian, with a portion resembling a farm silo, but the interior is made up of sophisticated laboratories in modular form, flexible and adaptable to individual research needs.

Closely connected to the university is the administrative and research complex, mostly related to agriculture, which has grown up on Stone Road West. Federal and provincial Ministries of Agriculture and private industry have all been involved. The centrepiece is the Ontario Ministry of Agriculture, Food and Rural Affairs at 1 Stone Rd. W. completed in 1996. Designed by the Toronto architectural firm, The NORR Partnership, this five-storey structure has two sweeping wings of stone and glass, joined by a dramatic atrium decorated with cherry wood walls. A noteworthy occupant of this building is the Land Registry Office, the repository for all records relating to land and subdivision development in the city, formerly located on Douglas Street. Other buildings of the Stone Road complex are relatively low, mall-like structures and include the recently completed Agriculture and Agri-Food Canada's Food Research Program at 93 Stone Rd. W.; the Health Canada Laboratory at 110 Stone Rd. W. built in 1986 and designed by Robbie, Young and Wright; and the Semex Alliance Building at 120 Stone Rd. W.

The Stone Road West area of Guelph has also become the major location of the shopping mall, that universal phenomenon without any local distinguishing characteristics. The Stone Road Mall was started in 1975 by Sifton Properties of London, on land leased from the University of Guelph for 99 years. The transfer of important commercial activity to the suburbs was symbolized by the move by Simpson-Sears from the downtown to the Stone Road Mall in 1977. This mall was upgraded with skylights and improved interior configuration in 1984, reflecting a trend in malls everywhere which no longer tried to imitate street scenes, but attempted to give the feeling of the outdoors, with more light, trees and fountains. An addition opened in 1990, bringing the number of shops to 130, including a five-theatre complex and a parking ramp. Additional shopping facilities of the strip mall type were built across Stone Road to the south and then across Edinburgh Road to the east as this area became an alternate commercial core to the downtown.

Smaller malls proliferated in various parts of the city. Many of these were designed by Karl Briestensky, including Campus Estates (1976) and Silvercreek Mall (1976), which bear the signature of his angular designs. Philip Gosling's Bullfrog Mall on Eramosa Road, built in 1982, is a good example of commercial development away from the downtown core. Land assembly from six owners took two to three years, but Gosling did not finalize the deals until he had secured a major tenant, an A & P grocery store. His re-zoning proposal met opposition from some local residents who feared a mall would negatively affect their lifestyles, and it took an Ontario Municipal Board hearing to decide in Gosling's favour. An A & P architect suggested a particular design for the store and Karl Briestensky was hired to design the rest of the mall in that fashion. A later

The old Speed Skating Rink (1882) in 1989.
Source: Stelter, 1989

The Speed Skating Rink burns in 1991.
Source: Donald Coulman, 1991

The completed arts centre, the "River Run."
Source: Dave Carter, 1999

example, the Hartsland Market Square Shopping Plaza on Kortright Road West, developed and built by Orin Reid, in partnership with Russell Cox, in 1992-1993. The neo-colonial style complex was designed by Toronto architect John Stark and has won several design awards.

Imitating the suburban commercial model became a fashionable North American solution to downtown decline in the late 1970s and Guelph's city officials followed this trend. In 1979 the city hired the Toronto architectural firm, Crang and Boake, to develop a conceptual plan for the downtown. They recommended redeveloping Quebec Street East. A Toronto developer, Chuck Magwood of Chartwood Development, worked out an agreement with the city, the province and Co-operators Insurance, under an urban revitalization program. The result was a small version of Toronto's Eaton Centre, a two-level mall anchored by an Eaton's department store and 83 other stores. It duplicated the artificial, placeless character of the suburban malls. Norman Harrison says that the planning department at City Hall was unsuccessful in getting the developer to visually connect the new complex with Guelph's traditional downtown, or to indicate in some way that the mall covered one of the radial streets of Galt's original town plan. While the opening of the Eaton Centre seemed to stimulate downtown activity for several years, Eaton's abandonment of their store precipitated the virtual commercial death of the mall by the late 1990s. A hockey arena is replacing the Eaton's space, with the future of the rest of the mall still very much in doubt at the time of writing.

Building a Performing Arts Centre

The most controversial building in Guelph's history, a performing arts centre, was finally constructed in the 1990s after several decades of discussion following the demise of the Royal Opera House. Earlier plans had appeared promising but never came to fruition. For example, in 1957 city council set up a civic centre committee which reached the stage of commissioning drawings from Richard Pagani of a civic centre designed as a group of separate buildings, including an auditorium building to hold 1,500. In 1974 Edith Kidd was appointed to do a feasibility study and recommended a hotel and civic centre complex at the foot of Wyndham Street at York Road Council felt the city could not afford it. More than 20 years later council appointed a citizens' committee headed by Peter Brazolot and Guelph Arts Council president Barbara Connolly. They recommended the site of the old Speed Skating Rink, built in 1882, on Woolwich Street by the Speed River, which had long been used as a railroad freight warehouse. City council approved of this plan in July of 1987.

The ensuing controversy appeared to reveal a major fault line running through the community, with competing visions of what kind of city Guelph should be. The opposition charged that the city's expected contribution of $ 4 million (later $4.7 million) of the total of $12 million was for the benefit of only a small arts-oriented elite. They managed to delay the project by a decade which substantially increased the costs. As well, a fire which destroyed the former skating rink/ warehouse in early 1991 forced a change to plans for an entirely new building. At this stage, the drive for the new centre was led by an indomitable trio: Margaret Mackinnon, the citizens' committee chair; Edwina Carson, director of the fundraising campaign; and Nancy Coates, the building committee chair, who reportedly remarked that "we'll have to name it Phoenix, I guess, rising from the ashes." Political support came from former Member of Parliament Jim Schroder, and successive mayors Norm Jary and John Counsell. Business leadership became crucial in fundraising, led by developer Douglas Bridge, who was able to get 50 people within two weeks to pledge $10,000 each. This support came from a wide spectrum of the business community, including many developers and builders, demonstrating strong interest from beyond what is usually thought of as the arts community.

In 1990, the building committee chose the distinguished Toronto architectural firm, Moriyama and Teshima, from a short list of six. This firm was known internationally for the Ontario Science Centre and the Canadian Embassy in Tokyo, and locally for the Arboretum Centre at the university (1973) and the Macdonald Stewart Art Centre. The performing arts centre's eventual design was the product of long consultations between the local committee and architect Ted Teshima. The site itself was daunting, featuring a parking garage and a car wash on the Woolwich Street side and a railroad track on the river side. But it also had exciting possibilities, since it was adjacent to the original founding site of Guelph, immediately to the south-east, and its neighbours included two of Guelph's finest heritage buildings, the County Court House and St. George's Anglican Church. The exterior design is primarily functional and spartan except for a great curved wall of glass which provides spectacular views from the inside and which becomes a major attraction from the outside at night when the activities inside are put on display. The interior is based on current concepts of community centres which stress multi-purpose rather than single-purpose use. The major auditorium is the 800-seat du Maurier Theatre, a smaller space is the 220-seat Co-operator's Hall. The spectacular lobby, the Canada Company Hall, is large enough to host special events in its own right. Facing the street entrance is a copper wall designed by Guelph artist Peter Johnston, with 35 panels depicting impressions of Guelph's past. The long-awaited facility finally opened to the public in 1997, named the "River Run Centre," symbolically tying the building to the river that gave Guelph its original reason for existence.

HOSPITALS

Hospital redevelopment was also a contentious issue with 17 formal proposals in 20 years. These finally culminated in 1992 when the provincial government accepted the report by a committee headed by businessman William Blundell. The central recommendation of the report was a call for a rationalization of hospital services in the city from the existing system of two acute care hospitals. An expanded General Hospital, to cost $69 million, was to become the sole acute care centre; a new St. Joseph's, costing $44 million, would concentrate on long-term care. The General's redevelopment was designed by Parkin Associates of Toronto. A large addition was completed by April, 1999; since then, work is progressing on renovations to the old wings. The addition re-focussed the entry away from Delhi Street to a parking lot on what was formerly the rear of the building. The new portion houses the hospital's high-tech functions including the critical care unit (coronary and intensive care); the family birthing unit, with delivery facilities now located in each room; and seven state-of-the-art operating theatres. The new St. Joseph's, designed by Crang and Boake, is an entirely new building and is being constructed to the rear of the old hospital.

INDUSTRIES

The expanded scale of local manufacturing has led to the construction of dozens of new industrial buildings in the city. At least three corporations have made their headquarters in the city. The most obvious is that of the Co-operators, whose nine-storey tower dominates the eastern portion of the downtown at Priory Square on Macdonell Street. One of Canada's insurance giants, the Co-operators was the product of the merger of several smaller companies in the West, Ontario, and the Maritimes. In 1965 they moved their general insurance headquarters to Guelph from Toronto (their life insurance headquarters is located in Regina). Their rather plain, modern building was designed by Toronto architect Gordon Adamson. A large addition, designed by Karl Briestensky to match the original, was built from 1976 to 1978. More than 600 employees are housed in the combined structure.

Another Canadian headquarters is McNeil Consumer Healthcare, a subsidiary of the American firm, Johnson & Johnson, who established an office in Guelph in 1978. The original building at 890 Woodlawn Rd. W. was a two-storey structure designed and built by Finley McLachlan Construction of Toronto, featuring a combination of glass and reinforced concrete coated with a quartz pebble aggregation. McLachlan also landscaped the 55-acre park-like grounds. When the company became the Canadian producer of Tylenol acetaminophen products in the early 1980s, the Kitchener architectural and engineering firm, Walter, Fedy, was commissioned to build a large addition which effectively matched the original building.

Linamar Corporation headquarters.   Source: Stelter, 2000

Another example is the headquarters of the Linamar Corporation, completed in 1999 at the corner of Speedvale Avenue and Silvercreek Parkway. Linamar, which manufactures a wide range of products including auto parts in 20 plants in the city, was founded by Frank Hasenfratz who migrated from Hungary. According to his daughter Linda, the current president, the family wished to have a more traditional, European look for their corporate headquarters, a look that would make a statement about the family's origins. They interviewed three architectural firms and felt that the designs of Paul Roth, of Roth-Knibb, Architects, Toronto, most corresponded to the style they preferred. The classical design, in brick with stone lintels, is in sharp contrast to the modernistic designs of most local corporate buildings. The family connection carried over into the construction phase which was handled by Kiwi-Newton Construction, a Guelph firm owned by Linda's husband.

CHURCHES

The churches built in the last quarter of the century reflect the suburbanization of the city. These new churches usually began as mission churches, subsidized by established congregations. Early meetings took place in schools, plazas, other denomination's buildings, or even a movie theatre. When they did construct their building, it was usually designed as a multi-purpose facility, closely connected to the everyday needs of their neighbourhood. Some of the suburban churches are Parkview Pentecostal Church (1976) on Speedvale Avenue; Kortright Presbyterian Church (1984) on Kortright Road; St. Matthias Anglican Church (1986), on Kortright Road; St. Paul's Lutheran Church (1987), on Silvercreek Parkway; and Westwood United Church (1987, 1993) on Willow Road West.

The experience of Westwood United Church is typical of the trend. As a mission, worship services were held at Westwood Public School from 1976 and in 1982 a store-front church was opened in the Westwood Court Plaza. A small building was completed in 1987, but a significant expansion began in 1993, designed by Hamilton architect Trevor Garwood-Jones. The result is a community-oriented, multi-function structure with a convertible sanctuary and several other spaces for activities that take place throughout the week.

St. Paul's Evangelical Lutheran Church, on the other hand, is an example of an established downtown congregation moving to the suburbs. Their old church at 200 Woolwich St. had been designed by Henry Langley in 1894 as the Second Baptist Church, and became a Lutheran church in 1909. By the 1980s it was proving increasingly impractical, according to Pastor Jon Fogelman, for there was a lack of parking, a difficult entry to the sanctuary via a dramatic spiral staircase, and little room for expansion. A desired move to more spacious suburban quarters required a good price for the old church and a reasonable price for new land. The first was provided by John Lammer, who purchased the church and converted it to condominiums in 1987-1988. The second involved land on Silvercreek Parkway owned by T.T. "Jack" Skov. Pastor Fogelman was able to convince Skov to sell the necessary three acres to the church at cost. A large building committee carefully outlined the congregation's needs and dreams, which included a 34-unit senior-citizens' residence. The committee interviewed three architectural firms and chose the Waterloo group of Snider, Reichard and Marsh to design a modern space with a traditional church look. Karl Briestensky designed the senior-citizens' residence now known as Lutheridge.

SCHOOLS

Like the churches, schools were built to accommodate the increased population of the outlying suburbs. In the public system, the city helped to finance schools like Westwood (1976), which were designed to facilitate community use. During the energy crisis of the late 1970s and early 1980s, many of the older schools like Edward Johnson had their large, modernistic windows filled in with bricks, with aesthetic results which would have horrified the architects of the 1950s. When new schools were again built, starting in 1989, they represented a substantial improvement in quality and design from those of the previous era. The Toronto firm of Moffat and Duncan designed three schools in two years: Fred A. Hamilton

 June 17, 1995 – Bishop Macdonell High School closes after 135 years in spite of protests from many Guelphites. The building has since accommodated the continuing education program.

Fred A. Hamilton School.   Source: Stelter, 2000

Ecolé St-René Goupil.   Source: Stelter, 2000

(1989), Jean Little (1990) and Taylor Evans (1991). These were handsome structures, enhanced with the latest architectural fashions such as dramatic entrances and interiors. They also included sophisticated computer equipment, special music and science rooms, and day-care facilities.

Similar trends were apparent in the separate school system. At the high school level, Bishop Macdonell was closed in the early 1990s and students moved to expanded versions of St. James and Our Lady of Lourdes schools. New schools included St. Michael School (1990) at McElderry Drive, designed by William Jarrett. This had two levels, to allow for more space for playing fields, and featured pyramid skylights and sloped glass at the stairwells. A French language school, L'Ecole St. René Goupil, established in 1978, was attached to St. Patrick School on Victoria Road. In 1990 this school got its own building on Scottsdale Drive designed by Karl Briestensky. He remembers being encouraged by school officials to produce something out of the ordinary. The result was a profusion of rounded and pyramidal shapes quite unlike anything else at other Guelph schools.

A New Attitude to the City's Heritage

During the 1970s a new appreciation of the city's architectural heritage became evident in the public's attitudes and this was parallelled by changes in thinking by political and business leaders. Heritage conservation became a significant feature of the city's official policy with the passing of a height bylaw in 1975. This involved the preservation of a relatively low profile townscape in the old core of Guelph dominated by the Church of Our Lady. The initiative came from the city's planning department. Norman Harrison, then a senior planner with the city,

recalls learning that Toronto developers were assembling land in the block bounded by Quebec Street and Church Lane, with the intention of putting up a 20-storey apartment block. The same firm had earlier put up the 13-storey Park Mall tower at the corner of Yarmouth and Quebec streets. The planning department went into emergency mode, as Harrison puts it, preparing a bylaw which would protect the sight-lines to the Church of Our Lady by restricting the heights of any other buildings along those lines. In addition, in the tradition of medieval towns, the height of other buildings in the downtown could not exceed that of the bottom of the rose window of the church. The bylaw was taken to the planning board, and recommended to city council, where it passed without much comment. When some of the local real estate interests became aware of the real significance of the bylaw, they mounted a vigorous attack at council and launched an appeal at the Ontario Municipal Board. A citizen's group hastily formed by Professor Gordon Couling encouraged an increasingly wavering city council and helped win the case at the Ontario Municipal Board.

The mechanism for the city's official involvement in heritage protection was set up after the height bylaw controversy. The Province of Ontario Heritage Act in 1975 enabled municipalities to create committees of local residents to advise council on heritage matters. Guelph's committee was set up in 1977 using the act's rather cumbersome title of Local Architectural Conservation Advisory Committee and is generally referred to simply as LACAC. Gordon Couling was its first chair and served until his death in 1984. Norman Harrison of the planning department became its secretary in 1977, serving as the committee's staff and as the liaison between the planning department and the committee until he was succeeded by Karen Rolfe in 1996. Since its inception, LACAC has carried through designations of over 60 local buildings as being of architectural and historical interest.

Local architectural heritage has also been a major interest of the Guelph Arts Council, created by city council in 1974. Under Sally Wismer's direction, the arts council's work in this area has been designed to increase public awareness of the city's heritage in at least two ways. The first is through the publication of walking tours such as *Where Guelph Began* (1979), and *Downtown Walkabout* (1982), which Gordon Couling wrote and illustrated. Since then Florence Partridge has written several more, including *The Slopes of the Speed (1990)* and *Altar and Hearth in Victorian Guelph (1994)*. Together, these publications form the basis for the arts council's popular guided walking tours each summer. The arts council has also actively encouraged the restoration and renovation of private homes and businesses through their annual awards.

Gordon Couling, 1913-1984

Born and raised in Guelph, Couling studied art at the Ontario College of Art in Toronto. As art teacher, as artist, as local historian, and as heritage conservationist, Couling had a major impact on Guelph's conception of itself as a community. He taught art to a generation of students, first at the Macdonald Institute and later as the founding chair of the University of Guelph's fine art department. He also taught art to adults through the Guelph Creative Arts Association, which he helped to create, and through the Central Ontario Arts Association. As an artist, he did hundreds of drawings and paintings, many depicting local scenes. He illustrated Guelph's history in several large murals, such as those in the cafeteria at GCVI and at St. Joseph's Senior Citizens' Lounge. His work in decorating churches is best seen in the stained glass windows of Paisley Memorial United Church, where he was an active member, and the entry doors at Sacred Heart Church. His art and his interest in local history became central features of his leadership of the local heritage movement. He was the first chair of the Local Architectural Conservation Advisory Committee (LACAC). His inventory of Guelph buildings long formed the basis of what should be protected from demolition. And he made the public aware of the value of Guelph's architectural heritage through his enthusiastic public lectures and through his walking tours.

Photo source: Couling Collection, University of Guelph Library Archives

Other groups and institutions that have actively promoted an interest in Guelph's past include the Guelph Historical Society and the Guelph Civic Museum. The historical society had acted as a lobby group in the 1960s whenever another significant building was threatened, but their chief function has been the publication of local history, through an annual journal, *Historic Guelph*, and through their commissioning of Leo Johnson's *History of Guelph, 1827-1927 (1977)*. The Guelph Civic Museum, located in a fine restored building on Waterloo Avenue at Dublin Street, displays artifacts from Guelph's pioneer days and runs a large educational program with school children. It also operates the McCrae

House at 108 Water St., dedicated to the preservation of the memory of Dr. John McCrae and his involvement in the First World War.

THE CANADA TRUST ISSUE

The opposing views of "progress" and "conservation", as well as questions of economic feasibility and community identity, collided head-on in 1979 during the debate on the future of the Canada Trust building. That September, Canada Trust officials announced that they planned to demolish their buildings at the corner of Wyndham and Cork streets and replace them with modern structures designed by local architect William Jarrett. LACAC recommended that the city designate the buildings, or at least, their facades, because the buildings represented an important part of one of the few complete pre-Confederation blocks still standing in Canada.

In a close vote, council moved to begin the designation process. City planners provided ideas for retaining the stone facades on the modern bank structure, but Canada Trust officials were adamant in their opposition to any preservation plans. Company president Mervyn Lahor argued that preserving the facade would increase costs by 10 to 15 percent. He was later quoted in the *Mercury* as saying that the building had "few, if any, redeeming features from an architectural point of view." Local opposition to the demolition included the Guelph Historical Society. President Ruth Pollard presented council with a petition of more than a thousand names. But the issue went far beyond the city. At the provincial level, architect Anthony Adamson, a director of the Ontario Heritage Foundation, and architect Kent Rawson of the Architectural Conservancy of Ontario, both went before council. At the national level, Pierre Berton, chair of the Heritage Canada Foundation, wrote several strong letters to council.

Still, city council was split on the issue. The advocates of preservation included Margaret MacKinnon who was quoted by the *Mercury* as saying that "to destroy this facade would be like shooting the last whooping crane." Ken Hammill argued that "Canada Trust has the responsibility to retain... the uniqueness of this pre-Confederation block." But at the November 19, 1979, meeting of council, Mayor Norm Jary voted against designation, which led to a tie vote and thus the motion was lost. A demolition permit was then granted. A last minute attempt to buy the building, by a citizen's group led by lawyer Alex Moon, was rebuffed by the company and the building was demolished in May, 1980. Moon pointedly contrasted Canada Trust's action with that of the Toronto-Dominion Bank at the

The old Canada Trust building in May, 1980.
Source: Stelter, 1980

The new Canada Trust building.

Source: Stelter, 2000

the necessary zone change by the city and by the Ontario Municipal Board because of one neighbour's objections. After a concerted editorial campaign by the *Mercury*, and strong support from Norm Harrison and the planning department, the OMB reversed its decision in 1973 and allowed Veri to operate his business. Restoration of the building was a slow process, as funds permitted, and was eventually completed by 1978, with William Jarrett as the architect and Umberto Staniscia in charge of restoring the interior and exterior stonework.

Another example of effective re-use is the Guelph Civic Museum, 6 Dublin St. N. Erected about 1847, this large commercial building was one of the finest examples of mid-19th century stone work in Guelph, with its ashlar (cut stone) facade, its symmetrical proportions and its parapet gables. The building went through many uses, including a store and a boarding house, and was long occupied by the Knights of Columbus. It was purchased in 1977 for use as the museum, with Peter Stokes as the restoration architect. It opened as the Guelph Civic Museum in 1980.

A major turning point in the re-use of heritage buildings in Guelph came in 1978 with the saving of the Wellington Hotel, even while the final countdown was on for the Canada Trust building. The Wellington, designed by the talented Victor Stewart, was built in 1877 at the intersection of Wyndham and Woolwich

other end of the block, whose building had been restored, not demolished. The Canada Trust case demonstrated that a determined property owner could demolish a building regardless of the public's wishes. The Ontario Heritage Act, it should be noted, is still a remarkably weak instrument for preserving buildings. Even if council had designated the building, demolition would have been possible after a wait of six months. With the advantage of hindsight, it must also be conceded, that compared to other local demolitions and replacements with modern structures, Jarrett's design actually was quite sensitive to the rest of the block in terms of the new building's height and its window treatment.

SAVING HERITAGE STRUCTURES

Despite the loss of the Canada Trust case, the success rate for saving heritage structures since 1975 is really quite remarkable. The preservation process is sometimes extremely complex, often requiring the co-operation of several levels of government and of entrepreneurs willing to break away from the common assumption that constructing new buildings is more economical than restoring the old. Guelph still has a distinctive look because so many heritage structures have been restored or have been renovated and used for new purposes.

One of the earliest examples of "adaptive re-use" involves the Bullfrog Inn, 414 Eramosa Road, which Freddy Veri converted from a rooming house to a hair salon. The Bullfrog, a two-storey limestone structure with the traditional gothic gable over the front door, was built about 1847 as one of a series of "farmers' inns" along the Eramosa Road. Its most noteworthy operator had been the eccentric poet, James Gay. Veri purchased the building in 1969 but was refused

Norman Harrison, 1938-

Harrison grew up in Preston, Ontario. He studied architecture at the University of Manitoba and then switched programs, graduating as a geography major with an interest in planning in 1964. He joined the planning staff at City Hall in 1968 when Robert Hall, the director of planning, was the only other member of the department. With the creation of LACAC in 1977, Harrison became its secretary and served in that capacity until his retirement in 1996. He feels that the planning department always allowed him to pursue his interest in heritage preservation in addition to his regular planning assignments. As a result, he has been involved in most of the heritage preservation projects since the 1970s including the restoration of the Wellington Hotel, the creation of Goldie Mill Park, the renovation of the County Courthouse and the preservation of the Bullfrog Inn. He continues his activities in this field as a citizen member of LACAC. Photo source: Stelter, 2000

The Wellington Hotel during a fire in 1975.
Source: Donald Coulman

The restored Wellington.
To the right of the Wellington are the Masonic Block and the Alma Block, also restored. Source: Fred Dahms, 1984

The renovated County Courthouse. Source: Stelter, 1989

streets, and provided a Parisian look to Upper Wyndham, with its triangular shape and Second Empire, Mansard roof. In 1975 a fire gutted the interior and destroyed the roof, leaving only the stone walls standing.

The Wellington's unlikely renovation represents a model of how some notable structures can be saved. The cast of characters included planning officials Ken Perry and Norman Harrison, who pursued several options while local businessmen called for the removal of what had become an eyesore on their street. Developers Douglas Bridge and Chester Carere had originally purchased the building in order to tear it down but were persuaded by the planners to at least consider restoration. According to Bridge, the project became viable when Royal Bank manager John Counsell provided interim financing and federal and provincial politicians helped negotiate long-term leases for federal and provincial office space, making possible a long-term mortgage. The developers were able to hire Herb Clough, who had experience in reconstructing buildings in London, England, after the war. Clough worked out a system for removing the rubble and installing the new steel interior structure from the top, over the walls. Karl Briestensky, who was working on several other restoration projects at the time, was the architect in charge. He recalls inventing the construction system as they went along. The developers decided to recreate the sophisticated copper roof of the original, instead of merely installing a flat roof. The dormers were crafted by Mario Crenna of Guelph General Millwork. The result was an outstanding

restoration of the building as the anchor of Upper Wyndham Street. Bridge and Carere also bought and restored the next two buildings along Wyndham Street – the Masonic Block, Nos.137-145 , which had also been designed by Victor Stewart, and the Alma Block, Nos. 127-135, an attractive commercial building with a series of segmented arches, designed in the 1860s by Toronto architect James Smith.

One of the most significant buildings in the city, the Wellington County Courthouse on Woolwich Street, was effectively restored and added to in 1981. Designed by Toronto artist and architect Thomas Young in 1841, this structure has had additions made to it over the years, but county officials seriously considered

John Lammer, 1941-

Lammer was born in the southern Austrian city of Graz and apprenticed in the building trades before coming to Canada at the age of 24. In Kitchener he worked in the heating and air conditioning business but his real interest has been the renovation of older buildings. His first project in Guelph was completed in 1979 and proved that restoring heritage buildings could be economically feasible. After several successful renovation projects he became disenchanted with what he considered to be an inflexible attitude to downtown redevelopment at City Hall and turned his attention to work in Cambridge for almost 10 years. In the late 1990's he returned to Guelph where he is working on several conceptions for downtown renewal. Photo source: Stelter, 1990

The renovated Raymond Sewing Machine factory on Yarmouth Street. Currently housing 20 bachelor apartments and The Other Brother's Restaurant. Source: Stelter, 1992

The former St. Paul's Lutheran Church on Woolwich Street. Converted to condominiums. Source: Stelter, 1986

The renovated Kelly-Petrie building on Wyndham and Macdonell. Source: Stelter, 1995

moving their operations to more spacious quarters, perhaps in a community more central to the county than Guelph. City officials at several levels took action, including the city administrator and the mayor. On behalf of LACAC and the planning department, Norman Harrison suggested ways in which they could increase their space. These efforts must have been convincing for Simcoe-based architect Carlos Ventin was hired to restore the original and add new space. His solution clearly distinguished between the original and the new office addition at the southerly end, and enhanced the visual impact and the usefulness of this historic structure.

The most active renovator of older buildings in the downtown core has been developer John Lammer. He describes his philosophy of renovation in simple terms: the interior must end up being a new building, in order to get the services up to standard. Therefore he usually guts the entire interior, keeping only the outer shell of the older building. Lammer converted his first building in 1979, creating six townhouses called "The Stone Terrace", at the corner of Woolwich and Norwich streets. He described his "first big project" as the renovation in 1980 of the Raymond Sewing Machine factory at 37 Yarmouth St. This superb factory building had been designed in 1875 by Victor Stewart, but the building had been used as the Cooke and Denison machine shop for many years and was quite dilapidated. Lammer's research indicated that Guelph needed bachelor apartments downtown. In this case, he saved most of the interior structure. The result was 20 bachelor apartments and the La Cucina Restaurant (now The Other Brother's Restaurant).

Other Lammer projects which resulted in the creation of residential space included the 1986 conversion of the Tolton Textile factory on Commercial Street into apartments and the Stone Store. As with other Lammer conversions, he says he had difficulty with the city's bureaucracy, especially the engineering department, because the property could not provide enough parking spaces. He was also expected to pay development charges that were later dropped from downtown re-development. Another example of adaptive re-use was his conversion of the old St. Paul's Lutheran Church at 200 Woolwich St. in 1988 by imaginatively building seven two- storey condominiums into the former church sanctuary.

Lammer was also involved in the restoration in 1983-1984 of the Kelly-Petrie building at the corner of Wyndham and Macdonell streets. This prominent structure had been designed by local architect John Hall in 1882 in an eclectic mix of Victorian styles that was typical of most of his buildings. Lammer says that he convinced developers Denzil Williams and Clark McDaniel to purchase the building from the Wolfonds. He became the contractor and Kitchener architect John Clinkett did the restoration designs. The interior was partially saved, including the third floor ceilings where they found and restored elaborate paint and plaster decorations done by the Independent Order of Odd Fellows who had earlier occupied this space. The building now houses commercial uses on the first floor and five luxury apartments and an office for the developers on the upper floors.

After several major projects in Cambridge, Lammer again became active in Guelph in the late 1990s. A recent example of his work is 83 Neeve St., generally referred to as the Danby site, a two-storey stone factory built in 1873 which became the Guelph Carpet factory. The building was badly damaged by fire in 1994 and became a vacant derelict. As part of LACAC's search for a way to save a part of Guelph's industrial heritage, Norman Harrison approached Lammer about 1996, suggesting he consider it as another of his projects. Lammer eventually agreed, completing the conversion to apartments in 1999 by adding a third floor and a corner tower.

A number of other conversions from industrial to residential use have protected some of Guelph's earliest industrial buildings. A few examples give an idea of the process. Between 1976 and 1978, Karl Briestensky joined partners Sev Peloso and Guido Gatto in converting an old pea mill at 97 Farquhar St. into elegant apartments. In 1980, Robert Johnston renovated 196 Arthur St. N., a foundry going back to the 1850s, into a complex of two-storey townhouses he named "Millside." Ike VanSoelen converted the old Colonial Whitewear factory, 40 Northumberland St., built in 1911, into apartments in 1988. Two features of the factory were retained – the very high ceilings and the huge industrial windows. In 1991 local contractor Mike Rao renovated the former Phoenix Mill, 358 Waterloo Ave., into apartments. The mill had been built in 1870, and was the only remaining water-powered mill in the city. In a conversion from industrial to prestige office space in 1993, Briestensky renovated the former Gooderham and Worts storage facility, 111 Farquhar St., with partners Peloso and Gatto. The added space above the original building was used as Briestensky's architectural firm, with striking views of the city's downtown.

Two conversions on the university campus merit mention. In 1978-1980, the old Macdonald Consolidated School on Gordon Street was renovated to become the Macdonald Stewart Art Centre. The plain, functional school, built in 1904, had been designed by Toronto architect George M. Miller for the benefactor, Montreal tobacco magnate, William Macdonald. A descendant, David Macdonald Stewart, provided the naming grant to enable the building to be converted into an art gallery, to be owned by a unique combination – the Wellington County Board of Education, the County of Wellington, the City of Guelph and the University of Guelph. Architect Raymond Moriyama maintained the facade and the front porch, added two wings, and designed a three-storey sky-lighted central gallery as the focal point of several galleries.

A more controversial preservation in 1989-1991 involved Zavitz Hall which had been slated for demolition as part of the 1960s master plan, for it sat in

the middle of Branion Square, designated as the central square of the new campus. The English Cottage-style building constructed in 1913 had been the site for much of the pioneering research on Canadian crops by Dr. Charles Zavitz and his department early in the century, but in the 1980s university officials were determined to clear the

The renovated former Guelph Carpet factory at 83 Neeve St.
Converted to apartments with the main floor used as a parking garage.
Source: Stelter, 2000

square. Students and faculty, however, convinced a new president, Brian Segal, to renovate the building for the fine art department which was already using it at that point. The Toronto architectural firm, Lett-Smith, left most of the exterior unchanged, except for a new side entrance and a two-storey glassed-in sculpture court on the front. Inside, they made use of the heavy timber trusses and high ceilings to create distinctive painting and drawing studios.

The success of the preservation process often depends on the possibility of effective co-operation between local government and local entrepreneurs. The restoration of The Boathouse on the Speed River at the Gordon Street bridge in 1997-1998 is a useful case in point. The background of the building is uncertain, but the city-owned site had long been associated with a rental boathouse belonging to the Edward Johnson family. Although the building was in very bad shape, LACAC regarded it as a good example of recreational pavilion architecture with its low profile, and prominent bell-cast roof with dormers. LACAC also pointed to the "downtown gateway" location and the possibilities of enhancing the recreational use of the river as reasons for preservation. The result was a city agreement with a private business which renovated the building with some city help and leases it for a nominal fee. The Boathouse has become a popular eating and meeting place, and has become an important part of the city's return to the river which originally gave the community its life.

Two developments as the century ended reflected imaginative approaches to commercial expansion and a sensitivity to the particular character of the

The Boathouse during renovation.
Source: *Guelph Mercury,* 1997

The renovated Boathouse.   Source: Stelter, 2000

The expanded Bookshelf.   Source: Stelter, 2000

downtown core. Barb and Doug Minett, the innovative owners of the Bookshelf, enlarged their varied operations at a time when independent bookstores elsewhere were in decline. Their business, marked by their distinctive tower on Quebec Street, has been a dynamic element in the downtown for two decades, with its combination of bookstore, restaurant, cinema and bar. In what they billed as "the great leap sideways," the Minetts expanded into the building next door where they relocated the restaurant. This allowed them to double the size of the bookstore and they also added a pool hall and an Internet café.

The conversion of the old Woolworth's store on St. George's Square into commercial space and two floors of apartments has reintroduced a 19th century look to the square. The Woolworth's store property, owned by Milan Lesic, was characterized by a massive, modernistic blank facade. Elora architect James Fryett designed a set of windows which effectively matched in style and scale the windows on the mid-19th century buildings on Wyndham Street.

 December 29, 1976 – Mary Jane Harrison becomes the first female president of the Guelph and District Real Estate Board. She was only the third person to be elected president since 1941.

BUILDING HOMES

The city's expanded population was reflected in the increased amount of housing being produced. While a substantial number of apartment blocks were built, the emphasis has been on single-detached houses and townhouses. Much of the apartment building was for condominiums. Examples include three projects designed by Karl Briestensky: the Marilyn Drive Apartments, 150 units, built in three phases between 1978 and 1988, considered by many to be some of the finest multiple residences in the city; the Waterloo Avenue Apartments, 86 units, 1985-1986; and the Christopher Court Apartments, 56 units, 1987-1988, with their distinctive gothic-like gables.

A major addition to downtown housing was the building in 1995-96 of the 70-unit Matrix Centre, 141 Woolwich Rd. This was "social," or "affordable" housing, and was already under construction when the new Conservative provincial government cut funding for this sort of program. According to Edward Pickersgill, Guelph's leading advocate of affordable housing, the need for this type of housing was enormous. In a *Mercury* interview, he pointed out that "I could fill it four times over without blinking. The waiting list is phenomenal." The apartment block fits in effectively with its prestigious neighbour across Woolwich Street, the Wellington building. Local architect A. Lloyd Grinham designed it with a modern version of a mansard roof and with artificial stone of a texture and colour that matches the Wellington.

Compared to the period before 1975, the scale of building operations greatly increased as local building firms became larger and built more homes each year. The

The Matrix Centre.   Source: Stelter, 2000

Orin Reid, 1952-2000.
Source: Stelter, 2000

The clubhouse in the Village by the Arboretum.   Source: Stelter, 2000

house-building business continued to be dominated by locally-based firms, especially by the companies formed by the sons of the original three Reid brothers from the firm Reid and Laing. Thomasfield Homes, Verdone Homes, Pidel Homes, Brazolot Homes, Gatto Homes, and others have all been part of the building boom. Some of these firms also built extensively in other communities in Southwestern Ontario. In contrast, only a few outside firms, such as Claysam of Cambridge, have been active, especially in the single-family detached house market.

The story of housing in Guelph in the last several decades of the 20th century is to a large extent the story of a second generation of the Reid cousins, the sons of Melville, George and Albert Reid who had formed the most successful house-building firm of the previous generation. After Reid and Laing was dissolved in 1970, two of the brothers continued to operate separately into the 1990s as George Reid Construction and Albert Reid Construction. The second generation of Reids slowly took over from their fathers and created several new companies. Melville's sons, Richard and Raymond, created Reidco, which specialized in inexpensive first buyer homes; Richard continued with Reidco while Raymond formed a new firm, Wood Creek Homes. Orin, the son of George, worked with his father and then founded Reid's Heritage Homes in 1979. His sudden death in the summer of 2000 shocked the entire community. Carson, the son of Albert, created Carson Reid Homes in 1982, and also continued to work closely with his father until about 1997. A third generation of Reids has recently entered the home building field. Orin's son, Scott, worked with his father but has also formed his own company, Brooklyn Homes. Orin's daughter, Charlotte, and her husband, Tim Blevins, both worked for Orin's firm and have also started a new company, Sherwood Homes.

Orin Reid's Heritage Homes is the biggest home-building firm in the region with a staff of over 200 and is also associated with many subcontractors who work primarily for that company. By the end of the century, Orin Reid's firm, and others he was associated with, were producing more than 1,000 housing units per year in Guelph, Cambridge, Kitchener-Waterloo, Brantford and London. In some cases, as in the Eastview Road area, he purchased serviced lots from a developer, but mostly he acted as his own developer, subdividing the land into lots and providing services. Much of his construction focussed on townhouses. His first big project was 180 Marksam Rd., where he built 98 units in 1986-1987; another was a 91-unit complex off Victoria Road, just south of the Victoria Recreation Centre, in 1991. Sixty townhouses as well as 250 detached houses were built in 1992-1993 in conjunction with his Hartsland Market Square Shopping Plaza in the Kortright Road area. In 1992-1993 he also constructed 60 non-profit townhouse units in the Stone Road Mall area.

Orin Reid's Village by the Arboretum on Stone Road East is a special kind of subdivision. Reid had been constructing this gated retirement community since 1992 in conjunction with the University of Guelph which developed the concept and has retained ownership of the land. Over 400 houses and townhouses have been built, as well as a 28,000 square foot clubhouse with a large swimming pool, an auditorium, a library and an exercise room. House purchasers pay a premium in order to cover the cost of these facilities and they also pay an annual fee for general property maintenance by Reid's Heritage Homes. Plans are underway for extended care facilities so that as residents age, they will be able to stay in the community. The houses have a traditional look. Early models were designed by

Toronto architect Ken Viljoen and more recent versions by Reid's in-house architect, David Parrish. Landscaping has been a more significant feature than in most local subdivisions, with designs by Hilton Foster, Landscape Architects.

Orin Reid's largest subdivision project, in partnership with industrialist John Wood, was just underway as the century ended. Westminster Woods is a 400-acre site off Gordon Street South which will eventually hold 3,000 units and supporting commercial facilities. A special feature of this development will be the re-creation of the Hanlon and Clair family farmhouses which dated back to the 19th century. These had deteriorated beyond restoration, and Reid worked out an agreement with LACAC to measure and reproduce them as new, usable homes at the formal entrance to the development.

Carson Reid, with a staff of 17 and a regular group of subcontractors, has operated at the modest scale of the former Reid and Laing company. From the mid 1980s to the late 1990s, he and his father have built about 1,200 single family homes in Guelph, specializing in custom infill on lots purchased from developers such as Armel and University Village. Some examples of their work in the mid 1980s are three architecturally designed houses on Palmer St.(Nos. 67, 73, and 79), on part of the Ker Cavan property then owned by Toronto developer David Medhurst. Examples from the 1990s include six houses on Brady Lane in the city's south end (Nos. 22 to 27). Carson Reid is also building a substantial number of houses in the Clairfields subdivision, on lots purchased from the developer, Victoria Woods, where he, like other builders, offers a variety of models on lots ranging from 30 to 50 feet. Occasionally Carson Reid has also acted as a developer, as at Whitetail Court, where he purchased 10 acres next to a wetlands area and laid out 35 lots and built houses between 1995 and 1997.

Beyond the Reids, another leading Guelph builder and developer is Thomas Krizsan who founded Thomasfield Homes in 1977. After an MBA from the University of Western Ontario, Krizsan ventured into business on his own at the age of 25. Since then, as he told the *Mercury*, he has built about 4,000 homes in Guelph, Kitchener-Waterloo, Cambridge and Burlington. Two projects in particular are outstanding. His Pine Ridge subdivision on Gordon Street South emphasizes green space for recreational purposes and water management. In another, related endeavour, he built and owns (and operates) the Springfield Golf and Country Club which opened in 1990.

DESIGN TRENDS

The trends in house design in late 20th century Guelph have essentially been those that were typical of North American communities in general. The first of these trends is the predominance of the garage at the front of the house, resulting in what has been derisively referred to as the "snout house." This type of house has made many suburban streets look like a row of garages, with houses attached at the back as though the homes are only secondary features. One of the reasons for the style, of course, is our society's strong commitment to the automobile and the desire for a two-car garage. Carson Reid points out that this type of house is the result of two conflicting trends – the smaller, narrower lots, and the desire to have a large main floor oriented toward the backyard. This contrasts with the earlier generation of houses which had picture windows facing the street.

A second trend is the reorganization of interior space, especially in larger homes. Front halls have become spacious and bathrooms and kitchens have become special places, not just service areas. Separate dining rooms are disappearing as they are incorporated into "the Great Room," which also encompasses the family room and living room functions.

A third trend is the popularity of vernacular styles based on traditional, rather than modern, architectural shapes and detailing. In general, these vernacular styles are known as Neo-eclectic, for they are a very free interpretation rather than a precise copying of traditional styles. According to architectural historians, the Neo-eclectic movement first was introduced by the builders of modest houses who sensed the public's new interest in more traditional forms. Several subtypes of this approach are discernable in Guelph, but it must be emphasized that builders have offered a large variety of models and have readily mixed components to suit a particular client.

The first version of the Neo-eclectic to become popular in Guelph was the Mansard, named for its characteristic roof. A good example from the late 1970s is 40 Waverley Dr., built by Albert Reid. This version was also popular on public buildings, malls and townhouses. A second version is the Neo-Colonial, lightly based on American east coast design from the colonial period. This style often features prominent dormers on second-floor windows. Many examples can be found among fairly modest houses; a more sophisticated rendering is the clubhouse at the Village by the Arboretum. A third version of the Neo-eclectic, the Neo-French, has became very popular during the 1990s, particularly for the larger houses of the south end, and in the rural-like settings of the Bridle Path, just

A street of garages: Borland Drive. Source: Stelter, 2000

The Neo-eclectic house: Neo-Victorian on Monticello Street.
Source: Stelter, 2000

resource community, but is a diversified industrial and university city with close ties to its agricultural roots. Also included would be the origins of its people. While Guelphites were once heavily British, especially English, in background, they later came from a variety of places, as indicated by the birthplaces of many of those who have shaped the modern city.

Guelph's character was also determined to a large extent by the built environment. We shape our cities and then our cities shape us. The process of building the 20th century city can be regarded as a combination of large-scale continental trends and of local activity through dynamic individuals and

beyond the southern reaches of the city. The Neo-French is characterized by a steeply pitched, hipped roof. Doors and windows are often rounded, or with segmented arches. Many of these houses are built in the modern forms of artificial stone. The Neo-Tudor, a fourth version, can be shaped like that of the Neo-French, but features prominent front-facing gables, with decorative half-timbered detailing. Modest examples abound on almost every recently built street. More imposing types, resembling medieval mansions, can be seen at some of the rural retreats to the south of the city. A fifth version is the Neo-Classical, which ranges from the modest symmetrical house with a pedimented portico, to the larger homes with imposing columns (No. 66 Monticello), or projecting frontispieces (No. 25, Hands Drive). A sixth version is the most eclectic and is usually referred to as the Neo-Victorian. This includes a variety of touches, from Queen Anne rounded towers, to rounded windows, and front porches in the New Urbanism mode. Most of these elements can be seen on almost any suburban street built since 1980 such as Monticello or nearby at the Village by the Arboretum.

groups. These combined forces are apparent in several aspects of city-building. First is the process of de-centralization. All cities have become suburbanized in the 20th century and Guelph is no exception. Its population has spread in every direction, first to the north, later to the west and recently to the south and east. Much of the city's commercial activity has moved from the downtown core to the suburban malls such as those on Stone Road West. In this respect, Guelph is indistinguishable from other regional cities.

Second, local design and building trends have reflected larger changes in North American consumer tastes. In the early 20th century, architects William Mahoney and Frye Colwill represented two poles of thinking – the functional and the aesthetic – about how to design buildings. As in most other places, the functional prevailed. The introduction of the modernist International style at mid-century was exemplified by Allan Sage's schools and other buildings. By the 1960s a more individualistic approach was initiated by Richard Pagani and John Haayen. The popular forms of the North American suburban house were effectively constructed by local builders such as Reid and Laing. By the last quarter of the century, a post-modern trend was represented by Karl Briestensky's designs. As elsewhere in North America, Victorian styles re-emerged on public buildings, homes and even shopping malls. We have come full circle from the Queen Anne of the 1890s to the Queen Anne of the 1990s.

Third, is the question of how to deal with older buildings when shaping a modern city. By the 1960s Guelph was typically North American in displaying its disdain for its 19th century architectural heritage. Many important symbols such as

V CONCLUSION: BUILDINGS AND A COMMUNITY'S CHARACTER

In conclusion, what kind of city is Guelph? Any portrait of the city must begin with its scale, its relatively modest size in comparison with other Canadian cities. It would have to take into account the city's proximity to Toronto, Canada's major metropolis, for Toronto's influence has always been apparent in everything from political and economic activities to the latest in architectural styles. What the city does for a living is part of the picture, for Guelph is not a one-company, or one-the Customs House were demolished and replaced with modern structures. Fortunately, a large stock of Victorian buildings still exist, probably because the local pressures for development were not as strong as in some neighbouring communities such as Kitchener. By the 1970s a new respect for the past was represented by Gordon Couling's organization of a preservation movement. Since then, a remarkable number of older buildings have been restored or renovated and adapted to new uses by John Lammer, Douglas Bridge, Chester Carere and many others. Public attitudes have changed, from a rejection of heritage to a recognition that what we have is a precious, if fragile treasure. There once was a Guelph look. In some respects it continues to shape our idea of what kind of community Guelph should be.

SOURCES

The major sources for this chapter have been the *Guelph Mercury* and interviews with many of the participants in the city-building process. Very little has been published in this area. For that matter, the topic is largely unexplored for most communities.

I wish to acknowledge the assistance of Norman Harrison, a retired senior planner with the city, who has provided invaluable information and advice. Karen Rolfe, planner and LACAC co-ordinator, was helpful in researching specific heritage projects.

INTERVIEWS

Len Ariss	Margaret MacKinnon
Suzanne Bone	John Mogk
Douglas Bridge	Robert Oakes
Peter Brazolot	Richard Pagani
Karl Briestensky	Albert Reid
Jon Fogelman	Carson Reid
Phil Gosling	Orin Reid
John Haayen	Allan Sage
William Hamilton	Elio Stradiotto
Linda Hasenfratz	Freddy Veri
Harold Jackson	Alan Whitworth
John Lammer	Mel Wolfond

CHAPTER 5

THE GROWTH AND PLANNING OF GUELPH IN THE TWENTIETH CENTURY

FRED DAHMS

THE LEGACY OF THE PAST: 1827 TO 1900

The Physical Basis

Site, situation and physical features have been major determinants of the early success of many settlements. Only later, when physical factors gave way to social and economic forces did the actions of boosters and entrepreneurs become more important. When Guelph was established in 1827 by John Galt and Tiger Dunlop, water for power and drinking, access to potential markets and potential farmland were of paramount importance. Guelph's situation between the eastern edge of the vast undeveloped Huron Tract and York was ideal. Its site at the confluence of the Speed and Eramosa rivers promised excellent potential for waterpower for its planned mills and workshops. Beyond the river flats, a series of gravel terraces and drumlins from the Wisconsin glaciation provided interesting relief and a variety of building sites safe from spring floods. Heavy stands of mixed woods, including oak, maple, ash, cedar, elm, spruce and pine provided potential raw materials for building and fuel. The Guelph formation of the Lockport Dolomite, which outcropped along both rivers, would eventually be quarried to construct Guelph's numerous limestone buildings. Its site provided potential resources, but it also channelled and constrained the settlement's physical growth at its foundation and long thereafter.

Guelph's initial growth was almost entirely along the west bank of the Speed River because of the large drumlin and gravel terraces blocking any growth to the east. Development to the west of Gordon Street was also inhibited by the drumlin now crowned by the Church of Our Lady. By 1850, the settlement was bounded on the east and south by the loop of the Speed River. It nestled comfortably on the relatively level land as far west as what is now Yorkshire Street and stretched north to London Road. It was punctuated by the major drumlin just west of the square. This pattern was encouraged and perpetuated by Galt's original plan which specified a series of streets radiating from the bend in the river behind the River Run Centre.

From the very beginning, Guelph was the product of deliberate planning, first by John Galt and the Canada Company and later by a series of transportation plans and land-use regulations. Galt carefully prepared the economic base and physical layout of the city to make it the headquarters for the sales of Canada Company land in the Huron Tract to the west. His untimely recall to London by his employers began the end of early planning, while the coming of the railway ensured that his grand design for streets and squares would survive only in a truncated form. This was the beginning of what became an almost constant struggle between concern with the quality of life in the city and its real or imagined transportation requirements. The Grand Trunk Railway disrupted the integrity of Galt's plan in 1857. Its requirement of a low gradient along the river resulted in the truncation of Waterloo Avenue at what is now Gordon Street and in a new barrier to expansion south of the original site. The band of steel also bisected City Hall square. Transportation infrastructure in the form of the railway changed the street patterns, channelled growth to the north and forever influenced the built environment of the Royal City. Early in its history, the works of people and nature had conspired to set the stage for Guelph's subsequent physical expansion and economic development.

Galt's Plan and Subsequent Growth

John Galt's original plan for Guelph complemented the local topography by skirting the hills and using level land. Woolwich Street ran along the riverbank and eventually climbed the sides of the hills. Macdonell Street, confronted by the steep side of the drumlin at its western end, simply stopped. Others such as Waterloo, Market and Quebec streets climbed the drumlins diagonally or went around them. After 1832 however, Galt's layout was supplemented by the standard grid pattern, which ignored topography and marched directly over the tops of the hills. This checkerboard pattern became the standard for the community until the development of "designer suburbs" with their winding streets, loops and cul-de-sacs after the Second World War. Nevertheless, Galt's plan provided a lasting legacy in the central areas, while its junctions with the subsequent grid resulted in a number of bizarre and complicated intersections that

The Site of Guelph: Topography

309 Spot elevation

Contour interval = 1 metre

Source: Dept. of Planning and Development

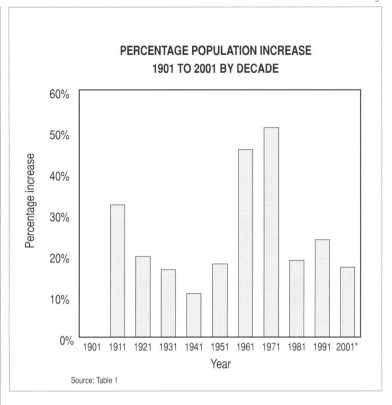

PERCENTAGE POPULATION INCREASE
1901 TO 2001 BY DECADE

Source: Table 1

continue to haunt the traffic engineers. Especially in its central area, Guelph's morphology has been affected profoundly by the local topography and by the pattern of roads and railways initially developed there.

THE GROWTH OF GUELPH

As indicated in the population graph, Guelph grew rather slowly before the Second World War, accelerated considerably from 1951 to 1971 and then slowed to a rate slightly greater than that before Second World War.

By 1906, both roads and railways had influenced the city's physical expansion. Railways, which effectively blocked access to the east and south, now surrounded the old Central Business District, which had been around Market Square. From origins around Gordon and Farquhar streets on the southeast corner of Market Square, the Central Business

District was cut off from places to the south by the tracks and subsequently migrated north of the river and the railways. The Grand Trunk had split Guelph's central square and forced the construction of subways and bridges to facilitate safety. The drumlin and river terraces between the centre of the city and the Eramosa River inhibited growth in that direction, while large tracts of land owned by the Roman Catholic and St. Andrew's churches beyond Exhibition Park blocked expansion to the west. The land immediately west of the core was generally too hilly for industry, which slowed population and industrial growth there until the turn of the century.

An example of one of the many handsome Guelph buildings that once graced St. George's Square: the old Bank of Montreal and the manager's residence, to the right, c. 1920. Source: Guelph Public Library

By 1900, the results of the industrial revolution were having a major effect on Guelph. The street railway and the increasing use of motor vehicles facilitated residential growth beyond walking distance of the early places of employment. The city began to expand along the Dundas Highway (Gordon Street), Eramosa Road and along York Road towards the new industrial area paralleling the Eramosa River. Distinct sectors of similar land uses developed, with industry expanding along the river and railroad corridors. New higher income residential developments spread north along a linear sector over the hills along Eramosa Road. Because of war and depression, both Guelph's physical and population growth were slow from 1906 to 1945, with little new residential development except north of the Eramosa River to Victoria Road, and between Beverley and Grange streets, east of Stevenson. Another area that grew was south of the Speed River from Water to Forest Street. In most respects, the map of Guelph in 1906 is almost identical to that in 1945. Some new industry had come to the city, a small amount of new development had occurred on the edges, but most population growth was accommodated by infilling of areas settled by the turn of the century. Small contractors and individual builders were responsible for most of the residential construction.

THE CHARACTER OF THE CITY TO THE SECOND WORLD WAR: 1901 TO 1939

Despite the fact that growth was slow from 1900 to 1945, Guelph was considered an extremely desirable location by industry and citizens alike. The 1903 souvenir edition of the *Evening Mercury* boasted that Guelph was "bound to become one of the most important cities in the province." With a population over 11,000, the "streets of the city are broad, well paved and lined with handsome public and private buildings and beautiful residences, while the business section is well supplied with substantial business blocks tenanted by the leading firms in commerce and finance."

By 1915, Guelph had an area of 3,200 acres and assessed property valued at $11,213,464. Among its attractions, the *Evening Mercury* listed a free public library, two daily and two weekly newspapers, free postal delivery, 18 churches, an agricultural college, a business college, a collegiate and public and separate school systems. The city owned its own street railway, gas system, electric light system and waterworks. A modern fire fighting force and sewage system completed the picture. "Standing 1200 feet above sea level, Guelph is an ideally healthy spot, with two hospitals, a sanitarium and Aged Peoples' home." The publication *Guelph Ontario 1915, Commercial Progressive and Industrial Edition*, boasted that the city owned its own utilities and had 65 miles of granolithic (concrete) sidewalks. Its industrial base was varied, comprising almost 100 industries, some small but of an excellent variety and quality. The Wellington Hotel contained 60 guestrooms, was steam heated, had the best dining in the city and was known by travellers throughout Canada for its excellent accommodations.

In addition to his flowery praise of the city, A.W. Drummond provided some statistics on its economic development in 1923. In that year more than 50,000 farmers visited the Ontario Agricultural College, and an active Chamber of Commerce and progressive city council encouraged businesses to invest in Guelph. As a result, building permits for the year ending 1923 were $571,484 while

 1911 – Guelph decides to get tough on reckless driving on paved and city roads. The matter is taken to the city council and they decide to take action. Several men are charged with speeding and fined $5 for exceeding the speed limit of 10 miles an hour.

 January 5, 1922 – Olive L. French becomes the first female Deputy Returning Officer in the Guelph election as Mr. A. Cordiner had fallen ill.

$43,699 was spent on waterworks. The assessment increase was $1,523,266. "Labour troubles are unknown in the city ... and homes for the labouring class may be had at low rental, or purchased on government loan of 90 percent of the cost price." Despite, or possibly because of its relatively slow growth, between the turn of the century and 1945, Guelph developed an excellent infrastructure and a quality of life that was the envy of many other Ontario communities.

By 1945, Guelph was beginning to share in post-war prosperity and population growth. Despite the havoc wreaked by the railway lines, Galt's early plans continued to add character to the older areas of the city and by example guided the growth of subsequent subdivisions. A civic publication in 1945 described the city as "a centre of natural scenic beauty....its views well watered and rolling. The visitor to Guelph is impressed with its wide streets, modern stores and well-kept houses in shady residential districts." Colourful flowerbeds,

 1933 – After voting for it in a bylaw election, Guelph becomes the only city or town in Southwestern Ontario to accept daylight savings time for the summer months.

A tree-lined street in one of Guelph's older residential districts: Park Avenue, off Exhibition Park. Source: Fred Dahms, 1999

gardens and lawns are a prominent feature of this city of "congenial and comfortable" living. A typical citizen's comment to a visitor was "mister, Guelph just hasn't any slums; why our people wouldn't stand for them."

THE BEGINNING OF PLANNING IN GUELPH – 1945

The end of the Second World War saw not only a period of renewed growth and prosperity for Guelph, but also the beginning of formal planning that would guide it for the next 50 years. The publication *Why We Chose Guelph*, (1945), provided statistical information on the city and proclaimed that "continuing the policy of progressive planning, the City Planning Commission has projected plans to control zoning, and to provide additional parks, subdivisions in outlying districts and a general overall plan for future development."

Planned Progress – Policies in Guelph's First Official Plan

Guelph: Planned Progress for the Next Fifteen Years, 1945, Guelph's first official planning document, was prepared by consultants Culham, Dryden and McDonald for the Guelph Planning Commission. Gordon Grierson was chair of the Guelph Planning Commission and G.F. Koch had been chair of the Guelph Board of Trade Housing Committee, whose report on housing conditions in Guelph led to the formation of the planning commission. The housing report raised issues leading to objectives for planning, road building, land use and zoning in Guelph. Despite their origins in an era of rather unsophisticated planning, many of the policies and concepts introduced in *Planned Progress* have affected Guelph to the present day.

Guelph city council and the planning commission were concerned with costs as well as with planning matters. The general plan that they devised was "designed with close reference to the city's ability to pay for improvements over a period of 15 years, and to comply with the requirements for a post-war program of construction of much-needed public works and housing under the National Housing Act." The planning commission suggested that "a levy of two mills per annum would be adequate to finance their suggestions and that half the revenues should be kept in a special fund for larger projects when unemployment warrants." They also promoted citizen participation by ensuring that every property owner in the city received a copy of the plan. Others would be made available to government agencies and for "advertising purposes," since this was "among the first to be prepared in the province and likely to be in demand by other municipalities for reference."

In its historical background to the plan, the commission referred to Galt's problems with the Canada Company, which was unhappy that he tried to plan for the future rather than "their very natural preference for a quick realization of profits." The commission criticised surveys subsequent to Galt's for ignoring Galt's vision of the future and creating streets that were "dead-ended or were extended by very narrow widths at dangerous grades." They desired to "recapture the inspiration of Galt's plans for the achievement of an even greater sense of responsibility for these human needs." The city's river valleys and green hills were noted as among its greatest attractions, to be preserved and enhanced as "playgrounds for the people," while hilly residential areas would be free of heavy traffic. The plan was to preserve Guelph's natural and historic assets, but stressed the ability of good planning to attract new industry and additional housing to the city.

Wartime housing, 1945, at Lemon Street and Winston Crescent.
Source: Fred Dahms, 1999

Major Recommendations in *Planned Progress*

The philosophy and proposals in *Planned Progress* have affected the growth and development of Guelph since they were adopted. City councillors have subsequently embraced many of the attitudes expressed by the authors, business people and those involved with planning. Inadvertently or otherwise, the emphasis on physical solutions to Guelph's perceived problems provided the engineering department with major influence over the form and function of the city. Traffic problems have at times seemed to be the most important considerations in the development of Guelph. The city's fiscally responsible (frugal) approach to planning is also emphasized in this document, which pointed out that most planning costs could be recovered from those who received benefit, and that "over 80 percent of planning accomplishment is achieved by regulation at no cost to the taxpayer."

Traffic

Street widenings and improvements were the first major policy to be mentioned in the plan (**See *Planned Progress* map**). The Guelph Planning Commission felt constrained by the barriers presented by Guelph's topography and Galt's original layout of the city. Essentially the Central Business District (CBD) was confined within a narrow triangle from which it was not expected to emerge. Existing streets effectively funnelled all traffic through this small, congested area. In Guelph, the mixing of local and through traffic was believed to cause accidents, and according to John Sutherland & Sons Insurance Company, contributed to higher insurance rates in the city. Guelph was seen as a major gateway to the north, receiving traffic from the Queen Elizabeth Way bound for Muskoka. The mixing of local and "fast moving and often bulky through traffic in central Guelph" was "exacting a heavy toll from citizens and merchants in increased liability insurance, and seriously blockades the local traffic flow with a harmful effect on shopping. It also adds a heavy burden of maintenance to city pavements." Several solutions to projected traffic problems were suggested, and a number of the plan's proposals were ultimately implemented. The key component of a ring-road scheme was to be the new Memorial Parkway, linking the western edge of the city to Victoria Road by

 1923 – Guelph drivers form the Guelph Automobile Club on May 12 stating, "the organization promises to prove useful to the public at large and not to motorists only."

Planned Progress and The Memorial Parkway
The Guelph City Plan 1945

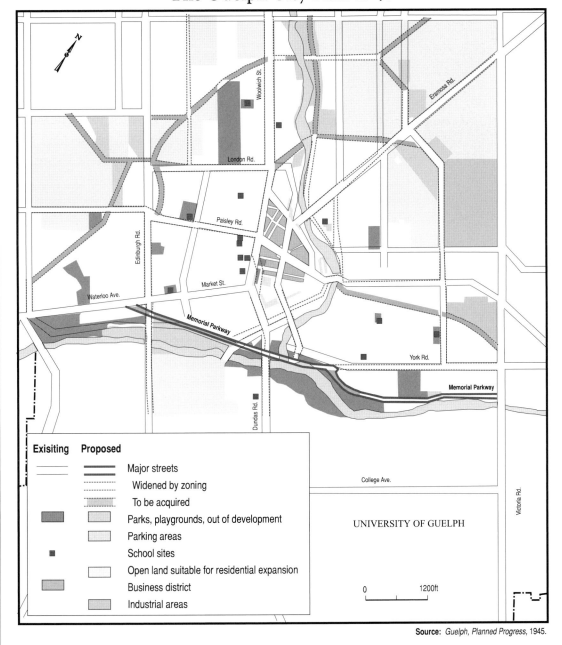

Exisiting | Proposed

Major streets
Widened by zoning
To be acquired
Parks, playgrounds, out of development
Parking areas
School sites
Open land suitable for residential expansion
Business district
Industrial areas

0   1200ft

Source: *Guelph, Planned Progress,* 1945.

following the Speed and Eramosa rivers. The idea of the Memorial Parkway has been resurrected as recently as 1997.

The Business District

The plan suggested that there were too many small stores serving local customers in the Central Business District. It encouraged the migration of small stores to neighbourhoods to make room for larger businesses downtown that would serve customers from outside Guelph. The commission proposed new shopping frontages with better accessibility, improved environment and adequate, carefully located parking for out-of-town shoppers. They proposed a ratio of 25 feet of store frontage per 100 potential customers instead of the 34.4 feet per 100 population existing in the city. Given a total effective business frontage downtown of 14,000 feet, they reckoned that at 25 feet per 100, Guelph could serve 56,000 people. This seemed feasible given expected growth in nearby communities if Guelph merchants would co-operate to achieve this objective.

Guelph's First Plan for its Central Square –The Civic Centre

The commission proposed a new civic centre (essentially a square), which was to be the focal point of Guelph's rail and road transportation at the lower end of Wyndham Street. Improvements in the street pattern, with a new subway at Gordon to Norfolk and a realignment of Wilson through to Cork Street, were to be established. Much needed parking and a bus terminal would be created at the site of the old Winter Fair building adjacent to the railway station. The commission argued that it was a firetrap that should be removed. An auditorium, tree-lined boulevards, a new location for the market and parks would complete the civic centre. The plan read:

> The enhancement of land values by the release and safety of
> traffic flows was, of course, your Commission's first
> concern… So many of the features of the Centre are existing.
> John Galt chose the imposing site for the Church of Our
> Lady on the commanding hill at the head of Macdonell
> Street. The Norfolk Street Church terminates the important

cross axis and between it and the proposed site for a new City Hall lie a group of old buildings which should never stand in the way of a project so expressive of the civic aspirations of all the citizens of Guelph.

The proposed new city hall would be at the end of a boulevard on Carden Street, but the plan did not mention the fate of the existing structure. Was it one of the "group of old buildings" to be removed?

Parks, Playgrounds and Other Open Spaces

Parks followed street widening in priority. Areas with "fine natural features" would be acquired near residential areas, but the majority of parkland would be "low-lying lands, unsuitable for residence because they would be likely to attract sub-standard dwellings." Since the majority of potential parkland fell into the second category, the acquisition would not be expensive.

The commission recommended that low-lying lands along the Speed and Eramosa rivers eventually become a continuous belt of park through the "most densely populated parts" of the city. Since much of it had been filled with ash, and was also prone to flooding, it could be acquired at a reasonable cost. It also recommended that parks and playgrounds be constructed near areas of new residential growth so that children would not have to walk more than a quarter mile to play.

Industrial Expansion

The commission recommended industrial development to the east between Stevenson Street and Victoria Road, in locations which might be expanded through annexation. This easterly location was easily served by the railway and would allow smoke to blow away from the city. It was also adjacent to large areas suitable for workers' housing. Westerly expansion of industrial areas was not

Swimming at Riverside Park, early 1960s.

Source: J. Keleher

recommended at this time. The commission suggested that the city acquire potential industrial lands, which it would subsequently sell at reasonable prices to prevent speculation by private landowners. This policy was implemented and has continued to the present day.

Housing

As a result of the Depression, war, and subsequent slow growth, Guelph's Board of Trade Housing Report called for 100 new houses a year for 10 years. New National Housing Administration regulations insisted on high building standards and protection of the environment, requiring that subdivisions be designed carefully and conform to the *Official Plan*. An urgent call was made for the extension of water and sewage services and sufficient accepted plans of subdivision. The commission wanted a large reserve of well-trained building tradesmen and common labourers to construct the required houses. The plan stressed that new subdivisions should be adjacent to existing housing and not allowed to sprawl indiscriminately. There was concern that Guelph's economic and population growth might fall behind that of its rivals, so the commission urged rapid implementation of its recommendations. At this early juncture, growth became a major goal of politicians in Guelph.

 1935 – Thomas Nichol, Guelph's first superintendent of parks, appointed on April 14, 1909, retires from his work improving Guelph's park system. He was particularly noted for Exhibition, Lyon and Riverside parks. However, before his advent, St. George's Park was a cow pasture. He personally felt that his "most oustanding achievement" was Royal City Park. His grandson, Howard Grasley (well-known himself as "the ramblin' yodeler" for his musical endeavors in the 1930s and 40s), recounts:

"When the river wall was being constructed in Royal City Park, relief workers were sent to work on the project. Seeing some holes in their shoes, etc., Grandpa Nichol would accompany them back to City Hall to have them outfitted with proper clothing to suit the conditions they would be working under. He was adamant that they be dressed for the elements."

Subdivision Regulations

The *Planning Act* of 1945, Section 24, set out regulations for subdivision control. *Planned Progress* recommended that Guelph incorporate a bylaw as part of its *Official Plan* to prevent the sale or transfer of land by metes and bounds and to make subdivision approvals in accordance with Section 24. Recommendations to council on subdivision approval included consideration of the following:

Small-lot development in St. Patrick's Ward before 1945.
Source: Fred Dahms, 1999

Conformity with the *Official Plan* and adjacent land uses

Agreement with owners of adjacent land on subdivision uses

No building on poorly drained land

Designation of highways and internal circulation to discourage through traffic

Avoidance of dead-end streets and layout respecting contours in hilly areas

Land set aside for parks and preservation of large trees where possible

Provision for local stores

They also specified that streets should join at right angles and that lot lines should be perpendicular to street lines. Probably the most important recommendation affecting the subsequent form of Guelph was the stipulation that lots "must have a frontage of at least 40 feet for inside lots and 50 feet at corners, and an area of at least 4,000 and 5,000 square feet respectively." Surveys with smaller lots than these should be re-plotted.

This provision would eliminate small-lot development such as that in St. Patrick's Ward. It was the first step to neighbourhood-based "designer suburbs" as suggested by the architect Clarence Perry in the United States in 1929. Perry felt that automobile traffic was becoming dangerous and should be kept out of residential areas. He also felt that people should be linked with each other and their environment within well-defined subdivisions. To accomplish this he recommended that neighbourhoods be organized in units of 64 hectares with a maximum walking distance of 500 metres for children to an elementary school.

An example of a designer suburb, after the ideas of architect Clarence Perry's neighbourhood unit.   Source: Fred Dahms, c. 1997

Arterial roads would skirt and define each neighbourhood, while a system of curving streets and cul-de-sacs would discourage through traffic. Shops and services were to be on the arterials at the periphery. The total population of one of these neighbourhoods would be about 1,500 families or 5,000 to 6,000 people.

Variants of this scheme have been used over and over in North America, producing traffic-insulated communities from 3,000 to over 12,000 people. Perry's neighbourhood unit has become one of the most enduring ideas in planning, subsequently repeated extensively in Britain and North America. Ultimately, Perry's ideas as translated by the *Planning Act*, local official plans and city bylaws had a profound effect on the physical form and extent of residential growth in Guelph after 1945. Guelph's adoption of *Planned Progress* in 1945 and the provisions of Section 24 of the *Planning Act* were the first steps in this process.

PLANNING, GROWTH AND CHANGE FROM THE 1950S TO THE 1970S

Between 1951 and 1971 Guelph grew at a rate more rapid than at any comparable period before or since (**See population table on page 230**). In the 10 years after 1951 the population increased by 45.5 percent and from 1961 to 1971 by 50.8 percent. This prompted the annexation of land to accommodate the unprecedented growth.

 November 1947 – Elizabeth Mowatt Heron becomes the first woman to sit on city council. She had not been elected, but was next in line when another councillor retired.

Annexations 1854-1993

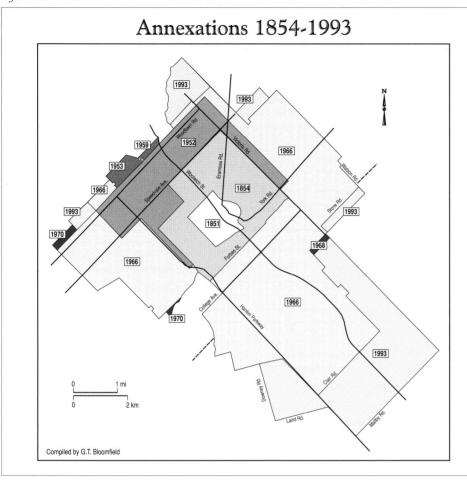

Compiled by G.T. Bloomfield

Annexations

One of the first major events in Guelph after 1951 was the annexation of 2,500 acres of land from Guelph Township in 1953. This acquisition provided additional relatively level land for the development of industry and residences in the northwest quadrant of the city, adjacent to Highway 7 and the CPR line. A small additional annexation added land to the north in 1959 east of Highway 6. In 1955, the Guelph City Planning Board responded to eight years of land use regulation under the bylaws in *Planned Progress* and to two years of study after the 1953 annexation. The addition of so much developable land provided the impetus to update and refine the earlier attempts at planning and zoning in Guelph.

 December 5, 1955 – Elvie R. Lowell is the first woman elected to council.

Table 1	Population of Guelph 1901 to 2000		
Year	Population	Change	%Change
1901	11496		
1911	15175	3679	32.0%
1921	18128	2953	19.5%
1931	21075	2947	16.3%
1941	23273	2198	10.4%
1951	27386	4113	17.7%
1961	**39838**	**12452**	**45.5%**
1971	**60087**	**20249**	**50.8%**
1981	71207	11120	18.5%
1991	87976	16769	23.5%
2001*	102818	14842	16.95

*Estimated.
Source: Statistics Canada, Census of Population, 1901-1996;
City of Guelph, Department of Planning and Development,
Statistical Summary, 1991

As with similar documents of this era, the new zoning bylaw (1955) was intended to "make the greatest possible contribution to the employment opportunities and the health, comfort and living amenities of its citizens." It provided for "ample room for industry in the new Industrial Basin and elsewhere where commuting to work was convenient. It protected the "vital central business area," designated appropriate locations for shopping and school areas and "created areas of ample size to prevent overcrowding. Its street pattern was designed to prevent undue traffic hazards; existing park and recreational zones are conserved and new play areas are set aside for future expansion." The other major intent of the zoning bylaw was to "give permanence to property values by preventing the intrusion of uses incompatible with those existing in the respective zones, and by placing such unwanted uses in zones which permit their operation." Exceptions to zoning were to be allowed after consultation with neighbours and hearings by the planning board, city council and Ontario Municipal Board.

The bylaw set minimum standards for lot sizes, setbacks, side yards, building size, accessory buildings and of course, land uses in each zone. A series of maps designated zoning on existing areas and for undeveloped lands in the city. As a result, all residential, commercial and industrial growth in this period of rapid population increase was strictly controlled. Beyond the already built-up areas, the ideas of Clarence Perry manifested themselves in suburbs with wide streets, 25-foot setbacks and curvilinear patterns cut off from other areas by even wider arterials. John Galt's original plan and the subsequent gridiron pattern of streets were being surrounded by the latest fashion in planning which eventually became indistinguishable from that of other large scale developments in Don Mills, Mississauga or Bramalea.

The Bylaw of 1955

The bylaw of 1955 was considerably more comprehensive than its predecessors. It designated 10 land use

zones and specified that its intent was to:

> prohibit the use of land in the City of Guelph for or except for such purposes as are set out
> in the bylaw; to prohibit the erection or use in the City of Guelph of buildings or structures
> for or except for such purposes as are set out in the bylaw; to regulate the type of construc-
> tion and the height, bulk, location spacing, external design, character and the use of
> buildings or structures to be erected within the City of Guelph and the minimum frontage
> and depth of the parcel of land and the proportion of the area thereof which any building
> or structure may occupy; and to divide the city into areas or zones for such purposes.

Detailed regulations for each zone were specified and a series of 14 maps showed exactly where each zone was located and to which lots each zone applied. This was the city planning board's most powerful and comprehensive document to date, allowing close control and monitoring of all subsequent proposals for land development in the city. It was just in time to cope with the rapid residential, industrial, institutional and business growth that was soon to occur.

THE 1960S

By 1960, the planning board and council were concerned enough about the prospect of rapid growth that they commissioned a series of planning studies to guide what they saw as a busy future. In the province, a new *Planning Act* was adopted in 1955 and the Ontario Water Resources Commission was established in 1956. TransCanada Pipelines Ltd. was now bringing western natural gas to Ontario, and by 1960, the Trans-Canada Highway had also been completed. The economic recovery after the late 1950s recession was underway as Guelph began to participate in national economic growth.

The *City of Guelph Planning Studies* 1960 was a comprehensive look at the factors that were anticipated to affect Guelph for the next 20 years. Its population projections suggested that the city would reach 76,800 by 1980, for an increase of 99 percent in the two decades after 1960. Much of the anticipated growth was to be the result of major immigration by Italians to a city which had attracted a large Italian population for many years. Guelph had the advantages of a flourishing Italian community and appropriate employment to attract additional Italian immigrants. The actual population change from 1961 to 1981 was 71,207, for an increase of 78.7 percent, somewhat less than the optimistic forecast, but impressive nonetheless. Based on this projection, the document examined contemporary and anticipated land uses and recommended a series of policies to guide the expected growth. This very thorough study captures the character of the community in 1960, just before the period of its most explosive development.

In 1960, much of Guelph consisted of solid single-family residences. Multiple residential uses were found primarily around the central business area and north and west of the business section. A considerable amount of such development was the result of the conversion of older large single family dwellings into multiple use establishments. Recommendations were made for "properly controlled conversions" of older homes to multiple uses as well as for the construction of and zoning for apartment units in new areas of the city.

The extent of the Central Business District (CBD) continued to be restricted by the rivers, railways and drumlins that had always dominated the site. Some growth was forecast to the north along Woolwich Street, but the planners suggested that the CBD continue to be a compact and convenient central retail focus for the city. Smaller neighbourhood plazas were recognised as necessary in areas of new residential growth, but it was suggested that any large retail developments be required to apply for a zone change, an *Official Plan* amendment and undergo economic impact and feasibility studies. This was to preclude any negative impact on the downtown. Industrial development had traditionally followed the railways, but since the 1953 annexation, gravitated to the new northwestern industrial area. The foresight of Fred Woods, who was the city engineer and became the city administrator, provided Guelph with a large and inexpensive pool of land for new industrial growth. He convinced council to purchase a number of farms at very reasonable prices long before industry became interested in the newly available area. When they did require land there, the city made it available from their industrial land bank, which greatly facilitated industrial growth in the 1960s and 1970s. Relocation of older industries to the newer area was anticipated as their plants became obsolete and their sites became cramped. Such trends were subsequently encouraged by the planning department and city council.

The economic survey accompanying the planning studies assessed the city's labour force and manufacturing potential and compared them to Ontario averages. By 1960, Guelph had 121 establishments in "Primary and Manufacturing and Constructional" categories, employing 9,000 persons. Their gross wages were $27,000,000 and the gross value of their products was $100,000,000. A comparison of Guelph's industrial sector with that of the province showed that Guelph was considerably under-represented in food and beverage manufacturing and processing, with only 350 persons in that category. Since this was the third most important category in Ontario, the study recommended that Guelph attempt to obtain more such enterprises. In Guelph, 50 percent of the total manufacturing labour force was employed in 19 factories, distributed as follows: Metal Fabrication - 8; Textiles - 5; Electrical products - 3; and one each in Food and Beverages, Plastics and Tobacco. The study urged the city to attempt to attract more industries in the manufacture of paper products, chemical and food and beverage products and to concentrate on medium size enterprises. This would balance the economy and bring it more into line with provincial norms.

In the Guelph of 1960, the location of automobile service stations continued to be an important planning issue. Special sites were designated for their peculiar requirements, necessitating a separate zoning category. Open space was concentrated along the Speed River away from the centre of the city, but it was anticipated that eventually the park belt would extend along the river through the central business area where railways then dominated. A detailed inventory revealed that in general building conditions in Guelph were good, with only a few classified as fair. However, in the opinion of the consultants, the number of homes of only fair quality was not great enough to constitute a threat to the overall calibre of housing in the city, but policies to improve substandard structures were recommended. Major population growth had taken place in St. George's Ward between Eramosa Road and Elizabeth Street. Conversely, St. Patrick's Ward which had been a major recipient of Italian immigrants grew very slowly during this period. Nevertheless, because of its size and earlier growth, population densities remained highest in St. Patrick's Ward and directly west of the CBD, but were slightly lower in adjacent areas. The lowest densities were found in the rapidly growing northeast sector and to the northwest. To some extent, densities radiated from the centre and decreased towards the edge of the city.

During this period, the Wolfond family owned large tracts of land on the western edge of the city. By 1966, they began to develop what would ultimately be known as the Willow West area, and the shopping plaza of the same name. Many homes and apartments were constructed by their Armel Corporation, which continues to build and develop in Guelph. The Wolfond family also owned a wrecking yard, and while they were building on the outskirts of the city, they had been hired to demolish buildings in the centre. Their machines destroyed the Carnegie Library and the old Customs House, as businessmen replaced the old with the new. The Goldie Mill was scheduled for demolition, but a concerted effort by City Administrator Fred Woods, Director of Planning Ken Perry and

Senior Planner Norman Harrison saved the structure. These three interacted with the Grand River Conservation Authority to delay the demolition, and co-operated with Gus Stahlmann of Parks and Recreation to create Goldie Mill Park. This quiet oasis near the centre of Guelph will ultimately be integrated into the river system walkway, which has been part of city planning for years.

Transportation Planning

The *Major Street and Traffic Plan* 1959-60 prepared by A. D. Margison and Associates, resurrected the Memorial Parkway as the Silvercreek Parkway which was to run as a controlled access, four-lane highway along the route of Silvercreek Road from Woodlawn Road to Waterloo Avenue. From there it was to follow the Speed and Eramosa rivers. In effect, a four-lane concrete barrier was to isolate both rivers from their neighbours and usurp the river valleys for cars and trucks. This road plan was completely at odds with *Planning Studies* 1960 which recommended that a park belt eventually extend along both the Speed and Eramosa rivers. The conflict between engineering and planning agendas has continued till the present, with council generally favouring engineering recommendations.

The major impact of this plan was to design all roads designated as provincial highways as major arterials and recommend that they become at least four lanes wide. The same fate was recommended for streets on the city's boundaries and for those circumventing the central area. Many intersection improvements and new road links proposed by the study were never completed because of their cost, but Victoria Road was eventually widened and was provided with an underpass below the CNR where many accidents had occurred.

THE 1966 ANNEXATIONS

A planning study by Dryden and Smith, the city's consultants, was commissioned to serve as background for the annexation and for yet another transportation study. Guelph was deemed to be in excellent financial condition with a capacity to fund growth from taxes and other revenue sources without incurring excess debt. Compared to neighbouring municipalities, the city financed a large proportion of its capital expenditures from current revenues. One potential problem with the annexation was that the balance among industrial, commercial and residential assessment would deteriorate. Because of the large proportion of residential uses in the townships, Guelph's ratio would change from 54.8 residential, 21.3 commercial and 22.6 industrial before annexation to 67.7 residential, 18.6 commercial and 11.1 industrial after annexation. The consultants suggested that Guelph would need to attract a higher proportion of industrial assessment if it were to afford rapid growth without placing an undue tax burden on homeowners. On the other hand, it would possess ample additional land for both residential and industrial expansion after the annexation.

In May 1965, the Technical Committee on Annexation, chaired by R. L. Shoemaker, submitted an urgent report to Guelph Mayor Ralph Smith and to council. It recommended that as of January 1, 1966, the city annex 9,759 acres of land from the townships of Guelph and Puslinch to add to the existing 5,604 acres within the city limits. Of this, some 5,600 acres

The Hanlon farm, once part of Puslinch Township, sits at the busy Guelph intersection of Hanlon and Kortright.   Source: Fred Dahms, 2000

was developable land that could be used for housing and industrial purposes, effectively doubling the area of the city. This recommendation was made on the advice of Dryden and Smith who had made a careful study of the possible 15,000 acres that had originally been considered for annexation. A number of factors led to this report, the most important of which was the projected growth of the University of Guelph and its anticipated effect upon demand for services and housing in the city.

Eventually an agreement was reached to annex the lands, an area that was probably much larger than needed at the time, but one that was later expanded to include even more of the adjoining townships, especially in the south to accommodate planned industrial growth for Guelph.

Another Traffic Study

After the 1966 annexation, Guelph's leaders were again concerned about the impact and movement of vehicular traffic through and around the city. By then, the city had grown to 51,377 from the 1961 figure of 39,838, for a 29 percent increase. Since many of the earlier traffic report's recommendations had not yet been implemented, another more comprehensive analysis was undertaken: the *Guelph Area Transportation Study* by Read, Voorhees and Associates, 1967. This

would update the earlier work and take into account the large increase in area, and subsequent population growth resulting from the annexation.

The Memorial Parkway was once again resurrected, this time in the form of the Silvercreek Parkway. The major new addition to the road network was to be the Hanlon Parkway to skirt the western edge of the city from Highway 7 to Highway 401. Detailed design criteria and alternate routes were proposed for this road without a single mention of the potential harm that it might inflict upon the environment. Its proposed route took it through sensitive wetlands surrounding the Hanlon Creek. In fact, the term "environment" does not appear in the *Area Transportation Study* that was intended to solve Guelph's traffic problems, and revitalise its downtown. To this end, major new parking garages and downtown bypasses were proposed, along with numerous road widenings and other changes that were considered to be improvements throughout the city. Little citizen participation or consideration of the environment was expected or encouraged, but soon a number of events conspired to alter the direction of decision-making and to involve the people of Guelph in determining the future of their city.

GROWTH AND DEVELOPMENT IN THE 1960S AND 1970S

Guelph reflected growth in Ontario's economy, but after 1964 when the University of Guelph was established, population and business numbers benefitted from the swift development of what was to become the city's largest employer. However the university's growth never reached the magnitude envisioned by its founders, rendering worthless many optimistic earlier projections of population and traffic. Nevertheless, it had a major impact on the economy, and initially at least, did grow quickly.

During this period of rapidly increasing population, Guelph also attracted new industries. In 1966, 1967 and 1968, 7, 16 and 12 new industries came respec-

 June 10, 1970 – Guelph Pollution Probe is formed of some 50 citizens.

tively. Additions then dropped until 1973 when 25 new industries were established. Some 777 acres had been developed for industrial purposes, leaving 845 acres open for future use. Projections suggested that an additional 1,167 acres would be required by 2001, given an average of 49.2 acres per year being developed for industrial purposes.

Water and Sewage Concerns

In 1966, Dryden and Smith, the city's planning consultants had done some background work that at least recognised the potential impact of urban growth on the local environment. They examined many factors that might affect the future physical and population growth of Guelph, and as part of this study, probed the potential supply of groundwater. They concluded that there was a sufficient supply of groundwater in the Guelph area to sustain growth to a population of 100,000 and that enough additional groundwater might be located to support 200,000 persons. They recognised that the major aquifer south of the Eramosa River was the most important source of local water and should be protected by discouraging development on the "porous overburden of sand and gravel." It was recommended that trees and grass continue to be the only cover on this important source. Another aquifer south of the Speed River was not considered useful as a potential water supply because industries and a school had already been built over part of it. The remainder of Guelph's water came from an aquifer in the Lockport Dolomite supplying Guelph, Galt and Preston, estimated to contain 22 million gallons of water per day.

Although water quality in Guelph was generally good, several wells had become saline by 1966 and others had high iron and sulphur content. Most wells also supplied rather hard water. The Ontario Water Resources Commission, which regulates water supply in the province, stated that it would be prepared to consider a pipeline if Guelph's growth warranted such a move, but the cost would be very high. The consultants were more concerned in the short term about the ability of both the groundwater and the local rivers to absorb an increasing amount of effluent from Guelph's residential and industrial sewers. While water supply was then not considered a crucial limiting factor in Guelph's growth, sewage capacity was and remains a constraint today. Recommendations on water use and supply suggested that the existing groundwater sources must be protected from pollution, especially from industrial sources. By this time, the Guelph dam, which was planned to regulate spring run-off and ensure a steady

summer flow in the Speed, had received provincial approval. It would create Guelph Lake to regulate the capacity of the river to receive effluent from the Guelph sewage treatment plant, thus reducing a definite constraint on future growth. The dam would also ultimately provide recreational facilities for swimming, boating, fishing and camping in the new lake close to the city limits. This study is one of the first planning documents in Guelph that explicitly recognized the harm that growth could do to the physical environment, and conversely, the limitations that the physical environment might ultimately place upon projected growth. It also recognised the potential to use the environment to enhance the city's quality of life. This was but the tip of the iceberg.

New Blood

Faced with the prospect of major areal expansion through annexation to accommodate the expected new industries and population, a number of studies were commissioned to prepare the Royal City for unprecedented change. University faculty often played key roles as expert advisers, as members of the planning board and as study committee members. As their involvement increased and their expertise was recognised, faculty became more influential and increasingly involved in the affairs of the city.

One of the first major planning studies involving faculty and other citizens was the *City of Guelph Urban Renewal Scheme Report* of 1968. The City of Guelph hired a number of consultants to probe the health of its central business area. The Citizen's Advisory Committee was chaired by Prof. Victor Chanasyk, while Prof. Jack Milliken was a member of the city's planning board at the time and eventually became chair.

The Urban Renewal Scheme, 1967 - 1968

In 1967 and 1968 detailed studies documented assessment, tenancy, occupancy, conditions and uses within the central business area, where it was suspected that renewal would be required. Every conceivable factor that might affect the future of the study area was examined and evaluated. Recommendations included plans and policies along with suggested phasing for implementation. They drew on this report as well as on the 1960 *Planning Studies* and *Street and Traffic Plan*. At the same time, the city and its traffic consultants were compiling the *Guelph Area Transportation Study* which also had recommendations for the Central Business District (CBD).

The *Urban Renewal* findings suggested that Guelph's CBD had suffered "major deterioration" in its physical, social and economic structure. The reasons for this deterioration were the "lack of a plan to guide the area's development and an increasing number of dilapidated and obsolete buildings occupied by undesirable uses that diluted the commercial mix and drove appropriate uses from the area." As vacancies increased and physical and economic environments suffered, buildings continued to deteriorate, further exacerbating the decline of the core. Excess vehicular traffic combined with a lack of convenient parking spaces were believed to discourage use of the core by shoppers.

Recommendations suggested that public funds should be made available to purchase and assemble sites appropriate for CBD uses. Improved parking, pedestrian walkways, amenities, traffic access routes and public services were also required. Four major parking garages were envisioned at the edges of downtown. One for 400 cars was projected as part of a new hotel-motel complex between Wyndham and Baker streets. By 1985, three other garages to accommodate another 1,100 cars "should be built" to provide a total of 3,400 parking spaces in the area. Finally, it was recommended that additional retail space for high-order comparison shopping be concentrated exclusively in the core, rather than being allowed to disperse to suburban malls. This was strong and potentially expensive medicine for what was seen as an ailing business district. Many of the report's observations on traffic and transportation as well as on the importance of the CBD in the city mirrored those made earlier in *Planned Progress* (1945).

Guelph's *Urban Renewal Scheme* recommended that the *Official Plan* contain policies to protect the CBD from excessive commercial and office competition from peripheral areas, and to encourage those businesses in the core which should be strengthened and remain the focus of the community. Detailed plans for all aspects of renewal were provided, along with recommendations on priorities and phasing. Examples of design improvements for streets and buildings were included, as was a suggestion to preserve important sight lines; a recommendation implemented in 1975.

As a result of excessive population projections, all other estimates such as buying power and demand based upon these statistics were considerably overstated. Similarly, estimates of the amount of space required for shops and offices both in and beyond the core were also too high. Nevertheless, the report identified a number of real deficiencies of the CBD, established the principle that public money should be invested to assist with core rehabilitation, and led to

Official Plan policies to protect Guelph's core as the pre-eminent shopping, office and entertainment area. Unfortunately, few of the urban renewal recommendations were implemented.

THE HANLON WATERSHED STUDY–
THE BEGINNING OF ENVIRONMENTAL PLANNING IN GUELPH, 1971 - 75

The *Hanlon Creek Ecological Study* was almost a panic reaction to the *Guelph Area Transportation Study* which recommended that a major four-lane highway pass through the sensitive wetlands of the Hanlon Creek and its tributaries. Since there was virtually no development in this pristine area that harboured deer, skunk, voles, raccoons, trout and muskrat, provincial traffic engineers considered it an excellent potential right-of-way for the new highway. Fortunately for the citizens of Guelph, a number of concerned faculty at the university saw the potential destruction of a priceless part of our natural heritage. Despite the absence of any discussion of environmental impacts in the 1967 *Transportation Study*, these individuals mobilised support from citizens and from key personnel in the city's engineering department.

Planning on the Back of an Envelope

According to Prof. Jack Milliken who was then a member of the City of Guelph Planning Board and later chair, much of Guelph's planning in the late 1960s and early 1970s was still "done on the back of a brown envelope." Members of the planning board were appointed by city council, which was lobbied by builders, developers and real estate agencies to have their candidates chosen. In one instance a member was chosen on the recommendation of a newspaper reporter. The planning board reviewed schemes proposed by builders and developers, but public input was virtually unknown. Citizens were neither encouraged to attend planning board meetings, nor were they encouraged to participate if they did attend. For a number of years, the board operated almost as a private club, the members of which were selected by horse-trading among city councillors.

Very few planning consultants were involved in planning decisions, which were normally discussed by the planning board and then by council with builders, developers and planning staff. The prevailing attitude in the city seemed to be that no change was a good solution to most local problems. While this may have been the general consensus, the growth of the university was bringing major change, and planning board members were often lobbied by those involved in accommodating the pressures for growth and development. A major new planning initiative involving the city and the university was stimulated by the proposal for the Hanlon Expressway which was to connect the western edge of the city to Highway 401 which had been completed south of Guelph between 1958 and 1961. It eventually became "Main Street Ontario" and has attracted city growth to the south since its opening.

Beginnings of Environmental Awareness

Several factors conspired to initiate the *Hanlon Creek Ecological Study*. First, a number of faculty in the school of landscape architecture (Jack Milliken, Owen Scott and R.R. Forester) and engineering (Peter Chisholm, Gord Molnar); departments of botany (G. Hofstra), horticulture (Glen Lumis) land resource science (Dave Elrick, Irv. MacIntosh) and zoology (R. J. Brooks, J. Sprague) became concerned that the expressway plans would disrupt the drainage, flora and fauna of the Hanlon Creek. It was apparent that run-off and silt during construction would have an adverse effect on the water quality and that the expressway itself would alter and possibly reduce the groundwater discharge that sustained the flow of the clean, clear creek.

For the first time in Guelph, The Grand River Conservation Authority and the Ontario Department of Highways also became concerned about the potential impact of the construction. Eventually the City of Guelph and these organizations agreed that a study should be conducted. Jack Milliken, who was then chair of the Guelph Planning Board, became chair of the study team which developed a proposal to undertake an assessment of the possible effects of the highway on the Hanlon Creek.

One of the major factors that led to the acceptance of the study was its low proposed cost. By using graduate students, faculty advisors and university computing facilities, work that would have cost far more if done by consultants was promised for $10,000; a major bargain. On February 1, 1971, the Hanlon Expressway Technical Advisory Committee accepted the terms of the study sponsored by the City of Guelph and the Ontario Department of Transportation and Communications. It was to be directed by the university team with the co-operation of city staff and the Grand River Conservation Authority.

The study examined the major natural systems that might be affected by the construction of the expressway. Detailed chemical analyses, fieldwork and mapping were done as appropriate. Public attitudes towards the Kortright Waterfowl Park

and eventual use of the Hanlon area were solicited through a questionnaire survey. Eventually, a 66-page report presented the team's findings. Its crucial conclusions were that the expressway could have major impacts on water quality and flow, especially during the construction phase. It also had the potential to disrupt vegetative cover and wildlife habitats in the area. Much of the study was breaking new ground, making it difficult to predict precisely the expressway's ultimate impacts. Nevertheless, a number of recommendations were made to guide construction. The extreme choices for the Hanlon Creek were for it to become a storm drain or a rehabilitated trout creek protected from additional urban impacts. The study team favoured rehabilitation over the storm drain option.

Recommendations

After a very detailed analysis of all possible effects of the proposed construction, a number of realistic recommendations were made to guide construction and road design. It was recommended that a series of ditches be built to guide construction runoff to siltation ponds before water percolated back into the watershed. Slopes should be protected by mulch and then seeded to reduce run-off to a minimum until natural cover became established. A series of retention ponds was to be constructed to catch sediment run-off from the road after its construction, to filter harmful sediments before the groundwater was recharged.

As much care as possible was to be taken to avoid damage to natural vegetation during construction, and salt tolerant species were recommended for planting along the new road. Every effort was to be made to retain as much plant diversity as possible to sustain the habitats of wildlife living in the area. A system to monitor the effects of the road was to be initiated to ensure that safeguards were effective and to suggest additional mitigating measures. Since this was a pioneering study, its results would lead to improved design criteria and savings when future construction in environmentally sensitive areas was contemplated elsewhere.

Planning Over a Beer

The *Hanlon Creek Ecological Study* illustrates the effect of personal relationships and trust in a scheme of this magnitude. Initially, Bill Taylor, City of Guelph engineer, had planned to route major water and sewage pipes along the bed of the creek itself, but over a beer in a local pub, Jack Milliken convinced him to run the services beside the creek, thus sterilizing it from any further development. Despite the fact that this was considerably more expensive than the original proposal, Taylor accepted arguments that the environment was worth preserving for the future residents of Guelph.

At the time of the study, little was known about the details of siltation catchment or sediment movement, so engineer Peter Chisholm's best guesses became part of design criteria for the drainage schemes. Similarly, the use of bales of hay to impede construction runoff and siltation was an innovative and pioneering idea that worked extremely well. In one instance, a swamp above the expressway was sealed with clay to prevent its drainage as the road was built. Ultimately, these leaps of faith paid off and the expressway was completed with minimum impact on the environment. Local newspapers gave the scheme extensive coverage, city council supported the work, and feedback from the public was generally positive. Several controversies developed, but ultimately almost everyone benefitted and "town and gown" began much closer co-operation. Almost all the study's recommendations were incorporated into the construction of the expressway with excellent results and very little additional cost. The Hanlon Parkway officially opened in June of 1972.

LEADERS IN ENVIRONMENTAL PLANNING

Immediately after the opening of the Hanlon Parkway, Phase B of the *Hanlon Creek Ecological Study* was conducted by the same team in co-operation with the city and the Grand River Conservation Authority. Now that the parkway recommendations had been accepted, it looked more generally at the implications of urban development for the whole Hanlon Creek watershed. The team recognised that the city could not afford to sterilise development throughout the whole area, so compromises would have to be made between the economic health of the city and the ecological health of the study area. Ultimately, this joint effort put Guelph into the forefront of environmental management in Ontario. The City of Guelph and the Grand River Conservation Authority eventually acquired 845 acres of land in the Hanlon watershed. The cost was $1.2 million with the city's share being 32 percent, or about $400,000 while the province covered the remaining 68 percent. With this acquisition, the Niska Waterfowl Research Facility and Kortright Waterfowl Park were protected and no urban development could occur within the most sensitive areas of the watershed. This area which was protected forever from urban encroachment because it was owned by the conservation authority, became a nature refuge in the centre of what was to become the fastest growing district of the city.

A siltation pond in the Hanlon Watershed. An example of environmental management and sustainable urban development.   Source: Fred Dahms, 1999

Because compromises were made between urban growth and the protection of the environment, development was allowed on the margins of the conservation area, but only with special provisions for storm drainage. Traditional storm sewers discharge directly, carrying water and impurities rapidly to the streams and eventually out to the Speed River. To preserve the cleanliness of the water in the Hanlon area, new urban developments on the margins of the watershed were served by special run-off schemes employing siltation ponds similar to those designed for the expressway. Water from roofs and roads, sometimes laden with salt and pesticides was taken to ponds where it seeped slowly back into the ground and eventually into the creeks. During this process, sediments and impurities were left behind in the ponds while the pure water provided a continuous supply to the streams, rather than running rapidly off in floods after heavy rains. This system ensured a much steadier flow of water all year round and helped to retain the purity of the urban streams.

Despite the fact that the construction of retention ponds and their associated drainage cost slightly more initially, homes around the Hanlon Watershed (**See Guelph map 2000 endpaper**) are more valuable because of their proximity to an almost pristine wilderness in the middle of a growing city. Guelph thus became a leader in environmental management and sustainable urban development long before these terms became popular. The policies developed by the *Hanlon Creek Study* were eventually enshrined in the *Official Plan* and spelled out more completely in the *Hanlon Planning District 9 Plan.* Subsequently there have been controversies about the form of development in the watershed area, but in general the original intent of the study team has been honoured.

THE ROLE OF THE GUELPH PLANNING BOARD

During this period, the Guelph Planning Board took a leading role in guiding the growth of the city. Under the *Planning Act*, planning boards were responsible for considering *Official Plan*s, approving zone changes, suggesting planning policy and reviewing subdivision applications. Despite the fact that city council had the final authority to pass zoning bylaws and approve planning policy, it consulted closely with the planning board and took its advice on most matters. Since Prof. Jack Milliken was both chair of the planning board and director of the Hanlon Study Team, they worked very closely on this project. Many of the recommendations of the Hanlon study became environmental guidelines for planners assessing requests for subdivision approval and preparing *District Plans*. During this period, public involvement in the planning process increased, to some degree as a result of the publicity generated by the Hanlon study. It was also a period when planning board and council worked together closely to devise policies that would affect the growth of Guelph and the protection of the environment for years to come.

Despite the close co-operation between council and the board on some matters, there was considerable controversy about its composition and about the process by which council appointed its members. This was particularly apparent from 1972 to 1975, when the "town-gown split" seemed to remain a problem with some members of city council. After Prof. Milliken retired, he was replaced by an urban sociologist who resigned after a short period on the board. This left no representation from the university after the important contributions of its faculty to the Hanlon study. Spirited debate erupted at council when a local realtor was proposed, but arguments that lay people rather than experts were needed on boards and commissions eventually prevailed. There had been others associated with building, mortgage financing and development on the board over the years, and council seemed to have no problem with conflicts of interest. As a result, many potential members of the planning board with planning expertise were refused appointments by narrow votes. One applicant to the planning board was told by a councillor to "join the Country Club and meet with us socially, and then you may be appointed." Only after a civic election replaced some old guard politi-

cians with additional reformers was the appointment process improved and planning board membership became more a function of one's expertise and qualifications than of one's connections.

PROVINCIAL PLANNING INITIATIVES 1968 - 1971

Between 1968 and 1971, the Province of Ontario took unprecedented steps to analyze and plan for growth and economic development. The first was the *Metropolitan Toronto Region Transportation Study* (MTARTS) in 1968, which was to predict population change, traffic patterns and road building in the greater Toronto area. A comprehensive regional plan based on MTARTS and on a series of subsequent studies and consultations called *Design for Development: Toronto-Centred Region* (*TCR Plan*) was prepared. It was to become the planning centre-piece for the conservative government of the day, and in ways not visualised by its proponents, has affected Ontario until today.

The 1970 concept plan suggested that Guelph would reach between 100,000 and 200,000 by the year 2000. A parkway belt, roughly paralleling Highway 401 was to contain the urbanised lakeshore district and divide it from areas to the north. With increasing traffic on Highway 401 and the Hanlon Parkway linking Guelph to Highway 401, some feared that Guelph might become a commuter dormitory for the urbanized lakeshore area.

LOCAL GOVERNMENT RESTRUCTURING: A NARROW ESCAPE

The provincial government originally intended to restructure local government in Ontario on the basis of the regional planning suggested in the *TCR Plan* and a number of related documents. During this period, many studies of transportation, economic development, location for a new Toronto airport and future land use options were in progress, and Guelph was near the centre of the area suggested by some for major new growth. A series of local government reviews was undertaken to determine whether Guelph and Wellington County should become part of a new regional municipality. The *Wellington-Guelph Area Study* directed by Howard Smith of Dryden and Smith Planning Consultants in Kitchener, employed planners from the Kitchener area as well as Jim Forbes, then an MA student in the geography department at the University of Guelph. In response to the province's predictions that a new industrial revolution would occur along the 401-development corridor, places like Guelph were expected to produce strategies for coping with major growth in population and economic activity. The *Wellington-Guelph*

Area Study surveyed many factors, including Guelph's trade area or sphere of influence, which was delineated in Forbes' thesis. He demonstrated that Guelph had a trade area covering much of Wellington County, with close social and economic links to the city. But this area was quite distinct from Kitchener-Waterloo's trade area or hinterland.

Based on Forbes' and other studies, the new Regional Municipality of Waterloo excluded Wellington County and Guelph, which had a separate hinterland. However, it included Waterloo County and its constituent municipalities. Most former municipalities in Waterloo County were amalgamated and absorbed into the Regional Municipality of Waterloo. Guelph and Wellington County remained independent municipalities without regional government. Thus the history of Guelph from this time to the present continues to be the story of events within its municipal boundaries and in areas that were annexed. Had regional government evolved here, this history would have been distinctly different. If the Waterloo Region is an appropriate parallel, a two-tiered system of government and planning would have been developed: police, fire and other services would have been regionalized, new bureaucracies would have been created and Guelph's development would have been very different from what actually occurred. The results of the *Wellington-Guelph Area Study* had a profound and lasting effect on Guelph's subsequent evolution. The planning and economic development studies of the late 1960s and early 1970s determined Guelph's course for the next 20 years.

Design for Development spawned many other local planning studies, one of which was the *Waterloo-South Wellington Area Studies* which were to re-evaluate regional development patterns in response to the provincial document. *Strategy for Growth* was released by the Area Planning and Development Co-ordinating Committee in June 1972 and contributed to Guelph's growth debate by predicting that the city would reach 117,000 by 1991. Given recent trends, this did not seem unreasonable at the time. After a decade (1961 to 1971) marked by expansion of the university, annexations of large tracts of land from the adjacent townships, increasing concern with the environment and a population increase of 20,248 (50.8 percent), residents of Guelph were understandably concerned about growth. The provincial and local studies added to the debate because they all predicted increasing pressures on Guelph to accommodate growth generated by Toronto and the 401 corridor. This was also a period of major debate about the impact on the food supply of excessive conversion of agricultural land to urban uses. Critics

of growth saw some of the most productive soils of Ontario to the north and west of Toronto being paved and covered with buildings.

THE GREAT GROWTH DEBATES

Growth debates were often polarized between faculty members from the university who advocated little growth or carefully controlled growth, and leaders of business, industry and development who saw growth as the answer to their economic prayers. At times, the pro-development lobby called opponents "fanatics" while the no-growthers argued that the developers' agenda would degrade the environment while making money for builders, developers and mortgage lenders.

City council scheduled a debate on growth for April 8, 1974, which was relatively low-key, despite the packed gallery. Council voted to ask planning staff for a series of studies on possible alternative growth policies. At times during these years, passions ran high and debate was hot, but in the end, events conspired to slow population growth without conscious controls.

One very positive result of the growth debates was an increasing awareness by citizens of development and planning issues in the city. Gone were the days when a small group of influential business people and city staff were the major force shaping Guelph's development. Citizen participation was becoming more important and more accepted at all levels of civic government, even as the "town-gown" animosity was beginning to diminish.

SLOW AND CAREFUL PROGRESS: 1971 TO 1981

Provincial cuts to its funding slowed the development of the university in the 1970s, while improved birth control and a slight economic downturn decreased the rate of population growth. By 1981, when earlier projections in the City of Guelph *Urban Renewal Study* put Guelph's population at 118,300, the actual figure had risen to only 71,207, for an 18.5 percent increase from 1971. This was a far cry from the 46 and 51 percent growth in the previous two decades, and much lower than the projection which would have been 97 percent. The pace of residential and economic development decreased commensurately, thus relieving the city of some of the pressure that had been experienced earlier. Nevertheless, major new residential growth had occurred south of Stone Road, west of the Silvercreek Parkway and in the northeast quadrant of the city around Waverley Drive School. The prices of houses rose considerably south of the Speed River as competition for locations close to the university drove the market upwards. Almost identical bungalows south of the Speed were selling for over $5,000 more than their counterparts in the northeast. Needless to say, many new staff found accommodation north of the Speed, while areas to the south were more heavily populated by deans, administrators and senior faculty members.

Just as John Galt's original plans left a lasting legacy in the physical layout and subsequent development of Guelph, the planning studies and policies of the 1970s set the pattern for many years. Given the growth predictions of the late 1960s and early 1970s, local politicians, planners and developers were determined to channel development in the most efficient and beneficial directions, although they didn't always agree on which path to take. Under the leadership of Ken Perry, the director of planning, a major series of studies was commissioned to ensure that this happened. Each study was prepared by planning staff, perused by the planning board, and after possible amendment, sent to council to be approved and become policy. Citizens were encouraged to participate during planning board meetings, and if not satisfied, attended when council considered the documents.

The Impact of the *Official Plan* of 1969

The basis of much of the planning in the 1970s was the *Official Plan* for the Guelph Planning Area approved by council on June 6, 1969, to replace the plan approved in 1953. The 1969 plan was the culmination of a major series of studies conducted by Dryden and Smith Planning Consultants of Kitchener. Howard S. Smith, the firm's president, had been a major force in the planning of the Kitchener-Waterloo area and Guelph. To this date, most studies and policy directions for the city had originated with this exceptional individual. The new *Official Plan* was designed to "recognize...in an area of explosive growth and rapidly changing technology...that policies must continuously be reviewed and amended to recognize changing circumstances." It would therefore be the subject of "continuous review and amendment as required." It was flexible, relatively straightforward, and provided the framework for much of the planning analysis to follow in the seventies and beyond. In 1971, the zoning bylaw was amended to conform to some provisions of this plan.

More Transportation Planning Studies

Despite slower residential growth, by 1972, the need for road improvements in the Royal City was again being assessed. Even though it was reported that there were

no major problems then, high population projections for Guelph and the surrounding area prompted yet another major traffic study and plan. Given the experience with the Hanlon Expressway, an attempt was made to involve citizens through meetings with eight groups and a questionnaire survey, but the response was poor. By the time the plan was completed, some 18 meetings had been held and extensive media coverage had been generated. Unfortunately, much of the consultation consisted of meetings where the public was invited to respond to scenarios created by the consultants, rather than having input at the inception of the process.

The *City of Guelph Transportation Plan to 100,000 Persons and Beyond*, 1974, was prepared by the Toronto firm, Marshall, Macklin, Monaghan Limited, in conjunction with the city's planning and engineering departments. The study was essentially an update of projections based on a telephone survey conducted in 1965, combined with recent population projections, land use projections and traffic counts. Much of the report dealt with improvements to existing streets and intersections, although it did consider and recommend a pilot bicycle path project, parking improvements and continued investment in public transit. Nevertheless the primary objective (as in all previous traffic studies) was the maintenance and amelioration of vehicular flow in the city. This emphasis was now being questioned by a number of local citizens.

A committee of the Guelph and District Community Service Council, chaired by the author, analyzed the *Transportation Plan* in detail and questioned many of its assumptions. It found that the plan would have the city spend $1.14 million per mile to reduce possible congested roads by 37 miles by 1981. Essentially, the *Plan* catered to the 82 percent of trips made by car in the three traffic peaks at morning, noon and late afternoon. The committee asked the city not to adopt the *Transportation Plan* as part of the *Official Plan*, but to consider alternate strategies to encourage public transit and bicycle use to improve traffic flow and accessibility in the city. The committee's report caused considerable controversy, but the *Plan* was eventually adopted. Nevertheless, the interest generated by this exercise made many citizens aware of transportation planning and its implications for the future of the city.

As almost all earlier transportation studies, the 1974 *Plan* was based on unreasonable population projections for Guelph (100,000 by 1991 and 130,000 by the year 2000), which led to high traffic estimates for most major arteries. The standard solution was to widen roads and build new links to shorten travel times. Budget restraints eliminated many of the proposed solutions, such as an extension of Woodlawn Road to Highway 24 and the reincarnation of the Memorial Parkway linking the Silvercreek Parkway to York Road. However, the Wellington Street bypass, realignment of the Hanlon-Silvercreek interchange and various intersection improvements were completed. In addition, bicycle paths were designated and bus use was encouraged, but no major effort was made to shift travel from motor vehicles to other modes of transport. Essentially the 1974 *Plan* repeated many of the questionable assumptions of its predecessors, but like them was never fully implemented.

Housing

By 1975 significant housing shortages had occurred in Guelph, especially for the elderly, students and those with low incomes. The situation prompted a series of studies by the department of planning and development, which examined the situation for various groups and then proposed policy options. The major problem was not one of availability, but rather one of cost. As a result of the rapid growth of the city in the 1960s, much of Guelph's single family housing was becoming too expensive for young or low-income families. The desire of many to move to Guelph because of its perceived quality of life and the increasing student population exacerbated the situation. Land prices escalated much faster (150 percent) than building costs (60 percent) from 1971 to 1975, putting many of Guelph's new homes out of financial reach of its citizens. Essentially the market cost of housing in the city more than doubled from $24,500 to $48,700 in four years.

The situation in the rental market was not much better, since the trend had been for the construction industry to concentrate its efforts on the more profitable single-family category. The building of condominium townhouses at a somewhat lower cost enabled many average households to purchase a dwelling unit at a time when new single family detached units were doubling in price. Given the projections of household formation and housing demand, Guelph planners concluded that an increasing proportion of young families would be forced to purchase attached dwellings to meet their needs. The problem was not any shortage of developable land in the city,

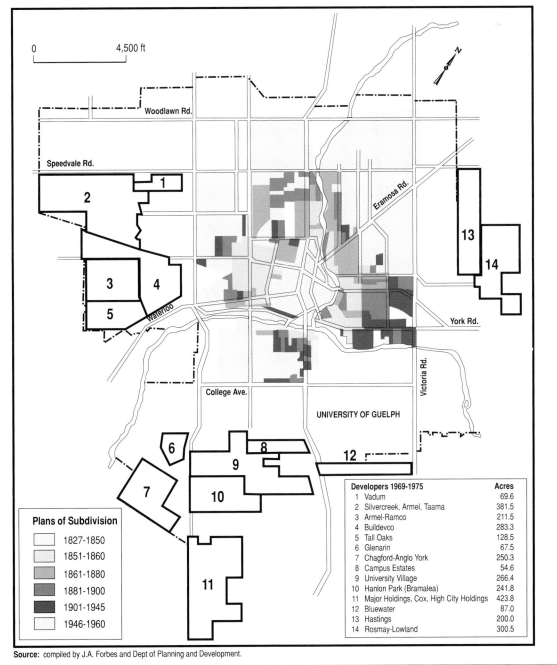

Plans of Subdivision 1827-1960 and Development Land Transactions 1969-1975

0   4,500 ft

Woodlawn Rd.

Speedvale Rd.

Eramosa Rd.

Waterloo

York Rd.

College Ave.

Victoria Rd.

UNIVERSITY OF GUELPH

Plans of Subdivision

	1827-1850
	1851-1860
	1861-1880
	1881-1900
	1901-1945
	1946-1960

Developers 1969-1975		Acres
1	Vadum	69.6
2	Silvercreek, Armel, Taama	381.5
3	Armel-Ramco	211.5
4	Buildevco	283.3
5	Tall Oaks	128.5
6	Glenarin	67.5
7	Chagford-Anglo York	250.3
8	Campus Estates	54.6
9	University Village	266.4
10	Hanlon Park (Bramalea)	241.8
11	Major Holdings, Cox, High City Holdings	423.8
12	Bluewater	87.0
13	Hastings	200.0
14	Rosmay-Lowland	300.5

Source: compiled by J.A. Forbes and Dept of Planning and Development.

but rather one of supply and demand. Developers were catering to the profitable upper and middle-income market rather than to the low end of the spectrum. As attempts were made to provide affordable housing, "Not In My Backyard" (NIMBY) reactions became increasingly common, both at the planning board and city council. Owners of single-family dwellings did not want townhouses or apartments in their neighbourhoods.

The rental market was more stable. Rents had not increased as quickly as purchase prices for homes. Between 1973 and 1976, the average two-bedroom apartment rental increased from $173 to $324 in large buildings, while comparable town house units rose from $195 to $285 in the same period. A planning department survey of privately-owned apartment buildings showed an increase in rent from $158 per month in 1971 to $220 per month in 1976. Unfortunately the "relatively poor return on rental housing has discouraged development and ... suggests a shortage of rental housing in the near future." Detailed analyses of housing costs, needs and household incomes in Guelph suggested that an increasing proportion of its residents would require rental assistance or subsidized housing in the future. Especially at risk were low-income seniors, with some 890 senior citizens needing housing assistance in 1976, while only 490 units were available. The other major problem was with student housing, as about 10,000 students sought accommodation each fall. Projections showed a shortfall of several hundred student places per year, but a slight over-supply of condominium apartments and townhouse units, combined with commuting and living at home averted any major crises in student accommodation in most years. At one point it was assumed that the ultimate size of the university would be limited by the ability of Guelph to supply student accommodation, but this was not to be as government funding was cut, slowing the university's development. Nevertheless, on several occasions during this period, "tent cities" were erected on the front campus in September, and residence rooms became crowded with additional beds.

Even with slowed university growth, Guelph experienced excessively high housing costs in the seventies and reduced opportunities for those of moderate incomes. The *Guelph Housing Study* noted that: "Speculation on the availability of municipal services and development potential has resulted in exorbitant residential land prices." While municipal planning policies and regulations slowed the approval process and raised prices to some extent, final prices were determined by developers charging "all that the market would bear." This

made the 1970s a difficult and expensive period for those of moderate incomes who desired to live in Guelph. Fortunately, provincial and federal governments eased the situation with a number of programs designed to provide low cost loans and grants to those needing financial assistance. Nevertheless, the reality and perception of high residential costs in Guelph during this period had a dampening effect on its population growth, especially as compared to the two preceding decades.

Between 1969 and 1975, 14 developers built 8,550 dwelling units in Guelph, 38 percent of which were apartment units, 35 percent single family dwellings, 22 percent townhouse units and the remainder semi-detached. A number of major companies including Armel, Buildevco, Major Holdings and University Village developed large areas west of the Hanlon Expressway between Speedvale and Waterloo avenues, south of Stone Road and east of Victoria Road. During the period of rapid growth ending in the early 1970s, the character of Guelph was transformed from a relatively compact city of primarily single family homes into a sprawling and more cosmopolitan community. The recently developed areas beyond the old boundaries of Woodlawn, Edinburgh, Stone and Victoria roads contained a greater mix of townhouses and large apartment blocks than the historic city. Despite the slowing of construction and rising prices after 1971, the character of the city had been altered forever as new trends of suburban expansion were established.

Government Housing Initiatives

Fortunately for seniors and moderate-income citizens, Guelph took advantage of provincial housing programs during this difficult period. So successful were these efforts that the Ministry of Housing devoted most of the January/February 1980 issue of *Housing Ontario* to its role in Guelph. Detailed articles about its mayor, planners, business people and major developers followed a brief history of the city. The historic legacy that had been preserved in Guelph's limestone architecture was discussed, as were the combined efforts of city and province to alleviate local housing shortages.

Between 1977 and 1984 the Ontario Home Renewal Program assisted 126 citizens (mostly seniors) to invest in major home repairs, thus raising the standard of accommodation in the city. The Ontario Housing Corporation instituted a program to enable occupants of rental housing in the Green Meadows subdivision (Vancouver Drive area) to purchase their homes at very favourable rates. The

Wellington and Guelph Housing Authority administered the building of many additional townhouse units for seniors and those of moderate income between 1952 and 1980. Rent supplements encouraged private owners to lease accommodation to those who could not afford market rates. By 1980, the Authority administered 975 units in the city and 312 in the county. The majority was for seniors and families while 98 received rent supplements.

The Hadati Farm Subdivision in an excellent example of how the city and province co-operated in the Home Ownership Made Easy (HOME) program. The plan limited costs to $17,000 per unit and the Ontario Mortgage

Subsidized seniors' homes at Norwich and Dublin streets.
Source: Fred Dahms, 1999

The Hadati homes, part of the Home Ownership Made Easy (HOME) program. Upton Crescent. Source: Fred Dahms, 1999

Corporation provided most mortgages which required down payments as low as five percent. Lots could be leased for 50 years with an option to purchase at market value after five years. Speculation and escalating prices caused some problems with the plan and eventually it was combined with the Federal Assisted Home Ownership program and direct sales of provincial land at the low end of market value. In 1968, Ontario Housing Corporation (OHC) purchased 66.3 hectares for $335,000 and proceeded to develop housing in the new Hadati subdivision for low to moderate-income families. By 1972, 373 housing units had been marketed and the city began the Victoria Road Recreation Centre. By 1977, 62 condominium units were sold and by 1987, a seniors' building housing 89 occupants was completed. Projections for Phase Two called for 685 additional housing units, but a combination of decreased growth and overbuilding by private developers in 1974 caused the project to be reduced to 175 units and later phases to be delayed till the market improved.

The University of Guelph also took advantage of government support for student housing. The Ontario Student Housing Corporation (OSHC) helped it to add 2,212 residence beds and 140 married students' units. The South Residence ("The Complex") was built in an "X" shaped configuration as several halls with greens in the centre. Wellington Woods on Stone Road was the first married students' housing built in Guelph. It pioneered economical residence design and was constructed from factory-built modules, which were publicized first at

Expo 67. While innovative and quickly constructed, these buildings developed leaks and other defects over the years. The rents of the attached two-storey townhouses in a wooded setting were originally $250 per month for a unit with basement, two bedrooms and a study. Even then however, there were complaints about lack of day care, no common room and poor recreational facilities. The Wellington Woods experiment was the first and last in prefabricated residence development in Guelph. Nevertheless, government programs did help students and lower-income citizens to find affordable housing in Guelph during the 1970s.

By mid-1970s, the city had felt the full effects of rapid growth of population and industry. A few major developers built large numbers of houses on the peripheries of the historic city. The total value of building construction reflected both the residential construction and the growth of the university. This was also the beginning of a period of housing shortages and rapid escalation in housing prices because of land speculation.

ADDITIONAL ATTEMPTS AT DOWNTOWN RENEWAL 1971 - 1980

Between 1968 and 1978, housing, transportation planning and urban renewal were important issues for Guelph's politicians and planners. Following the major Central Business District (CBD) renewal study in 1968, the federal government withdrew funding for downtown renewal, resulting in no action on the recommendations of the 1968 study. Thereafter, the fate of the downtown continued to be discussed, culminating in another major series of studies beginning in 1971. At that time district plans were being developed for all areas of the city and a major discussion paper was produced to explore the problems and prospects of the city's core. Once again, significant collaboration among city staff, consultants and university faculty contributed to the planning process. The 1971 discussion paper proposed a number of approaches to renewal and suggested policies to preserve and enhance the heritage and economic status of the CBD. This was soon followed by a series of studies sponsored by the planning department, setting out design guidelines, development strategies, and finally, in 1979 a proposal for a joint enterprise including the city, the province and Chartwood Developments to build the Eaton Centre.

Downtown Guelph: Evaluation of Land-Use and Development Strategies was written by the Department of Planning and Development with considerable citizen participation. The Community Planning Association distributed 5,000 questionnaires to residents, producing an excellent response. Nine of 35 community organizations contacted responded, while only 18 of 600 property owners in the CBD replied. It appeared that citizens cared more about the CBD than those with financial interests there. The CBD study reviewed growth trends, noting that most residential development had occurred in the south and west of the city. This led to the establishment of the Willow West and Stone Road malls in the early 1970s, both of which competed directly with the CBD. By 1979 the new malls had added 325,000 square feet of retail space while Phase Two of Stone Road would contribute another 210,000 square feet. This total of 535,000 square feet would exceed that of downtown by about 35,000 square feet. On the other hand, the CBD contained an additional 400,000 square feet of office space, but had lost industry to the suburbs.

Once again the assets and disadvantages of the downtown were assessed and a number of redevelopment scenarios were evaluated. The one chosen emphasized the CBD's primary position as a comparison shopping destination for high-order goods as well as its role as an office location. New zoning designations were proposed to allow retailing almost everywhere, but to encourage offices or residential uses above ground-level retailing. Sensitive commercial zones were designated along Norfolk and Woolwich streets where land uses had been in transition from residential to offices and retailing. To achieve the desired improvements in buildings and parking, the report recommended an application to the Ontario Downtown Revitalisation Program. Before this could be

successful, the city also had to pass a *Maintenance and Occupancy Standards Bylaw* which ultimately was done. Four areas were considered for renewal by demolishing and replacing existing buildings. These were the Eaton Centre location, the Baker Street parking area, the area around Trafalgar Square and the area south of the CNR tracks from Gordon to Wellington and Wyndham streets.

At this time a civic centre located at the old CPR freight building was considered, as was a series of pedestrian walkways linking streets in the core. Another planning department study, *Townscape Analysis and Proposal for Guelph Central Business District*, provided details of landscaping, protected sight lines, building improvement and parking arrangements. Positive and negative aspects of each area were delineated with recommendations for action following. At about the same time, Landplan Collaborative Ltd. which included faculty from the university's school of landscape architecture and an architectural firm, prepared an improvement manual to help revitalize the downtown. The Downtown Business Section of the Guelph Chamber of Commerce with the co-operation of the city planning staff sponsored it. It detailed ways in which buildings and streetscapes could be improved to enhance the attractiveness of the downtown. Ultimately only the Eaton Centre location was chosen for the renewal program which would assist with up to two-thirds of the approved cost of the project.

The Eaton Centre

On August 13, 1979, Chartwood Developments presented their Downtown Redevelopment Scheme to Guelph city council. It was to contain a two-level full-line Eaton's department store of about 100,000 square feet, along with a major food store of 35,000 square feet and 60 other retail stores. Two parking garages were to accommodate about 1,000 cars. The centre would link with the existing Co-operators building and replace the businesses and bus terminal on Quebec Street East. The project would cost approximately $23 million and would be jointly financed by the city, Chartwood and the Ontario Downtown Revitalisation Program. It was contemplated that the centre would have 400 full-time and 250 part-time employees and generate approximately $725,000 per year in realty, business and school taxes. The parking garages would be built and owned by the city while the mall would be leased by the city to Eaton Centre-Guelph Joint Venture on a net-net basis for 60 years.

The Eaton Centre was built and opened but not without initial problems.

Because of high costs and the difficulty of transporting groceries to cars, the food store never materialised. Attempts were made to induce a theatre chain to locate there, but they preferred suburban locations and ultimately went to Stone Road Mall. Eaton's never seemed to reach its full potential and there was significant turnover among other tenants. The project did provide much-needed parking in the CBD, and cleaned up Quebec Street East, but some argued that it "sucked business off Wyndham Street." There is no doubt that it did employ many workers, but the Eaton Centre never became the major catalyst for downtown renewal envisioned by all the earlier redevelopment studies.

The 1970s were a period when urban renewal meant replacing the old with the new. According to those involved, during this period, some business people and the Chamber of Commerce wished to erase our "one horse town" image and "get rid of the old junk" in central Guelph. Fortunately, little money was available from council for large-scale urban renewal and only minor changes such as brick along wider sidewalks and the demise of angle parking downtown were introduced. St. George's Square was rebuilt to its present configuration, much to the chagrin of some who dislike the large expanses of concrete lined by idling buses spewing diesel fumes every half hour.

The atrium in the former Guelph Eaton Centre.
Source: Fred Dahms, 1990

THE BEGINNING OF HERITAGE PRESERVATION - 1970S

In 1974, the Ontario Heritage Act was passed, giving local preservationists a tool with which to save prominent buildings. A Local Architectural Conservancy Advisory Committee (LACAC) was established, but little action was taken in Guelph until 1977 when the city began to designate significant buildings, and later "heritage areas." During this era, the former Canada Trust building fell to the wreckers' ball, while the Toronto-Dominion Bank building was saved. Private developers contributed to the renovation of several downtown buildings.

The Red Barn and the Height Bylaw

By 1975, pressures were mounting to increase densities in downtown Guelph and to construct ever-higher buildings. Things were brought to a head by proposals to construct a towering structure on the site of the Red Barn restaurant at the corner of Paisley and Gordon streets. If allowed, this would have obstructed the view of the Church of Our Lady, Guelph's most prominent landmark. After studies by the planning department and many debates at council, a height bylaw was passed. It designated important sight lines within which building heights were restricted to the bottom of the rose window in the Church of Our Lady. Despite complaints from some developers that the bylaw was inhibiting downtown growth and renewal, it remains in place and has preserved the relatively low profile of central Guelph. Taller buildings are allowed in peripheral areas, but the ambience of the core was preserved effectively by this piece of legislation.

The Auto Mall

For many years, Wellington Street between Gordon and Woolwich streets had been the primary location for automotive sales and service facilities. This was complemented by a Canadian Tire store and Wellington Motors nearby on York Road. Planners felt that this extensive use of space so near to the CBD was not appropriate, and actively encouraged car dealers to move to a new planned auto mall on Woodlawn Road, between the corner of Elmira Road and the city limits. Moves were slow at first, but over time each dealer moved out. Canadian Tire relocated to Woodlawn Road, and later built another branch near Stone Road Mall.

Wellington Street was eventually widened to become the official bypass for downtown, and retail strip malls and fast food outlets slowly replaced the auto-related activities. The Wellington Street strip has housed video component shops, waterbed stores, hairdressers and ice cream parlours, but its tenants are less persistent than the fast food outlets which seem to have taken permanent root. Visually, it is no more attractive than similar areas in Kitchener or Cambridge, and is now being considered for redesign.

Meanwhile, the new auto mall has become a bright, well-landscaped entrance to the western side of the city. Most major car dealers have located there along with ancillary repair and supply businesses. The availability of ample supplies of reasonably priced land and high volumes of passing traffic assured its success. Today it is a one-stop-shopping destination for those comparing car prices and models. At night the glow of its lights can be seen for miles. This is an excellent example of conscious land-use planning changing forever the form and function of the city.

GUELPH'S GOLDEN AGE OF PLANNING AND ITS DISTRICT PLANS 1970 - 1990

Under director Ken Perry, the 1970s were a golden age for Guelph planning. A group of bright and enthusiastic planners conducted studies and made recommendations that affected the development of the city for many years to come. Morale was high, the environment was becoming an important issue and Guelph's citizens were becoming increasingly interested and involved with the growth of their city. Delegations appeared regularly at the planning board meetings, and if they did not receive satisfaction there, reappeared at city council when the board's recommendations were being discussed. Growth and development in this era were steady, controlled and generally the result of reasonable debate. At times NIMBY (Not In My Back Yard) attitudes opposed specific projects, but the building of new subdivisions, commercial plazas and industrial enterprises proceeded consistently and with little controversy. This process was facilitated considerably by the district plans that had been developed for each area of Guelph.

The *Downtown District Plan* (District 4) was completed in May 1978, in time to affect the Eaton Centre development. District plans were intended to "provide the necessary direction for implementing the *Official Plan* through public administrative decision-making and development or redevelopment proposals..." A bylaw was passed requiring economic impact analyses for any peripheral shopping development proposals that might threaten the Central Business District. Council came down firmly on the side of the downtown as the retail and commercial heart of Guelph.

District plans filled in the blanks in the *Official Plan*. Each was based on a number of careful background studies on matters such as transportation, ecology, industry, commercial development, and parks and public transit undertaken since 1971. Although they did not have the legal status of the *Official Plan*, district plans were used to guide growth and development in each area for a number of years.

By the end of the 1970s, a new era of citizen participation and environmental awareness had begun. Provincial policy stated that planning documents should be reviewed constantly and revised every five years, although this was seldom accomplished. Somewhat slower growth in the late 1970s and early 1980s allowed planning staff to prepare an excellent series of studies as background to the most comprehensive revision of the *Official Plan* ever undertaken. This exercise culminated in a number of reports that ultimately were adopted and became an integral part of the new *Official Plan*.

THE 1987 *OFFICIAL PLAN*

The *Official Plan for the City of Guelph* approved by the province on May 5, 1987 was the most complete statement on the future growth and character of Guelph. It considered a number of factors that had previously been omitted or given very little consideration in official plans. Their inclusion reflected extensive citizen participation during which the city held open houses and public meetings to ensure that the aspirations and attitudes of its citizens were reflected. A number of innovations such as the Vision Statement that had been developed through public meetings, and detailed policies on issues such as open space and aggregates were also included. Ultimately, the 1987 *Official Plan for the City of Guelph* and its successors became powerful influences on the city's development over the next decade. The population for 2000 was now forecast to be 102,818 with 39,000 households. An average size of 2.64 persons per household expected for 2000 was down considerably from the 2.78 average in 1986.

In addition to these innovative policies, the *Official Plan* contained a number of detailed statements on the form of commercial and industrial development, transportation planning (still based on the 1974 *Transportation Plan*), the role of the CBD, a possible civic centre and staging of growth. It was also the first planning document to include population projections that were reasonably accurate. Its effect was to alert builders and developers to the environmental and quality-of-life considerations thought important by the citizens of Guelph, and to provide council with some enforceable constraints on projects that did not meet *Official Plan* criteria. During the plan adoption process, a number of delegations argued that the new constraints would greatly hamper development while others strongly supported the new policies that were being proposed.

Guelph's *Official Plan* vision statement was especially significant because it reflected a real commitment to maintaining and enhancing the quality of life rather than dealing primarily with economic development. Its vision of the city was developed with considerable citizen participation and became the guiding force for future development. Statements on the quality and characteristics to be encouraged in the city were an excellent reflection of citizen aspirations for their community. As an integral part of the *Official Plan,* it had legal authority, but recently, has been more ignored than emulated.

Between 1981 and 1991, the city grew from 71,207 to 87,976 (23.5 percent) which was five percentage points more than what had occurred in the previous decade and some 3,000 higher than the 1987 *Plan* projection for 1991. A slightly revised version of the *Plan* was released in 1991. It contained provincially approved amendments and some mapping corrections. Most of the amendments were to expand lists of uses in commercial and residential zones and to alter residential densities in some areas. The general intent of the 1987 document was not materially altered by these changes.

HOUSING IN THE 1990S

While growth continued to be a major issue on the periphery of the city, the quality, cost and quantity of existing housing remained a major concern in the Royal City. Because of its accessibility to the Toronto area via Highway 401, Guelph's housing prices remained higher than those of the Waterloo Region and availability for those with modest incomes continued to be difficult. The other concerns were for residential densities, the possibility of infilling and the condition of homes in some older areas. In 1992, the city commissioned Hemson

Innovative policy statements in the *1987 Official Plan*

Vision Statement	Community Renewal
Heritage Conservation	Residential Care Facilities
Energy Conservation	Group Homes
Floodplain Policies	Housing Policies
Aggregate Extraction	Energy Conservation
Development Policies	Barrier Free Environment
Open Space	Environmentally Sensitive Areas
Waste Disposal	Development Controls
Maintenance and Occupancy	Public Participation
Standards	Commercial Nucleations
Businesses in Residential Zones	

Consulting to address these issues and to propose appropriate policies for the future. The reports addressed the general issue of intensification, intensification in the central area and future land-use strategies for Ward 1 ("The Ward"). Such initiatives were encouraged by the NDP provincial government which was in the process of revising the *Planning Act* and had released a policy statement on land-use planning for housing, the intent of which was to make housing more accessible to everyone.

Vision Statement from *1987 Official Plan*

While it is far too complex to describe in detail here, the Plan's *intention is captured by the Vision Statement which possesses the legal authority to be the guiding philosophy affecting all planning decisions made in the city. The Vision Statement was developed with considerable citizen participation, and closely reflects their desires for Guelph's future development. It was accepted and passed by city council as part of the new* Official Plan. *Unfortunately, it has often been ignored in the process of political decision-making. Nevertheless, it does capture the collective thinking of the many persons involved in formulating the* Official Plan *and faithfully reflects the public mood when it was being written. Some of its major provisions are as follows:*

- The city's future depends on a careful balance of yesterday's legacy, today's needs and tomorrow's vision. By respecting the history that enriches local architecture, preserving the nature that adorns the landscape, and promoting an atmosphere of innovation and creativity, that balance will be achieved.
- Guelph's beauty lies in its compact, small-town character. …. Continued preservation of significant natural areas and water courses will add to Guelph's unique environment. ….
- By the year 2000, Guelph is expected to be a city of about 100,000. Growth will be moderate, steady and managed to maintain a compact but human scale city. At the same time, flexibility will be maintained to ensure ample opportunities for industry, commerce and housing…
- The downtown will continue to mature as the commercial and civic heart of the community. Its landmarks and unique architecture provide an identifying focus for civic pride; while, a performing arts centre, offices, housing, related service facilities and improved access to the area will make it an even stronger and more vibrant city centre…
- The city will provide a wide range of living accommodation for both owners and renters, including the special needs of physically disabled, senior citizen and low income households. Development will complement the overall private-home scale of residential areas. The limestone heritage architecture that enhances older neighbourhoods will be respected…
- The Plan strives to maintain the quality of life in Guelph and to ensure that Guelph grows strategically rather than impulsively to become an even better place to work and live.

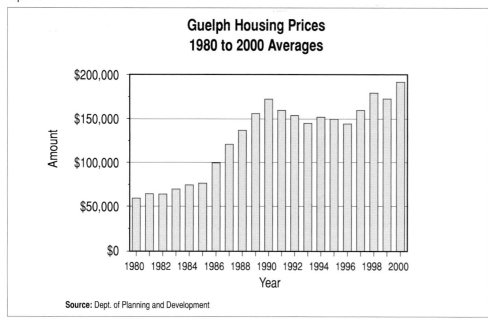

**Guelph Housing Prices
1980 to 2000 Averages**

Source: Dept. of Planning and Development

In their general recommendations, the consultants suggested that intensification could help to alleviate housing shortages for some individuals with modest incomes and was feasible through infilling in several older neighbourhoods. They recommended new *Official Plan* policies and major revisions to outdated and restrictive zoning bylaws which tended to thwart the more permissive *Plan* policies. While no more than five to 10 percent of housing needs could be met through intensification, it was a worthwhile goal. They recommended encouragement of coach houses and granny flats as well as apartments with appropriate regulation and control. By the time these recommendations found their way into the revised zoning bylaws, the newly elected Conservative government had once again revised the *Planning Act*, making it more difficult to implement a number of the innovations suggested earlier by the NDP.

The downtown intensification study concluded that there were modest opportunities to intensify housing there. Most are already recognised and encouraged by the *Official Plan*, but incentives might encourage additional small-scale developments. The study encouraged mid-rise developments that complement existing downtown uses. It also suggested that the mass and bulk of buildings should be controlled rather than placing limits on densities per hectare. It recommended that a facilitator be appointed to encourage central residential development.

In January 1992, Hemson produced a major document on future land use strategy for "The Ward"; one of Guelph's oldest mixed industrial and residential areas. This very comprehensive report recommended the continuation of mixed uses within the area and the encouragement of stable low-density residential areas along with some intensification. A variety of compatible housing types would be encouraged along with complementary non-residential uses. Some areas would be mixed industrial-residential. A key recommendation suggested traditional main street commercial and office uses along major arteries such as York Road and Elizabeth and Wyndham streets. This would promote low-rise buildings close to the street and encourage a community atmosphere along arteries that would accommodate pedestrians and shopping. Unfortunately, these recommendations were in direct conflict with transportation plans recommending major four-lane arterials with wide setbacks on the same streets. Once again, planning for people was clashing with planning for vehicles. Only the future will indicate which faction is ultimately successful.

GUELPH IN THE 1990S

By 1991, Guelph had a population of 87,976, well below estimates from earlier projections, but close to that of the *Statistical Summary* 1991. The population was aging as 16.4 percent were over 60 in 1990, an increase from 12.8 percent in 1961. Housing prices continued to be a problem, as did vacancy rates in apartments. By 1990, the building of single-family homes became less prevalent than that of attached and apartment units. This was reflected in the age composition of Guelph housing stock when the greatest number of apartments and row houses were post-1970. The largest group of single-family homes dated from 1941 to 1970. Despite their increasing numbers, multiple dwellings remained in the minority.

By 1991, both the composition and location of building activity in Guelph had changed from earlier patterns. University, Edinburgh, Hanlon and Willow West districts attracted new construction. Most of Guelph's new apartments were built in the Edinburgh area whereas townhouses predominated in the University and Hanlon districts. Willow West led in single-family construction. In southern areas, apartment units and condominiums helped to alleviate the shortage of student housing. Higher density townhouses and taller structures were slowly surrounding Guelph's old low-rise core, but overall residential densities remained relatively low.

The Guelph Non-Profit Housing Corporation was incorporated in 1988 and by 1992 operated 383 units in six projects across the city. One of the main problems for all non-profit housing providers was the scarcity of appropriately zoned land for such developments. Unfortunately, senior governments stipulated maximum unit prices which were far too low in the Guelph market and made it impossible to purchase suitable sites. The limits were raised in 1990, and by 1991, approval had been received for 383 additional units; a good start, but not nearly enough to satisfy the demand.

By 1999, Guelph's housing shortage had again become acute. Despite the fact that 1,000 new residential units were added in that year, the privately owned rental apartment vacancy rate was only 0.5 percent. This represented a major decline from the 1998 rate of 1.6 percent. For those on low incomes, the situation has become desperate. The Wellington and Guelph Housing Committee reported that there is a 10 to 20-year wait for non-profit apartments in Guelph. The Victor

The Victor Davis apartments on Neeve Street.
Source: Fred Dahms, 1999

Edward Pickersgill

Edward Pickersgill has been described as "Guelph's foremost affordable housing advocate" and as a housing activist. This is not a misnomer. Since his arrival in Guelph in 1970 he has become totally involved in ensuring that even the poorest of people has a chance to obtain the very rudiments of shelter.

Ed Pickersgill was born in Glasgow, Scotland on October 11, 1944. He arrived in Canada at age 11 in August 1957. Eventually he found his way to Guelph and began a career that has focussed on the three key components of his philosophy: employment, literacy and housing. To reach this end he first became involved with the Centre for Employable Workers in 1983. Three years later he helped found two other important groups locally: Action Read and Matrix Affordable Houses.

Matrix Affordable Houses was launched in the International Year of Shelter for the Homeless with a goal of 250 units by 1992. Its name, like the date of its founding, was deliberately chosen. The word "matrix" is Latin for the original home – the womb. Matrix's intent was to help the disadvantaged groups in Guelph's community to have what every Canadian deserves: clean and affordable housing. To ensure that people knew about the project and the availability of housing Pickersgill held monthly information meetings at Knox Presbyterian Church. Here, he talked to people who felt that any home, let alone a suitable one, was out of reach.

By 1990, the first building undertaken by Matrix Housing was up and running. Located at the corners of Verney and Woolwich streets this development was intended to house single women. In spite of some opposition, the 20-unit townhouse community opened in August of that year. This was followed by two more structures: in 1992, the apartment at 213 College Ave. was completed and a townhouse community, located at 264 College Ave., opened its 43 units in April 1993.

The last building project to date was completed three years later. It was in December 1996, that Matrix Housing finally fulfilled a plan to build housing within a block radius of downtown. Matrix Centre rose on the grounds of the old Mueller shop at 141 Woolwich. Originally intended as a seven-storey structure with 75 units, it was scaled down to five with 70 units to fit specific community demands. Pickersgill and his supporters saw this as not only a means of providing housing but also as a way of revitalizing the downtown core.

Matrix over the years has spawned an increased interest in adapting housing to meet the needs of the less fortunate sector in society. UpBuilding! Non Profit Homes, was a group of different denominations of churches that was co-ordinated originally by Ed Pickersgill. It entered the housing support market in 1990 with a west-end housing development. In 1991, Room For Us was launched to provide clean and safe rooms for the disadvantaged.

Fresh Start is a housing centre with a difference that evolved from the defunct Housing Help Centre in 1995. Ed Pickersgill was instrumental in ensuring that this group did not, like its predecessor, fail. Located on Wyndham Street and sharing facilities with the Anishnabeg Outreach Centre and Matrix, Fresh Start shares the Matrix mandate of being a community body that responds to the housing crisis in as humane and open a way as possible. Their goal is simple but ambitious: "to do something real and practical" in order to alleviate the housing crisis for those people who need help.

In 2000, Pickersgill ran as the NDP candidate in the federal election.

– Bonnie Durtnall

Victor Davis

The Victor Davis Pool in the Victoria Road Recreation Centre, opened in 1984, was named in honour of the young athlete Victor Davis. Born in the city in 1963, Davis was a member of the Guelph Marlins Aquatic Club in his early teens. His natural talent as a swimmer led the young competitor to a list of international swimming achievements including the gold medal and world record in the 200-metre breaststroke in the Commonwealth Games in 1982. This led to a gold medal and world record in the 200-metre breaststroke and silver medals in the 1984 Olympics. Davis won gold and silver medals in the 1986 Commonwealth Games and gold and silver medals in the world championships in Madrid. In 1988 he won a silver medal in the 4 x 100-metre medley relay and fourth in the 100-metre breaststroke in the Seoul Olympic games. The young Olympian announced his retirement from competitive swimming just weeks before he was killed by a car in Montreal in November 1989. In death, Davis proved once again to be a champion: his organs were donated so others could live.

– Ceska Brennan

Davis facility which is currently full, receives an average of 28 applications a month, but the provincial freeze on funding has stopped construction of rent-to-income accommodation.

Retirement Communities at the Millennium

By 1999, several developments were available to accommodate the increasing number of ambulatory seniors in the city. The first of these was the Ellridge, built adjacent to the Elliott nursing home on Metcalfe Street in 1989. The Ellington was built on the same site a few years later, to cater to persons requiring prepared meals and some nursing care. The Elliott continues to provide full nursing-home care, and a new building is now planned. It will have underground parking and complement the other facilities on the site.

A major retirement condominium has been built on Woolwich Street adjacent to the Evergreen Seniors' Centre and many of its suites have views of the Speed River and Riverside Park below. Another large development is on Woodlawn Road by the Speed River, while a number of former mills, factories, schools and offices throughout the city have been converted into nursing or retirement homes.

The largest seniors' project is the Village by the Arboretum on Stone Road which offers a wide variety of accommodation from townhouses to large bungalows. Properties are leased while homes are purchased. It has become a very popular up-scale retirement option for Guelph and currently attracts people from distant locations, including Toronto.

By the end of the 1990s, Guelph was changing from a relatively compact low-density city punctuated by high rises along its peripheral arterial roads to a sprawling community. Increasing numbers of townhouses and small, detached dwellings proliferated in the outer suburbs. High housing costs forced some builders to serve the condominium and rental or small single market, but others began to concentrate on very large and expensive homes. Many of these are in the south of the city where access to Highway 401 makes them attractive to commuters employed in Cambridge, Toronto, Mississauga or Brampton.

PLANNING INITIATIVES IN THE 1990s

Guelph's development has always been affected by the economy, and by provincial planning legislation. During the late 1980s and 1990s, as legislation was being rewritten, citizens became increasingly involved in the planning process in Guelph. At times, their participation was a result of incomplete information or misunderstanding of city policies and the *Planning Act*. Because of the rapid growth that had affected some areas, more and more instances of NIMBY (Not In My Back Yard) became apparent in the city. Controversies arose over businesses in residential areas, new housing in environmentally-sensitive regions and road improvements in many parts of Guelph.

The *Sewell Commission Report on Provincial Planning* in 1993 recommended considerably more protection for environmentally-sensitive areas, improved citizen participation and more planning power for local municipalities. The commission's hearings attracted massive public involvement, resulting in a greatly changed *Planning Act* and volumes of regulations. The reforms inspired some changes in local planning practice, but before they could be implemented fully, a provincial election in 1995 returned a Conservative government. It reversed most of Sewell's policies and introduced a much shorter planning document which led to some confusion about provincial planning priorities.

By 1991, a number of amendments had been incorporated into the 1987 *Official Plan*. This major review was intended to reflect the socio-economic conditions and attitudes of the nineties and to produce a new set of user-friendly bylaws that would guide the implementation of planning policies for many years to come.

Zoning Bylaws and Urban Design

During 1991 and 1992, the planning department developed a series of recommendations for Guelph's new comprehensive zoning bylaw. In addition to public forums where interested parties could react to preliminary recommendations, the process included interest groups which helped to develop policies on bylaw revision. The end result was a series of zoning bylaws that reflected the realities of the nineties and the interests of a large proportion of Guelph's citizens.

The revised bylaws use diagrams rather than long explanations to illustrate definitions and some regulations. The wording is greatly simplified and allows home occupations in some residential areas. Zones were created where it is possible to build closer to the street on smaller lots than previously allowed. Provision is made for "granny flats" on some of the larger properties in the city. Regulations set standards for lodging houses and group homes. Protection for natural areas and the environment is also built into the document.

The city produced a set of urban design guidelines in 1995 which were paralleled by *Making Choices*, an Ontario government publication on alternative development standards. Both studies reflected trends in the province towards energy efficient and compact urban development similar to that proposed by the "Neo-Traditional Planners" or "New Urbanists." This movement suggested that the traditional small town with narrow streets in a grid pattern with porches, lively main streets, corner stores and pedestrian interaction, was the best model for new subdivisions. Although several experimental communities such as Seaside in Florida and Montgomery Village in Orangevillle, Ontario have experienced great success and acceptance, Guelph has been slower to adopt the Neo-Traditional model.

Guelph's design guidelines and revised bylaws encourage developers to orient new construction to natural areas such as rivers, and to accommodate innovative building styles. Provisions are suggested to preserve sight lines, accent landmarks and encourage transit-oriented development. The bylaw contains progressive policies on floodplains, natural heritage features, parks, day-care centres and aggregate extraction. Proposals to reduce setbacks between buildings

 May 5, 1995 – The 16th annual Speed River Clean-up fills two city dump trucks - the largest haul yet.

Bonnie McCallum

Bonnie McCallum, born in 1940, stood up for what she thought was important. She was a trailblazer in the quest to introduce recycling to Guelph, fighting against the stigma of its unpopularity in doing so. Bonnie, from Calgary, first met her husband Bruce when they were both students at the University of Guelph. In 1974 they made Guelph their home when Bruce was offered a position at the university. Bonnie worked on their cattle farm. She was an active mother and an avid camper who soon identified the need to make her community aware of recycling issues. Among the many people involved in environmentalism, McCallum stood out. She appeared many times before city council to speak about recycling. At a time when council meetings were broadcast on the radio, she had a unique way of keeping the public's and council's attention. McCallum convinced friends to attend meetings and to bring tin cans in bags. During her speeches she would have them shake the bags to help make her point. Thanks, in no small part to her efforts, Guelph is a leader in waste management in Canada.

Guelph's first volunteer-run recycling depot was established on property beside the covered bridge. Bruce McCallum recalls the day the first recycling depot opened. It was a freezing cold day in January and a band of eager volunteers, waiting for the first car, huddled in a trailer trying to keep warm. When the first car arrived, a hoard of people descended on the vehicle. The family inside was startled and quickly handed over their refuse. Garbage sorting had never been so much fun!

The city then moved forward to curbside and backyard recycling programs and then to a wet/dry recycling program.

Bonnie died of cancer in 1989. In recognition of her work, the Ontario Public Interest Research Group (OPIRG) created the Bonnie McCallum Award to recognize other individuals who have also made a difference to our environment in Guelph.

– Ceska Brennan

and roads were sometimes opposed by the engineering department, as were attempts to reduce road allowances and delete road widenings listed in the *Official Plan*. Nevertheless, despite the demise of the *Sewell Report* recommendations, Guelph went a long way towards more environmentally-sensitive and people-oriented planning during the 1990s.

More Transportation Planning

Along with the revision of the zoning bylaws and urban design guidelines,

Guelph commissioned yet another report - the *Guelph and Area Transportation Study*, 1994 to update the 1974 transportation plan that had been used in the latest *Official Plan*. Like its predecessors, this study relied on projections of population growth and employment and on the gravity model to forecast future travel demand. Unlike its predecessors, it outlined steps for environmental assessments that would be required for "needs assessment and justification of transportation improvements." The revised transportation process included environmental assessment approval before design or implementation of transportation recommendations. A major step forward was the inclusion of recommendations for bicycle lanes and improved bus service. Unfortunately, the implementation of these recommendations has been slowed by a lack of funds for bicycle lanes and the province's frugal policies on funding bus transportation.

THE GREEN PLAN

The development of Guelph's *Green Plan* paralleled studies for the zoning bylaw revision. In 1990, the city engineering department suggested that the Guelph Round Table on the Environment and Economy solicit public input and ultimately prepare a plan to integrate environmental sustainability into all city planning decisions. By November of that year, council had approved the concept and a steering committee was established, including councillors, staff and the Ontario Public Interest Research Group (OPIRG), which made major contributions to this plan and to many related debates on planning and environment during this period.

The *Green Plan* was given wide publicity with more than 1,000 persons participating in a process to bring local environmental sustainability to international levels through education and integration with Guelph's *Strategic* and *Official Plans*. The primary focus was to be on land use, water and energy consumption, and alternative modes of transportation. The *Green Plan* was adopted by council on September 12, 1994. At times it appeared that council paid little heed to the *Green Plan* when making decisions on zone changes and subdivision approvals, even though many of its recommendations were relevant.

CITY OF GUELPH *STRATEGIC PLAN* 1993

While the *Green Plan* was being prepared, the city was also working on a strategic plan entitled *The Royal City Looking Ahead* which was to complement the *Official Plan*. Studies were also commissioned on economic development, the downtown, replacement of Memorial Gardens, several environmental assessments, transportation and water supply-sewage treatment evaluations. They assessed the city's economic strength and residential growth prospects in an attempt to produce "controlled quality growth and development." In contrast to the *Official Plan* and *Green Plan*, the objectives of the *Strategic Plan* were to be implemented through the budget process. It predicted major new residential growth in the south, northwest and northeast which could add 7,000 new housing units by 2001, and it suggested annexation of 1,750 hectares from Puslinch Township, primarily for industrial and commercial uses. Objectives were to recognize our heritage and the environment and be responsive to requirements for community services through "innovative management" of city departments.

In 1994 *Strategic Economic Directions: A Proposal to Ensure Controlled Quality Growth and Development* was adopted by the city. This document was intended to facilitate the implementation of the *Strategic Plan* through a co-ordinating group which would represent each municipal department and businesses in Guelph. It was intended to streamline the economic development process, develop small business capacity, ensure quality growth and make available adequate land for business and industrial expansion. It also recommended action to revitalise the CBD, to encourage redevelopment and to stimulate the tourist industry. When Mario Venditti was replaced as the director of planning in 1995, his successor, Tom Slomke became the director of planning and economic development, essentially filling two roles. Many informed citizens and local experts saw this combined role as an inherent conflict of interest, but it did reflect the thrust of recent planning initiatives supported by city council.

BARRIERS TO GROWTH: THE SEARCH FOR A LANDFILL SITE

It is difficult to assess the impact of the *Green Plan* on transportation planning or residential development, but it did lead to major innovations in waste disposal for Guelph. Guelph and the County of Wellington recognised that their waste would have to be disposed of in an environmentally-sensitive manner and adopted a *Waste Management Master Plan* in 1983. In January 1993, the City of Guelph and County of Wellington adopted an updated *Waste Management Master Plan* to guide future refuse disposal policies. Guelph had already been a pioneer in this area, having adopted drop-off recycling in 1982, blue box curbside recycling in 1987,

November, 1991 – McDonald's on Gordon Street becomes first restaurant in Canada to launch a wet/dry pilot project.

and in 1995, wet-dry recycling. For this purpose the province assisted financially with a pilot plant that would recycle dry waste and compost wet waste which was to be sorted by home owners. Hazardous and noxious wastes were to be treated separately. This system greatly reduced the amount of material deposited at the Guelph landfill site which had been licensed only till 1993, with an extension to 1998. Despite the reduction in waste however, Guelph and Wellington had to search for a new landfill site to replace the Eastview facility.

The *Waste Management Master Plan* was also intended to identify a landfill site for the disposal of waste that could not be recycled or composted. After many meetings and the expenditure of millions of dollars, the City and County Joint Steering Committee recommended a strategy for waste disposal for the next 25 years to both councils. The county accepted this recommendation which included a landfill site called N-4 in Nichol Township near the Speed River. Well-organized protests from neighbours and environmental activists, led by artist Ken Danby whose studio was adjacent to the site, claimed that effluent from the dump would pollute the Speed River watershed. On January 11, 1993, Guelph council agreed with the protesters and rejected the N-4 recommendation. Both councils then accepted the other waste management plans, most of which were ultimately implemented. This resulted in the Guelph wet-dry facility, a hazardous waste depot in Guelph and other plans to minimize waste in the city and county.

Because Guelph had rejected N-4, the county withdrew from the process and Guelph attempted to find a landfill site within city limits. A committee chaired by Prof. Stephen Rodd commissioned a lengthy study which attempted to involve as many citizens as possible in the search for a suitable location in Guelph. This process resulted in the expenditure of another $6 million, considerable citizen involvement and controversy about the process of information sharing and decision-making. In 1994, four possible sites were identified but none were deemed acceptable and the life of the Eastview dump had to be extended to 1998. Now a major constraint on Guelph's future growth is its ability to find a site for its waste. No suitable alternative to Eastview has yet been identified and neighbours have been pressing for its termination. At this point, its life has been extended again and council is paying compensation to some neighbours who had expected it to close in 1998. Numerous meetings between city staff and those opposing any extension of the landfill's existence have been held and it is scheduled to close.

 September 10, 1986 – The 'Neighbourhood Watch' program gets underway in Guelph.

The other equally important constraint on any future growth is the capacity of Guelph's sewage treatment plant and the Speed River to handle the effluent produced by its citizens and businesses.

River Valley Planning

One of the keys to Guelph's delightful ambience and excellent quality of life has always been the river valleys meandering through the city. The *Hanlon Watershed Study* led to the preservation of significant wetlands in the southern section of the city. Nevertheless, both the Speed and Eramosa rivers are lined with businesses, industries and railways through much of the city. Late in 1993, council approved the

Alfred Hales

Born in 1909, Alfred Dryden Hales dedicated his life to Guelph and Wellington County. He was director of the YMCA in 1938 and, over the years, was involved in the Chamber of Commerce, the Reserve Navy, the Guelph Transportation Commission, Waverley Lodge, Guelph Kiwanis Club and the Grand Valley Conservation Authority. "Community service is the rent we pay for a place on Earth," he said.

Hales served as a city alderman in 1956 and 1957. In 1957, he became the Progressive Conservative MP for Wellington South - a position he held until 1968 when the riding became Wellington. He was re-elected. He grabbed national headlines as chairman of the public accounts committee when he exposed government overspending on a contract to refurbish the HMCS Bonaventure. A picture of Hales on the ship beside a $25 medicine cabinet that had cost $258 to repair became a national symbol for government mismanagement at the time.

In the 1970s, the Italian-Canadian Club in Guelph appreciated Hales so much he was made an honorary life member, the first non-Italian to be so named. In his later years, he was active in both the Col. John McCrae Birthplace and Guelph Historical societies. An accomplished athlete and a former Toronto Argonaut, Hales was inducted into the University of Guelph Sports Hall of Fame in 1990. He received the Certificate of Merit for Outstanding Volunteer Service given to the Red Cross in 1992 and, in 1993, was awarded the Commemorative Medal of the 125th Anniversary of the Confederation of Canada.

"My years of public service, although demanding, have been among the happiest in my life," Hales said when he retired from parliament in 1974. "My greatest satisfaction has been doing things for people."

Alf Hales died in 1998. On July 24, 2000 a dedication ceremony was held for the Alf Hales Memorial Trail and Overlook.

– Ceska Brennan

The Alf Hales Memorial Trail behind the
River Run Centre.   Source: Fred Dahms, 2000

Wide roads at Grange Street and Starwood Drive.   Source: Fred Dahms, 2000

planning decisions because of potential flooding and because of conservation authority regulations, the master plan adds municipal authority to initiatives to enhance and preserve this outstanding civic asset.

RENEWED GROWTH AND PLANNING CONTROVERSIES

As suggested in the *Strategic Plan*, pressure for development has come in Eastview and in areas annexed from Puslinch Township. Proposals for major new "big-box" commercial developments in the Woodlawn-Woolwich and Edinburgh-Stone Road areas have caused confrontations and Ontario Municipal Board hearings. A court challenge to the OMB's order that Wal-Mart divulge sales figures has delayed final OMB deliberations. The forces of growth versus slow growth are again clashing, as are supporters of the CBD and proponents of suburban commercial development.

River Systems Management Study, chaired by Prof. Hugh Whiteley, which examined all land contiguous to the two rivers. Its objectives were to preserve environmental integrity, ensure continuity of connections along river trails, encourage compatibility of development beside the rivers and promote a variety of land uses on the riverbanks. Major public consultation was conducted to ensure that all interested parties were included in the deliberations. These initiatives reflected the renewed interest in ecology, sustainability and the natural environment.

The *River System Study* eventually resulted in a master plan for the valleys through the city. It proposed the removal of all dams and weirs, the naturalization of the riverbanks, extension of riverside trails, policies for urban design along the rivers and viewing corridors in some areas. Ultimately, the Speed and Eramosa rivers are to be flanked through the city by pedestrian and bicycle paths. Since much land along the rivers is privately owned, its acquisition is slow and expensive, but major strides have been made in developing the river corridors. When zone changes are requested the city attempts to acquire land along the river. In 1999, it finally managed to purchase the CPR line along the Speed behind the River Run Centre. Work has begun with the Grand River Conservation Authority for major beautification of this area with the Alf Hales Memorial Trail and Overlook. A number of the *River System Master Plan* recommendations tied in closely with new zoning bylaws and urban design guidelines. Although the rivers have always been considered in

For years, development in the area east of Victoria Road was delayed because sewage would have to be pumped to the treatment plant. As a result of discussions between developers and city officials, the *Official Plan* was amended in 1991 to incorporate the *Eastview Secondary Plan* which would guide the growth of this expanding area. Servicing for Eastview was upgraded allowing earlier development than previously anticipated. To facilitate development, municipal trunk sewers and water mains are being extended into the area and a storm water management plan was prepared. Anticipated additional traffic required a traffic study and implied major road and intersection modifications for areas outside Eastview. The extension of Watson Road became Watson Parkway bisecting a cedar forest in the process. Environmental impact studies were required for a number of areas as was the construction of a new municipal pumping station to service the area north of Eastview Road.

While the secondary plan attempted to be sensitive to the environment and to control commercial development, its transportation recommendations were questioned by many. A number of major road and intersection improvement recommendations are being debated in the context of a transportation study update. Nevertheless, development that may ultimately accommodate some

Development in south Guelph.   Source: Fred Dahms, 2000

The new arena being built on the site of the former Eaton's store.
Source: Fred Dahms, 2000

10,000 persons is well underway. Previously open fields are now dotted with a mixture of small single-family homes, townhouse complexes, duplexes and a few larger singles. Some units back on woodlands and drainage corridors, but many have very little private open space with few trees in sight. Crescents and cul-de-sacs are reasonably narrow, but streets such as Grange and Starwood have unusually wide road allowances, despite the fact that houses line them.

Relatively high densities have been achieved with few of the advantages of the new urbanism. Corner stores and heterogeneous land uses are nowhere to be found, necessitating the use of vehicles for almost every trip. Signs indicate that since local capacity does not exist, children will be bused to schools at distant locations. Road design will ensure that arterials become very busy. Rather than being dispersed through a grid allowing access by many routes, all traffic is funnelled from local streets, to collectors to arterials. The arterials inevitably become congested at rush hours when they provide the only access to subdivisions. They are designed to accommodate peak traffic flows for the hour or so per day when this is necessary. At other times, they are lightly travelled but their size and disposition encourage speeding.

South Guelph Proposals

For years, Guelph had been expanding south, but was blocked by Puslinch Township between it and Highway 401. The strong attraction of Highway 401 provided a major impetus to annexation from the township, since it is now considered the main street of Ontario. Commuters desiring to live in Guelph and potential businesses are attracted to the south of the city by the access to the Toronto and Cambridge areas offered by the highway.

After a series of studies beginning in 1982, the Joint Fringe Area Planning Program was established to discuss development proposals, boundary issues and future land use policies for Guelph and Puslinch Township. In 1989, Wellington County established a committee to review county government which eventually considered potential land transfer to Guelph. In July 1990 the most-recent report, *Wellington County Study - Future Land Needs* was adopted by all parties and became the basis for Guelph's 1993 annexation of 1,488.5 hectares from Puslinch Township. In 1998, a secondary plan for the area was prepared and was adopted as an amendment to Guelph's *Official Plan*.

The amendment is intended to guide the growth of the area to the year 2016 when Guelph is expected to have a population of 130,000. In addition to recommending locations for residential, commercial and industrial uses, the amendment sets out environmental constraints and recommends a bicycle path network. A major new component of the plan is corporate business parks in highly visible locations along the Hanlon Expressway. The significant wetlands and watersheds are designated and protected "due to the importance of these features within the community."

The plan establishes a user-friendly approval process, but will "provide resourceful and sensitive stewardship of natural systems." The area will become an important "gateway to the city." Special efforts are to be made to preserve historic farmsteads and to protect the city's drinking water sources in the Arkell Springs area. Existing residential development on septic systems and wells will be recognised, but all new development and infilling will require full municipal services. As in the Eastview area, major road widenings and intersection improvements are recommended, but these are already attracting attention from environmentalists and others concerned with the quality of life in the city. On the other hand, sustainable development polices encourage mixed uses, a dense network of local streets, diversity of design and compact urban form.

More Downtown Redevelopment Proposals

After years of studies, the building of the Eaton Centre and its apparent lack of success in revitalising the CBD, the city produced yet another document analyzing downtown prospects. This was the *Guelph Downtown Economic Strategic Plan Background Information*, 1996. It suggested a number of possible options for redevelopment of the City Hall/Memorial Gardens area. These ranged from better co-ordination of policies to suggestions that Memorial Gardens be removed from the area, to designs for an enhanced civic square, to suggestions that parking be improved in the central area. With the closing of Eaton's store in early 1998, many of these ideas will have to be re-thought. The opening of the River Run Centre in 1997 added impetus to downtown redevelopment, while the closing of Eaton's created much uncertainty.

An agreement was concluded between the city and Nustadia Corporation in November 1998 to build an arena where the Eaton's store had existed. This facility will be used for hockey, entertainment, and conventions and is hoped to inspire additional economic development in the downtown. It will be operated by Nustadia Corporation, and theoretically is being built at no cost to Guelph taxpayers. Some have suggested that a proposal to move the library to the Eaton Centre might have been more appropriate, but the sporting lobby won on this issue.

Elsewhere on Wyndham Street, new apartments are being built over some of the stores while various schemes have been considered for the Baker Street parking lot. The city would like this area to be used for additional apartments and possibly a parking garage to encourage greater use of downtown shops and facilities. Seniors' housing has also been considered for the CBD, and several groups including Friends of Guelph are seeking to transform the area into a place in which to live, work and be entertained. Many would like to include a grocery store in any downtown redevelopment, but the cost of space and the amount of parking required make this difficult. While the downtown arena facility is being built, construction is continuing on another arena, fire hall and library branch in the west end. This too generated considerable controversy and heated debate at council.

The plaza at Edinburgh and Kortright in south Guelph.   Source: Fred Dahms, 2000

Peripheral Development

While efforts were being made to preserve and revitalise the CBD, growth in the southern section of the city has helped to weaken its position as the premier retail centre in Guelph. Stone Road Mall expanded and South City Centre has continued to develop with major shopping facilities south of Stone Road. The building of many new homes and apartments in the area supplied a major market which is now served by additional businesses east of Edinburgh Road at Stone, and at the intersection of Edinburgh and Kortright roads. Despite vigorous citizen opposition and negative recommendations from the Department of Planning and Business Development, council supported applications for "Big Box" facilities in the north and south of the city. Now much of Guelph's development is far away from the traditional core. The opening of the new YM-YWCA at the corner of Kortright Road and the Hanlon Parkway has exacerbated this spread.

The new YM-YWCA at Kortright and Hanlon; far from Guelph's traditional core.
Source: Fred Dahms, 2000

Guelph now seems to be divided between the traditional city surrounded by Victoria, Edinburgh, Woodlawn and Stone roads, and new peripheral areas around this core. The compact, tree-lined community of the *Official Plan* continues to exist within the old boundaries, but it is rapidly being swamped by treeless Mississauga/Brampton-like development on the periphery. The Eastview area is quickly joining the traditional city's outer suburban rivals. For many, Guelph is in a major fight to preserve the old-world character and charm that initially attracted its residents. Citizens confronted by constant proposals for growth, faster arterial roads, additional industry and low-density subdivisions often feel that they are fighting a losing battle.

From Micro-Management to the Ascendancy of Technical Standards

During the late 1980s and 1990s, Guelph city council moved towards "micro-management" of planning in the city, which led to a decline in initiatives taken by staff. After the abolition of the Guelph Planning Advisory Committee in 1994, all planning disputes were resolved at council meetings, sometimes through long and acrimonious proceedings. Rather than producing bold policies and district plans, planners were often involved in fighting brush fires arising from zone change requests and demands of developers. At times, some councillors failed to support staff in public meetings while others have gone as far as to attack public servants and accuse them of conflicts of interest.

After almost a decade of micro-management in Guelph planning, more citizen participation was forced upon reluctant councils, and planning began to change again from rigid plans to a process involving many participants. Meetings of council became even longer as increasing numbers of voters questioned decisions on everything from landfill selection to traffic flow. On many occasions, the gallery was packed with irate citizens demanding changes in policy and procedure. During these tense encounters, animosity between councillors became apparent. Some citizen delegations were subjected to hostile inquisitions by councillors, making decisions increasingly difficult to consummate. The end result was a very different approach (which is still evolving) to planning in Guelph.

From "Planning" to "Process"

In 2000, Guelph's population is over 100,000 and both politics and planning have changed forever. Both positive and negative effects have accompanied downloading by the provincial Conservative government. On the positive side,

many formerly provincial decisions have become local. Council may now approve *Official Plan* amendments and plans of subdivision. This should speed the planning process and enable development to respond to local requirements. On the negative side, the province has gutted ministries that formerly assisted municipal professionals and granted provincial approvals. City of Guelph staff members are now expected to become experts on environmental impacts, ecology, law, traffic, pollution and anything else that might be involved in a development decision.

Given municipal budget restraints, staff members are expected to accomplish their tasks with declining resources. There is pressure to complete everything quickly, despite personnel shortages. Does this reflect Guelph's new official slogan: "Taking Care of Business," which replaced "Cosmopolitan Countryside" on city letterhead and publicity brochures? When possible, consultants are retained for major projects, and are required for important traffic planning. Occasionally they are unfamiliar with local circumstances and produce little that is helpful. As a result, some specifications for infrastructure have been made on the basis of wildly optimistic projections, questionable data and superficial analyses.

A corollary of the recent approach to planning is the question of plan versus process. In the past, staff prepared carefully documented background studies which were translated eventually into zoning bylaws, policies and official plans. These reflected a long-term set of objectives intended to consummate the Vision Statement in the *Official Plan*. Recommendations by professionals and decisions by council generally reflected this careful preparation. Recently, and especially since budget cuts reduced staff capabilities, planning has become more process than planning. Now the strategy is to present a general outline of a policy or idea that will affect the city and invite interested groups to participate. This has happened recently for the south city plan, the Victoria Road plan, the landfill debate and the proposed Woolwich Street widening. Workshops and drop-in centres are organized and attempts are made to reconcile opposing views before conflict develops. When all views have been heard, staff revise plans or reports which are often considered again. This enables citizens to have early input to policy and is often successful, but it can also increase acrimony and is generally very time-consuming.

Given adequate budgets and resources, the process method has the potential to result in excellent planning, but with inadequate resources, it can drain staff time, lead to superficial research and capitulation to pressure groups. On many occasions, small groups of well-organized citizens have stopped or altered proposed policies. The N-4 landfill controversy is probably the most significant recent example. On other occasions, massive public input has been generated, and in the case of the proposed Woolwich Street widening, resulted in a superior design. Nevertheless, close votes by council have occasionally ignored recommendations generated by process planning.

CONTINUING PLANNING CONTROVERSIES

Since the mid-1990s, citizens of Guelph have questioned many policies of city council, and have been especially critical of recommendations based on the *Guelph and Area Transportation Study*, 1994. The perception of people living along Edinburgh Road South, Kortright Road West, Dean Avenue, the Cardigan Street area, and in St. Patrick's Ward is that traffic is too heavy and too fast. They have made many submissions to city council and to the traffic department to reduce, slow, and calm traffic in their areas. Many of the problems are the result of insisting on arterial roads with wide paved areas through residential neighbourhoods. As a result of heavy lobbying and many meetings with traffic personnel, lane changes have been made "on an experimental basis" to slow traffic on Edinburgh and Kortright roads. Traffic calming measures have been implemented on Dufferin Street and Dean Avenue, but the concerns of people in "The Ward" have not yet been addressed. Despite the fact that Guelph has the appropriate technology, budget cuts have delayed the synchronization of traffic signals, adding considerably to driver frustration. Throughout the city, speeding, running red lights and road rage have been increasing, with little meaningful response from city council. Cameras at key traffic lights have been suggested by the police and some councillors, but have been prevented by provincial government opposition.

Citizen Activism

Several major confrontations brought transportation issues to a head in 1995, resulting in some of Guelph's most widespread activism. A proposal to widen Gordon Street from Wellington to Stone Road met sweeping opposition. A coalition of environmentalists, university faculty, residents of the street and bicycle enthusiasts fought the scheme. Residents and environmentalists were particularly concerned about the loss of mature trees along the route. Bike riders objected to the reliance on wider roads for cars at the expense of pedestrians,

The Hanlon-Wellington Street interchange.   Source: Fred Dahms, 1999

bicycles and public transit. University faculty demonstrated that projections in the *Transportation Study* were unrealistic because they ignored the unique situation of pedestrians, bikers and bus users on Gordon Street. After numerous public meetings and presentations at council, a compromise was accepted that saved most of the trees, provided bicycle and turn lanes, and essentially preserved a two-lane road up Gordon Street hill.

During the debate about Gordon Street, marches were held, demonstrations took place at City Hall, and councillors were lobbied extensively. Several individuals were charged for painting the roadway but never convicted. As a result of such controversies and concern about the expenditure of tax dollars, Citizens Urging Responsible Budgeting was formed to monitor and hopefully influence the city's budget process. For two years it attempted to monitor and influence city budget decisions, and succeeded in convincing council to hold public meetings to discuss the budget. CURB has now ceased its activities although individuals continue to address council on specific issues.

Another major controversy erupted over the provincial Ministry of Transportation's decision to build a controlled access interchange at the corner of Wellington Street and the Hanlon Parkway. Traffic accidents were cited as the major reason for providing this facility, despite several proposals to improve the intersection with relatively minor signal and lane alterations. Delegations argued that the interchange was unnecessary, that it would disrupt fish and wildlife habitats and create noise and pollution for nearby residents. Despite these arguments, council accepted the interchange "because it was provincial money," ignoring the fact that provincial taxes come from everyone. Consultants warned that methane from a former dumpsite might cause problems in the future, but this did not deter council from accepting a provincial gift.

For the last two years, traffic at the interchange has been disrupted, the environment has been despoiled and residents have suffered from constant dust and noise. In July 1999, construction halted completely because of a legal dispute between the contractor and the Ministry. Because of Ministry downsizing, engineering was left to consultants who made major errors that increased the cost by more than $2 million. The courts supported Bot Construction in the dispute, but the Ministry threatened to appeal. By mid-July, Bot and the Ministry had reached a compromise on the additional cost of the $20 million project, but it will not be completed until 2001 or later.

A proposal to widen Woolwich Street between Speedvale Avenue and Woodlawn Road by some 17 metres in July 1999 also encountered stiff citizen opposition. After several public meetings, a compromise design was selected. It included tree plantings, bicycle paths and intersection improvements. Although not everyone was satisfied, the plan ultimately approved by council provides a much more pleasant entrance to the city than the original proposal. The process that led to this compromise was a model of effective citizen participation.

DOWNTOWN PROBLEMS, POTENTIALS AND PROPOSED SOLUTIONS

In August 1995, the city commissioned the *Goldie Mill Secondary Plan Study* to resolve conflicts over redevelopment proposals suggesting high-rise apartments near the banks of the Speed River on the fringes of the CBD. **(See map on endpaper)** Existing policies encouraged high-density (up to 350 units per hectare) development which could be achieved only through high-rise buildings surrounded by open space and parking. Given the low-rise character of the area, such an approach was incompatible with existing structures and clearly unacceptable to the residents, many of who loathe the high-rises on Cardigan Street. The study concluded with recommendations for amendments to the *Official Plan* which would encourage sensitive and compatible development in this key area.

Important Recommendations: *Goldie Mill Secondary Plan Study*, 1995

The character, flora and fauna of the river valley should be preserved

New development should be low-rise and compatible with existing buildings

Design guidelines on building massing and configuration, rather than density controls should guide the scale of redevelopment

River trails should be maintained wherever possible

Heritage buildings should be retained and enhanced

Natural recreational areas and parks should be developed along the river

Streets should be kept narrow and traffic minimized

Incompatible industrial uses should be eliminated

Existing buildings should be reused whenever possible

All developments should be sensitive to the local environment and to their proximity to the CBD

The *Goldie Mill Study* incorporates many of the issues that were being addressed in the revision of the *Official Plan* and zoning bylaw revisions. It summarized much contemporary thought on redevelopment and suggested policies that reflected the opinions of local residents, sound design and ecological approaches. In a sense, it delineates the old technological approach to planning from the new environmentally-aware attitudes suggested by the river systems study and increasing citizen participation. It places people and the environment ahead of motor vehicles and wider roads.

Essentially, the *Goldie Mill Study* suggests that any development in the area must respect its unique natural and cultural characteristics while being sensitive to the wishes of its residents. It is a direct result of

Goldie Mill.   Source: Fred Dahms, 2000

continuous political action led by Julia Amies and the Goldie Mill Neighbourhood Association, formed originally to oppose high-rise development on the former Stewart Lumber site on Cardigan Street. What began as a negative reaction seems to have ended in positive recommendations.

Guelph at the Millennium

As we enter the 21st century, Guelph is a vibrant, rapidly growing city with great potential. It has world-class musical, cultural and artistic activities, and an active little theatre. The River Run Centre is an outstanding venue for all types of meetings and performances. Ball diamonds, soccer fields, arenas, swimming pools and exercise facilities are widely available. Its wet-dry facility is on the cutting edge of recycling. Miles of tree-lined trails along its rivers provide excellent opportunities for walkers and bicyclists. In 2000, they were linked with the Trans Canada Trail. Guelph still enjoys many pleasant residential neighbourhoods and some of the best water in the province. According to the 1999 issue of *Maclean's Magazine*, the University of Guelph is now the top comprehensive university in Canada.

On the other side of the ledger, much of Guelph is being developed like the suburban sprawl of Brampton or Mississauga. Vast suburbs on the periphery are thrown up after all vegetation has been removed and the land has been levelled. Wide arterial roads slice through these areas, with the threat of more wherever predictions suggest that there may be heavy traffic. This mechanistic approach has provided some ugly entrances to the city, the problematic Wellington Street overpass and speedways like Woodlawn, Victoria, Eramosa, Kortright and Edinburgh roads. Despite pleas from residents to slow dangerous traffic, every major new area being developed contains such arteries, which are often built before anyone is present to object. "Big Box" proposals supported by council at both ends of the city threaten to obliterate what remains of our local plaza infrastructure.

Who Pays for Development?

On March 15, 1999, Guelph city council passed a bylaw that effectively forces homeowners to subsidize new industrial and commercial development. Development charges were reduced from almost $19 per square metre for new industrial construction to $10. To compensate for this potential loss of revenue, the city will increase water bills up to $8 per year for four years to total $32 for the average homeowner. A combination of growth mentality among councillors and lobbying led to this decision. Representatives of Linamar Corporation, one of Guelph's largest employers, threatened to build their new facilities outside the city if the development charge was not reduced. The major business lobbies in the city supported them. Councillor Bill McAdams demonstrated that during the next five years, residents would subsidize new business development by $3.5 million. Despite this argument, council supported its earlier decision to revise both charges in an effort to increase the rate of growth in the city. Little consideration was given to the ultimate cost of schools, roads, policing, fire protection and social services, not to mention stresses on water supply and sewage treatment capacity to be generated by accelerated growth.

Growth and Water Supply

After a dry winter and spring in 1999, the city experienced severe shortages of water. Because of low water table levels, the Eramosa River could not be used to recharge the Arkell Springs aquifer. Reserves of water dropped to dangerously low levels, requiring several wells with poor quality water to be brought into service. In August, contamination from industrial runoff and lawn care products caused five other wells to be shut down. With more growth, such incidents will continue and increase. On a number of occasions, alternate day watering and outright bans on lawn watering were imposed. Similar situations had occurred in previous dry years, but this was the most severe occurrence to date.

The availability of ample supplies of high quality water has always been a major attraction for both industries and homeowners in Guelph. Unfortunately, the city's rapid growth and climatic change have created a potential water supply crisis. Thousands of new residential units have been approved in the south and east of Guelph, while the Department of Business Development actively pursues new industry and council approves plans of subdivision. Guelph has lost its leadership in environmental protection that originated with the *Hanlon Creek Study*. Neighbours in Kitchener-Waterloo have now surpassed Guelph in environmental preservation. At some point, council will be forced to choose between quality of life and continued population and economic growth. Theoretically, Guelph could tap into a pipeline to a lake or use river water, but only for a very large financial commitment and a major sacrifice in the quality of local water. This and the disposal of sewage may be the greatest challenges facing city council for the foreseeable future.

THE FUTURE

Rapid industrial and residential growth are straining all our facilities to the limit. Somewhere, the *Official Plan's* vision of Guelph as having a "careful balance of yesterday's legacy, today's needs and tomorrow's vision," has disappeared. Where in the present approach are we "respecting the history that enriches local architecture, preserving the nature that adorns the landscape, and promoting an atmosphere of innovation and creativity"? Guelph's Vision Statement went on to say "Guelph's beauty lies in its compact, small-town character." Has this vision been buried by "Taking Care of Business," the city's new official slogan?

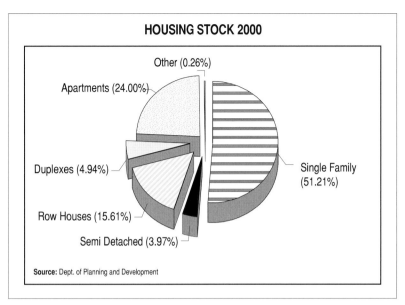

HOUSING STOCK 2000

Other (0.26%)
Apartments (24.00%)
Duplexes (4.94%)
Row Houses (15.61%)
Semi Detached (3.97%)
Single Family (51.21%)

Source: Dept. of Planning and Development

In their approach to decision-making and obsession with growth, council (and some staff) seem to have lost sight of the qualities that attracted people to Guelph in the first place. This is indeed unfortunate, since these qualities are enshrined in the *Official Plan*, which is supposed to guide the future development of the city. Within the boundaries of Woodlawn, Edinburgh, Stone and Victoria, real neighbourhoods flourish, corner stores may still be found, people walk to the library or to the market and some of traditional Guelph is preserved. Outside these boundaries lies a mix of modern residential enclaves and pods of industry, shopping, commerce and recreation linked by busy arterials designed to carry all vehicular traffic beyond the collectors. In older neighbourhoods, congestion is decreased and speeds are slower because the grid pattern of streets offers many choices of routes between areas.

Growth, Growth, Growth

Guelph has continued to grow as we approach the millennium. According to city officials, "there doesn't seem to be a downside to the city's expanding fortunes, unless you're against steady growth." Since 1998, Guelph's rate of growth has exceeded that of its rivals, Kitchener-Waterloo and Cambridge. In 1998, the city recorded total construction valued at $173.5 million, down slightly from the $202.3 million in 1997, which included the $48 million General Hospital development. On average, Guelph has experienced a $20 million per year increase in construc-

tion over the past five years. Building permits in 1998 totalled 2,204, up from 1,893 the year before. Residential construction was most common with a value of $100 million as against $70 million for other sectors. Single-family homes led the way at $74.8 million, with multiple units at $24.3 million. The growth trend continued through 1999 when 85 more homes were constructed than in 1998. Much of the development was in the Eastview and southern areas of Guelph on previously open land, some adjacent to sensitive wetlands. The building of multiple units, and especially townhouses has increased dramatically since 1994. Their prices make them competitive with resale homes of similar size. As a result of all this development, Guelph's population passed 100,000 well before the millennium.

When potential growth is examined, the scenario is even more alarming than that suggested by past statistics. By September 1999, 8,270 dwelling units had received draft approval. Of these, about 42 percent were for single and semi-detached dwellings and 58 percent were for apartments. Assuming a conservative 2.5 persons per unit, this could lead to population growth of 20,675. In addition to the draft approved units, there is potential on undeveloped land in the city for up to an additional 18,000 dwelling units. Building department reports show that some could be accommodated on vacant or redeveloped infill sites, while others might be adjacent to provincially significant wetlands. Approval for those would be contingent upon successful environmental assessments, which in the prevailing political climate might not be too difficult. The bottom line is that within Guelph's recently extended boundaries, some 26,000 new dwelling units or over 65,000 additional people might be accommodated. Has anyone analyzed the effect of this influx upon the city's water supply, environmental quality, traffic, school capacity, police and other service costs, or are we just "Taking Care of Business"?

Which image will be the future for the 21st century? With careful, slow, environmentally-conscious development, Guelph still has the opportunity to retain some of the outstanding qualities that attracted growth in the first place. If present policies continue, sewage capacity will be exceeded and waste disposal problems will multiply. Water shortages will become chronic, speeding traffic will increase, and school capacity shortages will continue. Ultimately, much of Guelph could become yet another anonymous suburban wasteland. The ultimate solution lies with voters who must elect councillors with vision, compassion and intelligence. Guelph needs those who will think beyond immediate "growth" and increasing tax revenues to the long-term costs and consequences of their policies.

RETROSPECT AND PROSPECT

In conservative Ontario of 2000, local city officials have the power to approve plans of subdivision, amend the *Official Plan* and set

Towne Lattice Footbridge in Royal City Park.　　　　Source: Fred Dahms, 1999

policies for the future. Guelph's staff is now functioning with almost no provincial support or expertise. Because of council's concern for balanced budgets and tax reduction, no department has the in-house expertise to cope with the workloads thrust upon them. Occasionally, expensive consultants are hired to provide solutions to difficult problems. Council now acts as its own planning advisory committee, wasting valuable hours on sometimes trivial planning disputes that should have been resolved by a committee or by staff. There is often little

consensus or vision of the city among this group of councillors, with many crucial votes being decided by a majority of one.

Ultimately, Guelph's future lies with the electorate. If someone can articulate a realistic vision and intelligent priorities for the city, and then get elected on such a platform, the future could be bright. The successes of the Hanlon Watershed, the district plans, the wet-dry recycling program and the preservation of our riverlands could be duplicated and multiplied. *The Hanlon Watershed Study* became a model for environmental preservation and regulation in the province. When they had adequate resources, our planning and engineering departments were pioneers in this and other innovative developments.

Once again we are at a crossroads between fiscally-driven technological solutions and those based on vision and humanity. Guelph's legacy of beauty and careful growth can still be preserved and projected. However, if present political and administrative trends persist, the once proud Royal City could become nothing more than a clone of the suburban wastelands surrounding most large North American communities.

SOURCES

Allen, David, *Guelph and its Early Days,* 1924.

Bloomfield, G., Samuel Carter 1859 - 1944: An outline biography, *Historic Guelph,* 32, 1993, 22-45.

Bloomfield, G.T., Map of City of Guelph Boundary Changes, 1851 to 1993.

Center for Resources Development 1971, *Hanlon Creek Ecological Study Phase A,* University of Guelph, Publication 50.

Chartwood Developments Ltd., *Eaton's Centre - Guelph, Ontario,* Toronto, 1979.

City of Guelph, *Zoning By-Law No. 4000,* 1955.

—, *Planning Studies 1960,* Kitchener, Dryden and Smith, 1961.

—, *Zoning By-Law No. 5418,* 1962.

—, Report -Technical Committee Re Annexation, Guelph, 1965.

—, Assessment Department, *Annual Report for the Year Ending 1966,* 1967.

—, *Urban Renewal Scheme Report,* Candeub, Fleissig and Associates, 1968.

—, *Official Plan for the Guelph Planning Area,* 1969.

—, Eight Briefs to City Council on Growth Issues, 1974.

—, *City of Guelph Transportation Plan to 100,000 Persons and Beyond,* 1974.

—, *Commercial Planning Policy,* 1984.

—, *Retail Study,* 1985.

—, *Official Plan for the City of Guelph,* 1987.

—, *Official Plan,* 1991.

—, River Systems Management Study, Progress Report on the Preparation of the Management Plan, 1992.

—, *Official Plan,* 1994.

Cox, J.L Planning Consultants, Inc., *Eastview Secondary Plan, City of Guelph,* 1991.

—*Goldie Mill Secondary Plan Study: City of Guelph,* 1995.

Department of Planning and Development, City of Guelph, *City of Guelph Park Study,* 1969.

Annual Reports and Building Permit Summaries, 1973 - 1999.

—, *District Plans: 1. Riverside; 2 Willow West; 3. Edinburgh; 4. Downtown; 5. Eramosa; 6. Eastview; 7. University; 8. Southview; 9. Hanlon,* 1973 - 1975.

—, *The Guelph Correctional Centre Surplus Lands Study,* 1974.

—, City of Guelph, *Housing Policy for the City of Guelph, Initial Statement,* 1975.

—, *Housing needs in Guelph: An Analysis and Targets,* Guelph, 1976.

—, *Townscape Analysis and Proposals, Guelph Central Business District,* 1977.

—, *Downtown Guelph: Evaluation of Land-Use and Development Strategies,* 1977.

—, *Analysis and Projection of Guelph's Population 1976 - 2001,* 1980.

—, *Group Homes and Other Residential Care Facilities, Proposal for Official Plan Policies and By-Law Amendments,* 1981.

—, *Retail Study,* 1983.

—, *Heritage Conservation Planning policy: A Discussion Paper,* 1984.

—, *Residential Planning Policy: A Discussion Paper,* 1984.

—, *Industrial Planning Policy,* 1984.

—, *Community Improvement, A Discussion Paper,* 1985.

—, *Population Study of Guelph 1986 - 2006,* 1988.

—, *Statistical Summary,* 1991,

—, *Commercial Planning Policy, A Discussion Paper,* 1994.

—, *Urban Design Guidelines,* 1995.

—, *Zoning By-Law No. (1995) - 14864.*

—, *Guelph Downtown Economic Strategic Plan, Background Information,* 1996.

—, Modifications to Official Plan Amendment Number Two: South Guelph Secondary Plan, 1998.

Drummond, A.W. *Guelph the Royal City,* Guelph, 1924.

Drummond, I.M. 1987, *Progress Without Planning: The Economic History of Ontario from Confederation to the Second World War,* Toronto, U. of T. Press.

Dryden And Smith, Planning Consultants, *Economic Survey, City of Guelph,* Kitchener, 1960.

—, *Background Studies for the City of Guelph Transportation Plan,* Kitchener, 1966.

Evening Mercury, Souvenir Industrial Number Descriptive of and Illustrating Guelph, "The Royal City of Canada," Guelph 1903.

Guelph City Planning Commission, *Guelph, Planned Progress for the Next Fifteen Years: A General Plan for the City of Guelph, Ontario,* 1945.

Guelph Landfill Site Search, Position Paper No. 1, 1995.

Guelph Non-Profit Housing Corporation, *1991-92 Annual Report,* 1992.

Guelph Transportation Study Committee; *Stage 1: A Transportation Planning Policy Framework,* Guelph, 1972.

Government of Ontario, *The Planning Act,* Statutes of Ontario, 1955.

—, *The Planning Act,* Revised Statutes of Ontario, 1970.

—, *Bill 159, An Act to Revise the Planning Act,* 1983.

—, *Bill 163, An Act to Revise the Ontario Planning and Development Act and the Municipal Conflict of Interest Act and the Municipal Act and to amend other statutes related to planning and municipal matters,* 1994.

—, *Bill 20, An Act to promote economic growth and protect the environment by streamlining the land use planning and development system through amendments related to planning, development, municipal and heritage matters,* 1996.

—, *Provincial Policy Statement,* 1996.

Hemson Consulting Ltd., *City of Guelph Ward One Area: Future Land use Strategy,* Toronto, 1992.

—, *City of Guelph Downtown Housing Intensification Study,* Toronto, 1992.

—, *City of Guelph Housing Intensification Study,* Toronto, 1992.

Landplan Collaborative Ltd., *Revitalization, Downtown Guelph, Improvements Manual,* nd.

Margison and Associates, *Guelph Major Street and Traffic Plan 1959 - 1980,* Toronto, 1960.

Ministry of Housing Ontario, The Ministry's Role in One Municipality (Guelph), *Housing Ontario,* Vol. 24,1, 1980.

—, Special Edition, Ontario Renews for the 80s, *Housing Ontario,* Vol. 24, 4, 1980.

Ministry of Housing and Ministry of Municipal Affairs, Ontario, *Alternative development Standards, Making Choices, Guideline,* 1995.

Monteith, Jean and Associates Ltd. *Final Report: Joint Fringe Area Planning Program, Wellington-Guelph, nd.*

Rae, K.J. 1985, *The Prosperous years: The Economic History of Ontario 1939 - 1975,* Toronto, U. of T. Press.

Reed Vorhees and Associates, Ltd., *Guelph Area Transportation Study,* 1967.

Rogers, D.C. The Geography of Retailing for the City of Guelph, B.A. Thesis, Department of Geography, University of Guelph, 1975.

Schull, J, *Ontario Since 1867,* Toronto, McClelland and Stewart, 1978.

Stanczyk, P.J. Guelph, A Locational Analysis of Industrial Development, B.A. Thesis, Department of Geography, University of Guelph, 1975.

The Guelph Daily Mercury, Assorted Articles and Editorials, 1900 - 2000.

Thoman, R.S. *Design for Development in Ontario: The Initiation of a Regional Planning Program,* Toronto, Allister, 1971.

Thomasfield Homes Ltd., *Pine Ridge, Guelph,* nd.

Waterloo County Area Planning Board, *A Strategy for Growth, Final Report,* Kitchener, 1972.

Wellington-Guelph Area Study Committee, *Some Major Regional Considerations: The Wellington-Guelph Area,* Kitchener, 1970.

INTERVIEWS (1999)

Ruth Dempsey

James Forbes

Ann Godfrey

Carl Hamilton

Norman Harrison

Margaret MacKinnon

Jack Milliken

Rajan Philips

Nancy Shoemaker

ACKNOWLEDGEMENTS

My sincere thanks to Marie Puddister and Mark Haennel for their assistance with cartography.

Appendix A

SOURCES: 'PROFILES: PEOPLE OF GUELPH' by CESKA BRENNAN and GUELPH ANECDOTES by BONNIE DURTNALL

Bernardi, Guiseppe 1931- : interview with nephew Peter, July 1999.

Bernardi, Valentino 1927-1994: interview with son Peter, July 1999.

Bradburn, Lenna 1960- : personal interview, Aug. 1999.

Clark, Jock 1913-1973: *Guelph Tribune*, May 6, 1992 pg. 7, June 11, 1997 pg. B1; *Guelph Mercury*, Sept. 13, 1973, June 18, 1993, pg. A10; Handout, Guelph Parks; Guelph's Floral Clock - Fact Sheet.

Cutten, Arthur 1870-1936: *Guelph Mercury*, Jan. 19, 1957, "A Picture History of Guelph," p. 164; "City View" *Guelph Mercury*, July 10, 1992; "History in Homes" The Golden Triangle, July 10, 1986; *Guelph Magazine*, Aug. 1981 pgs. 6, 7 & 8; James Cutten interview, Oct. 1999.

Davis, Victor 1964-1989: *Guelph Tribune*, Nov. 15, 1989; *Guelph Mercury*, Nov. 14, 1989.

Donnell, Robert 1920-1990: various undated *Guelph Mercury* articles and a clip "The Poppy Patch"; Guelph Historical Society Publication Vol. VI 1966 No. 6 contributed by Miss F. MacKinnon.

Hales, Alfred 1909-1998: *Guelph Mercury*, March 5, 1998 p. A1 & A3; personal interview, 1998.

Hamilton, Fred A. 1909-1989: *Guelph Mercury*, Dec. 16, 1967, June 1989; *Guelph Tribune* May 1988; personal interview with daughter, Aug. 1999.

Hammond, Fred 1912-1999: *Guelph Mercury*, John Roe's People, Oct. 30, 1992; *The Canadian Amateur Magazine*, Fred Hammond VE3HC . . . by Harold Braun, June 1997; Hammond Manufacturing release.

Jary, Norman 1929- : *Guelph Mercury*, May 7, 1994, March 15, 1994; personal interview, July 1999.

Jensen, Arnold 1918-1993: *Guelph Mercury*, May 3, 1993, June 29, 1993; interview B. Monaghan, Oct. 1999.

Leyser, Christine 1931- : *Guelph Mercury*, June 21, 1996; *Guelph Tribune*, May 18, 1999.

Little, Flora 1902-1991: *Guelph Mercury*, July 13, 1991.

Little, Jean 1932- : *Guelph Tribune*, 'Trib Trivia,' Dec. 9, 1992, June 11, 1997; *Guelph Mercury* Profile, May 22, 1993, May 9, 1992 p. 9, Dec. 1, 1992, June 3, 1997 p. A5; undated *Guelph Mercury* article by Alexandra Paul and Family by Helen Brimmell and Rosemary Anderson; personal interview, 1999.

Mack, Horace 1895-1961: *Guelph Historical Society Publication* Vol. VIII, No. 9 - 1969; *The History of Guelph* Vol. I, Robert Stewart; p. 115 reprinted article *Guelph Mercury*, June 14, 1975.

McCallum, Bonnie 1940-1989: 'Caring for Our Rivers,' OPIRG Guelph; Bruce McCallum interview, Sept. 1999.

Pickersgill, Edward 1944- : articles from *Guelph Mercury* dated July 15, 1993, May 12, 1990, Jan. 18, 1995; Matrix Project Rental Housing brochure; *Guelph Tribune*, July 5, 1995; interview by Bonnie Durtnall, Aug. 16, 2000.

Singh, T. Sher 1949- : personal interview, Aug. 1999.

Sleeman, John W. 1953- : *Toronto Star*, Dec. 27, 1994, Guelph Profile 1990, B1; Information provided by Sleeman office, Aug. 1999.

Stewart, Richard "Dick" 1943- : *Guelph Mercury* Oct. 11, 1994 p. A3, July 13, 1994; *Guelph Tribune*, June 1, 1994 p. A9; personal interview, Aug. 1999.

Winegard, William "Bill" 1924- : *Guelph Mercury* May 4, 1988, Oct. 30, 1998 p. B1; *Wellington Advertiser* Feb. 8, 1988 p. 3; 'Winegard Times,' self promotional piece 1988.

Worton, Harry 1921- : undated *Guelph Mercury* article by John France; "Official press release Harry Worton, M.P.P." *Guelph Mercury*, June 11, 1980; *Guelph Historical Society Publication* Aug. 1984; personal interview, June 1999.

 *Additional Guelph Anecdotes by Bonnie Durtnall – *Guelph Mercury*, issues from 1900 to 2000.

Appendix B

MAYORS OF THE CITY OF GUELPH 1900 - 2000

1900	R.E. Nelson	1933-1934	R. Beverley Robson
1901-1902	John Kennedy	1935-1936	Harry Mahoney
1903-1904	John H. Hamilton	1937	David E. Kennedy
1905-1906	George Sleeman	1938-1942	William G. Taylor
1907-1908	John Newstead	1943-1944	R. Beverley Robson
1909-1910	George Hastings	1945-1949	Gordon L. Rife
1911-1912	George John Thorpe	1950-1951	James A. Clare
1913-1914	Samuel Carter	1952-1955	Harry Worton
1915-1916	Harry Mahoney	1956-1957	Harold L. Suitter
1917-1918	John Newstead	1958-1960	David E. Hastings
1919-	J. E. Carter	1961-1962	William E. Hamilton
1920	H. Westoby	1963-1967	Ralph W. Smith
1921	C. H. Burgess	1968-1969	Paul Mercer
1922	F. Howard	1970-1984	Norman Jary
1923-1924	William Stephens	1985-1995	John Counsell
1925	George A. Drew	1995-2000	Joe Young
1926-1931	R. Beverley Robson	2000-	Karen Farbridge
1932	Ossian G. Lye		

Appendix C

MEMBERS OF THE CITY COUNCIL

ALDERMEN

1900	Penfold, Geo Dunbar, C. L	Kennedy, John Walker, Hugh	Thorp, Geo. J Hastings, Geo	Petrie, A. B Newstead, J	O'Connor, T Peterson, C	White, W. W Brill, G. J	Drew, J. J	Barker, G. A	Hamilton, J. H	Carter, S	Kilgour, J. W	Barber, Robt
1901	Stull, H. H. O Dunbar, C. L	Taylor, W. E Hastings, Geo	Thorp, G. J Ryan, Jas	Day, Jas. E Anderson, Jas	Petrie, A. B Crowe, R	White, W. W Slater, Wm	Barker, G. A	Hamilton, J. H	Carter, S	Barber, Robt	Kilgour, J. W	Scott, J. A
1902	Newstead, J Barber, W. F	Stull, H. H. O Hastings, G	Taylor, W. E Mahoney, J. J	Drew, J. J Crowe, R. H	Day, J. E Irvine, T	White, W. W Slater, Wm	Barker, G. A	Carter, S	Hamilton, J. H	Barber, Robt	Kilgour, J. W	Scott, J. A
1903	Barker, Geo. A	Carter, Samuel	Crowe, R. H	Johnston, Robt	Mahoney, John J	Malone, Hugh	Newstead, John	White, W. W	Rumford, Asa	Scott, John A	Stull, H. H. O	
1904	Barber, Robt	Barker, Geo. A	Carter, Samuel	Crowe, R. H	Hastings, Geo	Higgins, G. L	Mahoney, J. J	Newstead, J	Penfold, Geo	Scott, John A	Struthers, J. M	
1905	Newstead, John	Higgins, G. L	Cray, M. F	Penfold, Geo	Gemmell, T. H	Barker, Geo. A	Barber, Robt	Barber, Wm. F	Struthers, J. M	Cunningham, Jno	Hamilton, J. H	
1906	Macdonald, D. E	Lyon, James W	Nelson, R. E	Newstead, J	Penfold, Geo	Howitt, Chas. E	McCrea, J. A	Cray, M. F	Ryan, Geo.B	Higgins, G. L	Stewart, Alex	
1907	Rudd, D. E Barber, W. F	Thorp, G. J McMillan, R	Kennedy, John Struthers, J. M	Lyon, J. W Cunningham, Jno	Hewer, Jas McAteer, John	Nelson, K. E Carter, J. E	Hamilton, J. H	Higgins, G. L	Denyes, J	Simpson, Robt	McCrea, J. A	Messenger, D
1908	Bennett, E. J Stewart, R. D	Thorp, G. J Ryan, Jas	Penfold, Geo McMillan, R	Hewer, Jas McAteer, John	Nelson, R. E Humphries, R	Kennedy, John Carter, J. E	Hamilton, I. H	Pequegnat, J	Denyes, J	Callandar, H. B	Mahoney, H	Simpson, R
1909	Johnston, Jas Ryan, Jas	Rudd, D. E Rogers, T. C	Taylor, W. E Yeates, C	Mackinnon, R. L Barber, Albert	Calvert, S Cheevers, Matt	Waters, F Shaw, Jos	Kelly, C. W	Pequegnat, J	Rundle, S	Callandar, H. B	Mahoney, H	McCrea, J. A
1910	Rudd, D. E	Thorp, G. J	Carter, J. E	Mahoney, H	Taylor, W. E	Pequegnat, J. W	Kelly, C. W	McMillan, R	Rundle, S	Cheevers, M	Penfold, S	
1911	Carter, J. E	Nelson, R. E	Pequegnat, J. W	Kelly, J	Howard, F	Occomore, H	Kelly, C. W	McLean, H. C	Mahoney, H	Penfold, S	Calvert, S	
1912	Lawson, J	Kelly, J	Carter, J. E	Brydon, R. H	Penfold, S	Calvert, S	Mahoney, H	Pequegnat, J	Howard, F	Occomore, H	McLean, H. C	
1913	Barlow, D. H	Brydon, R. H	Carter, J. E	Doughty, W. T	Hannigan, T. J	McMillan, Robt	Newstead, J	Occomore, H	Parker, W. B	Penfold, S	Steele, H. C	
1914	Barlow, D. H	Brydon, R. H	Burgess, C. H	Doughty, W. T	Hannigan, T. J	Mahoney, H	Newstead, J	Occomore, H	Penfold, S	Ryan, Jas	Steele, H. C	
1915	Rundle, S	Steele, H. C	Martin, D	Dunbar, G	Crawford, E	Calvert, S	Stull, H. H. O	Carter, J. E	Hewer, Jas	Newstead, J	Rowen, O. E	
1916	Barlow, D. H	Brydon, R. H	Dunbar, G	Henry, G. M	Howitt, J. R	Lawson, J	Martin, D	Rowen, O. E	Rundle, S	Steele, H. C	Westoby, H	
1917	Buchner, A. A	Dunbar, Geo	Henry, G. M	Howard, F	McHugh, H. J	Payne, R. A	Rowen, O. E	Rundle, S	Steele, H. C	Stratton, Wm	Westoby, H	
1918	Buchner, A. A	Rundle, S. R	Stratton, Wm	Howard, F	McHugh, H. J	Payne, R. A	Henry, G. M	Penfold, S	Crawford, E	Barlow, D. H	Cowan, W. A	
1919	Macdonald, E. A Quarmby, H	Carter, J. E Barlow, D. H	Newstead, John Howard, F	Stephens, Wm Hoover, J. B	Brydon, R. H Walker, G. W	Hood, W. G Penfold, S	Hannigan, T. J	Burgess, Chas	Westoby, H	Henry, G. M	Cowan, W. A	Simpson, J. H
1920	Penfold, S Hannigan, T. J	Howard, F Burgess, Chas	Barlow, D. H Westoby, H	Wing, R. H Henry, G. M	Buckner, A. A Cowan, W. A	Quarmby, H Simpson, J. H	Macdonald, E. A	Carter, J. E	Newstead, John	Stephens, Wm	Brydon, R. H	Hood, W. G
1921	Burgess, C. H Macdonald, E. A	Grenside, F. C Carter, J. E	Tyson, A. W Mahoney, H	Evans, W. P Stephens, Wm	McElroy, H. J Brydon, R. H	Yeates, Chas Hood, W. G	Penfold, S	Howard, F	Barlow, D. H	Wing, R. H	Buchner, A. A	Quarmby, H

1922	Jaffray, Alex / Penfold, S	Drew, Geo. A / Howard, F	Stephens, Wm / Barlow, D. H	Baldwin, A. E / Wing, R. H	Mahoney, H / Buchner, A. A	Oakes, J. W / Quarmby, H	Burgess, C. H	Grenside, F. C	Tyson, A. W	Evans, W. P	McElroy, H. J	Yeates, Chas
1923	Howard, F / Burgess, C. H	Penfold, S / Grenside, F. C	Armstrong, J / Tyson, A. W	Brydon, R. H / Evans, W. P	Coady, M / H. J McElroy	Finnie, J. A / Yeates, Chas	Jaffray, Alex	Drew, Geo. A	Stephens, Wm	Baldwin, A. E	Mahoney, H	Oakes, J. W
1924	Evans, W. P / Jaffray, Alex	Bain, Alex / Drew, Geo. A	McElroy, H. J / Meldrum, G. E	Dempsey, C. W / Baldwin, A. E	Robson, R. Bev / Mahoney, H	Cunningham, L / Oakes, J. W	Howard, F	Penfold, S	Armstrong, J	Brydon, R. H	Coady, M	Finnie, J. A
1925	Mahoney, H / Howard, F	Jaffray, Alex / Penfold, S	Barlow, D. H / Armstrong, J. A	Baldwin, A. E / Brydon, R. H	Bentley, D / Coady, M	Stuart, W. W / Finnie, J. A	Evans, W. P	Bain, Alex	McElroy, H. J	Dempsey, C. W	Robson, R. Bev	Cunningham, L
1926	Penfold, S / Evans, W. P	McNiven, A / Bain, Alex	Stuart, L. M / McElroy, H. J	Grundy, R. H / Dempsey, C. W	Rundle, Sam / Coady, M	Howden, Ben / Cunningham, L	Mahoney, H	Jaffray, Alex	Barlow, D. H	Meldrum, G. E	Bentley, D	Stuart, W. W
1927	Bain, Alex / Mahoney, H	Grenside, F. C / Jaffray, Alex	Ramsey, F. R / Barlow, D. H	Brown, L / Meldrum, G. E	Wing, R. H / Bentley, D	Cunningham, L / Stuart, W. W	Penfold, S	McNiven, A	Stuart, L. M	Grundy, R. H	Rundle, Sam	Howden, Ben
1928	Frank, A.J / Rundle, Sam	Dempsey, C.W / Penfold, S	Taylor, W.G / Stuart, W.W.	Bain, Alex / Hammersley, H.T	Cunningham, L / Meldrum, G.E	Brown, Louis / McNiven, Angus	Ramsey, F.R	Bentley, D	Howden, B.F	Grundy, R.H	Stuart, L.M	Wing, R.H.
1929	Frank, A.J / Ibbotson, G.L	Dempsey, C.W / Penfold, S	Taylor, W.G / Stuart, L.M	Bain, Alex / Ritchie, A.E	Cunningham, L / Meldrum, G.E	Brown, Louis / Berry, Wm H	Ramsey, F.R	Bentley, D	Rae, Alex	Grundy, R.H	More, J.E	Ward, R.B
1930	Murphy, Fred	Dempsey, C.W	Ward, R.B	Bain, Alex	Cunningham, L	Brown, Louis	Lye, O.G	Newton, J.C	Rae, Alex	Penfold, S	Stuart, L.M	
1931	Frank, A.J	Dempsey, C.W	Taylor, W.G	Bain, Alex	Berry, W.H	Brown, Louis	Lye, O.G	Newton, J.C	Rae, Alex	Mahoney, H	Stuart, L.M	
1932	Frank, A.J	Dempsey, C.W	Barber, W.L	Mahoney, Harry	Hayes, W.W.J	Kennedy, D.E	Ramsey, F.R	Templeman, Wm	Rae, Alex	Howard, Frank	Brown, Louis	
1933	Frank, A.J	Dempsey, C.W	Barber, W.L	Mahoney, Harry	Hayes, W.W.J	Kennedy, D.E	Lye, O.G	Templeman, Wm	McArthur, G.C	Howard, Frank	Cowan, W.A	
1934	Frank, A.J	Dempsey, C.W	Taylor, W.G	Mahoney, Harry	Hayes, W.W.J	Kennedy, D.E	Fulton, C.E	Brown, Louis	McArthur, G.C	Howard, Frank	Cowan, W.A	
1935	Frank, A.J	Dempsey, C.W	Taylor, W.G	Brydges, A.J	Rife, G.L	Kennedy, D.E	Freudeman, F.L	Greenaway, W.J	McLaughlin, A.C	Graesser, F.A	Stratton, R.W	
1936	Frank, A.J	Dempsey, C.W	Taylor, W.G	Brydges, A.J	Rife, G.L	Kennedy, D.E	Freudeman, F.L	Smith, W.P	McLaughlin, A.C	Graesser, F.A	Stratton, R.W	
1937	Frank, A.J	Dempsey, C.W	Taylor, W.G	Brydges, A.J	Rife, G.L	Rudell, Dr. J	Freudeman, F.L	Smith, W.P	McLaughlin, A.C	Graesser, F.A	Stratton, R.W	
1938	Frank, A.J	Dempsey, C.W	Bennett, Phil	Brydges, A.J	Rife, G.L	Rudell, Dr. J	Freudeman, F.L	Smith, W.P	Mahoney, Harry	Graesser, F.A	MacGowan, M.C	
1939	Woods, H	Dempsey, C.W	Bennett, Phil	Brydges, A.J	Rife, G.L	Rudell, Dr. J	Freudeman, F.L	Wilson, John	Kenyon, Richard	Mahoney, H	Fulton, C.E	
1940	Frank, A.J	Dempsey, C.W	Bennett, Phil	Mahoney, Harry	Rife, G.L	Griffenham, C	Freudeman, F.L	Wilson, John	Kenyon, Richard	Graesser, F.A	Penfold, H.J	
1941	Frank, A.J	Dempsey, C.W	Howard, Frank	Brydges, A.J	Rife, G.L	Griffenham, C	Freudeman, F.L	Mahoney, Harry	Kenyon, Richard	Templeman, Wm	Penfold, H.J	
1942	Frank, A.J	Dempsey, C.W	Howard, Frank	Brydges, A.J	Rife, G.L	Griffenham, C	Freudeman, F.L	Mahoney, Harry	Kenyon, Richard	Graesser, F.A	Penfold, H.J	
1943	Frank, A.J	Dempsey, C.W	Barber, R.O	Brydges, A.J	Rife, G.L	Worton, H. W	Freudeman, F.L	Bennett, Phil	Kenyon, Richard	Jones, L.E	Mahoney, Harry	
1944	Frank, A.J	Owen, Len	Barber, R.O	Brydges, A.J	Rife, G.L	Thain, W.B	Freudeman, F.L	Bennett, Phil	Kenyon, Richard	Jones, L.E	Allan, C.H	
1945	Frank, A.J	Owen, Len	Barber, R.O	Brydges, A.J	Bennett, James	Thain, W.B	Freudeman, F.L	Bennett, Phil	Kenyon, Richard	Worton, Harry	Allan, C.H	
1946	Frank, A.J	Leggett, L.H	Bennett, James	Brydges, A.J	Goad, John	Keefe, Doug	Freudeman, F.L	Owen, Len	Burbridge, N.A	Worton, Harry	Thain, W.B	
1947	Frank, A.J	Leggett, L.H	Bennett, James	Brydges, A.J	Clare, James A	Keefe, Doug	Freudeman, F.L	Goad, John	Burbridge, N.A	Worton, Harry	Jones, L.E	
1948	Frank, A.J	Heffernan, J.P	Bennett, James	Brydges, A.J	Clare, James	Keefe, Doug	Freudeman, F.L	Smith, John R	Burbridge, N.A	Sanders, J.C	Hosking, Henry A	
1949	Frank, A.J	Heffernan, J.P	Bennett, James	Little, J.L	Clare, James	Keefe, Doug	Oaks, J.D	Sanders, J.C	Bubridge, N.A	Toole, G.W	Hosking, Henry A	
1950	Frank, A.J	Heffernan, J.P	Worton, Harry	Little, J.L	Mennie, David	Sanders, J.C	Oaks, J.D	Robinson, C.V	Burbridge, N.A	Toole, G.W	McFadzen, D. E	
1951	Frank, A.J	Heffernan, J.P	Worton, Harry	Dixon, Fred W	Mennie, David	Wood, W.C	Oaks, J.D	Robinson, C.V	Burbridge, N.A	Toole, G.W	McFadzen, D. E	
1952	Frank, A.J	Heffernan, J.P	Smith, Ralph W	Dixon, Fred W	Kemp, G.C	Wood, W.C	Oaks, J.D	Robinson, C.V	Laing, A. M	Wells, A.J	McFadzen, D. E	
1953	Frank, A.J	Heffernan, J.P	Smith, Ralph W	Dixon, Fred W	Kemp, G.C	Pinch, Dr C	Oaks, J.D	Robinson, C.V	Suitter, Harold	Wells, A.J	McFadzen, D.E	
1954	Frank, A.J	Mayes, Jim	Smith, Ralph W	Dixon, Fred W	Kemp, G.C	Pinch, Dr C	Suitter, Harold	Robinson, C.V	Laing, A.M	Wells, A.J	McFadzen, D.E	
1955	Frank, A.J	Mayes, Jim	Smith, Ralph W	Dixon, Fred W	Laing, A	Pinch, Dr C	Suitter, Harold	Robinson, C.V	McFadzen, D.E	Wells, A.J	Vince, C	
1956	Frank, A.J	Mayes, Jim	Smith, Ralph W	Hastings, D.F	Rife, G.L	Pinch, Dr C	Hales, Alfred	Robinson, C.V	Lowell, Elva	Wells, A.J	Vince, C	
1957	Frank, A.J	Mayes, Jim	Smith, Ralph W	Hastings, D.F	Rife, G.L	Hamilton, Wm	Hales, Alfred	Robinson, C.V	Lowell, Elva	Wells, A.J	Vince, C	
1958	Frank, A.J	Mayes, Jim	Suitter, Harold	Pinch, Dr. C	Rife, G.L	Hamilton, Wm	Laing, A.M	Robinson, C.V	Lowell, Elva	Wells, A.J	Vince, C	
1959	Frank, A.J	Suitter, Harold	Smith, Ralph W	Dixon, Fred W	Rife, G.L	Hamilton, Wm	Laing, A.M	Robinson, C.V	Lowell, Elva	Wells, A.J	Vince, C	

1960	Frank, A.J	Suitter, Harold	Smith, Ralph W	Dixon, Fred W	Rife, G.L	Hamilton, Wm	Laing, A. M	Robinson, C.V	Lowell, Elva	Wells, A.J	Vince, C	
1961	Frank, A.J	Suitter, Harold	White, F.J	Dixon, Fred W	Rife, G.L	Leaman, C.F	Laing, A.M	Robinson, C.V	McAdorey, Robt	Wells, A.J	Vince, C	
1962	Frank, A.J	Hammond, C.M	Smith, Ralph W	Dixon, Fred W	Leuthard, J.L	Farmer, D.H	Laing, A.M	Robinson, C.V	Lowell, Elva	Rife, G.L	Suitter, Harold	
1963	Frank, A.J	Hammond, C.M	Rife, G.L	Dixon, Fred W	Armstrong, Paul	Farmer, D.H	Hammill, Ken O	Robinson, C.V	Lowell, Elva	Laing, A.M	Mercer, Paul	
1964	Laing, A	Hammond, C.M	Frank, A.J	Dixon, Fred W	Armstrong, Paul	Farmer, D.H	Hammill, Ken O	Robinson, C.V	Lowell, Elva	Rife, G.L	Mercer, Paul	
1965	Jary, Norman	Hammond, C.M	Laird, A.L	Dixon, Fred W	Armstrong, Paul	Smith, Ralph W	Hammill, Ken O	Robinson, C.V	Lowell, Elva	Wells, A.J	Mercer, Paul	

TWO YEAR TERM OF OFFICE BEGINS

1966	Jary, Norman	Hammond, C.M	Laird, A.L	Dixon, Fred W	Stephens, Russell	Hamilton, Wm	Hammill, Ken O	Robinson, C.V	Lowell, Elva	Valeriote, D.M	Mercer, Paul	
1967	Jary, Norman	Hammond, C.M	Laird, A.L	Dixon, Fred W	Stephens, Russell	Hamilton, Wm	Hammill, Ken O	Robinson, C.V	Lowell, Elva	Valeriote, D.M	Mercer, Paul	
1968	Jary, Norman	Slinger, J.E	Smith, R.W	Dixon, Fred W	Hamilton, Wm	Hanlon, Pat F	Hammill, Ken O	Robinson, C.V	Armstrong, Paul	Valeriote, D.M	McFadzen, D.E	
1969	Jary, Norman	Slinger, J.E	Smith, R.W	Dixon, Fred W	Hamilton, Wm	Hanlon, Pat F	Hammill, Ken O	Robinson, C.V	Armstrong, Paul	Valeriote, D.M	McFadzen, D.E	
1970	Jary, Norman	Slinger, J.E	Murphy, G.H	Dixon, Fred W	Hamilton, Wm	Hanlon, Pat F	Hammill, Ken O	Robinson, C.V	Hamilton, Carl	Valeriote, D.M	Mercer, Paul	
1971	Brazolot, Peter	Slinger, J.E	Murphy, G.H	Howitt, J.F	Hamilton, Wm	Hanlon, Pat F	Hammill, Ken O	Mercer, Paul	Hamilton, Carl	Patterson, C.J	Valeriote, D.M	
1972	Brazolot, Peter	Slinger, J.E	Murphy, G.H	Howitt, J.F	Hamilton, Wm	Hanlon, Pat F	Hammill, Ken O	Mercer, Paul	Hamilton, Carl	Patterson, C.J	Valeriote, D.M	
1973	Brazolot, Peter	Hammond, C.M	Murphy, G.H	Howitt, J.F	Scammell, Robert	Hanlon, Pat F	Hammill, Ken O	Love, Les	Hamilton, Carl	MacKinnon, M	Valeriote, D.M	
1974	Brazolot, Peter	Hammond, C.M	Murphy, G.H	Howitt, J.F	Scammell, Robert	Hanlon, Pat F	Hammill, Ken O	Love, Les	Hamilton, Carl	MacKinnon, M	Valeriote, D.M	
1975	Brazolot, Peter	Hammond, C.M	Murphy, G.H	Kendrick, D.E	Cochrane, Mel	Hanlon, Pat F	Hammill, Ken O	Valeriote, D.M	Hamilton, Carl	MacKinnon, M	Godfrey, Ann	
1976	Brazolot, Peter	Hammond, C.M	Murphy, G.H	Kendrick, D.E	Cochrane, Mel	Hanlon, Pat F	Hammill, Ken O	Valeriote, D.M	Hamilton, Carl	MacKinnon, M	Godfrey, Ann	
1977	Brazolot, Peter	Hammond, C.M	Murphy, G.H	Kendrick, D.E	Marett, Clara	Hanlon, Pat F	Hammill, Ken O	Valeriote, D.M	Hamilton, Carl	MacKinnon, M	Godfrey, Ann	
1978	Brazolot, Peter	Hammond, C.M	Murphy, G.H	Kendrick, D.E	Marett, Clara	Armstrong, P	Hammill, Ken O	Valeriote, D.M	Hamilton, Carl	MacKinnon, M	Godfrey, Ann	
1979	Brazolot, Peter	Hammond, C.M	Murphy, G.H	Kendrick, D.E	Valeriote, D.M	Armstrong, P	Hammill, Ken O	Marett, Clara	Hamilton, Carl	MacKinnon, M	Godfrey, Ann	
1980	Brazolot, Peter	Hammond, C.M	Murphy, G.H	Kendrick, D.E	Valeriote, D.M	Armstrong, P	Hammill, Ken O	Marett, Clara	Hamilton, Carl	MacKinnon, M	Godfrey, Ann	
1981	Ferraro, Rick	Cochrane, Mel	Valeriote, D.M	Kendrick, D.E	MacKinnon, M	Armstrong, P	Hammill, Ken O	Marett, Clara	Hamilton, Carl	Whitechurch, James	Godfrey, Ann	
1982	Ferraro, Rick	Cochrane, Mel	Valeriote, D.M	Kendrick, D.E	MacKinnon, M	Armstrong, P	Hammill, Ken O	Marett, Clara	Hamilton, Carl	Whitechurch, James	Godfrey, Ann	

THREE YEAR TERM OF OFFICE BEGINS

1983	Ferraro, Rick	Young, Joe	Counsell, John	Kendrick, D.E	MacKinnon, M	Valeriote, D.M	Hammill, Ken O	Marett, Clara	Hamilton, Carl	Whitechurch, James	Godfrey, Ann	
1984	Ferraro, Rick	Young, Joe	Counsell, John	Kendrick, D.E	MacKinnon, M	Valeriote, D.M	Hammill, Ken O	Marett, Clara	Hamilton, Carl	Whitechurch, James	Godfrey, Ann	
1985	Ferraro, Rick	Young, Joe	Counsell, John	Kendrick, D.E	MacKinnon, M	Valeriote, D.M	Hammill, Ken O	Marett, Clara	Hamilton, Carl	Whitechurch, James	Godfrey, Ann	
1986	Peacock, Don	Young, Joe	Pate, Dr. John	Lennon, Linda	Jary, Norman	Kendrick, D.E	Hammill, Ken O	Marett, Clara	Hamilton, Carl	Whitechurch, James	Gaw, Adam	
1987	Peacock, Don	Young, Joe	Pate, Dr John	Lennon, Linda	Jary, Norman	Kendrick, D.E	Hammill, Ken O	Marett, Clara	Hamilton, Carl	Whitechurch, James	Gaw, Adam	
1988	Peacock, Don	Young, Joe	Pate, Dr. John	Lennon, Linda	Jary, Norman	Kendrick, D.E	Hammill, Ken O	Marett, Clara	Hamilton, Carl	Whitechurch, James	Gaw, Adam	
1989	Peacock, Don	Young, Joe	Pate, Dr. John	Lennon, Linda	Jary, Norman	Kendrick, D.E	Hammill, Ken O	Marret, Clara	Hamilton, Carl	Whitechurch, James	Gaw, Adam	
1990	Peacock, Don	Young, Joe	Pate, Dr. John	Lennon, Linda	Jary, Norman	Kendrick, D.E	Hammill, Ken O	Marett, Clara	Hamilton, Carl	Whitechurch, James	Gaw, Adam	
1991	Peacock, Don	Young, Joe	Pate, Dr. John	Lennon, Linda	Jary, Norman	Kendrick, D.E	Hammill, Ken O	Marett, Clara	Hamilton, Carl	McAdams, Wm	Gaw, Adam	

FIRST ELECTION BY WARDS

1992	Carere, John	Young, Joe	Maine, Frank	Walton, Gary	Jary, Norman	Stafford, Theresa	Kovach, Gloria	Sinclair, Jim	Hamilton, Carl	McAdams, Wm	Bilanski, Walter	Pate, Dr. John
1993	Carere, John	Young, Joe	Maine, Frank	Walton, Gary	Jary, Norman	Stafford, Theresa	Kovach, Gloria	Sinclair, Jim	Hamilton, Carl	McAdams, Wm	Bilanski, Walter	Pate, Dr. John
1994	Carere, John	Young, Joe	Maine, Frank	Walton, Gary	Jary, Norman	Stafford, Theresa	Kovach, Gloria	Sinclair, Jim	Downer, Catherine	McAdams, Wm	Bilanski, Walter	Pate, Dr. John
1995	Carere, John	Farbridge, Karen	Farrelly, Sean	Walton, Gary	Jary, Norman	Schnuur, Dan	Kovach, Gloria	Sinclair, Jim	Downer, Catherine	McAdams, Wm	Bilanski, Walter	Pate, Dr. John
1996	Carere, John	Farbridge, Karen	Farrelly, Sean	Walton, Gary	Jary, Norman	Schnuur, Dan	Kovach, Gloria	Sinclair, Jim	Downer, Catherine	McAdams, Wm	Bilanski, Walter	Pate, Dr. John
1997	Carere, John	Farbridge, Karen	Farrelly, Sean	Walton, Gary	Jary, Norman	Schnuur, Dan	Kovach, Gloria	Cumming, Phil	Downer, Catherine	McAdams, Wm	Billings, Christine	Prior, Linda
1998	Furfaro, Rocco	Farbridge, Karen	Farrelly, Sean	Walton, Gary	Jary, Norman	Schnuur, Dan	Kovach, Gloria	Cumming, Phil	Downer, Catherine	McAdams, Wm	Billings, Christine	Shapka, M
1999	Furfaro, Rocco	Farbridge, Karen	Farrelly, Sean	Walton, Gary	Jary, Norman	Schnuur, Dan	Kovach, Gloria	Cumming, Phil	Downer, Catherine	McAdams, Wm	Billings, Christine	Shapka, M
2000	Furfaro, Rocco	Farbridge, Karen	Farrelly, Sean	Walton, Gary	Jary, Norman	Schnuur, Dan	Kovach, Gloria	Cumming, Phil	Downer, Catherine	McAdams, Wm	Billings, Christine	Shapka, M

Selective Index

Contributors

Ceska Brennan - Author, 'Profiles: People of Guelph'

Ceska is an artist and writer who lives in Guelph with her husband Scott and their sons Tobin and Kelsy. Ceska is a memorial designer and the counsellor at historic Woodlawn Cemetery in Guelph. Ceska is a past president of the Guelph Creative Arts Association and is a principal in the historical walking tours and the popular Spirit Walk event held in Woodlawn Cemetery.

Gloria Dent - Author, Chapter One

A resident of Guelph for the past forty years, Gloria has participated in several aspects of the city's cultural life, including its Arts Council, Creative Arts Association, Spring Festival, Civic Symphony and Chorale, the university orchestra and the Wellington County Historical Society. She wrote a history of the Guelph Spring Festival for *Guelph and its Spring Festival*, a book she edited with Leonard Conolly, and an historical account of 'The City on Stage' in *A Place to Call our Own*, the souvenir program for the opening of the River Run Centre. She holds an Honours BA in Philosophy and English from the University of Toronto and an MA in History from the University of Guelph.

Bonnie M. Durtnall - Research Assistant and Author

Bonnie, BA, MA in History, is a local historian and researcher. She is a member of the Guelph Historical Society for whom she has written several articles. Bonnie is an instructor at Conestoga College and elsewhere on Celtic religion (past and present), herbalism, plant lore, rituals and modern nature religions.

Ted Mitchell - Author, Chapter Two

Ted is a fifth-generation member of the Mitchell family in the Paisley Block. The Mitchell family emigrated from Suffolk County, England in 1832. Ted attended SS No.6 Guelph Twp, GCVI, University of Western Ontario (BA) and University of Waterloo (MA). He taught at Parry Sound and at Guelph. From his family, he learned to value rural traditions, primarily the necessity of well-directed work and incidentally, a love of nature. He and wife Elizabeth, a recently retired professor of human nutrition at University of Guelph, live in the Mitchell family farmhouse.

(L-R, front row)

Ross Irwin

Ross was president of the Guelph Historical Society from 1995 to 1999. He initiated the writing of this history book.

Dawn Matheson - Managing Editor/Design

A media artist and editor, Dawn grew up in Guelph and graduated in English and Drama from the University of Toronto. She has worked at a myriad of creative jobs in theatre, and in radio and television documentary for the CBC. Locally, Dawn has worked on the Guelph Social History Project video series and for the *Guelph Mercury*. She is an active member of EdVideo, GIRC and the Canadian Media Guild. Dawn's home is in Guelph, but her wanderlust has taken her on many international adventures.

(L-R back row)

Fred Dahms - Author, Chapter Five

Fred is professor, founding member and former chair of the Department of Geography, University of Guelph. He has published widely on urban geography, urban planning and on the changing functions of rural service centres. In addition to having been an advisor to the Guelph Planning Department since 1968, he was a member of the Guelph Planning Advisory Committee for eleven years and its chair for two. Fred is now writing a series of books on small Ontario towns for James Lorimer Publishers.

Donald Coulman - Project Manager

Don taught electronics, mathematics and communication technology at J.F. Ross CVI for almost one-third of a century. He completed his teaching career as technical director at the school. Don wrote the book, *Guelph: Take a Look at Us!*, as part of Guelph's sesquicentennial celebrations in 1977. As well as having presented many illustrated talks to a variety of groups about the history of Guelph, Don has written numerous self-guided Guelph walking tours for school classes, service organizations and the Guelph Museums.

Steve Thorning - Author, Chapter Three

A lifelong resident of Elora, Steve Thorning is a graduate of the University of Guelph. Following an eight-year stint as an accountant with CIBC, he graduated from McMaster University with a PhD in 1994. He is a specialist in business and railway history, but has been fascinated with local history for many years. His popular weekly column, "Valuing Our History," began in 1991 and now appears in the *Wellington Advertiser*. He has served seven years on the Village of Elora council; the last four as deputy reeve.

John W. Keleher - Photo Resource

John, a member of an old Guelph family, was educated in local schools, served in the Canadian Postal Corps during the Second World War and, in 1957, joined the staff of the Guelph Post Office. He is a member of the Guelph Stamp Club and the Royal Canadian Legion. He has a collection of over 2,000 photos of Guelph.

Rosemary Anderson - Editor

Rosemary has been involved in journalism since Centennial year, 1967, when she started as a junior reporter at the *Orillia Packet and Times*. She and her husband moved to Guelph in 1972, when she started work at the *Guelph Mercury* where she is currently lifestyle editor. She lives with her daughter, April, and granddaughter, Cassandra, and enjoys exploring Ontario, reading mysteries and writing a weekly column.

David Mowat

David is the president of the Guelph Historical Society.

Gilbert Stelter - Author, Chapter Four

Gilbert is university professor emeritus at the University of Guelph where he continues to teach urban history in the graduate program. In 1998 he won the John Bell medal for outstanding teaching. He is president of the Urban History Association, an international organization based in the United States. He has published a number of books and articles in the fields of Canadian urban history and his current research is about the connections between urban theory and urban history. His local interests include research and publications about Guelph architecture (with several articles in *Historic Guelph)* and he is a member of LACAC. He and his wife Sally are frequent international travellers and avid gardeners.

Ryan Price - Printmaker

Ryan is a printmaker and illustrator. Originally from the London area, he studied at BealArt before moving to Guelph in 1993 where he co-founded and continues to help run the printmaking studio 'room twenty-three' in the downtown.

Dave Carter - Photographer

Dave, a life-time resident of Arkell, Ontario, has been a photographer for over 40 years, working for the *Guelph Mercury* for most of them. Dave has taken photos of all the Prime Ministers of Canada visiting Guelph since John Diefenbaker. He has also taken photos of most major storms and fires in the Guelph area and many celebrity sports figures throughout his career.

Not Pictured:

Hilary Stead - Proofreader

Hilary is a Guelph journalist.

Jeff Whyte - Index

Jeff is the former archivist at the Guelph Public Library.

Guelph at the Turn of the Century – Land Uses and Policy Areas

General Residential

Medium Density Residential

High Density Residential

Central Business District

Regional Commercial Centre

Community Commercial Centre

Neighborhood Commercial Centre

Service Commercial

Service Commercial/Special Development Area

Mixed Office - Residential

Commercial Mixed Use

Corporate Business Park

Industrial

Mixed Industrial - Residential

Major Institutional

Urban Reserve

Open Space

Areas of Natural and Scientific Interest (ANSI)

Provincially Significant Wetlands (PSWs)

Waste Management

Aggregate Extraction

Institutional / Research Park

Special Study Area

Special Policy Area

CITY OF GUELPH
PLANNING AND BUSINESS DEVELOPMENT
Planning Division

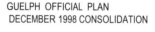
GUELPH OFFICIAL PLAN
DECEMBER 1998 CONSOLIDATION

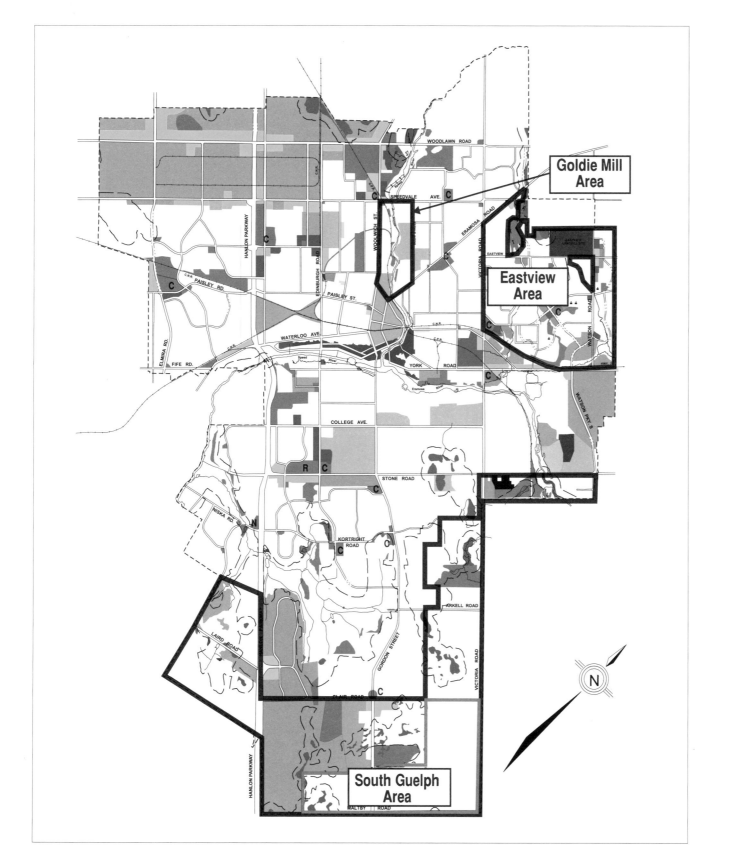